ADVANCE PRAISE FOR *THE GOSPEL OF*

"Prepare to be inspired, as John Dear guides you on a journey into the grounded in Jesus and his Way of Love. Along the way, you will enc fast fearlessness of figures like Gandhi, Martin Luther King, Jr., D Romero . . . and find yourself ready to join them in this holy work."
–The Most Rev. Michael B. Curry, Presiding Bishop of The Episcopal Church

"John Dear's is a beautiful message of peace!"
—Anne Lamott, author, *Traveling Mercies* and *Almost Everything*

"Each time I consult this magnificent commentary for insight into a particular gospel passage, I am drawn further into the nonviolent teachings of Mahatma Gandhi and Martin Luther King, Jr. As John Dear convincingly demonstrates, Jesus was their inspiration. *The Gospel of Peace* lovingly confronts us all with what it means to follow Jesus in all dimensions of life. It is a master class on Christian discipleship."
—The Rt. Rev. Mariann Edgar Budde, Bishop, Episcopal Diocese of Washington, D.C.

"Father John Dear's commentary on the synoptic gospels from the perspective of nonviolence is needed especially now. With the Third World War being fought piecemeal, as our Holy Father Pope Francis regularly reminds us, and the violence of handguns and assault weapons daily taking the lives of God's children in the U.S., we Christians need to be reminded that the Gospel of Jesus is about peace. Father John Dear's book helps us reflect on Jesus the Peacemaker and assists us in becoming blessed peacemakers ourselves."
**—Bishop John Stowe, OFM Conv.,
Bishop of Lexington, Kentucky, and Bishop-President of Pax Christi USA**

"A thoughtful, deeply challenging reflection on the synoptic Gospels that captures the complexity, depth, and nuances of nonviolence in the word and witness of Jesus. It will be a valuable resource for all who seek to understand and to live the nonviolence that Jesus taught."
–Marie Dennis, Pax Christi International and Catholic Nonviolence Initiative

"John Dear is one of the few towering figures in the Christian Nonviolent Freedom and Peace Movement in our time! This powerful book should not be missed!"
—Cornel West

"Father John Dear's passion for peace illumines every page of this book. Recognizing the Beatitudes and the Sermon of the Mount as a blueprint for the life of Christ, John Dear demonstrates how the gospels are a blueprint for peace, inviting believer and nonbeliever alike to follow the Prince of Peace by living the Beatitudes and the Sermon on the Mount."
–Most Rev. Archbishop John C. Wester, Archdiocese of Santa Fe, New Mexico

"John Dear's work shows the deep connections between nonviolence and the gospels. This study is crucial for understanding the heart of Christian faith. This fresh study will be useful for all people who have a passion for justice." **—Rev. Malcolm Young, Dean,
Grace Cathedral, San Francisco**

"Father John Dear's *The Gospel of Peace* is a landmark book. The Church has begun to reclaim gospel nonviolence. As Pope Francis has taught: 'To be true followers of Jesus today includes embracing his teaching on nonviolence.' John Dear has solidly anchored that turn to Jesus' nonviolence in this book. It is the first complete commentary on the synoptic gospels that shows Jesus' all-embracing nonviolence. Illumined and inspired by the examples of Gandhi and Martin Luther King, Jr., Father John Dear opens the gospels for us anew."
—**Terry Rynne, author, *Gandhi and Jesus: The Saving Power of Nonviolence***

"No living person has done more to root Jesus' message of nonviolence and peace in scripture than John Dear. He understands so clearly that humans live inside the stories that we claim together or, better, that claim us. Follow John's lead through Matthew, Mark, and Luke and, like those disciples on the Emmaus Way, your heart will be set afire with excitement to tell others the Good News!"
—**Wes Howard-Brook, author,**
"Come Out, My People!" God's Call out of Empire in the Bible and Beyond

"A profoundly important work that liberates Christ from the scribes and screeds of violent empire and returns Him to us as the Light of Peace, the Prince of Peace, the living embodiment of active nonviolence. In a world of acquiescence to endless wars and human suffering, this book summons us to follow Christ and carry out our own ministry of nonviolent resistance born and nurtured by the deepest love of humanity."
—**Brad Wolf, editor,**
A Ministry of Risk: The Selected Writings of Philip Berrigan

"With scholarly, masterly, and simple elegance, Fr. John Dear reminds us that the heart of God is love and that Jesus, as the image and true servant of God He is, summons us into the revolution of God's nonviolent love in the world. Nonviolence is not only the style—the way we serve humanity and creation; it *is* the Gospel—the 'good news' for a world that is so enamored with violence. Christians everywhere need to reawaken to this Gospel."
—**Rev. Emmanuel Katongole,**
Professor of Theology and Peace Studies, University of Notre Dame

"This book is a masterpiece, opening the door anew to the revolutionary Good News of Jesus, his life and death and teachings."
—**Rev. Matthew Fox, author and teacher**

"Reading the Gospels in jail can alter one's hermeneutic. Such a location frees your perspective. Witness what's been elicited here, a spiritual thread so long, so thoroughgoing, so relentless. John Dear has pulled that thread, producing a resource for mission and movement much overdue. Following the best of scholarship, he brings into focus the gospel of nonviolence embedded within the synoptic gospels—too long unseen, unsought, unwelcome, and above all, unimagined—now visible and in the light. Look and see. It's the remedy we need to heal our history and transform what's to come. Thanks be!"
—**Bill Wylie-Kellermann, editor,**
William Stringfellow: Essential Writings

THE GOSPEL OF PEACE

THE GOSPEL OF PEACE

A Commentary on Matthew, Mark, and Luke
from the Perspective of Nonviolence

JOHN DEAR

ORBIS BOOKS

Maryknoll, New York 10545

Founded in 1970, Orbis Books endeavors to publish works that enlighten the mind, nourish the spirit, and challenge the conscience. The publishing arm of the Maryknoll Fathers and Brothers, Orbis seeks to explore the global dimensions of the Christian faith and mission, to invite dialogue with diverse cultures and religious traditions, and to serve the cause of reconciliation and peace. The books published reflect the views of their authors and do not represent the official position of the Maryknoll Society. To learn more about Maryknoll and Orbis Books, please visit our website at www.orbisbooks.com.

Library of Congress Cataloging-in-Publication Data

Names: Dear, John, 1959- author.
Title: The gospel of peace : reading Matthew, Mark, and Luke from the
    perspective of nonviolence / John Dear.
Description: Maryknoll, NY : Orbis Books, [2024] | Includes bibliographical
    references and index. | Summary: "A comprehensive commentary of the
    synoptic gospels from the perspective of nonviolence"— Provided by
    publisher.
Identifiers: LCCN 2023026957 (print) | LCCN 2023026958 (ebook) | ISBN
    9781626985339 (trade paperback) | ISBN 9781608339907 (epub)
Subjects: LCSH: Bible. Gospels—Criticism, interpretation, etc. |
    Nonviolence—Religious aspects—Christianity. | Peace—Religious
    aspects—Christianity.
Classification: LCC BS2555.52 .D415 2024 (print) | LCC BS2555.52 (ebook)
    | DDC 226/.06—dc23/eng/20230808
LC record available at https://lccn.loc.gov/2023026957
LC ebook record available at https://lccn.loc.gov/2023026958

Mohandas Gandhi

"Devotion to nonviolence is the highest expression of humanity's conscious state."

"Jesus was the most active resister known perhaps to history. This was nonviolence par excellence."

"Nonviolence is the greatest and most active force in the world. One person who can express nonviolence in life exercises a force superior to all the forces of brutality. My optimism rests on my belief in the infinite possibilities of the individual to develop nonviolence. The more you develop it in your own being, the more infectious it becomes till it overwhelms your surroundings and by and by might oversweep the world."

"The Kingdom of God is nonviolence."

Mairead Corrigan Maguire
Nobel Peace Prize Laureate

"The way of Jesus is the way of active nonviolence against evil. He does not use evil means to fight evil. As a Christian, I repent that we Christians have not taught or lived the full gospel message of Jesus' nonviolence and love for enemies. I am convinced, however, that we are evolving into a new age, and that in time, the Christian church will again proclaim a theology of nonviolence as the norm for Christian life."

Walter Wink

"Nonviolence is a characteristic of the coming Reign of God, and a foretaste of its transcendent reality."

Romans 6:13–14

"Put on the armor of God that you may be able to resist on the evil day and having done everything, to hold your ground. Stand fast with your loins girded in truth, clothed with righteousness as a breastplate, and your feet shod in readiness for the Gospel of Peace."

CONTENTS

Contents

Contents

MARK
The Radical Discipleship
of Nonviolent Resistance to Empire   **148**

LUKE
The Grassroots Campaign of Peace, Nonviolence, and Compassion   **222**

INTRODUCTION

I've always been stirred and challenged by the Gospels, but also by the lives and teachings of Mahatma Gandhi and Rev. Dr. Martin Luther King Jr., the legendary apostles of nonviolence. As I study these two giants, I hear their urgent pleas to humanity to end its pandemic of violence and to learn the ancient wisdom and way of nonviolence. Their call has influenced the way I read the Gospels and my understanding of Jesus himself.

Indeed, I've come to the conclusion that the more we study Gandhi and Dr. King, the better we will understand Jesus and the Gospels.

If Gandhi and Dr. King are the greatest practitioners of nonviolence in modern history, then the Gospels portray Jesus as the greatest practitioner of nonviolence in all of history. Gandhi described Jesus as *nonviolence par excellence*. Reading Jesus through Gandhi's and King's lens of nonviolence opens up new avenues of insight and depths of wisdom. Every word, teaching, and action of the nonviolent Jesus makes more sense. In turn, we realize that Gandhi and King were right: nonviolence is the way forward on every level—personally, communally, spiritually, nationally, politically, and globally. Nonviolence, we realize, is the way of God, the law of nature, the wisdom of creation, and the hope of humanity. It must become our common practice if we are to have a future.

These days, however, when I look around at the Christian community, I'm dismayed to see how far we remain from that ancient wisdom. Somehow or other, we Christians have become mean, judgmental, argumentative, and condemnatory. Worse, we carry guns, advocate racism and sexism, support war and nationalism, build nuclear weapons, chase after money, and place our trust in all kinds of idols. It's as if Christians don't read the Gospels, much less understand them from a Gandhian/Kingian hermeneutic of nonviolence. (Hermeneutic just means "interpretive lens" or perspective.) Worse, it's as if we have perverted Christianity into some kind of false gospel of violence and war, where some kind of false god blesses war and warmakers, encourages us to kill the enemies of our nation, and wants us to be rich, successful, and powerful, at the expense of billions of impoverished sisters and brothers. This heretical Christianity actually promotes a kind of anti-gospel.

Many people might say that I exaggerate the case, but even if the vast majority of Christians are praying and trying to follow Jesus, nearly every single one stops short at nonviolence. Many people try to be kind, and many even try to do charitable works for the poor—to donate to relief organizations, or pitch in at the local homeless shelter or soup kitchen. Even though they practice this Gospel mandate to "do unto others as you would do to me," they still blindly support U.S. militarism, the latest war, the national "defense," and our nuclear arsenal. The gospel of peace outlines a journey of service to the poor and needy, followed by critical reflection on why there are so many poor and needy people (billions upon billions in today's world), which then leads to passionate work for social, economic, racial, and environmental justice, which leads to further critical reflection on where all the world's money is going if not to the poor and needy (and the shocking discovery that trillions of dollars have been spent on war over the last century by the U.S. Pentagon, the world's militaries, and the weapons manufacturers and their multinational corporations), which leads us to passionate advocacy for national, global, and nuclear disarmament, which leads to further reflection about how to reorganize a disarmed world based on institutionalized nonviolent conflict resolution and global justice. If you pursue that path, you end up like Gandhi, Dorothy Day, and Dr. King, committed to total nonviolence. Few make the entire journey into the holistic nonviolence of Jesus, what Matthew calls, in the Sermon on the Mount, the "narrow path" or the "narrow gate," and that is precisely why we are so violent and on the verge of destroying the planet.

Gandhi thought Matthew's Sermon on the Mount was the greatest writing on nonviolence in history, so he read from it every day for over forty years. He thought that Jesus's prohibition of violent retaliation and killing enemies required that his followers live unarmed and work for justice and peace for all humanity through creative nonviolence. The only way Gandhi could maintain this spiritual path, he concluded, was to use the Sermon on the Mount as a daily handbook, as a personal guide to living nonviolence on a day-to-day level and as a plan for the disarmament of humanity. In that way, the Gospel offered far more than a private religion between me and God alone. It opened an urgent, specific way of life that puts us at the service of humanity and creation so that everyone might live in God's peace.

Gandhi and Dr. King invite us to read the Gospels from the perspective of nonviolence so that the nonviolence of Jesus might disarm us, guide us, and direct our lives, and together, disarm the human family to live in peace as one with creation. If we lived according to Gospel nonviolence as they did, we might become as nonviolent as they were, and together create a more nonviolent world.

How can that be? The Gospels focus on a brown-skinned, Jewish rabbi who was poor, homeless, and a refugee, who walked through ancient Palestine, a backwater of the Roman Empire, preaching and practicing unconditional love, compassion, and justice for the poor and disenfranchised. This Jesus points to the living God as a God of peace and nonviolence, announces God's reign as eternal peace and universal nonviolence, welcomes God's reign of peace and nonviolence here on earth, practices meticulous nonviolence even as he was brutally killed, and commands his followers to practice meticulous nonviolence and build movements of nonviolence to the ends of the earth. Jesus's witness of nonviolence, understood within the examples of Gandhi and Dr. King, is, to say the least, staggering.

Apparently, Jesus was so nonviolent that all you had to do was touch him and you would be healed. I think that's because he didn't have a trace of violence within him. He loved everyone, even as he showed it in different ways. He served the poorest and the disenfranchised, resisted the rich and powerful, spoke the truth with love, denounced injustice and empire, and called everyone to follow him out of the culture of violence into God's reign of nonviolence. One of the first steps he took was to gather a group of followers and form a community of nonviolence around him. He taught and trained these disciples in his way of nonviolence, then sent them ahead of him in pairs on a campaign of nonviolence throughout the Palestinian countryside in a grassroots march toward the holy city of Jerusalem, where the religious authorities cooperated with the Roman occupiers in the name of God to maintain their occupation, control the population, and steal as many resources as they could.

It was in the temple, the center of Jerusalem and Judaism itself, that Jesus turned over the tables of greed and injustice as the final act of his campaign. Such revolutionary civil disobedience could result only in arrest and trial. He was condemned by the authorities, tortured, and executed—yet he remained steadfast in his nonviolence to the bitter end.

Of course, the Gospels are understood as faith testimonies of the early communities that survived Jesus. Their survival alone proves that something unique happened. They say it plainly: he rose from the dead and came back just as nonviolent—and as subversive—as ever. Jesus appeared to his friends and sent them forward all over again to carry on his campaign of creative, disarming, troublemaking nonviolence. Apparently, they did this. His ragtag gang spread their gospel of nonviolence throughout the region and the world, inviting everyone to put down the sword, take up the cross, and become citizens of God's reign of peace, compassion, and universal love. That campaign continues today.

Perhaps the only reason it continues today is because of the Gospels. Through their amazing stories, the Spirit of God has touched people for two thousand years, despite the overwhelming forces of violence, war, and death. For the first three centuries, the early church kept the Pentecostal flame of nonviolence alive as an illegal underground grassroots movement. After Emperor Constantine's supposed "conversion" and his legalization of Christianity, the church began to conform to the surrounding culture of empire, rejecting the nonviolence of Jesus and allowing for violence, killing, and participation in warfare. Some fled to the desert to keep the Gospel way alive. From these desert fathers and mothers came various monastic traditions in which peace was taught and lived. Eventually, St. Francis and St. Clare reclaimed the nonviolence of Jesus. Later, remnant churches such as the Quakers, Anabaptists, and Mennonites put Gospel nonviolence at the center of their traditions. These new communities of nonviolence gave birth to the Abolitionists, Suffragists, and Transcendentalists, and the writings of Leo Tolstoy, Henry David Thoreau, Dorothy Day, and eventually Gandhi and Dr. King.

While most Christians today do not understand the life and teachings of Jesus as a broad vision of daring nonviolence, more and more are beginning to understand that Jesus was nonviolent, not violent, and that every Christian is called to practice Gospel nonviolence.

Four decades ago, I set out to study, research, and discover the insights of nonviolence in the Gospels. I've been speaking about them around the country and the world ever since. This apostolic project of promoting Gospel nonviolence has meant that nearly every day of my life, for over forty years, someone has told me how misguided I am, how violent Jesus actually was, how justified warfare indeed is, and in particular, how holy American warmaking is. If one takes up Gospel nonviolence today, I submit, one had better be prepared to be assaulted on all sides with the myth and lies of the false spirituality of violence.

Recently, however, the Catholic Church took a giant leap forward when Pope Francis published the first statement on nonviolence in the history of the Church. On January 1, 2017, he published his message for the Fiftieth World Day of Peace entitled "Nonviolence:

A Style of Politics for Peace," in which he encouraged everyone to reclaim the nonviolence of Jesus and start working for a new culture of nonviolence.

"Jesus marked out the path of nonviolence," Pope Francis wrote. "To be true followers of Jesus today includes embracing his teaching about nonviolence." He was building on Pope Benedict's statement, calling the command to love our enemies in the Sermon on the Mount "the magna carta of Christian nonviolence. It does not consist in succumbing to evil, but in responding to evil with good and thereby breaking the chain of injustice."

Inspired by Pope Francis's breakthrough, I offer my own little contribution. This book is probably the first ever commentary on the Gospels from the perspective of nonviolence, as lived and taught by Mahatma Gandhi and Martin Luther King Jr. As with other commentaries on the scriptures, I will walk through each Synoptic Gospel, chapter by chapter and verse by verse, but unlike in other commentaries, I will point out the nonviolence of Jesus, his lessons of nonviolence, and its implications for us today. The individual chapters can be read consecutively or kept nearby and consulted during our readings of the Gospels. The strength of this approach is its insistent, persistent, and consistent focus on the total nonviolence of Jesus as a way to break us out of the cultural acceptance and view of violence.

Why Gandhi and King?

Mahatma Gandhi and Martin Luther King Jr. were the greatest teachers and exemplars of active, creative nonviolence in modern history, and both insisted that Jesus was totally nonviolent. Gandhi took the ancient word "*ahimsa*," or "nonviolence," to describe the spiritual life, the path to God, and the best methodology for resistance to tyranny and oppression that can transform cultures of violence into cultures of justice and democracy without using violence or killing anyone. He applied the methodology of nonviolent resistance and social transformation in South Africa and India, where he led a nonviolent revolution to independence from Britain.

In preparation for my book *Mohandas Gandhi: Essential Writings*, I read all of Gandhi's collected works and discovered a vast vision of creative nonviolence that few, if any, have grasped since he was assassinated on January 30, 1948. While India and the world continue to reject his way of nonviolence, his vision and example remain because he was right: nonviolence is the way of God and is therefore at the heart of the spiritual life and every major religion.

"Nonviolence means avoiding injury to anything on earth in thought, word, or deed," Gandhi said, pointing to a seemingly unreachable ideal. For Gandhi, nonviolence is not just the refusal to hurt or kill: it is active love and truth as a force for positive social change. Since he saw it as the force of God, the method of God, the power of God at work for good among the human race, he concluded that nonviolence is more powerful than all nuclear weapons combined. If billions of ordinary people would practice his aggressive nonviolence, with creative, peaceful campaigns against war, nuclear weapons, poverty, racism, injustice, and environmental destruction, then positive social transformation, including nuclear disarmament, the abolition of war and poverty, and true environmental sustainability would occur. Nonviolence always works, he said, because it uses the power of the people to withdraw their consent and cooperation with systemic injustice, violence, and tyranny and to nonviolently demand a new culture of justice, democracy, and nonviolence, even to the point of accepting suffering without retaliating in truth and love to disarm every opponent and oppressor so that all might receive the gift of peace.

"Nonviolence is the greatest and most active force in the world," Gandhi wrote. "One person who can express nonviolence in life exercises a force superior to all the forces of brutality. . . . My optimism rests on my belief in the infinite possibilities of the individual to develop nonviolence. The more you develop it in your own being, the more infectious it becomes till it overwhelms your surroundings and by and by might oversweep the world." Gandhi's vision of active nonviolence was so broad and all-encompassing that he eventually concluded that "Devotion to nonviolence is the highest expression of humanity's conscious state."

When he was a seminarian in Philadelphia, Martin Luther King Jr. was first exposed to Gandhi. Young King attended a lecture on pacifism by the legendary leader of the Fellowship of Reconciliation, A. J. Muste. Inspired, he attended another lecture not long afterwards by Mordecai Johnson, president of Howard University, on the life and philosophy of Mahatma Gandhi. Johnson had just returned from fifty days in India, which included meetings with Gandhi, and spoke of Gandhian nonviolence as a way of life and a proactive methodology for positive social change. That lecture changed King's life. The next day, he bought six books on Gandhi, including Louis Fischer's classic biography, *The Life of Mahatma Gandhi*, which remains one of the best.

King pondered Gandhi as he finished his doctoral studies in Boston and moved to Montgomery, Alabama, where he became pastor of the Dexter Avenue Baptist Church. When Rosa Parks was arrested on December 1, 1955, for refusing to give up her seat on a segregated bus, he was quickly named the new head of the committee to coordinate a citywide boycott to end segregation on buses. From day 1 of the boycott, King intentionally used Gandhi's language and methodology of nonviolence mixed with the teachings and call of Jesus to motivate and encourage the boycotters. This novel approach electrified and empowered the African American community to build a grassroots movement of disarming nonviolence that became a tidal wave of peaceful transformation.

Two months after the start of the bus boycott, King's home was bombed and his wife and baby nearly killed. As a crowd gathered and called for violent retaliation against white people, King gave a spontaneous speech on the ruins of his porch invoking Jesus and Gandhi's way of nonviolence as the only positive response. "We cannot solve this problem through retaliatory violence," he said that night. "We must love our white brothers no matter what they do to us. We must make them know that we love them. Jesus still cries out in words that echo across the centuries: 'Love your enemies; bless those that curse you; pray for them that despitefully use you.' This is what we must live by. We must meet hate with love." This spontaneous speech disarmed the crowd and saved the lives of the white police officers, they later testified.

After the boycott ended successfully with the integration of public transportation, King and Coretta journeyed to India, where they were welcomed by Prime Minister Jawaharlal Nehru and Gandhi's colleagues as Gandhi's heir apparent. From then on, King was wholly committed to active nonviolence and would teach it, preach it, and experiment with it publicly throughout the civil rights movement until the day of his assassination in Memphis on April 4, 1968.

In his book *Stride toward Freedom*, Dr. King outlined six principles of active nonviolence. First, it is a way of life for courageous people; it is not passive, it actively resists evil. Second, it does not seek to defeat or humiliate the opponent, but to win friendship and understanding. Third, it attacks the forces of evil rather than the people who do the evil; it seeks to defeat evil, not people. Fourth, unearned suffering is redemptive; it trains us to accept suffering without retaliating with further violence as we struggle for justice, disarmament, and peace. Fifth, it refuses external physical violence and internal violence of spirit; at its center is the principle of *agapē*/love. Sixth, it believes that the universe is on the side of justice, that we have cosmic companionship, that God is leading us to justice (King, *Stride toward Freedom*, 83–88).

"Gandhi was probably the first person in history to lift the love ethic of Jesus above mere interaction between individuals to a powerful effective social force on a large scale," King wrote. Jesus furnished the spirit, while Gandhi showed how it could work, he added. "The command to love one's enemy is an absolute necessity for our survival," he said later. "Love for enemies is the key to the solution of the problem of our world. Jesus is not an impractical idealist; he is the practical realist."

That last sentence is a paradigm shift in our historic understanding of Jesus. King suggested that we are wrong to read the Gospels as pious platitudes solely for individual practice; rather, they should be read as a practical, down-to-earth, realistic social and political methodology intended for the whole human race. As a Christian deeply rooted in the scriptures, King unpacked Jesus's way of nonviolence in astonishing campaigns against racism, segregation, poverty, and war, first in the South and then throughout the nation. As he was threatened, arrested, and denounced for disturbing the peace, betraying Jesus, and misleading people, he began to unpack new insights into nonviolence that help us understand the Gospels better. We are only now beginning to grasp the theological and spiritual implications of his life and teachings.

For example, Dr. King distinguished between "negative peace" and "positive peace." Negative peace is no peace at all, he said, but a kind of false peace, a veneer of peace, an absence of tension that comes at the expense of justice, which sweeps issues under the rug and maintains an air of civility and the pretense of peace in the midst of systemic injustice, warfare, widespread violence, racism, poverty, nuclear weapons, and environmental destruction. Negative peace leads to complacency and the normalization of violence.

Positive peace, on the other hand, seems loud, messy, disruptive, tense, risky, and frightening as it publicly resists systemic injustice, agitates for justice, and tries to reconcile and create "the Beloved Community." It does not look or feel peaceful at all, because it engages systemic injustice and violence and exposes fear, hostility, hatred, and division in the process of social transformation. It is the peace of peaceful means engaging the culture of violence and war for peaceful ends, and so it demands our full attention, faith, fearlessness, mindfulness, commitment, steadfastness, and forgiveness. In the short term, there seems nothing peaceful about positive peace; but, in the long term, it brings new depths of lasting social peace based in justice.

One of Dr. King's greatest examples of creative nonviolence was his 1963 direct action campaign in Birmingham, Alabama. Thousands of African Americans, mainly teenagers, were arrested by white police officers for marching against segregation. They kept coming forward, even marching into the face of the fire hoses, and one day, a miracle happened— the white firemen put down their fire hoses and let them march. When that happened, segregation fell. King himself spent Easter week behind bars where he wrote his "Letter from a Birmingham Jail," perhaps the greatest document in U.S. history. "We are caught in an inescapable network of mutuality, tied in a single garment of destiny," he wrote in his jail cell. "Whatever affects one directly, affects all indirectly."

> Nonviolent direct action seeks to create a crisis and establish such creative tension that a community which has constantly refused to negotiate is forced to confront the issue. It seeks to dramatize the issue so that it can no longer be ignored. . . . The creation of tension is part of the work of the nonviolent resister. . . . I have earnestly worked and preached against violent tension, but there is a type of constructive nonviolent tension that is necessary for growth. The purpose of direct action is to create a situation so crisis-packed that it will inevitably open the door to negotiation. . . . We who engage in nonviolent direct action are not the creators of tension. We merely bring to the surface the hidden tension that is already alive. We bring it out in the open where it can be seen and dealt with. Like a boil that can never be cured as long as it is covered up but must be opened with all its puss-flowing ugliness to the natural medicines of air and light, injustice must likewise be exposed, with all of the tension its exposing creates, to the light of human conscience and the air of national opinion before it can be cured.

In his letter, Dr. King explained active nonviolence as an organizing methodology and people-power grassroots movement aimed at confronting and transforming injustice, tyranny, oppression, and war into new cultures of justice and peace. King called people to become "nonviolent gadflies who create the kind of tension in society that will help men and women to rise from the dark depths of prejudice and racism to the majestic heights of understanding and brother and sisterhood."

In his description of creative tension, King showed how we can follow the nonviolent, revolutionary Jesus today, by provoking and agitating for God's reign and the end of injustice and empire. His letter brings the Gospels to new life and helps them make sense today. With the help of his letter, we recognize how all that Gospel talk of carrying the cross, proclaiming peace, and renouncing fear makes sense if we are publicly trying to resist the culture of violence and death and welcome God's reign. Every day, King urged movement activists to take up the cross as active nonviolent resistance to structured injustice, perhaps as no one else in U.S. history had ever done before. To his opponents, he said, "We will match your capacity to inflict suffering by our capacity to endure suffering. We will meet your physical force with soul force. Do to us what you will, we will still love you, yet still we cannot in conscience obey your unjust laws. . . ." With these insights, King taught nonviolence as a way of discipleship that can be used in grassroots movements to end the greatest injustices; and, at the time of his death, he spoke of new movements that would emerge around the world to end poverty, racism, war, and nuclear weapons. He was only thirty-nine when they killed him, and still just beginning to unpack the implications of Gospel nonviolence. For example, a few hours before he was killed, he said to Bernard Lafayette,

"Make a note that when this campaign is over, we start to institutionalize and internationalize nonviolence." That work has been left to the rest of us.

Gandhi and King taught and practiced meticulous nonviolence in thought, word, and deed, and insisted that, if we organize together in strategic grassroots movements of daring, public nonviolence, we can transform ourselves, our nation, and the world. Along the way, they both insisted that their spectacular, visionary nonviolence came from Jesus, even though there were few, if any, books suggesting that Jesus was nonviolent or that Christians should be nonviolent. Together Gandhi and King help us understand the Gospel and everything Jesus said and did, and demonstrated that the Gospel was meant to be lived and put into practice for the disarmament of every heart and the entire world.

What Is Nonviolence Anyway?

The Bible never uses the word "nonviolence." Jesus never used it, St. Paul never used it, St. Francis never used it—no one did until Gandhi starting talking about it and writing about it in South Africa. Most people then and now have been confused by this clumsy word. A literal interpretation might mean "avoiding physical violence against others"; and, while many people might avoid physical violence and consider themselves "nonviolent," they would not come close to Gandhi's and King's grand vision of nonviolence. Some might interpret the term to mean refraining from violence or any form of coercion or domination against others, even refusing to condemn or shame others. Others confuse "nonviolence" with "civil disobedience," and think it means peacefully breaking unjust laws to uphold a higher law. Civil disobedience, however, is only one tool in the arsenal of nonviolence, which also includes boycotts, public fasts, vigils, strikes, marches, symbolic actions, and the use of art and music.

My friend Kazu Haga teaches nonviolence to prisoners and distinguishes between hyphenated and unhyphenated nonviolence. "Non-violence" with a hyphen is not what we are talking about. He defines "non-violence" with a hyphen as the absence of physical violence, the lack of physical violence in one's life, a kind of passive pacifism that is unrealistic, unresponsive, reactive at best, and complicit with the culture of violence. The refusal to use violence or any form of coercion or domination against others is definitely part of nonviolence, but just the beginning. If it remains passive and silent, and does not involve active non-cooperation and resistance to the culture of violence and death, then it is not only not helpful; it is part of the problem, if not the very problem itself.

"Nonviolence" without a hyphen, Haga says, refers to something much bigger—the force, power, and Spirit of God's love and truth at work within us and among us communally and globally to disarm our hearts, disarm our world, and welcome the fullness of God's peaceful presence with justice and mercy on earth.

For decades, I've taught that active nonviolence begins with the truth that all life is sacred, that we are all equal sisters and brothers, all children of the God of peace, already reconciled, all one, all already united, and so we could never hurt or kill another human being, much less remain silent while wars wage, people die in poverty, and nuclear weapons and environmental destruction threaten us all. As we deepen into this vision of our common unity, we come to understand that we are one with all humanity, all creatures, all creation, and God. So nonviolence is much more than a tactic or a strategy; it is a way of life that is based in the oneness of creation, the unity of life itself. It is not passive but active love and truth that seek justice and peace for the whole human race and all of creation, and so resists systemic evil and violence, persistently reconciles with everyone, works to create new cultures of justice and peace, yet insists there is no cause however noble for which we support the killing of any human being. Instead of killing others, we work to stop the killing and are even willing to be killed in the struggle for justice and peace.

The visionary nonviolence taught by Gandhi and King flows from our disarmed hearts, from our inner depths, where we renounce our inner violence, let God disarm us and cultivate interior nonviolence, then moves us to practice meticulous interpersonal nonviolence with our families, neighbors, co-workers, communities, cities, nation, all creatures, and Mother Earth. As we face the structures of violence head on with the power of organized nonviolence, we build grassroots, bottom up, people-power movements to end tyranny and injustice and institutionalize nonviolent democracy and social, economic, racial, and environmental justice. When organized on large national and global levels, active nonviolence can peacefully transform entire societies, even the world, as Gandhi demonstrated in India's revolution, as the civil rights movement showed, as the growing women's, LGBTQ, and environmental movements demonstrate, as the People Power movement showed in the Philippines, and as Archbishop Desmond Tutu and the churches of South Africa showed against apartheid. Gandhi said that nonviolence, when it is harnessed, becomes contagious and can disarm the world.

A few years ago, social scientists and scholars Erica Chenoweth and Maria Stephan published a groundbreaking book, *Why Civil Resistance Works*, which studied massive data about every conflict, violent revolution, and war from 1900 to 2006 and concluded that where nonviolence was used, it almost always brought about a more nonviolent, more just, democratic, and lasting outcome than violent methods of resistance. Their research has proved that everything Jesus, Gandhi, and King taught was correct. Nonviolence really does work when it's organized on a mass scale to bring about justice and disarmament.

In an effort to define nonviolence, I proposed in my book *The Nonviolent Life*, that the holistic nonviolence of Gandhi and King demands three simultaneous attributes: we have to be nonviolent to ourselves; at the same time, we have to be nonviolent to all people, all creatures, and Mother Earth; and also at the same time, we have to be part of the global grassroots movement of nonviolence. We can't just pick one or two of these attributes; we have to practice all three at the same time, otherwise it's not the holistic, authentic nonviolence of Jesus, Gandhi, and King.

The Synoptic Narrative of Active Nonviolence

In light of the teachings of Gandhi and King, we will read the three Synoptic Gospels—Matthew, Mark, and Luke—from the perspective of nonviolence for clues about the nonviolence of Jesus. In this new light, we will see him form a community of nonviolence, lead a nonviolence training and teach-in with his Sermon on the Mount, then organize a grassroots movement of nonviolence from Galilee to Jerusalem, where he confronts the imperial establishment and engages in nonviolent civil disobedience, only to be arrested, tortured, and killed, and then rise from the dead to urge his followers to carry on his grassroots campaign of nonviolence to the ends of the earth.

Matthew presents Jesus as the new Moses, the new lawgiver, who gives us something far greater than the Ten Commandments, a whole new series of commandments of nonviolence outlined in the Sermon on the Mount that turns the ways of the world upside down. Mark describes Jesus in daily, ongoing nonviolent resistance to the empire, to violence and death itself, creating tension everywhere he goes to expose latent violence and call everyone to repent and welcome God's reign of nonviolence. Luke presents Jesus as a teacher of compassion, a servant of the poor but, most of all, a movement organizer who trains his followers, building a grassroots campaign of nonviolence that marches to Jerusalem in a final showdown of nonviolent resistance against the structures of injustice. When all hope seems lost, he appears to the downcast disciples, tells them the story of God's nonviolence moving throughout history, and inspires them to carry on his illegal campaign of revolutionary nonviolence.

Written decades after the Synoptics (probably in the 90s, but possibly as late as the 110s), the Gospel of John describes an altogether different story, one that begins with the dramatic civil disobedience in the temple and culminates in the raising of Lazarus as a symbolic, dramatic image of the God of life calling the entire human race, which is stuck in the culture of violence, the tomb of death, back to new life. In this book, I will investigate the nonviolence of Jesus in the Synoptic Gospels. Those who are interested in John's Gospel might want to read my book on John called *Lazarus, Come Forth!*

The Gospels present a vision of nonviolence from the world's greatest visionary of nonviolence, which has never been surpassed and rarely been attempted. At its bottom line, Gospel nonviolence says we are not allowed to kill or support killing or warfare, no matter what the reason, no matter what the authorities declare, no matter how grave the threat we face. There is no cause for which we ever again support the taking of a single life. Instead, the Gospels commend steadfast nonviolence, persistent reconciliation, and all-encompassing inclusion; constructive work for structured justice, disarmament, and equality; lifelong resistance to systemic, nationalistic, imperialistic violence balanced with universal love toward every human being as one's sister and brother and all creatures and creation itself.

If we engage in active nonviolence as the nature of God and the methodology of God as Jesus did, then we will discover that nonviolence is infinitely creative. There are vastly more creative alternatives with nonviolent resistance to evil and injustice than with violent resistance. One might conclude that there is always a nonviolent alternative, including going to our deaths nonviolently as opposed to trying to kill others, or being angry and violent. So, for example, for many people, this challenge comes down to the question, Is self-defense justifiable? When seen through the lens of Gospel nonviolence, we realize, as Gandhi did, a better question is, Is violent self-defense justifiable? The answer becomes no. Nonviolent self-defense is the only justifiable response to violence, according to the Gospel of Jesus. This is the scandal of Jesus, God, and the Gospels. Jesus and the God of Jesus described in the Gospels want us to learn the lessons, methodology, and wisdom of nonviolence.

From the perspective of creative nonviolence, the Gospels present a new image of what it means to be human. In the life of Jesus, we discover that to be human is to be nonviolent, to be nonviolent is to become, like Jesus, fully human. Instead of the inhumanity of violence, which diminishes those who wield it while killing those who suffer it, nonviolence leads us to the fullest possibilities of humanity—to becoming people of universal love, universal compassion, universal solidarity, universal peace, indeed, total nonviolence. That's why Gandhi concluded that nonviolence is the highest form of human consciousness. What is more, he believed that Gospel nonviolence could be applied to communities, nations, and the entire world, and when every human being finally embraces total nonviolence as a way of life, God will reign on earth exactly as God reigns in heaven. "The kingdom of God is nonviolence," he said. This is a profound theological insight that needs to be explored.

A Note about Terms and Language

I have used only the New American Bible as my source. I consider it one of the best translations, if not the best, of the New Testament. It has two sets of excellent footnotes, and I highly recommend it. Before we jump into Matthew, let me mention a few thoughts about inclusive language.

By and large, I have tried to use inclusive language, and I have, on occasion, slightly adapted the text of the New American Bible in this respect. In general, I have tried to avoid male pronouns for God and deliberately tried to use the term "*the God of peace,*" instead of the word "God." I base this entire premise on the Sermon on the Mount, where Jesus makes the scandalous announcement that God is a God of peace and universal love. We read this in his two foundational statements: "Blessed are the peacemakers, for they shall be called the sons and daughters of God" (Mt. 5:9)—and so, "the God of peace"; and, "But I say to you, love your enemies and pray for those who persecute you, that you may be sons and daughters of your heavenly God, for God makes the sun rise on the bad and the good, and causes rain to fall on the just and the unjust" (Mt. 5:44–45). These statements are the basis of the Synoptic Gospels and of my entire argument: God cannot be both warlike and peaceful, violent and nonviolent. God is peaceful, universally loving, and totally nonviolent.

The use of this term, "*the God of peace,*" is in keeping with the Synoptic Gospels and helps us better understand the God being described—not our commonly misconceived image of a violent, warlike, vengeful, punishing God, but a nonviolent, peaceful, universally loving, and compassionate God. I could also have said, "the God of universal love" or "the God of active nonviolence." I'm highlighting this term right up front because I'm not trying to be deceptive or manipulative. You will notice it, for example in the infancy narratives, especially Luke's story of Mary. The danger in using this phrase is that it can project our limited understanding onto the mystery of God to whatever advantage we want, just as if I said "the God of America," "the God of socialism," or "the God of free enterprise," throughout this book, and then wrote, "See how the Gospels support America, socialism, or free enterprise."

Some may object, but I note that St. Paul and many saints used this term, "the God of peace." Pope Francis has even said, "God's name is peace." I find that this term helps us better understand the profound message of Jesus. To me—and I dare say to many, including

Gandhi, Dorothy Day, and Martin Luther King Jr.—it is clear that the message of peace, nonviolence, and universal love pervades the Gospel, that a new way of understanding and naming God is being announced, one that has been so thoroughly ignored and rejected for nearly two thousand years that it sounds like I'm making it all up and describing something new. Instead, with Pope Francis, I'm trying to get us back to the radical message of the Synoptic Gospels: God is totally nonviolent, peaceful, and universally loving and created us to be the same, to be God's beloved sons and daughters who are freely, equally, and totally nonviolent, peaceful, and universally loving.

One of the breakthroughs that a hermeneutic of nonviolence can offer besides a new way of understanding the nature of God is a new understanding of the kingdom of God—as a realm of total nonviolence, where there is no more violence, war, racism, sexism, injustice, hunger, or killing. It is beyond anything we have ever imagined—a place where everyone lives in universal love, universal compassion, and universal peace, in the presence of the God of universal love, compassion, and peace. It is even harder to imagine Jesus's announcement that this otherworldly realm is near and available to every one of us right now. Perhaps that is why the question most frequently asked by Jesus in the Synoptic Gospels is, "To what can I compare the kingdom of God?" Even Jesus didn't know how to explain it! He didn't have the word "nonviolence," so he used parables to describe it and left everyone confused, beginning with the male disciples. It is for this reason that Gandhi came to the brilliant conclusion that "the kingdom of God *is* nonviolence."

So I continue to use the limited and problematic term "the kingdom of God." Sometimes I say, "the reign of God," but both words are rooted in exclusive male language and patriarchy. I do not like the phrases others have tried, such as "the kindom of God," "the community of God," "the family of God," even "the empire of God." Dr. King spoke of "the Beloved Community," which some prefer, but I do not think any of these terms captures the broad, universal vision of Jesus's term or the sharp political semantics featured throughout the Synoptics, especially in Mark. I thought seriously about using the original Greek word employed by the Synoptics—*basileia*—because then no one would be offended, even though that word, too, has overtones of patriarchy. So I have kept Jesus's problematic term, and I am consoled knowing that Jesus himself had difficulty talking about what he most wanted us to know about.

You will also notice that instead of the mysterious phrase "Son of Man" from the book of Daniel, which Jesus uses to refer to himself, I use the term, "*Son of Humanity*," which is slightly more inclusive. As Walter Wink and Ched Myers have written, this term, as I understand it, refers to "the fullest human being," as if to say, "the one who is most truly human, and therefore, the human being most like God." They translate it as "the Human One," or "the Human Being." I believe this mysterious phrase is trying to get at the total nonviolence of Jesus, as both human and divine. So I have used the expression "Son of Humanity" in the hope that it might be a little more palatable to readers, but I agree that it too is clumsy.

In addition, Jesus clearly used the phrase "Father" or "Abba" (meaning "Daddy") to refer to his intimate, beloved God, and nearly every scholar agrees that this was an original teaching of Jesus of Nazareth; no one had ever said this before in history. For many, that patriarchal phrase is another stumbling block, and I have tried in general not to use it, though that too is problematic since it was so original to the text. As we jump into the Synoptics and the ongoing struggles of noninclusive language, the ancient scriptures, and current studies, sensibilities, and awareness, my hope is that we not let our translation problems prevent us from hearing and embracing Jesus's spectacular vision and teachings of total nonviolence and universal love.

Further Points to Keep in Mind

One of the dangers of Gospel commentaries is that, by their very nature, they are repetitive. So scholars agree that the Gospel of Mark was written first, and that Matthew and Luke drew much of their material from Mark, but also from another common source, commonly known as "Q" (from the German word *Quelle*, "source") consisting mainly of sayings, as well as from their own unique sources. Each of the Gospels was composed for a particular audience, and each was shaped by the theological perspective of the individual evangelist. Thus, Matthew and Luke (but not Mark) contain accounts of Jesus's birth, but with different details.

For our purposes, I have tried to highlight the subtle distinctions within the framework of Gandhian/Kingian nonviolence between the three Gospels, but we are inevitably going to return to the same stories and sayings again, some of them occurring in all three Gospels. So a certain amount of redundancy is unavoidable when writing and reading a commentary, and it gets especially challenging by the time we get to Luke, although there is much exciting original material there. So, I urge the reader to be patient and generous and to use my efforts as a help to stir your own reflections on these big Gospel themes and questions about violence, nonviolence, universal love, compassion, discipleship, the cross, resurrection, God, and the person of Jesus. I do not expect most readers to read this book straight through; few people read commentaries straight through. Instead, commentaries become reference books that you keep and refer to for the rest of your life. You can also pray with this commentary over time as you read the Gospels; that is my hope, that it will help you in your reading of the Synoptics and draw you closer to understanding and knowing the nonviolent Jesus.

Over the decades, as I have studied and taught the Gospels and Jesus's nonviolence, I have seen thousands of students, retreatants, and congregation and audience participants project our violence, anger, resentments, hurts, and wounds onto the person of Jesus to varying degrees. We presume that Jesus in this or that instance was angry, yelling, and violent. I propose the shocking alternative that he never succumbed to that behavior. I think he was fully human and fully nonviolent, and that he believed any of us could reach his heights of nonviolence. He was gentle and slow to anger, like Gandhi and Martin Luther King Jr., and my friend the Buddhist Zen master Thich Nhat Hanh. Once, Jesus is described as frustrated by his disciples (after his transfiguration); on another occasion, in response to the harassment of the religious authorities, he lets out "a deep sigh." In the Sermon on the Mount, as we shall see, Jesus clearly forbids anger in the first of the six antitheses in the Sermon on the Mount. I think Jesus did not resort to anger because he saw there the deep hidden roots of violence, but, more importantly, he found a way beyond anger and fear into the grief and joy of creative nonviolence that few have explored. Indeed, there is only one moment in the Synoptic Gospels where we're told that Jesus is "angry" (Mk. 3:5), but, as I write, this is due to a bad translation from the Greek; he was deeply upset and disturbed, which I think is different than anger.

More often than not, Jesus is grieving throughout the whole narrative, which is how I understand Gandhi and King over the course of their public struggles, and my own life experience of public experimentation with nonviolence. There's a profound difference between a grieving, nonviolent Jesus and the projection of our anger onto him, though few seem to consider or understand this. I invite readers to withhold their judgment on this portrayal but instead to meditate with me on the depths of Jesus's gentleness, nonviolence, grief, and unconditional love, and how we might take new steps into his profound nonviolence. (For this insight, I thank my friend Archbishop Desmond Tutu. Once during a visit with him in Cape Town, South Africa, he fell into my arms sobbing, trying to describe to me the nonviolence and grief of Jesus and God. That day, he embodied it to me and demonstrated it. He taught me personally the Gospel path beyond anger and fear through grief, empathy, and nonviolence, to universal compassion and joy, and how that way is far more fruitful and blessed.)

I share these reflections because over the decades, I have been accused of being an absolutist with regard to nonviolence. Let me say up front that this is precisely my point: I am not an absolutist about nonviolence or anything because I am not willing to kill for my beliefs! By its very definition, I submit, absolutism is rooted in violence. That is why I am offering this book. The whole point of this hermeneutic is non-absolutist; people kill one another over their absolute and ideological principles. I am arguing precisely against that, and propose a new hermeneutic that is truly nonviolent, non-ideological, and non-absolutist. That's the good news of the Gospel of universal love and visionary nonviolence.

A major problem I wish to avoid is perpetuating any stereotypes from these texts. As the reader will see, I focus on the narrative and themes embedded in the Gospel stories, not historical-critical interpretation. Of course, I acknowledge that these texts were written decades after the events they describe, and that they were written in part to address the situation and the concerns of the communities that received them. One of the great historical problems with the interpretation of these texts over the past two thousand years has been the horrific rise of antisemitism by Christians. Much of the blame can be placed on John's Gospel, with its regular naming of "the Jews" as the ones who wanted to kill Jesus, which makes no sense since nearly all the characters are Jewish. As Wes Howard-Brook points out, the problem has its source in a mistranslation; the word should have been translated "Judeans."

For the Synoptics, the problem begins with the growth of the early church from the community of Jesus's original Jewish disciples into an increasingly Gentile church. By the time the Gospels were written, they were employing a "supersessionist" theology, or "replacement" theology, which saw the new Christian church as replacing the Old Covenant with Israel, with the Jewish people as the chosen people, the people of God. Today, we roundly reject any notion that the church has replaced Judaism or "superseded" the Jewish people as the people of God. I do not agree with supersessionism and want to avoid any hint of the prejudice and ideology that led to the historic, horrific rise of Christian antisemitism. That goes against the very nonviolence, compassion, and universal love that Rabbi Jesus taught. That means, with this commentary, we want to embark with other scholars and students of the Gospels on a new post-supersessionist reading of the Gospels to find the deeper meaning of Jesus and his message of universal love and nonviolence.

Almost everyone in the Gospels, including Jesus and his disciples, is Jewish. In the Sermon on the Mount, Jesus speaks within the lineage of the Jewish prophets and teaches that his call of universal love and total nonviolence is the point of the law and the prophets. The Hebrew Scriptures and Judaism itself are essential to understanding Jesus and what it means to be a person of peace and nonviolence. The Hebrew Scriptures remain the word of God, the Jewish people remain the chosen people, and we name Jesus as the Messiah, only here we are naming him as a Messiah of total nonviolence, which no one ever expected.

In particular, the Synoptics feature harsh criticism of the Pharisees, to the point that it raises questions about Jesus's own nonviolence. This presumption has led to many grievous misunderstandings, a distorted view of Jesus that contradicts his own teachings, and the demonization of the Jewish people and the rise of Christian antisemitism. The conflicts we read between the Pharisees, scribes, and religious authorities and Jesus have more to do with the situation at the time the Gospels were written, when there was a widening conflict between what became rabbinic Judaism, based in the synagogues, and the emerging church—both of these essentially offshoots of the temple-focused Judaism of Jesus's time. The Pharisees were actually closest to Jesus among the many movements of the time; some scholars have even speculated that Jesus was himself a Pharisee. Although Pharisees did not survive beyond the first century, at the time the Synoptics were written the growing Gentile church began to project onto this group the embodiment of legalism, juridicism, spiritual narcissism, and hypocrisy. Over time, these became attributes projected onto Judaism itself, whereas the evangelists most likely intended their portrayal of the conflict as a warning and cautionary teaching against such tendencies in the church. Actually, Jesus himself calls his disciples to surpass the high bar of righteousness set by the Pharisees. He calls for "perfection," not them; he is the one who makes the Torah even more demanding. While he challenges instances of hypocrisy, he teaches his disciples to adhere to their teachings. Luke even portrays the Pharisees as hospitable and solicitous to Jesus. (For further study, I recommend *The Pharisees*, edited by Joseph Sievers and Amy Jill-Levine [Grand Rapids: Eerdmans, 2021]; for a synopsis, see Chris Seeman, "Scholars Outline History of the Pharisees and Roots of Harmful Anti-Jewish Stereotypes," *National Catholic Reporter*, November 19, 2022.)

We reject any and every trace of anti-Jewish prejudice; reject any projection of attributes such as hypocrisy onto Judaism or Jewish people in general; renounce antisemitism and supersessionism; honor Judaism and the Jewish people; seek to practice nonviolent universal love toward one and all; and lift up the spectacular, prophetic Jewish vision of shalom that is at the heart of Jesus's life, teaching, death, and resurrection. We simply want to explore how Jesus responded to every challenge and trace of violence with loving nonviolence, particularly the harassment he faced from the religious authorities who were rightly threatened by his prophetic stand, revolutionary movement, and widespread popularity.

As we seek to avoid these dangers and pitfalls, we can eventually get beyond the clumsy word "nonviolence" itself and discover, as I have along the way, that the Synoptic Gospels are ultimately about God and present a radical new image of God and God's sovereignty as total nonviolence and universal love announced in the life, teachings, and actions of the nonviolent Jesus. It is this breakthrough vision that I hope we can stay focused on, and all the rich implications it holds for our lives, hearts, souls, politics, and world.

Because they insist that Jesus and God are totally nonviolent, the Gospels demonstrate that Jesus and God, by their very nature, cannot force any human being to disarm and practice nonviolence. With this insight, we step into the mystery of God's gift of free will, which makes much more sense within the framework of Gandhian/Kingian nonviolence. Nonviolence cannot be forced upon anyone; we cannot force people to convert to nonviolence. Like Jesus, we can only invite, persuade, and call one another to the wisdom and way of nonviolence, using every reasonable nonviolent approach possible, including public action and civil disobedience to systemic injustice, and ultimately disarming us and winning us all over through creative, redemptive, suffering love, and innocent martyrdom—the paschal mystery of the cross.

The Gospels portray Jesus as living out the call of Deuteronomy 30:15–20: "I have set before you life and death . . . choose life that you and your descendants may live." Since we are given the choice to accept or reject the fullness of life through God's will of total nonviolence and universal love, it becomes clear through the story and history how we have rejected God's will of nonviolence in favor of our own self will, individually and collectively, which has led us down the endless cycle of violence into war, hostility, hatred, injustice, and now, the real possibility of planetary destruction through nuclear war and environmental destruction. In other words, we are free to choose "death," the culture of violence and war, if we want, and we have done so repeatedly. This is why Dr. King ended his famous "I've been to the mountaintop" speech, delivered the night before he was assassinated, with the declaration: "The choice is no longer violence or nonviolence; it's nonviolence or non-existence."

As we begin to ponder the narrative and teachings of Jesus within the framework of nonviolence, we begin anew to understand the implications of this choice between God's will and our own stubborn, egocentric, self-centered wills, individually and globally. We begin to understand perceived threats of eternal punishment in hell, especially in some of the parables, as "consequence." This does not mean God is violent or unfair; we're being given a choice and it's up to us to choose wisely God's will of nonviolence. The idea of karma is simply about cause and effect—every action leads to a response, a reaction; if you do this, that will happen. In the Sermon on the Mount, Jesus teaches, as Gandhi and Dr. King later insisted, that the means are the ends *in progress,* that you reap what you sow, that what goes around comes around, that every violent deed leads to the inevitable consequence of further violence down the road, including one's own further entrapment in violence.

Another way to consider these difficult passages is to see them simply as warnings. Any loving parent tells their little child not to place her hand on a stove because if she does, it will get burned by the heat of the fire. The parent is not threatening the child but protecting the child. The parent simply does not want the child to get hurt. From this angle, we see how Gandhi and Dr. King never spoke in threatening terms but consistently warned everyone of the consequences of their violence, racism, and warmaking. We see this most dramatically perhaps in the consistent warnings and calls for repentance (as opposed to threats of divine punishment) made by Archbishop Oscar Romero in the months before he was brutally assassinated at the altar while presiding at Mass.

As we read through the text, I invite us to keep in mind the eschatological implications of Gospel nonviolence, and to hear the Gospels as hopeful, good news. Jesus calls us to practice nonviolence in thought, word, and deed, so that everything we do will lead to a nonviolent reaction, so that we will be held safely in the arms of the God of peace while speaking prophetically God's word of peace to the culture of violence and war, and so that our lives will bear the good fruit of creative nonviolence in new levels of disarmament, justice, equality, and an ever-widening universal love.

We are just beginning to apply Gandhian/Kingian nonviolence to ourselves, our communities, our politics, and our world. Likewise, we have hardly begun to develop a theology and spirituality of nonviolence. We need a new generation of scripture scholars to read and teach the Gospels from the perspective of creative nonviolence, and I urge Christians around the world to take up this exciting new approach to the Gospels, the church, and life itself.

My only qualification for daring to attempt this reading is that I am a lifelong activist: I have forty years of experience with experimenting in creative nonviolence at every level, including participating in hundreds of nonviolent protests, getting arrested some eighty-five times, standing in court hundreds of times, and spending many long nights in jails around the country, as well as in war zones around the world. It's my lifelong passion and belief in Gospel nonviolence, coupled with my profoundly hopeful experiences on the ground with creative nonviolence, as well as my faith in the God of peace, the nonviolent Jesus, and the many teachers and practitioners of Gospel nonviolence who have sustained me, that gives me the courage to present the Synoptic Gospels from this fresh perspective. In a world on the brink of destruction, now more than ever, I am learning, the Gospels offer truly good news.

My hope and prayer are that every Christian from now on will read the Gospels from the perspective of Gandhian/Kingian nonviolence, and that with this fresh perspective, we might all choose Jesus's way and wisdom of active nonviolence, that we might carry on Jesus's bottom-up, people-power grassroots campaign of creative nonviolence for global disarmament, justice, and environmental sustainability. May these commentaries inspire you to dig deeper into the Gospels and discover your own insights, that you might follow the nonviolent Jesus ever more faithfully and help spread his way and wisdom of loving, disarming, revolutionary nonviolence far and wide.

Pentecost, 2023

MATTHEW

The Mountaintop Sermon on Nonviolence

Blessed are the peacemakers, for they shall be called the sons and daughters of the God of peace. (Mt. 5:9)

You have heard that it was said, "An eye for an eye and a tooth for a tooth." But I say to you, offer no violent resistance to one who does evil. (Mt. 5:38–39)

I say to you, love your enemies, and pray for those who persecute you, that you may be sons and daughters of your heavenly God, for God makes the sun rise on the bad and the good, and causes rain to fall on the just and the unjust. (Mt. 5:44–45)

*   *   *

Most scholars agree that the Gospel of Matthew was written specifically for the growing community of Jewish Christians and with the intent of presenting to Jews and new Jewish Christians the good news that Jesus of Nazareth is the Messiah who has come to fulfill the law and the prophets. Furthermore, Matthew announces that, contrary to popular expectation, this Messiah is totally nonviolent and, instead of waging a messianic war against the pagan empire, he heralds an entirely new realm of justice, love, and peace.

Matthew describes Jesus as the new Moses who brings new commandments down from the mountaintop, indeed, a new way of life as taught in the Sermon on the Mount. This Messiah refuses to use violence, advocate violence, teach violence, or espouse revolutionary violence to overthrow the Roman Empire and establish the new Jerusalem. On the contrary, he models a new law and new covenant of nonviolence.

Jesus the nonviolent Messiah advocates universal love, universal compassion, and even universal nonviolence. As the fulfillment of the law and the prophets, he proclaims God's reign of nonviolence in which there is neither Jew nor Gentile, male or female, old or young, slave or free, where all are equal, all are loved, and all are welcome—indeed, where every human being is now beheld as a beloved son or daughter of the God of peace. This is the fulfillment of, or end of, institutional Judaism, depending on your perspective.

At the heart of Matthew's Gospel stands the clearest collection of Jesus's teachings on nonviolence in all four Gospels, which we call the Sermon on the Mount. This collection of teachings and sayings outlines the rules, boundaries, guidelines, and vision of nonviolence. It begins

1

with Jesus's eight Beatitudes, then his six antitheses, then a collection of sayings that culminate in the command "Seek first the kingdom of God and God's justice and everything else will be provided for you."

At the center of the sermon are the climactic commands: "Offer no resistance to one who does evil" and "Love your enemies," which I submit are the core of the Gospel, the fundamental centerpiece commandments of Jesus's life. Without these foundational teachings on nonviolence, Jesus's whole argument, life, and death crumble. But because of them, his life stands as the most spectacular manifestation of nonviolence in history. Further, with his call to love our enemies—that is, those targeted by one's nation for death—comes the announcement that those who practice this universal, nonviolent love are truly sons and daughters of the God of universal nonviolent love.

Matthew contains many passages that are unique to his Gospel, such as his infancy narrative (1:18–25; 2:1–23); Peter walking on the water (14:28–33), being given the keys to the kingdom (16:17–19), and being told to find the coin in the fish's mouth to pay the temple tax (17:24–27); Judas's suicide (27:3–10); the dream of Pilate's wife (27:19) and the moment when Pilate washes his hands (27:24–25); the opening of the tombs of patriarchs after Jesus's death (27:52–53); and the guards at Jesus's tomb (27:62–66; 28:11–15).

Matthew's Gospel is filled with references from the Hebrew Scriptures, such as how Jesus's mission work in Galilee fulfills Isaiah (4:13–16) and how his entrance into Jerusalem fulfills Zechariah (21:5). Matthew's original parables include comparing the kingdom of heaven to a field sown with weeds (13:24–30), to a dragnet (13:47–50), to treasure hidden in a field and a pearl of great price (13:44–46). With so much talk about the kingdom of heaven, Jesus will eventually say that it will be given to other people outside the chosen ones, if his commandments are not heeded (21:43). Other parables include the unforgiving servant (18:23–35), the laborers in the vineyard (20:1–16), the two sons (21:28–32), and the wise and the foolish virgins (25:1–13). Matthew alone names Peter as first among the apostles (16:17–19), has the strongest criticism of the scribes and Pharisees (23:1–36), but also praises scribes trained in the kingdom (13:51–52).

Matthew includes a touching invitation of Jesus: "Come to me all you who labor and are heavy-burdened and I will give you rest" (11:28) and the powerful parable of the last judgment by which Jesus teaches how the great king in the kingdom will say, "Whatever you did to the least of these, you did to me" (25:31–46). He also offers specific instructions of reconciliation (18:16–20); and the observation that some people will practice celibacy "for the sake of the kingdom of heaven" (19:10–12).

At first, Matthew sees Jesus as the new Moses, the new lawgiver, come to fulfill the Torah and save the chosen people, to the point that early on, the disciples are told not to go the Gentiles or Samaritans but to "the lost sheep of Israel" (10:5–7). By the end of his Gospel, however, all that has changed. Jesus abhors the hypocrisy of institutional, legalistic religion and demands active solidarity with the poor and outcast, universal love and mercy toward everyone, and the pursuit of justice through steadfast faith, so that, in the end, he extends his arms, his commandments, and his mission to embrace the whole human race.

In the only such resurrection account of the four Gospels, the risen Jesus appears to the disciples back in Galilee once again on the mountaintop where perhaps he first gave his great sermon. *This time he commissions the remaining eleven disciples to go forth and preach and teach his commandments and to baptize everyone and "make disciples of all the nations" (28:16–20). Jesus's visionary, universal love has become a mission for his followers. With a promise that he will always be with us, every follower is sent to practice Jesus's mountaintop sermon commandments of peace, love, and nonviolence, to teach Jesus's mountaintop sermon commandments, and therefore to make disciples of everyone everywhere, even all the nations of the earth, so that every human being might become totally nonviolent, so that God's reign of nonviolence might be fully realized on earth, so that God's will of nonviolence might be done and God's gift of universal peace be welcomed. The story ends there with the Great Commission. We are being sent to make everyone a practitioner of Sermon-on-the-Mount nonviolence.*

Journey to the Mountain: Preparing a Way for the Nonviolent Jesus (1:1–4:25)

The Lineage of the Nonviolent Jesus (1:1–17)

Matthew starts right off in the first sentence telling us that Jesus of Nazareth is a direct descendant of King David and therefore a direct descendant of Abraham. By giving us Jesus's lineage here at the start, Matthew indicates that Jesus is in line to be the Jewish Messiah. Our curiosity is piqued about this person, but we'll soon be in for a surprise when we discover what kind of messiah he is.

By verse 17, we're told "the total number of generations from Abraham to David is fourteen generations; from David to the Babylonian exile, fourteen generations; from the Babylonian exile to the Messiah, fourteen generations." There is a direct line from Abraham to David to Joseph and his betrothed Mary, the mother of Jesus. But this child, we will soon find out, is born in poverty, probably in an animal shed, to impoverished, homeless refugees in remote Palestine on the outskirts of the Roman Empire. How can this helpless child of refugees be born the Messiah?

For Matthew, the lineage of Jesus is crucial. For readers of Matthew's Gospel today, the lineage back to Jesus is crucial—and that's the main point for us. Just as Matthew traces Jesus's lineage back to David and Abraham, we need to trace our lineage back to Jesus. Indeed, toward the end of the Gospel of John, written perhaps fifty years after Matthew's introduction, Jesus will say *you cannot be my follower if you are not part of my lineage*. We know now that this means being part of the lineage of a whole new way of life, one that would express its power through nonviolence.

So as we read these opening sentences filled with ancient names, the question becomes, What is our lineage? How are we connected to the saints and martyrs of nonviolence who trace their lineage back to the nonviolent Jesus?

Practitioners of Gospel nonviolence are those who carry on the lineage of the nonviolent Jesus, from the first apostles and the early peacemaking church to those who upheld nonviolence among the desert fathers and mothers and the early monastics, to the Franciscan movement of nonviolence to the Abolitionists and the peace churches, to the Suffragists and civil rights movements, to the anti-Vietnam War movement, the women's movement, the environmental movement, the anti-nuclear weapons movement, and the thousands of non-violent movements that struggle for justice, disarmament, and a healthy creation today. All of us who join the nonviolent struggle are part of the biblical lineage of the nonviolent Jesus.

To put it another way, as people who live out the Sermon on the Mount and Matthew's Gospel nonviolence, we live so that our lives resemble the lives of the saints and martyrs of nonviolence, from St. Peter and St. Paul, to St. Maximilian and St. Justin Martyr, to St. Francis and St. Clare, to Mary Dyer and Frederick Douglass, Elizabeth Ann Seton and Thérèse of Lisieux, and Adin Ballou to Leo Tolstoy, Mahatma Gandhi to Dorothy Day, Franz and Franziska Jägerstätter, Anne Frank and Etty Hillesum, Abdul Gaffer Khan and Jerzy Popiełuszki, Howard Thurman and Rosa Parks, Martin Luther King Jr. and Fannie Lou Hamer, Daniel and Philip Berrigan, Thomas Merton and Thich Nhat Hanh, Steve Biko and Archbishop Desmond Tutu, Oscar Romero and Ita Ford, Maura Clarke, Jean Donovan and Dorothy Kazel, Ignacio Ellacuría and Dorothy Stang, Dom Hélder Câmara and Mother Teresa, Henri Nouwen and John Lewis, and so many more.

From the opening lines of Matthew, we are invited to explore our own roots and discover how we are directly connected, despite all appearances, to the lineage of the nonviolent Jesus. Or better, we're invited to choose to become part of his lineage of nonviolence. That's the challenge from the start of Matthew's Gospel. Do we want to be part of the lineage of Jesus, this nonviolent yet revolutionary Messiah?

The Epiphany of the Nonviolent Jesus (1:18–2:23)

Matthew's infancy narrative shows how the birth of Jesus fulfills the scriptures, how he is born of the Holy Spirit, how he actually is the Messiah, and how he threatens the empire. In effect, the life of the nonviolent Jesus is previewed in this unique infancy narrative, which is actually an "Epiphany" not only for the holy Magi but for us as well. From the get-go, Jesus relives the exodus experience on the way to becoming the new lawgiver of nonviolence. But if we read the fine print, we realize that, even at the start, we are in the presence of the God of peace.

We're told that Joseph is "a righteous man"—that is, one who keeps the Mosaic law—and "a son of David." In a dream, an angel tells him not to be afraid to accept Mary and the child. Dreams and angels are common in the Hebrew Scriptures, and here they reinforce the unique holiness of the child. Altogether, we are told he is the savior of all people from their sins, Emmanuel in whom "God is with us," the newborn king of the Jews, and the Son of God. Now we know that the prophecies of the scriptures have all led to this holy child. All of this is preparation: we now know that whatever he says and does as an adult is to be taken with the utmost seriousness.

Then we're told that when Jesus is born, the whole world reacts. Creation itself responds with a bright star hovering in the dark sky over the village of Bethlehem. Magi bearing gifts arrive from the East, following the star, to do homage to the newborn king. Right away, we understand that Jesus's message and mission are universal, for the whole human race, not just the chosen people.

Then we're given the news that the tyrant King Herod has heard rumors about this "new-born king" and is greatly disturbed along with "all of Jerusalem." The birth of the powerless child is already a threat to the most powerful, warmaking person in the region, as well as to all who live in fear under the status quo. The tyrant gathers together the religious authorities, whom he keeps under his control, and asks for the birthplace of this "holy" Messiah, and they name Bethlehem. Herod claims to want to do homage himself, but, as we know, like a typical ruler, he lies. His sole intention is to kill the child. Tyrants always want to kill those who threaten their power—even unarmed, helpless, powerless infants. But what Herod doesn't know is that the unarmed child has come to end the entire global cycle of imperial violence, injustice, and war.

The Magi rejoice when they see the star. They follow it and find Mary and the child, where they prostrate themselves in homage and offer the child gifts. Note that we're never told there are three Magi, only that they offered three gifts.

The strangeness and the politics continue. In a dream, the Magi are warned not to return to Herod, so they go home a different way. Joseph is warned in a dream to flee from Herod's armies, so he takes Mary and the holy child and journeys to Egypt. Herod is furious to discover that the Magi deceived him, so he issues an order to kill every boy age two years and younger in Bethlehem and its surrounding area. Here we see the policy of every government and imperial leader in history: to murder anyone who threatens their power. From this we conclude that this child is born to begin the nonviolent transformation that will end the killings and give birth to a global reign of nonviolence. Later, Joseph will take Mary and the holy child back to Israel, but instead of returning to Judea, he will settle them in Galilee—that is, in the middle of nowhere, in the village of Nazareth.

The story of the visitation of the Magi has become known through the ages as "the Epiphany," that quintessential moment when we suddenly realize we are in the presence of God. The Epiphany of the Magi sums up Matthew's Gospel story of our journey to the nonviolent Jesus. Like these wise men, we're on a journey, a holy pilgrimage throughout our lives to find the holy Christ. In their story we see the three movements of the spiritual life: the journey to Christ, the Epiphany of our encounter with Christ, and how that Epiphany changes the direction of our lives.

In the first movement of the spiritual life, we, like the Magi, set out on a pilgrimage in search of the Christ. From the start, we read that the spiritual life, the journey to Christ, the path of universal love and total nonviolence, has political implications. The wise men follow the "rising star," the "rising" light, and fearlessly ask to meet the horrible King Herod to inquire about "the newborn king." Herod is "greatly disturbed along with all of Jerusalem" about a rival king, and he summons the Magi and asks them about the star and the holy child and pretends to be religious and interested in God. Unfortunately for King Herod, the wise men actually are devout and serious, and they are determined to seek this new holy Messiah, so they go ahead with their journey and follow the star, and that's what we have to do! Like the holy Magi, we have to decide that, no matter what anyone else says, no matter what the culture says, no matter what the president says, no matter what the political consequences are, we are going to seek the holy Christ, worship him, do what he says, live our lives according to him and his Gospel—and disregard everything else!

The wise men are from the Persian priestly caste in the East, present-day Iraq and Iran. They are seekers, wisdom figures, and they are Gentiles, non-Jews. With their arrival, we know now that this holy child is a *universal* person, destined to save all people, not just the chosen people. The first thing these Eastern priests do is confront King Herod: "Where is the newborn king of the Jews?" From the start, this is a political story involving confrontation with the ruler. "We saw his star at its rising and have come to do him homage," they say. The famous Magi are saying, "We do not worship you or the emperor but God's incarnation among the poor, the Messiah." This is not going to go over well with Herod.

Herod and "all of Jerusalem" are troubled when they hear this. Political rulers cannot bear not being divine. They think they have the power to do whatever they want and to kill whomever they want. In particular, empires and government leaders despise children, as we see today in the way millions suffer in poverty and hunger. So they try to co-opt the Magi. Herod calls the Magi secretly to find the time of the star's appearance and says he wants to worship the child. Of course, he's lying. He tells them, "Go and search for the child. When you have found him, bring me word, that I too may go and do him homage." He's suddenly pious, but he's planning to murder the child, which is what he will do to protect his power over the poor. Here we see the outward, false piety of government officials, military rulers, and the murderous, inner violence that rules their hearts. This, in a nutshell, is the way of the world.

So the Magi set out, see the star in the sky, and follow it. It's as if the whole universe points to the holy Christ. The Gospel invites us to take a contemplative stance toward creation, to pay attention to the sun, the moon, the stars, and all God's creation, and to follow the light. If we look closely, we will find God in them and be led to the holy Christ. But we have to open our eyes, take a risk, take a step forward, look for the "rising" light and follow where creation will lead us, which is usually out of our comfort zone.

If you open yourself to creation and its path to Christ, you will discover a much bigger picture than the narrowness of government, nation, rulers, and the ever-present violence used to maintain power and wealth. Suddenly, the universe becomes real, and you feel the presence of God. If we dare follow the "rising" light of creation with all our hearts, Matthew suggests, we will meet the Christ.

The second movement of the spiritual life is the encounter with the newborn king, the "epiphany" of meeting Christ. An "epiphany" is a sudden realization that we are in the presence of God. The Magi enter the stable, see the holy child with Mary his mother, and are filled with joy. They immediately praise God and worship God. They prostrate themselves and do the child homage. They offer three gifts: gold (which is what you give a king); frankincense (which is what you give a high priest); and myrrh (which is used to care for a dead body. I've often wondered how Mary felt receiving the gift of myrrh at the birth of her child).

Like the Magi, each of us can set off on a spiritual journey to Christ and have an epiphany moment when we realize we are in the presence of Christ, when our hearts are filled with joy, we worship God, and we give our gifts to Christ. I think the point of life is to seek Christ and to be ready for those epiphany moments, to be on the lookout for Christ and to prepare for epiphanies.

The third movement of the spiritual life is how our lives change after we meet Christ, how, like the Magi, we go home a different way. We have changed, our worldview has changed, and so our direction, our journey, has changed. Once we meet Christ, we no longer cooperate with the empire or the rulers or King Herod or the president. Once we meet Christ, our allegiance has shifted. From now on, our allegiance is solely to Christ. As people on the spiritual journey, we worship the Christ and do what he says—and live a new pilgrimage in his light.

When the Magi refuse to go back to Herod and turn toward home on a different route, they commit nonviolent civil disobedience. They disobey the ruler and could be killed for this unlawful behavior. Their disobedience infuriates Herod, who wants to kill his rivals and maintain his imperial power. The Holy Family flees to Egypt, while Herod sends out his troops to massacre every little boy under two years of age in Bethlehem and its vicinity. He wants to destroy anyone who might threaten his power, even a helpless, vulnerable baby. Just as the Magi disobey the ruler in order to obey God, so all who have encountered the holy Christ from now on are willing to disobey imperial rulers who order massacres, wars, and bombing raids. From now on, our allegiance is to the nonviolent Christ we have met and experienced, and we accept all the social and political implications of that encounter. Once we meet the God of nonviolence, our first act is an act of worship and our second act is to disobey the false gods of violence and the imperial ruling authorities who kill and wage war, then and now.

Why do we disobey the ruling authorities of the world, no matter what our nationality? Because we are Sermon-on-the-Mount people who practice universal love, and therefore we oppose all wars, killings, and injustice. We, too, have heard the cry of Rachel in the desert, weeping for her children, in the village of Ramah (Jer. 31:15). Rachel's lament can be heard all the way to Jerusalem. Today, her cry can be heard around the world. Only the deaf cannot hear her—or those who have hardened their hearts.

Today, our country and other countries continue to kill the holy innocents around the world. As people who worship and obey the holy Christ, our task is to non-cooperate with the rulers who kill the innocents and to resist them, to defend the children, and to stop their slaughter. If we are epiphany people who have met Christ, we are no longer on the side of murderous rulers or warmakers. We live according to the nonviolent Christ we have met, and we adhere to his teachings on universal love and active nonviolence.

Here are a few conclusions about the birth of the nonviolent Jesus and the Epiphany of the Magi. First, God does not come to the rich and powerful but to the poor and powerless. That is as true today as it was then. If you want to meet God, go to the poor and powerless. Second, God is not found in the center but on the margins. Here lies the fundamental mistake of history. We presume that God dwells at the center, with the rich, powerful, famous, and beautiful. No. God is on the margins with those no one else wants to be with. Third, God is born among homeless people, refugees, migrants, the undocumented, immigrants, those with no country, those with no security, those with no money. Also, God is born in nature. Therefore, God is found in nature. Therefore, nature, creation, points to God. With the story of the Magi, we know that God is for all people, for the Magi are not the chosen people but Gentiles, and they are the ones who receive the holy child.

Further, epiphanies happen at night. They are journeys toward God, but they take place in the dark. The sudden spiritual experience of God's presence comes after a long journey at night. Epiphanies require following stars, attending to creation, which means risking appearing foolish in the eyes of the world. In other words, we have to become contemplatives if we want to have an epiphany.

Epiphanies require community. Notice that the Magi travel together, not as individuals. They seek the holy child together as a community. They worship together as a community. They share joy in the presence of Jesus together as a community, and they disobey the warmaking government as a community.

Epiphanies are political. They become acts of nonviolent resistance to empire and warmaking. They lead us to the God of peace, and the experience of God leads us away from the warmaking rulers. Thus, epiphanies are life-and-death journeys. They involve risk. They require dropping everything to go after the Holy. They are scary and take us into the unknown. Epiphanies get us in trouble. They disrupt our lives. That's what happens if we want to seek Christ. Our lives get disrupted.

And so, epiphanies are journeys into the margins of the world, among the homeless, the poor, and the refugees. Epiphanies call us to religious tolerance. Mary and Joseph are Jews, and they welcome the Magi, non-Jews; so, like Mary and Joseph, we respect all religions and all cultures. Epiphanies fill us with joy and lead us to worship God and offer gifts to God. When we meet God, we are filled with joy. These are contemplative experiences of prayer and praise because they are encounters with Christ.

The story of the Epiphany is a metaphor of our own pilgrimage through life to Christ. Matthew's infancy narrative and Epiphany story sum up the life of the nonviolent Christ. As we reflect on this text, we can ask ourselves: Where are we in the epiphany story? How are we seeking Christ in our lives? How does creation point us to God? When and where have we encountered Christ? What gifts do we bring to Christ? How has our encounter with Christ, our "epiphany," changed our lives? How has Christ set us off in a different direction, in opposition to the violence of the world? How do we disobey the political, warmaking authorities who kill children?

Eventually, after having relived the exodus experience, Joseph will take Mary and the child back to Israel—not to Judea, where Herod's cruel son now rules, but to the remote region of Galilee, to the tiny village of Nazareth, where the boy can grow in wisdom and peace.

John the Baptist, the Baptism of Repentance, and the Temptations of Violence (3:1–4:11)

Fast forward: Jesus has grown up, left home, and set off into the desert to be with God and to discern his vocation. Perhaps the reason he does this is because Elijah has appeared on the scene. Throughout the scriptures, we have been told that Elijah will reappear just before the coming of the Messiah.

Elijah is none other than John the Baptist. He appears in the desert dressed like Elijah, crying out to all who will hear, "Repent, for the kingdom of heaven is at hand!" This is the one whom Isaiah prophesied, we are told, the one who declares, "Prepare the way of the Lord; make straight his paths."

In fact, something is happening out there in the boondocks. People come from all directions to be baptized by the holy man. They are told to repent, and they do. In his presence, they return to God, receive forgiveness, and start their lives all over. This is a huge breakthrough.

To repent is to turn around; that is, we change direction. Presumably, we are realizing that everything in our former direction is a dead end.

What does the great man want us to repent from? Every trace of violence! From the entire culture of violence, from injustice, war, empire, and idolatry. Turn from all that, and walk toward justice and peace and the God of justice and peace.

John the Baptist is a fiery prophet of social justice in the long tradition of the Hebrew Scriptures. Compared to the Messiah who will soon appear, John seems a bit ambivalent about violence. He doesn't sound like a full-blown teacher of loving nonviolence. He seems angry and announces who's to blame: the religious authorities and their imperial backers. "You brood of vipers!" he tells them. "Who warned you to flee from the coming wrath? Produce good fruit as evidence of your repentance."

"Don't presume that Abraham is your father," he continues. Here he challenges their lineage. We readers know that Jesus is a descendant of Abraham, and we would presume that these religious authorities must be as well, but John challenges that presumption head-on with a teaching Jesus will repeat in the Sermon on the Mount: You will know them by their fruits. "Every tree that does not bear good fruit will be cut down and thrown into the fire," John says. Make sure your life bears good fruit. Do not bear bad fruit, rotten fruit, useless fruit. Bear good fruit.

Matthew's fiery John speaks of a baptism for repentance but points to the coming of Someone greater. "I am baptizing you with water, for repentance, but the one who is coming after me is mightier than I. I am not worthy to carry his sandals. He will baptize you with the Holy Spirit and fire." In this way, he models the life of every follower of Jesus to come: from now on all of us point to Someone mightier than ourselves: the nonviolent Jesus.

When Jesus arrives, John baptizes him, even though John is confused about his own role in the Mighty One's life. As Jesus rises from the water, the heavens open and the Spirit of God descends like a dove upon him. Then a voice comes from heaven saying, "This is my beloved Son, with whom I am well pleased."

This, I submit, is the key moment in the life of Jesus, the turning point, the occasion when he realizes who he is. From now on, he knows that he is the beloved of God. Unlike the rest of us, he accepts this calling as his true identity. Later, he will instruct us that God loves everyone universally and wants everyone to be God's beloved son and daughter. But as we see today and throughout history, few accept this calling as their core identity. I suggest that, unlike anyone else in history, Jesus accepts his fundamental identity as the beloved of God. "Okay," he says as he rises from the water, "I will be the beloved of God." From then on, he will be faithful to his beloved God. Because he encountered a gentle, loving God in his baptism, he taught, from then on, that we could trust God's gentle love with us, always. This, in a nutshell, is the entire Gospel.

So this moment by the Jordan River is the key, transformational moment in the life of Jesus, the beginning and explanation of everything to come. This is when he discovers who he is. This is when he commits to being who he is called to be. This is the moment he lived out until his dying breath on the cross—the moment of intimate relationship with his beloved God.

If we have ears to hear, this is the key moment in our lives too. If we want to be followers of this beloved Jesus, then we need to hear God tell each of us, "You, too, are my beloved, with whom I am well pleased," and claim this as our fundamental, spiritual identity. Later, in the Sermon on the Mount, Jesus will unpack this teaching. As God's beloved sons and daughters, we will strive to live exactly as Jesus lived. As we shall discover in our journey through the Gospels, this means we will become peacemakers.

Every Christian wants to rise from the waters of baptism with the peacemaking Jesus, and hear him call us "My beloved." With Jesus at the River Jordan, we too want to be included in that universal loving embrace, which means that we pledge to start acting as if we, too, are God's beloved sons and daughters, who live out the principles and passions modeled by Jesus. Here, at the beginning of Jesus's vocation, we find our own vocations as well.

With this shocking pronouncement, Jesus heads off into the desert to reflect on this calling to be God's beloved. There in the wilderness, he will feel it, explore it, test it, and discern it. He will realize that to be God's beloved is to act as God's beloved, which means he will have to embody universal, nonviolent love toward the entire human race. If we dare claim to be his followers, we too will have to learn the same lesson and strive for the same high ideal.

So Jesus is led by the Spirit into the desert, where he is forced to face the demons of doubt and violence. He fasts for forty days and nights, and is hungry. The tempter approaches him three times to get him to renounce his vocation as the beloved. Notice: each temptation begins with the phrase, "If you are the Son of God . . ." It is a challenge, a question, a doubt. How could you, you "nobody," you nothing, be the Son of God? The challenge confronts his followers as well.

This challenge holds the key to salvation. At the heart of the matter is the question of identity. *Who does he think he is? Who does he think God thinks he is?* As his followers, who do we think we are? This is the challenge of his baptism and our baptism. Who do we think we are? In fact, we dare claim to be followers of the nonviolent Jesus, and therefore sons and daughters of the God of peace, and so we dare go forth as people of universal love, universal compassion, universal peace, and total nonviolence. We know who we are.

Each of the three temptations is a temptation to violence. Jesus will reject each one of them, claim his identity as the beloved of the God of peace and love, and thus break new ground and pave the way for a future of nonviolence.

First, the tempter says, "If you are the Son of God, command that these stones become loaves of bread." Jesus replies, "It is written: 'One does not live by bread alone, but by every word that comes forth from the mouth of God.'" This is the temptation to despair, to seek immediate results, quick inhuman solutions, the temptation to play God. Think about it: if Jesus turned stones to bread, he could end world hunger! But then he would be just a magician and not like the rest of us. He would no longer be human.

Jesus is determined to be human, and he tells the tempter that the way to be human is to live by every word that comes from the mouth of the God of peace. We do not bring the results; God does. God feeds us, teaches us, and instructs us, and faithful humans follow God's lead. That's all that matters. (Later on, as we study his multiplication of the loaves and fishes, we will learn that the real miracle is how Jesus inspired the crowd of thousands to share the food they brought with everyone else around them! It wasn't magical at all, but a beautiful change of heart among people that came about because they first obeyed the word of God spoken by Jesus.)

Then we're told the tempter took Jesus to the holy city and made him stand on the parapet of the temple, and said, "If you are the Son of God, throw yourself down. For it is written: He will command his angels concerning you' and 'with their hands they will support you, lest you dash your foot against a stone.'" Jesus answered him, "Again it is written, 'You shall not put the Lord, your God, to the test.'"

This is the temptation to doubt, which always leads to violence and self-destruction. Notice that the forces of violence and death are always trying to harm or destroy Jesus, and all of us. We get tempted to doubt God every moment of the day, and every time we give in to doubting God, then we forget the meaning of life and how God calls us "My beloved," and we make bad decisions and give in to the culture of violence and its insanity. Throw yourself off a building and let's see if God catches you, if you really believe in God. If you have trouble understanding these connections—that's precisely the point! It's all crazy: doubting God, testing God's love, and throwing yourself off the temple in some spectacular public act of violence. Jesus knows that reality is not made like that. God created us to follow the boundaries of natural law, including the law of gravity, but also, the new law of nonviolence. We do not harm ourselves, or threaten ourselves, or test God. We do something much more radical: we trust God, and live according to God's law of love.

Finally, we're told that the tempter took Jesus up to a very high mountain, and showed him all the kingdoms of the world in their magnificence, and he said to him, "All these I shall give to you, if you will prostrate yourself and worship me." "Get away, Satan!" Jesus replies. "It is written: 'The Lord, your God, shall you worship and God alone shall you serve.'"

Here, we have the temptation to domination. It is a temptation to power, to be God, to rule over others—ultimately, to rule the world. And it comes with the loss of our souls. Once we choose worldly power for ourselves, we are no longer the beloved sons and daughters of the God of peace. We are sons and daughters of the culture of domination. We end up worshiping the idols of violence, war, and death.

The nonviolent Jesus will have none of it. "Get away, Satan!" he declares. "Satan" is code language for the Roman Empire, the culture of death. We could translate it today as "America," or any country with imperial pretensions. We worship the God of peace alone. We serve the God of peace alone. We do not serve any nation, any empire, any weapons of destruction, any kingdom, or even the whole world. We belong solely to the God of peace, which means that we worship no other.

If we are to reject the temptations of violence as Jesus did, we need to turn from the culture of violence and war and embark on his new Gospel path of nonviolence and peace. That will mean living off every word of his in the Gospel for the rest of our lives. That means we will not test God but trust God and stay within the law and boundaries of nonviolence. And that means we will reject worldly power, the power of violence, injustice, war, and death, and choose instead the power of nonviolence, which appears to the world as powerlessness but is actually the power of God to transform the world. We will not dominate or rule over anyone, much less the world. We will worship and serve the God of peace and nonviolence every day of our lives.

In a touching coda, we're told that the tempter left Jesus and angels came and ministered to him. The lesson for us is that if we choose nonviolence like Jesus, if we reject every temptation to violence, if we reject despair, doubt, and domination, the angels of God will likewise come and minister to us. Once you embark on the path of Gospel nonviolence in the footsteps of the nonviolent Jesus, angels will appear to you along the way to encourage your every step. This, too, is a law of nature.

Remembering that we are the beloved sons and daughters is the key to living Gospel nonviolence as disciples of the nonviolent Jesus. Once we know who we are, we see every human being on earth as our very sister and brother because they too are daughters and sons of the God of peace, and therefore we could never hurt anyone ever again, much less be silent in the face of war, injustice, or poverty. The minute we forget that we are God's beloved sons and daughters, then we no longer know who we are, and we no longer recognize other human beings as our brothers and sisters, and so we descend into violence and death. *That's why we can define violence as forgetting or ignoring who we are and who we are called to be.*

The Nonviolent Jesus Takes Up John's Announcement: "The Kingdom of Heaven Is at Hand!" (4:12–17)

As soon as he hears that his mentor John has been arrested, Jesus withdraws to a quiet place by the Sea of Galilee, where he decides to take up where John left off. There, in the village of Capernaum along the Sea, he will launch his global campaign of nonviolence. Matthew quotes the prophet Isaiah to say that "the people who sit in darkness have seen a great light, on those dwelling in a land overshadowed by death light has arisen." Light has come into darkness. Light has to come to the land overshadowed by death. Indeed, the light has risen. The shadow of death that overshadows the land is none other than the Roman Empire, its army and systems of local economic control. Jesus has come to shed light upon the darkness of empire and its systems, and call people out of empire, out of the darkness of violence and oppression, out of the culture of death. That is his mission.

"From that time on," we are told, Jesus began to repeat John's announcement and to teach about it: "Repent, for the kingdom of heaven is at hand."

This is the beginning of the disarmament and nonviolent transformation of the world. Here we are in one of the poorest places on earth, on the outskirts of the brutal empire, and we're told that here, of all places, "The kingdom of heaven is at hand." (Note that Matthew prefers to use the word "heaven" rather than "God.") As we hear this, we recall that after every Roman victory, the Roman troops would proceed to the next town and announce another great victory for Caesar, the gospel of Caesar, the good news. But here it's a different Gospel, a different kingdom, a different ruler. It's pure revolution. He might as well say, "The empire is over. The days of violence and war are over. Welcome into the new culture of justice and peace. Turn, and enter this new realm with me."

As followers of the nonviolent Jesus, we allow this announcement to outline the rest of our lives. From now on, we are people who repent; that is, we actively, consciously turn away from the culture of violence, war, and death, and actively, consciously turn toward the kingdom of God, a new culture of nonviolence, peace, and eternal life. From now on, our lives are about the kingdom of God—not our careers, not money, not success, not making a name for ourselves. Everything we do is at the service of the coming of God's reign of peace here on earth. We try to live in the presence of God and practice what we experience in God's reign: universal love, universal compassion, universal peace, and total nonviolence. That means, of course, our number-one task is to confront indifference, hate, war, and violence in all its forms.

We practice eschatological nonviolence; that is, we act as if we are already in the kingdom of God, here and now, on earth. This is the beginning of Gospel nonviolence. We now live and act first and foremost as citizens of the kingdom of God.

The Call to the Discipleship of Nonviolence (4:18–25)

Walking by the sea, Jesus throws out his net for his first catch. He calls two sets of fishermen brothers to follow him. "Come after me," he says, "and I will make you fishers of men and women." They take the bait. They drop their nets, leave their fathers and their families, walk away from their livelihood, and follow him—for the rest of their lives. They are the first of many.

The initiative always comes from the nonviolent Jesus. He calls everyone to follow him on the path of nonviolence into God's reign of nonviolence. The challenge is to hear his call and take the leap, and to continue the discipleship journey all the way to the end. In this world broken by violence, accepting the call of Jesus to enter his realm of nonviolence is the greatest thing we can do with our lives. That is why we remember the first disciples—because they dropped everything to follow Jesus. And he wants disciples. He needs a community of friends around him to carry on his campaign to make God's kingdom visible here on earth. If we dare join Jesus in his campaign, more will happen than if we tried to go on our own. Our lives are infinitely richer if we let go of everything and follow Jesus. Besides, there is no one else worth following who can compare with him. Even great saints like St. Francis and St. Clare, Gandhi and Dorothy Day, Dr. King and Oscar Romero would agree. Like St. Paul they would insist: don't follow me, follow the nonviolent Jesus wherever he is leading you. He's the only one worth following.

After Jesus calls them, he sets off on his walking campaign with the fishermen in tow. He preaches peace, love, and nonviolence everywhere he goes, to everyone he meets and invites everyone to seek the kingdom of God here and now. When sick people approach, he reaches out, touches them, and heals them. Overnight, word spreads and crowds gather. Huge numbers of people begin to follow him, seek his healing, and listen to his teachings. As his followers watch, he models the new life he wants for everyone, so that everyone practices peace, heals one another, and proclaims God's new reign at hand.

Disciples of the nonviolent Jesus spend their lives teaching nonviolence, healing the broken and wounded, and proclaiming the coming of the kingdom of heaven, God's reign of peace. As we translate this ancient announcement into today's language, that means we announce the abolition of war, poverty, racism, sexism, greed, gun violence, nuclear weapons, environmental destruction, and systemic injustice, and the pursuit of a new culture of justice for the poor, disarmament, nonviolence, and environmental sustainability. In this way, we give hope to people and inspire them to join Jesus's campaign to disarm and transform the world of violence.

As the number of disciples increases and more and more people gather around him, Jesus decides to sit them down and teach them everything about this new life. So he climbs a mountain by the Sea of Galilee and starts to teach them the vision, the details, the practice, and the new commandments of life in God's coming reign of peace, love, and nonviolence.

The Great Mountaintop Sermon on Nonviolence (5:1–7:29)

Jesus climbs the mountain, sits down with the disciples around him, and becomes the new Moses who issues a new set of commandments. Unlike those of Moses, these are not negative prohibitions but positive exhortations. Instead of "Thou shalt not . . . ," he says, "Thou shalt. . . ."

In the Sermon on the Mount, Jesus offers some of the world's greatest teachings on nonviolence. He starts with the Beatitudes, then the six antitheses, then a series of teachings on nonviolence, and, finally, a few parables. These three chapters offer the solutions to every problem and issue, personally and globally, from practices for personal peace to a social, economic, and political methodology for a new future of peace. There is simply nothing else like it.

Even so, relatively few people study the Sermon on the Mount. If this is Jesus's quintessential message, then the lack of attention to it is shocking. We can debate the words of Moses, Samuel, David, and Paul inside and out, and put them on the same plane as Jesus's words, or even give them greater import than Jesus's teachings. We take the Bible as a whole, with all its images and stories of violence, as if they equal the message of Jesus. Yet we do not give equal attention to Jesus's teachings on universal love, compassion, and peace. It's as if not one church in the world aspires to embody these core principles of Jesus, as if few have ever read them.

Except for Mahatma Gandhi. He read from Matthew chapter 5 pretty much every day of his life, during his morning and evening public, one-hour meditation. For him, this was the greatest instruction on nonviolence, almost like a handbook on how to be nonviolent, how to be human. For Gandhi, it was a text worth returning to every day. It laid out the guidelines of his life.

Gandhi offers a model for every one of us. He was not a Christian, but he lived his life according to the Sermon on the Mount and let the teachings shape his decisions. He demonstrated how every Christian should be living—according to the words of Jesus, starting with the great Sermon on the Mount. I propose that Christians around the world spend thirty years studying and practicing only the Sermon on the Mount and the Gospels; only then can they turn to Paul and other texts. We need to know the Sermon on the Mount inside out and try to experiment with it. Our goal should be to do what Gandhi did—to read from the Sermon on the Mount daily and let Jesus's teachings guide our day-to-day lives, determine our choices and decisions, and form us into authentic Sermon-on-the-Mount people. If we each tried to do this, we would be greatly blessed, and God's work of disarming the world could begin in earnest.

The Beatitudes of Nonviolence (5:3–12)

To understand the Beatitudes, it's helpful to remember that they were originally spoken in the ancient language of Aramai, not in Greek or Hebrew. In her book *Blessings and Woes: The Beatitudes and the Sermon on the Plain in the Gospel of Luke,* Megan McKenna suggests that instead of beginning with the familiar words, "Blessed are . . . ," each Beatitude should begin with the phrase, "Get up, get moving, and do something, you who are . . ." (20–22). In my book *The Beatitudes of Peace,* I conclude they should each begin with the phrase, "Arise and walk forth." Imagine how empowering Jesus's Beatitudes would be if in fact they each began: "Arise, get up, get moving, start walking, walk forth and do something, you who are poor, mournful, meek, hungering for justice, merciful, peacemaking, and persecuted!"

This sounds like the nonviolent Jesus: he empowers poor, oppressed, rural Galileans to get up and get moving and live out their calling as the sons and daughters of the God of peace, to live as if they were already in the kingdom of heaven. The Aramaic version includes hints of resurrection, walking, and discipleship. With this commandment to "Rise and go forth!" Jesus begins to send his followers out as sheep into the midst of wolves, as nonviolent campaigners commissioned to disarm everyone and prepare for God's reign of peace on earth.

"Blessed are the poor in spirit," Jesus begins, "for theirs is the kingdom of heaven" (5:3). The first words of his sermon concern the poor and the economics of God's reign. Luke's version says bluntly: "Blessed are the poor; woe to the rich." In each case, Jesus insists that the poor, the powerless, those empty of spirit, have one thing the rich do not have: the reign of God.

With these opening words, Jesus takes sides. He sides with the poor, the powerless, and those at the bottom of society, and he empowers them to live in God's reign in total trust of God. In doing so, he calls disciples and all of us to let go of power, prestige, privilege, possessions, and money; to share our hearts and lives with those in need; and to practice downward mobility for the rest of our lives as we surrender ourselves into the hands of God.

The poor already have the reign of God, Jesus says, so stand with the poor, side with the poor, and become one with the poor in spirit. As we live in solidarity with the poor and let go of power, privilege, prestige, and possessions, as we surrender our interior thoughts and goals and focus solely on God, we will enter a new peace and nonviolence not of this world. We will have moved out of the culture of dominance and empire into God's reign of mutuality and peace.

If we are rich, or rich in spirit, we don't need God. We have our money, our possessions, our weapons, and our armies to protect us. We live as full-on citizens of the culture of violence, injustice, and war. If we are poor, and poor in spirit, we need God. We have no money, no weapons, no armies to protect us; we place all our security in God and rely totally on

God. In that spirit of emptiness and nonviolence, we dwell in God's reign. The focus here is on total dependence and reliance upon God, not on wealth or power. That is the first step in the life of Gospel nonviolence that Jesus lives out every day until his last breath on the cross, where he dies in poverty of spirit, surrendering to God.

"Blessed are those who mourn, for they will be comforted" (5:4). Billions of people around the world spend their lives mourning because their loved ones have been killed by war, starvation, relievable illness, or systemic injustice. But in the "First" World, the empire, few mourn. Few are even permitted to mourn. Mourning is hidden. We are not encouraged to face the truth of our grief; rather, we're encouraged to be angry, afraid, depressed, despairing, helpless.

In this second Beatitude, Jesus instructs us about the emotional life of nonviolence. He will recommend that we do not cultivate anger or fear but says here at the start that we should practice grief; later, he will encourage us to cultivate joy. If nonviolence begins with the spiritual awareness that we are one with all 8 billion human beings alive, as well as all the creatures and Mother Earth, then as people of nonviolence we are always grieving because so many sisters and brothers are suffering and dying unjustly from violence, injustice, and war. We mourn for them, for the creatures, for Mother Earth. Jesus encourages us to mourn for our sisters and brothers. That grief will break our hearts and lead us to compassion and finally nonviolent action, so that we will work to stop the unjust deaths of so many sisters and brothers.

In other words, nonviolence begins with grief. If we mourn, Jesus promises, we will be comforted. Alas, the opposite is also true: if we don't mourn, we will not be comforted. If we do not grieve or mourn, we have lost ourselves to the culture of violence and injustice and have refused to enter God's realm of comfort and compassion.

"Blessed are the meek," Jesus teaches, "for they will inherit the earth" (5:5). Thomas Merton wrote that the word *meekness* is the biblical word for active, creative nonviolence (see his essay, "Blessed Are the Meek," in *Passion for Peace*). So here, Jesus is not blessing those who are passive and doing nothing; he's talking about people such as Martin Luther King Jr. and Dorothy Day, those who practice active, creative nonviolence.

Notice that Jesus connects the life of active, creative nonviolence with oneness with creation. He says that if we are actively nonviolent, we will be one with creation. I think the flip side is also true: if we are violent and support the culture of violence, then we will not be one with creation. Therein lie the roots of catastrophic climate change. We rejected Jesus's way of nonviolence, we disconnected from creation, and we started to destroy Mother Earth. A measure of our nonviolence, then, is our oneness with creation. The more we side with all humanity, especially the suffering and dying, as well as all the creatures and Mother Earth, the more nonviolent, loving, and compassionate we will become, like Gandhi, Dr. King, and Dorothy Day.

Over the past century, we have dug up fossil fuels, filled the atmosphere with carbon, which has raised the earth's temperature dramatically, caused the ice caps to melt, raised the sea level dramatically, leading not just to the hottest years on record but also to terrifying storms, hurricanes, droughts, blizzards, tornadoes, fires, and floods. Over the next century, hundreds of millions will have to flee coastal areas, and there will be many more wars over land and water. The only sane way forward is to immediately stop removing fossil fuels from the ground. The whole world must turn to renewable energy, solar and wind power, as well as to end war, which causes immense damage to the environment. The only way this can happen is through a global grassroots movement of active nonviolence, the likes of which the world has never seen, to end war and environmental destruction, and to heal Mother Earth. We are only three sentences into the Sermon on the Mount, and we can already see the way forward.

The life of nonviolence leads to oneness with creation, and as you start to work for oneness with creation, you enter the nonviolent struggle for justice, and so we have the next Beatitude: "Blessed are those who hunger and thirst for justice," Jesus says, "for they will be satisfied." (I prefer to translate the word "righteousness" as "justice," meaning social and economic justice.) Be passionate for justice, he tells us. Work for social, racial, economic, and environmental justice; hunger and thirst for justice, which is as important as our physical food and water. Work to end global, systemic, structural, institutionalized injustice; try to help bring justice to the poor, the oppressed, the creatures, and Mother Earth. When Jesus says we will be satisfied, I think he means that we will find meaning and purpose in our lives, that the most meaningful thing we can do is to side with justice. I hear this Beatitude as a call to join our local, national, and global groups working for justice, to pitch in, do our part, and even take to the streets in a demand for justice. Further, given the Beatitudes we have heard so far, we begin to realize that, for Jesus, hungering and thirsting for justice is part of the spiritual life, the contemplative life, life with God. As people who depend on God, grieve for suffering humanity and creation, and practice creative nonviolence in oneness with the earth, we cannot help but hunger and thirst for justice and stand up publicly for it.

Nonviolence and justice lead to mercy, hence the next Beatitude: "Blessed are the merciful," Jesus says, "for they will be shown mercy." While we struggle for justice on the one hand, Jesus says, we offer mercy on the other, especially toward those who have hurt us and seek our forgiveness, toward those who the culture says do not deserve mercy. Mercy is the very heart of God. Jesus tells us to be as compassionate, as merciful, as God.

Webster's dictionary defines mercy as "refraining from harming or punishing offenders, enemies, or persons in one's power. Also: kindness exceeding what may be expected or demanded by fairness; forbearance and compassion; imprisonment rather than the death penalty imposed on those found guilty of capital crimes; a disposition to forgive, pity or be kind; the power to forgive or be kind; clemency." Mercy means feeling empathy and pity for others, showing compassion to them, and practicing unconditional love for those who are unloved, poor, or marginalized. You might say that mercy means letting people off the hook. It means granting clemency to those who are deemed unforgivable; being kind and forgiving to those who we're taught don't deserve it. It means we don't retaliate or seek revenge. We forgive everyone who ever hurt us, we offer compassion to everyone, and we always grant others a second chance.

So we try to show mercy and compassion as Jesus showed it—to those who don't receive it from society: the poor, the sick, the weak, the elderly, the marginalized, the disenfranchised. We pursue the politics of mercy and try to institutionalize mercy. With this teaching, we

17

go forward to abolish the death penalty, racism, poverty, and war, to establish restorative justice and reconciliation, and to work for a new culture of mercy. As we show mercy, we sow seeds of mercy, which one day will wash back over us. Mercy becomes our way of being.

As we study the word "mercy," we find that Jesus points beyond the challenges of justice, consequence, and punishment. The New Testament Greek word for mercy, *eleos*, comes from the word for olive oil, which was used to treat wounds. According to Rev. James Popham, it was soothing, comforting, and healing, and that's how Jesus wants us to be to one another because that's the way God is toward every human being. The Hebrew word for mercy, *hesed*, means "steadfast love." Jesus wants us to practice the steadfast, consistent unwavering love of God toward one another, especially toward those we would prefer to reject or who are rejected by society. With these insights, we hear a call to radical mercy toward every human being, and all creatures and all creation, so that our very presence and every action are healing and so that the steadfast, nonviolent love of God works through us from now on toward everyone with no exceptions.

"Blessed are the clean of heart," Jesus says, "for they will see God." That fits with Jesus's public stand against the Jewish cleanliness laws. From day 1, Jesus repudiated and violated the Jewish cleanliness laws. By speaking out against them, and breaking them, he was committing civil disobedience and would have been punished. He challenged the hypocrisy of institutional religion, which set up rituals, rules, and traditions from which the religious authorities profited, which collaborated with systemic injustice and empire. Instead of cleaning our dishes and our hands, Jesus wants us to clean our hearts and give our hearts to God so that we can be God's instruments of universal love, compassion, and peace.

With Gandhi, I prefer the translation, "Blessed are the pure of heart, for they will see God." When Jesus calls us to purity of heart, he is calling us to the inner journey of nonviolence, the ongoing daily journey of disarming the heart, toward a nonviolent heart that keeps widening toward greater compassion and love. Purity of heart is the ongoing process of inner disarmament. Jesus is inviting us to explore and disarm the violence within us, to break open our hard, violent hearts, and to develop soft nonviolent hearts of love and compassion, to become tenderhearted, especially as people who struggle for justice and make peace. This Beatitude says that, while we work for justice and peace, we also do the inner work of justice and peace.

Jesus's active nonviolence flowed from the nonviolence of his heart. He had a pure heart, a clean heart, a nonviolent heart, what the church later called a sacred heart. At one point, he confides that he is "gentle and humble of heart." He didn't have a drop of violence in him. He said that all violence comes from within, so he wants us to have sacred hearts too, so that we too practice meticulous nonviolence and join his public campaign for a deep authentic place of interior peace. To begin the process of cleaning and disarming our hearts, we practice daily meditation with God. We sit with our God, hand over to God all our inner violence, hatred, anger, bitterness, and resentment; then we let God disarm and cleanse our hearts, let God fashion our violent hearts into new hearts in which the violence has been cleared away.

Notice how Jesus connects our hearts with our eyes. He says that, as we cultivate inner nonviolence of the heart and allow God to purify and disarm us, we begin to see God everywhere. Inner nonviolence helps us to see with the eyes of love, compassion, peace, and mercy, to recognize every human being as sister or brother, to see God in every other person. This inner work gives us a big vision. We see God everywhere: in the faces of children, in the creatures, in the beauty of creation, but more, in the poor and marginalized, even in our enemies. If we dare to plumb the depths of inner peace and nonviolence, Jesus says, we will receive the beatific vision right now.

This leads to the great climactic Beatitude, the call to become peacemakers. "Blessed are the peacemakers," Jesus says, "for they will be called the sons and daughters of the God of peace." (Notice my preferred translation of "children of God." This translation helps us to connect with, identify with, and understand Jesus, whom God calls "my beloved son" and reminds us that God is the God of peace.) I think this is the core of the Gospel, the heart of Christianity, the great mission of discipleship. We are called to become peacemakers. This is a great way to understand our lives: How have you been a peacemaker? What does it mean for you to be a peacemaker? How can you consciously live the rest of your life as a peacemaker? If Jesus calls us to be peacemakers, I think that means, first of all, that we can no longer be warmakers. We cannot support war, bless war, participate in war, pay for war, promote war, or send our kids off to war. Peacemakers work to end war and create peace. With this Beatitude, every follower of Jesus, every Christian in the world, is banned from participating in warfare and is called to work for peace.

Peacemakers are people of nonviolence. We are peaceful toward ourselves; we make peace with ourselves and steadfastly cultivate interior peace; we are also peaceful toward all those around us, all creatures, and all creation; and we do our part actively, publicly, to create a more peaceful world. We make peace by loving and reconciling with everyone, teaching peace and nonviolence, and supporting the movement of peace. We promote nonviolent alternatives and nonviolent conflict resolution and work to abolish war and nuclear weapons and the causes of war so that everyone can live in peace. Through various movements and political campaigns, we try to stop the building of weapons and funding for war preparations, and instead try to spend those trillions of dollars to provide food, clean water, housing, healthcare, education, employment, and dignity for every human being on the planet. We work to educate everyone at every age in every class in the methodology of nonviolent conflict resolution; our hope is to make this methodology the norm. All of this is achievable, if we set our hearts on it and put our political and spiritual will toward it.

What's truly shocking is that Jesus announces that God is a peacemaker. With this Beatitude, Jesus describes the nature of God as nonviolent and peaceful. He throws out thousands of years of belief in a violent god. He does away with any spiritual justification for warfare and the great lie that God might bless our troops or bless our wars. Instead, he opens our imagination to see the living God as peaceful and God's reign as a new world of peace. Then, even more amazingly, Jesus tells us who we are. From now on, he says, you are the sons and daughters of the God of peace. This is our true identity. We are beloved sons and daughters of the God of peace, so naturally we go forth and make peace.

If you stand up publicly for peace in a world of injustice and war, you are going to get in trouble. People don't want to hear it! That's why the last Beatitude is about getting in trouble for our work for peace and justice. "Blessed are they who are persecuted for the sake of justice, for theirs is the kingdom of heaven." (Note again that I prefer to translate "righteousness" into the clearer English sense of "social and economic justice.") Dorothy Day once said that we can measure our discipleship to the nonviolent Jesus by how much trouble we are in. In a world of total violence, war, and injustice, if you stand up for justice, disarmament, and peace, and try to change things, people will not thank you or honor you. Usually, they get mad at you and tell you to be quiet and not to rock the boat. But that's when we get to practice nonviolence and see how nonviolent we really are! If we keep at this public work for peace and justice, we will get in trouble, be persecuted and harassed, and maybe even arrested and jailed, as I've discovered. The nonviolent Jesus spoke out every day for justice and peace, resisted the Roman Empire, proclaimed God's reign of nonviolence, was constantly harassed, and eventually was killed. He says this is to be expected, but this active nonviolence is the greatest of blessings because the reign of God is ours.

Jesus expects us to rock the boat, to disrupt the culture of violence and war, as he did. He wants us to be nonviolent troublemakers, people who work for an end to injustice, poverty, and war, as did Dorothy Day and Dr. King, people who take risks for justice and peace. When we get in trouble, we maintain our nonviolence, forgive those who hurt us, and trust in God but speak truth to power. This is how positive social change occurs—through our participation in global grassroots movements of active, creative nonviolence for the sake of justice and peace. Through our nonviolent suffering love for the truth of justice and peace we share in the paschal mystery of Jesus, in the cross and the resurrection.

In the end, Jesus goes further and says, "And blessed are you when they insult you and persecute you and utter every kind of evil against you falsely because of me. Rejoice and be glad for your reward will be great in heaven. Thus they persecuted the prophets who were before you." If you are in trouble and put down because you speak out for justice and peace, rejoice and be glad, he says. Now you get to share in the blessings of the prophets. Now you get to be like the peacemakers who set an example for us.

As we study the Beatitudes and try to build our lives according to them, we hear again the empowering words of the Aramaic rendering: "Arise, get up, get moving, start walking and walk forth" all you poor in spirit; you who mourn; you who are meek and nonviolent; you who hunger and thirst for justice. Arise, get up, get moving, start walking and walk forth, all you merciful, you pure in heart, you peacemakers, you persecuted for justice. Rejoice and be glad." If all we had from Jesus were his Beatitudes, we would have enough to live by. Matthew summons us to become beatitude people who rise and walk forth, people of justice and mercy, God's beloved sons and daughters—peacemakers. These are sentences to memorize, ponder, and pursue for the rest of our lives.

"Those Who Obey and Teach These Commandments Will Be Called the Greatest in the Kingdom of Heaven" (5:13–20)

Between the Beatitudes and the following six antitheses, Jesus offers a series of powerful affirmations for those who live the Beatitudes.

"You are the salt of the earth," he says. In other words, you make all the difference in the world. You are the spice of the earth. You make the earth work. Without you, the earth has no spice, no flavor.

"You are the light of the world." Again, you make all the difference between night and day. The world is in the darkness of violence and death, but you dispel the darkness. You have a great responsibility. Let your light shine bright. Help everyone see. If you do, many others will be able to find their way to peace, God, and one another. They will see one another as sisters and brothers and discover the life of peace.

"You are a city set on a mountain." You are the ones everyone looks up to, the one safe place to which everyone aspires, the place that looks out over the whole world. You are set on high, above all that is. Be that city on the mountaintop.

"You are a lamp, set on a lampstand to give light to all in the house." You beatitude people give light to the whole house. "Just so, your light must shine before others," Jesus commands, "that they may see your good deeds and glorify your heavenly Father." Here he calls us not so much to be political as to be *public*, to go *public* with our beatitude light, our hunger for justice, our mercy, our peacemaking. We are told to let our light shine, and if we do this, we glorify the God of peace, which is the ultimate goal; in the end, it is the only goal that matters. St. Ignatius put it this way: try to go even beyond that and bring "greater" glory to God.

Notice that every one of these statements is a positive affirmation. Not once does he say, "You're all going to hell! You are all worthless!" There is no fire and brimstone in his talk; there is only affirmation, encouragement, and hope. This is critically important. Here, at the beginning of the historic sermon, Jesus affirms us and says we do make a difference. The challenge then is to take these affirmations to heart, to set aside our doubts and questions, and to live out his teachings. Along the way, as we strive to live like our teacher, we learn to affirm others too, and encourage them to let their light shine far and wide.

Then Jesus begins to explain his own place within these teachings, Judaic history, even salvation history. "Do not think that I have come to abolish the law or the prophets. I have come not to abolish but to fulfill. Amen, I say to you, until heaven and earth pass away, not the smallest letter or the smallest part of a letter will pass from the law, until all things have taken place."

Here Jesus announces that his teachings are the fulfillment of all Hebrew teachings. He declares that he is fulfilling the Torah and everything the prophets taught. This, too, is critically important. If we believe that Jesus is the Messiah, that he is also totally nonviolent, and that his teachings are the fulfillment of everything that came before—then we know now that the goal of life is to live these Sermon-on-the-Mount teachings. More, as we live them, study them, and teach them, we know that nonviolence is the way of God, that to be truly human is to be nonviolent, and that to follow the nonviolent Jesus is to practice, live, and teach the way of peace.

If we are to believe these verses, then we understand that the Hebrew Bible, which is the word of God, offers a slow revelation of God's nature. This has happened over a thousand years through more than a hundred authors and has gradually led to this breakthrough of divine nonviolence. The earliest books presume that God is violent like us. Then the Wisdom literature offers a change in tone, and we discover the feminine side to God. By the time of the prophets and their demand for justice for the poor, we are prepared for a God who engages the world in the struggle for justice and peace, even though we are still not clear about nonviolence. That breakthrough into new understanding happens right here in the Sermon on the Mount.

From now on, everything needs to be read through the eyes of the nonviolent Jesus and the sermon on nonviolence. The true living God can be met only through the lens of nonviolence. Everything in the law and the prophets leads toward the nonviolent Jesus and his new law of nonviolence. The scandal of Jesus, the scandal of Christianity, is that God is nonviolent. Perhaps it's because we do not want the nonviolent God of Jesus that so many Christians prefer to study violent characters such as Samuel and David and sacred texts filled with violence such as Chronicles and Kings, or even St. Paul, who was killed before the Sermon on the Mount was written. Perhaps the greatest need among Christians worldwide is to stop reading everything except the Gospels, particularly Matthew's Sermon on the Mount, so that we can know the nonviolence of Jesus as the early church did. What we are doing is not working, but the decision to study and meditate on the Sermon on the Mount helped Gandhi, so I hope more and more of us can study this sermon of Jesus as the fulfillment of everything that came before, including the law and the prophets.

The Jewish law, the Torah, set up limits and boundaries for us. "An eye for an eye" and "a tooth for a tooth" was a reasonable curtailment of our tendency to carry out vengeance out of proportion to the original crime. But with the coming of Jesus, those old standards are thrown out. Instead, we are summoned to the total nonviolence of God. Our new boundary is the prohibition of any violence in any proportion. When the world finally becomes nonviolent, it will seem like an entirely new world; the old world of violence will have passed away.

When the nonviolent Jesus speaks of heaven and earth passing away, he is not talking about an apocalypse of violence that will destroy everything, but rather about the fulfillment of God's reign on earth by which violence is abolished and all people can live in the freedom and peace of his total nonviolence. In light of God's nonviolence, Isaiah and the book of Revelation point to the coming of "a new heaven and a new earth," where everyone everywhere will live at peace in God's realm of nonviolence and universal love. That's why Gandhi concluded, "When the practice of nonviolence becomes universal, God will reign on earth just as God reigns in heaven."

Because Jesus's teachings in the Sermon on the Mount are the new commandments of God, the fulfillment of the Torah and the prophets, and the fullest revelation of the mind of God, anyone who breaks these commandments and teaches others to break them will be "the least," to put it mildly. We are to spend our lives according to these commandments and teach others to do so as well. This will earn the name "greatest" in the kingdom of heaven.

Life is a journey into God's reign of love, justice, compassion, and nonviolence. That's where we are headed. The question each of us must ask is, Do I help bring this reality to life by how I live? Or do I actually hinder the coming of God's reign here and now?

Many people want to be called great—especially religious people. We seem to do everything but teach these Sermon-on-the-Mount teachings of nonviolence, much less live by them. Yet here in black and white is the prescription for and promise of greatness. Want to be called the greatest in heaven? Great! Obey and teach every word in the Sermon on the Mount. This should become the new goal for every priest, minister, bishop, and Christian in the world.

Finally, before the six antitheses, Jesus offers a warning: "Unless your righteousness surpasses that of the scribes and Pharisees, you will not enter into the kingdom of heaven." The scribes and the Pharisees were good, devout people who knew the Torah inside and out, fasted twice a week, and followed the law to the letter. But none of that matters, Jesus suggests, if they remain part of the status quo—a system relying on dominance, and often lacking in mercy and compassion. This warning against violent fundamentalism still holds true today. We can be the most devout, strident religious person around, yet still not enter the kingdom of heaven. We do not want to be fervently religious and end up hurting others, even supporting war, domination, and empire. The goal is to enter the kingdom of heaven and help others enter as well. We need to reject any trace of violence in our religious practice, belief, spirituality, community, and church. Jesus does not want us to be religious fundamentalists who end up serving the very culture that treats people so brutally. Jesus summons us to a deep humility and the kind of mindset that sets others free, that blesses others rather than condemns them.

"You Have Heard It Said, But I Say to You": The Six Antitheses of Nonviolence (5:21–48)

The six antitheses that follow form the backbone of the Sermon on the Mount. Each one begins with the phrase, "You have heard it said, but I say to you. . . ." In each case, Jesus invokes a core teaching of Judaism, the Torah, and the Hebrew Scriptures, and then proceeds to transform and fulfill it in light of his way of radical love. These six antitheses are not pious platitudes or interesting phrases or friendly suggestions. They are commandments. They make up the new law of God. They are the fulfillment of Moses's Ten Commandments, and as such are meant to be taken as seriously as the Ten Commandments. Actually, they surpass and transcend the Ten Commandments. They are the concrete application of the Beatitudes, and they build up to the climactic fifth teaching against violent retaliation and the sixth teaching, the most revolutionary text in all of human history, the command to end war and love our enemies. They should be set in stone in our churches and our hearts.

With these new teachings, we make the historic transition from "Thou shalt not . . ." to "Thou shalt. . . ." They point to new, positive directions: "You shall love, you shall make peace, you shall be just, you shall forgive, you shall be totally nonviolent, you shall be as compassionate as God." The boundaries of nonviolence are still hard and difficult: no anger, no lust, no divorce, no violent retaliation, no war, no judging others, no condemning others. But what we might miss in the reading is that these boundaries of nonviolence open into the infinite *freedoms* of nonviolence.

Still, for some, the antitheses that follow seem impossible. I'm convinced, however, that Jesus would not have said these things if they were not possible to live. We see them lived out in the lives of the saints. If we make the Beatitudes and these teachings the primary focus of our lives, then they do become possible, doable, achievable, even welcome. For those who get stuck in the words that follow, the best solution is to keep your eyes on the nonviolent Jesus and go forward anyway; you will understand by doing as Jesus says, not by overthinking it. We say the ancient prayer, "Lord Jesus Christ, son of the Living God, have mercy on me a sinner," and get on with the work of discipleship. As we try to live Jesus's teachings and keep working at them one day at a time, we may find ourselves living into them and one day practicing them naturally without even realizing it. Until then, we "fake it till we make it."

First, "Be Reconciled" (5:21–26)

"You have heard it said, 'Thou shalt not kill,'" he begins, "but I say to you, do not even get angry." With this commandment, Jesus throws down the gauntlet and challenges us to go beyond the prohibition of war and killing. He wants us to dig out the roots of violence within us, which find their first expression in our anger, so that we never give in to hatred, violence, killing, or warfare.

Here Jesus instructs us in the emotional life of nonviolence. In the Beatitudes, he recommended that we cultivate two emotions: grief and joy. Now he urges us to avoid anger; later, he will instruct us to avoid fear as well. This is difficult because as people steeped in the culture of violence, we are taught to be angry and afraid.

For Jesus, anger leads to violence. The collective resentment and anger of people, even nations, leads to injustice, discrimination, racism, fascism, and war. Jesus wants us to look within, to find the roots of violence in our anger and resentment, and to surrender them to God every time we notice them. Only when we cease to be angry people can we act as authentic peacemakers.

The tragic history of violence and warfare proves that Jesus was right. Anger doesn't bring peace; it only breeds retaliation. Gandhi was one of the few public figures who cites this text as the reason why he "conserved his anger," in his words. Shortly before he died, he gave an interview in which he said it was the smartest move he ever made. It's easy to be a raging angry activist, he thought. The longer you live and work for justice, he realized, the more injustice you will face, and the angrier you can become. He did not want to spend his life in anger. Further, he presumed that Jesus knew better than he did, that Jesus had found a way to struggle for justice without cultivating anger. Gandhi wanted to be totally nonviolent, which meant going beyond anger into grief, joy, and peace. The greatest saints of justice and peace learned to let go of anger and fear, and taught themselves a new way of living, rooted in nonviolence, mindfulness, compassion, and reconciliation.

Jesus does not want us to waste time in anger. He's trying to form us into practitioners of nonviolence who transcend anger and join his campaign, even unto suffering and death, without any desire for retaliation or revenge, without even a trace of resentment. The public work he's training us for will lead to confrontations, disruptions, betrayals, harassment, persecution, even arrest and execution, as he and the early church experienced. If we are going to face this work in Jesus's spirit, then we have to learn to let everything go, even the putdowns, attacks, humiliations, insults, inconveniences, and hurts that make us angry, and to stay centered in the Holy Spirit of peace. In this training, we will be able to live out the last Beatitude—to rejoice when people insult and attack us because of our Christian witness. We will move way beyond anger into the ongoing practice of forgiveness and compassion that bring deep joy as we focus solely on God's reign.

Jesus was not an angry person. Even when he engaged in civil disobedience in the temple, as we shall see, he was acting not out of anger but out of grief. There are only two references in the four Gospels where it says he was angry: in Mark 3, the healing of the man with the withered hand; and John 11, the raising of Lazarus. But in each case, the actual Greek word denotes something different from anger, a kind of beside-himself, deep-down grief and disturbance. He becomes very upset, but he does not lash out in anger ever. We see this finally during his arrest, torture, and execution when he does not get angry but remains totally centered in faith in God, and maintains his forgiveness, compassion, and nonviolence to the bitter end.

The great modern peacemakers of history figured out how to work for justice and peace without resorting to anger and instead moving into a deep, mysterious sense of grief, peace, and joy, which allowed them to remain faithful to God's way of nonviolence until the end. We see this most especially in the extraordinary angerlessness of Gandhi and Dr. King. I have seen it up close my entire life in my great friends and teachers—Coretta Scott King, Mairead Maguire, Dom Helder Camara, Rev. Jim Lawson, Daniel Berrigan, Archbishop Desmond Tutu, Mother Teresa, Adolfo Perez Esquivel, and Thich Nhat Hanh. Each of them moved beyond anger, despite their having suffered the killings of their loved ones, even their own death threats. They were people of deep peace, compassion, and joy, and they encouraged me to pursue the unknown land beyond anger, the promised land of peace. Indeed, Archbishop Tutu, who was under near constant death threat his whole life, was famous for his joy and laughter, and I experienced it firsthand. Daniel Berrigan was one of the funniest people I've ever known, but so was Mother Teresa. It is possible to spend one's life confronting violence, poverty, and war without giving in to anger, despair, and fear. There is another way—a new path that Jesus is trying to teach us, a narrow path of peace beyond our understanding.

In his reference to judgment, Jesus simply explains the nature of things, the karma of violence. Those who live by violence will suffer and die by violence. He warns us not even to insult another person, starting with our brothers, because we will have to face the consequences of our violence. Jesus understands that if we reject anger; let go of hatred, bitterness, and resentment; learn to forgive everyone who ever hurt us; and refuse to retaliate, the roots of violence within us will dry up and we will begin to cultivate new depths of interior nonviolence, what he called "purity of heart" or "cleanliness of heart" in the Beatitudes.

But just when we think we might understand the teaching, there comes the new commandment: "*Be reconciled!*" This first antithesis goes on to say, whenever anger arises in you because of the way you feel you have been mistreated, not only do not respond with anger, hatred, resentment, or violence, but use the occasion to remember the people you have hurt, who hold something against you, and drop whatever you are doing and go "be reconciled" with the ones who are angry at you, the ones you have hurt.

What's even more shocking, Jesus says in effect, "Whatever you do, if someone has something against you, if someone is angry with you because you hurt them, do not go before God to worship God. Do not go to the altar to present your gift to God. Instead, go immediately to those you have hurt, apologize to them, and reconcile with them. Then, once you have reconciled with those you have hurt, bring your gift to the altar and worship God."

This is the new prerequisite for all worship of God. From now on, before we pray, or approach an altar, or worship the God of peace, we apologize to those we have hurt, ask them to forgive us, try to reconcile with everyone and forgive all those who have hurt us. We want to be reconciled with everyone on earth. From this new place of heartfelt humility, repentance, and reconciliation, we can approach the God of peace and reconciliation, and we will be reconciled with God. In the end, this instruction teaches us about the nature of God: God is nonviolent and is therefore always reconciling us with one another and to

God's Self. This should be the work of our lives, too—to constantly reconcile everyone with one another and with God; to become a reconciling, reconciled people. This is the work of the spiritual life; this is the path of peace.

Likewise, with Jesus's last antithesis, he commands us to "settle with our opponents on the way to court," while there is still time, before we foolishly end up in prison. Understand that compromise, forgiveness, reconciliation, and letting go are the tools necessary to protect your peace and help you maintain your nonviolence. Come to your senses, atone, and take action immediately before you suffer the consequences of your mistakes.

Gandhi spent most of his life praying through this first antithesis. He experimented with it with all his opponents, especially the British, and learned to love and make friends with his enemies. He became so disarming that his opponents in South Africa and Britain became his dear friends, including Prime Minister Jan Smuts of South Africa and Lord Mountbatten, the last British viceroy of India. Shortly before she died, Queen Elizabeth II told the current prime minister of India that her most cherished gift was a handkerchief Gandhi sent her on her wedding day. She kept it on her desk till the day she died. Peacemaking and reconciliation are possible, even for the staunchest enemies. This is the kind of total nonviolence Jesus teaches.

Second, Mind Your Heart, Change Your Lives,
Be Totally Nonviolent (5:27–30)

The prohibition on adultery in the second antithesis summons us to have pure, clean, nonviolent hearts like Jesus's. He is calling us to a life free from lust so that we look at and treat every human being on the planet compassionately as a sister or a brother, a child of God.

"You have heard, 'Thou shalt not commit adultery'; but I say to you, 'everyone who looks at a woman with lust has already committed adultery with her in his heart.'" Here he commands husbands not only to be faithful to their wives, but men not to look at women with lust. As he unpacks the boundaries of nonviolence, he commands every one of us not to give in to lust and never to look at another person with lust ever again. If we begin to look at one another through his eyes of respect and dignity, and learn to find God in one another, we will enter God's reign here and now, and that is always Jesus's goal. In this case, there would be no more sexual harassment, abuse, or violence against women or anyone. The nonviolent feminist Jesus here sides with women, protects women, and in effect, presages the #MeToo movement.

Mind the boundaries of sexuality and dignity, he counsels. Do not objectify others, do not violate others, do not hurt others. Examine your heart, protect your heart, mind your heart. For some people, the warning against lust in our hearts might sound preposterous; for others, it might sound inviting but impossible. But it is possible, otherwise Jesus would not have called us to this inner depth of nonviolence. Millions of people around the world who struggle with lust addiction have found relief through various Twelve Step programs in which members find community support to surrender their lust to God and live out the AA serenity prayer. As a priest who has counseled many people, I have seen people healed of all kinds of addictions, including lust, people who have found a new kind of peace through their sobriety.

For Jesus, this is all urgent life-or-death stuff. He wants us to make our inner transformation toward purity and nonviolence a priority, so that we do whatever we need to do to rid ourselves of violence, anger, hatred, resentment, lust, fear, and selfishness. To push us into the immediate work of reforming and disarming ourselves, Matthew's Jesus uses violent imagery to wake us up to the urgency of pure nonviolence toward all others, saying, protect your heart at all costs, even if it means suffering the loss of an eye or a hand.

> "If your right eye causes you to sin, tear it out and throw it away. It is better for you to lose one of your members than to have your whole body thrown into Gehenna. And if your right hand causes you to sin, cut it off and throw it away. It is better for you to lose one of your members than to have your whole body go into Gehenna."

The point here is to do everything we can to stop ourselves from sinning, that is, from hurting others and having to face the consequences of our violence. Jesus solemnly warns us about the consequences of all behavior. What goes around comes around. If you live by violence, you will suffer and die in violence. Gehenna is the hell of total violence, which is here and now for many people, either as oppressors or oppressed, victims or victimizers. Jesus wants us to do everything we can to enter the heaven of total nonviolence right now, which means taking drastic action to stop any behavior that is not the will of the God of peace and love.

As the embodiment of nonviolence, Jesus would never want us to hurt ourselves. But we spend our lives hurting others, participating in the social sin of mass murder (war), oppression, greed, and destruction, so he uses drastic language to wake us to the truth of our participation in the culture of violence, that this "sin" has eternal consequences for our souls. Therefore, he pleads, take urgent, drastic action to change yourself right now so that you never hurt anyone, anywhere ever again; so that you are not complicit in the culture of violence and headed toward the Gehenna of total violence; so that you do not think harm, including lustful thoughts, toward any human being ever again.

This passage is helpful, if we open ourselves to its wisdom and compassion. It expresses Jesus's urgent desire that we change whatever we have to change about ourselves so that we become like him, people of compassion and peace. He wants us to really do our inner work, to seek help if necessary, in order to root out every trace of violence, including anger and lust, so that the God of peace can dwell at peace within us, so that we can reclaim our humanity and live and die in peace with ourselves and others. As we take action to change our behavior, we learn all over again to become people of prayer, who rely on God every day, one day at a time, so that we never hurt anyone or anything and begin to experience the reality of God's reign of peace.

Third, You Men, Treat Women Respectfully as Equals (5:31–32)
In this antithesis on divorce, the nonviolent Jesus takes a stand in defense of women. Here he protects women and insists that women are equal to men, that men can no longer mistreat or disrespect women. This commandment is addressed to men: you must treat women with equality, dignity, respect, and nonviolence. This teaching, too, begins a nonviolent revolution in the sexist culture of violent patriarchy.

A close look reveals that Jesus is defending women who get blamed by men for everything. Men did not consider women to be equals; they were in effect subhuman, the property of men. If a husband was divorcing his wife, it was because she was to blame. Not anymore, says Jesus. Here, Jesus announces, every husband is equally to blame when it comes to divorce. This was nothing less than revolutionary! No man would say or believe such a thing in Jesus's time. Many men today are still so infected with sexism and patriarchy that they consider women to be less than equal. Jesus teaches here a new depth of nonviolence—that men and women are totally equal, and that men should treat women with total respect, nonviolence, and dignity, and that men should presume in fact that they are to blame because of the legacy of male violence, sexism, and patriarchy. By saying that men are equally to blame in matters of divorce, Jesus elevates women and tears down patriarchy. He points to the coming of a new culture of equality and respect.

This radical equality is at the center of Jesus's thinking and the beginning of feminism. The logic of his feminist nonviolence says, "You men, do not harass women, hurt women, verbally, emotionally, or sexually abuse women; do not rape women, do not be violent in any way to women, and work toward a new society in which all women are treated equally with men." This commandment for equality toward women is the beginning of the end of sexism, patriarchy, and male violence against women. It demands that men reject their tendency to dominate others.

Jesus is clearly against divorce because this teaching appears in other places in the Gospel. Within the wisdom of nonviolence, one presumes he wants marriages that remain faithful, peaceful, and lifelong; that husbands and wives live together in prayer and peace and raise children in a spirit of love and freedom. He does not want us to harm one another, much less to destroy a marriage, which will cause further harm. We can safely presume that he would want husbands and wives today to be doing their inner work, to practice nonviolence, to put the other before themselves, and to create marriages and families where God dwells in their midst in peace.

The so-called exception clause—"unless the marriage is unlawful"—seems to refer to a rare problem that was happening in Matthew's community, where some rabbis permitted marriages of incest, to one's relative. Gentile converts to Judaism who had married their relatives were permitted to maintain their marriages. Here, Matthew's Jesus addresses this question by saying that such marriages were not legal to begin with; Gentile converts to Christianity who had married within the familial bloodline were therefore not legally married.

Fourth, Speak Only Truth; Let Your Yes Be Yes
and Your No Be No (5:33–37)
"You have heard that it was said, 'Do not take a false oath,' but I say to you, 'Do not swear at all.'" Why does he say this? The purpose of an oath or a swear was to call upon God as a witness to our truthfulness. If you have to profess an oath or even swear to God that you are telling the truth, that indicates that sometimes you lie. For Jesus, thoughtful, loving relationships are rooted and grounded in truth, which means that you never lie. Nonviolence goes hand in hand with truth. In John's Gospel, Jesus will say, "I am the Way, the Truth and the Life." So Jesus instructs his followers: from now on, speak only the truth. There's no reason to swear to God to prove your truth-telling; you do not need to prove that what you say is true because you always speak the truth, no matter what. And you always speak

the truth with love and compassion. This is a requirement for Christian discipleship and nonviolence.

The teaching is short and to the point: "Let your yes be yes, and your no be no. Anything more is from the evil one." As truth seekers and truth speakers, we speak the truth and only the truth. That means our language can be simple, straightforward, and to the point. We do not need to say anything else. We speak the language of nonviolence, so we speak the truth in love.

In a culture of violence and war, you are required to lie. Lying is the language of violence. You are not allowed to say that every human being on the planet is your sister and brother, that we are all children of the God of peace. Instead, we objectify others, dehumanize people, and turn them into "them," the hated enemy, the "other," the "illegal alien," and so forth. One of the key requirements for a new culture of peace and nonviolence will be a new language of peace and nonviolence rooted in the truth of love and equality. The language of truth is desperately needed today as we descend into greater global violence. Now more than ever, our yes and no are greatly needed. In this Tower-of-Babel culture, from FOX News to social media, people say everything but yes and no. Matthew's Jesus invites us to learn how to speak the language of truth and nonviolence.

Later, when the nonviolent Jesus stands condemned before the Roman procurator, he will say, "All those who seek the truth listen to my voice." If we learn to disarm our language and speak only yes and no, then over time, we will become listeners instead of talkers. We will listen for the words of the nonviolent Jesus, for the truth, for wisdom, for the voice of God. This will eventually bring us to the peace of silence, to the silence of Jesus before the Roman court. In that silence, we deepen into contemplative nonviolence, contemplative peace, and contemplative truth. We enter a wisdom beyond the language of violence and discover the geography and language of peace. This listening and silence will make us ever better instruments of Jesus's peace.

Fifth, "Offer No Violent Resistance to One Who Does Evil" (5:38–42)
Here we reach the climactic fifth and sixth antitheses—the total prohibition of violence, the commandment to non-cooperation with those who do evil:

> "You have heard that it was said, 'An eye for an eye and a tooth for a tooth.' But I say to you, offer no [violent] resistance to one who is evil. When someone strikes you on [your] right cheek, turn the other one to him as well. If anyone wants to go to law with you over your tunic, hand him your cloak as well. Should anyone press you into service for one mile, go with him for two miles. Give to the one who asks of you, and do not turn your back on one who wants to borrow."

These words are pure revolution, for they launch a nonviolent revolution against not only war but violence itself. It is certainly one of the most important passages in the Bible, and in history, for it charts a way out of the downward spiral of violence into peace, justice, and reconciliation. That is why Gandhi read this verse every day for over four decades, why Leo Tolstoy spent the last twenty-five years of his life writing solely about this verse, trying his best to publicize this teaching. These great figures understood that this teaching holds the key to personal salvation and a more nonviolent world—if we dare to obey it, teach it, promote it, and organize around it.

Previously, the Torah had tried to regulate fair punishment so that the punishment would not exceed the injury. If you think of it that way, "an eye for an eye" marked a progressive step forward in the history of violence. Jesus will have none of it. He forbids all violence, even retaliatory violence in the face of violence, no matter how supposedly fair. He prohibits any form of violent punishment or violent retaliation or revenge. He advocates a new way: creative nonviolent resistance to oppression and violence.

The Greek word here is *antistēnai*, which theologian Walter Wink writes means "to resist violently, to revolt or to rebel with violence" (see Wink, *Engaging the Powers*, 184–93). "Offer no '*antistēnai*,'" Jesus commands; that is, do "no violent resistance to one who does evil." Do not use violence to resist evil. Do not continue the downward spiral of violence. Jesus wants us to break the cycle of violence by refusing to cooperate with it or retaliate with further violence. Violence in response to violence will lead to further violence, he teaches. "Do not repay evil for evil." Gandhi put it this way: "An eye for an eye only makes the whole world blind." Relying on Wink, I translate the phrase as "offer no violent resistance."

But just because we do not respond to violence with further violence does not mean we sit back and suffer violence passively. Jesus commands us to be creative, to disarm our opponent through nonviolent means. He does not teach that submission to violence or evil is the will of God; on the contrary, he commands active nonviolent resistance to evil. The culture of violence insists that there are only two options in the face of violence: fight back with violence or run away and do nothing. In *Engaging the Powers*, Walter Wink says Jesus offered "a third way": active nonviolent resistance. Jesus did not advocate passive resignation or indifference to evil or violent retaliation, but something entirely new. He taught and practiced active, steadfast resistance to every form of violence and injustice, with one catch: it must be nonviolent. He insisted that we stand up and resist all violence and injustice, in whatever form, whether at the personal, national, or global level, but we do not use the violent means of our oppressor; instead, we engage in nonviolent resistance so that everyone comes out unscathed. The only way to end the chain of violence is by refusing to become part of it. If you practice nonviolence, even in the face of violence, even through your own suffering love and insistence on truth and our common humanity, you will disarm the situation and literally end the violence.

The fifth antithesis in the Sermon on the Mount is the clearest teaching on nonviolent resistance to evil in all of history up until this point. But it has generally been misinterpreted to mean passivity. Scholars now agree that the text calls for creative, confrontational nonviolent action that disarms the oppressor without using the same means as the oppressor. Jesus wants us to resist evil with active nonviolence—to hold our ground, speak the truth, insist on our common humanity, disarm our opponent, risk suffering love, trust in God, and work for the conversion of our opponent—so that the one who does evil or supports systemic injustice disarms. The goal is not to hurt or kill our opponent but to transform him, to lead him to a change of heart, to win him over to the truth, to convert him to nonviolence, and to help him and others welcome God's reign of love and peace. Wink writes that Jesus's teaching on nonviolence "forms the charter for a way of being in the world that breaks the spiral of violence."

Jesus reveals a way to fight evil with all our power without being transformed into the very evil we fight. It is a way—the only way possible—of not becoming what we hate. "Do not counter evil in kind"—this insight is the distilled essence, stated with sublime simplicity, of the experience of those Jews who had, in Jesus' very lifetime, so courageously and effectively practiced nonviolent direct action against Rome. Jesus, in short, abhors both passivity and violence. He articulates, out of the history of his own people's struggles, a way by which evil can be opposed without being mirrored, the oppressors resisted without being emulated, and the enemy neutralized without being destroyed. Those who have lived by Jesus' words—Leo Tolstoy, Mohandas Gandhi, Martin Luther King Jr., Dorothy Day, Cesar Chavez, Adolfo Perez Esquivel—point us to a new way of confronting evil whose potential for personal and social transformation we are only beginning to grasp today. (Wink, *Engaging the Powers*, 189)

Like every good teacher, Jesus does not leave us just with the theory. He gives five concrete examples about how to do this. First, "when someone strikes you on your right cheek, turn the other one to him as well." Walter Wink was perhaps the first person to ask the obvious question: If you strike someone's face with your right hand, where's it going to land? On their *left* cheek. But Jesus specifically talks here about being struck on the *right* cheek. So what's he talking about? To strike someone on the right cheek would require using the left hand, but the left hand was only used for unclean work; you could be punished for using your left hand. So, the only way to strike someone with your right hand on their right cheek would be to use the back of your right hand. In other words, Jesus is not talking about a fistfight but top-down, violent humiliation, the behavior of a slave owner or Roman soldier toward an oppressed person who is kneeling down, struck with the back of the hand and humiliated. If you are a slave, or a peasant kneeling in front of a Roman soldier, and you turn the other cheek in the face of such humiliation, you would be asserting your dignity, equality, and humanity, and putting yourself on equal footing. You would be saying in effect, "I deny you the power to humiliate me. I am a human being just like you." As Gandhi said, "The first principle of nonviolent action is that of non-cooperation with everything humiliating."

Jesus does not want us to sit back passively and suffer the violence of our oppressors. He wants us to nonviolently resist their injustice, to take nonviolent action for our liberation and theirs. He tells us we are not helpless or powerless. The only problem is that his method is also risky. It means engaging the opponent right then and there, in the face of violence. It's scary, but he says, "Do not be afraid. Turn the other cheek and disarm your opponent." It's equally scary to fight back with violence, and the chances are you will most likely be really hurt or even killed; nonviolent resistance has a higher chance of a peaceful outcome. Furthermore, for Jesus, there is always a third party involved. It's not just the oppressed person and the violent oppressor about to strike, but God. God works through our active, creative nonviolence. If we respond nonviolently, the Holy Spirit of disarming nonviolence will be unleashed and will have a chance to disarm the oppressor. We see modern examples of this in the civil rights movement, when Black activists sat-in illegally at segregated lunch counters, refused to leave, were sometimes beaten, refused to retaliate, and eventually won the day and brought about desegregation.

A second example. "If anyone wants to go to law with you over your tunic, hand him your cloak as well." In that time, the poor were forever in debt. People wore outer and inner garments, but, as Wink writes, they were hauled into court and sued by landlords even for the clothes off their backs. Only the poorest, those Jesus addressed, would have nothing but an outer garment to give as a loan. So, when you find yourself in court and the authorities demand your outer garment as payment for your unjust landlord, he says, give them your inner garment as well. But if a poor person was sued in court for his outer garment and gave away his inner garment, too—what would that mean? He would end up naked in the middle of the courtroom. Now in those days, it was more shameful to see a naked person than to be naked in public, so Jesus is inviting his listeners to bold, creative nonviolent action—to claim their power, shame their oppressors, and liberate themselves without running away or being violent, but confronting the crisis nonviolently head-on. As Wink explains, the poor man has "transcended the attempt to humiliate him. He has risen above shame. At the same time he has registered a stunning protest against the system that created his debt. He has said in effect, 'You want my robe? Here, take everything! Now you've got all I have except my body. Is that what you'll take next?' . . . By refusing to be awed by their power, the powerless are emboldened to seize the initiative, even where structural change is not immediately possible. This message, far from being a counsel to perfection unattainable in this life, is a practical, strategic measure for empowering the oppressed, and it is being lived out all over the world today by powerless people ready to take their history into their own hands." (See Wink's analysis of these five examples in *Engaging the Powers,* 175–93.)

A third example. "Should anyone press you into service for one mile, go with him for two miles." In those days, as the Roman soldiers barreled through the countryside, burned people's huts, and stole their resources, they would then force the local men to carry their loot for them. But in those days, a new liberal Roman law forbade Roman soldiers from forcing these poor prisoners to walk more than one mile with their packs on their backs.

Go an extra mile, Jesus says. His audience would immediately understand that any soldier who made the people go an extra mile would be arrested for breaking the law and be imprisoned. Jesus is saying, if you did this, all the Roman soldiers themselves would be imprisoned, not you, because they violated their own law. Notice, he does not say, "Fight back and kill the Romans." He also does not say, "Run away, there's nothing you can do." In these teachings, we see Jesus leading a workshop in nonviolence just as Dr. King and the civil rights leaders did with movement participants. Jesus teaches them and trains them to respond to violence with creative nonviolent resistance and in doing so, to transform every dire situation. Use creative nonviolent action to end oppression and you will be free, he instructs. Rev. James Lawson, the great teacher of nonviolence and the main strategist of the civil rights movement, once told me that Jesus could teach this example because he himself had done it. He probably walked an extra mile with a Roman soldier, began talking with him, listening to his story, and disarming him in the process.

Once again, we note that, for Jesus and his own lifelong nonviolent, direct action, this is the methodology of God, the way God works and the way we are to relate with one another. Jesus is not speaking of some utopian world without conflict but a world with conflict in which we all can learn to resolve our conflicts nonviolently, as Wink explains:

Jesus does not encourage Jews to walk a second mile in order to build up merit in heaven, or to exercise a supererogatory piety, or to kill the soldier with kindness. He is helping an oppressed people find a way to protest and neutralize an onerous practice despised throughout the empire. He is not giving a non-political message of spiritual world-transcendence. He is formulating a worldly spirituality in which the people at the bottom of society or under the thumb of imperial power learn to recover their humanity. . . . One must be creative, improvising new tactics to keep the opponent off balance. To those whose lifelong pattern has been to cringe before their masters, Jesus offers a way to liberate themselves from servile actions and a servile mentality. He asserts that they can do this before there is a revolution. They can begin to behave with dignity and recovered humanity now, even under the unchanged conditions of the old order. Jesus' sense of divine immediacy has social implications. The reign of God is already breaking into the world, and it comes, not as an imposition from on high, but as the leaven slowly causing the dough to rise (Mt. 13:33/Lk. 13:20). (Wink, *Engaging the Powers*, 183)

"Give to the one who asks of you," Jesus says in his next example. Instead of making money and hoarding it, he teaches us to give to those in need. He calls his followers to lend money without expecting interest or even the return of the principal, as Wink explains. Be generous, selfless givers. This radical egalitarian sharing is the beginning of the oppressed peoples' own liberation. But it is nothing new, just a revision of the Jubilee Year outlined in the Torah, as Luke will explain further.

Finally, in the fifth example, he says, "Do not turn your back on one who wants to borrow." Lend to others; don't turn your back. Be generous. If we applied these Gospel economics socially and globally, we would end our hoarding, return the resources we have stolen from the poor, feed the hungry, house the homeless, and heal the sick. We would treat everyone with respect and dignity and make social and economic justice for every human being our first priority. Apparently, this egalitarian sharing became a hallmark of the early community, as the Acts of the Apostles testifies.

These five examples show us how to practice creative nonviolent resistance in the face of violence and systemic oppression. Later, Jesus will demonstrate his commandment time and again through his own fearless, daring nonviolence. If his life is read from the perspective of this commandment alone, we see that he practiced creative nonviolent resistance every hour of his public life and engaged in hundreds of disarming nonviolent actions. He is never passive, and he never uses violence or retaliates with violence, but instead stands up and engages in fearless nonviolent direct action each and every time.

Millions of people around the globe are engaged in grassroots campaigns of nonviolent resistance to oppression, war, and empire. As Gene Sharp, Walter Wink, Erica Chenoweth, Maria Stephen, and others have documented, more people are personally involved in local and global grassroots movements of nonviolence today than ever before in history. Perhaps despite the crises of the world, people are beginning to wake up to the teaching of Jesus here in the fifth antithesis, that we have the power to disarm our opponents through organized, thoughtful, steadfast nonviolent resistance. Perhaps humanity is waking up to the truth that

Jesus was right all along, that active, creative nonviolence works. Here's Wink's summary of these amazing teachings:

> Just on the ground of sheer originality the examples of unarmed direct action in Matthew 5:39–41 would appear to have originated with Jesus. No one, not only in the first century but in all of human history, ever advocated defiance of oppressors by turning the cheek, stripping oneself naked in court, or jeopardizing a soldier by carrying his pack a second mile. For three centuries, the early church observed Jesus' command to nonviolence. But nowhere in the early church, to say nothing of the early fathers, do we find statements similar to these in their humor and originality. These sayings are, in fact, so radical, so unprecedented, and so threatening, that it has taken all these centuries just to begin to grasp their implications. (Wink, *Engaging the Powers*, 184)

If we do not believe the ancient text, if we need further proof, then hear the teachings of the great practitioners of nonviolence, like Dr. Martin Luther King Jr. "Returning violence for violence multiplies violence, adding deeper darkness to a night already devoid of stars. Darkness cannot drive our darkness; only light can do that. Hate cannot drive out hate; only love can do that" (King, *Where Do We Go from Here: Chaos or Community?*, 64–65): Better yet, go and experiment with creative nonviolence in your own daily life. Attend a nonviolence training or organize one for your church or local community. When you join a vigil or demonstration, encourage everyone to adhere to the nonviolence of Jesus and Dr. King and watch how the power of nonviolence disarms everyone, including ourselves. Here's Wink's conclusion:

> Nonviolence must not be misconstrued as a way of avoiding conflict. The "peace" that the gospel brings is never the absence of conflict, but an ineffable divine reassurance within the heart of conflict: a peace that passes understanding. Christians have all too often called for "nonviolence" when they really meant tranquility. Nonviolence, in fact, seeks out conflict, elicits conflict, exacerbates conflict, in order to bring it out into the open and lance its poisonous sores. It is not idealistic or sentimental about evil; it does not coddle or cajole aggressors, but moves against perceived injustice proactively, with the same alacrity as the most hawkish militarist. The programmatic task of what we might call the "Jesus project" in the decades ahead will require moving from largely reactive, episodic, and occasional nonviolent actions to an aggressive, sustained movement. Our goal must be the training of millions of nonviolent activists who are ready, at a moment's notice, to swing into action on behalf of the humanizing purposes of God. (Wink, *Engaging the Powers*, 192)

Sixth, "Love Your Enemies; Then You Will Truly Be
Sons and Daughters of the God of Universal Nonviolent Love" (5:43–48)
The sixth antithesis is the climax of the Sermon on the Mount. In those days, writers put the key teaching in the center of the text, not toward the end. Everything in the sermon leads up to this verse, but in a way, everything in the entire Bible leads up to this verse: "You have

heard that it was said, 'You shall love your countrymen and hate your enemy.' But I say to you, love your enemies and pray for those who persecute you that you may be sons and daughters of your heavenly God, for God makes his sun rise on the bad and the good and the rain to fall on the just and the unjust."

These are the most radical, political, revolutionary words ever uttered. They are certainly the most radical words in the entire Bible, and the most profound spiritual teachings ever taught. For the last seventeen hundred years, we Christians have done our best to pretend Jesus never said them.

Here Jesus commands us to love the people targeted with death by our nation/state. This is the first point to note: he uses explicit nation/state language. He is not referring to a disagreeable neighbor or a difficult boss or a mean relative. The enemy here refers to that nation which is under attack by your nation. For North Americans, that would mean, over the past five decades, the people of Vietnam, El Salvador, Nicaragua, Guatemala, Panama, Grenada, Iraq, and Afghanistan. Jesus would want North Americans not only to stop the wars against these people but to actively love these people.

Instinctively we know that we would get in trouble from our government if we somehow sided nonviolently with the people our government wages war upon, and we do not want to get in trouble. We are afraid of the consequences. So we disobey Jesus, go along with our nation/state, sit by while our young people go off to kill or be killed, and support the culture of permanent war and hate. This is the way of the world but not the way of Jesus or God's reign of peace.

Throughout history, the nations have commanded us to hate and kill our enemies. When Jesus commands us to love the enemies of our nation/state, he uses the specific Greek word *agapē*, which is unlike any word in the English language. *Agapē* is unconditional, non-retaliatory, sacrificial, all-encompassing, all-inclusive, nonviolent love, a love by which one gives his or her life for the other—in this case, our enemy. Jesus commands us to practice the unconditional love of God and to do so in the most politically charged arena in the world. We cannot love people and at the same time wage war against them, so his commandment outlaws war, war preparations, killings, bombings, and the development of weapons of mass destruction. He's trying to get us ready to enter God's nonviolent reign of universal love, so he instructs us to see beyond our borders and embrace every human being as a sister and brother, to live in peace with everyone, especially those threatened by our nation/state.

Nowhere in the text does Jesus offer an exception to this commandment. He does not say, "Love your enemies, but if they're really hateful and violent, then you can kill them." There is no exception, no justification, no permission for killing. Killing our enemies is completely forbidden, because we are commanded to love them with *agapē*: unconditional love.

The so-called Just War Theory is never mentioned in the Sermon on the Mount or the four Gospels or the New Testament. It's like saying Jesus taught "just rape" or "just child abuse" or "just racism." It was created over time so that Christians could justify their participation in warfare, even though it is antithetical to everything the nonviolent Jesus taught and lived. In the various versions that exist today, a variety of conditions must be met for warfare to be "morally accepted," including the condition that no civilians will be killed. In today's warfare, however, 90 percent of all victims are civilians (as many UN reports confirm), so even the standards of the so-called Just War Theory cannot be met. But there is no such thing as a just war. In light of the Sermon on the Mount, it is heresy, and a blasphemy in the face of the God of peace. There is no just war.

Notice that the commandment reads, "Love your enemies and pray for your persecutors. . . ." If we start loving our enemies—that is, the people that our nation/state is trying to kill—then we are going to be persecuted, starting with our relatives, neighbors, and coworkers, and possibly even the ruling authorities. That's a sign that we've truly begun to follow Jesus: we are in trouble for making peace, practicing universal love, and walking the way of the cross. That's why Jesus follows the commandment with a second commandment. "Pray for your persecutors." This is the first time we are told to pray in the Sermon on the Mount! He is not saying, "Pray for your enemies." He does not say, "Pray for yourselves." He specifically commands us to pray for those who persecute us because we publicly show love for the enemies of our nation/state. He wants us to pray for them, that they too might be converted to Jesus's way of universal nonviolent love.

Followers of Jesus are eager to love everyone and should be happy to experiment with this universal, political nonviolent love. Life is short; we want to be citizens of God's kingdom of universal love, so we try to love everyone, including Russians, Iraqis, and Afghanis.

As we meditate on this commandment and try to put it into practice, we might ask why Jesus orders us to take this public, political stand of universal nonviolent love for our nation's enemies. Notice, he does not say, "Do it because it's right." He does not say, "Do it because it's moral." He does not say, "Do it because it's the only practical path to peace." He says, in effect, "Love your enemies because God loves God's enemies." This is the nature of God!

Jesus describes the nature of God in the simplest, clearest terms—God loves every human being no matter what, and if you want to worship, serve, and be related to this God, you must do the same.

This image of a God of nonviolence is a breakthrough in human history. It is the heart of Christianity and, as such, has been mainly rejected by most Christians. It challenges us to question our image of God. Is our God violent or nonviolent? Do we want the God of universal nonviolent love that Jesus tells us about? If we want to be sons and daughters of the living God, are we willing to practice the same universal nonviolent love as God and to accept the social, economic, and political consequences for our public stand? How do we love our nation's enemies? How do we stop our nation from killing our sisters and brothers in enemy nations? How can we help the churches practice universal nonviolent love?

Jesus does not end the six antitheses there. He asks a series of penetrating questions to try and persuade us of the wisdom of *agapē*/love. "If you love those who love you, what recompense will you have? Do not the tax collectors do the same? And if you greet your brothers only, what is unusual about that? Do not the pagans do the same? So be perfect, just as your heavenly Father is perfect." With these questions, Jesus addresses our very limited love, our conditional love, and how it serves the nation/state in the big business of war. Is there any reward for limited love? Is there anything unusual about limited love? Do not the tax collectors and the pagans practice limited love for those who love them, for their brothers?

For the ragtag group of impoverished Galileans listening to these teachings, there was nothing worse than being compared to a tax collector or a pagan. The tax collectors stole their meager resources and kept them in debt. The pagans were the Romans and other ruling authorities who oppressed and killed them. Jesus says, in other words, if you do not rise to the level of universal nonviolent love and be who you were created to be—the sons and daughters of the God of peace—then how are you any different from tax collectors or pagans?

Dr. King is, for me, the greatest teacher of *agapē* and nonviolence, and he once gave a sermon devoted to the theme of our loving our enemies. He said:

> Love is not this sentimental something that we talk about. It's not merely an emotional something. Love is creative, understanding goodwill for all men and women. It is the refusal to defeat any individual. When you rise to the level of love, of its great beauty and power, you seek only to defeat evil systems. Individuals who happen to be caught up in that system, you love, but you seek to defeat the system. . . . Hate for hate only intensifies the existence of hate and evil in the universe. If I hit you and you hit me and I hit you back and you hit me back, that goes on ad infinitum. It just never ends. Somewhere somebody must have a little sense, and that's the strong person. The strong person is the person who can cut off the chain of hate, the chain of evil. And that is the tragedy of hate, that it doesn't cut it off. It only intensifies the existence of hate and evil in the universe. Somebody must have religion enough and morality enough to cut it off and inject within the very structure of the universe that strong and powerful element of love. (Moore, ed., *Following the Call: Living the Sermon on the Mount Together*, 143)

The climax of Jesus's six antitheses comes when he questions our limited, conditional love to people like ourselves, our fellow countrymen and -women. "What's so unusual about that?" He's looking for unusual, outrageous love, the love that goes beyond all borders, politics, and expectations. Love should not be normal! It should not be the so-called love of our countrymen and -women that in fact upholds the culture of war and ends up supporting the death of people elsewhere in the world. The love Jesus calls for is bold, boundless, public, shocking, even dangerous; this is Godly love.

The final line of chapter 5 has caused problems for centuries. "Be perfect, as God is perfect." The word "perfect" means to have no flaws, no imperfections, no brokenness. And yet, every human being is flawed, broken, and imperfect. This mistaken call to perfection has led to much violence, judgment, and condemnation. The original Greek word, *teleios*, describes, instead, a call to go all the way to the end, to fulfill one's destiny, making everything "complete." Other translations suggest it means "maturity."

In the context of nonviolent universal love, this new understanding makes sense: we are called as weak, flawed, broken human beings to the fullness of nonviolent universal love, to go all the way to the very ends of complete, universal divine love. Jesus says we are to be like God. Luke's Gospel changes the complicated word "perfect" to compassionate or merciful. This helps unpack the original meaning. Be as compassionate, as merciful, as nonviolent, as universally loving as God. That's the goal of our lives. That's the teaching of the Sermon on the Mount in a nutshell. Do this, and you will be sons and daughters of God.

Be Real, Avoid Hypocrisy: Prayer, Fasting, Almsgiving, Forgiveness (6:1–18)

Chapter 6 offers a series of teachings on prayer, almsgiving, fasting, and forgiveness as basic practices to prepare us for Jesus's new commandment to seek first the kingdom of God. These four practices are presented as the key necessary ingredients for the life Jesus models for us. Jesus insists, contrary to current practice, that these four practices should be done with humility and secrecy, that our prayers should be made in the silence of our hearts, that we should give away money to the poor without anyone knowing it, that we should fast regularly without anyone knowing it, and that we should forgive everyone who ever hurt us over and over again, every day, for the rest of our lives. Religious practices, he insists, should not be performed to make us feel righteous or look holy before others, but should be done for God alone and God's kingdom of love and peace. Jesus does not want us to be hypocrites. He hates hypocrisy. He wants our faith to be authentic as we engage with our loving God in the privacy of our hearts.

Each of the short teachings urges us to avoid hypocrisy but it also sheds more light on the nature of God. Do not perform righteous deeds to be seen, Jesus says; then God will not reward you. Apparently, God rewards those who do good deeds sincerely in secret, without ego and without seeking any praise. Give alms to the poor, but do not let anyone know you are doing it, he commands. It must be a total secret. Why? Because the God who sees in secret will then repay you. God secretly sees everything you do, so do good things secretly, solely for the good of the poor person and to please God. Regarding prayer, he insists we go to our "inner room," close the door, and pray in secret, without anyone else knowing that we pray, so that we are people who have an intimate relationship with God, so that we are focused solely on God, not on achieving the respect of others, not for our egos and pride. Furthermore, do not say long prayers, he teaches, because God "knows what you need before you ask him." This is very consoling. God knows what we need; ask God for what we need, as a child would ask its mother or father, and trust that God will give us what we need. That is the basic nature of prayer.

Then Jesus teaches us exactly what to say. After two thousand years, the Lord's Prayer has become so rote to many that it might have lost its bite. Nonetheless, it still has immense revolutionary power if you stay with it and pray it, one word at a time.

It begins in the first-person plural: *Our*. We say this together; it's the prayer of the whole human family. Since we now know that God is a God of peace and universal love, and we are sons and daughters of this God of peace and universal love, he teaches us to address God as our common "Father." The prayer begins: "Our Father in heaven." We are praying as children who call upon our beloved Father. In the patriarchal world of Jesus's time, a Jewish father was revered as honorable, loving, and just, the one who deserves utmost respect. Jesus invites us to call upon God as our loving, gentle, wise, and just Father. This is how we are to relate to God—with intimate love, childlike trust, and total devotion. "Hallowed be your name," we proclaim. Everything about God is holy and deserves our utmost respect and reverence, including the very mention of God's name.

Then comes the heart of the prayer, the number one request every human being is to make of the living God of peace and nonviolence: "May your kingdom—of infinite peace, universal love, and total nonviolence—come, and may your will for infinite peace, universal love, and total nonviolence be done right now, here on earth, from now on, as it is done in heaven." That prayer sums up the prayer of Jesus and every peacemaker. May God's reign come to earth, God's will be done on earth, right now, by all of us. We have learned that God is a God of peace, so we beg that God's will and God's reign be done, by all humanity here and now, and that this reign be fully realized here and now on earth.

If we say these words and beg for God's will and God's reign to be realized here on earth, that means we have to look beyond our nation and its borders. We no longer consider ourselves citizens of our nation. From now on, we act as citizens of God's reign, and we beg for God's new world to become reality. Thus, we renounce our national identity and recognize our true identity as a son or daughter of the God of peace, our beloved Father (and Mother), and a brother or sister of every human being on earth. That's why this prayer is the most political of all prayers: it summons us beyond the limits of nationalism into the vision and practice of what Martin Luther King Jr. called the Beloved Community. Christians need to help other Christians understand the political nature of this prayer for the coming of God's reign on earth, and then practice the Sermon on the Mount to do their part to help make the prayer come true.

Next, we beg God for bread so that we never go hungry, so that no human being on the planet goes hungry. In John's Gospel, which does not contain this prayer, Jesus announces that he is the bread of life, so besides begging for bread for every human being, we are begging for the bread of life, for Jesus himself, to be our nourishment. Today in a world where millions are starving, and thousands die every single day from hunger and hunger-related disease, we realize that this is the prayer of the poor. Since we seek to live in solidarity with the poor, this prayer reminds us to do our part to help end hunger and poverty, that everyone might have food, water, housing, healthcare, education, and dignity, that hunger itself might end and everyone might be sustained by Jesus, the bread of life.

Then, we forgive everyone who ever hurt us. The wording is important. We ask God to forgive us to the exact same extent that we forgive those who have hurt us. That means, if there is anyone who has hurt us, we forgive them. If we do not forgive them, we cannot expect God to forgive us. If we do not forgive unconditionally, then we should not pray the Lord's Prayer.

Forgiveness is a critical ingredient in the life of nonviolence. It is a requirement. It will be the final act of the nonviolent Jesus as he dies on the cross. Each of us has hurt somebody and each of us needs to be forgiven. Over the course of our lives, we have probably hurt many people. As participants in the culture of violence, racism, injustice, and war, we have actually participated in hurting millions of people through our support of the violent status quo. In varying degrees, we have been racist, sexist, classist, greedy, and unjust. We have supported warmaking, the maintenance of nuclear weapons, and the ongoing destruction of the earth. We need to be forgiven. We need God to forgive us. We want God to forgive us for all the ways we have offended God and hurt God, including our participation in social sin. Basically, when the crucified Jesus begs God from the cross to forgive us, notice that he says, "Forgive them, for they know not what they do." That means all of us. We all need to be forgiven—especially for the grave wrongs we do not even know we are doing.

Jesus places a condition upon us: we will only be forgiven for the harm we have done if we forgive all those who have harmed us. If we want complete forgiveness, we have to offer complete forgiveness. Likewise, we need to forgive all those who have hurt us, and that means making forgiveness a daily mantra. I forgive everyone, I forgive everyone, I forgive everyone. With this mantra, recited daily and throughout our day, we forgive everyone every day for the rest of our lives—starting with our parents, siblings, relatives, friends, neighbors, co-workers, our nation's enemies, even those in our nation.

Forgive them all—and you will be forgiven all. Do not forgive them—and you will not be forgiven. This is so important that Matthew adds an addendum to make sure that we have clearly understood the teaching: "If you forgive others their transgressions, your heavenly Father will forgive you. If you do not forgive others, neither will your Father forgive your transgressions."

The prayer ends with a plea that we not be tested or tempted, that we be delivered from evil. This last verse has been glossed over, but we need to attend to it. It addresses head-on the question of evil. May we not be tempted to do evil. May we be delivered from evil. May we all be liberated from evil of every kind. We are all stuck in the culture of violence, war, and death—whether we are gang members in a city neighborhood or shareholders in a multinational company whose policies harm the world. Jesus has come to liberate us and teach us how to liberate ourselves and others by recognizing evil in its many forms and rejecting it. With this prayer, we pledge not to give in to any temptations to evil, and we ask for our deliverance from all evil, promising in effect to do our part by refusing to cooperate with evil and do only good.

With that, Jesus warns us about fasting publicly in order that others will see us and admire us for being holy and ascetical. When he fasted for forty days, he did so alone in the desert. Unlike the religious authorities of his time, he was not showing off or seeking his own glory. He wants us to fast and at the same time he wants us to avoid hypocrisy, even in such a simple but important spiritual practice. We can fast to repent from the culture of violence and deepen in nonviolence, for example, but we are not to let anyone know that we are fasting. Fasting should be done in private, so that only the God who sees in secret will know about our fast. Jesus gets specific in his practical suggestions: anoint your head, wash your face, and do not appear to be fasting. In that way, "Your Father who sees what is hidden will repay you." So the teaching is: fast as a way to repent, but do not do it for attention. Let no one know. Make it a private prayer to the God of peace for the coming of God's reign.

"Seek First God's Kingdom and God's Justice and Everything Else Will Be Provided for You" (6:19–34)

Now we know that the God of peace sees everything, including what is hidden. The point therefore is to do everything we do for the God of peace and universal love. Our focus is not on money, success, career, ego, honor, pride, but solely on the God of peace. Because we focus solely on God, we do not "store up treasure on earth." Instead Jesus urges us to store up treasure in God's kingdom. Renounce the treasures of the world, which lead only to selfishness, idolatry, violence, and spiritual death, and instead keep your eyes on God and do everything for God. "Store up treasures in heaven," we read, "where neither moth nor decay destroys, nor thieves break in and steal. For where your treasure is, there also will your heart be." Here Jesus urges us to set our hearts solely on God and God's kingdom. This is the spiritual journey and the meaning of life. Set your heart completely on the God of universal love, universal compassion, and universal peace. That is the only investment that lasts.

Because our hearts, minds, and lives are set on God and God's kingdom of peace, we renounce every aspect of violence, greed, and war. We live as if we are already in the kingdom of God, so we let the things of the world fall away. That's why Jesus's next teaching makes sense: "You cannot serve God and money." If we focus on money, we are not focused on God. Money becomes our primary goal, the literal treasure of our heart. But we are Sermon-on-the-Mount people. We set everything else aside to focus solely on God and God's kingdom of peace.

To help us pursue this Gospel call of downward mobility and total trust in God, St. Francis and Dorothy Day advocated voluntary poverty. They urged us to renounce money, possessions, storing up wealth, and the violence and wars that come with greed. When we enter a state of "precarity," our faith grows and we learn to trust more profoundly in God to protect us and provide for us. Here Jesus invites us to the fullness of life in God, to be like St. Francis and Dorothy Day, to "hate" money, to give it away to the poor, to simplify our lives, to practice universal love and compassion, and to focus our time, attention, and energy on the God of love and peace.

Of course, we can take his logic further and say, "You cannot serve both God and country. You cannot serve both God and war. You cannot serve both God and nuclear weapons. You cannot serve both the God of life and the false gods of death. It's one or the other." Every day, the choice stands before us. The nonviolent Jesus urges us to choose the God of peace.

All these teachings in chapter 6 lead to the climactic new job description for the Christian life of nonviolence: "Therefore, I tell you, do not worry about your life, what you will eat or drink, about your body, what you will wear. Is not life more than food and the body more than clothing?" So Jesus gives us another commandment: do not worry about your life, food, drink, or clothes. Trust God to take care of you, even down to the smallest detail. "Look at the birds in the sky. They do not sow or reap, they gather nothing into barns, yet your heavenly God feeds them. Are not you more important than they?" Jesus calls us to observe how God provides for little creatures, and to trust that God will provide for us, God's beloved children, even more. We are more important than the birds; so the Creator will provide for us, take care of us, and protect us. There is nothing to worry about ever again!

Then Jesus makes an astonishing declaration: God has numbered every hair on your head. God knows everything about you. God is inside every cell in your body, with you every second of your life, surrounding you with grace and light at all times. God loves you wildly, unconditionally, infinitely, madly, lavishly. God will protect you. Believe in this doting parent and trust in God. The more you trust in God and God's unconditional love of you, the more you will let go of all worry, anxiety, anger, fear, and violence. You are wildly loved and cared for, so you can relax into the peace of God and surrender to God and God's will. You have nothing to fear ever again: God is the best, most devoted, most gentle and kind parent of all.

"Can any of you by worrying add a single moment to your life span?" Jesus asks. The answer is no. No one can add a single moment to one's life span by worrying. "So stop your worrying," he says. With this commandment, he urges us to put into practice what we know with our reason, that worrying is useless. Concentrate instead on what's most important: God, God's reign, God's justice for the poor, God's mercy and compassion. Trust in God and let God take care of you. This has to become our daily spiritual practice if we want to follow Jesus.

"Why are you anxious about clothes?" he asks. "Learn from the way the wildflowers grow. They do not work or spin. But I tell you that not even Solomon in all his splendor was clothed like one of them. If God so clothes the grass of the field, which grows today and is thrown into the oven tomorrow, will God not much more provide for you, you of little faith?" Again, Jesus instructs us to learn how to live in God by studying nature. This is the ancient practice of all indigenous peoples of the earth. They study how God cares for nature, and they bend their lives according to ways of nature so that God will care for them too. Here Jesus invites us to be contemplatives who gaze mindfully at the wonders of creation—in this case, the wildflowers—to see the hand of God at work in our midst, to gain insight, strength, and understanding of God's care of us.

"So do not worry and say, 'What are we to eat?' or 'What are we to drink?' or 'What are we to wear?' All these things the pagans seek," he concludes. "Your heavenly God knows you need them all. But seek first the kingdom of God and God's justice and all these things will be given you besides." This is the great commandment of the Sermon on the Mount. *Seek first the kingdom of God and God's justice, and all these things will be given you besides.* Focus on God and God's reign. Don't waste your life in pursuit of money, possessions, privilege, or the false security of weapons. God will take care of you, so get to work seeking God's kingdom of peace and God's justice here on earth.

If you seek God's reign and God's justice wholeheartedly, all your needs such as food, clothing, and shelter will be met. Everything will be provided for you. It's a new law of nature, like the law of gravity. As you serve God by seeking God's kingdom, everything you need will be taken care of. At the end of your life, you will rejoice that you spent your life seeking God, God's reign, and God's justice.

Once again, the key to understanding this teaching lies in the meaning of God's reign and God's justice. Given the vision of universal love, universal compassion, and universal peace that Jesus has been presenting, we know God's reign and God's justice as an entirely new culture of justice, compassion, and peace. To put it negatively, it means a new culture without war, poverty, hunger, racism, sexism, gun violence, nuclear weapons, and environmental destruction. It means, from now on, every Christian must spend his or her life working for the abolition of all violence, war, poverty, hunger, racism, sexism, gun violence, nuclear weapons, and environmental destruction. This is the job description of the follower of the nonviolent Jesus. This is how we seek God's reign and God's justice here and now with our lives.

"Enter through the Narrow Gate" (7:1–14)

In the concluding chapter of the sermon, the nonviolent Jesus reminds us that, since we are all hypocritical, violent people, none of us can make any claim above anyone else. No one can think themselves better than another. Eventually, he will invite us to be the last of all and servant of all. So, he teaches, let go of any trace of self-righteousness, judgment, condemnation, or any other form of ego comparison. From now on, show compassion toward everyone else, and take a stand of humble nonviolence. He insists that our strength is our humility, gentleness, and vulnerability.

Here Jesus offers a series of teachings about the requirements of a life worthy of God's reign: "Stop judging, that you may not be judged. For as you judge, so will you be judged, and the measure with which you measure will be measured out to you." For the rest of our lives, we practice non-judgmentalism. To do this, it helps to learn Buddhist mindfulness, centeredness, and letting go. We do not judge others; instead, we look upon every single human being with love, kindness, and compassion. We accept people, appreciate them, try to imagine walking in their shoes, and so serve them and help them on their journey to peace. We can judge the unjust systems of violence and war, but we no longer judge other people. We love everyone and, like Jesus, go forward, inviting everyone to join his campaign of nonviolence and universal love. As we give up judging others or condemning others, we discover a new humility and serenity and enter the spectacular way of Jesus.

"Why do you notice the splinter in your brother's eye, but do not perceive the wooden beam in your own eye? How can you say to your brother, 'Let me remove that splinter from your eye,' while the wooden beam is in your eye? You hypocrite, remove the wooden beam from your eye first; then you will see clearly to remove the splinter from your brother's eye." This is one of the quintessential teachings of the Sermon on the Mount. In this graphic parable, Jesus explains why we can no longer judge others—because our condition is worse than anyone else, and we don't even know it.

We all want to correct and improve those around us—starting with our parents, our brothers and sisters, our children, our relatives, our co-workers, and our friends. There you are, stewing about some relative and why he or she doesn't get their act together, when all along, according to Jesus, you are in much worse shape. You are the one who needs to get his or her act together. It's a profound teaching, one that we need to work on for the rest of our lives. We start by presuming that Jesus is talking about us. Take this teaching personally. Presume you have a two-by-four in your eye and drop your immediate concern about the splinter in your brother's eye. Get to work removing the two-by-four!

Imagine having a splinter in your eye! Imagine the pain! We couldn't do anything until someone took it out. It would be total agony. Now imagine having a two-by-four piece of lumber in your eye, how it sticks out of your head, from either side. Imagine the pain! You would be in agony! Indeed, you would be dying, if not dead already.

So, Jesus says, there you are, trying to remove the splinter from someone else's eye, when all the while, you have this two-by-four sticking out of your head. First remove the two-by-four from your head; then, he says, you can remove the splinter from your brother's eye. "Then, you will see clearly," Jesus says. Seeing clearly is critical for the nonviolent Jesus. The only way we can see clearly is if we remove the violence within us, the two-by-four sticking out of our heads. Then we will recognize everyone as a beloved sister and brother, as if everyone were entering God's reign of peace and nonviolence. Only then can we see God in others. Only then can we be of service to others and offer real help, healing, and release.

"Do not give what is holy to dogs, or throw your pearls before swine, lest they trample them underfoot, and turn and tear you to pieces." Here he warns us to beware of those who would do us violence and kill us. Stay away from them, don't give your wisdom to them, don't tempt them to hurt you or kill you. This parable invites us to be mindful and centered always in God and the love of God, but, as Jesus will later say in Luke, to be wise as serpents as well. In the world, we want to be peaceful, calm, quiet, and careful, even as we serve others and work for peace and justice. But we also do not want to lead others to do violence, to commit social sin, against ourselves and anyone.

Next, he invites us to live in relationship with God, as a loving child toward its doting parent. Ask, seek, and knock, he says, and everything will be provided for you. "Ask and it will be given to you; seek and you will find; knock and the door will be opened to you. For everyone who asks, receives; and the one who seeks, finds; and to the one who knocks, the door will be opened." These teachings are a promise, ones that we should experiment with. Ask God for special graces. Why should God give us special graces if we don't ask for them? We need to *ask* for blessings. Seek God out, and he promises, you will find the loving, nonviolent God. Knock on God's door, and it will be opened for you. If you do not knock on someone's door, including God's, how will they know you are there? How will they ever invite you in? You have to ask, seek, and knock.

These teachings push us to engage God every day of our lives as a loving child who asks for help, food, safety, and security. God wants to help us, but in many ways God is shy and humble, so we need to ask, seek, and knock. God wants us to engage God. All the time.

Jesus goes further, then, and insists that God would give us only good things if we dare ask God. "Which one of you would hand his son a stone when he asks for a loaf of bread, or a snake when he asks for a fish? If you then, who are wicked, know how to give good gifts to your children, how much more will your heavenly Father give good things to those who ask him?" We know how to give good things to our children (even though we are wicked!), Jesus says. Imagine the good things God will give to us (since God is totally loving, nonviolent, and good). Jesus poses a question: "How much more will your heavenly Father give good things to those who ask him?" We need to sit with this question and mull over it for weeks and months and years. Do we believe it? If we dare choose, we can ask God for good things, and trust that he will give us good things. That's the promise. That's the life of faith. That's the way we are to live from now on.

"Do to others whatever you would have them do to you. This is the law and the prophets." The Golden Rule, as this teaching has long been called, appears in every major world religion, going back thousands of years. It is the basic law of decency and should be the basis for all common goodness. Jesus says that this rule sums up "the law and the prophets." We want to be treated with love, peace, respect, dignity, and nonviolence; if so, then, we need to treat every human being with love, peace, respect, dignity, and nonviolence.

We're all taught the Golden Rule in kindergarten, but somewhere along the way we get brainwashed by the culture of violence to do unto others whatever we want, however cruel or violent we might be. It's permissible to wage war, build weapons of mass destruction, ignore human suffering, maintain racism and segregation, steal the resources of others, and support the destruction of Mother Earth. Most everyone rejects the Golden Rule and looks the other way about the culture of violence and death, though few would admit it. That's why this bedrock Sermon-on-the-Mount teaching is best understood within the boundaries of nonviolence. If we live within the boundary lines of nonviolence, we want only the best for every human being on earth, which means we have our work cut out for us. We have to step up to the plate and do our part to ease human suffering and end systemic violence.

"Enter through the narrow gate; for the gate is wide and the road broad that leads to destruction, and those who enter through it are many. How narrow the gate and constricted the road that leads to life. And those who find it are few." This teaching on the narrow gate and the constricted road that leads to life sums up the entire sermon and the entire Gospel. Nearly everyone enters the wide gate of greed, nationalism, materialism, and militarism; nearly everyone walks the broad road of violence, war, and destruction, as if violence were perfectly normal, permissible, moral, and even holy. Few people wake up to the reality of global violence and turn around and head off on the unknown, long-ignored, hard-to-find narrow path of nonviolence.

Here Jesus instructs us again to go against the grain, to walk the narrow path of nonviolence, and to seek out the narrow gate of nonviolence. If we do, our lives will not end in violence, death, and destruction. Instead, we will discover peace, love, compassion, and the fullness of life for ourselves and others. We will find the freedom not to hurt or kill others or support the culture of violence. This, he teaches, is the spiritual journey of life: the journey along the narrow path of nonviolence through the narrow gate of nonviolence into God's realm of nonviolence.

We have not been taught to walk the narrow path of nonviolence; we have been urged to pursue the broad avenue of violence, war, and nationalism, as if this was the will of God. Most of us do not even realize that we are journeying along the highway of violence, war, and death. The only way to ensure which path we are taking is to seek the fullness of nonviolence as Jesus has taught and embodied, to renounce every trace of violence, and to support the culture of nonviolence. It means speaking out against the culture of violence despite the cost. Matthew invites us to take Jesus at his word and walk that narrow path from now on. For the rest of our lives, we will be people who do not kill or wage war, who try to stop the killings and wars, who work for a new nonviolent world where no one is ever killed again.

Jesus moves toward his conclusion by urging us to avoid the teachers and preachers of violence, whom he calls "false prophets." Have nothing to do with them, he says. We are people of total nonviolence, and so we avoid and disbelieve every teaching of hatred and war, especially when dressed up in religious language. From now on, we listen only to teachers, preachers, and prophets of total nonviolence.

"Beware of false prophets, who come to you in sheep's clothing, but underneath are ravenous wolves. By their fruits you will know them. Do people pick grapes from thornbushes, or figs from thistles? Just so, every good tree bears good fruit, and a rotten tree bears bad fruit. A good tree cannot bear bad fruit, nor can a rotten tree bear good fruit. Every tree that does not bear good fruit will be cut down and thrown into the fire. So by their fruits you will know them."

Notice the fruit of other people's action. If they bear the good fruit of peace, justice, compassion, and nonviolence, then they are true prophets, people of nonviolence through and through. But avoid anyone, including ministers, priests, or bishops, who espouse war, whose hearts are full of violence, whose actions support hate.

At the end, Jesus says, *"Not everyone who says to me, 'Lord, Lord,' will enter the reign of heaven, but only the one who does the will of my God in heaven. Many will say to me on that day, 'Lord, Lord, did we not prophesy in your name? Did we not drive out demons in your name? Did we not do mighty deeds in your name?' Then I will declare to them solemnly, 'I never knew you. Depart from me, you evildoers.'"* Jesus wants us to enter the narrow gate and walk the narrow path of nonviolence to life, even if everyone else supports some kind of violence, war, greed, racism, and imperial domination. He wants us to enter God's reign of love and peace now. Even more, he wants to know us personally as his friends. He seeks disciples, friends, and companions to join him on his journey of active nonviolence. But we cannot be with him if we do evil. As the psalms teach, we must renounce evil and do good. Otherwise, he will tell us that he never knew us.

This is an important and mysterious announcement that invites deep reflection. Does Jesus know us? How does he know each one of us individually? Matthew teaches that those who practice nonviolence and universal love and do good like Jesus are known by the nonviolent Jesus. He wants to live in relationship with us, so we have to be like him, doing good and walking the narrow path of nonviolence. Then we will know Jesus and he will know us. Living in personal relationship with the nonviolent Jesus while we practice loving nonviolence in the end becomes the real goal of our lives, and our quiet inner peace and joy.

Here's the conclusion: *"Everyone who listens to these words of mine and acts on them will be like a wise person who built her house on rock. The rain fell, the floods came, and the winds blew and buffeted the house. But it did not collapse; it had been set solidly on rock. And everyone who listens to these words of mine but does not act on them will be like a fool who built his house on sand. The rain fell, the floods came, and the winds blew and buffeted the house. And it collapsed and was completely ruined."* These are the last words of the Sermon on the Mount.

Notice that Jesus does not say, "Whoever acts on these words will not suffer rain, floods, or winds." In both cases, people are hit by a disastrous storm. The rains fall, the floods come, the winds blow, and everyone's house is shaken. This is going to happen to us all. For Jesus, the question is not whether we will be hit by a storm during our lives, but whether we will be able to withstand the world's violent, destructive storms. The only way to survive these stormy times is by practicing the teachings of the Sermon on the Mount, by experimenting with Jesus's way of active nonviolence and universal love, by putting the teachings into action and making them the basis of our lives as Gandhi did. If we do, our house will not collapse; we will stand on solid rock and be able to withstand anything the world throws at us.

The difference between the two cases is simple: some of us hear these words and act on them, while others of us hear these words and do not act on them. But notice, everyone hears God's word, Jesus says. The key is whether we act on his teachings. Jesus announces that our very survival depends on acting upon the Sermon on the Mount.

Matthew invites us to study and practice Jesus's Sermon on the Mount as the main guidebook and handbook for our lives. If we surrender ourselves completely to the God of peace, live according to the teachings of the Sermon on the Mount, build our lives on the solid rock of Gospel nonviolence, and hang on to the nonviolent Jesus for dear life, then not only will we survive and never again give in to violence, fear, hatred, war, judgmentalism, worry, anxiety, or self-righteousness, but we will be known personally by Jesus and be welcomed into God's kingdom of universal love and peace. In the end, all will be well.

Jesus Models the Teachings on Nonviolence That He Just Preached in the Sermon on the Mount (8:1–9:38)

In the following chapters, Matthew's Jesus models the teachings of nonviolence that he just taught in his great sermon. He takes the best of the Judaic law of neighborly love combined with his call to creative nonviolence and demonstrates how to be human, how to be a Sermon-on-the-Mount person, beginning with his first encounter as he descends from the mountain into the midst of the crowds.

There he meets a leper, one of the most despised, disenfranchised people, someone banned from society and considered cursed. Lepers were unclean, so you could not go near them, much less, God forbid, touch one. If you did, you violated the law and would also be declared unclean and face excommunication. In other words, it was illegal to go near lepers. To touch one would be an act of civil disobedience. In this first encounter after the sermon, Jesus demonstrates in one perfect act every word of boundless love and compassion he just preached.

We're told that the leper approached, did him homage, and said, "Lord, if you wish, you can make me clean." Jesus responds immediately. He stretches out his hand and physically touches the leper, saying, "I do will it. Be made clean." With that, the leper is healed, and Jesus has broken the law. *He* could now be ostracized and treated like a leper. Notice that Jesus practices compassion regardless of the consequences to himself. In this one act, he is willing to give up his entire life for this poor person. It is the height of nonviolent love. He touches the leper to affirm his humanity and to bring him justice.

Notice, too, that he tells the healed man, "See that you tell no one, but go show yourself to the priest, and offer the gift that Moses prescribed; that will be proof for them." This refers to Leviticus 13 with its detailed rules for the purification of a leper. Jesus wants the former leper made totally whole, which can only happen when the healed leper is fully welcomed back into the community. Jesus does not want the former leper to be marginalized anymore; he does not want any human being to be marginalized. He wants the full social, economic, and political implications of healing, so that a new culture emerges in which no one is marginalized, and everyone is welcomed.

In the next encounter, Jesus ups the ante not only by healing a poor person, but also by demonstrating active love for the enemy by associating with none other than a Roman centurion. Here again he breaks the law of Judaism and demonstrates *agapē* love for the enemy of his people: a Roman military official. This man—a Gentile, by the way—is in charge of one hundred men who represent Rome's oppression of Jesus's people.

"Lord, my servant is lying at home paralyzed, suffering dreadfully," he tells Jesus. "I will come and cure him," Jesus responds. But the hated enemy surprises Jesus with a bold account of faith. "Lord, I am not worthy to have you enter under my roof; only say the word and my servant will be healed," he says. "For I, too, am a person subject to authority, with soldiers subject to me. And I say to one, 'Go,' and he goes; and to another, 'Come here,' and he comes; and to my slave, 'Do this,' and he does it."

Jesus is amazed. "Amen, I say to you, in no one in Israel have I found such faith. I say to you, many will come from the east and the west, and will recline with Abraham, Isaac, and Jacob at the banquet in the kingdom of heaven, but the children of the kingdom will be driven out into the outer darkness, where there will be wailing and grinding of teeth." Jesus affirms the centurion's faith in him and announces that God's universal reign of love is open to every human being, not just the chosen people. Moreover, many of the chosen will not enter God's reign because they reject the teachings of God's universal love, while Gentiles of every race and description from around the planet will dwell in heaven with Abraham, Isaac, and Jacob. This shocking statement goes against the expectations of the Jewish people and the ruling authorities. God's love is open to everyone, Jesus declares, if you only believe with a faith-filled commitment that leads to compassionate action. "You may go; as you have believed, let it be done for you," he tells the centurion, and we're told that the servant was healed.

This dramatic encounter with the Roman enemy does not suggest, however, that Jesus supports the Roman Empire and occupation, or militarism or warfare for that matter, as many have concluded. Nowhere does it say that just because he healed the centurion's servant does he approve of the centurion's violence and domination. The centurion was managing the Roman occupation of Galilee and would be hated by the locals, including the disciples. He was probably involved in killing many people. The nonviolent Jesus is adamantly against the Roman occupation, empire, and its warmaking, so much that eventually the empire will execute him as a threat. Instead, the encounter shows how Jesus practices nonviolence even toward the Roman centurion and offers him disarming love. Remember: the real target of Jesus's love is the centurion's poor slave, whom Jesus heals.

The healings continue, with the brief mention of Jesus healing Peter's mother-in-law. Note: Peter was married and probably had children. Jesus simply touches the mother-in-law. He shows warmth, kindness, and real compassion, and she is immediately restored and starts to serve him. She was probably overwhelmed anyway by the arrival of her son's guru and his wild band of followers. No wonder she took to her bed! But Jesus's kindness heals and disarms her. He treats her with such dignity and humanity that she is restored to the fullness of life and health.

In the evening, Jesus continues to heal all those who are possessed or sick. Later, he will instruct the disciples to do the same. In effect, he is liberating everyone from the demons of empire, nationalism, violence, hatred, and addiction. Likewise, he is healing all those who are victims of the culture of violence—the poor, the sick, the marginalized.

Matthew then cites, of all passages, Isaiah 53 to point out that Jesus is the Messiah, just not the kind of Messiah the Jews were expecting. He is a nonviolent Messiah, the Suffering Servant described by Isaiah "who takes away our infirmities and bears our diseases." This brief note signals to us that Jesus is deadly serious about his Sermon-on-the-Mount nonviolence and will practice it all the way to the end to heal and help the human race enter God's reign of universal love.

Journey "To the Other Side" (8:18–9:8)

The encounter with the Roman centurion seems to have emboldened Jesus. He is determined to live out his Sermon-on-the-Mount teachings, so he gets ready to make a trip—to the other side of the Sea of Galilee—right into enemy territory. There, he will show his disciples how to love their enemies. He will walk among the hated enemies of Galilee and heal them and proclaim the good news. Perhaps, he thinks, they will welcome him and believe in him as the Roman centurion did.

So, we're told, "When Jesus saw a crowd around him, he gave orders to cross to the other side." This is an important sentence. These trips "to the other side" occur several times in each Gospel. They are stories of Jesus's universal love in action. It is hard for us to grasp the meaning of these sea crossings, but for North Americans, it would be like flying to Iraq, Afghanistan, or Palestine—right into the enemy lands where we have waged war and killed thousands of people in recent decades.

As Jesus sets off, we're told of two encounters he has with potential disciples. One is a member of the scribes, the religious authorities who knew the Jewish law inside out and could draft legal documents (such as contracts for marriage, divorce, inheritance, and the sale of land), but whom Jesus calls "hypocrites" because they do not do what the scriptures say. "Teacher, I will follow you wherever you go," he says to Jesus. "Foxes have dens and birds of the sky have nests, but the Son of Humanity has nowhere to rest his head." Here, Jesus makes himself vulnerable and reveals the reality of his life to this powerful, religious authority: *I'm a homeless person, and I will be ostracized and rejected by many.* In effect he asks the scribe, Are you willing to join my walking campaign of God's reign, to let go of everything you hold dear in life, to discover what real authority is, not the fake authority of copying some other author's writing? We never hear from the scribe again.

Then, upon hearing this, one of his disciples says to Jesus, "Lord, let me go first and bury my father." The greatest duty of a Jewish son was to serve and obey his Jewish father until his father dies, and then to give him a holy burial. In effect, this disciple is saying, "I will follow you, Jesus, once I have fulfilled my duty to care for my father. After he dies, I'll come back and follow you." That could be many more years. Jesus does not conform to the culture by making sacred the ties of family and blood. He wants everyone to follow him now. He demands full and total allegiance immediately. There is no part-time discipleship. There can be no delay in discipleship. There is urgent work to be done. There is no time to waste.

"Follow me, and let the dead bury their dead," he says. The main point is the call to discipleship. Leave the dead to bury the dead, he says. Those words sound harsh, maybe even cruel, but this is nonviolent truth-telling, compassion in action. They are actually life-saving words of love. "Let those stuck in the culture of death, acting as if they are dead, be with the dead and bury the dead," he says in effect. "You join me in my campaign of life, and live life to the full here and now." If you sit with his shocking statement and hear the power of Jesus's loving invitation, you can hear echoes of resurrection. He does not want us dead; he wants everyone fully alive and getting ready for resurrection here and now. Turn away from the culture of death, even from those who have given in to the culture of death, he insists. The only way to do that, Matthew shows, is by following Jesus. He has nothing to do with death because he is the fullness of life.

49

We do not know how the man responded. In Matthew's mind, the call is addressed to us readers as well. Follow Jesus and live life to the full, he tells us. Turn away from the culture of death; don't be dead but rise to new life by following Jesus in living out the Sermon on the Mount.

And so, the journey across the sea "to the other side," to enemy territory, begins. Each sea crossing "to the other side" in the various Gospel accounts is portrayed as a terrifying, life-or-death experience for the disciples—but not for Jesus. Loving enemies is easy for Jesus. It is scary for the rest of us. But he's trying to train us to be people who love even those we're not supposed to love, the people we should hate and want to kill, the people "on the other side."

In this account, a violent storm comes up suddenly on the sea, the boat is swamped by waves, and the terrified disciples think they are about to die. They cry out, "Lord, save us! We are perishing!" The whole episode becomes a parable. They are scared to cross "to the other side" and love their enemies. It's as scary as being in a boat during a storm.

For Jesus, however, traveling "to the other side" to love and serve human beings is perfectly normal. There's nothing to fear. In fact, the sea crossing offers him a chance to catch up on some much-needed sleep, and so he takes a nap. Elsewhere, we're told he slept on a cushion—he finally has somewhere to lay his head. The contrast between the peaceful, sleeping Jesus and the screaming, terrified disciples brings into focus how far we all have to go to renounce fear and live out the full social and political implications of universal, nonviolent love.

They wake him up, and he asks them point blank, "Why are you terrified, O you of little faith?" The answer is obvious: because we're about to drown! But for Jesus, it is equally obvious: our beloved God will protect us, there is nothing to fear, all will be well. He rebukes the winds and the sea, and a great calm comes over the sea, leaving the disciples amazed. The question they ask is meant for us to ponder: "What sort of man is this whom even the winds and sea obey?"

On the other side, in enemy territory, two demoniacs approach him, coming out from the tombs. (Mark's original version is longer and more detailed, with just one demoniac.) After the call to discipleship earlier, the call out of the culture of death, we now recognize that these two people are completely caught up in the culture of death, symbolized by their living in the tombs and being "savage," violent, deadly.

"What have you to do with us, Son of God?" they ask. "Have you come here to torment us before the appointed time?" Notice that they know who Jesus is and address him properly as Son of God. Because they know only violence and death, they presume he will treat them violently and kill them, that the Son of God must be a god of violence and death. They ask to go into the swine, he commands them to do so, and the whole herd of swine runs off the cliff. Their healing, their conversion to the sanity of nonviolence, their return to the fullness of life comes with an enormous economic price: it will cost the entire community its livelihood.

Matthew emphasizes that, since the people are raising pigs, they are not Jews; they are Gentiles. They are disturbed, even frightened, at the destruction of the pigs, not understanding that this is the price of liberation. They ask Jesus to leave. Would they have preferred that he not heal the poor demoniac? Was the herd of pigs worth more than a person's life? Whatever the case, they chose to turn away their liberator—something we still do today. So Jesus crosses back over the sea to his community base in Galilee.

Back in Capernaum, people bring to Jesus a paralytic lying on a stretcher. We're told that when he saw their faith in him, he said to the paralytic, "Courage, child, your sins are forgiven." The scribes said to themselves, "He is blaspheming." Jesus could see their outrage and asked them, "Why do you harbor evil thoughts?"

This is a critically important question that we need to hear and sit with. Whenever we see anything good—any act of love, kindness, healing, forgiveness, reconciliation, and selfless service—we should rejoice and praise God. Why do we mumble and "harbor evil thoughts"? Jesus asks non-judgmentally. His question points to a new alternative behavior—that we spend our lives harboring not evil thoughts but good, loving, compassionate thoughts. If we harbor good thoughts and nourish and maintain good thoughts, then we will more likely speak good words and do good deeds. This was the whole point of his great sermon. With this question, Jesus invites us deeper into his way of mindfulness and nonviolence. He does not want us to cultivate negativity and ill-will but positivity and goodwill, that we can learn to see the good in others and to be a force for goodness.

This leads to another provocative question: "Which is easier to say, 'Your sins are forgiven,' or 'Rise and walk'?" The crowd does not answer, and neither could we. We cannot make either of these statements. It's impossible for us to say to a paralyzed person, "Rise and walk," just as it's impossible for most people to forgive those who have hurt them the most. But the nonviolent Jesus can do anything. He wants us to know who he is, "that the Son of Humanity has authority on earth to forgive sins." He has "authority on earth," unlike the religious officials or imperial rulers, so he tells the paralytic, "Rise, pick up your stretcher and go home." He rises, goes home, and they all glorify God "for giving human beings such authority." With this subtle turn of phrase, Matthew tells us that God has now given people, starting with Matthew's church community, the authority and power to forgive each other's sins. Like the crowd, we begin to recognize that Jesus has real "authority" and he will share it with his disciples.

"Go and Learn the Meaning of the Words, 'I Desire Mercy, Not Sacrifice'" (9:9–38)

As Jesus walks along, he sees Matthew sitting at his customs post and calls out to him, "Follow me." All we're told is that Matthew gets up, leaves his post, follows Jesus—and then throws a big party in Jesus's honor. Matthew would have been hated by the religious elite and others because he charged an oppressive fee for legal permission to travel from one territory into another. He's friends with tax collectors and "public" sinners, and they gather in his house to toast the holy rabbi. When the religious authorities see Jesus among these low-life people, they accuse him, in effect, of violating the Judaic laws of cleanliness and ritual purity. Jesus is breaking the law once again, so they question his disciples for an explanation.

Jesus hears them and offers a simple summary of his mission. "Those who are well do not need a physician, but the sick do. Go and learn the meaning of the words, 'I desire mercy, not sacrifice.' I did not come to call the righteous but sinners." Here, Jesus sees himself as a doctor who heals the sick, as one who comes to help those in need. His mission is to call sinners out of the culture of death into God's reign of love and life, God's reign of universal mercy. He models that mercy by associating with those who need it most. Oddly enough, these "sinners" celebrate Jesus with a party, and show mercy to him. The righteous religious authorities, however, only question and condemn him, and show no mercy. They fulfill the letter of the law by offering ritual sacrifices in the temple—slaughtering countless animals in a festival of blood. Here, Jesus calls for an end to these temple sacrifices and summons us instead to the spiritual heights of universal mercy.

Jesus says, "Go and learn the meaning of the words, 'I desire mercy.'" This instruction is enough to pursue for the rest of our lives. In his great sermon, he taught us the meaning of the words "I desire mercy." He explained how we could be people of mercy. We are to show unconditional, soothing compassion and steadfast love. Those who are caught up in the culture of death, especially professional religious people stuck in the illusion of power, fundamentalism, and righteousness, need to go and learn mercy. At every point for the rest of his life, Jesus models and tries to teach universal mercy, and summons us to pursue a new culture of mercy. Alas, few have taken up his challenge to "go and learn," but the mission remains today. As we "go and learn . . . mercy," we discover ever-new insights into the infinite mercy of God, how even God's "judgment" is a merciful act for everyone's good.

With all this talk about righteousness versus mercy, the disciples of John the Baptist ask why Jesus's disciples do not fast. With Jesus, every question is an opportunity to testify about who he is and the truth he taught in his sermon. He responds to their question with a question, as all great teachers do: "Can the wedding guests mourn as long as the bridegroom is with them?" The answer is no. By shifting their question of righteousness to the image of a wedding feast, where he is the bridegroom to be honored and celebrated, he opens a whole new way of imagining what he is doing, what his presence means. He implies that he is the God of life, here in their midst, the God of unconditional, universal love. This reality should fill us with joy and gladness, as we might feel at the wedding party of a beloved relative. Every day in his presence should be a day of celebration, praise, wonder, and gratitude, the fullness of life itself. Alas, wherever he went, people attacked him, challenged him, and rejected him. Even here, John's disciples do not understand him.

"The days will come when the bridegroom is taken away from them," he announces. "Then they will fast." (This time has come for the community for which Matthew writes his Gospel, as they mourn the death of Jesus.) Then Jesus offers two small parables. You do not patch an old cloak with a new piece of cloth, for the tear will only worsen. Likewise, you do not put new wine into old wineskins. New wine is poured into fresh wineskins so that it will last.

We are starting all over. From now on, with Jesus, everything is new. We are going to have to go way beyond the Mosaic law, with its traditions and customs, not to mention imperial Rome. His new teachings on love, compassion, and peace do not fit into these old ways of thinking and acting. If we are going to take seriously the call to total nonviolence, as he taught in his great sermon, we cannot live according to the old rules and standards, which maintain the culture of violence. Matthew is trying to help his community understand that they have set out on an entirely new way of life. New wine—therefore, new wineskins! The status quo of systemic violence and injustice is over.

"While he was still saying these things," we're told, an official came forward, knelt down before him, and asked him to come lay his hand on his dead daughter that "she will live." Notice that Jesus is always teaching his new way of life, the lessons of his sermon, and is constantly being interrupted. But he is so centered, mindful, nonviolent, and patient that he is not fazed or tossed one way or another. We're told, instead, "Jesus rose. . . ."

Then, while on his way, he is interrupted again by a woman with a hemorrhage who touches his tassel, knowing that if she merely touches him, she will be cured. Matthew gives a shorter version than Mark, but the point is made: Jesus sees her, heals her, and says, "Courage, daughter! Your faith has saved you." He calls this unclean, ostracized woman his "daughter." He affirms her beyond her imagining, probably to the scandal of all the pious men around him. And when he arrives at the official's house, he dismisses the crowd, saying, "The girl is not dead but sleeping," and faces their ridicule. This must have hurt him. They do not have the faith in him that the official or the ill woman have. But Jesus does not let their ridicule and rejection poison him. He is focused on his mission, on God, on serving those in need. So, he takes the girl by the hand and raises her.

Throughout this episode with its interruptions, declarations of faith, and rejection, Jesus remains a tower of strength and trust in God. His very presence is healing and transformative. He heals the sick woman, raises the little girl, transforms everyone's doubt into faith, and fills everyone with wonder. The male disciples were probably stupefied, but they were witnessing how to be fully alive and infinitely compassionate.

Matthew changes Mark's account of the healing of blind Bartimaeus into the healing of two unnamed blind men who call out, "Son of David, have pity on us!" They give Jesus the messianic title, naming Jesus correctly as heir to King David, which we readers already knew from the beginning of the story. No one else has called him "Son of David." But Matthew adds a pointed question for the two blind men and for us readers: "Do you believe I can do this?" They respond, "Yes, Lord." So, he heals them.

Jesus is seeking people who believe in him. Matthew is urging us to believe in Jesus as much as these blind beggars do, to go through life believing in him, trusting him, and doing exactly as he has instructed in the Sermon on the Mount. If we believe in him, then he will be able to heal us and work through us to do even greater things.

The question stands before us too: "Do you believe I can do this?"

Once again, Jesus touches them. This time, he touches their eyes and gives them the gift of vision, so that they can see him, the God of life in their midst. Their eyes are opened and they see Jesus before them. The lesson: if we believe and ask for vision, we will see Jesus and live. He will say to us as he said to the two blind men, "Let it be done for you according to your faith."

The coda here is that he tells them not to tell anyone about this, but they go out and spread word of him throughout all the land. Why does he warn them? Because Jesus prefers the one-on-one personal touch, the intimate act of faith and love between himself and the person he's dealing with. He knows that if word about him spreads, he will just become a spectacle; that the adoring crowds will just be fans, not disciples; and that the crowd spirit can easily turn to violence, as will happen at the end of the story.

Jesus has now healed a sick woman, raised a dead girl, and given sight to two blind men; next he heals a mute person who can now speak. The crowds are amazed, but the religious authorities attack him as evil, saying, "He drives out demons by the prince of demons." Why do they attack him? This will become the basic cycle for the rest of the story; it's a serious question. He poses a great threat to their power, control, and so-called authority. Why is he a threat? Because his healings have social and political implications. The Roman Empire and the religious authorities want to keep the status quo because it is in their favor, under their control. They want the blind to stay blind, the mute to stay mute, the sick to stay sick, the poor to stay poor, and the dead to stay dead. When Jesus heals these disenfranchised people, he is liberating them from a system. In a sense they are all victims of the culture of violence, which takes away their vision, their voice, their health, and even their very lives. Jesus has come to restore everyone to the fullness of life and to welcome them into God's reign of healing and life. He is also calling them out of the culture of violence and death, which means that the days of violence, occupation, and empire are numbered. The ruling authorities know only how to be violent; they are confounded by Jesus's nonviolence. So they respond by attacking him violently with harsh false accusations. Jesus, however, remains steadfast in his nonviolence and in his mission.

Instead of quivering with fear and doubt at the attacks against him, Jesus ups the ante and steps up his mission. We're told that he goes to "all the towns and villages, teaching in their synagogues, proclaiming the gospel of the kingdom, and curing every disease and illness." This becomes the job description of the disciple, just as it was his job description. He is in fact a threat to the status quo. You cannot run an occupation and brutal empire if someone is roaming across the land, healing everyone, proclaiming another reign, and even raising people from the dead. They have to stop him, or soon everyone will start believing him and the empire will fall.

The key to Jesus's transforming, healing, disarming power is explained in verse 36. His heart was moved with pity, filled with compassion for all the people. Unlike the religious authorities, local officials, or imperial rulers, who operate out of judgment rather than compassion, Jesus sees every person through the lens of God's love. He feels for these suffering, oppressed people. We're told that he felt compassion for them for they were troubled and abandoned, like sheep without a shepherd. Later, in John's Gospel, he will announce that he is their good shepherd. He therefore tells his disciples to ask the master of the harvest (meaning himself) to send out laborers for his harvest, to send out more workers who will teach the great sermon, proclaim God's reign, and heal the poor. Apparently, they did ask. In the next chapter, he sends them forth to live his sermon, practice it, and teach it just as he does.

"Behold, I Am Sending You like Sheep in the Midst of Wolves" (10:1–33)

With chapter 10, Matthew's Gospel makes a shift. First, we heard Jesus's great sermon with all his teachings on a radical and loving way to live. Then we saw him put these teachings into practice by healing many people, including people in enemy lands. He was love in action. With chapter 10, he sends out his disciples to do as he did—to go forth as practitioners of the way of God's loving reign. He is building a grassroots movement that will eventually reach the holy city of Jerusalem.

But Jesus begins to warn the disciples in no uncertain terms: their message, their healings, their work, and their proclamation of God's coming reign will not be well received. Prepare yourself for rejection. This is the flip side of the great sermon—most people will not want to hear about God's way of universal love and total nonviolence, so they will ignore you, reject you, and harass you, or worse, arrest and kill you. This is as true today as it was two thousand years ago. Nevertheless, Jesus still sends us out.

Matthew's version is focused on Jesus's Jewish audience, whereas Luke's version will focus on his Gentile audience. We're told that Jesus gathers twelve disciples; we're given their names; and he calls them "apostles": "those who are sent." He gives them "authority," real authority, not like the false authority of religious leaders interested only in power, control, riches, and honor. With this "authority," the authentic power of God among them, Jesus's disciples can drive out unclean spirits and cure everyone. They will expel the demons of nationalism, imperialism, militarism, and violence—those qualities that possess people— so that people can be free in God's reign, in God's way of being. Their goal is to find and heal the lost sheep of Israel. He's training his disciples to become, like him, good shepherds of peace.

The instructions are important. They show how Jesus is building an underground movement of nonviolence, like Gandhi organizing his Salt March in India, or Dr. King preparing the movement for desegregation in Birmingham, or the People Power movement that brought down the Marcos dictatorship in the Philippines in 1985, when a million people, led by nuns, took to the streets of Manila in a spirit of nonviolence and sat down in front of the dictator's tanks until the soldiers fled.

First, the disciples are to tell everyone they meet: "The kingdom of heaven is at hand." In other words, the days of empire are over; everyone is welcome to live in God's reign. A modern translation might be, "Come out of the culture defined by power and politics and instead live as people defined by their relationship to their loving God." Such an announcement was politically dangerous and subversive of the unjust status quo back then—just as it is today if it is understood correctly.

The disciples are to cure the sick, raise the dead, cleanse the lepers, and drive out demons. How do they do this? Just as Jesus did: by touching and praying over the sick and the lepers, by calling people out of the culture of death into the new life of resurrection peace, and by driving out the demons that bind people through unjust systems and idolatry. Jesus believes the disciples can do this work, just as he still believes each one of us can do this today.

It is an urgent mission, one that harks back to the exodus story. The disciples are to depend totally on God and on the good of people they meet, so they have no money, no luggage, no extra clothes, no walking stick. They are poor pilgrims of peace, sent off into the culture of violence and war. Their humble, simple presence will disarm and heal everyone because they will model life in God's reign. Because the Roman soldiers arrest and kill anyone who threatens them, Jesus warns the disciples to be careful and to stay with any loving, kind local person who offers hospitality. Make every step along the way, every word you say along the way, a step, a word of peace, he tells them. When you enter a house, wish everyone peace. Let your peace, which is my peace, rest upon them, he says. He wants people to learn from his peacemaking disciples to make peace as they go, to bring peace to households, and, in doing so, to help create new cultures of peace. If they do not receive your peace, shake the dust from your feet, he continues. In other words, don't let their rejection of you cling to you. Don't let it fester and infect you and fill you with resentment or bitterness. Let it go and move on. You did your best. Go forward and try to spread the gospel of peace elsewhere. Let God handle the rest.

"Behold, I am sending you like sheep in the midst of wolves, so be shrewd as serpents and as simple as doves." This is one of the most important sentences in the Gospels, echoed only in Luke's Gospel. This sentence sums up how any follower of the nonviolent Jesus is to live and act in our world of violence. We have been sent out into the culture of violence "like sheep in the midst of wolves." We are to be as unarmed, innocent, harmless, vulnerable, and peaceful as little sheep. That means we cannot have swords or guns, or support war or nuclear weapons, or wish harm on anyone. We have been taught the great sermon and have been formed by Jesus to be practitioners of nonviolence and noncoercion. As nonviolent people working publicly in a culture of violence—we will probably be eaten alive. We will be attacked and rejected and mocked and hurt and maybe even killed, and yet, we will never lift a finger, respond with anger, retaliate with further violence, or even wish ill upon anyone. Jesus is sending us, in Gandhi's description, as soldiers of nonviolence; in King's words, as people of militant nonviolence. We willingly give our lives for this mission. We will learn to accept suffering peacefully, with love, without a trace of the desire to retaliate with further violence, knowing that our steadfast nonviolent love will be transformative of others and redemptive, because Jesus did it all first.

We are not naïve, idealistic simpletons. We know what we are doing. We are shrewd as serpents who crawl through the desert and hide in the bushes. Perhaps that means we get to hiss periodically. We mind our business but hiss at the system. We are also as simple as doves, as innocent, pure, peaceful, and inspiring. We fly hither and yon, embodying peace, inspiring peace wherever we land.

We are missionaries of Gospel nonviolence and peace, who live and breathe peace, who speak only words of peace, who embody peace so that our lives, our very presence becomes a healing, disarming force that transforms all those we meet. This is the life of the Christian in a world of violence, to be a force of transforming nonviolence.

Few Christians understand this because the churches have been so co-opted by the culture of war and empire. Nonetheless, the nonviolent Jesus still wants to send us out as sheep in the midst of wolves to make peace in every situation possible.

Here, the text takes an abrupt turn. Jesus gives us an explicit warning. If you try to live out my great sermon of nonviolence in a world of total violence, you will be eaten alive. In a world of zombies, you will be the only sane non-zombie, and eventually they will get you. However, keep on going with steadfast nonviolence, no matter what.

"Beware of people," he warns his nonviolent followers. "They will hand you over to courts and scourge you in their synagogues, and you will be led before governors and kings for my sake as a witness before them and the pagans." As a longtime peace activist trying to follow the nonviolent Jesus, I can testify that all of that has happened to me. I've been hauled in chains by countless police before dozens of judges and politicians, brought to speak before several governors, congressional representatives, senators, various presidents, a queen, and a pope. The key word here is "witness." No matter what happens to us, whether we encounter a powerless homeless person or a powerful politician, we witness to the risen, nonviolent Jesus, and invite people into his reign.

And so, we go forward in the footsteps of Jesus, trying to practice nonviolence, come what may. We accept what happens. We speak out for justice, disarmament, and creation and leave the results in God's hands. We try at all times, but especially in the moment of nonviolent direct confrontation with ruling authorities, to live Jesus's teachings: do not worry, trust in God, practice nonviolence, love everyone, stay humble and peaceful, and speak the truth prayerfully from the heart. We try to do as he does and say what he says.

"Do not worry about how you are to speak or what you are to say," he continues. "You will be given at that moment what you are to say." Worrying is useless. If we surrender ourselves completely to Jesus and carry on his work, we know that God will be acting through us. The results are in God's hands.

That's when the rubber hits the road. None of this will be well received, he announces. Things are going to get worse. This is the part that we usually ignore. In these passages, Jesus describes what will happen if we live out his great sermon. We will rarely be praised or honored or even listened to; instead, we will be rejected, crushed, and destroyed—and eternally blessed. Get ready for this, he warns his followers. Expect the worst, but pray for the best, and trust that you are held close in the palm of the God of peace.

"Brother will hand over brother to death, and the father his child; children will rise up against parents and have them put to death," he says. All hell will break loose! Jesus seems to say, Be prepared for a hostile, even violent reaction, and be ready then and there, in the heat of that moment, to practice meticulous Gospel nonviolence, as I have shown you.

"You will be hated by all because of my name, but whoever endures to the end will be saved." This powerful sentence is worthy of contemplation. All those stuck in the culture of violence hate those who model public active nonviolence and radical love. When we personally get rejected for taking a stand for justice, we are actually sharing in the rejection he experienced. The point is to focus not on the rejection but on Jesus and his perseverance. This is a key teaching, rarely discussed. He wants us to persevere. Those who persevere in the way of Jesus, no matter what form of rejection and cruelty they face, will be saved by the God of peace, will be liberated from the culture of violence and welcomed into the eternal realm of God's love. That outcome is worth our steadfast perseverance.

Jesus also seems to advise us not to seek martyrdom, just to be careful and wise and on our toes at all times. "When they persecute you in one town," he instructs, "flee to another." Get out when you have to, move on, and try spreading the message in another place where you might receive a more positive welcome. There is enough work to do for the rest of your life. Even if you travel as far and wide as you can, you still will not have reached out to every living human being with the message of the great sermon. But keep trying. Keep on moving on, reaching out, speaking out, and spreading the good news of the kingdom of God.

"It Is Enough for the Disciple to Become like the Teacher" (10:24–33)

After telling us how rough it's going to be, Jesus reminds us again that it's going to be rough for him, and since we are his disciples, how could it not be rough for us too? Which raises the question: If we are not facing rejection, harassment, attack, even arrest and death threats, how can we claim to be followers of the nonviolent Jesus who was harassed, rejected, arrested, and executed? This is part of our job description: to practice his total nonviolence and to endure the same rejection he endures.

"No disciple is above his teacher," he explains. "It is enough for the disciple to become like the teacher." This too is a teaching worth pondering. Do we really want to be his disciples? Do we want to become like him, and, if so, will we expect to suffer the rejection he suffered? Or do we suppose that, somehow, we will escape it, that bad things won't happen to us? Do we would-be disciples subconsciously think that somehow or other we are greater than our Teacher? That's why he tells us right here at the start: If they called the master of the house evil, how much more will they attack those of the master's household, those who follow him? All of this is to be expected. All of this will provide an opportunity for us to speak out and witness to Jesus's way.

In fact, if we dare approach the level of the nonviolent Jesus, Matthew advises, we will have fulfilled our highest vocation and become our truest selves. That is the definition of the saint: to become like Jesus, another Christ-figure here on earth, right in the midst of public hate and war, sent out to disarm the world.

And so we arrive at this bold command: "Do not be afraid!" Do not be afraid of those who reject you, harass you, attack you, hurt you, or threaten you. Do not be afraid of anyone. Love them and pray for them and trust in God. We are people of faith who trust completely in the God of peace, who follow the nonviolent Jesus on the path to the God of peace, who proclaim the coming of God's reign—so we are way beyond any type of fear. We have reached what Gandhi called "fearlessness," that state of total nonviolence whereby we have surrendered our lives to the nonviolent Jesus and the God of peace, and are at peace whether we live, or suffer, or die; as long as we are following Jesus and doing God's peacemaking will, we are content, we are at peace, we are not afraid.

"Speak in the light, proclaim from the housetops," he urges us. In the end, everything will work out. So do not be afraid. Rather, be even bolder; go forth as heralds, witnesses, apostles, prophets, and peacemakers. Speak out about the reality of God's reign, that together we might welcome it and dwell within it.

"Do not be afraid of those who kill the body but cannot kill the soul," he explains. "Life is short," he seems to say. "You're going to die anyway; if you join my campaign of nonviolence and are martyred, do not be afraid. Then you are following me all the way to the cross." Be afraid of the One who can destroy your soul in Gehenna. Focus on God, your Creator, your Higher Power, who has total power over you. Serve God. Do God's will. Practice God's way and you will live on.

This seems contradictory, but it isn't. We need never again live in fear. There is nothing to be afraid of. We focus on God, hold God in awe, bow our heads before God, and try only and at all times to do God's will. That is all that is required of us—and we can do this!

While this might sound frightening, Jesus hastens to console us. God loves us, cares for us, and knows everything about us. We are loved infinitely, wildly, unconditionally—each and every one of us—and personally as well, beyond our wildest expectations. If God is an infinitely loving parent, as Jesus teaches in the great sermon, then we have nothing to fear. We have a God who dotes on us, who holds us, consoles us, even spoils us. This nonviolent loving God—get ready!—knows so much about us that he even knows every single hair on our heads. God not only knows about us, knows every detail about our lives (as the best loving parent might), God knows every cell in our bodies. This is the greatest love of all. To be known through and through with total love. This is who God is, Jesus tells us. So why be afraid? We have nothing to fear!

In that same spirit, Matthew reports a promise: If we dare stand on the side of the nonviolent Jesus—that is, NOT on the side of some nationalist Jesus, pro-war Jesus, pro-rich Jesus, pro-greed Jesus, pro-money Jesus, pro-comfort Jesus, even pro-violence Jesus—if we stand on the side of the nonviolent Jesus, the nonviolent Jesus will one day in the new life of God's reign stand on our side. It's a promise made in faith that demands a response of faith. Matthew says, in effect, Okay, he will be for you if you are for him, so stand by him and everything will work out in the end.

"Whoever Loses His or Her Life for My Sake Will Find It" (10:34–11:24)

Then we have one of the most important statements in the Gospel—and one of the most misunderstood. "Do not think that I have come to bring peace on earth," he says. "I have not come to bring peace but the sword. For I have come to set a son against his father, a daughter against her mother, and a daughter-in-law against her mother-in-law; one's enemies will be those of one's own household."

If you read the four Gospels from the perspective of active nonviolence, in the tradition of Gandhi and King, then you realize, of course! Jesus came to bring peace on earth! When he was born, we are told, the angels sang about the coming of peace on earth. When he spoke his great sermon, he announced that God is a God of peace, a peacemaker, who calls us to make peace. In every action he took, he made peace among people. When he sent his disciples out, he deliberately sent them to make peace among people. Everything Jesus does is about peace.

So when he says, "Do not think that I have come to bring peace upon earth; I have not come to bring peace but the sword," he means this: My very peacemaking presence in a world of war, my nonviolence in a culture of violence, will be divisive, like a sword. Instead of seemingly bringing peace, I will bring division! That is what it means to bring peace into a culture of war. Those who bring peace will be misunderstood and will appear to be divisive. Yet the *way* to peace, the method of peacemaking, is itself peaceful.

If we dare accept this difficult teaching, that we are called to stand up publicly for peace and nonviolence in a spirit of peace and nonviolence, and that we will be rejected and attacked, then, Jesus declares, we are on the same path as he is, the path of nonviolent suffering love that can end only in the cross of suffering love and ultimately bring us to resurrection and a truly transformed life.

So he says, "Whoever loves father or mother more than me is not worthy of me, and whoever loves son or daughter more than me is not worthy of me; and whoever does not take up his cross and follow after me is not worthy of me. Whoever finds his life will lose it, and whoever loses his life for my sake will find it."

With this, we hit the bottom line of discipleship. We are called to follow the nonviolent Jesus with our all might, strength, spirit, soul, will, mind, body—with our very being. He summons us to join his spiritual journey of nonviolence into the face of imperial violence, come what may. It's not that we hate anyone, much less our parents or children. Matthew's dramatic language tries to shake us into giving our entire allegiance to Jesus and his beautiful nonviolence, his stunning glory, his universal love, his campaign of infinite peace for all humanity. If we join him, even our parents and children and our friends will one day join us. That's part of the unsaid blessing.

Jesus grew up in an occupied territory, where the Roman Empire arrested and executed any rebel. The empire killed its opponents in a brutal public fashion as a deterrent to any future opposition. They nailed the rebels naked to crossbeams and let them die slow, painful deaths, for all the passersby to see. Jesus would have seen many people die by crucifixion on the roads around Nazareth. This was the horrific world in which he grew up. Perhaps even his father Joseph had been crucified on the road outside of Nazareth. Some biblical scholars assume that Joseph was dead before Jesus began his public ministry. We don't know the manner of death, but we know that any opposition to Rome brought swift and harsh consequences. And Joseph was chosen by God to be the earthly father of Jesus, a man who could teach his son a truly holy way of life. It's not so far-fetched to imagine Joseph's integrity and holiness putting him in harm's way.

This verse (10:38) is the first mention of the cross in Matthew's Gospel. Jesus calls us to live peacefully in a violent culture, and such living will lead to confrontation, even crucifixion. So follow me and be prepared to take up your cross, he says. Face your death, let go of your life, trust in God, and go forward in the way of peace.

In the same spirit, Matthew has Jesus encourage those he's sending out with the good news of love and peace with the promise that, however people treat them, they will be treating him in the same way. If they receive them, they will receive Jesus. In an occupied land where Roman soldiers are patrolling and arresting and killing rabble-rousers, Jesus's generous attitude toward those who receive a prophet, a righteous person, or a disciple makes sense. Anyone who welcomes someone who stands against the empire will also face suspicion and possible arrest and execution by the authorities. You would risk your life to welcome a prophet, a righteous person, or a disciple of Jesus, so Jesus says that anyone who welcomes them will share their reward. The teachings end with the note that Jesus continued on, traveling to other towns, to teach and preach as many as possible.

After all these teachings, including this new insistence on taking up one's cross, John the Baptist enters the story again. He's in prison for teaching and preaching. He exemplifies the instructions Jesus just gave about renouncing one's family and one's very life, taking up the cross, serving God, and speaking out prophetically. Yet John has doubts about Jesus. We're told he heard of the works of Jesus but wonders about him, so he sends his disciples to Jesus with the question, "Are you the one who is to come, or should we look for another?"

Notice that Matthew calls Jesus the "Messiah." John's expectations of the Messiah, like every other devout Jew of their day, were the complete opposite of the life and teachings of the nonviolent Jesus. John and everyone else expected a violent messiah who would overthrow the Roman Empire and establish God's kingdom here on earth through violent force as a political power, stronger than all the other empires. Jesus was not mobilizing an army or talking about a violent takeover of anything, and this confused everyone, including John the Baptist.

Through the teachings of Gandhi and King, we can now see Jesus as a nonviolent messiah that no one expected. There are few scripture passages that allude to a messiah of nonviolence—most notably Isaiah's Suffering Servant. No one understands the kind of salvation Jesus is offering—eternal life in God's reign of compassion, inclusion, and peace, not just in heaven, as is commonly taught in the churches, but on earth as it is in heaven.

If this was the teaching of Jesus, any ordinary person would ask, How can a person of nonviolence be the emissary of the All Powerful, Almighty God? How can nonviolence save us, the chosen people? How can nonviolence overcome the Roman Empire? Don't we need a military to save us?

When Jesus hears about John's doubts, he sends John's disciples back with an unusual message: "Go and tell John what you hear and see: the blind regain their sight, the lame walk, lepers are cleansed, the deaf hear, the dead are raised, and the poor have the good news proclaimed to them." Here is the description of Jesus's messianic nonviolence in a nutshell.

The culture of violence, war, and empire brings only suffering and death to people. It makes people blind, takes away their vision, makes people lame and deaf, keeps lepers ostracized, proclaims the bad news of despair, poverty, and domination, and most of all, kills people, whether through the slow process of neglect or the outright murder of warfare. The culture of violence uses death as a methodology. The nonviolent Jesus does the exact opposite of the culture of violence, war, and death. He gives sight to the blind; heals the lame, the deaf, and the leper; proclaims good news to the poor, that their poverty is not the will of God; and raises the dead. He has come that everyone may have life, that they may live healthy and whole in a new culture of nonviolence. No one had ever done this before, and this report of his actions must have convinced John and his disciples that the messianic revolution had begun, that the means as well as the ends of the messianic revolution would be nonviolent.

Then Jesus offers a new beatitude: "And blessed is the one who takes no offense at me." Blessed are they who trust me no matter what, even if they have questions, even if they are confused, even if they do not understand, even if their expectations are not met. Trust me, trust the evidence of the good works of nonviolence, and you will be blessed, he says.

After John's disciples leave, Jesus speaks to the crowd about John the Baptist, calling him a prophet. He asks, "Why did you go out to the desert to see John?" You went, he says, because you wanted to see and hear a real prophet. Everyone was expecting a new prophet of God to come forth, the return of Elijah, and they recognized John as an authentic prophet. But

Jesus goes further and explains that John is more than a prophet; he is the messenger sent by God ahead of Jesus to prepare the way for Jesus.

Then he gives John the highest possible compliment: there is no one greater than John the Baptist; yet even the least person in the kingdom of heaven is greater than he. John is the greatest person who ever lived except the Messiah, Matthew says, but goes further to explain that in the kingdom of heaven, everyone practices Jesus's holy way of peace. Even John hasn't reached the heights and depths of the Sermon-on-the-Mount teachings. He's still looking for a violent messiah, someone who will take over, bring revenge, and dominate the world, by force if necessary. John never heard the Sermon on the Mount, so he is confused. We, on the other hand, have no excuse for our confusion: we have read the Sermon on the Mount, we know that saints and prophets of peace and nonviolence, from St. Francis to Dorothy Day, have lived Jesus's teachings, so we need not be confused. Matthew urges us not to take offense at Jesus but to take him at his word, even if we don't understand him. Like John the Baptist, let's see the fruit of his actions, and follow him.

Then, Matthew gives us an original, difficult saying that has confounded readers for centuries. "From the days of John the Baptist until now, the kingdom of heaven suffers violence, and the violent are taking it by force," Jesus says. "All the prophets and the law prophesied up to the time of John. And if you are willing to accept it, he is Elijah, the one who is to come. Whoever has ear ought to hear." I think this strange teaching makes sense only from the perspective of loving nonviolence. Jesus is trying to explain that throughout history up until his coming, even in the Torah and all the prophets, everything has been about violence—the culture, the empire, our religious practices, our religious teachings, our religious authorities—everything is rooted in violence. In his great sermon, he taught about the coming of God's reign as universal love and total nonviolence. With his teaching, in his presence, any justification for faith-based violence is thrown out. Jesus introduces God's reign as a new world and a different way of functioning, a completely different methodology. And so, from now on, religion, beginning with Judaism, has nothing to do with violence. "From now on," he says to those of us who have ears, "we are not to take the kingdom of heaven by violence, but to practice this new way that changes people's lives, that heals people and creation itself, through compassion, gentleness, justice, and love."

"To what shall I compare this generation?" he asks the crowd. This is the plaintive voice of one who has tried every nonviolent avenue to teach us, help us, and lead us—to no effect. He speaks of children who played the flute for people in the marketplace, only to find the people ignoring them; or the children who sang a dirge in the marketplace, only to find the people ignoring them. With this parable before us, he explains that John "came neither eating nor drinking," so they attacked him, saying he was possessed by a demon. Jesus comes eating and drinking among everyone, only to be attacked as "a glutton and drunkard, a friend of tax collectors and sinners." You can't win, he says. If this was true for Jesus, then it is true for us today. "But wisdom is vindicated by her works." Wisdom, the feminine image of God, the Holy Spirit, will eventually be proved right, he promises. With that promise, Matthew urges us to carry on our Sermon-on-the-Mount mission, whether we are successful or not. In the end, if we all follow Jesus, someday everyone will realize the wisdom of nonviolence.

Jesus then reproaches all the towns where he performed "mighty deeds," which were done in the hope that all the people would repent and follow his new way. Chorazin and Bethsaida lie in ruins by the Sea of Galilee today, along with Jesus's home village of Capernaum. He laments that they have not "repented in sackcloth and ashes." If Jesus was upset at these towns, what would he say today about cities where we build nuclear weapons (such as Los Alamos, New Mexico; Livermore, California; and Amarillo, Texas); where we execute people (Huntsville, Texas, and Angola, Louisiana); where we manage warfare (the Pentagon in Washington, D.C./Northern Virginia and the "School of the Americas" in Columbus, Georgia)?

"I Am Meek and Humble of Heart" (11:25–12:49)

The next passage begins with a prayer of praise for God, an explanation of Jesus's intimate relationship as God's son, and an invitation to learn from Jesus. First, we notice that five times Jesus calls upon God as his beloved Father. He models the intimate relationship that he desires for every human being to have with God. He names his Father as "Lord of heaven and earth."

Why does he praise God? He had just denounced the cities that witnessed his mighty deeds but did not repent in response. Then he praises God because God has "hidden these things from the wise and the learned and revealed them to the childlike; such has been your gracious will." From the perspective of nonviolence, this is a profound passage. We might ask, Doesn't God want cities and nations to repent and be converted to God's way of universal love and total nonviolence? Why doesn't God make it happen? Why does God let us get away with systemic injustice, warfare, even plans to destroy the planet with our nuclear weapons and environmental destruction?

If Jesus's teaching in the Sermon on the Mount is true, that God is a God of peace and universal love—then the only way for God to be truly nonviolent to all God's children, the whole human race, is if God gives us free will. God gives us the freedom to reject God and God's way of love. God does not impose God's Self upon us. As we ponder the nonviolence of God, the astonishing gift of free will that God gives us, we begin to understand just how "gracious" God has been to humanity. And if we look long and hard, we begin to glimpse the eternal suffering of God, who suffers through our ongoing rejection of God and God's way. God does not intervene to stop us. God sends the Holy Spirit, raises up prophets, gives us the word of God, and tries to inspire us to live at peace through the wonders of creation. But God does not use violent force; God will not force us to wake up and repent; and so, because we have so clearly rejected God's gift and way of peace, God weeps over our violence, killings, and wars. If we loved God as Jesus demonstrates by praising his "Father," we would do what we can to repent of violence and try to practice nonviolence just to ease God's pain and please our loving "God." Through God's suffering love, embodied in the nonviolent Jesus, God invites us to freely choose the wisdom of nonviolence for ourselves, our city, our nation, and our planet. That is the way God works, and Jesus is the first to praise God precisely for the gift of God's nonviolence and our free will.

Then, Matthew announces that the nonviolent Jesus is the only one who truly knows God. "All things have been handed over to me by my Father," he says. He has been given everything, but this does not mean money, possessions, houses, or worldly power. Jesus has been given all the graces and wisdom he teaches in his great sermon. Because he is the embodiment of God's love, compassion, and nonviolence, he is not mean, violent, cruel, or domineering. Instead, he is the true son of "Abba," which makes him childlike, gracious, and humble. Unlike the so-called wise and learned, the arrogant and powerful, he does not act with violence, domination, arrogance, or intimidation. It is precisely his gentleness, compassion, nonviolence, and loving-kindness that mark his power. He shares what he knows of God with the poor, the childlike, the meek, and the humble, not the rich, the violent, the warmakers, and the powerful. This reveals his sonship with a gracious God.

After this explanation comes the invitation. Here, the nonviolent Jesus echoes the Wisdom literature, and we begin to recognize him as filled with Holy Wisdom, *Hagia Sophia*. "Come to me, all you who labor and are burdened and I will give you rest," he says. The call is to the poor, the workers, those struggling for justice, the peacemakers, those burdened by the world; it is not a call to the rich, comfortable, powerful, and elite. He offers rest, which means an end to the perpetual enslavement to an oppressive world.

"Take my yoke upon you and learn from me," he says, "for I am meek and humble of heart; and you will find rest for yourselves. For my yoke is easy, and my burden light." Matthew's Jesus invokes the invitation of Ben Sira that we might learn wisdom and take up her yoke (Sir. 51:23, 26). We need no longer bear the heavy yoke of the law, the yoke of empire, the yoke of injustice and violence. Jesus invites us to take up the yoke he outlined in his great sermon. His yoke is the way of the gentle and wise. We need never hurt anyone again; instead, we love everyone and live in peace with everyone, come what may. It's an easy yoke, a light burden.

The reason we can trust that Jesus's yoke is easy and his burden is light is because, he tells us plainly, he is "meek and humble of heart." The biblical word for nonviolence, according to Thomas Merton as we noted earlier, is "meekness." Jesus here announces that he is nonviolent through and through. He is nonviolent and humble of heart. He is not egocentric, narcissistic, power-hungry, domineering, bossy, or arrogant. His gentleness comes from the depth of heartfelt humility. His heart is unarmed, vulnerable, all-encompassing, all-inclusive, and all-embracing. His heart, unlike ours, is wide open to the fullness of universal love. If we go to him and take up his yoke and burden—that is, if we live out his great sermon—we will find rest, and know ourselves as blessed and loved.

This is one of the clearest, most touching and compelling invitations in the four Gospels. I suggest we all take Jesus at his word, accept his invitation, learn his wisdom, and try to become meek and humble of heart like him.

It's the sabbath again, and this time, as Jesus and the disciples walk through a field of grain, his disciples begin to pick the heads of grain to eat. Of course, the religious authorities condemn him for this violation of the sabbath. "Your disciples are doing what is unlawful to do on the sabbath," they say. What follows is one of Jesus's first blatant defenses of nonviolent civil disobedience. It reveals his basic stance of nonviolent resistance to anything that dehumanizes or oppresses anyone. From the perspective of Gandhian civil disobedience, we begin to realize that much of what Jesus did was considered illegal.

"Have you not read what David did when he and his companions were hungry?" he asks, referring to the scriptures, "how he went into the house of God and ate the bread of offering, which neither he nor his companions but only the priests could lawfully eat? Or have you not read in the law that on the sabbath the priests serving in the temple violate the sabbath and are innocent?" He defends his disciples, and uses the scriptures to show that life is more important than the law.

"I say to you, something greater than the temple is here." This is his subtle, humble way of telling the authorities that they are missing the point. Then he repeats his theme: "If you only knew the importance of this statement: 'I desire mercy, not sacrifice'—you would not have condemned these innocent people." He calls on the religious authorities once again to put mercy first and foremost, rather than condemnation. This call rings true today more than ever. Matthew's Jesus still calls us to be people of unconditional mercy, not condemnation. That, Matthew emphasizes, *is* the spiritual life. No more condemning people, personally, socially, collectively, or globally. We are called to put mercy first in our relations with others and to institutionalize mercy as a social policy.

Then, the clincher: "The Son of Humanity is Lord of the sabbath." That mysterious designation from the book of Daniel, of the holy figure in the fiery furnace in the midst of the three nonviolent resisters, is now the way Jesus refers to himself. He is the Son of Humanity, the Lord of the sabbath, the one who stands with all persecuted nonviolent resisters, the human being with the fullest nonviolence, as I suggested in the introduction. The ruling authorities are shocked, and their outrage and resentment deepen.

Matthew then tells a politically charged healing story that Mark put at the beginning of his narrative. Jesus is speaking in the synagogue, notices a man with a withered hand, and heals the man then and there, on the sabbath no less, much to the horror of the law-abiding religious authorities. They challenge him, "Is it lawful to cure on the sabbath?" They always want to catch him in violation of the law. They're like religious vigilantes, a trap that many people still fall into today. Jesus is so famous, rebellious, wise, and notorious that they want to catch him red-handed at any moment to quash his influence before he builds a movement that threatens the status quo. They want to arrest him so they can get rid of him.

Here Matthew adds a later Markan reference to an image of the chosen people as sheep. "Which one of you who has a sheep that falls into a pit on the sabbath will not take hold of it and lift it out?" Jesus asks. "How much more valuable a person is than a sheep. So it is lawful to do good on the sabbath." The point of the sabbath, the point of the law, the point of life is to do good, to serve others, to heal others, to bring justice and peace—to serve human life. When Jesus heals the man's hand, the authorities are furious. They should have rejoiced that someone had been healed, especially in a synagogue on the sabbath. Instead, we're told, they "went out and took counsel against him to put him to death."

So we see what Jesus is up against—an unjust system, a ruling class that brooks no change, a wall of hatred and resentment. This outcome becomes a recurring nightmare for Jesus: no matter how wise, how helpful, how miraculous he is, the authorities respond with anger, resentment, plots, and death threats. This mythic story shows us not only the power, compassion, and divinity of Jesus, but how good deeds so often unveil the violence within us and among us. The story invites us to heal any poor person in need, beginning with those in our own religious communities. Moreover, it challenges us not to be like the violent religious authorities but to let go of resentment, anger, power, and control, and join Jesus's works of healing mercy and compassionate love.

Note that, of course, these religious authorities are human beings who believe in what they are doing, are totally corrupted by the power and wealth they've gained from the empire, and will kill to uphold God's name and the religious establishment as we see all over the world today in all the religions. How would Gandhi have dealt with this? In fact, for forty years he faced down Hindu fundamentalists who threatened him, charged him with blasphemy, threatened to kill him—and eventually did kill him. As Jim Douglass brings out in his unique book *Gandhi and the Unspeakable,* Gandhi was in much the same predicament as Jesus. Gandhi knew the Hindu fundamentalists who killed him, and today, over seventy-five years later, their heirs are now the main political force in India, where they continue to persecute Muslims and Christians and denigrate Gandhi. Jesus tries every nonviolent method possible to reason with his religious opponents, even using strong, clear language as we will see later, as in an alcoholic intervention, but to no avail.

Still, Matthew insists, we are called to show mercy as Jesus does and to heal those in need, regardless of the consequences to ourselves. This is what true, holy, religious behavior looks like. We never condemn anyone, especially someone who is doing good. We support every act of kindness, mercy, compassion, disarmament, and healing, even if we do not fully understand it.

"Whoever Does the Will of the God of Peace Is My Brother or Sister" (12:15–49)

With that, Jesus withdraws into solitude. But the crowds follow him and bring their sick, so he cures them all but urges them "not to make him known." Jesus knows how nonviolence works, and that the crowd mentality can turn violent at a moment's notice. He is a personalist; he seeks not mass crowds but a true nonviolent movement where each member has been trained in his methodology of nonviolence. Matthew adds that this inclination to "not make him known" fulfills the prophet Isaiah's vision of a nonviolent messiah, one who will bring the victory of justice but without resorting to even a trace of violence. "Behold my servant whom I have chosen," he quotes from Isaiah. This beloved one will "proclaim justice" but not do violence or cry out or be a clanging voice; instead, he will be gentle and compassionate, and even the Gentiles will place their hope in him, the quote concludes. With this commentary, we know that Jesus is the Beloved of God who has come to bring justice through the power of meticulous nonviolence, and that the religious authorities are dead wrong about him.

Jesus then heals a blind, mute demoniac. At the touch of Jesus, he can suddenly see and speak. He opens his eyes and sees Jesus and speaks words of praise for God. This is what happens when Jesus heals us and expels the demons that possess us—we see him and praise God. The crowds are astonished and ask if this is the Son of David, which once again provokes the fury of the religious authorities. They denounce him with the crazy logic of violence: "he drives out demons by the power of the prince of demons."

And so begins a long commentary from Jesus on their condemnation. "Every kingdom divided against itself will be laid waste," he says. "No town or house divided against itself will stand. If Satan drives out Satan, he is divided against himself; how, then, will his kingdom stand? And if I drive out demons by Beelzebul, by whom do your own people drive them out? Therefore they will be your judges." His questions cannot be answered, because he is sane and uses the logic of nonviolence and truly tries to do God's will and shows only compassion and love. With these comments he proves that in fact he is working to bring down Satan's kingdom on earth. "If it is by the Spirit of God that I drive out demons," he tells them, "then the kingdom of God has come upon you." This is the heart of the matter: all their logic and attacks make no sense and expose their desire for control, power, and domination. But if, as Jesus asserts, their charges are false, and since they have all witnessed his miraculous power to drive out demons and heal people, then he announces, "The kingdom of God has come upon you."

This great announcement should be a cause for rejoicing. God's reign of peace is here among us! But instead, the authorities want to kill Jesus for it. We can easily dismiss them all these years later for their failure to understand Jesus, but I recommend that we take care. We need to ask ourselves, Do *we* really want God's reign among us? Do we really want the end of our culture of comfort, entertainment, and privilege so that there can be an equal distribution of wealth and resources around the world, so that everyone can have what they need as well as justice, dignity, and peace? Do we really want to dismantle our weapons and our military and live according to Jesus's Sermon-on-the-Mount rules of nonviolence? If we can prayerfully say yes to such questions and give our lives in pursuit of Jesus's new culture of justice and nonviolence, then the kingdom of God has come upon us too.

With the parable of the strong man's house, Jesus describes himself as the stronger, more powerful one, the one who enters the culture of violence, empire, and death, and binds it up and tears it down. He has set out to disarm the culture and dismantle the empire. No wonder he is perceived as a threat! He *is* a threat! "If you are not with me, you are against me," he says. Jesus is here to liberate everyone from all that is opposed to the thriving of human life and creation itself. Because he knows that deep down, most want to be liberated, he is able to forgive everyone. Every sin and blasphemy will be forgiven, he announces—with one exception: blasphemy against the Holy Spirit.

Blasphemy against the Holy Spirit is the unforgivable sin. What is that? This is a mysterious statement worth pondering. I suggest that blasphemy against the Holy Spirit is any word or action done in the name of God, in the name of Jesus, in his Holy Spirit by "religious" people that supports violence, injustice, and death itself. That would include nationalism disguised as religion, greed disguised as service, hate disguised as love, evil disguised as goodness, warmaking disguised as peacemaking, racism and sexism disguised as democracy—but done in the name of Christ. The Holy Spirit is Jesus's spirit of universal love and cannot have anything to do with violence, war, or killing. Jesus sends forth his disciples in his spirit to spread his way of nonviolence, convert everyone to his way of nonviolence, and transform the culture of war and empire into a new culture of peace. Soldiers, generals, rulers, even the most violent can all be forgiven, healed, and converted to his way of nonviolence. But if professional religious people spend their lives teaching and promoting violence, hatred, war, and empire in the name of Christ, then they are harming many people and are working directly against Jesus's spirit. That will be unforgivable because they have chosen to reject his true spirit of nonviolence and universal love, and in doing so, they have thoroughly rejected Jesus.

In other words, Matthew is talking about religious leaders then and now. Blasphemy against the Holy Spirit happens when religious leaders "mislead" the faithful by teaching and promoting the false spiritualities of violence, war, nationalism, and empire, in Jesus's name. They do irreparable spiritual harm to people when they do this, to the point where millions of people engage in warfare as if this was the will of God, a requirement of faith, the Spirit of God leading us. This "unforgivable sin" is therefore addressed to all those who work full time as religious leaders and warns them against teaching anything other than the Sermon on the Mount, the way of universal love. If religious leaders mislead the people to go against Jesus's spirit of nonviolence as he taught in the Sermon on the Mount, then they blaspheme his spirit and lead people away from the God of peace, and God's reign of peace coming to earth.

Matthew is addressing the religious authorities who deliberately lead people to follow the law, adhere to their cultural rules, and obey the Roman Empire and the false god of Caesar and his reign of violence. In doing so, they lead people away from the living God of peace and God's spirit of nonviolence to serve instead the false gods of the culture of war and empire all so they can gain wealth and power for themselves. Anyone who mixes faith and violence, God and war, Jesus and nationalism is playing with fire—not the holy fire of the Holy Spirit. That's why he concludes, "Whoever speaks a word against the Son of Humanity will be forgiven; but whoever speaks against the Holy Spirit will not be forgiven, either in this age or in the age to come."

The unforgivable sin continues today as so many religious voices urge people of faith to support war, nationalism, violence, and idolatry, as if that were the will of the God of peace or the nonviolent Jesus. It would be better if such religious leaders had not undertaken any public ministry, for they have betrayed the nonviolent Jesus and his holy spirit and spread the unholy, demonic spirits of violence, war, and nationalism. The best way to avoid the "unforgivable sin" is to take seriously the Sermon on the Mount and adhere strictly to Jesus's specific teachings on universal love and nonviolence, even if all the faithful support the troops, the latest war, and the latest weapons. All those who would be religious leaders need to be humble servants of the Holy Spirit of peace who teach the nonaligned, nonviolent Jesus and his reign of nonviolence. Our goal is not to gain wealth or power for ourselves but to be vessels of his Holy Spirit, that the Spirit may touch and disarm many and lead more and more to the coming of God's reign of peace on earth.

So Jesus offers a beautiful image from nature to help us understand ourselves and one another. Good trees produce good fruit, he teaches. Good people bring forth good out of their inner store of goodness. Be like that, he says. Do not produce evil fruit; let your hearts be disarmed of hate and greed and claim your inner goodness so that throughout your life you produce only good fruit. He wants our lives to bear the good fruit of mercy, love, compassion, and peace, so that goodness spreads far and wide because of us, because of our time on earth.

Jesus calls the religious authorities "a brood of vipers." They are trying to catch him, arrest him, and kill him, so he's in serious danger, yet I do not hear him saying this in anger.

I do not imagine Jesus screaming at the top of his lungs as he says this. Just the opposite. I imagine him, the one who is meek and gentle of heart, almost whispering this with grief. A brood of vipers is a collection of poisonous snakes ready to attack and kill at any moment. Jesus is trying to wake them up, to show them how they're acting, to put a mirror up to them so they can see the harm they threaten. He calls them—and all of us—to claim the fullness of goodness and love that lies deep within our hearts, so that our words and deeds will be peaceful, merciful, and loving. "I tell you, on the day of judgment, people will render an account for every careless word they speak," he announces. "By your words you will be acquitted, and by your words you will be condemned." Here he simply explains again the law of consequence—what goes around comes around. He invites us to speak out of love and mercy and therefore carry out deeds of love and mercy. In this creative way, he calls these religious death squads to repent and to heed his great sermon. Of course, they miss the point—but most often, so do we.

They never hear Jesus's call to inner transformation, as few of us do, but he tries nonetheless to reach out to them. You could make the case that the people Jesus spends the most time with are the very poor and ostracized—and the religious authorities, the scribes and Pharisees. In response to his teaching, they say, "Teacher, we wish to see a sign from you." The totally wrong thing to say! This only saddens Jesus further. He says that no sign will be given, but at the same time, he promises "the sign of Jonah the prophet," by which he means his resurrection. Here Matthew compares Jesus, who will rise after three days in the tomb, to the great prophet Jonah who emerged from the whale after three days in its belly.

Then he goes further and references Jonah's spectacular preaching to the people of Nineveh. When Jonah called the people of Nineveh to repent, the entire city repented. "At the judgment, the people of Nineveh will arise with this generation and condemn it, because they repented at the preaching of Jonah," Jesus says, "and there is something greater than Jonah here." Notice how humble Jesus is when referring to himself. He does not say, "I am far greater than Jonah" (even though he is); rather, he says, "there is something greater than Jonah here."

What is there in Jesus that is greater than Jonah? I consider Jonah the greatest of all the Hebrew prophets simply because he's the only one who ever succeeded in converting an entire people! What is greater than Jonah is the total nonviolence of Jesus! Jonah threatened violence and punishment from God, and people repented because they feared God, God's wrath, and violent destruction. Furthermore, when God did not punish the people with death and destruction, Jonah grew angry with God and lamented that God was "gracious and merciful, rich in clemency" (Jonah 4:2–4). Jonah threw a temper tantrum because God was nonviolent; he wanted the people to be destroyed.

The nonviolent Jesus, on the other hand, is gentle and humble of heart, as we just heard (11:29). He does not threaten fire and brimstone; he does not say that God is a God of violence, punishment, or war. He does not want the people to repent out of fear but out of love for the God of love and peace. He wants them to become as nonviolent as he is and to live in God's reign of total nonviolence and universal love. If anything, Jesus simply warns everyone that there are consequences to their violence and complicity with systemic injustice, war, and empire. Even though they reject him and eventually kill him, Jesus will prove his nonviolence to the end by never once getting angry or throwing a temper tantrum like Jonah. So it is true: in his nonviolence, Jesus is far greater than everyone else, including Jonah the greatest of the prophets, and every great prophet and saint since, including Gandhi and Dr. King. In this, he is the true son of the God of peace, the epitome of God among us.

"At the judgment the queen of the south will arise with this generation and condemn it, because she came from the ends of the earth to hear the wisdom of Solomon," Matthew's Jesus continues, "and there is something greater than Solomon here." We agree immediately that the wisdom of Jesus, which is the wisdom of total nonviolence and universal love that we heard explained in fine detail in the Sermon on the Mount, is far greater than anything Solomon ever said, or that anyone else has said since. Moreover, Jesus embodies the nonviolence and universal love he teaches (unlike the wise King Solomon who led armies, waged war, and killed people—not to mention his seven hundred wives and three hundred mistresses). Solomon, the son of David, was considered the wisest of all wise men, but Matthew's Jesus humbly hints that, because of his nonviolence, there is something far greater here. For those who have ears, he says, please consider this. The finger of God is upon him, Matthew tries to tell us. God's reign, wisdom, and vision of total nonviolence and universal love—indeed, the God of peace—are here, right now, in our midst. Wake up and believe the good news of peace, he quietly insists.

"When an unclean spirit goes out of a person, it roams through arid regions searching for rest, but finds none. Then it says, 'I will return to my home from which I came.' But upon returning, it finds it empty, swept clean, and put in order. Then it goes and brings back with itself seven other spirits more evil than itself, and they move in and dwell there; and the last condition of that person is worse than the first. Thus it will be with this evil generation." This is a spectacular teaching on the spiritual journey. Despite our best efforts, we continue to sin. We continue to do evil. In other words, we are addicted to sin. Every human being is addicted to sin; to put it another way, sin means addiction—to ego, pride, selfishness, greed, resentment, anger, lust, and ultimately to violence and death. As the Twelve Step programs teach, we need to admit our powerlessness, turn to our Higher Power, ask for help from a community of friends, make amends to those we have offended, hand over our lives to our Higher Power, and let our Higher Power run our lives and begin the journey of sobriety toward healing and reconciliation.

Matthew, like the other evangelists, is a storyteller. Just as he offers these profound teachings, we're told, "Jesus's mother and brothers and sisters appear outside, hoping to speak with him." While this might sound touching, as we reflect on the political mess that Jesus has exposed and confronted, we realize that they have not come to support him but to try to stop him from speaking out and causing such trouble. His response to them sounds, at first, cold and mean. "Who is my mother? Who are my brothers and sisters?" he asks. Stretching out his hand toward his disciples, he says, "Here are my mother and my brothers and sisters." He summons us to break the bloodline of family ties. It no longer matters to whom we are physically related. We are called to align ourselves with Jesus and with the reign of God. Each of us is called to be Jesus's mother, his brother, or his sister. This is the invitation of universal love, compassion, and peace. Come, be my family, he says with a welcoming hand of friendship.

"Whoever does the will of my heavenly Father is my brother and sister and mother." This is one of the great teachings. If we can do the will of God, then we are indeed the brother, sister, mother of the nonviolent Jesus. "Whoever does the will of the God of peace is the brother or sister of Jesus," Matthew declares. From now on, if we want to be close to Jesus, if we want to be connected to him, if we dare to even want to be related to him, we must do the will of God, which means, as far as Matthew is concerned, to live, enact, and teach Jesus's great sermon. The mature spiritual life requires that we become Sermon-on-the-Mount people, the family of Jesus.

"A Sower Went Out to Sow" (13:1–58)

"On that day, Jesus went out of the house and sat down by the sea." Here's a seemingly ordinary sentence well worth pondering. Imagine this scene in your quiet meditation. Sit down by the sea with our friend and teacher Jesus. Notice how he sits and what he does. Note that he is fully present, at peace, centered, one with creation, looking out at the beautiful Sea of Galilee, praising the Creator of this peace, seeing everyone through the lens of universal love. We can return to this image for the rest of our lives. Whatever we are going through, we can always return in our meditation to this scene by the sea with the nonviolent Jesus. This peace foreshadows his gift of resurrection peace, when he will return risen, alive, ready to send us forth in the power of his peace.

With that scene, the story turns. The crowds appear, and Jesus starts to tell them stories. We're told he got into a boat, sat down, and spoke to the crowd as they stood listening along the shore. Each parable as Matthew writes it has one specific point. We as listeners must find the point.

He begins: "A sower went out to sow." He proceeds to describe what happened as the sower sowed his seed. "Some seed fell on the path, and birds came and ate it up. Some fell on rocky ground, where it had little soil. It sprang up at once because the soil was not deep, and when the sun rose it was scorched, and it withered for lack of roots. Some seed fell among thorns, and the thorns grew up and choked it. But some seed fell on rich soil, and produced fruit, a hundred or sixty or thirtyfold. Whoever has ears ought to hear."

What's unusual with this passage is that Matthew provides an explanation. Even if we have heard it a hundred times, this parable remains provocative. Why is Jesus talking about a sower? Why does he bother pointing out the seed that gets eaten by birds, or the seed that falls on rocky ground, or the seed that falls among thorns, before he tells of the seed that lands in rich soil?

In the traditional style of the Synoptics, we have the sandwich outline of A, B, A, where A is the parable; B is a commentary; and A retells the parable. The disciples ask him, "Why do you speak to them in parables?" They ask because they do not understand a word he is saying, and they want to sound intelligent. His answer sounds harsh at first, but it is a gentle truth. "Because knowledge of the mysteries of the kingdom of heaven has been granted to you, but to them it has not been granted." Some people have been given the gift of understanding the mysteries of God's reign, but not everyone. If you listen to Jesus's teachings and take them to heart and try to put them into practice, then you have been granted entrance into the mysteries of God's reign.

Matthew cites Isaiah to try to explain why some people refuse to accept Jesus's teachings or the mysteries of the kingdom of God. Some people are so broken, wounded, and sick that they cannot see their way toward universal love, compassion, peace, and justice for the poor. Jesus realizes that many people are unconcerned about his wisdom or his way. He knows they are incapable of listening, much less understanding. If we dare to look around us—or look at ourselves—we see what he means. It seems easier to close our ears to wisdom, compassion, and nonviolence. It's easier to remain stuck in our many harmful ways of thinking.

So Matthew cites Isaiah: "You shall indeed hear but not understand; you shall indeed look but never see. Gross is the heart of this people; they will hardly hear with their ears. They have closed their eyes, lest they see with their eyes and hear with their ears and understand with their heart and be converted, and I heal them."

But Jesus does not leave it there. He offers a beatitude of encouragement: "Blessed are your eyes, because they see, and your ears, because they hear. Amen, I say to you, many prophets and righteous people longed to see what you see but did not see it, and to hear what you hear but did not hear it." Notice how kind and affirming he is. That's the hallmark of Jesus. He always tries to encourage us.

"Hear then the parable of the sower," he goes on. "The seed sown on the path is the one who hears the word of the kingdom without understanding it, and the evil one comes and steals away what was sown in his heart. The seed sown on rocky ground is the one who hears the word and receives it at once with joy. But he has no root and lasts only for a time. When some tribulation or persecution comes because of the word, he immediately falls away. The seed sown among thorns is the one who hears the word, but then worldly anxiety and the lure of riches choke the word and it bears no fruit. But the seed sown on rich soil is the one who hears the word and understands it, who indeed bears fruit and yields a hundred or sixty or thirtyfold."

Here Jesus describes human life in a nutshell. He says, in effect, that every human being "hears the word of God." Everyone. At some point, we all hear the deep-down truth that we are all one, created by God to spend our lives and eternity in God's reign of peace. Some of us don't understand this truth but we hear it at some point on our journey. Some of us have no roots; we have no practice to maintain God's way. Others of us give in to anxiety and riches, and bear no fruit. But some rare people take this word to heart, and let it sink it, and spend our lives practicing the way of Jesus, discovering at the end that we have indeed been fruitful through steadfast faith in God's way of universal love and total nonviolence.

As readers of this parable, we might ask where we are—what kind of seed we are. Most of us have been every type of seed Jesus describes here. Nonetheless, the parable is an invitation. Jesus wants us to hear the word of God, take it to heart, root ourselves in God's reign of peace, and spend our lives bearing the good fruit of peace, love, and justice for the greater glory of God. This is doable. At any moment, we can choose to respond to God as good seed responds to the soil and sun.

One way to approach this parable is through prayer: to ask daily for the grace to become people of good soil who bear good fruit for God, a hundredfold or sixtyfold or thirtyfold. We need not get discouraged, thinking we are bad soil or rootless or permanently given over to anxieties and riches. There's always time to change and set out anew as Jesus's faithful disciples. In prayer, we can ask to be people who make the word of God a priority, as Gandhi did with the Sermon on the Mount. I recommend taking time every day to read a passage from one of the four Gospels, so that over time, we come to know the nonviolent Jesus better. We enter his story, and his story becomes our story too, and we live more and more as Jesus did, and we do what he wants us to do, thus bearing good fruit as he did.

Matthew then offers an original parable, using the same image of a sower sowing seed. This time, however, we hear of an enemy who comes at night and sows weeds in the sower's wheat fields, so that the field grows up with both wheat and weeds. The owner tells his servants to let them grow up together, so that his treasured wheat is not destroyed. At harvest time, he says, I will tell the harvesters to collect the weeds for burning, and then gather the wheat into my barn.

Here Matthew's Jesus explains the reality of life for his disciples who follow his way in a world opposed to his way. Matthew will offer an explanation, because neither we nor the disciples understand the parable. Once again, he uses the sandwich structure of A, B, A and inserts two other parables about the kingdom of God, before returning to the explanation of the weeds and the wheat.

The great recurring question for Jesus throughout the Synoptic Gospels is, "To what can I compare the kingdom of God?" In these two brief parables, he speaks about the tiny beginnings of the kingdom, and how it spreads far and wide to encompass the whole earth and to include everyone. First, it's like a mustard seed. "The kingdom of heaven is like a mustard seed that a person took and sowed in a field. It is the smallest of all the seeds, yet when full-grown it is the largest of plants. It becomes a large bush, and the 'birds of the sky come and dwell in its branches.'" In this famous parable, Matthew cites Jeremiah's image of the mustard bush. Its seed is the smallest, and yet it becomes a large plant that welcomes all kinds of birds. Jesus sows the seed of the kingdom of God with his teachings and his life, then the seed falls to the ground and dies, then bears fruit by leading billions of people from all nations, like birds from every corner of the sky, to the kingdom of God.

Next, he compares the kingdom to the yeast a woman uses to bake bread. "The kingdom of heaven is like yeast that a woman took and mixed with three measures of wheat flour until the whole batch was leavened." The small amount of yeast mixed into the large amount of flour (three measures can feed a hundred people!) leavens and transforms the flour into bread. Jesus is the yeast of the kingdom which God, a woman, mixes into the world, thereby transforming humanity and the world into God's kingdom. By Jesus's proclamation and teaching about the kingdom of God, even though he is one tiny person in history, he begins the process of global transformation. His disciples will continue the process so that the kingdom of God may be realized here on earth. We are told that he spoke this way in parables to the crowds to fulfill the prophets and the scriptures, as a way to announce what had been hidden.

Finally, Matthew returns to the parable of the weeds and the wheat. Jesus dismissed the crowds and "went into the house." This would probably be Peter's house in Capernaum, which has now become the community house. From here on, Jesus focuses on teaching and forming his disciples. They do not understand his parables, and ask for the explanation.

"He who sows good seed is the Son of Humanity," he explains. "The field is the world, the good seed the children of the kingdom. The weeds are the children of the evil one, and the enemy who sows them is the devil. The harvest is the end of the age, and the harvesters are angels. Just as weeds are collected and burned up with fire, so will it be at the end of the age. The Son of Humanity will send his angels, and they will collect out of his kingdom all who cause others to sin and all evildoers. They will throw them into the fiery furnace, where there will be wailing and grinding of teeth. Then the righteous will shine like the sun in the kingdom of their Father. Whoever has ears ought to hear."

This sounds terrifying! When we consider it in the context of the Sermon on the Mount, however, and when we remember that parables have one specific point, then we realize that Jesus is teaching us once again that all of us are called to be children of God in God's kingdom of peace and nonviolence. We are the sons and daughters of the God of peace and universal love. This is who we are. Further, we are the light of the world. And so, as people who have already entered eternal life here and now, we shine like the sun with all the qualities of God's kingdom. God wants everyone to be a child of the kingdom, to be good seed—and every one of us already has that potential within us. Every one of us already is a beloved child of God.

I hear this parable telling us not to be afraid, to be ourselves, to be who we were created to be, and to know that we are headed to the fullness of life in God's kingdom because we are God's beloved children. If we dare claim our true identities as Jesus taught us in the Sermon on the Mount, then this is a positive, affirming, and hopeful parable. That is the point of the parable. So I invite readers of this parable to pray to be good seed that grows and brings a good harvest of peace and justice; that is what each one of us was created to do, so that is our vocation and the focus of our attention. We try to be part of the harvest of peace.

If that doesn't work for you, think of this parable, like so many other teachings, as the effect of "consequentialism." Everything we do has consequences, so be mindful, nonviolent, peaceful, and careful about what you do. When a loving parent warns her four-year-old not to put her hand on the stove, telling her that she will burn her hand if she does, she doesn't want the child to burn her hand. She is not angry, yelling, or threatening—just explaining the way things are, as I suggested in my introduction. The child might be terrified by that warning, but the parent doesn't mean to terrify the child, just encourage it to be careful and stay safe. If you put your hand on a stove, it will burn, so don't do that. Likewise, Jesus tries in every gentle way possible to tell us not to do certain things because they can harm us. His loving-kindness cannot help but warn us to avoid sin, violence, hatred, and war; if we take his warning seriously, because we love and trust him, we will be fine. All will be well. We will not get burned later on. We will be the light of the world. We need not be terrified by his warnings; instead, we can appreciate them as the direction of a loving parent to us as innocent children who don't yet fully understand reality.

In this parable, we hear one of the first references to an interesting and unusual phrase about those in the fiery furnace where there will be "wailing and grinding of teeth." This phrase will appear in other difficult parables in the Synoptics. From the perspective of nonviolence, I find it helpful. In my opinion, this phrase, here and elsewhere, is simply reminding us that one sign that we are not living here and now in God's reign of universal love and total nonviolence, which is the urgent call of Jesus in the Synoptics, is if we are "wailing and grinding our teeth," that is, if we are miserable, unhappy, mean, self-centered, and stuck within ourselves in violence. We don't even realize that we are miserable, that we have not stepped into the possibilities, here and now, of universal love and total nonviolence! We are unconscious of our own predicament, powerless over our inner violence, and stubbornly refuse to budge or to change; and so, we remain at rock bottom in our own stew of violence. This is the message of Gandhi, Dr. King, Thich Nhat Hanh, and so many others: we can step out of the cycle of violence within ourselves and in the world, and step into the new life of nonviolence, peace, and universal love right this very minute, and practice peace and love toward all others and ourselves, and in the process, become happier, more peaceful, even joyful.

From the perspective of nonviolence, then, we can read this parable and others like it from a post-supersessionist interpretation, reaffirm Jesus's teaching that God is nonviolent and hear it as an urgent call to repent of violence and live from now on in God's reign of peace and nonviolence. In this light, even this parable becomes good news.

Matthew's parables about God's reign keep on coming. Here are three short ones: "The kingdom of heaven is like a treasure buried in a field, which a person finds and hides again, and out of joy goes and sells all that he has and buys that field. Again, the kingdom of heaven is like a merchant searching for fine pearls. When he finds a pearl of great price, he goes and sells all that he has and buys it." These two parables stress that once we understand the kingdom of heaven, once we grasp and put into practice the teachings of the Sermon on the Mount, we will drop everything to surrender our lives to God's way, and we will experience a deep joy in the process. The third parable, comparing the kingdom to a net thrown into the sea that collects fish of every kind, explains "the end of the age," when the angels will come and collect the righteous. That is the point to focus on: despite the struggles and difficulties we face, if we follow Jesus's way, God will send the angels to bring us one day into the fullness of God's peace. There is hope, there is cause for rejoicing, there is reason to persevere on the journey.

Whenever you hear a great question, the poet Rainer Maria Rilke advises, do not rush to answer it. Sit with it, for years if necessary, until you live your way into the answer. Thus it is with the question Jesus asks next: "Do you understand all these things?" We might probably say no. But if we sit with Jesus's teachings every day and practice the mindset of Jesus consistently, then we will live into the yes. Notice that the disciples answer yes to Jesus's pointed question. Jesus seems to affirm them and encourage them. They are slowly learning, they are teachable. Matthew then offers a saying unique to his Gospel, that everyone instructed in the kingdom of heaven, even a scribe, is like "the head of a household who brings from his storeroom both the new and the old." All those "learned" in the kingdom of heaven, all those who live according to the word of God, will go forth and teach the ancient wisdom, using the old stories and the newest insights to help everyone on earth. Anyone of us can become, like the disciples, "learned in the kingdom."

After all these astonishing teachings about God's reign, Matthew concludes this section with Jesus's return to his native village, Nazareth. There he teaches, and there he finds stiff opposition if not outright hostility. Who does this guy think he is? they ask themselves.

"Where did this man get such wisdom and mighty deeds? Is he not the carpenter's son? Is not his mother named Mary and his brothers James, Joseph, Simon, and Judas? Are not his sisters all with us? Where did this man get all this?" They cannot believe that this ordinary man, whom they've known since childhood, who has four brothers and many sisters, and an ordinary mother, could speak with such wisdom and do such mighty deeds. Because he is wise, eloquent, and authentic, which seems to frighten them, they question him and harass him, and Matthew says pointedly, "they took offense at him."

This is significant. One would expect a happy, proud response: "Hometown boy makes good!" "The pride of the village!" "Welcome back, hero!" In a culture of violence, empire, and war, it never works that way. People are suspicious, envious, and usually take offense at those who stand up publicly for the good, for the God of peace. They do not want "such wisdom" or "mighty deeds," because they do not want trouble with the authorities, and neither do we. Jesus responds with his famous dictum: "A prophet is not without honor except in his native place and in his own house." And we are told that "he did not work many mighty deeds there because of their lack of faith." For those of us who care about the nonviolent Jesus, we feel his grief at the hard-heartedness of those who knew him best.

This Gospel passage shows us that the rejection of Jesus's message of peace and nonviolence begins with those who know him best—his own hometown family and neighbors. This does not discourage him to give up his campaign. Likewise, we can expect our public work of peace and social transformation to be rejected by our families and hometown neighbors, but that should not discourage us. Like the nonviolent Jesus, we continue onward, even if our message is rejected. We pray for those who reject it and even persecute us, and we carry on our campaign. We are not responsible for making people accept the teaching of Gospel nonviolence; our task is simply to live out the teachings and proclaim them as far and wide as possible. The outcome is in God's hands. In the end, we too are sowers of peace, and we hope and pray that one day God will reap a great harvest of peace.

"Take Courage, It Is I; Do Not Be Afraid!" (14:1–16:28)

Matthew's account of King Herod's brutal execution of John the Baptist reads like an insane horror film featuring a wild party, dancing, and a beheading. Because Jesus has already warned us that his campaign will not be tolerated by the ruling class, we are somewhat prepared for this terrible outcome. What we do not know is that this horror story is actually a warning of what lies ahead for the nonviolent Jesus and for all those who live his Sermon-on-the-Mount teachings in an anti-Sermon-on-the-Mount world.

John had preached against Herod for marrying the wife of his brother, so Herod arrested John and put him in prison. He didn't dare kill him because John was revered as a prophet by the people. But after Herod's daughter performed a spectacular dance at his birthday party, he promised, in front of all his guests, to give her anything she wanted. His wife, who hated John because of his preaching against their marriage, told their daughter to ask for the head of John the Baptist on a platter. John was killed, his head was given to Herod's daughter, and she gave it to her mother. This horrifying outcome shows us what happens to people stuck in the systems of violence and death. They have no sense of decency, goodness, or love; they kill with impunity, for the sport of it, for revenge. They do not know the living God and so they are controlled by hatred, resentment, fear, and brutality.

After John's disciples bury his corpse, they find Jesus and tell him the shocking news. Herod is known as a mass murderer, but this brutal execution shakes them to the core. "When Jesus heard of it," Matthew writes, "he withdrew in a boat to a deserted place by himself."

As we read through Matthew's story of the nonviolent Jesus, it's worth pausing to ask periodically, What is going through Jesus's mind? How does he feel? How is he coping with this roller-coaster public campaign, between the crowds, the disciples, the sick, the religious authorities, and the death squads? One way to enter the nonviolence of Jesus is to study his feelings. As we reflect on that and sit with him and meditate on his feelings, we can learn how to fashion our own lives and feelings after his and deepen our interior nonviolence. In this instance, Jesus is grieving the execution of his friend and cousin, John the Baptist. Earlier, Jesus taught us in the Sermon on the Mount to reject anger and fear but to cultivate grief and joy. Here we see him retreating alone into the wilderness, deep in grief. As his followers we learn to go away with him, to retreat into solitude with him, and to grieve with him. He does not get angry at John's murderers; there is no talk of revenge or retaliation. Indeed, if we look deeply, we know Jesus will forgive them, that he has already forgiven them. But he does grieve for John, and his grief widens his heart to ever greater compassion.

As he disembarks from the boat to make his retreat into solitude, he finds a vast crowd waiting for him, and we're told "his heart was moved with pity for them, and he cured their sick." Jesus was tired from grief and crying, but he felt great compassion for these poor people, who were looking to him for healing and wisdom, so he got to work. He set aside his personal feelings, his need for solitude and privacy, and healed all those in need. His compassion is active, public, and helpful for everyone. Once again, he models for his disciples then and now the life of active love and universal compassion.

The disciples tell Jesus to dismiss the crowds because it's late, so they will have time to go to the nearby villages and buy food. When I read this, I hear the male disciples actually trying to figure out how *they* can get some food because they themselves are tired and hungry. But here again, in the famous episode of the multiplication of the loaves, Jesus gives them a demonstration of compassion in action. It begins with a command. "There is no need for them to go away. Give them some food yourselves." Notice the imperative verb tense. *You go and feed these people.* That is God's will for us—that we ourselves go and feed the hungry. In a world of global starvation, this is a new commandment that every disciple is ordered to obey. These words point to an egalitarian politics of food, whereby every human being has access to healthy food.

The disciples tell Jesus that they have only five loaves and two fish. He orders the crowd to sit down on the grass, takes the loaves and fish, looks up to heaven, says the blessing, breaks the loaves, and gives them to the disciples, who then distribute them to the crowds. "All ate and were satisfied," Matthew reports. "Twelve wicker baskets were needed to pick up the leftovers." Then, in classic patriarchal language, we're told that the crowd was made up of five thousand men, "not counting women and children."

There are two ways to look at this great miracle: the first way to approach the story is to accept it as the miraculous action of God in Jesus changing five loaves and two fish into enough loaves and fish to feed thousands of people. Jesus is the God who feeds the hungry and the poor, so that all are satisfied, so much so that he himself will become our bread. In this way, the feeding symbolizes the Eucharist, whereby Jesus gives us his body in the form of bread and feeds humanity. The invocation—taking, blessing, breaking, and giving—reminds Matthew's community that they are continuing the tradition of Jesus when they share the Eucharist together. It also fulfills the exodus story (Exodus 16) of the feeding of the crowds with manna from heaven. The problem with this way of reading the event, as we noted earlier, is that this is precisely the kind of magic, inhuman solution the tempter proposed to Jesus in the first temptation in the desert (4:3–4). Jesus rejected the spectacular miracle of turning "stones into bread" and instead demanded that we obey the word of God and do what God commands.

More and more scholars and theologians, therefore, are reading this famous passage in a new way, not as a spectacular magic act but as a spectacular miracle of everyone in the crowd who has food sharing it with those who do not so that everyone gets fed. This second way to read the story begins with the last sentence. The crowd had five thousand men, "not counting women and children." In this patriarchal world, women did not count, literally. If there were five thousand men following the holy rabbi, you can bet there were twenty-five thousand women and children. No woman, no mother, would traipse out into the wilderness with her kids without bringing food for the day. When the crowd is ordered to sit down, and they see the Master lift up loaves and fishes and break bread and distribute food, they in turn take out their own food and share it with all those around them who do not have any.

From this perspective, the miracle is that Jesus inspires thousands of people to share their food with those who do not have any so that no one goes hungry. That would never have happened before, and it rarely happens now. The culture of greed has a tight grip on all of us; we hoard our food and ignore the starvation of millions. But in the presence of the nonviolent Jesus, we let go of our fears and anxieties and freely share our food and possessions with everyone in need, with no thought of service in return. But from my perspective, it would have been the faithful women in the crowd who followed Jesus and helped save the day.

But in light of the first temptation in the desert (4:3–4), where the tempter tells Jesus to turn stones into bread, and Jesus responds by announcing that we do not live by bread alone but by every word that comes from the mouth of God, we now realize that thousands of people have been listening to the word of God all day, and suddenly start practicing it and living according to it! Jesus has been teaching the crowd all day to show love and compassion to one another, to share what they have with one another, and, in doing so, to practice justice and equality and welcome God's reign here and now on earth. They are hearing the word of God spoken by Jesus, so when they see him share food with the crowd, they do likewise and share what they brought with the hungry strangers around them. This second interpretation is more consistent, then, with the whole trajectory of Matthew's teachings on faith, obedience, and nonviolence. The miracle is the free sharing of food with the hungry. In today's world of hunger, that miracle must become the norm of Christian behavior.

After this episode, Jesus dismissed the crowds and sent the disciples off in a boat again to the other side. Remember, he's still grieving, so he retreats alone to a mountaintop to pray. "When it was evening," we are told, "he was there alone." This is an important image to sit with. Jesus's friend John has been killed, and, instead of going away to grieve, Jesus ends up teaching and feeding thousands of people. Now he retreats alone to a mountaintop, where he rests in solitude and silence in the beauty of nature, and there communes with God his Father. In this solitude of prayer, he is healed, renewed, and reenergized to carry on the journey. This little detail presents a crucial aspect of the life of Gospel nonviolence: we serve the poor, and we also take time alone in nature to commune with God and restore our own peace and strength. By doing this, we can maintain our nonviolence, our compassion, and our mission. We are not meant to get burned out.

Meanwhile the boat is tossed about by a windy storm at sea and, once again, the disciples must have been terrified. This time, they are by themselves. They have been sent to the other side—to enemy territory—on their own, without Jesus. Their mission is to bring peace, love, healing, and the kingdom of God to this enemy land, which is a terrifying mission. It feels like a struggle between life and death.

But not for Jesus. Crossing to the other side, loving the enemies of one's nation, reconciling peoples together, is simply his way of living. For Jesus, such active nonviolence and reconciling love are easy. And we're given a shocking, stunning image to demonstrate how easy it is to practice universal love and creative nonviolence. In the middle of the night, at the fourth watch, we're told, Jesus "came toward them, walking on the sea." The terrified disciples cried out and screamed. It must be a ghost, they thought. No living person could walk on water.

"Take courage, it is I," Jesus called out to them. "Do not be afraid." These are the key words of Jesus to every disciple who dares to follow him on the way of creative nonviolence. They are words that we need to hear over and over again as we engage in public, prophetic nonviolent action for justice and disarmament. He commands us to have courage—to be brave, strong, steadfast, and fearless. He tells us he's right there by our side, with us through every moment of active public peacemaking, no matter how dark the situation, no matter how rough the waters. And he commands us not to be afraid. Every disciple loves and trusts the nonviolent Jesus, so once we know that he is with us, then we're fine. There is no reason to be afraid. We can face anything—even a stormy sea, even death.

Peter is as bold as ever. "Lord, if it is you, command me to come to you on the water," he says. "Come." Jesus replies. Peter gets out of the boat and begins to walk on the water toward Jesus. But just then the strong wind blows and he becomes frightened and starts to sink. He cries out, "Lord, save me!" Immediately Jesus stretches out his hand and catches Peter.

Notice that Peter is able to walk on water, too! Why? Because he keeps his eyes on Jesus. If we keep our eyes on Jesus, then crossing to the other side to engage in peacemaking becomes possible even for us ordinary, terrified people. All we have to do is keep our eyes on Jesus. The moment we take our eyes off Jesus, we start sinking. We notice the waves, the wind, the storm, we become afraid, and we start drowning. Jesus is always there to rescue us, but he wants us to walk on water with him, to discover how easy it is to cross to the other side, to do what we used to believe was impossible. If this seems impossible, look at it this way: all we have to do is keep our eyes on the nonviolent Jesus right now, in this present

79

moment. As we live moment by moment, one day at a time, we shall spend our entire lives looking at Jesus and following him.

"O you of little faith, why did you doubt?" Jesus asks Peter. I always presume Jesus is smiling when he asks this. Peter is speechless; he is so dumbfounded he cannot form the words to answer the great question. Neither can the other disciples. Once they're back in the boat, Matthew adds a unique detail: they all did him homage, saying, "Truly, you are the Son of God." Again, Jesus encourages us to have faith in him, not to doubt him, and to keep on walking on his path. If we do, we will recognize him in our midst and do him homage.

And there, on the other side of the sea, in the heart of the enemy Gentile country, people started bringing him all their sick relatives and friends, and we're told that everyone who touched the tassel of his cloak was healed. The disciples, who had just worshiped Jesus, were witnesses to his healing activity and were beginning to learn that Jesus really wants us to practice active, universal love toward all human beings, especially those we hate, ostracize, marginalize, and even wage war against.

Jesus has fed thousands of people and healed the sick of the enemy territory, and how do the powerful religious authorities respond? They attack him and try to trap him. "Why do your disciples break the tradition of the elders?" they ask him. "They do not wash their hands when they eat a meal," they continue, charging Jesus's disciples with illegal activity, violating the Mosaic law. Earlier he tried to reason with the religious officials. This time he questions them in return and cites the scriptures while doing so: "Why do you break the commandment of God for the sake of your tradition? God said, 'Honor your father and your mother,' and 'Whoever curses father or mother shall die.' But you say, 'Whoever says to father or mother, "Any support you might have had from me is dedicated to God," need not honor his father.' You have nullified the word of God for the sake of your tradition. Hypocrites, well did Isaiah prophesy about you when he said: 'This people honors me with their lips, but their hearts are far from me; in vain do they worship me, teaching as doctrines human precepts.'"

Jesus exposes their own violation of God's law, in this case, the commandment to honor one's parents, and calls them hypocrites. Matthew cites Isaiah again to explain how these religious officials do not worship God from the heart. In doing so, Matthew urges us to worship God with all our hearts. This is a requirement for the Sermon-on-the-Mount life of nonviolence. As you read these passages, do not assume that Jesus is angry. There's no evidence that he's angry or in any way violent. He maintains his nonviolence but speaks truth with love. If anything, he's grieving the loss of John and the religious officials' refusal to accept his wisdom. He wants all of us to follow divine precepts, not human precepts. The divine precepts he refers to are the new commandments of love, compassion, peace, and nonviolence outlined in the Sermon on the Mount. He does not want his disciples to be like these power-hungry, hypocritical religious officials in their blind civil obedience but to practice nonviolent civil disobedience to the culture of violence and divine obedience to God's reign of peace. That is the dedication, the heartfelt worship that he seeks.

Matthew uses the sandwich technique to split Jesus's teachings. The disciples ask Jesus a serious question: "Do you know that the Pharisees took offense when they heard what you said?" In effect, they ask, "Didn't you hurt their feelings? Is that nonviolence? Aren't you being rude and insulting?" What they fail to understand, and we do as well, is that Jesus speaks from a heart of nonviolent, compassionate love. He loves the religious authorities so much that he tries every nonviolent tactic possible to wake them up, even the tough language of naming their hypocrisy. He is not angry, mean, or violent, but he does name their hypocrisy in no uncertain terms. Of course, they take offense at him, but they should not. They should humbly accept the truth and say, "You're right, Jesus. We have been hypocritical. From now on, we will worship God with all our hearts."

Jesus tells his disciples that hypocrisy in the name of God has consequences: "Every plant that my heavenly Father has not planted will be uprooted." Then he tells them to avoid these religious authorities and, in effect, carry on the mission of nonviolence he has given to them. "Leave them alone," he says. "They are blind guides of the blind. If a blind person leads a blind person, both will fall into a pit." This parable speaks to our condition today as well. If our guides cannot see, and we continue to follow them, we will all fall into a pit. Instead, Jesus urges us to find good guides, visionaries who can see the way forward to God's reign. For us today, that means that we should follow only visionary guides of universal love and active nonviolence. And if we want to be guides of others, we need to delve deep into the attributes of Jesus himself so that we can help others see the path forward to God.

In the midst of this exchange, Jesus gathers the crowd to teach them and begins with the imperative: "Hear and understand." He wants us to hear what he says, take it to heart, understand it, and know it by heart, that we might live out his teachings. "It is not what enters one's mouth that defiles that person; what comes out of the mouth is what defiles one." Of course, they don't know what he's talking about. Peter says, "Explain this parable to us." "Are even you still without understanding?" Jesus asks him. Peter and the others do not understand, and the truth is, neither do we. We have to go slow judging Peter because we are even slower to understand than he was.

"Do you not realize that everything that enters the mouth passes into the stomach and is expelled into the latrine?" he asks. "But the things that come out of the mouth come from the heart, and they defile. For from the heart come evil thoughts, murder, adultery, unchastity, theft, false witness, blasphemy. These are what defile a person, but to eat with unwashed hands does not defile." In this teaching, Jesus does away with ritual cleanliness practices saying, "Do not be concerned about what comes out of the body; be concerned with what comes from your heart." He names the various forms of violence that come from within us: evil thoughts, murder, adultery, unchastity, theft, false witness, and blasphemy. The way to avoid these harmful practices is by cultivating a pure heart, which means living according to his Sermon on the Mount. The goal is not to follow religious observances for their sake but to transform yourself, to have "a gentle and humble heart" like the nonviolent Jesus.

"O Woman, Great Is Your Faith" (15:21–16:12)

After this exchange, Jesus goes away to the Mediterranean coast, I submit, to get a few days of R and R. I think he was exhausted and, dare I add, frustrated at his disciples for their lack of understanding. Matthew's version of Jesus's encounter with the Canaanite woman is shorter than other accounts, but it is one of the most important episodes in the Gospels to understand Jesus's nonviolence. This unnamed Gentile woman calls out to Jesus with great respect, begging for healing for her daughter. "Have pity on me, Lord, Son of David! My daughter is tormented by a demon." Whenever anyone calls out to Jesus with respect with such a request, he immediately proceeds to heal the person in need. Here, however, he deliberately does not heal the daughter. In fact, he appears to be rude, mean, almost violent in his response.

First, he is cold to her and does not answer her. Then his clueless disciples tell him to "Send her away, for she keeps calling out after us." Finally, he gives the two meanest responses in the entire Gospel. "I was sent only to the lost sheep of the house of Israel." We know from various other episodes, especially from his boat crossings to the other side, that in fact he had learned to tend all sheep, Jew and Gentile, even the enemies of his people. So, something deeper is going on.

Matthew says she does him homage, and begs, "Lord, help me." He says in reply, "It is not right to take the food of the children and throw it to the dogs." In the face of this derogatory comment, she does not give in, but insists, "Please, Lord, even the dogs eat the scraps that fall from the table of their masters." "O woman, great is your faith!" he says to her. "Let it be done for you as you wish." And her daughter was healed from that hour.

I think Jesus sensed immediately that this Canaanite woman was one of the greatest people he had met so far. She clearly had a deep, strong faith in him and in God. So, in this episode, Jesus acts like an ancient Buddhist Zen master—who speaks harshly to someone, knowing they can handle it, for the sole purpose of instructing the bystanders, his clueless male disciples! I imagine Jesus with a slight smile saying these harsh things to the Canaanite woman, knowing that she has the wit and strength to stand her ground. When he finally grants her request, which he intends to do all along, he has taught his male disciples an important lesson: they can and should be open to changing their minds, just as Jesus here has apparently changed his mind. He lets himself be seen as being converted by one of the poorest persons on the planet: a Canaanite woman. He shows himself as someone who is not totally closed-minded but teachable; he does this so that in the future, the disciples will be open to changing their minds and widening their hearts in compassion for the poor.

After this, Jesus walks all the way back to the Sea of Galilee, climbs the mountain, sits down, and cures everyone—"the lame, the blind, the deformed, the mute, and many others." Matthew notes that "the crowds were amazed when they saw the mute speaking, the deformed made whole, the lame walking, and the blind able to see, and they glorified the God of Israel." By siding with the poor and healing them, Jesus practices creative nonviolence and heralds the coming of God's reign of abundant life for all, beginning with those who suffer the most. He summons his disciples and says, "My heart is moved with pity for the crowd, for they have been with me now for three days and have nothing to eat. I do not want to send them away hungry, for fear they may collapse on the way." Again, we note that his heart is full of compassion for these needy people. As he taught the disciples earlier, he wants them to have hearts full of compassion for the poor, too, that they might take action on their behalf and bring them justice.

"Where could we ever get enough bread in this deserted place to satisfy such a crowd?" Jesus said to them, "How many loaves do you have?" "Seven," they reply, "and a few fish." For the second time in Matthew, he orders the crowd to sit, takes the loaves and fish, offers thanks, and gives them to his disciples, who distribute them to the crowds. Once again, "all ate and were satisfied." The leftovers fill seven baskets. This time, we're told there were four thousand men, "not counting women and children." This second multiplication of the loaves and fish again combines the image of Jesus feeding the early community with the Eucharist, inspiring everyone to live according to the word of God and, in doing so, to share what they have with one another, calling his disciples to show active compassion to the poor, and unveiling the mystery of who he really is to those who believe.

Then Jesus gets into the boat and journeys to the district of Magadan, where the Pharisees and Sadducees confront him and ask him for "a sign from heaven." This is the second time they demand a sign, only this time Matthew adds that it be "from heaven." The religious authorities would not invoke the name of God, so with Matthew's reference to "heaven," we know that they are demanding proof that he is of God. They challenge him to prove he is of God, and presuming he is not, try to humiliate him and dismiss him and his miraculous feeding of the crowd. You can tell the weather by the appearance of the sky, he says, but you cannot read the signs of the times. "An evil and unfaithful generation seeks a sign, but no sign will be given it except the sign of Jonah." With that, he walks away. He says he will not give them a sign, but in the end, he does give them one: the sign of Jonah, referring again to Jonah's three days in the belly of the whale and how he returned. Jesus refers to his resurrection, but they don't know what he is talking about. But with this hint of a sign, with this talk of Jonah, we know there's more to the story than meets the eye. Indeed after all we have seen and heard since the last time they demanded a sign, we know for sure there is "something far greater" going on here.

Once they're back in the boat and approaching the other side again, the disciples realize they forgot to bring bread. They're hungry. That's all they can think about. They've long moved on from any talk of signs or Jonah. And so again begins a comedy of misunderstanding. "Beware of the leaven of the Pharisees and Sadducees," Jesus tells them. Try to avoid these powerful, religious authorities. Their teachings and example will only lead you astray. The disciples hear the word "leaven" and think he must be talking about bread. "It is because we have brought no bread," they mumble to themselves. When Jesus becomes aware of this, he says, "You of little faith, why do you conclude among yourselves that it is because you have no bread? Do you not yet understand, and do you not remember the five loaves for the five thousand, and how many wicker baskets you took up? Or the seven loaves for the four thousand, and how many baskets you took up? How do you not comprehend that I was not speaking to you about bread? Beware of the leaven of the Pharisees and Sadducees." He has to remind them over and over again what they saw him do, and ask them if they remember, to get them to focus on his message. Eventually they begin to understand that he is warning them against the teachings of the religious authorities. Likewise, we too are clueless and have difficulty hearing Jesus's warnings and remembering his example. We have to be open to his challenges and questions if we want to be his disciples. More, we have to be careful to follow religious leaders today who base their teachings on the Sermon on the Mount. We do not want the leaven of organized religion that merely supports the status quo of racism, violence, greed, and nationalism.

"I Will Give You the Keys to the Kingdom of Heaven" (16:13–28)

This exchange leads Jesus to question them further. It's as if he notices that they are mindless and clueless, so he presses the point with the ultimate question about his identity. "Who do people say that the Son of Humanity is?" he asks. They speak of John the Baptist, Elijah, Jeremiah, or one of the prophets. Then Jesus looks at them and asks them point blank: "But who do you say that I am?"

This is one of those quintessential Gospel moments when Jesus turns to his disciples and asks them who *they* say he is. Such a question confronts every disciple at some point in his or her life. After all we have seen and heard, after a lifetime of prayer and discipleship, at some point he wants to know who we think he is. He's probing to see if we have learned his teachings.

Simon Peter speaks up. Notice we're still given his pre-discipleship name. He is not yet fully a disciple. "You are the Messiah, the Son of the living God," he tells Jesus. He still cannot comprehend what it truly means that Jesus is the Messiah. He expects, like all of Judaism, a messiah who will liberate the chosen people from the Gentiles and the Roman Empire by overthrowing them in Jerusalem in a holy war that will establish God's reign on earth through violence. While Jesus is the Messiah who will liberate them, his liberation comes about through active, loving nonviolence. And he has to liberate not just the chosen people but all humanity from slavery to violence and all other acts that harm humanity.

Despite Simon Peter's misunderstanding, Jesus encourages him, as he encourages everyone who speaks up for him. The difference in Matthew is that Simon Peter also calls Jesus the Son of the living God. This is new, and shocking, and most scholars see this account as a resurrection story. What with Jesus's baptism experience and his teachings in the Sermon on the Mount about being sons and daughters of God, perhaps Simon Peter does understand Jesus.

"Blessed are you, Simon son of Jonah. For flesh and blood has not revealed this to you, but my heavenly Father. And so, I say to you, 'You are Peter, and upon this rock I will build my church, and the gates of the netherworld shall not prevail against it. I will give you the keys to the kingdom of heaven. Whatever you bind on earth shall be bound in heaven; and whatever you loose on earth shall be loosed in heaven." The Aramaic word for rock, *kêpā'*, is poetically close to the Greek word for Peter, which is *Kēphas*. So, he calls Simon Peter his rock, the foundation of his church. This is the one of only two times the word "church" appears in the four Gospels (the other being Mt. 18:17). The Greek word *ekklēsia* probably means community, not a building. Given Jesus's earlier instructions, this community would be made of people who live according to his Sermon-on-the-Mount teachings. And this community, the church, is not the kingdom of God or something we build. God is the one who builds it. Simon Peter will hold the keys to that kingdom, because he will be a caretaker of Jesus's Sermon-on-the-Mount teachings.

The netherworld is where the dead live, so Jesus adds that death itself shall not prevail against his community. As we will eventually learn in his resurrection account, life is stronger than death, love and peace are stronger than hate and war, nonviolence is stronger than violence, so death will not win out.

When Jesus speaks of binding on earth, he's talking about the ties of community. Those you bind together in community will be bound together in community; those who aren't part of the community, aren't. (This simple truth about Jesus's community of peace and love will later feature in John's resurrection account—and be misunderstood for two thousand years.) He "strictly orders" his disciples to tell no one that he is the Messiah because, despite everything he has taught them, he knows they simply cannot grasp his way, not yet.

From then on, Jesus teaches the disciples in bold, clear language what his way of nonviolence involves, what kind of nonviolent messiah he is, and what it will cost to be his nonviolent disciple. He must go to Jerusalem, he explains, suffer greatly from the rulers, be killed, and then rise. He is leading a campaign of nonviolence to confront the violence of the world, the Roman occupation of Jerusalem and the temple, and he will do so actively, publicly, but nonviolently, thereby calling for nonviolent resistance to the empire itself. He doesn't want to be killed, nor is he trying to commit suicide. He's publicly, boldly, nonviolently denouncing and resisting the entire culture of violence and death, and he knows that, sooner or later, the ruling authorities will nab him. In such an oppressive, imperial city as Jerusalem, his illegal nonviolent insurrection can only lead to his arrest, torture, and execution—and this is precisely the path he says he has accepted, the path that anyone who would dare to follow him must choose as well. Jesus goes forward with his campaign knowing the inevitable consequence of martyrdom, as Gandhi, Dr. King, Sophie Scholl, Franz Jägerstätter, and Oscar Romero later do. Jesus knows too, as Martin Luther King Jr. taught, that "unearned suffering love is redemptive," that his nonviolence will disarm and eventually win over everyone.

"God forbid, Lord!" Peter says to him, as he rebukes Jesus. "No such thing shall ever happen to you." Here we see how Peter, the community—and all of us, too—reject Jesus's way of the cross. We don't want a nonviolent messiah who suffers arrest, torture, and execution; we prefer a revolutionary who is successful, effective, powerful, dominating, even at the cost of a little "collateral damage." We prefer the use of violence to gain power, and we prefer to justify it, bless it, and consecrate it as God's will.

Peter, like nearly every disciple since, has no understanding of the nonviolence of Jesus. In a world of violence, the person of nonviolence will be crushed by imperial violence, because that's how the system always responds to insurrection. The world of violence always seeks to crush movements of nonviolence and their charismatic leaders.

Jesus turns and chastises Peter: "Get behind me, Satan! You are an obstacle to me. You are thinking not as God does, but as human beings do." The one whom he just called his rock, to whom he gave the keys, he now calls "Satan," the power of death itself, a synonym for the Roman Empire and the way of war. This exchange is worth our deep reflection. Jesus does not want us to think or live according to the world's way of violence. To think not as people do, but as God does, means to think not with the mind of war or empire but with God's mind of peace and freedom, and to live according to God's rules and boundaries of peace and nonviolence. St. Paul will later call this, in my translation, "putting on the mind of the nonviolent Jesus" (see Rom. 12:2; Phil. 2:5; 1 Cor. 2:16; Eph. 4:23).

As the story takes a turn, we begin to realize how serious Jesus might be about all this talk of nonviolence. So he tells us plainly what it means to follow him:

> "Whoever wishes to come after me must deny himself, take up his cross, and follow me. Whoever wishes to save his life will lose it, but whoever loses his life for my sake will find it. What profit would there be for one to gain the whole world and forfeit his life? Or what can one give in exchange for his life? For the Son of Humanity will come with his angels in his Father's glory, and then he will repay everyone according to his conduct. Amen, I say to you, there are some standing here who will not taste death until they see the Son of Humanity coming in his kingdom."

The condition for following Jesus is denying ourselves, our desires, our plans—indeed, our very lives—and joining his campaign. If we lose our lives for him on the way of the cross, by carrying on his public grassroots movement for disarmament, justice, and peace, we will find life. This is the way to fullness of life—to surrender ourselves to him, to God's will, to God's reign, to God's peace movement coming on earth. It is the most important thing we can do with our lives. If we live according to the world of violence, selfishly seeking power and domination through the ways of greed, violence, war, and empire, then we lose our souls, here and now. We find ourselves spiritually lost, unhappy, and miserable, no matter how much wealth and power we have. Likewise, if we follow Jesus, we enter the fullness of life here and now; we discover the freedom of peace, love, compassion, and nonviolence found in doing God's will and serving God's reign.

Some of you will live to see these promises come true, he tells them. His announcement of the coming of the Son of Humanity has nothing to do with the hokey *Left Behind* novels, where some people disappear in a flash and are taken up into the Rapture. Such crazy notions are untrue first of all because they have no connection with the cross, with joining Jesus's grassroots movement against empire, injustice, and war. Instead, Jesus hints here at his resurrection—and the promise that discipleship will be worth any denial, sacrifice, or suffering that comes along the way. They will see the Son of Humanity in all his fullness when he overcomes death and returns with his resurrection gift of peace. Anyone who accepts his resurrection gift of peace and carries on his mission of resurrection peace through their support of his ongoing grassroots movement of nonviolence for justice, disarmament, and peace will see the risen Son of Humanity along the way.

"This Is My Beloved Son . . . Listen to Him!" (17:1–18:35)

The story of the transfiguration is the great revelation of the Gospels: that the nonviolent Jesus truly is the blessed One of the God of peace, that his way is correct, that he is the one humanity should listen to and follow. Many have suggested that this revelation foreshadows his resurrection. Though the various accounts differ slightly, I believe otherwise, as I wrote in my book *Transfiguration*. This momentous epiphany, where Jesus is revealed as the light of the world, is actually an encouragement for him to continue on his journey of active nonviolence to the cross and his death, to lead humanity into the new life of resurrection peace.

Jesus took Peter, James, and John up Mount Tabor, where he was transfigured. His face shone like the sun and his clothes became white as light. And then Moses and Elijah appeared with him, representing the law and the prophets, the whole of Judaism. Luke will later tell us what they talked about: they encouraged Jesus on his journey to martyrdom. His disciples are not encouraging him. But Moses and Elijah confirm that he is doing God's will. This is the point of the revelation: the light of the world is the light of nonviolence, the light of peace, the light of universal love, and Jesus must carry on down the mountain as the light of the world.

Of course, the three disciples do not understand. Peter, in his fear and panic, tries to take control of the scene. "Lord, it is good that we are here." Think about it. He's saying, "It's a good thing we are here, Jesus, to take charge of this situation." What should he have said? "Lord, it is good that *You* are here!" They should have encouraged, comforted, and supported him, but they think only of themselves—as we do. It gets worse: they talk about building a retreat house so they can all stay there in safety, in peace and quiet, far from Jerusalem and the empire. "If you wish, I will make three tents: one for you, one for Moses, one for Elijah." Peter wants to remain there on the mountaintop for the rest of his life with God and with his heroes, Moses and Elijah. This is exactly what we want to do too, and this, according to Matthew, is exactly what not to do. We are meant to take up the cross and follow Jesus on his campaign of nonviolent resistance to our own Jerusalems.

Sometimes in life, you wonder why God doesn't just say something, just speak from the sky and tell us what to do. Here, on Mount Tabor, is that moment in history when the God of peace spoke from the sky. Matthew gives us details. A bright cloud cast a shadow over them, and then a voice spoke from the cloud saying, "This is my beloved Son, with whom I am well pleased. Listen to him." These are the same words of affirmation and encouragement that God spoke to Jesus at his baptism, only this time they are addressed to the male disciples. Then, God issues a new commandment. "Listen to him."

"Listen to him." If Jesus is the beloved Son of God come to earth, and he teaches us how to be human by practicing universal love and total nonviolence, and everyone ignores or rejects his teaching, what should God do? Here in this one instance in all of human history, God tells humanity: "Listen to the nonviolent Jesus."

This is one of the fundamental commandments of the Gospel: Listen to him. In fact, listen only to him. Do not listen to other voices. His voice is the only one that matters. Do whatever he says.

If you wonder what Jesus has to say, go back and reread the Sermon on the Mount. All the teachings of peace, love, and nonviolence are there in black and white. These words need to become the basis of our lives. "Blessed are those who hunger and thirst for justice. Blessed are the peacemakers. Be reconciled. Offer no violent resistance to one who does evil. Love your enemies. Be as compassionate as God. Seek first God's kingdom and God's justice and everything else shall be provided. Try to enter the narrow gate." Other teachings follow, most notably, "Take up the cross and follow me." These are the words we need to take to heart, this is what we need to listen to—not the bad news on TV, the Black Friday sales ads, the latest patriotic call to arms, the nation's support for war, or some Wall Street investment plan. We do not listen to those voices anymore but to the voice of Jesus, to his teachings.

The voice from the cloud terrified Peter, James, and John. They fell prostrate in front of Jesus and were as if dead. And here we see the real nonviolent Jesus: he came forward, bent down, and touched each one of them, saying, "Rise and do not be afraid."

"Rise and do not be afraid." That sentence alone is worth pursuing for the rest of our lives. The transfigured Jesus, just after the voice of God has spoken, touches us, commands us to rise from the dead, and no longer live in fear. These are some of the most important words we could ever take to heart.

For the rest of our lives, whenever we feel knocked out by the culture, when our efforts have only gotten in God's way, when we fall flat on our faces, when we give in to total despair, when the world becomes too much for us, we can imagine the nonviolent Jesus touching us and saying to us, "Rise and do not be afraid."

The story continues. As they walk down the mountain, he commands them not to tell anyone—"until the Son of Humanity has been raised from the dead." They don't know what he is talking about. Later, they will remember. But for now, they change the subject. "Isn't Elijah supposed to come first?"

An interesting question. In fact, the scriptures promise that Elijah will reappear before the appearance of the real Messiah. And Jesus tells the three that in fact, Elijah has come back, but no one recognized him. Also, the empire killed him, just as they will kill the Son of Humanity. They know he was speaking about John the Baptist, but they do not understand anything else, not to mention any talk of his death or resurrection.

Then, at the foot of the mountain, they meet a crowd of people who are arguing with the rest of the disciples. Some poor man, it seems, has a desperately sick child. He runs up to Jesus, kneels down, begs and pleads with Jesus to heal his child. "Lord, have pity on my son, for he is a lunatic and suffers severely; often he falls into fire, and often into water. I brought him to your disciples, but they could not cure him."

This is a rare bad moment for Jesus. He's at his wits end. He's just been transfigured; he's just dialogued with Moses and Elijah; God has just spoken from the clouds; he's raised his three friends from the dead—and now the other disciples cannot heal the child, and even the good father pleads with him to heal him—if he can.

"O faithless and perverse generation," Jesus says, "how long will I be with you? How long will I endure you? Bring him here to me." Jesus feels frustrated by the lack of faith that surrounds him, the unwillingness to believe him, the ineptitude of his best friends. Nonetheless, he doesn't let his negative feelings get the best of him. Instead, he keeps going forward, taking positive action for the good, serving and healing and teaching. So he asks for the child to be brought to him, expels the demon, and heals him. It's only later that the disciples sheepishly approach him and ask why they couldn't drive the demon out of the child. Jesus's answer, once again, is blunt and instructive: "Because you have so little faith."

So now we know: faith is the key to everything, and we have very little of it. We need to believe in Jesus, no matter what—really believe his teachings, really believe we can do what he tells us to do, really believe that God exists, really believe in God's love for us all, really believe that God can work even through us, and really believe that our lives can make a positive difference in the world.

"Amen, I say to you, if you have faith the size of a mustard seed, you will say to this mountain, 'Move from here to there,' and it will move. Nothing will be impossible for you." Here we have one of the greatest promises of the Gospel. In the context of peace activism, we can interpret it to mean that, if we believe in the God of peace, if we believe in the way of nonviolence, as Gandhi and Dr. King did, then we too can organize people and build a grassroots movement. If we believe in God and act according to Jesus's word in the Sermon on the Mount, we can move mountains—the mountain of despair, the mountain of war, the mountain of nuclear weapons, the mountain of environmental destruction. If we really believe that the God of peace is working through us, anything is possible. Indeed, nothing will be impossible for us. This is the challenge laid down by the nonviolent Jesus for each of us.

I say, let's take up the challenge and get to work with the task of moving mountains. There are no bigger mountains blocking the way into God's reign than permanent war, global poverty, racism, greed, fear, hunger, executions, nuclear weapons, environmental destruction, and violence of all sorts. Matthew urges us to take up the challenge and get to work moving these mountains.

This is what the saints did. Francis and Clare were ordinary people of extraordinary faith who moved mountains. The Quakers and some Evangelicals of England in the eighteenth and nineteenth centuries believed they could abolish slavery, and they gave their lives to accomplish that great task. Women Suffragists likewise believed they could take on patriarchy and sexism and achieve the right to vote, and so they did. Civil rights workers believed they could bring down segregation in bus stations, at lunch counters, and in department stores, and they did. There are a million examples of mountains of injustice being moved and transformed and thrown into the sea because of the extraordinary faith of ordinary people. That is what Jesus is calling us to do in this text.

With that, he tells us that he is soon to be arrested, tortured, and executed. After his transfiguration, the healing of the boy, and talk about moving mountains, this dramatic announcement stuns the disciples and leaves them speechless. "The Son of Humanity is to be handed over to men, and they will kill him, and he will be raised on the third day." They are overwhelmed with grief.

Then, they arrive back at the village of Capernaum along the Sea of Galilee, where Simon Peter and his wife and children have a home. And here we hear one of the most ridiculous, humorous episodes in the four Gospels, an absurdist tale worthy of Flannery O'Connor or Salvador Dali. Tax collectors approach Peter and ask if his teacher pays the temple tax. This is life-and-death stuff, so Peter answers, Yes, of course.

But the plot thickens. When Peter enters his home, which is now the community home, Jesus asks him a provocative question, and once again addresses him with his pre-discipleship name. "What is your opinion, Simon? From whom do the kings of the earth take tolls or census tax? From their subjects or from foreigners?" When he answers, "From foreigners," Jesus says to him, "Then the subjects are exempt. But that we may not offend them, go to the sea, drop in a hook, and take the first fish that comes up. Open its mouth and you will find a coin worth twice the temple tax. Give that to them for me and for you."

Jesus uses poetry, impressionism, even absurdity to answer the question. This is a joke! I think Simon would have laughed and gotten it, even though we don't. He would have understood that we do not pay taxes—temple or Roman. Jesus tries not to offend anyone, but later, he will offend many people with his truth-telling and illegal action, especially his civil disobedience in the temple, where he turns over the tables of the money changers. For now, Jesus is lying low.

We're not told if Simon went down to the sea and found a coin in the mouth of a fish. We are told that the other disciples are not included in this scenario. This is a rare bit of comedy used to mock the very idea of the temple tax.

"Whoever Humbles Himself or Herself like This Child Is the Greatest in the Kingdom of Heaven" (18:1–35)

Matthew then proceeds to offer various teachings for his community that will lead into a series of great parables. First, we're told that the disciples ask Jesus, "Who is the greatest in the kingdom of heaven?" The question reflects the typical male ego, arrogance, pride, and desire for honor. They want to be first, to be held in esteem, to lord it over others, an attitude that tempts religious and non-religious alike. Religious practice can lead to the delusion that those of us who do the practice are better than those who don't. That defeats the whole purpose of the spiritual journey. Jesus cuts to the chase with his brilliant demonstration and calls his disciples to the deepest humility.

He calls a child over and places it in the center of the group. Since we are in Capernaum, in Peter's house, I have always assumed it was one of Peter's children, probably his son Mark, who is referred to later in the New Testament and in whose name the first Gospel is written. There, with the child standing in the middle of the group, Jesus issues a great commandment: "Amen, I say to you, unless you turn and become like children, you will not enter the kingdom of heaven. Whoever humbles himself like this child is the greatest in the kingdom of heaven. And whoever receives one child such as this in my name receives me."

With these teachings about becoming as innocent, gentle, humble, and loving as children, Jesus turns the tables on the male disciples and us. Children were valued by their parents but had no rights, prestige, or power. Many of them did not live to adulthood. Yet Jesus saw in them a reflection of those who dwell in the kingdom of God. Children are full of awe and wonder. They play and love and enjoy life in the fullness of the present moment. And they cannot help but be humble because they are small, dependent, vulnerable, wide-eyed, new to the world. That, Jesus is saying, is the path into the kingdom of heaven. It's as if we already live the Sermon on the Mount, but as we grow, the culture of violence seeps into us, hurts us, and brainwashes us. We have to return to our original childlike state because the kingdom of heaven is intended for children—the children of the God of peace. So to be great is to be as humble as a little child. To love and serve children is to welcome Jesus himself because he is the ultimate child; he is the beloved Son of God.

As we ponder these teachings, we hear the call first to look deeply within at all the causes of our arrogance, privilege, self-righteousness, egotism, and false sense of superiority. In a spirit of peace and nonviolence, repentance, prayer, and confession, we try to root out all those defects in us and free the child within us, our true selves, that our hearts might widen, we might step more fully into the present moment, and live out our days humbly in peace, joy, love, service, worship, and wonder.

The journey toward humble, childlike wonder is one way to understand the Sermon on the Mount. We try to live here and now as if we are already in the kingdom of God, and so we try to cultivate love, compassion, and peace, and we turn away from anything that is opposed to those qualities of life. Even in times of grief, we can maintain humble, childlike wonder, especially as we enjoy the beauty of creation.

The more we ponder these teachings, the more we realize what a liberation, what a relief this is. We no longer have to put on airs, to try to be great or successful or famous according to the world's standards. We get to be our true selves, free to live in peace and joy with one another. As we choose the path of humility, we learn to surrender everything to our loving God as a trusting child does to a loving parent, and along the way we are freed to live in God's peaceable kingdom.

"Whoever causes one of these little ones who believe in me to sin," Jesus continues, "it would be better for him to have a great millstone hung around his neck and to be drowned in the depths of the sea. Woe to the world because of things that cause sin! Such things must come, but woe to the one through whom they come!" From the perspective of nonviolence, he's arguing that we must do whatever we can to avoid hurting others or leading them into sin. If we cannot do that, if we cannot change, Jesus says it would be better if we suffered some tragedy and were out of the picture altogether. He's trying to wake us up to the consequences of our violence, our harmful actions. We do not want to hurt anyone. Do no harm is the new bottom line.

And yet, today, we all participate in the social sin of systemic injustice and permanent warfare. We allow the deaths of tens of thousands of children each day from hunger and hunger-related diseases. So we are all guilty of hurting little ones and leading other little ones to participate in social sins and systemic oppression and violence. This will all come back to harm us one day, so we must repent of the culture of violence and be vigilant in our nonviolence, and practice nonviolence in thought, word, and deed, so that our lives do no harm, and spread peace and goodness.

"If your hand or foot causes you to sin, cut it off and throw it away. It is better for you to enter into life maimed or crippled than with two hands or two feet to be thrown into eternal fire. And if your eye causes you to sin, tear it out and throw it away. It is better for you to enter into life with one eye than with two eyes to be thrown into fiery Gehenna." In those days, and some places even today, violent revolutionaries kept order among themselves by maiming or crippling those in their company who betrayed them or hurt others. This violence was used by the IRA in Northern Ireland against those who betrayed or hurt others within their community; the Mafia follows the same logic of violence. Jesus again tries to shock us with drastic language and turn that image upon ourselves. Do whatever you can to stop yourself from hurting others, or sinning against God, or leading his little ones into sin. He wants us to live in the fullness of life now and forever, and that means paying strict attention to the boundaries of nonviolence.

Flannery O'Connor pursued this theme in her wild novel *Wise Blood*, in which the protagonist Hazel Motes founds "The Church Without Christ"—where the lame don't walk, the blind don't see, the deaf don't hear, the mute don't speak—and the dead stay dead. Hazel Motes mocks Christ, until his climactic change of heart. In a shocking act of repentance, he blinds himself, as Matthew's text suggests. Like Jesus, O'Connor doesn't want us to blind ourselves but to stop mocking Christ, hurting others, or being so self-righteous. Her dramatic language is a call to humble service, Gospel nonviolence, and faithful trust in God.

"See that you do not despise one of these little ones," Jesus says in summary, "for I say to you that their angels in heaven always look upon the face of my heavenly Father." We are called to show love, mercy, kindness, and compassion to children and all "little ones," all those who are small, ordinary, humble, vulnerable, poor, broken, in need, powerless, voiceless, and marginalized. God's eye is on them; ours should be as well.

Matthew next presents a short parable on the lost sheep. "What is your opinion?" Jesus asks. "If a man has a hundred sheep and one of them goes astray, will he not leave the ninety-nine in the hills and go in search of the stray? And if he finds it, amen, I say to you, he rejoices more over it than over the ninety-nine that did not stray." The answer, as we know, is that the shepherd will leave the flock, search for the lost sheep, and rejoice when he finds it. "In just the same way, it is not the will of your heavenly Father that one of these little ones be lost."

The image of Jesus as the Good Shepherd who protects his flock runs throughout the Gospels. Here, we focus on Jesus's effort to find every lost, broken, or marginalized person; to restore them to healing, life, and community; and to point out that this is the very will of God, and so it must be our primary focus as well. Given the context of the entire Gospel, however, one could extrapolate that every human being is at one time or another a lost sheep; and that, at one time or another, Jesus the Good Shepherd is seeking out each of us to heal us, to bring us to the fullness of life, and to restore us to the human family.

With these teachings, Jesus then proceeds to provide basic guidelines for his community of followers on how to deal with someone in the community who sins or hurts another. These guidelines seem like common sense, but unfortunately they have been practiced rarely by the Christian community down through the ages. Instead of practicing forgiveness, nonviolence, restorative justice, and reconciliation, we prefer anger, resentment, retaliation, and punishment, and end up becoming just like the religious authorities who attacked Jesus.

"If your brother sins against you, go and tell him his fault between you and him alone," he instructs. Right there, he's challenging us not to sit back and do nothing after a brother or sister in the community hurts us. Nonviolence is not passivity. We have to take action. We have to address the issue head-on. Talk to the person privately and tell them their fault. Say to them, "I was hurt." In nonviolent communication, the idea is to use "I" language instead of accusatory language. In this way, you might appeal to the person's heart. We do not repress our hurt to let it fester and come out in some other way.

"If he listens to you, you have won over your brother," Jesus teaches. "If he does not listen, take one or two others along with you, so that 'every fact may be established on the testimony of two or three witnesses.' If he refuses to listen to them, tell the church. If he refuses to listen even to the church, then treat him as you would a Gentile or a tax collector." Jesus is teaching here a methodology of nonviolent conflict resolution, truth-telling, restorative justice, and reconciliation. In doing so, we see how grounded Jesus is. He is not espousing some pie-in-the-sky utopia. He knows that conflict is inevitable and real, but it need not be resolved through violence or passivity. It can be resolved through the methodology of creative nonviolence. In each phase of the process, Jesus tells us to be nonviolent and loving. If it does not work, treat the sinning brother as an outsider, as "a Gentile or tax collector," he advises, which we know means that now we *really* love them because we remember how Jesus loves Gentiles and tax collectors. We up our nonviolent unconditional love until we win them over!

"Amen, I say to you, whatever you bind on earth shall be bound in heaven, and whatever you loose on earth shall be loosed in heaven." When Jesus speaks of "binding" on earth, he's talking about the creation of community, what Dr. King called the Beloved Community, and when he speaks of "loosing" here on earth, he's talking about loosening the chains and burdens of violence and the sin of injustice and war and forgiving one another as key ingredients to the creation of "the Beloved Community." This offers a viewpoint in keeping with Jesus's nonviolence.

The term "binding" refers to our nonviolent love for one another, our persistent reconciliation with one another, so that enemies become friends and friends become better friends, until we are all friends with one another here on earth as we shall be friends with one another in God's reign of peace. This "binding" in love, compassion, and peace with one another in small local communities spreads to regional communities and national communities toward the global community of the human family as it turns toward nonviolence that reveals the fullness of God's reign. We see this unfolding as Jesus forms a community around him, as he "binds" himself to the disciples and them to one another and himself, and then goes forth and widens this community of peace by calling others to join it, so that the binding in community spreads far and wide until it crosses the globe and God's reign begins to break through into a global human community of peace and nonviolence.

Likewise, he tells us that whatever we "loose" on earth shall be "loosed" in heaven. In other words, as we let go, relinquish, unbind, and loose the chains of violence, resentment, grudges, differences, division, and separation, as we forgive one another, establish restorative justice, and reconcile in peace, this loosening of the roots of violence and division between us, in a spirit of forgiveness and reconciliation as we pledge nonviolence toward one another, will permanently "loose" the chains of violence and resentment so that the God of peace and love begins to reign among us. As we move closer toward one another in reconciling nonviolent love, as we let loose the chains of violence, racism, classism, and war, as we disarm one another, forgive one another, and restore dignity toward one another, God's reign of peace, the eternal Beloved Community of universal love, comes to earth. In this eschatological vision of nonviolence, God creates a new heaven and a new earth in universal love and peace.

He continues his teaching on the workings of the Beloved Community: "Again, amen, I say to you, if two of you agree on earth about anything for which they are to pray, it shall be granted to them by my heavenly Father. For where two or three are gathered together in my name, there am I in the midst of them."

This is a profound promise to the community of faith. If you persevere in Jesus's way, and you pray for whatever grace you need, it will be granted. This is a promise worth pursuing and experimenting with. Furthermore, wherever two or more people who are Jesus's disciples gather, Jesus will himself be in their midst. This, too, is a promise that every community of nonviolence should experiment with. He dwells with those who espouse his way of life. He is not promising to be with those who remain outside his community by the way they live—in the context of this book, those who engage in warfare, violence, greed, killing, or injustice. He promises to be with those who truly follow him in the way of peace and justice. Following this promise, those of us who espouse and practice Gospel nonviolence should gather daily in Jesus's name, say our prayers, and trust that he is with us as we do our part for disarmament, justice, and creation.

"Lord, if my brother sins against me, how often must I forgive him?" Peter asks. "As many as seven times?" When Peter asks about forgiveness, he's being specific. He has someone in mind—perhaps his brother Andrew who annoys him. He feels hurt by Andrew. He harbors resentment. This is the usual human brokenness that we all experience. When Peter asks if he should forgive Andrew seven times a day, he's thinking that's an enormous amount of work. If someone close to us hurts us, it might take us a month to muster up the inner strength to forgive them, and we feel that it's a great accomplishment. To forgive someone every single day is hard work. To forgive someone seven times a day seems almost impossible.

For Jesus, unconditional forgiveness is the daily practice of the journey of loving non-violence. We forgive every day—morning, noon, and night. "I say to you, not seven times but seventy-seven times." Here is a new commandment. Jesus wants us to forgive those who hurt us seventy-seven times a day—that's a lot of forgiveness! The actual number is used poetically to show how there is no limit to our ongoing life of unconditional forgiveness toward others.

So the question becomes: How do we do that? As we watch the nonviolent Jesus deal with crowds and hostile religious leaders, we see that he doesn't cling to the hurt or to resent-ment, but moves on in peace, love, and compassion. He maintains his nonviolence first and foremost. He is solid as a rock. Interiorly, though, in the silence of his heart, he is forgiving everybody all the time. We can imagine him saying it like a mantra, under his breath: "I forgive you," or "Father, forgive them." This practice of forgiveness demonstrates that there is usually no "aha!" moment of pure forgiveness; it's a process, a journey of deepening into forgiveness, compassion, and nonviolence.

Why can we draw this conclusion? Because as he dies on the cross, Jesus asks God to forgive those who kill him. He forgives, and intercedes for God to forgive. The only way he could do that in one of the most horrifying torturous deaths is if he had been practicing for-giveness under his breath toward everyone who insulted him every hour of his public life. Jesus practiced what he preached and wants us to make forgiveness part of our normal daily prayer routine. Like Jesus, we forgive everyone who ever hurt us and so that we can instinc-tively say even toward someone who might kill us, Jesus's own words of forgiveness on the cross. As people of nonviolence, we forgive even those who take the lives of our loved ones; we do not seek vengeance, retaliation, or violent justice. We oppose the death penalty and try to break the downward cycle of violence with our steadfast forgiveness. We remember, too, the wisdom of the Sermon on the Mount: if we forgive those who have hurt us, truly, from the heart, then we will be forgiven, too.

Jesus then offers a parable to explain how entrance into the kingdom of heaven requires a life of steadfast, ongoing forgiveness and nonviolence.

"That is why the kingdom of heaven may be likened to a king who decided to settle accounts with his servants. When he began the accounting, a debtor was brought before him who owed him a huge amount. Since he had no way of paying it back, his master ordered him to be sold, along with his wife, his children, and all his property, in payment of the debt. At that, the servant begged for mercy until he paid it all back in full. The master was moved with compassion, and forgave the loan. So the servant went and found other servants who owed him, and tortured them as they begged for mercy. He imprisoned them all, only to be reported back to the original master. 'You wicked servant!' the master said. 'I forgave you your entire debt because you begged me to. Should you not have had pity on your fellow servant, as I had pity on you?' Then in anger his master handed him over to the torturers until he should pay back the whole debt."

The parable concludes: "So will my heavenly Father do to you, unless each of you forgives his brother from his heart."

Matthew is trying to shock us into forgiveness. He's saying in effect that the consequences of not forgiving are worse than the difficult process of swallowing our pride and forgiving those who hurt us. Not forgiving, holding a grudge, nursing lifelong resentment, even seeking revenge are like drinking poison to get back at your opponent: you're the only one it hurts, and it's our own fault. In other words, our own unwillingness to do God's will of nonviolence and forgive everyone here and now will eat away at us from within and torture us, even though we do not realize it, until we finally come to our senses, can't take it anymore, take right action, forgive everyone, pay up, do God's will, and put ourselves out of our misery. Matthew offers this parable with its tough conclusion to wake us up to our stupidity, so that we can get on with the task of forgiving every person who ever hurt us, beginning with our own brothers. Note too: Matthew writes not just of forgiveness in word but also forgiveness from our hearts, a complete and total granting of clemency and pardon to everyone who ever hurt us. Only then can we be guaranteed to receive complete and total forgiveness for the harm we have done.

"Come, Follow Me": The Turn toward Jerusalem (19:1–20:34)

The story subtly turns as Jesus leaves Galilee and enters Judea. His public walking campaign of nonviolence toward Jerusalem continues, and he's getting closer. Great crowds follow him. Think of Gandhi's famous Salt March to the sea. That's what he is doing as well. Along the way, he cures many people.

But with this turn begins his long confrontation with the religious authorities, which Matthew more than the other Gospels seems to dramatize. They attack Jesus relentlessly, and eventually he starts using strong prophetic language to denounce their behavior. This conflict will antagonize them even further and lead them to press the Romans to arrest him and execute him. The nonviolent Jesus, with all his talk of peace, love, and compassion, is a real threat to their power, corruption, and complicity with the Roman Empire. So they organize a full-scale attack on him and eventually do away with him.

And so we're told, in a typical episode: "Some Pharisees approached him, and tested him. . . ." In this case, they question him about divorce. But he returns the question with a question: "Have you not read that from the beginning the Creator 'made them male and female' and said, 'For this reason a man shall leave his father and mother and be joined to his wife, and the two shall become one flesh'? So they are no longer two, but one flesh. Therefore, what God has joined together, no human being must separate." Jesus cites the scriptures, points to the work of God, and answers gently that the way God made us makes it clear that we are intended for lifelong commitments between husband and wife.

His answer is wise and gentle, and so they can't leave it there. They are always trying to trap him and can't leave well enough alone. So they press him further, as they will time and time again: "Then why did Moses command that the man give the woman a bill of divorce and dismiss her?" His answer gets personal: "Because of the hardness of your hearts, Moses allowed you to divorce your wives, but from the beginning it was not so." In his answer, Jesus points to our interior disposition—"the hardness of our hearts." This inner spiritual malady is to blame for everything we do that goes against God's will of love. With this phrase, Jesus invites us to look within and try to soften and widen our hearts in compassion and love, like him. If they were sincere—if we are sincere!—they should have responded as we should respond as well: "Help us to soften our hearts."

"I say to you, whoever divorces his wife (unless the marriage is unlawful) and marries another commits adultery." His disciples respond, "If that is the case, it is better not to marry." He then speaks of those few people who renounce marriage "for the sake of the kingdom of heaven." Given the question of mandatory celibacy in the Catholic priesthood, which has been in practice for only some seven hundred years, not two thousand years, it's important to note that Matthew's point that the reason why some might choose to be celibate for God is not to get to heaven, not to be better than others, not to enter some superior human state—but solely to serve the kingdom of heaven, to work and witness for the coming of God's reign on earth. Still, as the church teaches, very few are called to the life of celibacy, but everyone is called to work for the coming of God's reign of peace and nonviolence on earth.

Just then, children were brought to him that he might bless them—and, of course, the male disciples object! They rebuke the adults who bring children to Jesus. This is precisely the problem, then and now: the effort to control Jesus, to make sure he does what we want, and to maintain the status quo. Jesus will have none of it and tells his disciples—and us—in no uncertain terms. "Let the children come to me, and do not prevent them; for the kingdom of heaven belongs to such as these." Everything we do is for the kingdom of heaven. Every act of discipleship should promote and welcome the kingdom of heaven. In particular, children are first and foremost the owners of the kingdom of heaven. It is theirs, right now. Jesus walks away and leaves the disciples shocked and perplexed.

"For God, All Things Are Possible" (19:16–34)

The encounter that follows is one of the most important in the Synoptic Gospels because it challenges all privileged, entitled, First World North Americans who would follow Jesus today.

Jesus is on his walking campaign, when someone approaches and asks, "Teacher, what good must I do to gain eternal life?" The question, of course, is entirely wrong. That's the first point to be pondered. Think about it: it's focused on ourselves, it's all about me, what must *I* do? . . . as if we rich, privileged, entitled people can decide whether or not we will gain eternal life. At the heart of the arrogant question is the presumption, "Hey Jesus—I deserve eternal life! I'm entitled! I'm important. I should gain eternal life." The minute we think that about ourselves, alarm bells should sound. That's a clue to how much we have misunderstood everything he has taught.

"Why do you ask me about the good?" Jesus asks. "There is only One who is good." Matthew changes Mark's wording but still poses the question. "Good is done by God; if you are asking me about the good, are you saying that I'm God?" We, too, ask him about the good we must do, which keeps the focus on ourselves and not on him. Instead, if we can dare accept it, all we can do is beg for his mercy for only he is good.

"If you wish to enter into life, keep the commandments," Jesus answers. He then proceeds to list them, but he adds one for good measure: "'You shall not kill; you shall not commit adultery; you shall not steal; you shall not bear false witness; honor your father and your mother'; and 'you shall love your neighbor as yourself.'" The last is the key to Matthew's Gospel. Love your neighbor as you love yourself. Here is the heart of the law, the prophets, the Sermon on the Mount, and Matthew's Gospel. If you do this, then you are doing God's will and will enter the fullness of life.

"All of these I have observed," the man answers. We're told he is young. "What do I still lack?" he asks. "If you wish to be perfect," Jesus answers, "go, sell what you have and give to the poor, and you will have treasure in heaven. Then come, follow me."

Here is the ultimate call of Jesus and Matthew's Gospel: sell your possessions, give the money to the poor, and follow the nonviolent Jesus for the rest of your lives into the kingdom of heaven. If you want to go to heaven, if you want to live life fully, if you want to follow Jesus, you have to let go of everything and surrender completely to Jesus. This is the challenge of the Gospels. What have you got to lose?

Alas, like so many, the young man heard this, turned around, and walked away sad. Why does he walk away sad? We're told in no uncertain terms: he had many possessions. He was rich! Possessions and riches are obstacles to spiritual growth and engagement in God's kingdom. They can trap us into selfishness and hardness of heart and prevent us from loving our neighbors and serving those in need. They tempt us into a false security that makes us feel that we will live forever, that we can take them with us, that we are in control of our lives. But in fact, we will die and no longer possess anything. Jesus is saying, get with the program. Prepare yourself for the fullness of the spiritual life to come. Pursue downward mobility, surrender your lives now to God, and follow me into the kingdom of God.

"Amen, I say to you, it will be hard for one who is rich to enter the kingdom of heaven," Jesus announces. "Again I say to you, it is easier for a camel to pass through the eye of a needle than for one who is rich to enter the kingdom of God." You cannot enter God's reign of universal love while you are clinging to worldly treasure; the load won't fit through the gate. Let go of everything if you want the kingdom of heaven. Life is short; don't waste it on possessions and money that pass away. As we ponder Jesus's instructions, we realize that the only riches worth pursuing are the spiritual riches of life in the kingdom.

When we connect this story of Jesus and the rich man who walks away with the Sermon on the Mount, we realize that for Jesus, there's an intimate connection between nonviolence and voluntary poverty. Jesus teaches us to practice the way of love and nonviolence, but money and possessions will clutter the way, making it hard for us to move forward. Once we acquire money and possessions, we must attend to them. We come to place our security in them, and we lose our passion for reaching out to others. Indeed, the richer we get, the more we try to protect what we have, and before long we are building fences and acquiring weapons to protect our wealth, as St. Francis of Assisi explained. Multiply this a trillion times, and we end up with the United States comprising less than 5 percent of the world's population but controlling 60 percent of the world's resources, and then building an arsenal with trillions of dollars that can blow the world up many times over to protect our interests. Seen in this light, everything Jesus taught makes sense.

"Who then can be saved?" the disciples ask Jesus. Remember they are discussing entrance into God's reign here and now on earth. The disciples, like us, focus on life after death, but Jesus wants everyone to be liberated now from the culture of violence, greed, and death, to enter God's reign now. He looks at them with love and offers one of the great truths: "For human beings this is impossible, but for God all things are possible." So there it is: *For God, all things are possible.* Do we believe this? You and I, as followers of the nonviolent Jesus, choose to accept this, believe it, and act on it. We know that, with God, all things are possible—even the seeming impossibility of rich people giving away their possessions and money to the poor and following Jesus on the path of compassion, universal love, and peacemaking. So we dare to believe and to let God lead us in that path of radical discipleship to Jesus.

"We have given up everything and followed you. What will there be for us?" Peter asks. "Amen, I say to you," Jesus answers, "you who have followed me, in the new age, when the Son of Humanity is seated on his throne of glory, will yourselves sit on twelve thrones, judging the twelve tribes of Israel. And everyone who has given up houses or brothers or sisters or father or mother or children or lands for the sake of my name will receive a hundred times more, and will inherit eternal life. But many who are first will be last, and the last will be first." Jesus promises the disciples not only life in the kingdom of heaven but their own thrones from which they will judge the twelve tribes of Israel. Every other follower throughout history is promised abundance. It's an odd paradox: if we give up everything to follow Jesus, including houses, brothers, sisters, father, mother, children, or lands, we will receive a hundred times more in this life and enter eternal life in the kingdom of heaven.

Then the punch line: the first will be last; the last will be first. If we dare experiment with Jesus's teachings, we will find that they are true. If we want to follow him, we try to be last, not first. The first are the rich, the successful, the powerful, the admired, the "one percent." We do not want to be in their class. That is not the way of Jesus; he ended up crucified as a revolutionary. Instead, we are downwardly mobile, headed to the bottom ranks, the last of all, the least important. We let go of everything, love everyone, serve everyone, surrender completely to God, and live by humble trust in God.

And so Jesus embarks on a parable about the last being first, a parable peculiar to Matthew alone.

"The kingdom of heaven is like a landowner who went out at dawn to hire laborers for his vineyard. After agreeing with them for the usual daily wage, he sent them into his vineyard. Going out about nine o'clock, he saw others standing idle in the marketplace, and he said to them, 'You too go into my vineyard, and I will give you what is just.' So they went off. He went out again around noon, and around three o'clock, and did likewise. Going out about five o'clock, he found others standing around, and said to them, 'Why do you stand here idle all day?' They answered, 'Because no one has hired us.' He said to them, 'You too go into my vineyard.' When it was evening the owner of the vineyard said to his foreman, 'Summon the laborers and give them their pay, beginning with the last and ending with the first.' When those who had started about five o'clock came, each received the usual daily wage. So when the first came, they thought that they would receive more, but each of them also got the usual wage. And on receiving it they grumbled against the landowner, saying, 'These last ones worked only one hour, and you have made them equal to us, who bore the day's burden and the heat.'"

This is where the plot thickens. He said to the one who complained, "My friend, I am not cheating you. Did you not agree with me for the usual daily wage? Take what is yours and go. What if I wish to give this last one the same as you? Or am I not free to do as I wish with my own money? Are you envious because I am generous?" Then again, the punch line: "Thus, the last will be first, and the first will be last."

The reaction of those first hired in the plantation-style rural economy of Jesus's day is understandable. No labor union today would put up with this landowner's actions. But in the society envisioned by the Torah, where everyone owns their own plot and cooperates with their neighbor, everyone would rejoice that each person working in the vineyard has their daily needs met. So Matthew's Jesus critiques the system and offers a glimpse of the economics of God's reign. He emphasizes the call to be the last, to serve everyone, to expect little, and to be grateful to God for everything. I may be jumping to conclusions, but I also hear a call to offer the same outlandish generosity of God, the fairness of God that blesses everyone. We have a just and generous God who honors everyone equally, and it shouldn't matter how long we served, or how short a time someone else served. We want everyone everywhere to be with God, so we rejoice with everyone. Most of all, we give thanks that we are able to serve God during our lives and only try to do better ourselves at loving and serving God and humanity. If only every person would accept God's invitation! If only everyone would celebrate that everyone else will be welcomed, whether we spent our whole lives serving God or only recently turned back to God. We want every human being to know the love of God and to share eternal life with God. Finally, we want to create a just society here on earth now that resembles the economics of God's reign, where everyone has an equal share of just work on the land, food, water, housing, healthcare, education, and dignity. The point is to welcome God's reign here and now and to bring God's generosity, equality, and justice everywhere.

After this great teaching, Jesus turns to the Twelve and for the third time tells them point blank that, when they get to Jerusalem, he will be handed over to the authorities, condemned to death, mocked, tortured and crucified, and be raised on the third day. We're not told how the Twelve responded, so we can presume that they are as speechless as we are. Who can take in such news? Once again, Jesus is not predicting the future as if he can see things we can't. He knows that he is going to confront the imperial system of injustice, which the religious authorities support, and that the only response to his nonviolent direct action in a society of total violence will be a deliberate crackdown and execution. The mystery actually lies in that strange pronouncement of the third day.

Elsewhere, when Jesus calls James and John to leave their boats and follow him, their father must have started yelling at them, which is why Jesus names them "the sons of thunder." Here, their mother enters the picture. Notice that she approaches him and does him homage. She takes her two boys with her and has a request of him. Again, notice that Jesus places himself completely at her disposal: "What do you wish?" She asks that her two sons sit next to him on his throne in the kingdom. The chutzpah! Jesus, however, does not rebuke her for her outrageous request. He remains gentle but turns solemn. "You don't know what you are asking," he replies. Think of it: he has just announced that he is to be tortured and executed—and she wants her boys to sit in power by his side in his kingdom.

Again, he does not chide the mother or sons but asks them how seriously they want to follow him. He puts his inquiry in the form of a question—one of the greatest questions in the four Gospels, one we all need to sit with and ponder: "Can you drink the cup that I am going to drink?" He is talking here about the cup of the new covenant, the cup of his blood, the cup of nonviolent suffering love that must be drunk if we are to fulfill his teachings. If we understood the depths of Jesus's question, most of us would answer no. But we can all pray for the grace and the courage to drink from his cup, to share his journey, to walk his path. This question is at the heart of our discipleship.

"We can," they answer confidently. Usually, the disciples struggle to understand Jesus, and even if they do not know what they are pledging themselves to, they say yes to Jesus, and that must be our response as well. Even if we do not understand, we always try to say yes to Jesus, to answer affirmatively to whatever he asks of us. After all, we know he is gentle and humble of heart, and trustworthy.

"My cup you will indeed drink," he answers, "but to sit at my right and at my left is not mine to give but is for those for whom it has been prepared by my Father." We know now who those spaces are reserved for—the violent revolutionaries who were executed next to him on the cross—one on his left and one on his right. James and John were not executed next to Jesus; they fled. Jesus sides not just with the poor but with those struggling for liberation and justice. He is nonviolent but is nevertheless mistaken to be a violent revolutionary and is executed as one.

When the ten other disciples heard about this, they became "indignant" at James and John. Why? They are jealous. They, too, want the power and prestige of being the leaders next to the king in his kingdom. Only moments before, Jesus has announced that he will be tortured and killed. They do not comfort him, console him, talk to him about it, or ask what they can do to help. Instead, they blow up at James and John. What a typical human response! Instead of focusing on the needs of Jesus, we focus only on ourselves. We consistently miss the entire point of the Gospel. Perhaps the disciples should have thought, with humility, "Whatever Jesus wants is what we want, too." No. They are self-focused, so they miss the meaning.

And so, Jesus has to start all over again and explain what he taught in his great sermon. "You know that the rulers of the Gentiles lord it over them, and the great ones make their authority over them felt. But it shall not be so among you. Rather, whoever wishes to be great among you shall be your servant; whoever wishes to be first among you shall be your slave. Just so, the Son of Humanity did not come to be served but to serve and to give his life as a ransom for many." These words sum up the Gospel in a nutshell. If we want to follow the nonviolent Jesus, we cannot dominate others, lord it over others, oppress others, or impose violent power over others. That kind of posture is the way of the world and the exact opposite of everything Jesus stands for and teaches.

Notice, he encourages us to be great, but the way to be great is by being servants of others. He encourages us to be first by being the slave of others, by taking the last place so as to serve others. Then he points out that he has come not to be served but to serve. He should have come to be served; he's the face of God. But no, he is infinitely compassionate, which means he has come to serve. He is 100 percent at the service of the human race—then and now. Such is the disposition of every authentic follower of Jesus.

Matthew adds the line that Jesus offers himself as a ransom for many. A ransom is the payment made to kidnappers who have kidnapped someone. In this case, the demons of violence have kidnapped the human race, and Jesus is giving his life as the ransom to free humanity. An innocent person, he undergoes brutal torture and execution in God's spirit of steadfast faith, truth, nonviolence, and universal love, and in doing so, offers a way for all of us to nonviolently resist the culture of death, bring it down, and welcome God's reign of peace on earth. As his followers, that is what we try to do as well: give our lives as a ransom for all who continue to suffer oppression, poverty, war, and destruction. We give our lives trying to end human suffering and violence and welcome God's reign in a new culture of justice and peace.

Next, we're told that outside of Jericho, two blind men cry out as Jesus passes by, "Lord, Son of David, have pity on us!" The crowd tries to silence them, but that makes them call out all the more, "Lord, Son of David, have pity on us!" Notice how these two beggars, the poorest of the poor, address Jesus. "Lord, Son of David, have pity on us!" Notice that the rich man, James and John's mother, and the twelve disciples do not address Jesus this way. In each case, their focus is on themselves, something they want for themselves. Here, the two blind beggars put all their focus on Jesus. They call him the Son of David, which is about the highest praise anyone could give another in those days. "You, Son of David, our Lord—you, please, have mercy on us." They know that only he can do anything. So they beg him.

This is instructive. This is the true disposition of an authentic disciple. All of us need to see ourselves as blind beggars in the sight of God who call out to Jesus for mercy. That is the basic attitude that we will take; anything else will get us in trouble.

Jesus responds by fulfilling the teaching he just offered his disciples. He places himself completely at the service of these two beggars. He is their slave. He stops, calls them, and asks, "What do you want me to do for you?" He acts as their servant and slave. Only these poor people know how to engage Jesus correctly. Calling him Lord again, they ask for vision, which is something Jesus can give. We're told he's moved with pity, filled with compassion for these poor blind beggars, and so he reaches out and touches their eyes. This act of touching two unclean people is a violation of the law, but Jesus does not care about the culture's rules and regulations, or the consequences of politically charged compassion. He is the ultimate servant of the poor, come what may.

Notice that the two are immediately healed, which means they suddenly can see Jesus, so they leave their positions as beggars and follow him. They have become his disciples. If we want to follow Jesus on the way, we too need to ask for vision. This means that we have to recognize that each of us is fundamentally a poor, blind beggar sitting by the road, waiting for Jesus to pass by. Only he can touch us, heal us, give us vision, and show us where he is going, that we might follow him from now on.

"You Shall Love the God of Peace with All Your Heart, with All Your Soul, and with All Your Mind, and Love Your Neighbor as Yourself" (21:1–23:39)

For months, Jesus has been marching toward Jerusalem. He is not a passive bystander but a rebel leader waging a nonviolent assault on the holy city. The Synoptic narrative describes a series of dramatic events: preparations for the Passover meal; Jesus's street-theater entrance into the city; his nonviolent civil disobedience in the temple; his confrontation with the religious authorities; the Passover meal; Judas's betrayal of Jesus; Jesus's arrest; his torture and execution. Each step of the way is aggressive, public, and truthful—and meticulously nonviolent. This is the way of the cross.

"Go into the village opposite you, and immediately you will find an ass tethered, and a colt with her," he tells two of his disciples. "Untie them and bring them to me. If anyone should say anything to you, reply, 'The master has need of them.' Then he will send them at once." Right away, we realize that we are dealing with an underground movement. The disciples—and readers like us—might wonder how he can predict where to find a donkey, much less, why he would need a donkey, but leaders of grassroots campaigns of nonviolence have contacts far and wide, then and now. As soon as the owner hears the words, "The master has need of them," he would send the creatures on their way. He would be one of the many anonymous followers of Jesus.

Why does Jesus need a donkey? To fulfill the scriptures. What scriptures? The vision of the coming of the Prince of Peace according to the prophet Zechariah 9:9, a text that everyone who is interested in creative nonviolence needs to learn and study. In that verse, written around 500 BCE, Zechariah's vision of the nonviolent Messiah entering Jerusalem sets the stage for the rest of the story and is critical to any understanding of the nonviolence of Jesus:

> Rejoice, heartily, O daughter Zion, shout for joy, O daughter Jerusalem! See, your king shall come to you, a just savior is he, meek and riding on an ass, on a colt, the foal of an ass. He shall banish the war chariot from Ephraim, and the warhorse from Jerusalem. The warrior's bow shall be banished, and he shall proclaim peace to the nations. His dominion shall be from sea to sea, and from the river to the end of the earth. (Zech. 9:9–10)

While the Roman procurator would have marched into Jerusalem for Passover Week accompanied by his full cohort of six hundred soldiers and hundreds of warhorses and swords, the nonviolent Prince of Peace rides in on a donkey, in a posture of humility and gentleness—the opposite of the imperial show of force, and yet a show of force of a new kind, the force of active nonviolence.

Jesus clearly chose this specific Hebrew oracle from Zechariah as the basis for his nonviolent entry into Jerusalem and the nonviolent action that followed. Note the word to describe him: "meek," the biblical word for loving nonviolence. Note the actions this king of peace will take: banning the war chariot, the warhorse, and war bow, then proclaiming peace to the nations and setting up a new dominion of peace to cover the whole earth. This is a stunning vision of a new disarmed, nonviolent world that Jesus chooses for himself. Everything he has done so far has led to the fulfillment of this vision of peace. Everything he will do in Jerusalem will flow from this. Everything we think about Jesus should come from the extraordinary vision of these two verses. They are critical to our understanding of Jesus—and yet, very few Christians know about them or know what Jesus was doing when he rode in on a donkey.

Matthew tells us that a large crowd spread their cloaks on the road, while others put down branches as Jesus rode past and then called out, "Hosanna to the Son of David, blessed is he who comes in the name of the Lord; hosanna in the highest."

"When he entered Jerusalem," Matthew writes, "the whole city was shaken and asked, 'Who is this?' And the crowds replied, 'This is Jesus the prophet, from Nazareth in Galilee.'" Jesus's nonviolent entry into Jerusalem fulfills Zechariah's ancient oracle. His dramatic nonviolent assault has power. It shakes the whole city. Everyone wants to know who he is. Everyone acclaims, "This is the prophet!" His powerful nonviolence is beginning to catch on and become contagious. If it goes unchecked, the ruling authorities will eventually conclude, it will spread like wildfire.

"My House Shall Be a House of Prayer, But You Are Making It a Den of Thieves" (21:12–22)

Jesus approaches the temple. It's hard to underestimate how central the temple of Jerusalem was and is. This massive structure was like St. Peter's in Rome, the Pentagon, Wall Street, the Mall of America, Catholic University, the U.S. Capitol, and the White House—all rolled into one. According to tradition, the God of Judaism lived only here in this massive structure, and the faithful were required to visit the temple once a year. But the temple was used by Herod the Great (who restored it) to make a fortune off the back of the poor as well as to control the population for the Roman Empire. To gain entrance to the temple, to worship God, people had to pay up, and for the poor, the price was high. Because the religious authorities claimed that Roman money was idolatrous (for it had an image of Caesar on it), they created their own "holy" money. People could change their Roman coins into temple coins, but they would be charged and taxed for this transfer. This entire operation symbolized the unjust economy that crushed the poor in the name of God and demonstrated the cooperation between the religious authorities and the Roman rulers. The elite religious authorities and the Roman rulers grew rich maintaining the temple, and so anyone who challenged it was threatening their wealth and security.

Jesus walked into the temple and turned over the tables of the money changers and those who sold doves for people to offer to God. With this dramatic civil disobedience, he symbolically overturned the unjust system that only benefited the elite religious authorities and the Roman ruling authorities. The authorities would have immediately seen him as a legitimate threat to the status quo.

Notice that Jesus does not use violence against people. He does not strike anyone or hurt them in any way. But he is fed up with systemic injustice. He will not be silent or passive in the face of this system that oppresses the poor in the name of God, so he disrupts the system.

Notice, too, that there is no evidence that he is angry. Everyone presumes that Jesus is raging mad as he undertakes this action. But as anyone who has ever done nonviolent civil disobedience knows, one does not take action from a place of anger or rage but from a place of love and grief. Jesus wept over Jerusalem, and those tears motivated him through compassion to take public action for justice for the poor. Likewise, he would not have been yelling or screaming. Rather, he would been have gentle and quiet, like Gandhi as he picked up the illegal salt by the sea and launched his nonviolent revolution; or Dr. King as he walked downtown into Birmingham breaking the segregation law and facing arrest; or the Berrigans as they stole draft files in Catonsville, Maryland, and burned them with homemade napalm to protest the Vietnam War. Public nonviolent action requires carefully thought-out action done peaceably and with mindfulness. Jesus will speak about prayer, so we can conclude that, instead of raging with anger or yelling or screaming, Jesus was praying for an end to this injustice in the House of God. We can presume that the money changers themselves responded not with violence but with stunned silence, because Jesus then proceeds calmly to start teaching.

Jesus's nonviolent direct action in the temple was good news for the poor. With this revolutionary turn of events, he demonstrates that no one has to pay to worship God, that God is freely available to everyone, that even the poor and marginalized can have full access to God. This action of civil disobedience, in effect, has the power to shake up the temple economic system. It was a small, symbolic act; the next day, if not within the next hour, the booths and banking tables were back up and running. Just as Gandhi's symbolic civil disobedience of picking up salt at the beach of Dandi foreshadowed India's independence and the Berrigans' burning of draft files with homemade napalm foreshadowed the end of the Vietnam War, this action foreshadows the end of the temple economic system. It could even change Judaism itself because it confronted the false theology that God belonged only to the rich, the elite, and the ruling authorities.

Matthew writes that Jesus quoted a scripture text to support his nonviolent action: "My house shall be a house of prayer, but you are making it a den of thieves." If we ponder this phrase "a den of thieves," we realize that Jesus is directly criticizing the religious authorities for stealing from the poor. He calls the religious leaders thieves. At the same time, he reclaims and lifts up an ancient image of the temple as a house of prayer. If the temple, and every structure used for spiritual purposes, was a real house of prayer, there would be no entrance fee, no requirement to buy something so that one's worship would be accepted by

God or perceived as worthy, and no control over people as they dwell in peace and silence with God. Everyone who entered the temple would be there solely to pray to God. No one would benefit economically just to be with God in this holy sanctuary.

With this action, Jesus proclaims, "No more injustice! This is a house of prayer. Be people of prayer. Welcome everyone. No one has to pay a penny to worship God. God is available freely to every human heart, and together, everyone can gather freely in prayer with open and loving hearts to God." Much of the problem stems from a false spirituality of violence, in which God is described as domineering, violent, and imperious. As Jesus taught in his great sermon, the living God is a God of peace; therefore, this house of prayer would be a place of peace and would inspire everyone to go forth in that same spirit of peace.

When Jesus engaged in this civil disobedience in the temple, he risked his life for his people and the people of Jerusalem. Once he turned over the tables of the money changers, his days were numbered. He would be labeled a subversive threat to Roman control over Jerusalem. The religious authorities would naturally seek to hunt him down and do away with him.

What does Jesus's dramatic act in the temple mean for us today? If Jesus gave his life in nonviolent protest against the injustice of the temple, what would he say about the Pentagon, or Los Alamos National Laboratory, or Lawrence Livermore National Laboratory, the Trident Submarine base in Bangor, Washington, or any of our global military and nuclear weapons installations where we prepare the end of the world? If he was anguished over the religious cooperation with imperial injustice in the temple, what would he say about our preparations for nuclear war, catastrophic climate change, systemic racism, corporate greed, and permanent warmaking? Like the nonviolent Jesus, we too will seek to dispel the den of thieves who steal from the poor and to make every house of God a house of prayer; indeed, make all of creation a house of prayer.

Matthew adds that the blind and the lame came to Jesus in the temple area, and he cured them. They would not have been allowed near the house of God because they were unclean, but already Jesus has transformed the house of God into a place of healing for the poor. This only further enraged the religious authorities, especially when they heard children calling out, "Hosanna to the Son of David." They angrily questioned Jesus about this, and he responded by questioning them, "Have you never read the text, 'Out of the mouths of infants and nurslings you have brought forth praise'?" We're not told their response, but once again, he would have silenced them.

Jesus is now leading an underground nonviolent movement. We see signs of it as he moves at night to stay in the outskirts of Jerusalem, in Bethany, where we're told later he had close friends, and in the Garden of Gethsemane, which was located across the valley from the city. The next day, as he returns to the city, he sees a fig tree by the road, stops to get some figs from it, notices there aren't any, and says, "May no fruit ever come from you again." Immediately the fig tree withered.

The fig tree is a symbol of Israel—that is, the organized religious system that has become corrupted and turned the temple into a den of thieves. When Jesus says, "May no fruit ever come from you again," he's addressing the temple system, with the prayer and hope of nonviolence, that the days of systemic injustice in the name of God are over. What he wants is a new spiritual, religious movement that bears the good fruit of peace, justice, compassion, and love for God.

Of course, the disciples do not understand any of this, and they ask him about the fig tree. Jesus, in response, starts talking about unwavering, steadfast, rock-solid faith. "Amen, I say to you, if you have faith and do not waver, not only will you do what has been done to the fig tree, but even if you say to this mountain, 'Be lifted up and thrown into the sea,' it will be done. Whatever you ask for in prayer with faith, you will receive."

This is one of Jesus's most important teachings, which he now repeats (see 17:20). Notice that he gives this instruction in the context of systemic injustice and his own nonviolent action to end it. If you have faith and act on that faith, anything for justice is possible, from ending the bad fruit of the unjust temple structure to throwing a mountain into the sea, that is, ending the bad fruit of any other system of social injustice. If you really believe in God and are seeking to bear the good fruit of peace and justice in his spirit of nonviolence, "Whatever you ask for in prayer with faith, you will receive."

The truth of his promise has been shown throughout history. For example, a handful of ordinary Quakers in rural England in the late 1700s started praying and organizing for an end to slavery—the horrific injustice that had always existed. They kept at it, converted the political leader William Wilberforce to their cause, and eventually ended slavery in England without a civil war. Likewise, ordinary women prayed, spoke out, and organized both in England and the United States for the right to vote in the early 1900s and won. Ordinary African Americans organized a bus boycott in Montgomery, Alabama, to stop segregation on the buses, and just over a year later, they won. Their effort led to the civil rights movement, which went on to move many other mountains. We could likewise cite the movements to end Communism, apartheid, the Berlin Wall, the Marcos dictatorship, and many other injustices. As we live out the Sermon on the Mount and struggle nonviolently for justice and peace, Jesus promises us, "Whatever we ask for in prayer with faith, we will receive." We need to test his promise by joining the campaign for change and asking for all these mountains to be thrown into the sea.

Jesus's civil disobedience in the temple is the most illegal, politically charged public action of his life. His healings, even raising the dead, stirred enormous public acclaim, but when he took illegal action in the temple, he provoked the ruling authorities and their system. Matthew in particular records a series of five confrontations that Jesus endured before he was finally arrested a few days later.

"The Kingdom of God Will Be Taken Away from You" (21:23–23:12)

The next morning, as soon as he arrived in the temple area, the chief priests and the elders confronted him, asking, "By what authority are you doing these things? Who gave you this authority?" They wanted to arrest him and do away with him, but they saw how the crowds admired Jesus. Indeed, some scholars have noted that Jesus was protected by the positive response he received from the crowds, so the authorities were scared to arrest him in public. But here, they would have been angry and hostile.

The word "authority" is important. It's sad that they had no idea with whom they were speaking, the Author of life! The disciples still did not understand who he was. In classic rabbinic fashion, Jesus responded by asking them a question: "I shall ask you one question, and if you answer it for me, then I shall tell you by what authority I do these things. Where was John's baptism from? Was it of heavenly or of human origin?"

Matthew's explanation of their conversation reveals their duplicity, insincerity, and wickedness. "If we say 'Of heavenly origin,' he will say to us, 'Then why did you not believe him?' But if we say, 'Of human origin,' we fear the crowd, for they all regard John as a prophet." When they tell him, "We do not know," he answers, "Then neither shall I tell you by what authority I do these things." Jesus understands their sinister motives, but he does not get angry or denounce them. Instead, he engages them and turns the question toward God. By asking them about the origin of John the Baptist, he invites them to see the work of God among us, but they are not interested in God. They are interested in their own authority, their power, control, and greed. The only authority they have, it turns out, is from the Roman emperor, his governor, and the troops who allow them to rip off the poor in the name of God. Turns out, they have relinquished any true authority, while Jesus is the only authority there is or ever was.

Jesus proceeds with a parable about two sons who have been told by their father to go work in the vineyard. We see again his gentle way of inviting us to a change of heart. He begins again with a question, this time addressed to all of us: "What is your opinion?" Like the authorities, we are asked to reflect on his short story and its meaning for us.

The short parable demonstrates brilliant psychology but his powerful explanation is shocking. A father with two sons asks the first to go and work in his vineyard; the son refuses, then changes his mind and goes. Then the father asks the second son to go and work in his vineyard; the son agrees but does not go. Jesus asks, "Which of the two did his father's will?" They answered, "The first." With this story, he's trying to show the religious authorities that though they have pledged to work for God, they are not doing so, while others who refused to do God's work actually are now doing so.

"Tax collectors and prostitutes are entering the kingdom of God before you," he tells them. This statement makes sense now, but at the time it would have been inconceivable to these self-righteous authorities. You couldn't get worse in their estimation than a prostitute or a tax collector, but Jesus says that these people are already entering the kingdom of God while supposedly holy people like them are not. "When John came to you in the way of righteousness," Jesus continues, "you did not believe him, but tax collectors and prostitutes did. Yet even when you saw that, you did not later change your minds and believe him." The parable challenges us as it did them: while we may think of ourselves self-righteously as doing God's work, we may very well not be doing so, while those we look down on for being poor and marginalized are in fact entering the kingdom of God right now. The minute we think we are doing God's will while certain other groups of ostracized people are not is the minute we refuse to enter the kingdom of God, even as they do. The point is to stop judging everyone, to stand with the last and the lowest, to renounce our hypocrisy and self-righteousness, to surrender our lives to the God of peace and universal love, to welcome everyone in an all-inclusive love, and to follow the nonviolent Jesus into the kingdom of God.

The invitation is to *actually do* God's work, whether we want to or not, whether we feel like it or not, or whether we judge others for their apparently Godless lives. We need to renounce every trace of hypocrisy, self-righteousness, privilege, and sense of entitlement and do God's work. What is the work we are called to do in God's vineyard? Matthew has been telling us throughout the narrative, beginning with the great sermon.

Next, Matthew's Jesus offers another parable, this one about a landowner who plants a vineyard and builds a tower, then leases it out to tenants and heads off on a journey. At vintage time, he sends his servants to the tenants to obtain his produce. But they seize them, beat them, stone them, and kill them. So, the owner sends more servants, but these too are beaten, stoned, and killed. Then he sends his son. The tenants say to themselves, "This is the heir. Come, let us kill him and acquire his inheritance." So, they seize him, throw him out of the vineyard, and kill him. The parable of course is the story of God's work to maintain God's creation. Over the years, God sends prophets to call humanity to justice, peace, and stewardship of creation, but the authorities seize them, beat them, stone them, and kill them. So, God sends his beloved Son, whom we know is Jesus, who will suffer the same fate. The parable is a wake-up call to the ruling authorities then and now to stop killing God's prophets and to end the legacy of violence and injustice.

"What will the owner of the vineyard do to those tenants when he comes?" Jesus asks the religious authorities. They answer him, "He will put those wretched men to a wretched death and lease his vineyard to other tenants who will give him the produce at the proper times." In saying this, they recognize themselves in the story and condemn themselves. But in Matthew's version, Jesus does not answer his question. He merely asks, "What will happen to the tenants?" It's a question that lingers today: What will happen to those who hurt and kill God's prophets, God's nonviolent peacemakers like Gandhi, Dr. King, Archbishop Romero, Jean Donovan, Sr. Dorothy Stang, or the hundreds of environmental activists who have been murdered in recent years? In other words, what will happen to all those who do violence? Why do we think there are no consequences to the violence we do, including those of us who think of ourselves as religious, spiritual, or good? The story pushes us again to choose Jesus's way of nonviolence and to side with the prophets of justice and peace.

Jesus continues his questioning: "Did you never read in the scriptures?" That alone is another shocking question. They are religious leaders; of course, they read the scriptures. And yet, on second thought, maybe not. Like today, many religious leaders do not read the scriptures, meditate, practice the wisdom they read, or care about the poor. They have a different agenda. In fact, few seem to read or know Matthew's great Sermon on the Mount. It is a question put to all Christians who support injustice or war. "Have you never read the Sermon on the Mount?"

Jesus continues: "'The stone that the builders rejected has become the cornerstone; by the Lord has this been done, and it is wonderful in our eyes.'" Here Matthew quotes Psalm 118:22–23 and points to Jesus as the cornerstone of all life, of the kingdom of God itself. He implies that the religious authorities do not know about the cornerstone just as they proceed to reject it out of hand even as it stands before them. But Matthew adds a coda: "The one who falls on this stone will be dashed to pieces; and it will crush anyone on whom it falls." Again he's speaking of consequences. If we reject the way of nonviolence, our own violence will come back upon us and crush us. It's an age-old story.

"Therefore, I say to you, the kingdom of God will be taken away from you and given to a people that will produce its fruit." For anyone with eyes to see, I think this is as true today as it was then. In a post-supersessionist reading, we note that everyone (eventually including the disciples) rejected Jesus because he was nonviolent and universally loving; that Matthew's community was warning people not to reject him because of his Sermon-on-the-Mount way of life; but that for centuries instead Christians have rejected Jesus's nonviolence, even though they claim to worship him. We pay him lip service, but we do not want to follow him on the way of the cross and get involved in the messy business of active nonviolence to disarm the world. No thank you. In which case, God's reign is given to anyone who is open to living the life of nonviolence; who resists systemic injustice through love and peaceful means; and who bears the good fruit of peace, justice, service, compassion, and equality.

We see that in the lives of Mahatma Gandhi and his Hindu community; Thich Nhat Hanh and his Buddhist community; Abdul Gaffar Khan and his Muslim community; the marginalized pacifist churches and indigenous communities around the globe, as well as atheists who practice engaged nonviolence in defense of the poor and the earth and work for disarmament and peace. Thousands of Buddhists live in peace, mindfulness, and total nonviolence across the world in sanghas organized by the Vietnamese Buddhist Zen master Thich Nhat Hanh. "We are trying to live right now in the kingdom of God," Thich Nhat Hanh once told me. Few Christians are trying to do that. Matthew adds that the religious authorities knew that Jesus was criticizing them and would have arrested him except for the crowds of people who regarded him "as a prophet."

Jesus continues with another parable that begins: "The kingdom of heaven may be likened to. . . ." Have you noticed how often Jesus refers to the kingdom of heaven, trying to describe it, inviting us to put it first and foremost, even as others oppose him? He tells of a king who gives a wedding feast for his son, dispatches servants to invite his best friends to the feast, but they refuse to come. So, he sends other servants to invite them to the feast, but most of them decline, while the rest kill the servants. Matthew adds that the king is enraged, sends out troops, kills the murderers and burns their city, then tells his servants to go out into "the main roads and invite to the feast whomever you find," which they do. The point: the invitation into the kingdom of heaven is urgent. Drop everything and go to the party, not just willingly but happily, otherwise you might lose your spot. Jesus hasn't killed anyone or threatened to kill anyone; he is simply trying to wake us up to the possibilities of life here and now in God's reign. He tries every nonviolent avenue he can think of, and keeps getting rejected.

Matthew adds a strange coda: the king sees a man in the crowd who is "not dressed in a wedding garment." "My friend," he asks the man, "how is it that you came in here without a wedding garment?" So, he tells his servants, "Bind his hands and feet, and cast him into the darkness outside, where there will be wailing and grinding of teeth." A post-supersessionist interpretation of this challenging parable, taken again within the entire context of Matthew's Gospel and the Sermon on the Mount, does not say that God is vengeful, violent, and punishing, but that our violence has consequences and that we need to turn away from our participation in the culture of violence and war and immediately enter God's reign of universal love and nonviolence right now, by practicing the Sermon-on-the-Mount way of life through nonviolent deeds of love, justice, peace, compassion, and a relentless search for God's reign. The one without the wedding garment does not refer to Jewish people as opposed to Gentile people but to all those who are not "dressed" in "the wedding garment" of peace, love, and Sermon-on-the-Mount nonviolence. As long as we reject the Sermon on the Mount and Jesus's peace, love, and nonviolence, we will remain in the dark, stuck in our violence, feeling absolutely miserable and helpless, "wailing and grinding our teeth."

The message is aimed at Matthew's community: If you want to join the party, if you want to enter the kingdom of heaven, you have to put my Sermon-on-the-Mount teaching into practice and live my specific way of life. And then Matthew adds, "Many are invited, but few are chosen." Every human being who ever lived is formally, cordially invited to enter the kingdom of God through the narrow door of peace, love, and nonviolence, but alas, few accept the invitation and join the party. To be chosen for the kingdom of God, you have to choose it. We're all invited, the parable announces. Don't be stupid, Matthew pleads. Accept the invitation, choose the nonviolent life outlined in the Sermon on the Mount, and come on in.

How do the religious authorities respond to this story? They immediately plot how "they might entrap him in speech." Not only do they ignore him, dismiss him, and hate him, but they start working out how they might kill him.

The story continues. The religious authorities step up their hateful attacks. In the next episode, they question him about the payment of taxes. "Teacher," they ask him, "we know that you are a truthful man and that you teach the way of God in accordance with the truth. And you are not concerned with anyone's opinion, for you do not regard a person's status. Tell us, then, what is your opinion?" Right there, we realize they are lying through their teeth. They smile through their vicious hypocrisy, flattery, and hatred. They even mock Jesus's previous question, "What is your opinion?" He, of course, can see right through them. So they ask, "Is it lawful to pay the census tax to Caesar or not?"

Jesus, of course, knows this is the beginning of the end, that with this question about taxes, they want to trap him and get him killed. "Why are you testing me, you hypocrites?" he asks them point blank. "Show me the coin that pays the census tax." They give him a Roman coin. He asks them again, "Whose image is this and whose inscription?" "Caesar's," they reply. And with that, he offers one of the most brilliant, subtle, poetic, political, revolutionary sentences in history—and lost upon all of history. "Then give to Caesar what belongs Caesar and give to God what belongs to God."

No faithful Jew would ever carry a Roman coin with the idolatrous image of Caesar on it, the emperor who claimed to be god. So Jesus exposes their hypocrisy and idolatry. For nearly two thousand years, everyone has concluded incorrectly that Jesus grants us permission to pay taxes to the empire or the nation/state. It was only since Dorothy Day wrote about it in her newspaper the *Catholic Worker* that this declaration of Matthew has been properly taught. "Once you give to God what is God's," Day explained, "there is nothing left for Caesar." Everything belongs to God, she taught. Nothing belongs to Caesar, the empire, the nation, the state, the military, or the president. Everything belongs to God, and God is the living God of peace. When the leaders heard Jesus's response, they were amazed and turned away.

With that powerful exchange, a new set of opposing religious authorities, the Sadducees, confront him. They do not believe in resurrection, so they question him about it with a crazy hypothetical question designed to discredit him. They begin: "Teacher, Moses said, 'If a man dies without children, his brother shall marry his wife and raise up descendants for his brother.' Now there were seven brothers. The first married and died and, having no descendants, left his wife to his brother. The same happened with the second and the third, through all seven. Finally, the woman died. Now at the resurrection of the seven, whose wife will she be? For they all had been married to her."

"You are misled because you do not know the scriptures or the power of God," Jesus answers them. If you imagine the meanness and hatred aimed at Jesus, and sit with his words, you will discover the depths of his nonviolence. He is humble, kind, and truthful to these people. He simply says they are "misled." This seems to be a key word for Jesus. Some people mislead others; he tries to lead people correctly. He wants his followers, his students, not to be misleaders but to be true leaders, good shepherds.

"At the resurrection," he continues, "they neither marry nor are given in marriage but are like the angels in heaven." This is an astonishing revelation. In the new life of resurrection, in God's reign of eternal peace, we will be like the angels. We will not have physical bodies but be free spirits overflowing with love and infinite peace. We will spend eternity befriending every other human being who ever lived and praising the God whose love brings us together.

"And concerning the resurrection of the dead," he asked them, "have you not read what was said to you by God, 'I am the God of Abraham, the God of Isaac, and the God of Jacob'? He is not the God of the dead but of the living." This is one of the key teachings of Matthew: God is not the God of the dead, but the living God of both the living here on earth and in the new life of the kingdom of heaven. This teaching might be better understood now, but at the time it was utterly new and shocking, and the crowds were astonished.

After this, both groups, the Pharisees and the Sadducees, joined to attack Jesus. Then a scholar of the law tested him: "Teacher, which commandment in the law is the greatest?" Jesus responded with an answer any five-year-old Jewish boy would know by heart: "You shall love the Lord, your God, with all your heart, with all your soul, and with all your mind. This is the greatest and the first commandment. The second is like it: You shall love your neighbor as yourself. The whole law and the prophets depend on these two commandments." No one could respond after this. His answer was both wise and childlike, both obvious and challenging.

Matthew's community is believed to have been made up primarily of Jewish converts to Christianity, so this text would hold tremendous power and remain a central teaching. The word "love" once again is *agapē*, unconditional, total love for the God of love. Matthew's version identifies three forms that this love for God should take. First, we love God with all our hearts. How do we do that? We have to make our relationship with God central to our lives, so that we feel intimate love and deep affection for God. To develop an intimate relationship of abiding love and trust with God, we make a formal check-in time with God every day. We sit in silent meditation and adore God, talk to God, and most importantly listen to God.

To love God with all our souls means to surrender our very beings to the God of love over and over again every day. It's not a onetime thing. Surrendering ourselves to God is a key aspect of Jesus's teaching. We surrender ourselves to God over and over again, every morning, noon, and night. We surrender the control of our lives to God, hand our very lives to God, and let God run our lives. We live for God and let God use us, guide us, and take care of us so that we belong to God through and through.

Then, we're told to love God with all our minds. Matthew invites us to be people of wisdom who put our minds to the service of God. We think about God, ponder the mystery of God, pursue the nature of God, and try to live the way God would want us to live. We read the Gospels and the lives of the saints and try to let the Sermon-on-the-Mount way of life form our minds so that we begin to think like the nonviolent Jesus. We want to put on the mind of Christ, to think like him, so that we act more like him, so that our lives are placed at the service of God and God's reign of peace.

The second commandment is like this first commandment: we love ourselves. To do that, we have to begin to act nonviolently toward ourselves. We non-cooperate with our own inner violence, make peace with ourselves, and are kind toward ourselves. We let God heal us and disarm us, and we create a space for the God of peace to dwell within us so that as we love ourselves, we love God. We practice nonviolence toward ourselves, so that we can go forward and be nonviolent to others. As we surrender into the universal love of God, we let our hearts widen with compassion and we start to practice God's love toward every human being on the planet, so that, in the end, there are no more enemies. There are only friends and neighbors, indeed, brothers and sisters. Our big all-inclusive love begins to reflect the universal love of God, and God's reign begins to shine here on earth.

Having silenced the authorities with his brilliant call to love God with all our hearts, souls, and minds, and for ourselves and our neighbors, Jesus turns on the religious authorities and starts to question them about the Messiah. "What is your opinion about the Messiah?" he asks. "Whose son is he?" This question would have been central to Matthew's community, but it's central to us today as well. We can translate it into the question, "Who is Jesus? What do we mean when we say that he is the Messiah, the Son of God?" In light of a Gandhian/Kingian perspective of nonviolence, we might say, "The Messiah is the beloved Son of God and thus is the embodiment of peace, love, and nonviolence who exposes our insane way of violence and invites us into God's reign of peace.

Whose son is the Messiah? "David's," they answer. Jesus continues, "How, then, does David, inspired by the Spirit, call him 'Lord,' saying, 'The Lord said to my Lord, "Sit at my right hand until I place your enemies under your feet"'? If David calls him 'lord,' how can he be his son?" His logic is brilliant. He silences each of them. Matthew emphasizes this: "No one was able to answer him a word, nor from that day on did anyone dare to ask him any more questions." So, the moral: Do not question Jesus, challenge Jesus, or doubt Jesus. Instead, accept him as the beloved Son of God.

In response to all these attacks by the misleading religious authorities, Jesus warns against following their bad example. "They have taken their seat on the chair of Moses," he says, affirming their position as religious leaders. They are teachers of the law, he says; so listen to them, "but do not follow their example."

"For they preach but they do not practice. They tie up heavy burdens hard to carry and lay them on people's shoulders, but they will not lift a finger to move them. All their works are performed to be seen. They widen their phylacteries and lengthen their tassels. They love places of honor at banquets, seats of honor in synagogues, greetings in marketplaces, and the salutation 'Rabbi.' As for you, do not be called 'Rabbi.' You have but one teacher, and you are all brothers and sisters. Call no one on earth your father; you have but one Father in heaven. Do not be called 'Master'; you have but one master, the Messiah. The greatest among you must be your servant. Whoever exalts himself will be humbled; but whoever humbles himself will be exalted."

Here is a direct critique of religious leadership that stands to this day. One way to ponder Jesus's critique is to ask what he expects from religious leaders. First of all, he says, they should practice what they preach. If they preach prayer, peace, love, compassion, and justice, then they need to live out those qualities every day. Religious leaders should not put burdens on people; rather, they should lift burdens off people. Their goal should be to liberate every human being to live in the freedom of God's reign of peace.

Religious leaders should not work to be seen as holy by others but should serve everyone in humility and put all the focus on God. They should not act pious to win the praise of others but should be holy, loving, and kind, even to the point that no one realizes that they spend all the time inside themselves praying to God, adoring God, loving God, and interceding with God. Next, he accuses them of widening their phylacteries, which were the miniature scrolls they wore on their wrists to remind them of the Torah. They made theirs look bigger to show off how holy and devout they were. Likewise, the tassels hanging from the four corners of their garments were meant to remind them of the commandments, but they made theirs longer to impress others with their devotion. For Jesus, the only one we should be trying to impress is God, and the best way to impress God is through heartfelt, humble, universal love that serves suffering humanity. All pious acts should be done solely for God, without anyone seeing them or knowing about them, beginning with prayer, fasting, and almsgiving. He points out, too, the leaders' explicit lack of humility in the ways they want to be seen and addressed as superior to others, and he gives us a bottom-line law of nature: if you exalt yourself, you will be humbled, but if you humble yourself, you will be exalted, so keep humbling yourself.

There in the midst of these teachings on religious practice, Jesus points to the essential heart of the matter: every human being is your brother or sister. Furthermore, God is your beloved Father, and God's Messiah is your teacher. As devout, religious people, our focus is on God, the nonviolent Messiah, and service toward every person as a beloved brother or sister. That's why he calls us servants; we are servants of all humanity, and God, and the Messiah, and all of God's creation.

"Woe to You" (23:13–39)

The section that follows is a gathering of Jesus's lamentations against the hypocrisy of the scribes and the Pharisees. The word "woe" could be compared to the word "alas." Most scholars agree that, while Jesus often engaged in disputes with the Pharisees, these sayings, which are unique to Matthew, represent the bitter conflict between the Pharisees and the later community for which Matthew was writing his Gospel. Many of the Pharisees working at the time the Gospel was written were good, faithful, and forward thinking, but here Matthew presents Jesus in the prophetic tradition of Jeremiah and Ezekiel with a list of seven "woes" upon the religious leaders. As I proposed in the introduction, these supersessionist passages have been misinterpreted across the centuries to indict Judaism and Jewish people in general, which was a grave misinterpretation. Originally, they were intended as a warning to everyone, especially Matthew's community, to avoid hypocrisy and self-righteousness. If we read the fine print, we can imagine Jesus naming these same faults against church leaders today as well. The main point, however, is to hear the pain, grief, and compassion in Jesus's voice as he indicts those who hypocritically dominate, oppress, and hurt others in the name of God.

While some may disagree, I suggest that Jesus remains nonviolent as he makes these apparently harsh statements. I do not hear him raising his voice in anger or screaming and yelling at the Pharisees. I do not see him waving his arms about and shouting like a maniac, as he is often imagined. I see the nonviolent Jesus practically whispering these lines. In other words, he remains gentle, peaceful, mindful, and compassionate, especially as he speaks truth to power. He has tried every type of nonviolent communication to teach and wake up people—from giving new commandments of nonviolence to telling engaging parables to pleading with the religious authorities to sighing and weeping. I hear these woes as the lamentations of someone who has just broken down and wept at the sight of Jerusalem, who has just announced that we are all sisters and brothers, who has called us to universal love and compassion.

I can imagine Mahatma Gandhi or Thich Nhat Hanh saying these woes because they too said harsh words yet with surprisingly soft-spoken gentleness. I knew well the Vietnamese Zen Master Thich Nhat Hanh for three decades. I can certainly imagine him saying, in that quiet voice of his, "Woe to you who build nuclear weapons! Woe to you who wage war! Woe to you who destroy Mother Earth and her creatures!" If you did not know him, you might read the text and think he would be shouting such words. On the contrary, he would be in tears, whispering, pleading, trying to wake us up to the consequences of our violence. I think we tend to project our anger onto Jesus as we read the Gospels, whereas anger is not the issue, but profound grief. These woes, I submit, are one last dramatic attempt by Matthew's grieving Jesus to wake up the religious authorities and the community itself—as well as us the readers. When this fails, Jesus will resort to two final forms of communication: his silence before Pilate, and his great cry as he dies on the cross.

"Woe to you, scribes and Pharisees, you hypocrites," he begins in grief. "You lock the kingdom of heaven before human beings. You do not enter yourselves, nor do you allow entrance to those trying to enter." Jesus says that authentic religious leaders should enter the kingdom of heaven and do everything they can to invite and welcome others into the kingdom of heaven.

"You traverse sea and land to make one convert, and when that happens you make him a child of Gehenna twice as much as yourselves." Jesus grieves that they struggle hard to gain a few followers, but instead of forming them in the way of universal love, compassion, and peace, they train them in arrogance, power, self-righteousness, and haughty hypocritical behavior that has nothing to do with the kingdom of heaven. In doing so, they train people for hell on earth, not peace on earth. This is a serious warning that needs to be heeded by faith leaders still. All young people, priests, and ministers should be trained in the Gospel art of universal love, compassion, and nonviolence; we should be training them to radiate the reign of God, not reflect the violence, anger, arrogance, divisions, racism, sexism, or warmaking of the culture.

"Woe to you, blind guides," Jesus laments. A guide is someone who knows the way, who can see the way forward, and who can lead others on that way forward, which means, in this case, to God. But if you are blind, you cannot see at all. When he calls them "blind guides," he's saying they are incapable of leading anyone anywhere. He wants people everywhere to see, and he's trying to form his disciples into being guides who can see the way forward. He's looking for people with vision. In a world where everyone is blind, visionaries are the only ones who can truly be helpful to others. To be a visionary is to live out his Sermon-on-the-Mount nonviolence, to get rid of the two-by-four in your head and see clearly the narrow path into God's reign of peace and love.

Jesus quotes their saying:

"'If one swears by the temple, it means nothing, but if one swears by the gold of the temple, one is obligated.' Blind fools, which is greater, the gold, or the temple that made the gold sacred? And you say, 'If one swears by the altar, it means nothing, but if one swears by the gift on the altar, one is obligated.' You blind ones, which is greater, the gift, or the altar that makes the gift sacred? One who swears by the altar swears by it and all that is upon it; one who swears by the temple swears by it and by him who dwells in it; one who swears by heaven swears by the throne of God and by him who is seated on it."

If you study these statements carefully, notice the focus is always on God. That may sound trite or obvious, but it is still very rare today to encounter someone, beginning with religious leaders, whose focus is entirely on God, not on finances or politics or whatever. These statements match Jesus's call to make the temple and its altar a house of prayer to God. Everything else is hypocrisy.

"Woe to you, scribes and Pharisees, you hypocrites. You pay tithes on the smallest herbs but neglect the far more important passages of the law: judgment and mercy and fidelity. But these you should have done, without neglecting the others." Again, he laments their attention to the tiniest religious duties while ignoring what truly matters—social, economic, and racial justice; mercy, compassion, and forgiveness; and fidelity to God. "Blind guides, who strain out the gnat and swallow the camel!" "You've missed the whole point," he says in effect. "You struggle to make sure a gnat doesn't get into your drink, while you eat the filthiest creature of all, a camel." It would be funny if it weren't so tragic.

"Woe to you, scribes and Pharisees, you hypocrites. You cleanse the outside of cup and dish, but inside they are full of plunder and self-indulgence. Blind Pharisee, cleanse first the inside of the cup, so that the outside also may be clean." All these statements flow from the great sermon, Jesus's own life, and his previous interactions with the religious authorities. This particular statement is central to Jesus's teaching. Clean your hearts and souls of all inner filth. Strive to be pure of heart. Through prayer, fasting, and almsgiving, wash away all inner violence and selfishness. That's the work of the spiritual life. If we do this, we can create a place of peace where the God of peace can dwell within us and, like Jesus, let our bodies become temples of God.

"Woe to you, scribes and Pharisees, you hypocrites. You are like whitewashed tombs, which appear beautiful on the outside, but inside are full of dead men's bones and every kind of filth. You work to appear righteous and clean on the outside, but inside you are full of unrighteousness, hypocrisy, violence, and evildoing." Here, he uses even more dramatic imagery. There was nothing more vile or unclean than a tomb, and Jesus compares them to tombs—full of dead bones and filth. The nonviolent Jesus is doing an intervention with them, trying to get them to acknowledge their mistaken focus on cleanliness laws and, instead, to focus on their inner cleanliness and integrity.

Jesus concludes by saying in effect that they are full of death, and so they carry on the works of death, killing God's holy prophets and supporting the unjust system that oppresses and kills the poor and disenfranchised. "Woe to you, scribes and Pharisees, you hypocrites. You build the tombs of the prophets and adorn the memorials of the righteous, and you say, 'If we had lived in the days of our ancestors, we would not have joined them in shedding the prophets' blood.' Thus, you bear witness against yourselves that you are the children of those who murdered the prophets; now fill up what your ancestors measured out!" If they were on the side of the prophets, they would have joined with John the Baptist and even become Jesus's disciples. Instead, they are ready to pounce on him and kill him. Repeating what he heard from John the Baptist, he calls them serpents and a brood of vipers, ready to bite, poison, and kill. "How can you flee from the judgment of Gehenna?" he asks. Notice he doesn't condemn them to death. He poses a question about eternal life and eternal death. He tries to get them to reflect on the seriousness of life and the spiritual consequences of their actions. By posing the question, he leaves the door open for a positive answer: they can fall down at his feet, repent, beg his forgiveness, convert to his way of loving nonviolence, and ask him to take them as his disciples. But, of course, they are blind, so they do not do that. They cannot see who it is who is talking to them.

"I send you prophets, wise people, and scribes," he says referring to his disciples. "Some of them you will kill and crucify, some of them you will scourge in your synagogues and pursue from town to town." Because of the violence inflicted on his nonviolent movement, he says, you will share in the consequences, the karma, of all those who have killed the saints and the prophets. This is the generation that was blessed to see the nonviolent Messiah, Matthew points out, but instead of welcoming him and converting to his great sermon, they have been dead set on killing him. Their plan to trap and kill the nonviolent Messiah is the culmination of *generations* of violence. They, like all of us, will have to answer before God.

Jesus turns to Jerusalem and grieves over the holy city itself. "Jerusalem, Jerusalem, you who kill the prophets and stone those sent to you, how many times I yearned to gather your children together, as a hen gathers her young under her wings, but you were unwilling! Behold, your house will be abandoned, desolate. I tell you, you will not see me again until you say, 'Blessed is he who comes in the name of the Lord.'" Notice how Jesus compares himself to a mother hen, one of the most devoted and caring of parenting animals. A mother hen can hold a dozen chicks under her wings where they feel safe and warm and loved. Jesus offers not just a feminine image of God but an animal image of God. God is like a mother hen. Like a mother hen, he yearns to gather everyone together—but everyone has refused. Because they refused his loving invitation into God's reign of peace here on earth, their violence will lead to their own self-destruction. Jesus can see that, and Matthew knows that, because his Gospel was probably written just after the destruction of Jerusalem by the Roman forces. Likewise, we too can see today that if we do not let the nonviolent Christ gather us under God's wings, if we do not dwell solely in God's love, then we will be doomed to suffer the consequences of our faithless and violent ways.

Again, I invite us to hear these lamentations not in anger or hostility but in terms of quiet grief and lamentation: "Woe to you hypocrites, blind guides, blind fools." I invite us to imagine the woes that the nonviolent Jesus would say to our generation: "Woe to you who build and maintain nuclear weapons. Woe to you who wage permanent war on the poor, on Mother Earth. Woe to you who invest in Wall Street and ignore the cry of the poor. Woe to you who live comfortably in a nice home with good food while your homeless neighbors freeze and starve. Woe to you who turn away the stranger and the immigrant at your border, who marginalize those of different race, nationality, religion, or sexual orientation. Woe to you who continue to dig up fossil fuels at the expense of Mother Earth, who lead creatures to extinction and set loose climate chaos. Hypocrites! Wake up and change your ways—by following the way of Jesus."

We might ponder how the scribes and Pharisees should have responded to Jesus's woes, but a more serious question is: How are we today to respond to Jesus's woes? I suggest we need to sit with them in silence, prayer, and grief, to feel the love and compassion behind their pleas, to contextualize them in our own global reality, to take them to heart and join Jesus's ongoing campaign to reconcile the whole world to God's forgiveness and peace.

I invite us to hear the nonviolent Jesus saying these words to us, not as condemnation but as invitation, as a call to conversion and repentance. Matthew urges us to summon the courage through prayer and love, to repent of our complicity in the culture opposed to God's reign of peace.

One way to respond to Matthew's woes is to return to the two blind beggars that we encountered a while back (20:39–34). Unlike the rich young man who walked away from Jesus or the scribes and the Pharisees who try to trick and trap and kill Jesus, these two blind beggars offer the best model of how to appear before the nonviolent Jesus. If we do not want to be hypocrites, blind guides, or fools who waste our lives supporting the unjust status quo, if we do not want to be the ancestors of those oppressive religious hypocrites who carry on the tradition of preventing others from entering the kingdom of heaven here on earth, then we need to recognize our blindness and our poverty and beg the nonviolent Jesus to have mercy on us and take us with him on his campaign to transform the world. If we dare wake up, change our lives, and get with the Gospel, we might see our way forward on the narrow path into the kingdom of heaven here and now.

"Whatever You Did for One of These Least Brothers and Sisters of Mine, You Did for Me" (24:1–25:46)

After Jesus's nonviolent civil disobedience in the temple, the attacks against him by the religious authorities, and his seven lamentations, Jesus walked out of the temple area knowing that his days were numbered. We are now a day or two from Passover. He is being hunted down, so he heads off to his hideaway in the hills across the valley from Jerusalem. In these last hours, Matthew offers a series of eschatological teachings and parables about life in the end times, teachings that culminate in the parable of the Last Judgment, which is unique to Matthew. There, Jesus will teach us that whatever we do or don't do to any other human being, we do or don't do to him.

As they walk away, the disciples point out the temple buildings. Clearly, they are in awe of this mighty structure with its large stones and interesting architecture. Jesus, we remember, has been here before, as a boy, and possibly in recent years as a practicing Jew for the three annual feasts. "You see all these things, do you not?" he asks them. "Amen, I say to you, there will not be left here a stone upon another stone that will not be thrown down." Jesus is not naïve or fatalistic or hopeless; he is pragmatic and realistic. In view of the rejection of Jesus's methodology of active nonviolence, people's passive acceptance of Roman occupation, as well as the revolutionary violence of the Zealots, can only lead to further violence, toward the inevitable destruction of the temple and all of Jerusalem. Violence and injustice lead to further violence, then and now. Jesus is simply pointing out the inevitable consequences of the culture's violence and warmaking. War begets war until everything is destroyed.

So they ask him, "Tell us, when will this happen, and what sign will there be of your coming, and of the end of the age?" His answer goes beyond the destruction of the temple to outline the history of violence and destruction to come unless humanity changes course. More, these eschatological instructions are intended for his disciples, for he teaches them privately. "See that no one deceives you," he begins. "Many will come in my name, saying, 'I am the Messiah,' and they will deceive many." The instruction is, "Do not be deceived." That means, do not be led into believing something that is not true. This is critically important. Followers of the nonviolent Jesus strive for truth, believe the truth, and seek what is true. We do not want to spend our lives believing in falsehood and leading others to do the same.

Alas, this is the story of humanity. We have all been misled and brainwashed to believe in untruth and the world's big lies: that empires and nations are noble and holy; that war leads to peace; that joining any military is a courageous, even holy vocation; that one race or gender or nationality or religion or sexual orientation is greater than another; that our leaders, generals, or violent revolutionaries have been sent by God to lead us, even to save our nations and empires; and that God wills that some people be poor, malnourished, and sick. None of this is true.

In fact, the world rarely acknowledges, much less promotes, truth. Untruth is the flip side of the world's violence, because to be violent and to wage war require that we believe the lie that some human beings are not our sisters and brothers. These days, untruth is broadcast far and wide; the idea of "fake news" is just the tip of the iceberg. To live the nonviolence of Jesus, we have to work hard so that we are not being deceived by anyone, no matter how popular or smart or powerful such voices are.

"You will hear of wars and reports of wars," he continues, telling us in direct language the inevitable consequences of the world's systemic violence, where nations fight one another relentlessly and sow the seeds for future wars. Two thousand years later, we live in a world of permanent warfare, where trillions of dollars have been spent over the last century killing over 100 million people, mainly civilians. Today, we have weapons of mass destruction beyond anyone's comprehension that can vaporize millions of people in a flash and blow up every city on the planet. On top of this, with television, news media, and social media, we can follow every war, every battle, 24/7 live on air as "breaking news." We go through life sitting in front of our screens, watching our wars, and eating and drinking as if we're watching a movie. War has become entertainment, part of the Big Lie.

"See that you are not alarmed, for these things must happen, but it will not yet be the end," he commands. This, too, is another key Matthean teaching: See that you are not alarmed. As he instructed us in the great sermon on nonviolence, we practice steadfast daily mindfulness. We live and breathe the holy spirit of the nonviolent Jesus, so we do not resort to anxiety, despair, worry, panic, anger, or fear. We are not alarmed. We remain steady, calm, and centered. We stay focused on the God of peace and practice the emotional life of nonviolence, as instructed, as Jesus does. We grieve, and we rejoice in the nonviolent struggle for justice and peace. By adhering to his teachings, we let nothing rattle our nerves. We are as steady as a rock, and fully alive in the present moment of peace.

"Nation will rise against nation, and kingdom against kingdom," he continues. "There will be famines and earthquakes from place to place. All these are the beginning of the labor pains." As he explains the inevitable violence to come, he is not being fatalistic, but rather, he calls us to be realistic, alert, and ready. Things are bad, but brace yourself—they're going to get worse, he says, but you have been formed in nonviolence and truth, and you are prepared for anything, even death. You will remain centered in me and my way.

But it's not going to be easy. Worse, this journey of nonviolence is going to require our very lives, just as it requires Jesus's life.

> "They will hand you over to persecution, and they will kill you. You will be hated by all nations because of my name. Many will be led into sin; they will betray and hate one another. Many false prophets will arise and deceive many; and because of the increase of evildoing, the love of many will grow cold. But the one who perseveres to the end will be saved. This gospel of the kingdom will be preached throughout the world as a witness to all nations, and then the end will come."

This, too, is one of the most important, albeit neglected, passages in the Gospels. We see how all these outcomes have come true in the lives of the martyrs and the persecuted peoples of history. For example, during the brutal war in El Salvador in the 1970s through the early 1980s, Archbishop Romero, the four U.S. churchwomen, eighteen priests, thousands of catechists, and seventy-five thousand other precious people were brutally tortured and killed by military death squads funded and trained by the United States.

Evildoing grows day by day, and so love grows cold everywhere. As we ignore systemic evil and allow it to spread, we stop loving one another. Nowadays, so many people do not know how to love. Many have never been loved and cannot comprehend the way of nonviolent love. The decline in love can be blamed on the church, which has so often failed to teach and practice universal, compassionate love. Yet even as things worsen and we head toward nuclear war and catastrophic climate change, universal nonviolent love remains the only practical way forward.

"The one who perseveres to the end will be saved," Jesus concludes. Here is the instruction: persevere to the end. Stay faithful to the God of peace, and therefore practice universal love and total nonviolence, come what may. "This gospel of the kingdom will be preached throughout the world as a witness to all nations," he says. That is our job description, as Matthew will repeat at the end of his Gospel. We are to preach the great sermon of universal love and nonviolence as a witness against the nations, that they may know there is another way, that God's way is contrary to theirs, that we could have chosen peace, if we had dared, and that it is never too late to repent of violence and war and turn back to the God of peace and love.

"When you see the desolating abomination spoken of through Daniel the prophet standing in the holy place (let the reader understand), then those in Judea must flee to the mountains." This critical teaching too has been largely ignored across the centuries, but now, during these end-times, we need to fearlessly reclaim it. Think of it like this: during the 1930s, as the Nazis took over every aspect of Germany, they recruited every priest, minister, and bishop, until before long, nearly every Christian and Catholic church was claimed by the Nazis. One of the first things they did was to hang a Nazi flag in the sanctuary. That meant that the church was now owned and run by Hitler himself, and it publicly supported his evil campaign to exterminate every Jew and take over the planet through unprecedented global violence. That Nazi flag, hanging in a German church, was, to quote the prophet Daniel, "the abomination of desolation." It was but one example of this. Matthew is saying to his original audience, When the Roman Empire has taken over the temple and every synagogue in Israel, when its Roman medallion and flag are placed in the holy of holies, run, for blasphemy has become the order of the day.

The deranged Syrian king Antiochus IV Epiphanes was as insane as Hitler, and he led a similar campaign of extermination and global violence. In 167 BCE, he desecrated the temple by setting up a statue of the false god Zeus. The prophet Daniel vehemently denounced and resisted the evildoer Antiochus IV Epiphanes and warned of the coming "desolating abomination" (see Dan. 12:11). The blasphemous event had already occurred, but Daniel wrote of it as a prophecy of worse things to come. Scholars suggest that Matthew considered the desecration of the temple by the Romans to be the fulfillment of Daniel's prophetic warning, that the worse that could ever happen has now happened—the idolatrous sign of the evil Roman Empire had been hung in the temple, replacing worship of the living God with worship of the false god Caesar and his empire of violence. No wonder the nonviolent Jesus risked his life in nonviolent protest at the temple!

"Let the reader understand." How much clearer could Matthew be? He cannot write: "Dear readers, when you hear me refer to the abomination of desolation, think ROMAN EMPIRE. Do everything you can to not cooperate with Caesar. Worship God, not Caesar.

Don't be taken in by the empire." If Matthew had written plainly like that, he knew the Romans would hunt down and round up every Christian everywhere. So he gives us readers a nudge to read between the lines. Alerted, we know he's referring to Daniel's prophecy, that Rome has now taken over the temple, that Caesar has replaced the living God, and that the time has come. Thus, we have a new commandment: Flee! One nonviolent response to the empire's takeover of our religious houses is simple and urgent: Run away! "Those in Judea must flee to the mountains!" With this commandment, he tells us to drop everything and run from the empire when it has taken control of our worship of God, whether then or now. It is better for you to remain faithful to the living God then go along with the blasphemy that has claimed the souls of so many.

That's why there should not be any flag or any sign of one's nation in any Christian sanctuary in the world. As long as we have a flag on the altar, we continue the legacy of blasphemy and the abomination of desolation. We do not need its symbol anyway; with the cross, we have a strong enough symbol to focus on.

"A person on the housetop must not go down to get things out of his house, a person in the field must not return to get his cloak. Woe to pregnant women and nursing mothers in those days. Pray that your flight not be in winter or on the sabbath, for at that time there will be great tribulation, such as has not been since the beginning of the world until now, nor ever will be. And if those days had not been shortened, no one would be saved; but for the sake of the elect, they will be shortened."

Here Jesus describes the urgency of the end-times, a new kind of flight into Egypt, a new time of exile, when we must drop everything to protect ourselves and our loved ones from the days of war and empire. Certainly, with the dropping of atomic bombs on Hiroshima and Nagasaki, where some two hundred thousand sisters and brothers were vaporized in 1945, those days are upon us. As the threat of nuclear warfare and climate chaos worsen by the day, we all face the possibility of having our lives upended by war, empire, and destruction.

"If anyone says to you then, 'Look, here is the Messiah!' or, 'There he is!' do not believe it," he teaches.

"False messiahs and false prophets will arise, and they will perform signs and wonders so great as to deceive, if that were possible, even the elect. Behold, I have told it to you beforehand. So if they say to you, 'He is in the desert,' do not go out there; if they say, 'He is in the inner rooms,' do not believe it. For just as lightning comes from the east and is seen as far as the west, so will the coming of the Son of Humanity be. Wherever the corpse is, there the vultures will gather."

Here he describes how many false spiritualties will spring up in the days of the abomination of desolation, when the empire has taken over the world, including any religious sanctuary. All kinds of false teachers and false prophets will spread their false teachings—anything and everything but Jesus's teachings of universal love. These false spiritualties will lead us not to question, resist, or renounce empire and war but will trick us into going along with

121

the big business of nationalism, war, and empire. Before we know it, we will be pawns to the forces of death and destruction without even realizing it. We will be spiritually dead serving the culture of death and surrounded by vultures, the servants of death, who will eat away at us. But someday, the Son of Humanity will appear like lightning from east to west, lighting up the darkness of the world for all to see and dispelling the power of death once and for all.

"Immediately after the tribulation of those days, the sun will be darkened, and the moon will not give its light, and the stars will fall from the sky, and the powers of the heavens will be shaken. And then the sign of the Son of Humanity will appear in heaven, and all the tribes of the earth will mourn, and they will see the Son of Humanity coming upon the clouds of heaven with power and great glory. And he will send out his angels with a trumpet blast, and they will gather his elect from the four winds, from one end of the heavens to the other."

This apocalyptic writing is not meant to frighten us. Rather, it offers hope. We know that the way of violence and empire will bring death and destruction to the world and will crush the nonviolent Jesus and his community of nonviolence. But he will return in glory, and all those who followed him will be welcomed into God's never-ending reign. One could argue that the end of the world, the darkened sun, moon, and stars, are Matthew's vivid poetic description of the Good Friday crucifixion just a few days away. Two thousand years later, as we threaten the earth with nuclear warfare, extinguish millions of species, and literally change the weather into chaos for the first time in millions of years, these apocalyptic images seem to be coming true fast. Nonetheless, the focus must remain on the nonviolent Jesus, the Son of Humanity. Whatever happens, whatever crisis we face, we keep our lookout for the Son of Humanity. If we want to be his faithful followers, to be part of his Beloved Community, the "elect," our focus is always on Jesus. So we are not alarmed. We stand ready, continuing to witness to his way.

"Learn a lesson from the fig tree. When its branch becomes tender and sprouts leaves, you know that summer is near. In the same way, when you see all these things, know that he is near, at the gates. Amen, I say to you, this generation will not pass away until all these things have taken place. Heaven and earth will pass away, but my words will not pass away." Now we know that Matthew is describing the execution of the nonviolent Jesus as the end of the world, but we are not afraid because we know he is near, we already know he is risen, and we trust that we will see him one day. Until then, we live according to his words and teachings.

"Of that day and hour no one knows, neither the angels of heaven, nor the Son, but the Father alone. For as it was in the days of Noah, so it will be at the coming of the Son of Humanity. In those days before the flood, they were eating and drinking, marrying and giving in marriage, up to the day that Noah entered the ark. They did not know until the flood came and carried them all away. So will it be at the coming of the Son of Humanity. Two men will be out in the field; one will be taken, and one will be left. Two women will be grinding at the mill; one will be taken, and one will be left. Therefore, stay awake! For you do not know on which day your Lord will come."

With his description of the days of Noah, when suddenly everyone was taken away by the flood except Noah and his community because they listened and obeyed God, Matthew's Jesus tries to warn us to "stay awake." Be alert, don't fall asleep, remain mindful, he warns us. Be ready for anything. This is not at all like the nonsense of the *Left Behind* novels, where people are randomly taken up into the Rapture. This is a call to mature radical discipleship, to be fully awake during these times of total violence. Of course, as we know, when the moment comes—in the Garden of Gethsemane—they will fail to stay awake and will sleep through Jesus's hours of agony. We do not want to do the same today. We do not want to sleep through the agony of Christ in the poor and oppressed and the crucifixion of creation. Rather we remain awake and do our part to serve Christ by carrying on his work of liberating the poor, bringing justice, making peace, and protecting creation.

"Be sure of this," Matthew adds. "If the master of the house had known the hour of night when the thief was coming, he would have stayed awake and not let his house be broken into. So too, you also must be prepared, for at an hour you do not expect, the Son of Humanity will come." By describing himself as a thief who breaks into one's house in the middle of the night, Jesus urges us to live out his teachings of prayer, fidelity, trust, and hope in God. If we grow slack and lazy, especially in these end-times, we will not only fail in service to those in need, we will fail to serve the nonviolent Jesus as he comes to us.

That is why Matthew then questions us about being faithful and prudent servants. "Who, then, is the faithful and prudent servant whom the master has put in charge of his household to distribute to them their food at the proper time?" he asks. Returning to the vision of the great sermon, Matthew adds a new beatitude: "Blessed is that servant whom his master on his arrival finds doing so. Amen, I say to you, he will put him in charge of all his property." We want to be faithful day in and day out, waiting to serve God and the nonviolent Jesus who comes to us in the poor, in the work for justice and peace, and in proclaiming God's reign of nonviolence to the nations. We want to be found carrying on Jesus's campaign. This may be the greatest beatitude, the greatest blessing of all.

"If that wicked servant says to himself, 'My master is long delayed,' and begins to beat his fellow servants, and eat and drink with drunkards, the servant's master will come on an unexpected day and at an unknown hour and will punish him severely and assign him a place with the hypocrites, where there will be wailing and grinding of teeth." Note that it is not God who is violent here: it is the person who should be following the nonviolent Jesus and serving God, who beats people, lives selfishly, and renounces the life of love toward all. The severe punishment is that the person of violence, the hypocrite who pretends to be holy but in fact is violent will not be welcomed into the house of peace. The consequence is wailing and grinding of teeth.

As the Gospel reaches its conclusion, Jesus offers three climactic parables about the faithful servants who persevere to the end and enter God's reign. He likens entrance into God's reign to ten virgins "who took their lamps and went out to meet the bridegroom." Five were wise, and five were foolish. The only difference was that the wise ones brought extra oil for their lamps, but the foolish ones did not. Since it was late, they all fell asleep only to be awakened at the arrival of the bridegroom. As they prepared to meet the bridegroom and got their lamps ready, the foolish ones asked the wise ones for some of their oil, but the wise ones said there wasn't enough and told them to go to the merchants and buy some. While they were gone, the bridegroom arrived "and those who were ready went into the wedding feast with him." Then, we're told, the door was locked. Later, when the foolish ones returned, they knocked on the door saying, "Lord, Lord, open the door for us!'" But the bridegroom answered, "Amen, I say to you, I do not know you." This parable insists that each of us must take responsibility for her or his own life. We will be held accountable for our lives and actions. If we are wise, we will live according to Jesus's teachings, and in that way, Jesus will recognize us, support us, and be with us. By offering universal love and compassion, hungering and thirsting for justice, making peace and seeking God's reign, we will be ready one day to meet Jesus, and, to our delight, we will recognize each other because we lived his journey. If we have not lived according to these teachings, Jesus will not recognize us. The supersessionist overtones of this passage are wrong; it is not a judgment on the Jewish people. The invitation here is to be ready for Jesus, to do his will, to put his teachings of universal love, peace, and nonviolence into practice—because we want him to recognize us and know us through and through that we might share in the fullness of life, love, and peace with him.

The ending of this parable is the same as the ending of the great sermon. Here, the bridegroom says what Jesus told us God will say when we die. Either we will be known for our faithful, persevering lives lived according to Jesus's teachings of love, compassion, and peace, or he will not know who we are. We will cry out, "Lord, Lord!" but by then it will be too late. The bridegroom will say, "I do not know you." We will not be able to rely on the wise people we have known who have lived according to the great sermon. No one else can share their oil with us; that is, no one can share part of their lifelong good deeds. It's too late for that. Instead, we want to be known by Jesus, recognized by him, welcomed by him, and that means that we live now as God's beloved sons and daughters, and model our lives after Jesus. As we do, he will say with a smile, "I know you, my friend. Welcome to the eternal feast." Matthew adds a moral to the story: "Stay awake, for you know neither the day nor the hour." From now on, we try to remain awake to the God of peace, to be ready to serve God at all times, to promote God's reign at all times, and to enter God's reign at a moment's notice. This is the most important work of our lives.

In Jesus's second-to-last parable, Matthew again describes God's reign in relation to those who have been faithful and persevered with the Gospel work of service, love, justice, and mercy. Before a landowner embarks on a journey, he leaves his possessions to his servants. "To one he gave five talents; to another, two; to a third, one—to each according to his ability." While he was away, the one with the five traded them and made another five. The one with the two invested them and received two more. "But the man who received one went off and dug a hole in the ground and buried his master's money." When the master returned, he called in the servants to see what they did with the money he left them. The one who had received five presented his additional five. "Well done, my good and faithful servant. Since you were faithful in small matters, I will give you great responsibilities. Come, share your master's joy." The master says the same to the one who had received two talents and presented his extra two as well.

Finally, the one who received only one talent appeared. "Master," he began, "I knew you were a demanding person, harvesting where you did not plant and gathering where you did not scatter; so out of fear I went off and buried your talent in the ground. Here it is back." "You wicked, lazy servant!" the master said. "Should you not have put my money in the bank so that I could have got it back with interest on my return?" Then he ordered the one talent to be taken from him and given to the one who has ten. "For to everyone who has, more will be given and he will grow rich, but from the one who has not, even what he has will be taken away. And throw this useless servant into the darkness outside, where there will be wailing and grinding of teeth."

Most scholars agree that Matthew stresses one key point here: faithful use of one's gifts for God and God's reign throughout one's life will lead to the fullness of life in God's reign of love. Not using our gifts for God and God's reign, not taking action as Jesus instructs for justice, peace, compassion, and service of the poor, and living out of fear and laziness will make us miserable and prevent our entering God's reign. Here again we hear about being stuck outside in the dark where we wail and grind our teeth. This telling detail alerts us again that Matthew's Jesus is urging us to recognize how miserable we are right now in our own lives as long as we do not invest ourselves in God's will and reign of universal love, justice, and peace. As long as we stay stuck in our selfishness, our own self-wills, we will remain in the dark, personally and collectively; we will be stuck in our own rock-bottom violence, individually and collectively; and we will not only have no peace, but we will have no joy. There will be no hope, no light, no meaning, no purpose, and perhaps most basically, no joy. A post-supersessionist reading helps us hear Matthew's urgent call to act on Jesus's teachings right now, to act as if we are already living in God's reign, to invest our resources and contribute—our time, talents, possessions, energy—in God's reign of universal love and peace. Then we will receive the greatest compliment and invitation ever: "Well done, my good and faithful servant," we will be told. "Come, share your master's joy." This is where we are all headed, starting today, if we step up and invest ourselves in Jesus's way of peace, love, and nonviolence.

Finally, we arrive at the climax of Matthew's Gospel. This original vision, unique to Matthew, is placed just before the passion, death, and resurrection of Jesus, but it could have been placed at the very end of the Gospel. I believe there is a direct line from Matthew 5 to this climactic story in Matthew 25. Here Matthew's Jesus calls us again to be faithful servants, but more, to recognize that whatever we did throughout our lives, we did to Jesus. If we served, loved, healed, and helped those in need, then we served, love, healed, and helped Jesus. If we did not, we did not serve Jesus in his need. This is a worthy climax to the visionary teachings of Matthew 5 and the great sermon.

The scene is shocking: it's the end of the world, we're at the gates of heaven, the Son of Humanity, the nonviolent Jesus, comes in all his glory, surrounded by his adoring angels, and sits upon his glorious throne, and all the nations of history gather before him—all of humanity, past and present. And we're told that he separates them "as a shepherd separates the sheep from the goats," with the sheep on his right and the goats on his left.

Then he says to those on his right: "Come, you who are blessed by my Father. Inherit the kingdom prepared for you from the foundation of the world. For I was hungry and you gave me food, I was thirsty and you gave me drink, a stranger and you welcomed me, naked and you clothed me, ill and you cared for me, in prison and you visited me." The righteous will ask, "Lord, when did we see you hungry and feed you, or thirsty and give you drink? When did we see you a stranger and welcome you, or naked and clothe you? When did we see you ill or in prison, and visit you?" And the king will say to them in reply, "Amen, I say to you, whatever you did for one of these least brothers or sisters of mine, you did for me."

Then he will say to those on his left, "Depart from me, you accursed, into the eternal fire prepared for the devil and his angels. For I was hungry and you gave me no food, I was thirsty and you gave me no drink, a stranger and you gave me no welcome, naked and you gave me no clothing, ill and in prison, and you did not care for me." They will ask, "Lord, when did we see you hungry or thirsty or a stranger or naked or ill or in prison, and not minister to your needs?" He will answer, "Amen, I say to you, what you did not do for one of these least ones, you did not do for me." They will go off to eternal punishment, we're told, but the righteous to eternal life.

Notice that these corporal works of mercy are the sole criteria for entrance in God's reign of love and peace. It does not matter whom you voted for, what color your skin is, what your sexual orientation is, how successful you are, how much money you own, or how pious you look. Everything regarding your entrance into eternal life depends on this: Did you feed the hungry, give drink to the thirsty, clothe the naked, house the homeless, welcome the immigrant, comfort the sick, or visit the imprisoned? Period. Matthew lists people who are suffering, and asks what we did to help them. What we do or do not do to relieve the sufferings of the poor and oppressed will determine our spiritual fate. Again, a post-supersessionist interpretation emphasizes not how the church has superseded the Jewish people, but rather, that we are all called to the urgent work of relieving the suffering and unjust deaths of sisters and brothers around the world, starting with those in need in our own vicinity. God is not a God of violence or punishment; again, we are simply being warned by the gentle, compassionate Jesus of the consequences of our refusal to love, serve, and do God's will of making peace and practicing nonviolence. As long as we do not serve the poor, the hungry, the naked, the homeless, the stranger, the sick, and the imprisoned, we will be stuck in our own selfishness, darkness, and violence. We will not know the joy of life in God's peace; rather, we will continue to wail and grind our teeth in misery.

At the heart of the great parable is the shocking revelation that Christ is present in all the poor, oppressed, suffering, and marginalized. "Whatever you did for one of these least brothers or sisters of mine, you did for me," the king will say. Matthew announces that Jesus is present in our world right now in the hungry, thirsty, naked, homeless, stranger, sick, and imprisoned. Whatever we do or do not do for them, we do or do not do for Jesus. No matter how pious or politically correct we may think we are, if we have not fed the hungry and ministered to the sick, imprisoned, or homeless poor, we have missed the whole point of life. We have not served Jesus here and now. We missed out on a golden opportunity. Dorothy Day and Mother Teresa both had personal struggles and issues, but they spent their lives serving the poor every day, which means they were serving Jesus every day. That is the call issued to each one of us in this great concluding parable. It means getting up, going to where the poor are, and getting to work ministering to them. That is what Matthew's Jesus wants.

Every time we do something "sheepish"—that is, gentle, peaceful, nonviolent, and loving—we move closer to Jesus and step into the reign of God. Every time we act like "goats"—that is, mean, selfish, violent, and bullying—we move away from Jesus and step away from God's reign. Matthew's Jesus uses all his storytelling powers here to urge us not to miss out on stepping into God's reign of universal love, peace, and joy here and now by going forth and serving him in the poor and needy.

What is so interesting is that no one on the left or the right claims to have seen this great king in all his glory ever before. They are astonished and shocked to hear that he came among us in disguise among the homeless, the refugee, the sick, the hungry, the thirsty, the naked, and the imprisoned. The whole story echoes the teaching of 10:40: "Whoever receives you, receives me."

In light of Matthew 5, the oracle takes on even more social, economic, and political overtones. Jesus calls us, in effect, to serve him in the hungry, thirsty, naked, homeless, immigrant, sick, and imprisoned. But as we look around the world then and now, we realize that the nation/state system, the warmaking empires, and war itself bring death upon countless sisters and brothers without any remorse or second thought. Reflection upon this oracle helps us understand that war makes people hungry, thirsty, naked, homeless, immigrants, sick, and imprisoned; it also kills them! War kills Christ with guns, bombs Christ in the enemy, poisons Christ with chemical weapons, and vaporizes Christ with nuclear weapons. War kills Christ. If we want to be welcomed into God's reign of peace, we can never participate in or support war. We must do everything within our power to oppose it, not cooperate with it, and resist it. Otherwise, according to this text, we are no different than the Romans who executed the nonviolent Jesus. That is why the great sermon on nonviolence is crucial to life, for if we practice the total nonviolence and universal love Jesus commands, then we will serve him well and be welcomed into God's reign of peace forever. As the Beatitudes teach and this parable promises, if we serve Christ in the poor and marginalized, if we do God's will of universal love, compassion, and nonviolence, we step into the fullness of life right now and begin to know a deep-down joy that no one can ever take from us, come what may. That is a promise worth pursuing.

The Arrest and Execution of the Nonviolent Jesus (26:1–27:66)

It's almost time for the Passover meal. Jesus sleeps outdoors on the outskirts of the city. One of his hideaway retreats is a garden across the valley. After his civil disobedience, he knows well, as anyone would, that the authorities are plotting to arrest him, and he keeps telling his disciples, who remain in denial and lack of understanding. The chief priests and the elders gather in the palace of Caiaphas the high priest, and they "consulted together to arrest Jesus by treachery and put him to death." They intend to do it secretly, because they fear the crowds.

One nearby village that Jesus seems to have frequented was Bethany. We're told that he was "in the house of Simon the leper," having a meal the night before Passover, when an unnamed woman approached him with an alabaster jar of costly perfumed oil and poured it on his head while they were reclining at table. The disciples were "indignant" and complained. While they were right to be concerned for the poor, as disciples their first concern should have been for Jesus and his mission. He told them earlier that he was about to be arrested and killed; no one is poorer than someone about to be executed.

"Why do you make trouble for the woman?" he asked his male disciples. Here we witness another aspect of Jesus's spectacular nonviolence: his radical feminism. When Jesus defends the unnamed woman, he directly rebukes the sexism of his male disciples. This is pure nonviolent revolution. In first-century Palestine, women were not considered equal to men. Jesus always treats women equally and risks his life to heal and liberate them. This defense of women is in effect an attack on patriarchy, yet it continues to be widely ignored by churchmen throughout the world today. Jesus's question should echo down through the centuries to every man stuck in systemic sexism. "Why do you make trouble for the woman?"

He goes on to explain the woman's good deed. "She has done a good thing for me. The poor you will always have with you, but you will not always have me. In pouring this perfumed oil upon my body, she did it to prepare me for burial." She is the first person to take seriously Jesus's word about his upcoming execution. She does not dismiss it, object to it, or ignore it. Unlike the male disciples, she accepts it and seeks to serve Jesus. So, she pours the expensive oil on his head and in doing so anoints him. This public action gives Jesus courage to go forward to his death in a spirit of dignity, holiness, and ever-deepening nonviolence. Decades later, John's Gospel will take this story further to show how Jesus adapted what the woman did for him. He will wash the feet of his disciples, not to model service but to anoint and prepare them for martyrdom, and will command them to anoint and prepare every disciple for our deaths in the holy spirit of nonviolence so that we can be part of Jesus's lineage. (See my book *Lazarus, Come Forth!*)

This nameless woman is one of the greatest figures in the Gospels. Her action far surpasses anything the male disciples ever do. That's why Jesus honors her by saying, "Amen, I say to you, wherever this gospel is proclaimed in the whole world, what she has done will be spoken of, in memory of her." The male writers, of course, do not name her, but they must have felt compelled to add this line because Jesus was adamant that she be remembered and honored.

I think this whole event must have challenged the male disciples' egos. They may have resented being chastised by Jesus. Remember they were "indignant" at her, and then Jesus sides with her. They were humiliated and had to swallow their pride to accept what Jesus was saying. Yes, they and we are called to serve the poor every day, but they and we need to serve Jesus as he gives his life in the nonviolent struggle for justice and peace. This will become ever more difficult in the hours to come until, instead, the disciples abandon him.

At this point in the story, Judas Iscariot leaves the community and begins the process of betrayal. I suggest that Judas Iscariot was the one who challenged Jesus about the wasteful expense of the women's oil used on Jesus. It makes sense to me that someone who is about to betray Jesus would attack Jesus with these words: "Why this waste? It could have been sold for much, and the money given to the poor." Judas doesn't care about the poor—and now we realize, he doesn't care about Jesus either. Jesus has just told them he is to be killed, and Judas calls this compassionate act by the woman toward Jesus "a waste." This would have been hurtful to Jesus. When he questions Judas, "Why do you make trouble for the woman?" Judas is humiliated. I submit this may have been the last straw for Judas, who was steaming mad and resentful, and so he immediately goes to the chief priests and tries to make money to hand Jesus over. "What are you willing to give me if I hand him over to you?" he asks them. "They paid him thirty pieces of silver," we're told, "and from that time on he looked for an opportunity to hand him over."

Without Judas's treachery, recent scholarship suggests, Jesus might have survived his nonviolent campaign in Jerusalem. In a certain way, his fame as a great prophet and respect among the crowds shielded him from possible public arrest. By hiding out at night in the countryside where the religious authorities would never go, he remained somewhat safe. He might have continued his daring attacks and public actions for weeks or months more, possibly even done civil disobedience against the Roman procurator. Judas Iscariot wrecked all Jesus's plans and paved the way for his speedy execution.

Passover arrives, and the disciples ask Jesus where he wants to hold the Passover meal. This is a nonviolent underground movement, and Jesus has connections that the others would not know about. "Go into the city to a certain man and tell him, 'The teacher says, "My appointed time draws near. I shall celebrate the Passover with my disciples in your house."'" So, they do, and that evening, Jesus joins them at the house for the Passover meal.

As they are eating, Jesus starts talking about betrayal. This is a critically important, though long neglected topic that needs greater attention in light of Jesus's teachings on nonviolence. Those who pursue radical Gospel nonviolence, who dare follow Jesus on the path when even the church supports war and nationalism and preaches a false spirituality of violence, I submit, will eventually be betrayed from within their Christian community. We hear such stories in the lives of so many Christian martyrs from Nazi Germany to El Salvador and Nicaragua to the Russian war on Ukraine, where Christians betray and kill fellow Christians. Just as nonviolent Christians will have to take up the cross to follow the nonviolent Jesus, as they share in the life, death, and resurrection of the nonviolent Jesus—they will also have to share in his betrayal.

"One of you will betray me," he tells them quietly. Deeply distressed at this announcement, the disciples begin to say to him one after another, "Surely it is not I, Lord?" He replies, "The one who has dipped his hand into the dish with me is the one who will betray me. The Son of Humanity indeed goes as it is written of him, but woe to that man by whom the Son of Humanity is betrayed. It would be better for that man if he had never been born." Even Judas tries to cover his tracks by asking, "Surely it is not I, Rabbi?" "You said it," Jesus answers.

Notice how none of the male disciples comfort Jesus when he announces that he will be killed, and likewise now, none of them comfort Jesus when he announces that he will be betrayed. Instead, they all speak about themselves. "It's not me, is it?" What should they have said? "Lord Jesus, we're so sorry! What can we do to help you? Tell us what you want us to do. We are here for you. How can we help you and comfort you? Let us protect you, or at least care for you." Jesus rarely gets the support he needs, which again makes the unnamed woman's anointing all the more remarkable. Lesson: from now on, stop focusing on yourself and instead try to support the nonviolent Jesus as he struggles for justice today.

As we ponder Judas Iscariot's betrayal of the nonviolent Jesus, and hear Jesus's comment that it would have been better had he not been born, we learn another lesson in Gospel nonviolence. Not only are we called to be nonviolent, but we are also called not to betray one another. This is difficult, but crucial. We don't want to continue the legacy of turning against sisters and brothers in Christ. We don't want to continue the sad history of letting the church be the place in which you get betrayed.

The New Covenant of Total Nonviolence (26:26–32)

At the Passover meal, Jesus does something shocking. He transforms the ancient Jewish ritual of the Passover meal to commemorate his own Passover, but in light of his visionary nonviolence, he uses it to announce God's new covenant of nonviolence. From now on, we will share that holy meal together and enter into the life and death of Jesus; but more, through our participation in this Passover meal, we pledge not to kill others but to lay down our lives for them. With this new covenant, he seals our participation in his methodology of sacrificial, loving nonviolence.

Jesus "took bread, said the blessing, broke it, and gave it to his disciples." With these simple acts, he offers the memorable words: "Take and eat; this is my body." Then he took a cup, gave thanks, gave it to them, and said, "Drink from it, all of you, for this is my blood of the covenant, which will be shed on behalf of many for the forgiveness of sins." For some two thousand years, Christians have broken bread and passed the cup to share in the life of Jesus. But, in light of the great sermon on nonviolence, it is possible that Christians have missed the entire point of Jesus's Passover meal.

If Jesus were a violent Messiah, come to save the chosen people, if he were to transform the Passover meal according to his wishes, what would he have said? He would have taken the bread and said, "Go break their bodies for me, like this." He would have taken the cup and said, "Go and shed their blood for me, like this." He would have used the bread and the wine to call upon his followers to join in his campaign of revolutionary violence to overthrow the Roman Empire and take over the world.

But Jesus takes the bread and says, "This is my body, broken for you. This is my blood, shed for you. Do this!" In other words, he transforms the Passover meal into his new covenant of nonviolence. Instead of killing to save humanity, he offers himself, his body and blood, and his followers, our bodies, our blood, for the sacrificial, nonviolent resistance and transformation of the human race. When we share in the bread and the cup of the Eucharist, in the body and blood of the nonviolent Jesus, we enter the methodology of the paschal mystery. We choose to give our lives for humanity instead of supporting the status quo of taking human lives and oppressing others for our comfort. The new covenant of nonviolence that Jesus initiates on the night he is arrested is the most important, most transformative, most crucial act in all of human history. Few people along the way have realized what he did or have chosen to enter his methodology.

"I tell you, from now on I shall not drink this fruit of the vine until the day when I drink it with you anew in the kingdom of my Father," Jesus says. They conclude by singing a hymn, and head out to their hideaway on the Mount of Olives. There he tells them bluntly, "This night all of you will have your faith in me shaken, for it is written: 'I will strike the shepherd, and the sheep of the flock will be dispersed'; but after I have been raised up, I shall go before you to Galilee." With this declaration, he tells his friends, "I know when they come for me, you will lose heart, be filled with fear, and abandon me, but I will be raised, and rejoin you in Galilee." Again, this is a disturbing pronouncement, yet, at the same time, he tries to give us hope by saying that he will rise and rejoin us.

"My Soul Is Sorrowful Even to Death. Remain Here and Keep Watch with Me" (26:33–46)

Peter tries to respond with concern, and he promises not to abandon Jesus. At least, he tries. "Though all may have their faith in you shaken, mine will never be," he pledges. It's one of the strongest pledges of fidelity in the Gospels, but Jesus can see that even the best of us have not understood or accepted what it really means to follow him. When push comes to shove, Peter will freeze. His faith will be more than shaken; it will abandon him, so he will abandon Jesus. "Amen, I say to you, this very night before the cock crows, you will deny me three times," Jesus says to him. What? He knows that when the threat of violence and death shows up in full force, Peter will flee, and then later deny even knowing Jesus. But Jesus has compassion on him, on them all, because he understands that he will be arrested as a revolutionary, and just knowing Jesus could be cause for their arrest and executions as well. What could Jesus have hoped for? That all Twelve would stand by him, nonviolently resist the Romans and the religious authorities, and say, "If you take him, you have to take me too"? Could Jesus have hoped that the Twelve would have been executed each on his own cross in solidarity with him? No, he knows they're not ready to lay down their lives nonviolently for him. But he also knows there's more to the story, and someday they might, and indeed, would.

"Even though I should have to die with you, I will not deny you," Peter declares. He insists that he will die for Jesus and never deny him. Again, at least he tries. Within minutes, however, while Jesus prays in agony, Peter falls asleep. He can't even stay awake with Jesus.

When they get to Gethsemane, Jesus instructs the disciples, "Sit here while I go over there and pray." He takes Peter, James, and John with him and begins to feel "sorrow and distress." Then he says the saddest words so far in the story: "My soul is sorrowful even to death. Remain here and keep watch with me." Jesus is consumed with grief. What should a devout nonviolent follower of Jesus do? Stay with him, be there with him, remain quiet and attentive, love and comfort him, and try to help in any way possible. Jesus went a little farther, fell prostrate in prayer, and said, "My Father, if it is possible, let this cup pass from me; yet, not as I will, but as you will." He turns to his beloved God, asks that the cup of suffering be taken away from him, but says, let me do your will, not mine. It may be the most important prayer ever uttered. Notice, his focus is entirely on God, to the point of solely doing God's will, which he does not fully understand and does not want to do. But by returning to God, he finds grace to live the prayer he taught in his great sermon: "Your will be done on earth as it is in heaven."

He returns to the disciples and finds them sound asleep. "So, you could not keep watch with me for one hour?" he asks Peter. A little while before, Peter pledged total solidarity and service to Jesus, and now while Jesus prays in agony, Peter sleeps soundly in the garden. "Watch and pray that you may not undergo the test," Jesus tells them. Watch and pray. Even now, as he faces imminent arrest and execution, he tries to teach his friends how to live the nonviolent life in the face of death: watch and pray. From now on, we readers know to keep watch like sentinels in the night, and to pray constantly. That is how we live into universal love and total nonviolence to our own deaths.

A second time he withdraws and prays again, "My Father, if it is not possible that this cup pass without my drinking it, your will be done!" When he returns, he finds them asleep again, "for they could not keep their eyes open." If your eyes are not open, then you cannot see, you cannot keep watch; in effect, you are blind. With this phrase Jesus sums up the condition of his disciples and all of us today. We cannot see, we remain blind, so we do not keep watch. The invitation is to wake up, open our eyes, see, and keep watch with the nonviolent Jesus.

A third time, he withdraws and prays, only to return later and find his disciples sound asleep. "Are you still sleeping and taking your rest?" This is a question addressed to every one of us. As Christ continues to be oppressed and killed around the world through poverty, war, and violence of every kind, we sleep tight and take our rest. He wants us to wake up and live out the nonviolent life that practices universal love so that poverty and wars cease and God's reign of peace dwells among us.

"Behold, the hour is at hand when the Son of Humanity is to be handed over to sinners," he announces. One way to understand the trajectory of Jesus's life is to realize that his whole journey was headed toward this hour. He knew this hour was coming, and all his years of practicing love and nonviolence led to this hour. He had walked toward this hour and willingly accepted it as the consequence of being who he was, the Beloved of God, the nonviolent Messiah come to save humanity from its slavery to violence and death. Notice how he practices what he preaches. Though he has prayed in agony, he remains calm, mindful, centered, nonviolent, even peaceful. He can do this because he turned to God in prayer.

"Get up, let us go. See, my betrayer is at hand." If they are sleeping, they are like the dead, so with these words, Jesus orders them to rise from the dead. Then he orders them to open their eyes and "see." He wants us all to "see" because he is looking for witnesses. An eyewitness is someone who takes the stand and tells what he saw: "I saw the Son of Humanity live in perfect nonviolence, even through his arrest and execution, and I saw that it is possible for the entire human race to become totally nonviolent."

"Put Your Sword Back into Its Sheath for All *Who Take the Sword Will Perish by the Sword" (26:47–56)*

Judas arrived with a large crowd of religious authorities and soldiers carrying swords and clubs. He walked over to Jesus and said, "Hail, Rabbi!"' and kissed him. Jesus was ordinary looking, no different from the other rag-tag Galileans. The soldiers would not know which one was the troublemaker, so Judas had arranged to identify Jesus by kissing him. It would have been common for men in this Mediterranean culture, and in Jesus's community, to offer one another a greeting of peace by kissing one another. But here, this intimate sign of friendship and affection is betrayed as well and used against Jesus. More, notice how Judas mocks Jesus as if he were Caesar, a king, saying "Hail, Rabbi!" Later, the Roman soldiers will mock and torture Jesus, likewise pretending he is a king. This shows us that Judas was completely on the side of the Romans and the authorities. He was no friend of the nonviolent Jesus.

Yet Jesus responds by calling him friend. Judas is now Jesus's enemy, persecutor, and betrayer, but Jesus addresses him without anger, resentment, bitterness, or hatred—only grief, love, and compassion. Jesus already mourns Judas because Jesus understands the spiritual consequences of Judas's violence, even though Judas does not. "Friend, do what you have come for," he tells Judas. Jesus accepts that his hour is at hand, and he lets go of all control of the situation. Instead of defending himself, fighting back, or putting up a show of power and protest, he surrenders nonviolently. And so, the soldiers come forward, grab Jesus, and arrest him.

In response, one of the disciples draws a sword and cuts off the ear of the high priest's servant. Only John's Gospel names this disciple as none other than Peter. Think for a moment: Peter had endless days of retreats on nonviolence, teachings on nonviolence, and the living example of the nonviolent Jesus. But, faced with the threat of violence, he responds with violence. It was like he hadn't heard a word Jesus said. That is exactly the way most Christians act today. At best, we might admire Jesus's teachings on love and peace, but when faced with danger, we would quickly strike with the sword, pull out a gun, raise an army, drop a bomb, or nuke the planet. We remain deaf to Jesus's teachings on nonviolence.

And what good did the disciple's violence do? So he cut off the ear of a slave; this individual wasn't even one of the ruling authorities, or soldiers. He was a victim, too. Jesus knew this instinctively and tried to stop the violence, knowing it would only bring harm to the poor. "Put your sword back into its sheath," Jesus said, "for all who take the sword will perish by the sword." This is one of the laws of nature, which Jesus teaches again even as he goes to his death. Those who live by violence will die by violence. Violence in response to violence only leads to further violence. It cannot bring peace and never will bring peace. It's futile and fatal. If you try to kill someone, in a world where everyone is brainwashed by violence to retaliate with further violence, they will respond by trying to kill you, and you'll both die. Instead, do not try to kill anyone, and people will not try to kill you. Jesus wants the violence and the killing to stop. He continues until his last breath to train his followers—and the rest of humanity—in creative nonviolence as a way of life.

More importantly, these words are the final words of Jesus to his disciples, to the church, before they all abandon him. "Put your sword back." In other translations, "Put down the sword," or "Put up the sword." After all he has taught and shown them about the universal way of nonviolence, he now resorts to the most primal teaching: *Put down the sword. Thou shalt not kill.* We are back to square one. I imagine the disciples looking at him in utter shock as they realize for the first time that he is deadly serious about his nonviolence, that he is not going to defend himself with further violence, and that they are never again allowed to use violence under any circumstances for whatever reason, no matter how noble the cause. For Jesus, the days of violence are over. We are not allowed to kill.

Jesus has many options, but he refuses to use them. He will be human and nonviolent. "Do you think that I cannot call upon my Father and he will not provide me at this moment with more than twelve legions of angels? But then how would the scriptures be fulfilled which say that it must come to pass in this way?" A Roman legion was two thousand troops; if twenty-four thousand angels suddenly appeared in the Garden of Gethsemane, everyone there would have a heart attack and die. It would be like a scene out of *The Lord of the Rings*. But Jesus refuses to play God, to act differently, to be extraordinary in his power. He chooses to be humble and human. And the disciples, understanding now that violence is out of the question, run away.

"Have you come out as against a robber, with swords and clubs to seize me?" he says to the religious authorities and soldiers. "Day after day I sat teaching in the temple area, yet you did not arrest me. But all this has come to pass that the writings of the prophets may be fulfilled." With that, "all the disciples left him and fled."

It's important to ponder why they fled. Put yourself in their position. They were scared to death of being arrested and killed along with Jesus. Their fear took over their faith, whereas Jesus's faith was preeminent and gave him the courage to trust God and God's way of non-violence, even in the face of impending death. The disciples probably ran away on instinct, without even thinking, without realizing what they were doing to Jesus. Remember, these men would have witnessed Roman brutality over a lifetime of living in the region. We would do the same thing. In fact, most of us would never put ourselves in such a situation—out late at night, associating with a known revolutionary, in hiding, underground, avoiding the authorities for fear of being arrested. This whole scenario resembles Black South Africans during apartheid, or church workers at the time of El Salvador's brutal war, or Black southerners in Mississippi hunted down at night by the Klansmen in the 1940s and 1950s. With this context in mind, we can see the infinite compassion of Jesus for his friends. Earlier he had even affirmed to them: "The spirit is willing but the flesh is weak."

Jesus is completely abandoned. He is arrested and led away by soldiers. In addition to feeling the emotions stirred up by this treatment, Jesus suffers the wound of a follower betraying him and the rest of his friends leaving him to suffer alone. Nevertheless, he turns to God in prayer and surrenders his will, heart, mind, and soul to God, so that while he is being manhandled, interiorly he is focused solely on God his beloved Father.

"From Now on You Will See the Son of Humanity Seated at the Right Hand of Power" (26:57–27:26)

He's taken to the palace of Caiaphas the high priest, where all the scribes, the elders, and the Sanhedrin are gathered and begin to make accusations against Jesus. Many "false witnesses" tell lies about him. When the high priest demands an answer from Jesus, he remains silent. Here we see Jesus use another form of communication: silence. As you enter the scene, you realize that Jesus is the judge and everyone else in the high priest's palace is on trial.

"I order you to tell us under oath before the living God whether you are the Messiah, the Son of God," the interrogator declares. "You said it," Jesus answers. "From now on you will see 'the Son of Humanity seated at the right hand of the Power' and 'coming on the clouds of heaven.'" With this statement, Matthew invokes the apocalyptic imagery of the prophet Daniel to speak of the power of the Christ. He is in chains and about to be executed but announces that they will see him at the seat of Power. Though totally powerless and vulnerable, he speaks of being with the power of God. While this talk would have been understood as blasphemous, if not downright insanity, we know what Jesus means. In light of the great sermon, Jesus says he is the fullest human expression of the power of love, compassion, and nonviolence; and therefore he is one with the God of peace, which is the only real power, the power of universal love and total nonviolence. As St. Paul will explain famously in his letter to the Philippians, Jesus emptied himself of power, humbled himself in total nonviolence, and, in doing so, was crushed by the principalities and powers of the world. Yet, because he is with the power of God, he will overcome the empire, its militaries, all violence, and even death itself. They cannot grasp what he is talking about, but after two thousand years, with the examples of great apostles like Gandhi and Dr. King, perhaps we are beginning to understand. Nonviolence calls for humbling ourselves and doing only God's will, and while we may be dismissed by the world as useless, incompetent failures, we are actually participating in the power of God who is disarming and transforming the world through our nonviolent actions, resistance, and grassroots movements.

"He has blasphemed!" the high priest shouts as he tears his robes. "What further need have we of witnesses?" They were false witnesses, probably paid to lie about Jesus. "You have now heard the blasphemy; what is your opinion?" Matthew aims this question at the reader as well as the assembly: What is our opinion of Jesus as he stands accused, powerless, in chains, and talking about being in the power of God? Whose side do we take? Where are we in the story? Have we fled like the disciples, or do we condemn Jesus like the religious authorities, or dare we seek to live out the power of his way and so one day stand at his side?

"He deserves to die!" they shout. They spit in his face and strike him, while some slap him, saying, "Prophesy for us, Messiah: who is it that struck you?"

Why do they hate Jesus so much? Why are they so intent on killing him? The scene is like out of the Nazi trials of Sophie Scholl and the White Rose resisters in Munich; or the Salvadoran death squads on the hunt to kill the four U.S. church women or the six Jesuit priests, their housekeeper, and her daughter; or the white racist Ku Klux Klansmen over the past two centuries who hunted down, tortured, and killed Black men in the rural South. In the end, violence has consumed them and turned them into zombies of death. I use such talk to wake us up to the horrors that the nonviolent Jesus faced and that continue today. When people are consumed by violence and militarism, they forget who they are; they have no understanding of themselves as beloved sons and daughters of God, and so they lose their humanity and do inhuman things. This is what happened to everyone in history who killed others and waged war: they lost their humanity, their true selves. The nonviolent Jesus offers the best example of anyone in history who held on to his calling to be God's beloved, and thus retained his humanity even in the face of the most horrific torture and cruelty. This is why in his great sermon he announces that peacemakers are sons and daughters of God;

this is the vocation of every human being, to be God's son or daughter, which means to be a peacemaker. If we are given over to violence, killing, and war, we lose our identities and become inhuman. The Gospel invites us to become as totally nonviolent as Jesus and to remain steadfast in our nonviolence, even in the face of violence and death.

It's as if his peaceful presence of peace brings out all the violence within us, especially among the powerful, the ruling elite, and those with the authority to kill. Jesus exposes our addiction to violence and death. It's almost as if he has to suck out all the violence from the authorities in order to heal them, as someone would suck out the poison from a snake bite, and spit it out, in order to heal the victim.

"He deserves to die!" The ruling religious authorities denounce Jesus for claiming to be one with God, and therefore for blaspheming. According to their law, this is a capital crime deserving of capital punishment. Such a crime threatens their entire structure of power and authority. They cannot have anyone running around healing the sick, teaching an alternative spirituality, and doing civil disobedience in their institution, without running the risk of the system collapsing. The status quo is threatened by this harmless, nonviolent vagabond, and because they are men of violence, they know only one way to deal with Jesus: kill him. And do it in the name of God.

Notice especially that these are the highest religious authorities in the land, and what do they do to this poor, powerless, unarmed man? They spit in his face, strike him, and slap him. These use terrible violence on him. All the while they mock him as if he were a prophet or the Messiah. When they taunt him saying, "Who is it that struck you?" they reveal, among other things, their complete lack of understanding of the holy prophets or even prophecy itself. They think it means predicting the future or some other kind of magic trick, as most people do today, when it means speaking truth to power in the name of God.

While this horror is unfolding in the high priest's palace, Peter has made his way into the grand courtyard and is sitting there, outside, among the servants, listening to the attacks on Jesus. One by one, people begin to recognize him as a Galilean, as one of the blasphemers' supporters. And instance by instance, he denies it, "I do not know what you are talking about!" he says. "I do not know the man." Finally, he begins to curse and swear and repeat his "innocence": "I do not know the man." As the cock crows, Peter suddenly remembers that Jesus foretold that he would deny him three times before the cock crows, and Peter "went out and began to weep bitterly."

Peter considered himself as the greatest and most faithful of the disciples. In later years, he must have received acclaim and praise from the early Christians who sought him out. By then, Peter had learned many hard lessons, and he clearly set the story straight. He passed on his failures for all the world to know and, in doing so, showed us not only how hard it is to follow Jesus all the way on the path of nonviolence, but that acknowledging and repenting of our failure is part of the journey, too. He sat comfortably in the courtyard while Jesus was mocked, struck, and spat on, and he did nothing. Further, he vehemently denied even knowing Jesus and swore up and down that he did not know the man. Just a few hours before he had pledged to die for Jesus; now he went out and wept bitterly over his betrayal, his total lack of faithfulness. As we ponder Peter's experience, we learn to feel compassion for him, as Jesus had compassion for him, and then we realize that Jesus has compassion for each of us. Nonetheless, we are summoned to walk with Jesus all the way and give our lives as he did in the nonviolent struggle for justice and peace.

In the morning, the authorities gathered again and made a plan to have Jesus executed. They had him bound, led away, and handed over to the Roman governor, Pilate. Here, Matthew inserts a brief story about the fate of the betrayer. He writes how Judas saw that Jesus had been condemned to death and "deeply regretted what he had done." He returned the silver to the religious authorities, saying, "I have sinned in betraying innocent blood." He threw the money into the temple and went off and hanged himself. His self-hatred and inner violence consumed him. Once again, we see how violence destroys everyone's life—the chief priests, the religious authorities, Peter, and Judas—and leads them to do harm, whereas Jesus's nonviolence allows him to maintain his innocence, his truth, his faith, and his power. Jesus is the only person in the story who has true stability of faith and character.

The chief priests collect the money and, suddenly feeling devout and pious, declare that it is not lawful to deposit this money into the temple treasury, "for it is the price of blood." So they use it to buy a field as a burial place for foreigners, thus fulfilling, we're told, the prophecy of Jeremiah. (Matthew uses this reference to show how the story of the nonviolent Jesus continues to fulfill the scriptures, although there is not an actual passage in Jeremiah that describes such a burial field.) Notice how the chief priests and religious officials mock, torture, and hand someone over to be killed but try to follow the letter of the law whenever it comes to money.

"Are you the king of the Jews?" Pilate asks Jesus. "You said it," he answers. Again, the chief priests and elders make charges against him, but after that one line, we're told that Jesus remains silent. These painful attacks and interrogations would have lasted for hours, and for nearly the entire time, Jesus said nothing. Even Pilate, we're told, is amazed at his silence. This is important to ponder. He did not plead for his life or make a long speech. Matthew and the other evangelists portray Jesus as the true judge, like a judge during a trial who watches and listens to everyone.

Next Matthew explains how the governor each year would release any prisoner that the crowd called for. A violent revolutionary named Barabbas, who would have killed Roman soldiers, was being held. Pilate asks the crowd which one they wanted him to release—Barabbas or Jesus "called Messiah." Matthew adds that he said this "because he knew that it was out of envy that they had handed him over." This clue adds another dimension to our understanding of the religious authorities' hatred toward Jesus: they are envious because he is popular, he teaches with authority, he gathers followers, and he can heal people; deep down they must wonder if maybe he really is the Messiah. Envy breeds violence in our hearts and can lead to murder and war. Nonviolence requires letting go of our selfish desires such as envy, anger, fear, or distrust and maintaining inner peace through prayer and trust in God. But the religious authorities, along with Pilate, were too concerned about maintaining their systems to consider what their hatred was doing to them.

The religious authorities stir up the crowds to call for Barabbas and "to destroy Jesus." "Let him be crucified!" they chant. Pilate's wife sends a message urging him not to have anything to do with Jesus, that she had a terrible nightmare about him. So, Pilate dramatically washes his hands and says, "I am innocent of this man's blood. Look to it yourselves." The crowd shouts back, "His blood be upon us and upon our children." Pilate released Barabbas, has Jesus whipped and tortured, and sends him over to be crucified.

We can infer here the controversy between Matthew's community and the Pharisees of his day, but this text does not blame the Jews for the death of Jesus. With the line from Pilate declaring his innocence over the case of Jesus, we might even begin to feel sympathy for him. Don't be fooled: Pilate ordered the execution of Jesus. The whole proceeding, in the end, was the work of the Roman Empire executing someone who was a threat to the local powers, and therefore to Rome. Pilate is not innocent. No one is innocent here, except the nonviolent Jesus. Everyone but Jesus is guilty, and through Jesus's steadfast nonviolent resistance, he begins the fall of empire, even the end of death itself.

"My God, My God, Why Have You Forsaken Me?" (27:27–66)

Earlier, the religious authorities mocked and tortured Jesus. Now Roman soldiers take their turn. It is critically important to understand that when the Roman governor entered Jerusalem for the feast days, he marched in on his warhorse in a big military parade with his cohort—which was composed of six hundred armed Roman soldiers. They made a show of force each year to impress upon the local population the total control of the empire over the holy city and its surroundings. That's why Jesus's riding in on a donkey and offering an image of peace and nonviolence is so striking; it was the complete opposite of the imperial parade and the emperor's representative riding a warhorse.

Inside the Roman governor's headquarters, Jesus is taken into a massive stone hall and surrounded by the six hundred Roman soldiers. It is easy to presume that they were bored to death, and perhaps even drunk, like the death squads of El Salvador, who were often bored, so they drank and did drugs until the time came for them to torture the innocent poor. The Roman soldiers strip Jesus so that he is naked, then throw a scarlet military cloak around him. Then they make "a crown of thorns" and put it on his head and place a reed in his right hand. Then they kneel before him, mock him, spit upon him, hit him with the reed, and shout, "Hail, King of the Jews!" Six hundred men crowd in and abuse him, mock him, and make fun of him as if he were a king. They must have laughed hard because this skinny wretch from the outback was about as far from being a king as anyone could possibly be.

Here the nonviolent Jesus stands mocked before the violence of the world, before the Roman Empire and its soldiers. He is mocked as a king and messiah, and he suffers their humiliations, abuse, and torture. In this scene, it's as if he stands before the armies, militaries, empires, and rulers of the world down through the ages. He is innocent as a lamb and is led to the slaughter. We have no sign that he got angry, fought back, retaliated, mocked them in return, cussed them out, or renounced his faith in God. With this scene, we see the full power of nonviolence confronting the Roman Empire. They mock him, attack him, and prepare to kill him, but he lets them. He is the one with real power and authority, not them. By maintaining nonviolence in the face of their violence, Jesus reveals that he is the strongest person there. He would have been clinging in interior prayer to his beloved God and even praying for these his persecutors, as he instructed us to do in his great sermon.

Afterwards, they lead him through the city. A Cyrenian named Simon is forced to carry

Jesus's cross. They take him to Golgotha and offer him wine, which he refuses to drink. He accepts suffering, but earlier he had said he would not drink again until he was in the fullness of the kingdom. They strip him naked, nail him to a cross, and raise it up on the wooden scaffold for the crowd to see. Crucifixion was a form of deterrent—capital punishment for those who would engage in violent revolution, a public display of torture and a slow, agonizing death that would terrorize the population so it would not support the violent rebels or engage in any resistance to the empire or its local ruling authorities. The soldiers cast lots for his clothes, fulfilling the text of Psalm 22, and they place a placard over his head, "This is Jesus, the King of the Jews." Two violent revolutionaries are crucified with Jesus, one on either side of him, so Jesus goes to his death mistaken as a violent revolutionary like them. He never killed or harmed anyone, yet he was legally tortured and executed as if he had.

Next, we're told about the passersby, those who walked by the torture and execution of Jesus. Imagine: they walk by, look up and see this naked man covered in his blood, and start mocking him. Their charge against him is instructive and brings the Gospel full circle: "If you are the Son of God, come down from the cross." They challenge his identity!

The story began with Jesus's revelation by the Jordan River that he was the beloved Son of God. He claimed that as his core identity and recognized that this identity meant a vocation of universal love and nonviolence, and so he rejected every temptation to violence and worldly power during his fast in the wilderness, temptations that tried to get him to prove he was the Son of God. Then in the great sermon, he taught us the way of nonviolence, saying that we make peace because we are all the beloved sons and daughters of the God who makes peace; we practice universal love because we are all the beloved sons and daughters of God. Each step of the way, Jesus clung to his fundamental identity and thus remained faithful to the God of peace and universal love. In the Garden of Gethsemane, he prayed hard to remain faithful to this vocation, saying, "Not my will but your will be done." Now, hanging on the cross, covered in blood, in agony, slowly suffocating, he is taunted because of his true identity. Just as the devil challenged him three times in the wilderness, saying, "If you are the son of God," these bystanders channel the devil by repeating his taunt, "If you are the son of God, prove it! Come down from the cross and we will believe you!"

At the heart of nonviolence is the question of our identity. Gospel nonviolence requires first that we accept our vocations to be the beloved sons and daughters of the God of peace and universal love, as Jesus taught in his great sermon. We then recognize every human being as our very brother and sister, and so we could never harm or kill anyone, or wage war, or be silent in the face of anyone's suffering. The minute we forget our true identities, we give ourselves over to the culture of violence and mindlessness. We forget that others are our brothers and sisters, and, before you know it, we are marginalizing, oppressing, and killing them. People of nonviolence claim their true identities and suffer through every attack upon their nonviolence. They also try to affirm every other human being's true identity as a beloved son or daughter of the God of peace. It is a lifelong mission that the nonviolent Jesus has called us to.

Here, in the minutes before his excruciating death, he shows us the depths of his fidelity, suffering endless attacks on all his claims about God and his identity as God's Son, and therefore, on his teachings that we can all become God's beloved sons and daughters. The attacks upon him are overwhelming, yet again, let me point out clearly, even though I am a broken record, Jesus does not show any sign of anger or hostility; he does not curse anyone or condemn them. He suffers in silence, as the judge and the king of nonviolence that he is.

The end of the world has come. The apocalypse he foretold is here. At noon, darkness covers the land. There is no sun, the world is now in complete darkness, until three o'clock. Then Jesus cries out in a loud voice, "My God, my God, why have you forsaken me?" What could be worse than this? Jesus is forsaken by God; is he now going to abandon his faith in God?

Not at all. Every devout Jewish Christian of Matthew's day would have immediately recognized these words as the opening line of Psalm 22. This intense psalm begins with the cry of a tortured person who feels abandoned and rejected by God as he goes to his unjust death but evolves into a hymn of hope and praise, knowing that God is there with him, that God is trustworthy, and that he will live on with God. It is one of the most amazing pieces of writing in all literature. Over the course of its verses, the tortured person announces that all will be well, the poor and the faithful will be cared for, and he shall live on in God's house, where everyone will praise God forever. Beginning with these words of apparent abandonment and hopelessness on the lips of Jesus, Matthew notes that Jesus is still focused on God, even as he suffers and feels God's absence. With this psalm of all psalms, Matthew hints that inside Jesus, he continues to trust God, praise God, and see that soon he will live on with God and lead the vast assembly in praise. With this psalm, Matthew points out that in the midst of his agony, Jesus looks toward the new life of resurrection.

And so, we hear in Psalm 22 (verses 7–9, 17–19) a description of Jesus's crucifixion and attacks from the passersby:

> I am a worm, not a man, scorned by men, despised by the people.
> All who see me mock me; they curl their lips and jeer; they shake their heads at me:
> "He relied on the LORD—let him deliver him; if he loves him, let him rescue him."
> A pack of evildoers closes in on me. They have pierced my hands and my feet. I can count all my bones. They stare at me and gloat. They divide my garments among them; for my clothing they cast lots.

Matthew has just described this horror for us, showing us how Jesus is the fulfillment of the scriptures, but we know the rest of the psalm. Following Matthew's lead, we read on and know that Psalm 22 (verses 20–30) turns into a plea to God for deliverance and then promise to praise God before all the world and fulfill his vows to God that all the nations of the world will turn to God and bow low before God. It's a spectacular turnaround that leads to an ecstatic vision of hope and fulfillment in God:

> But you, LORD, do not stay far off;
>   my strength, come quickly to help me.
> Deliver my soul from the sword,
>   my life from the grip of the dog.
> Save me from the lion's mouth,
>   my poor life from the horns of wild bulls.

Then I will proclaim your name to my brethren;
    in the assembly I will praise you:
"You who fear the Lord, give praise!
    All descendants of Jacob, give honor;
    show reverence, all descendants of Israel!
For he has not spurned or disdained
    the misery of this poor wretch,
Did not turn away from me,
    but heard me when I cried out.
I will offer praise in the great assembly;
    my vows I will fulfill before those who fear him.
The poor will eat their fill;
    those who seek the Lord will offer praise.
    May your hearts enjoy life forever!"
All the ends of the earth
    will remember and turn to the Lord.
All the families of nations
    will bow low before him.

With this renewed feeling of trust, hope, and praise, the crucified one gives his political analysis about God. God alone is the king of the world, the ruler of the nations: not Caesar, not Pilate, not Herod, nor their armies or weapons. Because God is a God of peace and love, God will raise up the faithful, and one day all the faithful will kneel before the living God of peace. To go from being mocked, tortured, and crucified, from inner despair and ultimate rejection, to such faith, hope, and ecstatic vision shows the triumphant resurrection of the nonviolent Jesus:

Kingship belongs to the Lord,
    the ruler over the nations.
All who sleep in the earth
    will bow low before God.
All who have gone down into the dust
    will kneel in homage.
And I will live for the Lord,
    my descendants will serve you.
The generation to come will be told of the Lord,
    that they may proclaim to a people yet unborn
    the deliverance you have brought. (verses 29–32)

Finally, we're told that "Jesus cried out in a loud voice and gave up his spirit." One of the many horrors of crucifixion is that you do not die from the agony or wounds or blood loss but from suffocation. Since you are nailed to a board and quickly lose any and all strength, your body falls due to its own weight, bringing further agony. In the process, you don't have the strength to breathe in air, and you slowly suffocate to death. Jesus knew this and felt this. He was also smart and committed to his mission of calling humanity back to God, even until his last breath. I submit that the nonviolent Jesus was always trying to do whatever he could that was humanly possible to wake up humanity. So, as he entered the last few seconds of his life, he undertook one last nonviolent action on behalf of humanity. Instead of quietly dying, he forced himself to take one big breath. The minute he did this, his life would end. With that one big breath of air in his lungs, he cried out in a loud voice. As he did this, all the oxygen in his lungs left his body and he died. By doing this, he offered one last form of communication for the whole human race: a loud cry of one being executed. This last nonviolent act calls us to reflect and meditate. It's Jesus's one last attempt to wake us up to the reality of suffering humanity and to convert us to his way of nonviolence and love.

As Jesus undergoes his crucifixion and death, he moves into solidarity with all humanity, but first of all the poor, the oppressed, and those who are killed by others, especially by the military establishment. In his universal love and compassion, he identifies with every dying human being in history and becomes one with them. In his loud cry, he calls out to the rest of us to stop the killings, stop the wars, stop the executions, and stop all violence. The loud cry is intended to be heard. If we do not hear it, and if we are not moved and cut to the heart and converted by that, what hope is there for us to be disarmed and become people of compassion and nonviolence like him? His loud cry continues today in the cry of all those being killed in war, by unjust disease and poverty, by starvation and racism, by gun violence and execution. Their loud cries are the ongoing loud cry of the crucified, nonviolent Jesus, calling us to put down the sword, disarm our hearts, and join his campaign to disarm the world and welcome God's new reign.

Notice, too, that Matthew chooses the words "gave up his spirit," to describe Jesus's death. With these words, Matthew says Jesus was still in control and consciously surrendered to God and God's will of nonviolent suffering love as the way to peace with God. With these words, we realize that Jesus perfectly fulfilled his mission and remained faithful to the way of nonviolence to the end. Likewise, even in his final act, he teaches us how to die well, not with weapons or anger or a sense of vengeance or a desire for retaliation, but with total trust in the God of peace and total surrender into the vast unknown of death, and, therefore, into God.

All hell breaks loose. Matthew reports that the veil of the sanctuary is torn in two from top to bottom, signaling the end of unjust, institutionalized, status-quo, money-making, empire-supporting religion. It not only foretells the destruction of the temple but also heralds a new day when every human being now has free access to God, not just the ruling authorities who control the holy of holies. An earthquake shakes the land, rocks are split, tombs are opened, holy people who had died appear to many around Jerusalem, and lo and behold, the Roman soldiers, not just the centurion, recognize the crucified Jesus as the Son of God.

Matthew also notes that "there were many women there, looking on from a distance, who had followed Jesus from Galilee, ministering to him. Among them were Mary Magdalene and Mary the mother of James and Joseph, and the mother of the sons of Zebedee." By honoring the presence of these women at the cross of Jesus, and their faithfulness and ministry to him since far back in Galilee, and by giving us their names, Matthew is also describing the end of patriarchy and sexism. Jesus's radical nonviolent feminism, his defense of women, and his illegal association and friendship with women have proved true and right.

The women emerge from the narrative as the true righteous people of their generation—far greater than Pilate, the Roman soldiers, the appalling male religious leaders, and even the male disciples who are nowhere to be seen. It is the women, and there are many of them, who are the faithful disciples, who live out Jesus's great sermon. Some scholars have suggested that no male disciple could have gone near Golgotha because they would have been arrested and executed as a comrade of Jesus, but no one would have cared about the presence of several crying women. They were not considered a threat to the empire or the male soldiers. Still, they ministered to Jesus every step of the way, according to Matthew, and they continued all the way to Golgotha, and witnessed his horrific suffering, something that few would choose to do. They did not turn away from suffering and pain; they stayed with the one who endured suffering, agony, and death, and they reached the greatest heights of compassion by standing near the one who was suffering. Keep in mind the shame that would have hung all around this scene; Jesus has been executed as an enemy of the state, and any loved ones brave enough to attend would be looked upon with scorn, might even suffer verbal abuse from others. But Jesus does not die alone; his women friends are with him, and that would have been a great help and encouragement.

One last key point about the women at the cross. Three are named: we know about Mary Magdalene, who was a devout follower, and Mrs. Zebedee, mother of James and John, two of Jesus's closest friends. She had previously asked Jesus if her sons could sit at his right and his left in the kingdom. She now sees him die with violent revolutionaries at his right and his left. But who is this "Mary the mother of James and Joses"? Many scholars are now concluding that this is Jesus's mother, Mary. Earlier in chapter 13 (verse 55), when the village of Nazareth rejected Jesus outright, one of the complaints was, in effect, "Who does this guy think he is? Isn't he the son of Joseph the carpenter? Don't we know his mother Mary and his brothers James, Joses, Simon and Judas, and his sisters [who are not named]?" By describing this "Mary" as the "mother of James and Joses," we know this is Mary the mother of Jesus, who has now become a faithful disciple like the other women. Matthew does not give her any special designation of reverence; rather he lists her as one of the faithful holy women. In doing so, he shows how every woman and man has to undergo a similar journey of transformation to become a true, albeit ordinary, disciple of Jesus by walking his path all the way to the end, to Golgotha.

Finally, Matthew's denouement features the story of a rich man from Arimathea named Joseph who is a disciple of Jesus. Joseph goes to Pilate, requests the body of Jesus, receives it, wraps it in clean linen, and puts it in his new tomb that he has hewn in a rock. Then he rolls a huge stone across the entrance to the tomb and departs. This is late in the afternoon that Friday, just as the sabbath is beginning. We're also told that Mary Magdalene "and the other Mary" (referring probably to Mary the mother of Jesus) "remained sitting there, facing the tomb." Notice how the women are the first disciples to do what Jesus commanded: they keep watch.

And so, the stage is set for what follows.

But not quite. Matthew adds a coda. The next day, the chief priests and the Pharisees go to see Pilate, show him reverence, and tell him that Jesus promised to rise from the dead after three days. "Order that the grave be secured until the third day," they ask the Roman procurator, "in case his disciples come and steal the body and then start saying, 'He has been raised from the dead.'" This would make the situation even worse than before, they state. So Pilate gives them the Roman guard and tells them, "Go ahead and secure it as best you can." What do they do? They secure the tomb, place Roman soldiers next to it to guard it, and put the imperial seal on the stone, saying, "We killed you, you're dead, now stay there! We order you, in the name of Caesar, to stay dead!"

Alas for soldiers, emperors, rulers, religious hypocrites, and all those who commit violence and wage war. They do not understand the truth of reality: death does not get the last word. Life always wins out, even if just by a slight edge.

Break Out! The Civil Disobedience Continues: The Illegal Resurrection of the Nonviolent Jesus (28:1–20)

All four Gospels report that on the first day of the week, a group of women went to the tomb and found it empty. John and Luke give detailed stories of the risen Jesus. In Mark's account, the shortest of the four, an angel at the empty tomb tells the women to have all the disciples meet Jesus back in Galilee. They take off running, frightened out of their wits, and the risen Jesus never appears.

Matthew emphasizes the drama of his resurrection account by beginning with an earthquake and describing the resurrection's political implications as an ongoing illegal threat to the empire and the law. For Matthew, if the execution of the nonviolent Jesus was meticulously legal, then the resurrection was just as illegal. The prisoner has escaped his punishment and legal custody in the tomb of death and his civil disobedience continues! The nonviolent Jesus is alive and well, on the loose, out roaming the countryside. He's gone underground all over again to stir up trouble for the culture of violence, war, and death. His illegal, underground campaign of active nonviolence and resistance to empire and the forces of death continues to this day.

Matthew's Gospel alone tells the details of the Roman guard who stood by the tomb, as well as the imperial seal placed on the rock so that everyone would know for sure that the Romans have killed Jesus and that Jesus is therefore officially dead. The message, as Daniel Berrigan wryly once pointed out, is, "We killed you, now you're dead, so stay dead."

Alas, even in death, Jesus disobeys the empire. Matthew's account announces that Jesus has risen from the dead and gone ahead to meet the disciples in Galilee. Matthew expands Mark's short narrative to emphasize Jesus's power over the empire and death itself, and so to highlight the triumph of nonviolence. With that, he affirms the great sermon on nonviolence and concludes his Gospel with the risen Jesus meeting his disciples back on the mountain in Galilee and missioning them to make disciples of all the nations, to teach every human being in the world the commandments of his great sermon, and thus to give their lives for the coming of God's reign of peace, love, and nonviolence on earth.

If Jesus has risen from the dead, as Matthew testifies, then all bets are off. Everything Jesus said and taught in the great sermon and throughout his life was true, and works, and is now proven right. Jesus's way is the only way to survive, transform, and overcome the forces of death. Those who live by the sword die by the sword, he said. Now we know that the opposite is true: those who do not live by the sword live, and live on forever. With the resurrection of the nonviolent Jesus, we too return to Galilee, hear the great sermon again, commit ourselves to practice Jesus's radical way, and start all over again on the journey of nonviolent resistance to the empire and in permanent proclamation of God's coming reign of peace.

Matthew begins by placing Mary Magdalene and the other Mary (possibly Jesus's mother) at the tomb as the sun rises on the first day of the week. Suddenly there is a great earthquake. Then, even scarier, an angel descends from heaven, approaches the tomb, rolls the stone all the way back, reveals the empty tomb, and sits on the stone. Matthew reports that his appearance was "like lightning and his clothing was white as snow." With this lightning suddenly shining from east to west (as we were told about previously), and the earthquake, and the empty tomb, the end of the world as we know it has happened, and a cosmic shift has occurred. Death does not get the last word. The way of nonviolence has won. History will never be the same.

"Do not be afraid," the angel tells the terrified women. "I know that you are seeking Jesus the crucified. He is not here, for he has been raised just as he said. Come and see the place where he lay. Then go quickly and tell his disciples, 'He has been raised from the dead, and he is going before you to Galilee; there you will see him.' Behold, I have told you." The angel comforts the women, acknowledges that they are here to see the crucified one, and announces that he has been raised from the dead and has gone to Galilee as he said he would. He then sends them on a mission: go and announce the resurrection of the nonviolent Jesus to his disciples.

Note: none of the four Gospels testifies that any of the male disciples was there with the women that Sunday morning at the tomb. That is why it is so important to note that women, and only women, are witnesses of the resurrection. Women, and only women, are apostles of resurrection. Women were the ones sent to announce the resurrection to the male disciples and the world. They are still trying to tell us men today that Jesus is alive and well, and we will meet him if we return to where he started and carry on his grassroots movement of transforming nonviolence.

This is the greatest honor given to any disciple, and Matthew says it went to two women named Mary. He adds that they ran quickly from the tomb, "fearful yet overjoyed." Along the way, they met the risen Jesus. Immediately they knelt before him, embraced his feet, and did him homage. They showed total devotion, love, joy, awe, and adoration. Like the angel, Jesus told them not to be afraid and sent them again on the mission to tell the male disciples to go to Galilee where they will see him. They obey him, and set off to tell the male disciples.

Meanwhile, Matthew tells us of the soldiers back at the tomb. They too must have been terrified. They return to the city, tell the chief priests that the body is missing, and are paid off by the authorities to tell everyone that Jesus's body was stolen by the disciples during the night. The religious authorities promise to protect them from Pilate, in case he makes trouble for them. Matthew concludes that this is the story that continues to circulate at the time of his writing. This story sounds reasonable, because who would believe that someone has risen from the dead, especially an executed revolutionary who broke through the seal of the Roman Empire? No one.

Matthew's account is brief, like Mark's, but he adds a final commission. The eleven disciples return to the mountain in Galilee. "When they saw him," Matthew notes, "they worshiped, but they doubted." The women never showed any signs of doubt. Their loving devotion made them true believers and, as such, true witnesses and true apostles. The men meet the risen Jesus but do not really believe it's him, that he is risen. Perhaps they too are scared, because they know that if it's true, then an executed martyr is now standing in front of them about to tell them to carry on where he left off—to continue his grassroots campaign of revolutionary nonviolence and risk their own executions.

"All power in heaven and on earth has been given to me," Jesus tells his disciples. He has been granted universal power, so he gives them a universal mission. "Go and make disciples of all nations, baptizing them in the name of the Father, and of the Son, and of the Holy Spirit, teaching them to observe all that I have commanded you. And behold, I am with you always, until the end of the age."

The mission is truly universal now—they are to make disciples of Jews and Gentiles, men and women, people of every race, religion, nationality, age, and description everywhere on earth for all time. This is the spiritual life, the work of the Christian. Matthew shares the Trinitarian baptism formula used in his community to welcome newcomers. After they baptize newcomers, they are to train the neophytes in the way of Jesus, teach them, demonstrate to them Jesus's Sermon-on-the-Mount commandments of universal love and total nonviolence, and send them forth to live in God's reign of peace and proclaim it, even if that means they too will one day be arrested and killed by the empire. As followers of the nonviolent Jesus, they no longer kill or support killing or the typical methods of empire; rather they are willing to be killed in the nonviolent struggle for justice and peace, and to proclaim God's reign of peace to the ends of the earth, come what may. They can do this because they know now that the nonviolent Jesus is with them, that their survival is guaranteed, and that they themselves have been given the full power of nonviolence to move mountains, end wars, and disarm the world.

Before we move on to Mark, I invite us to pause, take a deep breath, and offer a prayer of thanks and wonder at Matthew's Gospel. Like the Magi, we have had an epiphany in our encounter with the coming of the God of peace; like the shepherds of Bethlehem, we rejoice at the coming of peace on earth in the nonviolent Jesus. Matthew's Jesus gives us the Beatitudes and the great Sermon on the Mount as a blueprint for the rest of our lives. As followers of Jesus, we will be poor in spirit, mournful, meek, gentle, nonviolent, hungering and thirsting for justice, merciful, and pure in heart; we will be peacemakers, the sons and daughters of the God of peace, and we will rejoice in being persecuted for the struggle for justice, just as the prophets Mahatma Gandhi, Dorothy Day, and Dr. King were. We will try to follow Jesus on his path of meticulous nonviolence and public peacemaking to our own Jerusalems. We take to heart all his teachings of universal love and total nonviolence, leading up to his climactic parable to serve him in the hungry, thirsty, naked, sick, and imprisoned, to give our lives in the service of the poor, and in the nonviolent struggle for justice and disarmament for the end of war and injustice.

When we think of Matthew, we remember that Leo Tolstoy spent the last decades of his life teaching and promoting the Sermon-on-the-Mount commandment of nonviolence: "You have heard it said, 'An eye for an eye' and 'a tooth for a tooth,' but I say to you, 'Offer no violent resistance to one who does evil'" (5:38–39). We remember, too, how Gandhi read this verse daily for over forty years and tried to experiment with it publicly and applied it not just personally but nationally in his campaign of nonviolent resistance to British imperial rule. We, too, pledge to obey this commandment from Matthew and the entire Sermon on the Mount, and to commit our lives to practicing and teaching Sermon-on-the-Mount nonviolence, and to organizing new breakthroughs in grassroots movements of nonviolent resistance like Mahatma Gandhi and Dr. King.

Finally, we hear Matthew's risen Jesus send us forth to "make disciples of all nations," and we take that mission personally. We know now what we must do: we will spend our days calling everyone to follow the nonviolent Jesus on the way of universal love and total nonviolence that all might be disarmed and healed, that all wars, injustices, and systemic violence might end, and that all might welcome God's reign of peace. Amen.

MARK

The Radical Discipleship of
Nonviolent Resistance to Empire

Is it lawful to do good on the sabbath rather than to do evil, to save life rather than to destroy it? (Mk. 3:4)

Everyone will be salted with fire. . . . Keep salt in yourselves and you will have peace with one another. (Mk. 9:49–50)

Be watchful! Be alert! You do not know when the time will come. . . . What I say to you, I say to all: "Watch!"(Mk. 13:33, 37)

* * *

Mark's Gospel was the first Gospel written, probably a few years before the Roman military destroyed the holy city of Jerusalem. If Jesus was killed around the year 24 CE, and Jerusalem and the temple were destroyed by the Roman armies in the year 70, then Mark's Gospel was likely written around 67–68 CE. We know, too, that Rome burned down under Nero in 64. The empire was oppressing and killing Christians everywhere, and it's in this context that the community of Mark writes their call to action, a tale of radical discipleship and steadfast nonviolent resistance to empire.

Someone named John Mark is mentioned in the Acts of the Apostles, and many speculate that Mark was Peter's son. He could be the young man who ran away naked in the Garden of Gethsemane as the soldiers arrested Jesus. It would make sense that Peter confessed to his son all his doubts, his denials, and his failings. How else could we come to know Peter's brokenness, if he himself hadn't told someone close, like his oldest son? Mark probably grew up with Jesus and the community, eventually formed his own community, and then wrote down his memories and testimony with the help of his community members (including women) as a way for other Christians to carry on the campaign of nonviolent resistance that Jesus started. In any case, Mark changed the world because, through him and his community, we have the original story of the nonviolent Jesus.

Matthew's Gospel includes 90 percent of Mark's Gospel; Luke's Gospel includes 50 percent of Mark's. There are few stand-alone passages that are unique to Mark. But, given that this Gospel was written first, whatever material seems original to Mark was later passed over by Matthew and Luke, which says more about Matthew and Luke than it does about Mark. Mark features no infancy narrative, no Sermon on the Mount, no long farewell discourse as does John, and even no resurrection appearance of Jesus. But a cold reading reveals an intensity and an urgency unlike the other Gospels. It is not an ethereal spiritual treatise or an inspiring tale that leads to mystical prayer or a long hymn to peace and love. There are few teachings and few speeches. This Gospel is a call to radical, urgent action. It is a record of the deeds of Jesus, which are, to say the least, pure revolution. It says: if you want to follow the nonviolent Jesus, spend your life resisting the culture of war, the empire of violence, and the reign of death. This is the spiritual life in a nutshell: steadfast, meticulous nonviolent resistance to systemic, structured, institutionalized violence, war, and empire in pursuit of God's reign of justice and peace.

Right from the beginning, Jesus is targeted for death by the ruling authorities, and so, more than in the other Gospels, Mark tells a life-and-death struggle of ongoing resistance to the ruling class, the empire, and death itself. Compared to the other Gospels, Mark's narrative is written mainly in the historical present tense. Perhaps the word repeated most often is "immediately," which appears forty-one times. It keeps the narrative moving forward quickly, and keeps us on edge too, as if we're following a fast-paced action movie. Many biblical scholars agree that because of the poor Koine Greek used in this Gospel, it was intended to be told and retold orally, and that's probably what happened for centuries.

Some scholars believe that Mark's Gospel was written in Rome for the emerging church, to inspire faith-based resistance to the empire, and that unlike Matthew's Gospel, it was intended for non-Jewish readers. Because it was short and did not have as much teaching material as Matthew or Luke, it was almost ignored until the nineteenth century, when scholars concluded that it was the earliest Gospel written and therefore closest to the time of Jesus.

The best scripture commentary ever written on this Gospel is Ched Myers's masterpiece, Binding the Strong Man: A Political Reading of Mark's Story of Jesus *(Maryknoll, NY: Orbis Books, 1988; Twentieth Anniversary edition, 2008; throughout this commentary on Mark, references to Myers's book will be* BSM *plus the page number). Myers broke through the stagnation of academic commentaries and their absurd premise of academic detachment and brought Mark's Gospel to life as a call to permanent resistance in a world of permanent war and systemic injustice. As others have written, Myers's book is as revolutionary as the Gospel of Mark itself. A politically challenging, intellectual, and insightful work, it has been grudgingly acknowledged by the academy but widely studied by Christian activists across North America.*

Daniel Berrigan's lengthy introduction honors Myers's work by sharing how groundbreaking it was, how it shares with Mark himself a "new authority." He writes:

One senses in Myers' work a Jesus who would be accounted a stranger by many Biblicists of the Western world. But hardly new to the resisters of our lifetime, the base communities, the Christians hailed into courts and jails here and elsewhere, that noble "third world" that has invaded our own with its sublime evangel of liberation. A Jesus witnessed to in art and music and poetry and dance, the noble testimonies and testaments of the tortured and disappeared.

The glance He casts, that Jesus of Mark!, upon the world, in our direction too. A glance that takes much into account, that is both merciful and courageous, that ranges where it will, upon outcast, woman, child, the half-hearted, and the hero; upon harvest, coin, lurking scribe, snoops and parasites and betrayers, soldiers and their vainglorious superiors. A glance that rests with equanimity upon the powers that will destroy Him.

The glance rests on the disciples—nursing their pride, only half understanding, half-willful, boastful in good times and fretful and childish in the breach. All taken in, and taken into account. And then the end, or the purported end, the showdown. But on the third day . . . (BSM, xxiii).

I well remember Dan studying and presenting sections of Myers's work to our community and on various retreats in the 1980s as it was still being written. Dan was totally renewed and energized by Binding the Strong Man, *and his enthusiasm and renewed radical discipleship were contagious. I will refer to Myers's work and, like him, focus on Mark's call to repentance, action, and resistance to empire from a Gandhian/Kingian perspective of nonviolence, but I encourage readers to study Ched Myers's definitive commentary.*

I also encourage readers of Mark to engage in their own praxis of nonviolent direct action and resistance to our own deadly empire as they study Mark's Jesus and Myers's Mark. Experimenting with radical discipleship and public nonviolent action against the culture of war, greed, racism, nuclear weapons, and environmental destruction, as you are reading Mark, will lead to a deeper understanding of Mark's testimony and narrative, and it will take you beyond reading the written text into living the text and make the story come alive all over again. So if you are not involved in the global grassroots movements of nonviolence for justice, disarmament, and creation, pick a cause and get involved. As Archbishop Oscar Romero said the day he was killed, "No one can do everything, but everyone can do something!" Join the movement, get involved in ongoing nonviolent resistance to the culture today, and step into Mark's Gospel.

As we read Mark and engage in the revolutionary praxis he demonstrates, the risen, nonviolent Jesus will then live on in us, and his campaign of revolutionary nonviolence will spread farther, which is what he desires, and which is Mark's intention. That will be bad news for the military-industrial nuclear-weapons nations, but good news for the poor and oppressed and ourselves as well. All we have to do is enter the story, find our place in this nonviolent action thriller, and do our part to hasten the global grassroots movement of nonviolence.

The Campaign of Nonviolent Resistance and Civil Disobedience Begins (1:1–3:35)

"The Beginning of the Gospel of Jesus Christ" (1:1–13)

With that opening sentence, Mark throws down the gauntlet not just to the Roman Empire but to the world and all of history. As noted earlier, the proclamation of a gospel belonged solely to Caesar and his Roman military. After each slaughter and victorious battle, they rode into the next town announcing the gospel of Caesar. Mark co-opts the empire's announcement of victory in war to announce Jesus Christ's victory in peace, and an everlasting victory over death itself. This use of the word "gospel" to proclaim the new way of Jesus was a brilliant act of genius. Not only does it declare that Jesus is as victorious as the emperor—and far more so—it is an act of nonviolent resistance itself to the empire. One could be killed by the empire for saying, spreading, and teaching these words and, indeed, many were.

To introduce Jesus, Mark offers a brief description of John the Baptist and his message as the opening act. To place John the Baptist in biblical context, he cites Isaiah the prophet, who foretells a messenger who will be sent ahead of the Messiah to prepare the way.

John appears in the desert, far from the empire, in the middle of nowhere, "proclaiming a baptism of repentance for the forgiveness of sins." Crowds of people seek him out and are baptized "as they acknowledged their sins." We're told he wears camel's hair with a leather belt, and eats locusts and wild honey, images that lead us to wonder if this might be a new Elijah, the great prophet. "One mightier than I is coming after me," he tells them. "I am not worthy to stoop and loosen the thongs of his sandals. I have baptized you with water; he will baptize you with the Holy Spirit."

Luke will list many more details, but Mark's messenger stands in total resistance to empire and the culture of violence. He will have nothing to do with the way the world is run, with the way people live, with the common false presumptions about God. He rejects it all, names our common social sin, and demands a complete turnaround in everyone's life through baptism and committed repentance. He demands that everyone start their lives all over again, and symbolize their new spiritual/political beginning through the act of baptism, to wash away the old and start clean anew. This repentance requires ending all cooperation with the culture of violence and empire, and instead living an entirely new life devoted to God, loving service of others, and working for justice. He is determined to prepare us for the Messiah who is to come, and apparently there had never been anyone like him before, so the crowds trekked out into the boondocks to hear his call and be baptized.

We've hardly begun when the nonviolent Jesus appears in verse 9, center stage. He is baptized by John, and as he comes out of the water, as we read in Matthew and will read in Luke, he sees "the heavens torn open and the Spirit like a dove descending upon him, and a voice spoke from heaven saying, 'You are my beloved Son; with you I am well pleased.'" As with Matthew, this is the vocation moment in the life of Jesus, when God speaks directly to him and announces that he is God's beloved Son. This realization sets Jesus moving. Mark's Jesus is always on the move. "At once, the Spirit drove him out into the desert, and he remained in the desert for forty days, tempted by Satan. He was among wild beasts, and the angels ministered to him." (This reference to the wild beasts may be an encouragement to the early Christians who at that time were being fed to wild beasts in Rome by Nero.) It was then that news spread that John had been arrested and, on cue, Jesus enters the remote desert area by the Sea of Galilee "proclaiming the gospel of God." Note that Mark proclaims the gospel of Jesus, but Mark's Jesus proclaims the gospel of God; God is the real emperor and ruler of the world.

"For This Purpose Have I Come" (1:14–45)

From the beginning of Mark, we note several key ingredients of the Jesus movement. The first thing he does is call everyone to turn away from the unjust dominant economic social order run by the religious authorities for the empire, and to turn toward the kingdom of God, a new realm of justice, compassion, and nonviolence, which is as close as your hand (1:15). Second, he calls disciples to follow him and join his campaign (1:17). Then he demonstrates how the campaign works: through public, political exorcisms (where he expels the demons that keep people oppressed and submissive to the dominant order and empire, from the possessed man in the synagogue in a few verses to come to the Gerasene demoniac); public, political healings of the poor and marginalized (so that everyone is physically healed but also welcomed into a new social order of total equality, where no one is marginalized, where everyone is a sister and brother); and public, political teachings (about how to live and practice his way of love, compassion, and nonviolence), proclamations (of God's reign) and denunciations (of the anti-reign that keeps people stuck under the empire's heel).

"This is the time of fulfillment," Mark's Jesus announces. "The kingdom of God is at hand. Repent, and believe in the gospel." The *kairos* has arrived, the time of great urgency, when we should drop everything and turn away from the culture of war and empire; believe in the social, economic, and political liberation that God is bringing about; and welcome God's reign of justice, compassion, and peace. This announcement is pure revolution. He's saying in effect, "Today, the permanent revolution of Gospel nonviolence has begun! Join the campaign to disarm and transform the earth!"

With this announcement, Mark's Jesus hits the ground running. By the sea, he calls the fishermen brothers Simon and Andrew with the declaration, "Come after me, and I will make you fishers of men and women." He also calls the Zebedee brothers, James and John, who drop their nets and follow Jesus. These are poor fishermen on the outskirts of the empire, with no hope of ever breaking loose from their poverty and social and economic oppression. They literally drop everything and turn from their families to join Jesus's campaign of liberation from the current unjust social order.

It's in the fishing village of Capernaum, on the north side of the sea, that Jesus takes his first nonviolent direct action. Myers calls it his first direct assault on the established Jewish social order (*BSM*, 137). He teaches the people in the synagogue and astonishes them with his new "authority." Then, right there in the synagogue, a man cries out, "What have you to do with us, Jesus of Nazareth? Have you come to destroy us? I know who you are—the Holy One of God!" We're told he has an unclean spirit. Because he feels threatened by Jesus, he is taken to represent the entire social order and the religious ruling class, the scribes. The presence of the nonviolent Jesus in the synagogue in Capernaum is clearly a threat to the synagogue itself, which symbolizes the ruling establishment and helps maintain the unjust social order run by the empire through the religious authorities. The synagogue blesses in God's name the Roman occupation and the poverty and injustice that these poor desert people suffer, and in doing so keeps them subjugated and apathetic, thinking it's all God's will. (In the same way, the churches in Nazi Germany whether actively or passively supported Nazism with their silence, as the white churches of South Africa maintained apartheid in their silence.)

No one in the synagogue, Capernaum, or Galilee had ever witnessed a political exorcism, where a holy rabbi expelled everyone's fear and acceptance of the imperial occupation. No one had experienced a religious community publicly working against the unjust political order (as few have experienced today in North America, where most churches go along silently with the culture of war and nuclear weapons).

Notice how the possessed man has internalized the culture's violence and presumes that Jesus, the Holy One of God, has come to destroy him and everyone—because violence is all he knows. Jesus takes direct action, rebukes the unclean spirit, and orders it to come out of the man; it does so with a loud cry, to the amazement of everyone. He demonstrates the real power of the living God, the power of nonviolence to free the man (and the crowd) from his bondage to violence and expectation of destruction. By expelling the unclean spirit in the synagogue, Jesus frees the man and all the people into the new life and freedom of God's compassion and peace. "What is this?" people ask. "A new teaching with authority. He commands even the unclean spirits and they obey him."

In this first day, a day in the life of the nonviolent Jesus, he goes to the house of Simon and Andrew, with James and John. I imagine they all had many children. They immediately tell Jesus that Simon's mother-in-law is sick with a fever, so "he approached, grasped her hand, and helped her up." The healing begins with his extraordinary kindness to her, touching her and helping her stand. He waits on her, so she then waits on them all. We the reader recognize that Jesus takes care of everyone in need but especially anyone in his discipleship community. That evening, crowds of physically sick or spiritually possessed people come and are healed, with "the whole town at the door." By healing the sick and exorcising the demons, he makes everyone whole and free from the unjust dominant social order, which would have ostracized them and marginalized them. Jesus restores everyone to the fullness of life and the human community. He shows us what the kingdom of God looks like.

Next, we're told that Jesus goes off into a desert place before dawn to pray. Specifically, Mark writes, "Rising very early before dawn," which helps us see that Jesus acts as if he is already risen, that he rises above the culture of death that oppresses everyone else, and that part of his resurrection life includes quiet meditation with his beloved God. This quiet meditation gives us a clue as to how to live his steadfast nonviolence as well. From now on, we would-be disciples take time each day to meditate with the God of peace and the non-violent Jesus in the solitude of nature.

Simon and the others search for him, find him, and say, "Everyone is looking for you." Simon wants Jesus to return and enjoy his acclaim, but Jesus has been communing with God and he has a far different plan. "Let us go on to the nearby villages that I may preach there also," Jesus tells Simon and the others. "For this purpose have I come." With Simon, we learn that Jesus does not seek acclaim from crowds but seeks to build a grassroots movement that requires him to go to the impoverished villages throughout the region, so he can heal the sick, exorcise the demons, and preach Gospel nonviolence, justice, and liberation. That, he tells us, is his purpose, the reason he is here on earth. As would-be followers, we realize that we are being called to join his grassroots movement of nonviolent revolution, that we too must journey from town to town to spread the revolution of Jesus's way.

They set off, and the campaign takes off. Mark writes that he "went into their synagogues, preaching and driving out demons throughout the whole of Galilee." He's like Martin Luther King Jr., traveling throughout the South in the 1960s, preaching in every church, denouncing segregation, expelling the demon of racism, and calling upon the oppressed African

American community to rise up and engage in nonviolent civil disobedience to bring down segregation and racism itself, and eventually economic injustice and war. We see this kind of political exorcism in the Montgomery Bus Boycott (where everyone was liberated and inspired to walk to work rather than ride a segregated bus); in the Freedom Rides and lunch counter sit-ins (which broke through the subservient acceptance of interstate segregation and segregation in ordinary businesses); and in Selma, where the complicated race laws prevented African Americans from voting or holding office (until he helped liberate everyone to demand the right to vote, and publicly protest the system).

Word about the movement spreads. One of Mark's clearest signs that this call for healing, liberation, and empowerment of the poor was working is the appearance of a leper. He approaches Jesus, kneels down in front of him, and begs him, saying, "If you wish, you can make me clean." Lepers were probably the most ostracized people of Jesus's day. They were declared unclean and kicked out of synagogues and communities by the religious authorities. No one was allowed to go near one, and they were kept apart from the public. They were sent away to live in the wilderness and in caves far from villages and towns. Here, however, Mark presents a brave, fearless leper who walks right up to Jesus and shows him the utmost respect.

We're told that Jesus is filled with compassion, "moved with pity," and stretches out his hand and touches the leper. That was an illegal act. By touching the leper, Jesus broke the law. He too would have been declared unclean, but he does not care about the consequences to himself. He cares solely for the leper. He wants him healed, restored to the community, and fully empowered to join his campaign. "I do will it, be made clean," he says, healing the leper. Right away, we notice that Mark's Jesus, the nonviolent revolutionary, is radical in another aspect, too: he is sweet and kind. He is not mean, bossy, arrogant, or bullying. He doesn't have a mean bone in his body. This is a new kind of revolutionary—a nonviolent revolutionary who shows kindness and compassion to those in need. Anyone who is violent, whether on the far left or the far right, is still violent. Jesus's nonviolence runs deep and shines in his basic humanity and personalism.

Jesus instructs him not to tell anyone but to show himself to the priest in the synagogue, as the scriptures advise, so that he will be fully welcomed back into the community. In this case, the healed leper does not do that but goes away and tells everyone what happened. Perhaps he did not go to the priest because he suspected that the priest would never believe him or accept him back. Why does Jesus then stay in the wilderness? Not to avoid the crowds. After illegally touching the unclean leper, he's a marked man, Myers concludes (*BSM*, 154). So, he remains in wilderness areas. Even so, people seek him out to be cured.

"Why Are You Thinking Such Things in Your Hearts?" (2:1–28)

The story continues with a whirlwind of subversive actions. Jesus has turned Peter's Capernaum home into a base of operations, and when they return to the community house, it is mobbed. He sits and teaches the people, but, notice, Mark does not outline what Jesus taught; perhaps that is why Matthew added his long, detailed sermon on nonviolence. But from his actions, we can presume that Mark's Jesus would have talked about rejecting the unjust dominant order in all its forms, including its classism, violence, religious control, and the Roman Empire, as well as about welcoming all the poor and marginalized back into society and seeking God's reign with all our hearts.

It's during this scene at the crowded house, while Jesus is teaching, that men lower a paralyzed man down through Peter's roof on a stretcher and lay him right in front of Jesus, in the middle of Peter's house. What does Jesus do? He does not heal him. He announces that his sins are forgiven—that is, in the Greek, his "debts." Mark writes that he says this once he sees the faith of the paralyzed man's friends. Think about it: they have such love for this poor guy that they are determined to get him to the Holy One. So they take the trouble of climbing up the house, onto the roof, disassembling the roof, and lowering the poor man down into the crowd in front of the Holy One. Jesus is so moved by this expression of love and compassion that, when he says, "Child, your sins are forgiven," he's stating the obvious. These friends of yours love you so much, he says in effect, that they have forgiven any wrong you have done, any debts you may have owed, and I do the same. It's a beautiful affirmation of love, compassion, and forgiveness, which, for the nonviolent Jesus, mark the path of healing.

But there's more. Only the scribes can forgive debts in God's name; this is a direct affront to them, and they are indignant. "Why does this man speak that way?" they ask. They do not focus on love, compassion, or forgiveness but expend huge amounts of energy keeping people in line and the poor powerless. "He is blaspheming. Who but God alone can forgive sins?" Of course, Jesus can see them squirming and whispering. He can tell that they are appalled; he's beginning to get used to the idea that they do not want love, compassion, or forgiveness, much less the healing of social outcasts and marginalized peoples. The charge of blasphemy is a capital crime, and eventually they will charge him for it and seek capital punishment.

"Why are you thinking such things in your hearts?" Jesus asks them. It is a critical question that hovers in the air. Why do we think such things in our hearts? Why do we not affirm every act of love, compassion, forgiveness, nonviolence, and healing? Why do we support the dominant system that keeps the poor and marginalized down and out? Do we really care about God, seek to serve God, and know God anyway? What kind of God do we actually worship?

"Which is easier to say to the paralytic," Jesus asks them: "'Your sins are forgiven,' or to say, 'Rise, pick up your mat, and walk'? But that you may know that the Son of Humanity has authority to forgive sins on earth"—he said to the paralytic, "I say to you, rise, pick up your mat, and go home." The man rose, picked up his mat at once, and went away in the sight of everyone. They were all astounded and glorified God, saying, "We have never seen anything like this."

With his question followed by his action, Jesus challenges the resentful religious authorities not just about forgiveness and healing but about his own identity. He calls himself the "Son of Humanity," which Myers translates as the "Human One," that is, the ideal human being, the one who is fully open to God, universal love, compassion, and peace. Because he has no sin in him, that is to say, not a trace of violence in him, Jesus is filled with the Holy Spirit of God. Just touching Jesus brings healing. His very presence is disarming. At his word, the sick are healed and people are forgiven. In this case, his commandment to the paralyzed man begins with the loaded word, "Rise." In effect, he raises the man from the clutches of death. In doing so, he returns the poor man now fully healed and whole to his home, his family. This nonviolent action ultimately is aimed at the scribes, who claim to have authority, to show them who has real authority, and what it looks like. He has the authority to forgive sins and debts, heal the paralyzed, and even raise the dead because he is fully human and the One sent from God, whom John the Baptist foretold. The religious leaders were not looking for this kind of messiah—one actually opposed to their system.

By the sea, he calls Levi, a customs official, to discipleship with the simple words, "Follow me." Levi leaves his post and that evening holds a meal at his house in honor of Jesus, attended by tax collectors and publicly known sinners, those cast out by the religious authorities. The religious officials are there as well and watch in horror as Rabbi Jesus flagrantly violates the dominant order's rules and customs by eating "with sinners and tax collectors." They question his disciples about this behavior. Jesus tells them flatly: "Those who are well do not need a physician, but the sick do. I did not come to call the righteous but sinners."

This is one of the great teachings of Mark, aimed at the religious authorities but offering hope to all those on the margins. Jesus sides with all those in need—in need of healing, wholeness, justice, compassion, community, a human touch, protection from the culture of death—in short, all those who sincerely need and want God. This is a nonviolent savior who is not here for the rich and powerful, the establishment, the power brokers, the one percent, the generals, the rabid politicians, those in the center. He has come for all those under the boot of the culture, those being crushed, the excluded. He does not ask if they are worthy; he does not require any condition for healing. His compassionate action is generous and free to all in need. We can conclude that, for Mark, Jesus seeks out, stands with, and sides with all those who are ostracized, disenfranchised, and marginalized by the culture of domination. He is on the side of those ignored and pushed aside by everyone else. His healing touch is for them, not the rich or the powerful, those in authority who have no apparent need of healing.

We've only just begun the journey, but at every turn Jesus gets pushback. This will become the theme of Mark, even as Jesus ups the ante by resisting systemic injustice in every instance. "Why do the disciples of John and the disciples of the Pharisees fast, but your disciples do not fast?" they question him. He, of course, answers with his own question. "Can the wedding guests fast while the bridegroom is with them? As long as they have the bridegroom with them, they cannot fast. But the days will come when the bridegroom is taken away from them, and then they will fast on that day." In this image, he describes himself as the bridegroom at a wedding feast. Everyone should celebrate in his presence. If and when he is taken away, then everyone should fast and pray, as signs of repentance.

"No one sews a piece of unshrunken cloth on an old cloak," he continues. "If he does, its fullness pulls away, the new from the old, and the tear gets worse. Likewise, no one pours new wine into old wineskins. Otherwise, the wine will burst the skins, and both the wine and the skins are ruined. Rather, new wine is poured into fresh wineskins." With these parables, he announces the coming of a new day, the reign of God at hand, with new wine and new wineskins, symbols of the fullness of life, community, and joy. The hallmark of this new day, new time, new wine, and new wineskins is the new life of universal love, compassion, justice, and nonviolence, which has begun with Jesus's presence among us. He will continue to use every sort of imagery to impress upon us the coming of an entirely new world, to imagine it, and then to pursue it.

He and his disciples walk through a field of grain on the sabbath, and they start to pick the heads of grain and eat them. The Pharisees attack him for this unlawful activity on the sabbath. Jesus's disciples are engaged in nonviolent civil disobedience, violating the sabbath law. This is his new normal. We no longer obey the rules of the culture of violence and death, when human needs are not met. He doesn't flinch for a moment but challenges them with his own question: "Have you never read what David did when he was in need and he and his companions were hungry? How he went into the house of God when Abiathar was high priest and ate the bread of offering that only the priests could lawfully eat, and shared it with his companions?" He cites not just scripture but King David himself to point to a higher law, a human right.

What is at issue here? Human hunger. They are hungry, they need food. That's the bottom line for Jesus: no one should be hungry anywhere in the world. Everyone has the right to food and water, here and now and forever. That is what is at stake here—not the rules or laws of the establishment, even the holiest of duties, respect for the sabbath. "The sabbath was made for humanity, not humanity for the sabbath," he says, in a sentence unique to Mark. "That is why the Son of Humanity is lord even of the sabbath."

Myers helps us unpack this scene:

In all three episodes in which the Pharisees figure, Mark has focused upon some aspect of food consumption. First Jesus defended his (and his disciples') right to break bread with the socially outcast. Then he asserts their freedom to ignore ritual noneating practices; such piety, after all, was a luxury for the affluent, not for the poor for whom hunger was an involuntary and bitter reality! Now Mark escalates his attack: he justifies the disciples' right to break the law by procuring grain on the Sabbath in a situation of hunger. Mark is doing more than simply deflating the Pharisaic holiness code. He is implicitly raising a political issue of criticism by identifying the Pharisees with issues of "land and table."

The disciples' commandeering grain against Sabbath regulations must be seen as a protest of civil disobedience over the politics of food in Palestine. Jesus is not only defending discipleship practice against the alternative holiness code of Pharisaism; he is going on the offense, challenging the ideological control and the manipulation of the redistributive economy by a minority whose elite status is only aggrandized. Mark consistently argues that solidarity with the poor also means addressing oppressive structures. This may well mean breaking the law, but such action is legitimated by the Human One, who in overturning the authority of purity and debt codes is being revealed to the reader not only as "lord of the Sabbath" but lord of the entire "house" itself (13:35). (*BSM*, 160–61)

Recently, Dr. King's chief lieutenant, Andrew Young, made an insightful comment about the civil rights movement. He said that he and Martin were not running "a piety program."

They were not leading a contemplative movement of prayer, meditation, or monasticism. They were trying to change the country, so they were leading a grassroots campaign of nonviolent direct action, civil disobedience, resistance, and cultural transformation, to bring about justice, disarmament, and full human rights for every human being. This is an important way to understand Dr. King and the civil rights movement—and Mark's description of Jesus and his movement. It is not a piety program; it is a grassroots campaign of nonviolent civil disobedience aimed at bringing down the entire unjust dominant order and empire and heralding an entirely new kind of culture based in justice, compassion, inclusivity, and dignity for everyone.

"Stretch Out Your Hand!" (3:1–31)

And so, the civil disobedience continues. The nonviolent Jesus goes on full nonviolent attack. He enters a synagogue, and again, it's the sabbath. This is the house of God, where the faithful read and discuss the law. For Jesus, that means, in this house, everyone should be welcome; everyone should find wholeness, inclusivity, love, and community in God's house. And there, up front, as he is about to read from the scroll, he notices in the back of the room a man with a withered hand. This is one of the most provocative stories in all the Gospels. Jesus sees a man who is incomplete, not whole, on the margins, and he immediately takes nonviolent direct action. He calls the man to come forward and stand with him up in front of everyone. And then—nothing. A long dramatic pause. In other words, he does not heal him. He stands there up front with the poor guy at his side, with all eyes on him, in a long, drawn-out dramatic moment. The silence deepens, the tension mounts. He waits until he has everyone's complete attention.

Then, with everyone holding their breath, sitting on the edge of their seats, he poses the most hard-hitting question: *Is it lawful to do good on the sabbath rather than to do evil, to save life rather than to destroy it?* As Rainer Maria Rilke famously wrote about the great questions, it's best not to rush into an answer. Instead, sit with it, he suggested, even for years, and live your way into the answer. That certainly applies to this question. One could spend a year meditating over this scene, watching the nonviolent Jesus address the synagogue, asking this tough question, and enduring their cold silence.

"Who is talking about doing evil on the sabbath here in this synagogue?" the religious authorities must have thought. "How are we doing that? Who is trying to destroy life? Here we are debating the Torah. Who do you think you are? How dare you!" But, as the nonviolent Jesus knew well, they ran the system that prevented helping, healing, and serving the poor on the sabbath. Their crime was failure to heal the man's arm; healing and restoring everyone into community is the work of the Torah and the sabbath.

What should they have said? "Lord Jesus, you know well, it is not lawful to do evil on the Sabbath. It is only lawful to do good on the sabbath and every other day as well. It is not lawful to destroy life on the sabbath or any other day of the week. It is only lawful to save life on the sabbath, and every other day of the week." The purpose of life is to do good and to save life, not to do evil or destroy life, Jesus implies with his question.

Those in the synagogue remain silent. Their silence speaks volumes; they do not publicly agree with what he has said, neither do they defend themselves. Looking around at them with anger and grieved at their hardness of heart, Jesus tells the man, "Stretch out your hand." He stretches it out, his hand is restored, and immediately the Pharisees went out and "took counsel with the Herodians against him to put him to death."

Now we see the effects of Jesus's nonviolent direct action—the religious and ruling authorities feel threatened, set out to arrest Jesus, and intend to kill him. He is a danger to society, a threat to the ruling establishment, a disturber of the peace. It is no small thing that they now seek allies. Once they enlist the Herodians, the supporters of Herod Antipas, tetrarch of Galilee and Perea, they have set their course for the rest of the story, and we now know the outcome. I don't mean to demonize Jesus's opponents because Jesus doesn't, but we need to understand just how dangerous Jesus was to the ruling authorities, and how dead set they were against him.

This passage is one of the most important in the New Testament. In his groundbreaking book *Jesus and the Nonviolent Revolution*, the great French peacemaker and scholar André Trocmé called it "carefully staged political theater." Ched Myers explains:

> Jesus could presumably heal the man with the withered hand in private without pro-voking a reaction (as in 1:29) but chooses yet again to force the issue. Under the glare of media lights, as it were, with the hostile officials hovering, waiting for Jesus to "cross the line," Mark finally resolves the lingering subplot concerning healing on the Sab-bath. As in the modern practice of civil disobedience, which might break the law in order to raise deeper issues of its morality and purpose, so Jesus, just before "crossing the line," issues a challenge to his audience. Pitting his mission of compassion and justice to the poor against the imperatives of the dominant order, Jesus calls the entire ideological edifice of the law to account. He paraphrases the watershed question of Deuteronomic faith (Dt. 30:15ff) (in his question), drawing a sharp contrast between his messianic intentions and those of his opponents. (*BSM*, 162)

Notice that Jesus looks at them with "anger." This is the first time in the four Gospels we're told that the nonviolent Jesus gives in to anger. Remember, in Matthew's great Sermon on the Mount (5:22), he commanded us never to give in to anger. The only other time when this word is used to describe Jesus's emotion is in John's account of the raising of Lazarus (Jn. 11:33, 38), as he faces the same religious authorities who show no faith in him, only in the culture of death. The Greek word is commonly translated in John 11 as "deeply disturbed, incredibly perturbed, profoundly upset," which conveys something slightly different from anger. There's a sense of grief in this painful emotion. I think that's what Mark means—not anger rooted in hatred or violence but a state of being profoundly upset and disturbed by their hostility, to the point that Jesus is beside himself with grief.

It's easy to sit with this passage, side with the nonviolent Jesus, and be amazed at his risky, illegal nonviolent direct action to heal this poor man. But if we claim to be follow-ers of the nonviolent Jesus and apply this story to our world today, it's not so easy. If Jesus was profoundly upset that the synagogue was going about its business while someone in their midst was suffering, what would he say about our situation today—where billions live in subhuman poverty while corporate greed makes the one percent richer by the minute; where wars continue to destroy nations and kill children; where nuclear weapons threaten the destruction of the planet; where the mining of fossil fuels hastens catastrophic climate change; where we go about our business while those suffering in the world continue to die? Jesus tried to wake up the religious authorities that day in the synagogue; he continues to try to wake us up today to do everything we can to promote and do good, while resisting and stopping evil, to save life rather than destroy it. To be a Christian in today's world of total violence requires the total nonviolence of Jesus himself. Like him, we take nonviolent direct action to do good, stop evil, save life, and stop the destruction of life.

For sure, we can never again have anything to do with evil or destroying life, but that is no longer enough. As Jesus shows, we cannot just do good—*we have to resist evil*, and stop it. We have to do both, and that requires taking a public prophetic stand through nonviolent direct action, as he does.

Notice how public Jesus is and how different this is from being political. He takes public action because he is trying to wake everyone up, to get us to look deeply at the reality of our human situation and to choose compassion, faith, and love. The only way to do that is to *go public*. That's the key: as his nonviolent followers, we go public with universal love, universal compassion, total nonviolence, and steadfast resistance to death in all its forms.

Afterwards, Jesus withdraws to the sea. He's like a military commander, although his campaign uses daring nonviolence. The crowds follow him; he cures everyone and expels all unclean spirits. Then, we're told, he walks up the mountain. As with Matthew, Mark presents Jesus as the new Moses. There, on the mountain, he officially forms his community of nonviolent resistance to empire and death. He names twelve apostles and missions them to proclaim God's reign of peace publicly and drive out the demons of violence and empire as he does.

The attacks continue and get more serious. "He is possessed by Beelzebul," the scribes say. "By the prince of demons, he drives out demons." These powerful religious authorities feel threatened by him and seek to discredit him, and there's no greater charge than saying he is possessed by Satan. Mark reports that Jesus addressed the charges with parables. "How can Satan drive out Satan?" Jesus asks. "If a kingdom is divided against itself, that kingdom cannot stand. And if a house is divided against itself, that house will not be able to stand. And if Satan has risen up against himself and is divided, he cannot stand; that is the end of him." His logic, as usual, is impeccable and irrefutable. We see him using reason to invite faith in him, to address the accusations.

"No one can enter a strong man's house to plunder his property unless he first ties up the strong man. Then he can plunder his house." As Myers points out, Jesus identifies himself as a thief who breaks into a strong man's house to plunder his property. The house, meaning the world, is the property of the strong man—Satan—a.k.a. the empire—the culture of war and death—and Jesus has come to plunder his house, disarm it, and cleanse it of evil.

Then he speaks about what such accusations really mean. "All sins and all blasphemies that people utter will be forgiven them," he announces, "but whoever blasphemes against the Holy Spirit will never have forgiveness but is guilty of an everlasting sin." This teaching, too, is shocking. On the one hand, Jesus promises that in effect everything wrong we do will be forgiven, and we can take heart knowing this promise. The one exception, the sin against the Holy Spirit, or the blasphemy against the Holy Spirit, refers to speaking, teaching, and preaching about God, while in reality you go completely against God, promoting the spiritual life for your own gain, for wealth, and to support the culture of death. We can look to those who preached and taught racism, slavery, sexism, war, and nationalism, as if it were the will of God, as if these were requirements of Christianity, to see them as blasphemy against the Holy Spirit. We can easily judge, say, the priests and bishops who supported Hitler and Nazism, but the challenge of this teaching is to examine honestly our own beliefs and acts, to see if we are really following Jesus's teachings of nonviolence and resistance to empire, nationalism, and the culture of death, or if we too are guilty of identifying God with our own nation-state system, with all its violence. If we have anything to do with supporting violence, murder, weapons, or warfare, while publicly demonstrating faith in God, then we are sinning against the Holy Spirit.

Remember, as we ponder such episodes, that Jesus was a faithful Jewish rabbi upholding the Torah, fulfilling it in light of God's nonviolence and universal love. Do not be lured into the ancient trap of antisemitism as you read these confrontations between Jewish leaders, including Jesus. He has a broad vision of universal nonviolence that he draws from his tradition, the Torah and the scriptures, and is calling everyone—from the local poor and oppressed to all the religious leaders, and in the end even the imperial representative in Jerusalem—to embrace God's reign of total nonviolence and universal love.

In the middle of his confrontation with the religious authorities, Jesus is confronted by his own relatives. Mark is quite explicit: "They set out to seize him, for they said, 'He is out of his mind.'" Jesus's family thinks he's completely crazy. He threatens the dominant social and political order and faces the danger of excommunication and death, so they are afraid that they too might be killed. They think they are in danger. What sane person would bring on the wrath of the ruling authorities or the empire? Mark's word "seize" hints that Jesus's relatives are trapped like everyone else in the culture of violence and will not tolerate his active nonviolence. But they are right: the public campaign he has launched is dangerous. In a world where violence, war, and empire are perfectly legal, his underground movement against the violence and injustice of Roman occupation (and for the coming of a new culture of nonviolence) is illegal—then and now. Jesus's relatives want to protect their own lives, so their first natural act is to stop him, grab him, and take him away before he makes things worse.

Jesus would know his family well. He would not be surprised that they are shocked by his actions. They certainly do not act as if he is the Messiah. Like everyone in the story, and all Mark's readers, each one of us has to decide for ourselves how to respond, and whether we want to embark on the journey of radical discipleship.

Thus, Jesus is calm, cool, and collected. He doesn't react one way or another; there is no fear or codependency in Jesus. When he hears that his mother and brothers are outside the house, he simply asks the crowd a potent question. "Who are my mother and my brothers and my sisters?" We would expect the answer to be—your blood relatives, those people standing at the door, the ones you are forcing to wait outside. "Looking around at those seated in the circle he said, 'Here are my mother and my brothers. Whoever does the will of God is my brother and sister and mother.'" Jesus breaks the definition of the human family as our relatives and announces that his family are all those who do the will of God as our

161

beloved Father, who therefore live as brothers and sisters to one another and to him. In a tribal culture, family and bloodline are everything; Jesus's rejection of his family in this situation is certainly scandalous. But with his statements here, Jesus opens a new understanding of what it means to be human.

For Mark and Matthew, the will of God is discipleship to Jesus on the journey of universal love, universal compassion, universal peace, and total nonviolence. This is the will of God. As we practice universal solidarity with one another and all creation and Jesus himself, we become his brother, his sister, and brothers and sisters to one another. As we do, we start to recognize God in one another, pledge never to harm one another, and God's reign of justice and peace breaks through here on earth. So, this is not a tale of harshness toward Jesus's family; rather, it's a revolutionary openness to the meaning of life, the question about what it means to be human, and an invitation to see Christ in everyone and thus to consciously live and serve the human family.

"To What Shall I Compare the Kingdom of God?" (4:1–34)

Mark has two major teaching sections. The first, Ched Myers suggests, commands us to "listen," and the second to "watch." In this first sermon section, Jesus calls for "revolutionary patience," and then "revolutionary vision and hope despite the odds." As we sit with the teachings and parables, we see Jesus instructing the disciples that the gospel they are being sent to proclaim will not be well received, that, in fact, it will be rejected by many. Mark's Jesus is showing the disciples—and us the readers—that in varying degrees, our allegiance still resides with the dominant social order (*BSM,* 171–75).

Jesus sits in a boat on the sea, speaks to the crowd on the shore, and says, "Listen!" As Myers writes, this commandment is one of Mark's key themes. But as we witness the disciples' inability to listen and understand, we find ourselves doing the same thing. Few are really listening to Jesus today, including ourselves. To listen is to concentrate, to meditate, to ruminate on every word that Jesus says. That is how Mark wants us to approach the words and teachings of Jesus.

"A sower went out to sow." The parable of the sower tells how some seed fell on the path, others on rocky ground, others among thorns, and finally some on rich soil that produced a tremendous harvest. "Whoever has ears to hear ought to hear." Well, everyone has ears, so the emphasis is clear: Listen up and understand! There are great obstacles to accepting Gospel nonviolence in a world of violence! Few will take it to heart, but those who do will yield a large harvest of peace.

The disciples are clueless. Will people accept your gospel? they wonder. "The mystery of the kingdom of God has been granted to you," Jesus tells them. "You are witnessing the nature of God's reign in my universal love, steadfast resistance to the empire, and my way of nonviolence." I speak in parables, he explains, because everyone else is completely stuck in the culture of violence, domination, and empire. Mark cites Isaiah to critique the ruling authorities who will never comprehend Jesus's nonviolence. They are addicted to power, domination, imperial control, oppression of the poor, and systemic violence. They believe in the false god of domination and refuse to be converted to faith in the God of nonviolence and universal love, or to accept forgiveness for their complicity in death and destruction.

"Do you not understand this parable?" Jesus asks the disciples. *If not, how will you understand any of them?* he wonders. The question is meant for us too. We, Mark's readers, are granted access to the mysteries of God's kingdom along with the disciples, but we too remain clueless and in need of an explanation. Like the disciples, we want to know the mysteries of the kingdom of God; we want to understand them, live them, and pursue them. We no longer wish to be stuck in the world as it is but want to understand the mystery of Jesus's way of being.

So, the explanation: "The sower sows the word." When some hear it, the world of violence comes and takes it away. Others rejoice in it, but have no root, and quickly return to the dominant order of "the way things are." As soon as trouble or persecution hits them because of the word, they quickly fall away. The minute they get attacked for their gospel position, they give up in despair. Then there are those who hear the word, but "worldly anxiety, the lure of riches, and the craving for other things intrude and choke the word, and it bears no fruit." Finally, he explains, those "sown on rich soil are the ones who hear the word and accept it and bear fruit thirty and sixty and a hundredfold." Does this mean we are predetermined to fail in Gospel living? Not at all. It's an explanation of the life of Gospel living in an anti-Gospel world. The story is meant to encourage us to beg for the grace to be the faithful ones with rich soil who take the Gospel to heart and bear fruit "thirty and sixty and a hundredfold." We want to bear good fruit. So we determined to spend our lives studying the Gospel, changing our lives to live according to Jesus's teachings, and witnessing to the kingdom of God in love, regardless of the consequences to ourselves. That way, our lives will bear good fruit, like Jesus, who is the Word of God.

"Is a lamp brought in to be placed under a bushel basket or under a bed, and not to be placed on a lampstand?" he asks them. The answer of course: the lamp is meant to be placed on a lampstand. We do not sit in the dark and live in the dark—but, indeed, the world is full of darkness. Jesus is the light of the world, the Word is the light of the world, and he wants us to carry on his mission and light the whole house, to be the light of the world, not to be hidden away. If we do this, then our lives will bear great fruit. Bearing fruit is different from worldly success, effectiveness, and results. It's a slow, patient, natural, nonviolent image from nature, and it operates in the exact opposite way of the world but has a far more lasting, healing, and peaceful impact.

Everything hidden or secret will be made visible by the light, he continues. In his light, in the face of his truth, all hearts will be bared; more, the world of violence and hatred will be exposed as ungodly and will fall away. As we go forward as his light to the world, we will expose all forms of violence and the system of violence itself, as evil and ungodly, and his light will lead us all out of this world of darkness into God's reign of love, compassion, and peace. Everything Jesus says makes sense from his perspective of love, compassion, and peace. But if you believe in the world's violence, greed, and dominating systems, Jesus's teachings do not make sense. That's why he urges us again to listen hard and consider what he is saying. "Anyone who has ears to hear ought to hear," he says.

He repeats this message, but this time adds a warning. "Take care what you hear." In other words, choose carefully what you listen to. If you listen to the voices of the world of violence and domination, they will guide you; instead, listen to his voice of love, compassion, and peace, and let him guide you into the kingdom of God. "The measure with which you measure will be measured out to you, and still more will be given to you," he continues. "To the one who has, more will be given; from the one who has not, even what he has will be taken away." This teaching becomes clearer as we ponder life. What goes around, comes around, he says. If you show mercy, love, and peace, you will be shown mercy, love, and peace. If you are a mean, nasty, selfish, violent bully, then your violence will come back upon you. He repeats this later in the Garden of Gethsemane: "Those who live by the sword will die by the sword." Here, he offers the positive side: those who live Jesus's way of love will continue in it. But he adds that we will receive even more than the love and peace we give out to others, because that is the nature of the spiritual life, the way the universe is created.

The universe is ruled by love, compassion, and peace, so those who enter this spiritual way will receive even more blessings of love, compassion, and peace. If we can stay faithful to this path throughout our lives, we will be astonished at the blessings that will come upon us now, and in the new life to come. If we do not live by this Jesus way, then we will miss out on such blessings; further, the way of violence, hatred, and despair will rob us over and over again of any new blessings.

"This Is How It Is with the Kingdom of God" (4:26–34)

"This is how it is with the kingdom of God," he teaches. He wants to explain what the kingdom of God is like, but God's reign is so different from this present world of violence and death that it's a struggle to explain it.

In this parable about the coming of God's reign here on earth, Jesus uses the example of a farmer who plants a field and waits for the harvest. "It is as if a man were to scatter seed on the land and would sleep and rise night and day and the seed would sprout and grow, he knows not how. Of its own accord the land yields fruit, first the blade, then the ear, then the full grain in the ear. And when the grain is ripe, he wields the sickle at once, for the harvest has come." With this image Jesus describes his mission, and ours as well. Like him, we spend our lives sowing seeds of justice, compassion, and nonviolence, and live in peace, even taking our rest, until the day of harvest, when we make new advances of justice and peace. We do not know how God's reign comes on earth; we are not in control of it, we can't force it, we don't build it. It happens according to nature, and it depends on how many seeds we have sown. But the day of harvest will come.

Myers's comments are helpful. He says that Jesus counsels here both patience and hope:

Patience so that the apocalyptic militance of Jesus' "declaration of war" in 3:37 is not misconstrued. Mark sobers any illusion that change will be quick and triumphal. It is rather a matter of finding the right soil and trusting that the seed will grow, maintaining faith that the small seed will be "raised up" and the mighty brought down. *Hope*, because, according to the story so far, the results of Jesus' kingdom practice have hardly been encouraging: he has been abandoned by his family, driven out of the cities, and is hunted by the authorities. Mark wants to reassure the reader/disciple that the seed is being sown, and the harvest will surely come. . . . . The "way of the Sower" will subsequently be revealed as the way of nonviolence: servanthood become leadership, suffering become triumph, death become life. The lesson of the "unknowing farmer" is that the means of the kingdom must never be compromised by attempting to manipulate the ends. (*BSM*, 181)

Jesus goes on to explain the revolutionary nature of global transformation that is slowly coming about with the breakthrough of God's kingdom on earth. "To what shall we compare the kingdom of God, or what parable can we use for it?" His question is worth pondering, for he asks us to explain it for him, and tell stories about it. He wants us to ponder, understand, and teach what God's reign would look like here and now on earth. If we could imagine a world in which there is no violence, no racism, no war, no hunger, and no injustice; where everyone has equally what they need to live in peace; where everyone shares in life to the full and there is no harm done anywhere on earth; then we can begin to imagine what God's reign might look like on earth. This is what the disciples and the saints have done—to imagine God's reign of peace and love, and then to make that vision come true in their lives and work. With this question, we all need to turn our focus to the kingdom of God, and spend time imagining it and working to make it real on earth.

"It is like a mustard seed that, when it is sown in the ground, is the smallest of all the seeds," Jesus explains. "But once it is sown, it springs up and becomes the largest of plants and puts forth large branches, so that the birds of the sky can dwell in its shade." The tiny mustard seed resembles the littleness of God's kingdom as it is first announced by the nonviolent Jesus, but both will slowly grow into a global reality that transforms the world. With the seed planted by Jesus, over time new possibilities will emerge for humanity, so that all who have been ostracized, disenfranchised, and marginalized will now be welcomed and feel at home. In God's reign of universal love and peace, everyone is welcome—indeed, all the nations of the world. The image of the tree in which all the birds of the sky can rest comes from Ezekiel 1:23; 31:6; and Daniel 4:17–19. It points to the universality of God's reign, where no one will be excluded, where every nation, every type of bird in the sky, is welcome and can find rest.

Notice how these and other parables involve down-to-earth examples of life here and now on the earth. By using examples from nature, as any indigenous religious leader would, Jesus helps us to understand that the coming of God's reign of peace and nonviolence is not about life after death, but about life here and now on earth and, therefore, involves the way we treat Mother Earth and all her creatures.

Myers concludes this first narrative cycle of Mark by comparing Jesus's "messianic sociopolitical strategy" with Gandhi's satyagraha campaigns:

Gandhi repudiated the caste system, which segregated India's "untouchables." He founded a disciplined community which shared life with the poor. And he nonviolently assaulted the economic and political structures that undergirded an imperial system of privilege and exploitation. Because of his firm alignment with the poor and their interests, Gandhi too became a target, not only of the British but also the Indian aristocratic classes. Mark's narrative, like satyagraha, legitimizes militant, direct action, yet at the same time severs any absolute relationship between such action and historical efficacy.

It is up to the disciple/reader to sow the seed of the kingdom through nonviolent witness—but it is up to God to bring that seed to fruition. And by refusing to personify the enemy in the human face of the opposition, Mark affirms another cardinal characteristic of nonviolence, what Martin King called "the Beloved Community." The struggle for justice must always find a way to include its opponents in its vision of the future; just as no disciple is infallible, no adversary is "disposable." (*BSM*, 184)

And so, the journey takes a turn—"to the other side."

"Let Us Cross to the Other Side" (4:35–8:26)

It is evening, and Jesus tells his disciples, "Let us cross to the other side." They climb into a boat, head out to sea, and begin Jesus's first campaign of nonviolent action—into enemy territory. Crossing to the other side, as in Matthew's version, means going into the fearful, unknown, pagan territory, into the land of the Gentiles, the hated enemy. He is teaching them how to practice active nonviolence and love for enemy—not just by talking about it but by doing it with them. Jesus is setting off to reconcile Jew and Gentile, and to begin the reconciliation of humanity. In Mark's first sea crossing, a violent squall comes upon the sea, and the waves crash violently upon the boat and threaten to sink it. Jesus, however, remains sound asleep on a cushion.

It's one of the great symbolic images of the Gospels. All hell is breaking loose around him as they practice this dangerous, daring nonviolence, but he remains totally calm and peaceful because he knows he is doing God's will and he leaves the results to God. The disciples are terrorized, but Jesus catches up on some much-needed rest. Traveling into pagan territory to the other side, where the hated Gentile enemy lives, is illegal and could cost them their lives, they fear. It would be like sailing through a violent squall. Jesus, on the other hand, embodies universal nonviolent love, so he has nothing to fear. Love will carry him safely to the other side. That is the first lesson of universal love and total nonviolence. Those who practice it have nothing to fear. Those who do not practice it will always live in terror and will not know how to journey to the other side and love every human being as a sister or brother. Jesus wants us to be the calm in the eye of the hurricane, not to live terrified as if we are about to die in a hurricane.

"Teacher, do you not care that we are perishing?" they cry out to him. He wakes up, rebukes the wind, and orders the sea, "Quiet! Be still!" The wind ceases and, we're told, there was a great calm. With this image, we learn of Jesus's power over creation, his ability to make peace among people and in nature, even upon the seas, the storms, and the weather.

The disciples' fear reveals their lack of faith, so he asks them, "Why are you terrified? Do you not yet have faith?" These are questions we need to let Jesus ask us. We can sit with them in silence and let the kindness behind the questions touch us. What am I afraid of? Why have I not made the leap of complete faith in total surrender and trust to the God of peace, to the nonviolent Jesus? These are requirements of nonviolence and discipleship, yes, but I know deep down that God, that Jesus, is trustworthy, that I do not need to be afraid anymore of anything, that I can surrender my life to God and believe totally in God, and go forward as calm and peaceful as Jesus, even though a storm roars around me.

Mark is telling us that everything boils down to faith in Jesus. With faith, we have no fear. Without faith, we are easily afraid and therefore unable to practice nonviolence—or any other aspect of God's reign. When push comes to shove, we get terrified and fight back. The antidote to fear is faith. "Faith Not Fear" might have been the motto of the disciples from then on, but they remain clueless, and still do not understand what Jesus is talking about or who he is, though one day they will get it. Likewise, we readers and would-be disciples remain clueless. We do not know what he is talking about and have yet to step into the total faith that brings fearless nonviolence, the kind that crosses boundaries into enemy territory, where we put God's love into action. That's why I define this radical fearless faith in God more as "total reliance" on God. We see this fearless faith and total reliance on God time and time again in the daring-do of Gandhi, King, and other practitioners of active nonviolence. Anyone of us can shake off our fear and attain these heights of daring nonviolence if we only place our total reliance upon God and undertake public action for justice, disarmament, and peace as Gandhi and King demonstrated so well.

Mark's version of the encounter with the demoniac on the other side of the sea is one of the greatest episodes in Mark, and a much fuller account than what we read in Matthew or in Luke. When they arrive in the enemy territory of the Gerasenes, a man from the tombs who has an unclean spirit approaches them. Mark goes into great detail: he lives in the tombs; no one can restrain him; he can't be held even by a chain; he pulls apart his chains and shackles; no one is strong enough to subdue him; he cries out night and day and bruises himself with stones. Mark presents a horrific description of someone possessed by the culture of violence and death. He is out of his mind. Jesus is filled with God's spirit of nonviolence and life, and at once he starts saying, "Unclean spirit, come out of that man!" He orders the spirit of violence and death to leave him. As we saw in Matthew's shorter version, the man represents the entire Gerasene territory, which is occupied by the Roman Empire and has a garrison with two thousand Roman troops stationed there. The land and its people are occupied by the spirit of violence and oppression!

"What have you to do with me, Jesus, Son of the Most High God?" the man with the unclean spirit asks. "I adjure you by God, do not torment me!" Those filled with violence and used to violence, we notice, can relate only to violence; they are stunned by the power of nonviolence, and do not know how to respond. "What is your name?" Jesus asks. "Legion is my name," the man answers. "There are many of us." A "legion" is a division of two thousand Roman soldiers. Mark's story is clearly not only a story but rather a parable about Roman occupation and how Jesus's fearless nonviolence confronts imperial occupation with its side effects of violence and death. The unclean spirit named Legion asked to enter the herd of swine on a hillside, and Jesus allowed them to do so. Immediately, we're told, "the herd of about two thousand rushed down a steep bank into the sea, where they were drowned." Those in charge of the swine ran away, to the Roman authorities I presume, where they reported the incident. Crowds came out to see the man who had been possessed by Legion who was now "sitting there clothed and in his right mind." "And they were seized with fear," Mark adds. So, they begged Jesus to leave, and he does.

As he is getting into the boat to leave, the formerly possessed man pleads "to remain" with Jesus, but Jesus tells him instead, "Go home to your family and announce to them all that the Lord in his pity has done for you." Here we see Jesus once again restoring everyone who has been lost, broken, excluded from community, and consigned to death, even someone in enemy territory. The man went off and proclaimed what Jesus had done throughout the entire region. Jesus's mission at first seemed to fail, but now we see that it bore tremendous fruit: he healed the man, and if we follow the logic of Mark's imagery, expelled the Roman garrison from the region (at the price of getting kicked out). On top of this, the newly healed man proclaimed God's work to the whole region, which in some ways was better than Jesus doing it! Creative nonviolence, in the end, always works and bears tremendous, even unexpected, good fruit.

"Do Not Be Afraid. Just Have Faith!" (5:21–6:6a)

Jesus returns home across the sea. This time, there's no storm because there's no need to dramatize returning home. He is met by a synagogue official named Jairus, who falls at his feet and pleads for him to come and lay hands on his sick daughter and heal her. So begins one of the other key healing accounts of the Synoptic Gospels. As Jesus heads off to heal the girl, his mission is interrupted by another person, an ill woman, who prevents him from getting to the girl in time. It's this interruption and Jesus's untroubled, peaceful demeanor that make these healing stories transcendent.

As he walked to Jairus's house, the woman came up behind him in the crowd and touched his cloak. She had suffered hemorrhages for twelve years, we're told, and thought, "If I but touch his clothes, I shall be cured." She touched his clothes and knew immediately that she was cured.

But Jesus stopped. He knew something, too. We're told that he sensed that "power had gone out from him," so he turned around and asked, "Who touched my clothes?" The disciples chided him, but he persisted, until the woman approached "in fear and trembling," fell down before Jesus, and confessed how she had touched him and was cured. "Daughter, your faith has saved you," he tells her. "Go in peace and be cured of your affliction."

The woman had good reason to be terrified. Normally, a man, even a religious leader, might scold a woman or attack her for interrupting him, much less touching him. Jesus, instead, is as gentle as can be. He even addresses her as "Daughter," which is simply scandalous. That he was touched by an unclean, sick woman would mean his excommunication from the local synagogue nearby; that he calls her "daughter" would ensure it. Jesus is so kind and nonviolent that merely touching him brings healing. For him, the healing is complete only when he looks into her eyes and says, "You are my beloved daughter." He radiates the unconditional love he first experienced by the Jordan River.

Just then, people arrived to tell Jairus that his daughter has died. Jesus said to Jairus, "Do not be afraid. Just have faith." What?! Why does he tell Jairus to have faith? It's too late! The girl is dead. There is nothing that can be done. Here, we cut to the chase and get to the heart of the matter. Do we as disciples/readers believe in the nonviolent Jesus or not? Can anything be done? Can he do anything? What would happen if we had real faith in him? Aren't we too afraid of death or of making a scene in public or, dare we say it, of pursuing some kind of unimaginable resurrection? This teaching is central to Mark and is aimed at all of us. "Do not be afraid. Just have faith." He wants us to have the blind faith in him that the sick woman with the hemorrhage had. He does not want us to be afraid or faithless, like the male disciples on the stormy sea.

"Do not be afraid. Just have faith." That is the key to the life of active nonviolence in a culture of death.

Apparently, Jairus did not object to Jesus, so Jesus takes that as a yes. So, he summons his three closest friends—Peter, James, and John—and they arrive at the house, where people are weeping and wailing. "The child is not dead but asleep," he says to the crowd, and they "ridicule" him. Think of that: he's trying to prepare them; he's come to the rescue; and they all make fun of him. They simply do not live in his consciousness of God's endless love, of healing power, of a different way to live.

Jesus dismisses the crowd and takes the father, mother, and his friends into the room where the child lies on her bed. He takes her by the hand and says, "Little girl, I say to you, arise!" She immediately gets up and walks around, and he tells them to give her something to eat. They are shocked and astounded, and he tells them not to tell anyone. Remember that the authorities are already on the alert about him, and most people misunderstand his work and ministry. Since he is leading an underground movement of nonviolent resistance in a brutalized outpost of the Roman Empire, he has to be careful for himself and those he ministers to, so he asks them not to talk about it.

When we consider this unusual story of the healing of an unnamed "uppity" woman within the story of a powerful man whose daughter is dying, we realize that Mark is, as usual, inviting us to consider more than meets the eye, as Myers explains:

> The healing of Jairus's daughter, framed around the healing of the woman with the blood flow, addresses *class* status within Judaism, dramatizing what today is referred to in liberation theology as the "preferential option for the poor." . . . On the one hand, the synagogue ruler, Jairus (one of the rare named characters in Mark's story), makes an assertive approach to Jesus, as befits male social equals. This man was both "head" of his family (thus appealing on behalf of his daughter) and "head" of his social group (leader of the synagogue). The man falls down at Jesus' feet, a proper granting of honor prior to asking a favor. On the other hand, the woman who reaches out from the cover of the crowd, an ashamed and covert attempt to gain healing, is anonymous. When Jesus tries to seek her out, the disciples discourage him: "You see how the crowd is pressing around you and yet you say, 'Who touched me?'" The woman has no name, she belongs to the crowds—she is statusless, with no one to defend her (as Jairus defends his daughter). . . .
>
> This woman is doubly poor, doubly outcast. As a result of her physical condition of unarrestable hemorrhaging, she should—according to the Levitical purity code—be perpetually segregated. And she was a victim of exploitation as well. . . .

I would contend that the primary level of signification in this episode lies in the fact that Jesus accepts the priority of the ("highly inappropriate") importunity of this woman over the ("correct") request of the synagogue leader. His mission to "lay his hands on" Jairus's daughter is interrupted by the "touch" of the doubly poor woman, and now she is the one who falls at the feet of Jesus. The most important symbolic reversal here is the status of the destitute woman. . . . She herself has become the "daughter at the center of the story!" . . . Not only is her integrity restored, but she receives a grant of status superior to that of Jesus' own male disciples, who are "without faith"! (*BSM*, 198, 201)

The connotations of these two healings will deepen as the story goes on.

With that, Jesus heads off to his unnamed hometown village, where he teaches in his synagogue, much to the astonishment of the locals. We're told that instead of accepting Jesus's interpretation of the scriptures, instead of joining him with joy at God's fulfilled promises, "they took offense at him." "Where did he get all this?" they ask. "Is he not the carpenter, the son of Mary, and the brother of James and Joses and Judas and Simon? And are not his sisters here with us?" This is not a welcome-back committee. This sounds more like "Who do you think you are? How dare you?"

"A prophet is not without honor except in his native place and among his own kin and in his own house," Jesus says. With that declaration of truth, Mark reports that "he was not able to perform any mighty deed there," and "was amazed at their lack of faith."

I consider Jesus's public address in his hometown synagogue nothing less than another of his many nonviolent direct actions. Instead of winning the people over with his wisdom, he is rejected by his mother and entire family, and then the whole town. This seems to be the norm for all those who struggle for justice and disarmament, who publicly advocate God's reign of peace and nonviolence. It is rare that one's family, relatives, and childhood friends support one who publicly campaigns for justice, disarmament, and creation. It is almost natural to "take offense." "Who do you think you are?" is the common criticism. What's noteworthy is Jesus's hallmark of nonviolence. He tries to heal people and summon them to discipleship and the reign of God, even in the face of their rejection. He tries as hard as he can. He does not write them off; he loves them and teaches them. In doing so, he makes himself completely vulnerable and opens himself to the rejection of his loved ones, and the certain hurt to follow. Interiorly, we can only presume that he spent time, perhaps every single minute, forgiving them and praying for them, over and over again.

"His Heart Was Moved with Pity for Them" (6:6b–52)

After his failed attempt to win over his own family and townspeople, Jesus shakes off this debacle and launches his official public campaign of nonviolence throughout Galilee. In the verses that follow, Mark describes a nonviolent leader who organizes a public, daring, nonviolent, military-like campaign to undermine the Roman Empire and welcome God's reign of nonviolence. Jesus starts out by sending his twelve disciples two by two ahead of him. He gives them authority over unclean spirits and teaches them to anoint with oil all those who are sick. Mark's image is exodus. "Take nothing for the journey but a walking stick—no food, no sack, no money in their belts," he says. Do wear sandals but not a second tunic, he tells them. (He allows a walking stick, not for use as a weapon of violent self-defense, but to help through the arduous journey across the rocky desert landscape.) "Wherever you enter a house, stay there until you leave from there. Whatever place does not welcome you or listen to you, leave there and shake the dust off your feet in testimony against them."

These are basic organizing techniques, critically important to any understanding of Jesus as a global movement organizer. He wants us to go forth into the world of violence like labor organizers, people of nonviolence, full of passion for his teachings, on a mission to change everyone, to convert everyone, to transform any and every local culture into a new culture of nonviolence and love. They went off and preached repentance to everyone they met. They drove out many demons, they anointed with oil and cured many who were sick, they proclaimed the coming of God's reign, and altogether they were amazed and consoled and excited that this stuff actually works! We, too, as readers who aspire to be disciples, are astonished, excited, and challenged. Perhaps we can take up where they left off.

Just then, the story abruptly shifts. Here, Mark announces the horrific fate of the prophet John the Baptist. Everything seemed to be going well, but with his execution by King Herod, we are reminded, as we learned from Jesus's hometown reception, that the countercultural ways of God's reign are rarely welcome. We hear of John's arrest, of how Herod's wife hated the prophet, how her daughter danced at a party, pleasing Herod so much that he offered her anything she wanted, and how, at her mother's urging, the daughter asked Herod for the head of John the Baptist on a platter. And so, John was beheaded, and his disciples took his body and buried it. What a horrible demonstration of how the ruling class, which often assumes the mantle of leadership and the heights of civility, can act with insanity, cruelty, and impunity. Mark is trying to show us not only the inevitable outcome of a prophetic truth-teller in a culture of violence, but also the habitual behavior of those who lead the cultures of violence.

Everything John the Baptist did was prophetic, which means that he spoke truth to power and therefore was on track to suffer the consequences of his truth-telling. Jesus learned from John to speak truth to power, and with news of John's horrific execution, he could see the writing on the wall for his own impending doom. Perhaps that is why, when the disciples returned and reported all they had done and taught on their campaign of nonviolence, Jesus said, "Come away by yourselves to a deserted place and rest a while." They got into a boat and sailed off "to a deserted place." He wanted them to rest—because he cared for them, and he did not advocate workaholism but rather self-care. He was also grieving the death of his beloved friend and teacher, John, so he needed to get away from the crowds to mourn and pray.

It is in this context that Jesus's heart opened with infinite compassion for the crowd. They had been "coming and going in great numbers," Mark reports, and "had no opportunity even to eat." The crowd then followed Jesus on foot to the place where he was going by boat. As he disembarked and saw the vast crowd, Mark tells us, "His heart was moved with pity for them, for they were like sheep without a shepherd; and he began to teach them many things."

The disciples tried to get rid of the crowd, claiming they should be allowed to go and buy food for themselves. I read this again to mean that *they*, the disciples, were tired and wanted food for dinner. In response, Jesus issued one of the great commandments: "Give them some food yourselves." They objected, so he questioned them: "How many loaves do you have? Go and see." And when they found out, they said, "Five loaves and two fish."

They presented to Jesus this small amount of food in front of a huge and hungry crowd. What did he do? He told them to make everyone sit down on the green grass in groups of hundreds and fifties. He took charge, organized the crowd into small communities, and inspired them, against all odds, to share what they had with one another.

Mark's Jesus took the five loaves and the two fish, looked up to heaven, offered a blessing, broke the loaves, and gave them to his disciples to set before the people. He also divided the two fish. The next thing we know, everyone in the crowd has eaten their fill, and there are tons left over. "All ate and were satisfied," we're told laconically.

Mark notes that there were five thousand men. No one, in those days, would record the number of women. But we know there would have been women and children present, and if there were that many men, we can safely assume there might have been as many as twenty-five thousand women and children.

Mark describes how Jesus worked an astonishing miracle feeding some thirty thousand men, women, and children with just a few loaves and fishes, that God worked through him to feed the hungry. As we sit with the scene, we can see that the miracle is the inspiration he gave them to overcome their selfishness and greed and to share the little food they had brought for themselves with one another so that everyone would have plenty to eat. Thus, the laws of capitalism and consumerism evaporate in Jesus's presence. Instead of holding on to what you have earned, what you have, you let go and give away everything you have freely to those around you in need because you have compassion on them. The compassion of Jesus inspired the crowd to recognize the humanity of those around them and to show compassion toward one another. *This* is the miracle. The politics of compassion end hunger and lead to a just distribution of all resources, beginning with food.

We can safely presume that any woman who would have brought her children out into the middle of nowhere to hear the holy rabbi would have brought food for herself and her children. If they had spent the day listening to the Holy One talking about unconditional love, boundless compassion, and selfless service of the other, it seems reasonable to conclude that, by the end of the day, when they had all grown hungry, as they watched him up on the hill break bread and pass it around, they would have done likewise. They would have taken the bread and food they had brought for themselves, broken it, and shared it with those around them in their small group. Suddenly, everyone would be eating, everyone would have enough food, everyone would know life in community with sisters and brothers. "The only 'miracle' here," Myers concludes, "is the triumph of the economics of sharing within a community of consumption over against the economics of autonomous consumption in the anonymous marketplace" (*BSM*, 206).

Jesus makes the disciples get into the boat and proceed again "to the other side." He alone sends the crowd home. And we're told, "he went off to the mountain to pray." Why? He was in shock and grief over the news of John's brutal and senseless execution. He had spent the day teaching tens of thousands of people, then had proceeded, at the very least, to inspire them to share their food so that everyone would have enough to eat. Now he retreats alone into nature in grief and exhaustion to turn in prayer to his beloved God. This brief mention of prayer—the fact that he withdrew alone to spend hours in silent communion with God—is crucial to our understanding of Mark's nonviolent Jesus: he is able to resist the culture of death because, first and foremost, he knows well the God of life. Everything he does flows from this intimate relationship with his beloved God.

The disciples didn't want to go to the land of the Gentiles, but Jesus urged them to go and to go on alone. That evening, when the boat was far out on the rough sea during a high wind, at the fourth watch, in the middle of the night, "he came toward them walking on the sea."

"When they saw him walking on the sea, they thought it was a ghost and cried out," Mark writes. They were terrified, but he called out: "Take courage, it is I, do not be afraid!" He got into the boat with them, the wind died down, everything became peaceful, and they were utterly astounded. Then Mark adds his own commentary: "They had not understood the incident of the loaves. On the contrary, their hearts were hardened."

With this crossing narrative, once again the disciples face a life-or-death situation as they are tossed about in the rough seas in the dead of night. This is the second dramatic sea crossing in Mark's Gospel, trying to explain to us the life of peacemaking and reconciliation that Jesus is teaching his disciples, making them go "to the other side," the land of the Gentiles. They are terrified; there's a storm, but to make matters worse, a ghost comes walking on the water in full sight near their boat. This is just about the scariest thing one could imagine. But Mark is attempting to describe the life-or-death fear of the disciples—and of us the readers—at the thought of crossing to the other side. They do not want to go to the land of the enemy, nor do we. They don't understand what that has to do with Jesus's healing work or prayer with God. Why are we getting political all of a sudden? they must have wondered as they headed off alone in the boat. Peacemaking is scary, for them and for us. It's like being in a boat alone in the night during a storm; worse, it's like seeing a ghost come walking toward you on the water.

The ghost calls out to them in the dark, "Take courage, it is I, do not be afraid!" Once he gets into the boat, the wind stops, the sea becomes calm, and all is well. There is no need to be afraid in his presence. He is here, peace has arrived, we have newfound courage. It's Jesus, we know him, he is the embodiment of peace, so all will be well. Now, we know we can cross to the other side because he is with us; eventually, we will learn not to fear ever again, even in the face of our enemies or of death, because we have learned to live and walk and act like him. We know he is always with us.

"Hear Me, All of You, and Understand" (6:53–8:10)

When they reached the other side, crowds came running toward Jesus, bringing all kinds of sick people, and we're told that he healed every one of them. Anyone who simply touched the tassel on his cloak was healed. But then tension with the authorities started up again. The Pharisees and scribes who had come from Jerusalem to investigate him saw that his disciples did not wash their hands before eating and were thus violating the cleanliness laws. So they asked Jesus about this. Mark uses Isaiah to expose their hypocrisy:

"Well did Isaiah prophesy about you hypocrites, as it is written: 'This people honors me with their lips, but their hearts are far from me. In vain do they worship me, teaching as doctrines human precepts.' You disregard God's commandment but cling to human tradition." He went on to say, "How well you have set aside the commandment of God in order to uphold your tradition! For Moses said, 'Honor your father and your mother,' and 'Whoever curses father or mother shall die.' Yet you say, 'If a person says to father or mother, "Any support you might have had from me is *qorban*" (meaning, dedicated to God), you allow him to do nothing more for his father or mother. You nullify the word of God in favor of your tradition that you have handed on. And you do many such things.'"

Jesus's response is a sharp attack on hypocrisy. His charges are strong and truthful: your hearts are far from God; you do not offer true worship; you teach human precepts as if they were divine; you disregard God's commandments; you nullify the word of God; and you uphold the tradition itself as if that were divine. With these criticisms, he exposes the false intentions of the religious authorities, who do not seek the will of God but instead serve as religious police who enforce the dominant social order, as if that were God's will. Like the disciples and the crowd, we are warned not to repeat their mistakes. Jesus wants us to have hearts close to God; to offer true authentic worship of the living God; to teach only divine precepts, and to obey God's commandments and God's word.

Mark's Jesus then turns to the crowd to call them beyond hypocrisy to honesty, sincerity, and purity of heart. "Hear me, all of you, and understand," he tells them, and us. We are commanded to understand what he is saying. "Nothing that enters one from outside can defile that person; but the things that come out from within are what defile." Of course, his accusers have no idea what he is talking about. If he is saying what it sounds like he might be saying, then he has just dismissed the Hebrew laws of cleanliness and eating. Later, however, he's shocked to discover that even the disciples are clueless. We can laugh at them for not understanding, but we are just like them. "Are even you without understanding?" he asks them, and us. "Do you not realize that everything that goes into a person from outside cannot defile, since it enters not the heart but the stomach and passes out into the latrine?" Mark emphasizes the point: with that decree, "he declared all foods clean." "But what comes out of a person, that is what defiles. From within people, from their hearts, come evil thoughts, unchastity, theft, murder, adultery, greed, malice, deceit, licentiousness, envy, blasphemy, arrogance, folly. All these evils come from within and they defile."

With these teachings, Jesus gets to the heart of the matter: all the evils of the world come from within us, in our hearts, and that's where our focus should be. We need to purify our hearts, not our hands or our dishes. We need to disarm our hearts of every form of selfishness and violence. Jesus wants us to have hearts that are wide open, full of love and compassion for every human being, so that we can be instruments of peace and do God's will in the world.

How do we root out the causes of evil from within us? Prayer, fasting, almsgiving, repentance, and the inner work of learning Jesus's radical way of living. We are a constant work in progress, as we let God disarm us, heal us, expel the demons of violence and evil from within us, and cultivate God's love, which manifests in compassion and peace. We learn to surrender ourselves over and over to God and let God give us a previously unknown humility, peace, and serenity. If we do this, we can renounce once and for all any evil thoughts, unchastity, theft, murder, adultery, greed, malice, deceit, licentiousness, envy, blasphemy, arrogance, and folly. We can live in Jesus's Holy Spirit and become a force of goodness and transformation.

The lack of understanding Jesus encountered, as well as perhaps sheer exhaustion, seems to have gotten the upper hand. He heads off to the Mediterranean, to the village of Tyre, to get away, to be alone and rest. We're specifically told he entered a house and wanted no one to know about it. He was seeking solitude, silence, rest, and prayer. He was now in Gentile territory and would remain there for a while, traveling and speaking to the crowds. As usual, people heard that he was there. Mark proceeds with a story parallel to Jairus's appeal for his daughter, but this time, of all things, it's a woman who falls at Jesus's feet. She is a Greek, therefore, a Gentile, and a Syrophoenician, which means she's a pagan. How dare she enter the house of the Holy One and disturb him! She pleads for him to expel an unclean spirit from her daughter.

The exchange that follows is perhaps the toughest and harshest in the Gospels, but as I wrote about Matthew's version, I believe Jesus could see that this Syrophoenician woman was one of the strongest, most faithful people he had yet encountered, and that she could help him teach his clueless disciples that he had come not just for the Jews but for the Gentiles too.

"Let the children be fed first," he tells her. "For it is not right to take the food of the children and throw it to the dogs." It is the most insulting thing Jesus ever said! He calls her and her people dogs! Apparently, that kind of insult was common. But if Jesus remains consistently nonviolent, then we know there is more to the story. Perhaps he is smiling, and she is smiling too. She understands, even if the disciples do not, that he belongs to the Gentiles as well as to the chosen people. She doesn't miss a beat and gives it right back to him, the way close friends banter and joke with one another. "Lord, even the dogs under the table eat the children's scraps." It is the best comeback in the entire New Testament. Jesus was clearly testing her or maybe even kidding her, and he knew she had the faith to match his repartee. Her quip about the dogs eating the children's scraps wins Jesus over. "For saying this, you may go. The demon has gone out of your daughter." When the woman went home, she found the child lying in bed and the demon gone.

Not only did she fight for her daughter and acquire her healing, but she also allowed herself to be used by Jesus so that he could show himself to the disciples as someone who changed his mind, someone who was teachable, someone who was learning the universality of his mission. Jesus really wanted to impress the disciples that he had come for everyone, including the Gentiles. He wanted to change their minds and their mindsets. By acting this way with the Syrophoenician woman, he offered his disciples the example of him changing his mind, giving them permission to changes theirs too. I think, however, that he knew what he was doing all along, and the woman did too. From the moment they met, he was going to heal the daughter; they both knew it. I imagine them smiling and laughing together. They were trying to teach the male disciples, who afterwards were probably more confused than ever.

Then Jesus heads off into the Decapolis by way of Sidon; in other words, he tours the land of the Gentiles. We're told they bring him a deaf man with a speech impediment and beg Jesus to heal the poor fellow. Instead, Jesus takes him off "by himself away from the crowd." Mark gives us specific details: Jesus puts his finger into the man's ears, spits, and touches the man's tongue. Nothing could be more illegal, or just downright disgusting, to a law-abiding Jew than to touch an unclean deaf and mute person, much less a pagan—but to spit and touch the person with one's spit? This would have been unthinkable. It's as if Mark is pushing all our buttons to show how determined Jesus is to break every so-called ritual purity law to heal the broken and restore them to community; further, he does this among the Gentiles.

Jesus looks up to heaven and groans, saying in Aramaic, "*Ephphatha!*" ("Be opened!"). The man's ears are opened, his speech impediment is removed, and he begins to speak. Jesus orders him not to tell anyone, but the man and the crowd head off and tell everyone, and people everywhere are astonished. Mark concludes with the shocking proclamation of the Gentile people, "He makes the deaf hear and the mute speak!" As Myers points out, Jesus can do this even with the Gentiles, but apparently not with his own disciples! (*BSM*, 205).

Mark has offered parallel healing stories of Jesus among the Gentiles, and now he offers a parallel feeding story, like the two previous feedings of the masses of Jewish people, only this time, Jesus will feed thousands of Gentile people. Again, Jesus says that his heart is moved with pity for the crowd. He is filled with compassion and does not want them to go away hungry. The disciples think only of buying food; they lament being stuck out in the wilderness where there are no stores. Jesus finds that they have some loaves and fish; he orders them to sit down, takes the food, gives thanks, breaks the loaves and divides the fish, and tells the disciples to distribute them. Everyone eats until they are full, and there are seven baskets of scraps left over. Again, Mark shows how Jesus welcomes God's reign of equality and sharing here among the hated enemy people. A new social order is at hand, one rooted in justice, equality, food for everyone, and the peace and wisdom of the nonviolent Jesus.

"He Sighed from the Depth of His Spirit" (8:11–26)

They journey back to Jewish territory where immediately the Pharisees come forward and start arguing with Jesus, demanding that he give them "a sign from heaven." We the readers have just witnessed a sign from heaven, but it has been given to the Gentiles, not the religious authorities. They are testing him, Mark reports, just as Satan did at the beginning of the story. Here we arrive at a key turning point. Jesus has faced their obstinance, hostility, and attacks again and again. Despite his universal, compassionate love for the Jews and the Gentiles, for all the healings and feedings he has done, they demand "a sign." Mark writes: "he sighed from the depth of his spirit."

This sigh from the depths of Jesus's spirit is worth pondering. No matter how much goodness and love Jesus brings, the religious authorities respond only by attacking him. They are threatened by his steadfast truth-telling and persuasive hold over the crowds. They refuse to be touched or converted. Two thousand years later, this is still the hard-hearted attitude of many today. Despite all the goodness and love and steadfast nonviolence that have been demonstrated by the likes of St. Francis and St. Clare to Gandhi and Dorothy Day, to Dr. King and Thich Nhat Hanh, we continue to demand a sign, to test God, to attack Jesus's way of nonviolence. We continue to make the nonviolent Jesus sigh from his depths as he watches us. Instead of thanking him, serving him, and following him, we question him and attack him all over again, and cause him endless grief. I urge everyone to reflect on the way we live, the way we relate to the nonviolent Jesus. Do we test God and continue to make Jesus sigh from the depths? If so, how can we change our behavior, accept the Gospel testimony, believe in Jesus's way, and start following him so that he never again sighs from the depths?

"Why does this generation seek a sign?" Jesus asks the religious authorities. "Amen, I say to you, no sign will be given to this generation." With that, he walks away from them, gets into the boat, and heads off to the other side. Notice that, unlike Jesus in Matthew and Luke, Mark's Jesus makes no reference to "the sign of Jonah the prophet." For Mark, only unbelievers want signs. There are no signs from heaven because the signs are being done on earth: the blind see, the deaf hear, the mute speak, the lame walk, the hungry are fed. The only signs worth seeing that are authentic and unhypocritical are the concrete works for justice, mercy, compassion, and nonviolence (*BSM*, 224).

We are in deep waters now. They are in the boat, and the disciples "had forgotten to bring bread" and had "only one loaf" with them. Jesus, meanwhile, launches into a warning: "Watch out; guard against the leaven of the Pharisees and the leaven of Herod." He is telling them to stand against both the Jewish and Gentile systems that keep everyone oppressed and divided. But they have no idea what he is talking about and conclude that his talk of leaven must have something to do with the fact that they did not bring enough bread. Myers explains:

> Mark is reminding the disciple/reader of the two main political forces in Galilee hostile to the kingdom project of reconciliation between Jew and gentile. On the one hand the Pharisaic party opposes integration on grounds of social boundary and purity. On the other, the Herodian-sponsored program of Hellenization offers a style of "integration" based on cultural imperialism and collaboration with Rome. Those who resist such a program are disposed of, as in the case of John the Baptist. Either "leaven" will destroy the delicate social experiment of the "one loaf." (*BSM*, 224)

A key to understanding Mark here is the distinction between the plural "loaves" and the singular "loaf." The disciples' inability to understand the difference, and ours too, leads to Jesus's heated remarks:

> "Why do you conclude that it is because you have no bread? Do you not yet understand or comprehend? Are your hearts hardened? Do you have eyes and not see, ears and not hear? And do you not remember, when I broke the five loaves for the five thousand, how many wicker baskets full of fragments you picked up?" They answered him, "Twelve." "When I broke the seven loaves for the four thousand, how many full baskets of fragments did you pick up?" They answered him, "Seven." He said to them, "Do you still not understand?"

Even with the benefit of this written record of Jesus, we today struggle to understand just as those first disciples did. Jesus cannot fathom our lack of understanding, then or now. Jesus is uniting all humanity into himself, into one loaf. He is uniting the divided world of Jew and Gentile in his kingdom of one new humanity where all resources are shared equally, where all are healed, where all are liberated, where all live in love and peace together. Do you still not yet understand? he asks us. We do not. Don't you see? he asks them. They do not. And so, he goes forward next to give sight to the blind.

Back in their home territory, people bring him a blind man and beg him to touch him. Jesus takes him outside the village, which means, into the wilderness, puts spit on his eyes, and lays hands on him. "Do you see anything?" he asks the man. "I see people looking like trees and walking," he answers. He has eyes but cannot see clearly. This is an allusion to the disciples. They still do not see clearly, or understand, what Jesus is doing. So, Jesus has to lay hands on him a second time until his vision is completely restored. As with the blind man, Jesus will have to keep at it with the disciples until at last they begin to see. The same will be true with us.

"Take Up Your Cross and Follow Me!" (8:27–10:52)

Jesus turns to the disciples and asks the ultimate question: "Who do you say that I am?" It is a question for the ages, a question asked of each one of us. There are a million ways to answer. You are a very good person, we could say. You are a hero. You are a prophet. You are my idol. You're the greatest. None of these suffice. At best, they reveal that we are mere fans of Jesus, and Jesus is not looking for fans. He is looking for faithful disciples. At worst, they betray our complete lack of understanding about who he is, what he teaches, and what he has come to do.

"You are the Messiah," Peter responds. Every faithful Jew was expecting a messiah, but they were expecting a violent messiah who would overthrow Rome in a revolution and lead the chosen people to rule Jerusalem. Jesus knows that's what Peter and the gang are hoping for. He also knows that he has nothing to do with violence. He is a revolutionary, yes, but a nonviolent revolutionary who will lead a grassroots movement of nonviolent resistance against Jerusalem and the empire. For him, everything boils down to nonviolence, even to his understanding of self and God. Yes, he will save everyone from the evils of empire, but he will show them how to do that by following him every step of the way, on the path of nonviolence. For him, the means are the ends; all the way to heaven is heaven. But no matter how much he emphasizes the call to universal love, compassion, and mercy, the disciples cannot begin to grasp his way of nonviolence. So, he tells them not to tell anyone about him. He knows what lies ahead and that one day they will understand and be able to talk about him the correct way. But for now, they are not to talk about him publicly as the Messiah.

So, the instruction begins. He explains the way of nonviolence, and the consequences he will suffer for his nonviolent resistance to the empire. The Son of Humanity, he explains, "must suffer greatly and be rejected by the elders, the chief priests, and the scribes, and be killed, and rise after three days." Jesus knew the stories of the prophets, how Jeremiah, Daniel, Isaiah, and so many others were persecuted, even killed. He knew and loved John the Baptist. He could see that, if the authorities executed John, he didn't stand a chance. He would face the same outcome. He started to prepare himself for his arrest, torture, and execution. Part of that preparation was to begin preparing his disciples, too, to help them understand the inevitable outcome.

Jesus was not passive. That is something Mark makes blatantly clear. He was a man of action, someone who took risks, someone who stood up publicly, spoke out publicly, and sided publicly with the poor, the marginalized, the excluded, and the enemy. His was a bold, daring, creative nonviolence. By announcing the coming of God's reign of peace and, therefore, by publicly denouncing and resisting the empire's reign of domination, Jesus could face only inevitable martyrdom. He was not a fortune-teller: this future was clear for anyone with eyes wide open. It was clear to him, as it was to Gandhi, who knew he would be assassinated, just as Dr. King knew his days were numbered, just as Archbishop Romero knew that in a land of death squads he would be killed sooner or later. Arrest, torture, and execution are the normal, natural consequence of public revolutionary action that threatens the powers that be.

Peter will have none of it. He takes Jesus aside and begins to rebuke him. "Are you crazy?" he must have said. "You can't do that! You'll ruin everything. We can't let you get arrested, tortured, and killed! God forbid!" Jesus turns around, and "looking at his disciples," Mark tells us, rebukes Peter, saying, "Get behind me, Satan. You are thinking not as God does but as human beings do."

This is one of the most shocking, surprising statements in the Gospels. Jesus calls Peter none other than Satan, the ruler of the world of violence and death. The charge is that Peter is not thinking as God does. To think as God thinks is, of course, the only thing that matters. In our shock, we need to ask, how do we think as God thinks? To think as God thinks means to think with a mind of proactive love and compassion, active nonviolence, solidarity with the oppressed, yet in an attitude of faith and infinite peace. Learning this mindset and heart-set, we become more empowered to act as Jesus acts.

Jesus summons the crowd and says to everyone, "Whoever wishes to come after me must deny himself, take up his cross, and follow me." If you want to be a Christian, you have to deny yourself and follow the nonviolent Jesus on the path of peace and into universal redemptive suffering love, as you resist the structures of harm and oppression. Renounce your violence and comforts and join his campaign of nonviolent resistance to empire and steadfast allegiance to God's reign of peace.

None of these words do justice to the power of Mark's declaration. If you want to follow Jesus, you have to change your life and start working for a global nonviolent revolution and transformation, and that means you have to start preparing for your own death. Presume you are going to be killed. Get ready for martyrdom. The more authentic your discipleship, the more inevitable such an outcome will become. Because you are a disturber of the peace, like the nonviolent Jesus, the state will come after you, punish you, arrest you, imprison you, maybe even kill you. This is your job description.

Like everyone in ancient Palestine, Jesus would have seen men crucified along the roads by the Romans. Their horrific executions were intended to terrify the population and prevent them from joining various revolutionary groups to overthrow the empire. Jesus was determined to nonviolently resist the empire and proclaim God's reign of peace, and he wanted followers who would carry on his campaign. So, when he commands his followers to take up the cross, he's directing us to speak out publicly against the status quo of empire. He wants his followers to know what they are getting themselves into. He wants us to discover that the greatest thing we can do with our lives is to put aside our personal plans for success and join the work of God's reign.

The stark teachings continue: "Whoever wishes to save his life will lose it, but whoever loses his life for my sake and that of the gospel will save it. What profit is there for one to gain the whole world and forfeit his life? What could one give in exchange for his life?" Apparently, those who have gained every success, who rule the world, who have every luxury imaginable, are the greatest failures. Life in the world is only a prelude, he teaches. We have only a short time before we stand before God on the edge of eternity. Don't waste precious time in pursuit of power, prestige, money, or success in a world that crushes billions in violence and poverty. That will not count for anything in God's reign. That is not thinking as God thinks. Don't try to be rich, powerful, and domineering in this life, because you will end up with nothing. Rather, practice downward mobility. Seek voluntary poverty, powerlessness, nonviolence, universal solidarity, and love for the poorest and the enemy. As you let go of your life and follow what the nonviolent Jesus did with his life, you are entering eternal life. You will not have success in this world, but you will be honored and celebrated in the next as one of Jesus's faithful followers.

"Whoever is ashamed of me and of my words in this faithless and sinful generation," he concludes, "the Son of Humanity will be ashamed of when he comes in his Father's glory with the holy angels." Mark emphasizes that Jesus wants wholehearted devotion to his visionary nonviolence and to God. He does not want us to have any allegiance to or reliance on the world, its systems, its powers, and its militaries; rather, he wants us to rely solely on God and God's reign. If we shake our heads at such idealism, if we walk away from it, if we are embarrassed by it, Jesus will feel the same for us. It will be embarrassing to stand at the door of heaven having spent our time so fervently mocking it by our support of our nation's injustice and violence.

Mark is trying to impress upon us the karmic law of consequence from the perspective of violence and nonviolence. We reap what we sow. We gain what we give. If we reject Jesus and his way now, how can we expect to be part of Jesus's reign after we die? It is a provocative life-or-death question worth pondering.

The coda to the teachings: "Amen, I say to you, there are some standing here who will not taste death until they see that the kingdom of God has come in power." This is a hint of things to come: not just the crucifixion of Jesus but his resurrection from death as the fullest possible sign of the breakthrough of God's reign on earth.

"This Is My Beloved Son. Listen to Him" (9:2–32)

Mark's account of Jesus's transfiguration is more bare bones than Matthew's. Jesus takes Peter, James, and John up Mount Tabor, and he is transfigured. His clothes turn into dazzling white (the clothing of martyrs); Elijah and Moses appear with him (representing the law and the prophets); and Peter tries to take control of the situation. "Rabbi," he says, "it is good that we are here! Let us make three tents: one for you, one for Moses, and one for Elijah." Like everyone since then, he tries to control God, to grasp this "spiritual experience" and bottle it, and to build a shrine or at least a retreat house where they can stay safe in their "feel good" experience. But that is not the point at all. So, a voice speaks out from a cloud saying, "This is my beloved Son. Listen to him." The focus should always be on Jesus, not on us. We should not talk but listen to him, and him alone.

"Suddenly, looking around, they no longer saw anyone but Jesus alone with them." He told them not to tell anyone about this, until the day of his resurrection. That was no problem; they didn't know what just happened—or what he meant by such a day. "So, they kept the matter to themselves, questioning what rising from the dead meant."

They ask him about Elijah the prophet who is supposed to return just before the coming of the Messiah. Yes, Elijah will come first, he says, and he has come (in John the Baptist), and they jailed and killed him, but why, he asks, turning the question back on them, "must the Son of Humanity suffer greatly and be treated with contempt?" It is the question of all time. Why should this be the end for someone who loved so many, healed so many, taught so many, and worked so hard to stop violence and injustice and serve God? Why? Because anyone who speaks out against the abuse of power in an occupied land and who attracts a large following will be perceived to be a threat, and the powers will crush him.

When they arrive at the bottom of the mountain, they discover a large crowd standing around the disciples, who are arguing with the scribes. He asks them, "What are you arguing about with the scribes?" A man with a possessed boy approaches Jesus and tells him, "Wherever it seizes him, it throws him down; he foams at the mouth, grinds his teeth, and becomes rigid. I asked your disciples to drive it out, but they were unable to do so."

Jesus has landed right back into the world, dealing with a child filled with violence, his father, and the disciples who are unable to help the poor father or son and are arguing with the scribes. "O faithless generation, how long will I be with you?" he asks aloud. "How long will I endure you? Bring him to me." He has just been transfigured into pure white light and has conversed with Moses and Elijah, only to find everyone as faithless as ever. Jesus is looking for followers who really believe in him. We can read this text two thousand years later and tell ourselves, "I believe in him," but he's probably as frustrated with us as he was with the first disciples, the scribes, and the crowds. If we really believe in him, then we would do the works of mercy, healing, justice, and peace that he did. We would wield the power of Gospel nonviolence left and right, and our lives would give bold witness to our faith. We would do everything we could to please Jesus and welcome God's reign of peace.

When they bring the boy to Jesus, the boy is thrown into convulsions. He falls on the ground, rolls around, and foams at the mouth. Jesus questions the father, like a doctor seeking a diagnosis, so he can give the correct cure. "How long has this been happening to him?" "Since childhood," the father responds. "It has often thrown him into fire and into water to kill him." Mark alludes here to the fire of Pentecost and the water of baptism and refers to the intense turmoil of the early Christians and would-be Christians who struggle to believe, to deal with their baptisms and confirmation of the Spirit.

"If you can do anything, have compassion on us and help us." Jesus's frustration comes out again. "'If you can!' Everything is possible to one who has faith." The boy's father cries out, "I do believe, help my unbelief!" Jesus rebukes the unclean spirit, orders it to leave the boy, and the boy becomes "like a corpse." Jesus takes him by the hand, raises him, and the boy stands up. Mark shows us who this Jesus is, how he can raise those to new life who are baptized and confirmed, and maybe even killed by the empire for their faith.

The disciples look on in confusion. This time, instead of expressing awe or wonder, they ask why they could not drive out the demon. "This kind can only come out through prayer," Jesus tells them. Here we have the first reference to prayer addressed to the disciples so far in Mark's Gospel. We have heard the commandment to take up the cross, and we have seen how only faith can lead to healing and good works, but we still haven't learned, like the disciples, that authentic discipleship requires carrying the cross of nonviolent resistance to empire yet rooted in profound faith in and commitment to the nonviolent Jesus. Ched Myers expands on these new questions:

> What is prayer? When Jesus next returns to this subject (11:23), he will explicitly connect prayer to "the power of belief." To pray is to learn to believe in a transformation of self and world, which seems empirically impossible—as in "moving mountains" (11:23). What is unbelief but the despair, dictated by the dominant powers, that nothing can really change, a despair that renders revolutionary vision and practice impotent. The disciples are instructed to battle this impotence, this temptation to resignation, through prayer. "Keep awake and pray that you may not succumb to temptation!" Jesus later will urge them (14:38). The "strength" (or inability) to cast out demons is deeply connected to the "strength to stay awake" (14:37); tragically, the disciples will sleep while Jesus sweats in prayer in Gethsemane, and they will flee when he turns to face the powers. (*BSM*, 255–56)

Myers proceeds with a series of pertinent questions:

> Is not prayer the intensely personal struggle within each disciple, and among us collectively, to resist the despair and distractions that cause us to practice unbelief, to abandon or avoid the way of Jesus? And has not this demon, so embedded in our imperial culture, not kept us impotent, docile subjects of the status quo "since childhood" (9:21)? Yet just as the synagogue ruler's daughter, who was presumed lost (5:39) is raised, signaling a "future" for Israel, so too this boy, giving us hope for the future of the deteriorating discipleship narrative. To acknowledge that we are impaled on the contradiction of our belief and our unbelief is to take the first step toward healing. (*BSM*, 256)

The issue is the cross, which is rarely the center of our discussions. Few try quietly to follow that difficult path—spending their entire lives in steadfast nonviolent resistance to militarism, violence, injustice, and war. "How many generations of interpreters have insisted on spiritualizing the cross, transforming it from a strictly political to a strictly religious symbol?" Myers asks. The future of Christianity depends on our refusal to spiritualize the cross and instead practice it as the way of full-time resistance to our culture of death. Myers concludes:

How many still read the negation, rather than the affirmation, of martyrdom in the vision of the advent of the Human One and the transfiguration, despite the fact that Mark identifies both with the one moment of the cross? This is a longstanding conspiracy of hermeneutical suppression by those who have never stood in an earthly court charged with messianic subversion, those who are busy building booths to dead prophets rather than struggling with the demons that mute their own prophetic voice. But it cannot hide the truth of Mark's discourse: there is no discipleship to Jesus that does not take up the cross. (*BSM*, 256)

Myers's point—that prayer is based in a deep, profound faith in God that encourages our resistance to the culture and our practice of total nonviolence every step along the way of the cross—will become clearer later. For now, Jesus hides out from the crowds and tries to teach his disciples about the reality of the cross, his resistance to the empire, and the inevitable consequences. "The Son of Humanity is to be handed over to men and they will kill him, and three days after his death he will rise," Jesus tells them up front. They are going to kill me, but I will rise from the dead. Once again, Mark states the obvious: "They did not understand the saying, and they were afraid to question him." Not only do they have no idea what he is talking about, but they are afraid. It's the same with us. Two thousand years later, not much has changed. We do not understand the political, confrontational focus of the cross as nonviolent resistance to the culture of violence, and we're too afraid to think about it, study it, talk about it, much less practice it. And so we spiritualize the whole thing as a kind of private form of piety and take away its power to transform ourselves and our world.

"Be the Last of All and the Servant of All" (9:33–10:12)

In the lessons that follow, as Jesus continues on the road to Jerusalem, where he will engage in nonviolent civil disobedience and suffer the consequences, he teaches them that this way needs to touch every aspect of their lives. The community has to be nonviolent; we have to be nonviolent to one another; and we have to be nonviolent toward all those we meet. Furthermore, as disciples on the way of nonviolence, as we explore every avenue of this action, we challenge every cultural structure of violence and turn it upside down so that a new culture of peace can be born. Through our communal nonviolence the dominant social order will be turned upside-down, and every aspect of religious culture that supports the dominant order will be turned upside-down as well.

Jesus is talking about what lies ahead, how he is about to be killed, and what are they talking about? They are arguing among themselves about which one of them is the greatest! If this were a situation comedy, you would laugh. You couldn't make it up. They seemed to say and do the opposite of whatever the nonviolent Jesus says and does. By showing us their extreme misunderstanding, Mark hopes to shake us, the readers, out of our complacency and turn our attention to the nonviolent Jesus and his impending execution.

"What were you arguing about on the way?" he asks them. They are embarrassed and probably lower their heads in silence. He's about to die, and they're focused on themselves, arguing about which one of them is the greatest. If we want to surpass them, we to have stand against ourselves, let go of our egos and our narcissism, and focus solely on Jesus, his way of the cross, and God's will. The minute we focus on our greatness, we know we have lost the way.

"If anyone wishes to be first," he tells them, "he shall be the last of all and the servant of all." Then Mark describes how Jesus takes a child, places it in their midst, and puts his arms around it and says, "Whoever receives one child such as this in my name, receives me; and whoever receives me, receives not me but the One who sent me."

With this teaching and this symbolic act, Jesus upends the social order, including its oppression of everyone, beginning with children. If we are to follow Jesus's way, we must become the servant of all and the last of all. We do not seek to be served, or even have a trace of the desire for reciprocation when we do service. We reduce ourselves to zero, as Gandhi described it, humble ourselves, empty ourselves, put everyone else before us, and try our best to help relieve—even end—human suffering. Along the way, we plumb the depths of nonviolence, and even reclaim our inner child and become as free, innocent, wide-eyed, open, vulnerable, loving, and excited as a child. Our hearts open wide into universal love.

A little footnote: Paul mentions traveling with Peter's son John Mark. Some suggest that the only way the writer Mark could know so much, especially all the failings of Peter, is if he had heard them directly from his father, or perhaps even witnessed his father's failings at discipleship. More, perhaps the little child whom Jesus placed in the midst of his disciples was none other than a boy named Mark. Mark might be reporting his own experience!

The teachings about discipleship, leadership, and personal nonviolence continue. John complains about some other person who's proclaiming the gospel in Jesus's name, and he and the disciples are angry. Who does this other person think he is? He's not part of our group! They're trying to manage the Jesus movement, even to control Jesus, if possible. "Teacher, we saw someone driving out demons in your name, and we tried to prevent him because he does not follow us," John says. Notice: he and the other disciples are upset because this guy does not follow *them*! The focus is still on themselves, not Jesus.

This mistake has continued for two thousand years. We don't have to look far to see narcissism, control, abuse of power, and domination behind the actions of numerous church leaders today. We want to be in charge; we don't want anyone else getting any credit for proclaiming the gospel. We are jealous and want all the attention. "Do not prevent him," Jesus tells them. "There is no one who performs a mighty deed in my name who can at the same time speak ill of me," he continues. "For whoever is not against us is for us." This is the logic of nonviolence, the way of the nonviolent Jesus. We have to be humble and support one another—especially anyone else who does the work of nonviolence, who supports the nonviolent Jesus, who proclaims God's reign of peace. Anyone who proclaims the nonviolence of God and Jesus is doing the same work and on the same side as all others following Jesus's way.

"Anyone who gives you a cup of water to drink because you belong to Christ, amen, I say to you, will surely not lose his reward," he concludes. To give a cup of water to a nonviolent Christian in the first century was to risk one's life. That act showed solidarity with the campaign to resist the empire and proclaim God's reign of peace. We could translate this as follows: any Indian who supported Gandhi and gave him a glass of water was targeted by the British, but also rewarded by God—eventually. Anyone who supported Dr. King during the

1960s in Mississippi could be targeted by the Klan. Everyone who supports the prophets of justice and peace will share in the troubles and honors of the prophets themselves.

The opposite is also true. Those who harm or lead astray the followers of Jesus will suffer the consequences. In the examples that follow, we hear Jesus teaching his followers to be nonviolent even to those community members who fall away. The Zealots punished those who broke the rules or engaged in criminal behavior. The nonviolent Jesus teaches, however, that we do not punish our own people who fail, as the violent Zealots punished their own. Jesus is on the side of justice and teaches that there are consequences to all our actions, but his punishment always comes within the boundaries of nonviolence.

How can he impress this upon the disciples? He tries to explain how serious the calling of discipleship and nonviolence is, that we as his followers can never hurt any human being ever again, especially these little ones—children, minorities, the poor, the disenfranchised.

> "Whoever causes one of these little ones who believe in me to sin, it would be better for him if a great millstone were put around his neck and he were thrown into the sea. If your hand causes you to sin, cut it off. It is better for you to enter into life maimed than with two hands to go into Gehenna into the unquenchable fire. And if your foot causes you to sin, cut it off. It is better for you to enter into life crippled than with two feet to be thrown into Gehenna. And if your eye causes you to sin, pluck it out. Better for you to enter into the kingdom of God with one eye than with two eyes to be thrown into Gehenna."

Violent revolutionaries—from the Zealots to the Mafia to the IRA—have always had their own warped sense of justice rooted in violence and punishment. Often they would execute one of their own to protect themselves from the empire. If someone's hand hurts another revolutionary, they teach them a lesson by cutting it off. If someone's foot hurts another revolutionary, they cut it off. If someone's eye leads to hurting another revolutionary, they plucked it out. Jesus says, forget that: cut off your own hand or foot, pluck out your own eye before you dare hurt anyone else in the discipleship community! It's a shocking exaggeration intended to wake us up to the implications of the nonviolent lifestyle in our own community of faith.

"Everyone will be salted with fire," Mark's Jesus concludes. "Salt is good, but if salt becomes insipid, with what will you restore its flavor? Keep salt in yourselves and you will have peace with one another." Salt purifies and preserves food. Here he says the salt that will flavor us will be the fire of Pentecost, when his Holy Spirit of total nonviolence will come upon his community and disarm, purify, and preserve his followers. So, he urges us to stay salted, stay on fire with his passionate nonviolence, and be at peace with one another. If we remain salted, seasoned, and steadfast in his nonviolence, we will remain disarmed; practice universal love, compassion, and persistent reconciliation; and live on in communities of peace. All will be well if we do. If we stay salted, if we keep the fire of his spirit of nonviolence within us and among us, then, like him, we will always dwell in the peace of God and maintain that holy peace among us. As people of Pentecostal nonviolence, we will maintain communities of nonviolence even in the culture of violence and war. If we don't, we will not have peace among us. We will hurt and fight with each other, and will wage war and kill one another. Apparently, the early church remained salted with fire for the first three centuries, but then we lost our salt, renounced Gospel nonviolence, put out the fire of Pentecost, and have had no peace among us since then.

As Jesus continues his walking campaign, he teaches the crowd and faces the hostile interrogations of the religious authorities. This time, the Pharisees ask if it is lawful for a husband to divorce his wife. He responds with another question: "What did Moses command you?" "Because of the hardness of your hearts he wrote you this commandment," Jesus tells them. "But from the beginning of creation, 'God made them male and female. For this reason, a man shall leave his father and mother and be joined to his wife, and the two shall become one flesh. . . . What God has joined together, no human being must separate.'" Back in the community house, the disciples ask him what this means, because, of course, they cannot understand it. "Whoever divorces his wife and marries another commits adultery against her; and if she divorces her husband and marries another, she commits adultery." Jesus will not get into a legal debate, but uses the scripture to point to the equality between men and women. No one did that in those days, particularly not the patriarchal religious authorities. That's why Jesus's teaching on divorce was revolutionary. It's an attack on patriarchy itself and points back to the equality envisioned in Genesis. A careful study reveals that he does not make a blanket condemnation of divorce but rather questions why these religious authorities maintain the patriarchal, unjust status quo. Jesus is a feminist through and through, which means he insists on the totally equality of men and women.

"The Kingdom of God Belongs to Such as These" (10:13–16)

Mark tells of how people brought their children to Jesus that he might bless them, and how the disciples rebuked the parents. At this, he says, Jesus became indignant at the disciples. They have missed the whole point of accepting and blessing children. They are trying to be "holier than thou" like the religious authorities who just interrogated Jesus. Jesus is nonviolent but is frustrated with them. He can't seem to get them to understand his new way of life. "Let the children come to me; do not prevent them, for the kingdom of God belongs to such as these."

The kingdom of God belongs to children. Once again, with this saying, Jesus subverts the religious tradition and the surrounding culture because he places children first and foremost in the sight of God and at the center of his community. Mark writes specifically that he embraced the children and blessed them by placing his hands on them. He is gentle, loving, and welcoming of all children, for he sees the best of humanity in their openness, vulnerability, sweetness, wonder, innocence, trust, and joy.

With this act, Jesus insists that our nonviolence must go back to our roots, through our past, to childhood, and that we must raise our children so that they might grow into Jesus's way of life. "Whoever does not accept the kingdom of God like a child will not enter it." If we want to enter the kingdom of God—God's home of universal love and infinite peace—we have to start living as innocent children—full of wonder, curiosity, interest, laughter, and joy.

But Myers goes further. He argues that Mark is not idealizing childhood but calling the

Christian community to reverse the dominant social order by extending our nonviolence not just in resistance to empire but also in resistance to the status quo family structure, which is *domination*. Mark calls for a restructuring of social power at the most intimate level—the household.

> The war of myths rages even at the heart of the community: Jesus is committed to inclusivity, his disciples to exclusivity. Jesus' solemn pronouncement thus turns this seemingly minor skirmish into nothing less than a watershed challenge about participation in the kingdom! This episode for the second time illustrates the way of nonviolence by reversing the normal socio-cultural assumptions about status, elevating the "last" to "first." And certainly, the child represented the "least of the least." In a significant symbolic action, Jesus rescues children from the margins of the new community and places them at its center as a fundamental object lesson. (*BSM*, 267)

Myers argues that the child represents an actual class of exploited persons, that Mark understands the child as victim, and therefore Mark is not idealizing childhood but rather challenging us to raise children from birth to a life free from violence and subjugation.

> What if the "site" of the child, vulnerable, credulous and dependent, is in fact the very beginning point in the spiral of both exploitation and violence? Could it be that the discourse of Mark is arguing that if we are to forge a nonviolent way of life, we must weed out the structures and practices of violence at their roots? That the validity of nonviolence must pertain to the most basic building block of human social existence: the family? (*BSM*, 268)

> Myers cites the esteemed philosopher and psychoanalyst Alice Miller for insights into Mark's message. She argues that childrearing based in social domination and political violence is the root cause of our pandemic of violence. "It follows that nonviolence," Myers adds, "as a part of a radical practice that seeks to address structural injustice at its roots, must begin with the family system. It is then in this sense, I would argue, that we must comprehend the saying, 'Unless you receive the kingdom as a child, you cannot enter it.' A new social order cannot be constructed unless and until we have dealt with the very foundations of oppression [by ending all violence towards children]" (*BSM*, 270).

"Go, Sell What You Have, Give to the Poor, Then Come, Follow Me" (10:17–52)

Mark's one remaining teaching under the theme of the greatest and the least is the effect of economic class and privilege on Jesus's call to radical discipleship and nonviolence. In perhaps Myers's most brilliant analysis, he contrasts Mark's two extreme stereotypes: at one end of the spectrum, a rich landowner who rejects the call to discipleship, and at the other end, a poor blind man who eagerly follows Jesus "on the way."

Mark tells us that Jesus is walking on his journey when a man interrupts him, kneels before him, and asks, "Good teacher, what must I do to inherit eternal life?" Notice, he calls

Jesus a good teacher, not Lord or Master. This is just flattery, plain and simple. And like the disciples, the man's focus is on himself: what must *I* do?—as if he had the power to inherit eternal life! He thinks, like all rich, privileged, and entitled people do, that eternal life is his inheritance, his basic right, something he deserves.

Jesus immediately objects: "Why do you call me good? No one is good but God alone." He's trying to push the rich man and the rest of us to a deeper understanding of reliance on God. As we will soon see in the spectacular story of the blind beggar Bartimaeus, the only way to approach God is to kneel down in humility and say, "Have mercy on me." The focus of the action is on God, not ourselves, because there is nothing, in the end, that we can do. We are helpless and powerless regarding eternal life, and for that matter, birth and death, but God is not. God can do whatever God wants. Eternal life and the reign of God belong, first of all, to God. If we receive it or are welcomed into it, it is solely through the compassionate action of God. This is the mystery of faith and total reliance on God.

Jesus starts listing the commandments of the Torah, asking in effect if the man follows them, but what few realize is that he slips in one of his own making: "You shall not defraud." This means, "You shall not deceive people to deprive them of their wealth or possessions." Wealthy landowners would have normally done anything deceptive or oppressive to maintain their status and get ahead. Myers argues that Mark's Jesus is placing a judgment on the wealthy class. But the man insists he has observed "all of these" commandments.

Mark then writes specifically that Jesus looks at him and loves him. It is the only time in Mark that we're told that Jesus loves someone, using the Greek word *agapē* for unconditional love. Myers comments that Mark is making it abundantly clear that Jesus practices the great commandment of love, which he will discuss in an upcoming confrontation with the scribes (*BSM*, 273).

"You are lacking in one thing," Jesus tells the wealthy man. He then proceeds to give him four commandments: "Go, sell what you have, and give to the poor and you will have treasure in heaven, then come, follow me." *Go, Sell, Give, and Follow.* Because the privileged man has said he has kept God's commandments in the Torah, Jesus loves him and summons him into the fullness of God's reign through radical discipleship. Mark emphasizes this call to discipleship to those who think they are in control of their lives and their eternal destiny. This privileged person does not understand, as the blind beggar Bartimaeus does, that we can do nothing without God, that we need to be completely surrendered to God if we would reach the spiritual heights of the Torah, the prophets, universal love, and God's reign of peace. Jesus demands nothing less than a complete surrender to God and God's will. He knows that, even if we are surrendered some of the time to God, we are still running our own lives and thus hurting others and supporting the culture of death. For Jesus, it's all or nothing—let go of your life completely, give it to God, and live every moment from now on in God doing God's will, not one's own.

With these commands, the man's face falls and he walks away sad, we're told, because "he had many possessions." The Greek word used refers to people who owned large pieces of property. He is a rich landowner, and, even though he is loved directly by Jesus and invited to sell his possessions, give the money to the poor, and follow, he turns away sad. He's too attached to his money, his possessions, his land. Mark is telling us point blank that money, possessions, and land prevent us from following Jesus, and this addiction to wealth has spiritual consequences, eternal consequences.

Notice he tells the man to "Go." The Greek word is better translated as "Get up." This, according to Myers, is a common phrase in Mark's healing stories, so we can presume that Mark is describing here the call to be healed of the sickness of accumulating wealth (*BSM*, 273). It's also the same call issued to the fishermen who dropped their nets and left behind all their "assets." The only difference here is the command to distribute the wealth among the poor, which the man simply cannot do. "Landowners represented the most politically powerful social stratum" in Mark's Palestine, Myers points out. "As far as Mark is concerned, the man's wealth has been gained by 'defrauding' the poor—he was not 'blameless' at all—for which he must make restitution. For Mark, the law is kept only through concrete acts of justice, not the façade of piety" (*BSM*, 274).

"How hard it is for those who have wealth to enter the kingdom of God!" Jesus tells his stunned disciples. He repeats his statement, and in each case we're told how the disciples are amazed and astonished. "It is easier for a camel to pass through the eye of a needle than for one who is rich to enter the kingdom of God." With this sarcastic statement, the disciples are shell-shocked. The whole point of the Torah, the Word, the Bible is that God blesses the rich, they presumed. Wealth is the ultimate sign of God's blessing, isn't it? We hear it everywhere today, especially from the famous televangelists who preach "a gospel of prosperity." Making money is a sure sign that God is on your side, the culture of greed tells us. Baloney! Mark's Jesus declares. The exact opposite is true. The more wealth you have, the farther you are from God, and the more impossible it is to enter God's reign of universal love toward all.

"Who can be saved?" the confused disciples ask. "For human beings it is impossible, but not for God," Jesus declares. "All things are possible for God." With God, everything and everyone can be turned upside-down, and eventually will be. The last will be first, the least will become the greatest, the peacemakers will supersede the warmakers, the justice seekers will be satisfied, and the injustice builders will walk away empty. Here we have the revolution up close: the one percent who now own everything, control everything, decide everything, are far from God because God's reign is the exact opposite: a new world of emptiness, poverty of spirit, vulnerability, humility, voluntary poverty, and utter, total trust in God. Only those who are poor can be open to God's reign, as we heard in the first sentence of Matthew's Beatitudes. The rich do not need God and, therefore, will never fit in.

Shaken by all this talk of wealth as an impediment to discipleship, Peter speaks up in defense of the disciples. "We have given up everything and followed you," he says. Mark concludes with a list of ways the kingdom of God will be entered here and now on earth, for those who drop everything and follow him. "There is no one who has given up house or brothers or sisters or mother or father or children or lands for my sake and for the sake of the gospel who will not receive a hundred times more now in this present age—houses and brothers and sisters and mothers and children and lands, with persecutions, and eternal life in the age to come. Many that are first will be last, and the last will be first." His declaration promises that, if you are last, or choose to become last, in God's reign you will be first, even here on earth. All these blessings of houses, relatives, and land come through the Christian community, as Mark's community would have known well. Likewise, an authentic discipleship community would be engaged in ongoing campaigns of public nonviolent resistance and so would be persecuted by the empire, as Mark's community would also have known all too well.

"They were on the way," Mark writes, using the name of the early community of Jesus's followers—the Way—"going up to Jerusalem, and Jesus went ahead of them." The crowds were amazed to see him, while the disciples, knowing what they now knew, about downward mobility and the inevitable persecutions, were afraid. Once again, Jesus starts telling them in clear terms what lies ahead: "We are going up to Jerusalem, and the Son of Humanity will be handed over to the chief priests and the scribes, and they will condemn him to death and hand him over to the Gentiles who will mock him, spit upon him, scourge him, and put him to death, but after three days he will rise." The disciples can't take in any of this. They are expecting a violent messiah who will lead a hostile takeover of Jerusalem so they can all become rich and be saved, and he's saying the opposite of all that. This left them speechless, maybe even wondering if they had made the wrong decision by following him.

Not James and John. They step up and ask for a place of honor when he comes into his messianic glory. "Teacher, we want you to do for us whatever we ask of you," they tell him. "What do you wish me to do for you?" "Grant that in your glory we may sit one at your right and the other at your left," they answer. After all his instructions about becoming the least and the last, after explaining that he is not a military messiah who will take control of Jerusalem but a suffering servant about to be tortured and executed, they ask to sit by his side in the greatest place of honor. It's as if they never heard a word he said.

"You do not know what you are asking," Jesus tells them. "Can you drink the cup that I drink or be baptized with the baptism with which I am baptized?" This is one of the key questions of the Gospels. Can you drink my cup of nonviolent suffering love, or be baptized in nonviolent suffering love? Can you give your life in nonviolent suffering love for humanity? Can you give your life for humanity, like me? Surprisingly, they answer, "We can." That's good enough for Jesus. He can see that they will stay faithful to the public campaign of peace. "The cup that I drink, you will drink, and with the baptism with which I am baptized, you will be baptized; but to sit at my right or at my left is not mine to give but is for those for whom it has been prepared."

Two months before his assassination, Martin Luther King Jr. preached on this text. He pointed out that Jesus does not put them down for wanting to be up front in a place of honor. Dr. King thought it was important to recognize that Jesus, in fact, encourages their ambition by saying, in effect, "If you want to be first, if you want to be the drum major in the parade, wonderful! But be a drum major for justice, be a drum major for peace." If you want to do great things for God's reign, great! That was how King read this text. Go do great things for God's reign, which means, go be a leader for justice, equality, disarmament, and peace. Jesus affirms the desire to greatness but channels it into unconditional service and steadfast nonviolence for the coming of God's reign.

However, he is not the one to assign places near him in the kingdom. "Leadership belongs only to those who learn and follow the way of nonviolence," Myers comments about this verse, to those "who are prepared not to dominate but to serve and to suffer at Jesus's side" (*BSM*, 278). When Jesus tells them that he cannot name who will be on his left or his right,

James and John could not have imagined what he was alluding to. At the end of the story, Mark will speak of two men who are at his left and right—two condemned revolutionaries, one crucified next to Jesus on his left, the other on his right. If we want to be with Jesus at his right or his left, Mark is telling us, we have to stand with the poor, the marginalized, the oppressed, the enemy—and ultimately, the condemned.

The script is getting predictable. The other male disciples are "indignant" when they hear what James and John have asked. They want first-class seats, too. The disciples have clearly missed the point of everything Jesus has just taught; we probably have too. So he patiently instructs them all over again: "You know that those who are recognized as rulers over the Gentiles lord it over them, and their great ones make their authority over them felt," Jesus says. "But it shall not be so among you. Rather, whoever wishes to be great among you will be your servant; whoever wishes to be first among you will be the slave of all. For the Son of Humanity did not come to be served but to serve and to give his life as a ransom for many."

Here is the last and greatest teaching of his upside-down way of nonviolence. Those who are great are those who serve; those who are first are the last of all, and slaves of all. The Holy One has placed himself at the service of humanity, and, though he is really the first, he acts as the slave of all and, furthermore, gives his life as a ransom for humanity. The Holy One is perfect nonviolence, through and through. To be disciples of the nonviolent Jesus, then, means to serve everyone, especially the poor and those in need; to be the last of all and slave of all; and to give our lives for humanity. Nonviolence requires the giving of our lives, the art of suffering and dying, rather than the world's way of inflicting suffering and killing. We give our lives for suffering humanity, for an end to their suffering, for the coming of God's reign of justice and peace because we try to emulate the Son of Humanity who gave his life for humanity.

Myers adds an addendum. Notice, he says, that not only does Mark go out of his way to describe the ignorance of the male disciples, but there are few women mentioned, no married couples mentioned, and the women who are mentioned appear without husbands. He describes this as the intentional, subversive strategy of Mark, for at the end of the story, as we will see, it is only the women who stand with Jesus and serve unconditionally, and therefore it is only women who become witnesses to the resurrection (*BSM*, 280).

And so, we come to the last and greatest example of discipleship, the other extreme stereotype, the opposite of the rich landowner who walked away sad from Jesus. As they're leaving Jericho, a blind beggar named Bartimaeus, sitting by the road, calls out to Jesus and disrupts the procession with his shouting, "Jesus, son of David, have pity on me." We're told that many rebuke him, but of course, that would refer to Jesus's male disciples, who would have shouted right back at the poor fellow, telling him to "Shut up!" But their rebuke only makes him cry out all the more. All of a sudden, Jesus stops in his tracks. "Call him," he tells them. So they do, and this time, they are on his side, saying, "Take courage." Notice the blind beggar has been very courageous all along, not only interrupting the journey of the Holy One, but confronting the mean disciples. They are the ones who need to take courage.

Mark adds a strange detail: "He threw aside his cloak, sprang up, and came to Jesus." Why are we told this? Imagine the scene: he's a blind homeless man, sitting by the road, begging for alms. He would have laid his cloak on the ground in front of him. The cloak would have had many coins on it from the rich travelers who tossed him a coin as they passed by. In other words, the cloak held his entire livelihood, his entire bank account, all his possessions and savings! Without even thinking, he throws it aside at the word of Jesus! That is the kind of disciple Jesus is looking for: followers with total disregard for money, whose only focus is on him and his way.

"What do you want me to do for you?" Jesus asks the poor blind beggar. With this question, Jesus demonstrates infinite compassion and love for the beggar. The rich man interrupted him and demanded to know what he—the entitled rich landowner—had to do to inherit eternal life. In this scenario, Jesus places himself entirely at the disposal of the poor blind beggar. "Master, I want to see," the beggar says. This is something Jesus can give. "Go your way," he tells him. "Your faith has saved you." Jesus affirms the beggar's faith in him, and all at once, he can see. With that, Mark adds, Bartimaeus starts to follow Jesus "on the way."

When we contrast the Bartimaeus story with that of the rich man, Mark's radical demands of discipleship to the nonviolent Jesus become clear. The rich man is called but cannot leave his land and wealth and sadly turns away from Jesus. He is a member of the one percent, the upper-class elite, and he cannot follow. Bartimaeus, by contrast, is the poorest of the poor, the rock-bottom lowest class possible—a poor, blind, homeless beggar, with no one and nothing. When he hears the call, he throws away his cloak—and with it, any meager money he had—and jumps at the chance to follow Jesus. He will happily follow Jesus "on the way," and, since the next passage is Jesus's entrance into Jerusalem, Mark is showing us that the poor have joined in Jesus's final nonviolent assault on the dominant ideological order, as the rich have walked away downcast (*BSM*, 282).

Myers goes on to contrast the poor beggar's response with the clueless male disciples:

> Upon their approach, Jesus had asked James and John, "what do you want me to do for you?" To the beggar's petition, Jesus responds with exactly the same words. But how different the requests! The disciples wished for status and privilege; the beggar simply asks for his "vision." The one Jesus cannot grant, the other he can. It is Bartimaeus who is told to "take courage," as the disciples were told earlier during the dangerous crossing of the sea. And it is the beggar who follows. The narrative discourse of hope is now clear in this last discipleship/healing episode. Only if the disciples/reader struggles against the internal demons that render us deaf and mute, only if we renounce our thirst for power—in a word, only if we recognize our blindness and seek true vision—then can the discipleship adventure carry on. (*BSM*, 282)

Bartimaeus asks for vision, and Jesus is the only person in history with vision, precisely because he is not blinded by violence, wealth, imperialism, and fear. He can see; the rest of us think we can see, but actually we're all blind, beginning with the male disciples. We are blinded by our egos, our self-will, our wealth and possessions, whereas Jesus is completely surrendered to his beloved God and so he can see God completely and recognize everyone else as a beloved child of God, still stuck in the culture of death, which prevents us from understanding who we are or seeing God in one another. Bartimaeus knows he is blind, asks for vision, receives it, and what does he see? He sees Jesus standing before him, and thus he sees a vision of the way forward, for himself and the whole human race. Naturally, since he can see, he eagerly, happily, fearlessly follows Jesus "on the way." He becomes the model of radical discipleship to the nonviolent Jesus.

With the Bartimaeus story, the campaign ends where it begins: with the call to follow the nonviolent Jesus on the way of the cross—the way that touches every aspect of our lives and leads to a public campaign of resistance to the social order and the culture of domination and war. Peter couldn't grasp this early on, James and John couldn't grasp it, the rich man downright rejected it, the male disciples are terrified, the crowds are amazed—and Bartimaeus gets it and follows Jesus. He's glad to join the final nonviolent assault on the city of empire. This is good news for the poor and marginalized and bad news for the rich, the powerful, those who are first, and those who want to rule and dominate. And so, unlike Matthew's story with all his brilliant Sermon-on-the-Mount teachings, Mark presents a full-on drama, and we the readers are beginning to learn that following the nonviolent Jesus does not mean hearing the great teachings but engaging in the journey itself, joining in the narrative of nonviolent resistance, and taking public action with Jesus. This nonviolent direct action has now reached its climax as Jesus enters Jerusalem—leaving us each step of the way to choose whether we are going to join him.

"Entering the Temple Area, He Began to Drive Out Those Selling and Buying" (11:1–13:37)

Mark's Jesus is a nonviolent commando leading a nonviolent assault on Jerusalem and a nonviolent raid on the temple. There is nothing passive about him, yet there is nothing violent about him either. He's a conundrum, a new kind of human being, and a real threat to the dominant social order, including the Roman Empire itself.

It's hard for us to grasp the revolutionary nonviolence of Jesus when we have so spiritualized him and perverted his gospel into a private religion between "God and me," regardless of all the injustice and damage going on in the rest of the world. It's especially hard for us First World white, privileged, educated, entitled North Americans to understand him because everything he does goes against our complicity and participation in our own dominant social order. But it's not hard for the world's poorest, oppressed, marginalized, disenfranchised, and imprisoned people to appreciate him. For them, he makes perfect sense, and his nonviolent campaign is good news.

The greatest disciple and example of Jesus's dangerous nonviolence is Mahatma Gandhi, who led three hundred million people in a nonviolent revolution against the British Empire and eventually got the empire to leave peacefully. We romanticize Gandhi, too, and he has now been systematically dismissed by India's far right, but Gandhi's nonviolence was equally dangerous. It cost him his life.

The high point of Gandhi's campaign was his 1930 Salt March, when seventy-eight trained followers walked with him for nearly two months some two hundred thirty miles from his Sabarmati Ashram to the village of Dandi on the Indian Ocean, where they illegally made salt, thus sparking a civil disobedience campaign to break Britain's monopoly on salt and escalate a nonviolent revolution for India's independence. Millions of people immediately began to break the salt laws and violate the salt tax.

Gandhi himself was arrested and imprisoned the next day, while hundreds of other trained followers led a nonviolent assault on the Dharasana Salt Works. They marched up to the gate in rows of four or five in strict nonviolence, asked to enter, and in response were beaten with steel-like poles by Indians working for the British and the Salt Works police. Each Gandhian was severely beaten and injured, yet not one of them struck back or even lifted a hand in response. Several died, and nearly all of the hundreds of nonviolent marchers suffered broken bones and serious concussions. The whole of India, and the rest of the world, was electrified by the Salt March. The *New York Times* carried front-page daily reports. India and the world were equally horrified by the brutal British attack on the unarmed "satyagrahis" who marched on the Salt Works. With that, the tide of global opinion turned against Britain, and the journey to India's freedom began. By the early 1940s, at one point, Gandhi and over three hundred thousand Indians were serving long prison sentences for nonviolent civil disobedience. The British literally could no longer control the non-cooperating population. So in 1947, the British granted India independence and left.

Jesus was doing something similar. More than any other Gospel, Mark portrays Jesus as a nonviolent guerilla leader leading a grassroots movement of nonviolence made up of poor, disenfranchised, and outcast people to break the systemic injustice of the temple system and the oppressive hold of the Roman Empire. He wanted God's reign of nonviolence to come here and now, and he knew that in order to welcome God's reign, we had to undertake steadfast nonviolent resistance to the culture and the empire, regardless of the consequences to himself and his followers. Unlike the Zealots and other violent revolutionaries, he had no desire to create a new unjust system or to declare himself an emperor. He was not trying to reform the dominant social order, the temple, or the empire. He was mobilizing us to disarm our hearts and our world. He was rousing us, empowering us, and ordering us to create a new nonviolent culture of total equality, inclusivity, and justice. He's still doing that today.

The authorities, the elite, and those in power thought he was crazy, foolish, naïve, and hopeless, although his widespread popularity among the peasants threatened them. Who could disarm and transform the Roman Empire, or today, the British or American Empires for that matter? How could such a public campaign of resistance not end in arrest and execution, and thus total failure? Jesus, too, knew the inevitable outcome, but he was determined to be the seed that started a global grassroots campaign to disarm the world.

Two thousand years later, that global campaign of active nonviolence and steadfast resistance continues. Jesus understood, as Gandhi and King did, that the only human way to positive social change is through bottom-up, people power, grassroots nonviolent movements such as the Abolitionists, the Suffragists, the civil rights movement, the anti–Vietnam War movement, the women's movement, the environmental movement, the LGBTQ movement, the anti-apartheid movement, and countless other nonviolent movements for social change have shown. To ensure long-lasting nonviolent outcomes, with more just and democratic societies, only nonviolent means can be used, as Jesus and Gandhi demonstrate.

"Jesus comes to Jerusalem not as a pilgrim, in order to demonstrate his allegiance to its temple, but as a popular king ready to mount a nonviolent siege on the ruling classes," Myers writes:

> The long journey from the social and symbolic peripheries of Palestine (which began in the wilderness and the first direct action campaign in Capernaum) to its center is now complete. Jesus has arrived at the heart of the dominant order, and the time has come for a showdown in the war of myths. The Lord is now visiting his temple, as promised by Malachi since the beginning of the story (1:2, Mal 3:1f), and in his actions we will witness the one whom Gandhi referred to as "the most active resister known to history—this is nonviolence par excellence." (*BSM*, 290)

When they get to Jerusalem, Mark reports that Jesus tells his disciples to go into one of the villages and take one of the colts and bring it to him. If someone asks them why they are taking it, they are to answer that the Master needs it and will return it. This is one of the many clues that Jesus is running an underground movement, that he has connections all over the region with people sympathetic to him. Compared to Matthew, we note that, in Mark's earlier version, Jesus has taken the initiative, that he's the nonviolent general of this campaign. Jesus then sits on the donkey and processes into Jerusalem, while people spread their cloaks and leafy branches on the road and cry out, "Hosanna! Blessed is he who comes in the name of the Lord! Blessed is the kingdom of our father David that is to come! Hosanna in the highest!" Notice too that, compared to Matthew, Mark's crowd does not go so far as to hail him as a messiah, but more like the prophet of the messianic kingdom.

In either case, it is perfect political street theater, as Myers and others point out. Just as the nonviolent Jesus enters Jerusalem riding on a donkey, as a harmless symbol of humility and peace, the Roman procurator would have ridden into Jerusalem with his warhorse and chariot and six hundred Roman soldiers in a military parade. All of Jerusalem would have come to see this spectacle.

Jesus's entry into Jerusalem is recorded in all four Gospels, and because it precedes his nonviolent civil disobedience and the resulting execution, it must be understood as symbolic of everything to follow. Again, we realize how deliberately Jesus fulfills the ancient vision of Zechariah:

> Rejoice heartily, O daughter Zion, shout for joy, O daughter Jerusalem! See, your king shall come to you; a just savior is he, meek and riding on an ass, on a colt, the foal of an ass. He shall banish the war chariot from Ephraim, and the warhorse from Jerusalem. The warrior's bow shall be banished and he shall proclaim peace to the nations. His dominion shall be from sea to sea, and from the river to the ends of the earth. (Zech. 9:9–10)

No one as far as we know, either before or since, has cited this text, upheld this text, or reenacted this text. This is an original act based on a truly revolutionary vision by one of the ancient prophets. Not only is the nonviolent Jesus resisting and confronting the dominant social order, he is heralding a new one. Not only is he a nonviolent messiah, he's a nonviolent king whose kingdom is an eternal dominion of peace here on earth, a dominion that ends all wars and abolishes all instruments of war and killing. This symbolic act could not be more political for those with eyes to see. Of course, it sails over the heads of the disciples and the crowds as it does with us, but it marks the coming not just of the prince of peace but also of the king of peace.

With the image of Jesus as a king who will abolish all weapons of war and create a global culture of nonviolence, we need to reframe everything we have been taught about God, church, the spiritual life, politics, nationalism, and military might. This one image should disarm our theology and our understanding of God. No Christian and no Christian church anywhere in the world can ever again offer support for weapons and warfare. Rather, we are to do our part to make his peaceable kingdom come true. The churches must become places where Jesus's kingship and reign of peace flourish.

Jesus goes straight to the temple, looks around, and then leaves. He is "casing the joint," as anyone about to engage in illegal protest does. He wants to be prepared and think about what he is going to do. He wants to ensure that his action makes its point but does not hurt anyone. As someone who has engaged in well over a hundred nonviolent civil disobedience actions and been arrested about eighty-five times, I can say that, when one is about to break the law to uphold a higher law of justice and peace, it's essential to check things out beforehand, to be prepared, centered, and mindful. Jesus would have retreated and spent the night in meditation, prayer, and reflection, so that he was ready the next morning for his action in the temple.

As he was leaving the next day, he noticed a fig tree and was hoping to find some food, but found nothing, and he said in passing, according to Mark, "May no one ever eat of your fruit again!" For Mark, the fig tree symbolizes the temple-state system, which Jesus now confronts head-on. Here is Mark's dramatic account:

> On entering the temple area, he began to drive out those selling and buying there. He overturned the tables of the money changers and the seats of those who were selling doves. He did not permit anyone to carry anything through the temple area. Then he taught them saying, "Is it not written: 'My house shall be called a house of prayer for all peoples'? But you have made it a den of thieves." The chief priests and the scribes came to hear of it and were seeking a way to put him to death, yet they feared him because the whole crowd was astonished at his teaching. When evening came, they went out of the city.

Be careful not to presume that Jesus is angry and therefore violent; do not project your own anger onto him. As a veteran of many nonviolent actions, many with serious consequences, I can affirm that you cannot take such action in a spirit of nonviolence if you are angry, yelling, or threatening. On the contrary, in every nonviolent civil disobedience action I have participated in and witnessed, I have been, and seen others being, particularly peaceful, calm, mindful, and steady. We can tell that Jesus was calm and nonviolent because, after this action, he begins teaching the amazed crowd, using his normal procedure of asking questions. Notice, too, that Mark's tale, written probably in the late 60s before the destruction of the temple, has a fourfold plan of action: Jesus drives out those selling and buying; he turns over the banking tables; he does not permit anyone to carry anything; and he teaches them. The first three parts could have lasted all of five to ten minutes, whereas the teaching session could have lasted the rest of the day, until evening, we're told.

Many of my own actions of civil disobedience could be described in the same terms as Jesus's action in the temple. For example, during my first arrest, I sat down in the doorways of the Pentagon and read from the Sermon on the Mount. That's it. Thousands of people were trying to enter and walked past me, hearing me. (It was 1984, and anyone could walk into the Pentagon in those days.) The police came along and closed the entrance, so people had to take a long walk around to the other side of the building. You could say I blocked people from coming and going, and drove people away. I have done similar actions at the Concord Naval Weapons Station, various Trident submarine bases, Lawrence Livermore National Laboratory, the Strategic Air Command base, West Point, Congress, and the White House. In each instance, I was silent, peaceful, nonviolent, not angry, but quite disruptive.

Jesus's nonviolent raid on the temple is a dramatic call to end the big business of theft from the poor in the house of God. The question he asks is critical to our understanding of the event: Is this a house of prayer or a den of thieves? Which should it be? What kind of God do we worship, a God of universal love and peace available for every human being, or one who charges a hundred dollars per visit, like some kind of evil, neurotic, corporate Wizard of Oz? The temple system, Jesus declares, has been so co-opted by the imperial culture of greed that it has nothing to do with the living God and has everything to do with maintaining the power, domination, and wealth of the religious authorities. But underlying all this, Jesus sees how the empire uses the temple system and its authorities, bankers, and police to control the population, to keep them subdued, powerless, and malleable. Here are Myers's conclusions:

> Jesus attacks the temple institutions because of the way they exploit the poor. . . . His first target is the temple marketplace. The Jerusalem temple was fundamentally an economic institution, and indeed dominated the city's commercial life. The daily operation of the cult was a matter of employment for curtain makers, barbers, incense manufacturers, goldsmiths, trench diggers and countless others. . . . It is the ruling-class interests in control of the commercial enterprises in the temple market that Jesus is attacking. Mark considered the money changers suitable symbols of the oppressive financial institutions he so fiercely opposed. "Those selling doves" refers to the staple temple commodity relied upon by the poor. Doves were used primarily for "the purification of women," the cleansing of lepers and other purposes. Mark is not concerned with advocating lower prices for the poor or fair economic practices. Jesus has already repudiated the purity and debt systems themselves and its specific marginalization of lepers and women. Thus Jesus calls for an end to the entire cultic system—symbolized by his "overturning" of the stations used by these two groups. They represented the concrete mechanism of oppression within a political economy that doubly exploited the poor and unclean. (*BSM*, 299–301)

Mark's Jesus then cites Isaiah and Jeremiah when he asks, "Is it not written: 'My house shall be called a house of prayer for all peoples'? But you have made it a den of thieves." His reference to Isaiah 56:7 tells us that the temple should be "a house of prayer" that brings joy to those who are dispossessed. "The temple is supposed to embody inclusivity and community, with a special welcome to all who have been marginalized," Myers notes (*BSM,* 302). Instead of welcoming the poor, the temple system robs the poor. Mark also cites Jeremiah's attack on the temple state (7:11), which is significant because, unlike in other prophetic denunciations of temple injustice, Jeremiah does not call for the reform of the temple; he calls for its destruction based on its theft of the poor. That's why the immediate response to Jesus's action by the religious authorities is to plot how to kill him. They have to prevent him from destroying the temple system; otherwise, they will lose all their economic and political power and status.

Two thousand years later, Jesus's nonviolent civil disobedience is a direct challenge to each of us and our complicity with systemic injustice, empire, religious hypocrisy, and oppression of the poor. His dramatic nonviolence pushes those of us who claim to be his followers to take similar action against the institutions of violence today, which do far more harm than the temple did. Today, we face systems, structures, and institutions of violence that can literally destroy the planet, through nuclear weapons and environmental destruction, and that already kill millions through the slow torture of starvation, racism, extreme poverty, and disease. So the question is not, Did Jesus engage in violence in the temple? He did not. The question is, What nonviolent direct action are we going to undertake today as followers of the nonviolent Jesus, who took action against the unjust temple system? In a world on the brink of global destruction, discipleship to Mark's Jesus now requires nonviolent civil disobedience to systemic injustice and permanent warfare.

"Have Faith in God. When You Stand to Pray, Forgive" (11:20–26)

Mark then returns to the image of the fig tree. The next morning, as they were walking along, Peter noticed that the fig tree Jesus had cursed had now withered to its roots. This image represents the unjust temple system, which will die and wither. One might wonder what Jesus would say to Peter in response. It sounds simple and obvious, but once again it is pure revolution. "Have faith in God," Jesus says.

> "Whoever says to this mountain, 'Be lifted up and thrown into the sea,' and does not doubt in his heart but believes that what he says will happen, it shall be done for him. Therefore, I tell you, all that you ask for in prayer, believe that you will receive it and it shall be yours. When you stand to pray, forgive anyone against whom you have a grievance, so that your heavenly Father may in turn forgive you your transgressions."

These few sentences could be Mark's most crucial teachings. Coming right after Jesus's action against the unjust temple system, they point the way forward for every believer. Remember, in those days, the faithful were taught that God dwelt only in the temple, not in people, or among people, or in nature; therefore, if you wanted to be faithful, you had to visit the temple, the house of God, to worship God—and it's going to cost you a bundle. With Jesus's action in the temple, and the symbol of the withered fig tree as an image of the dying temple system, Jesus announces the good news that every human being, from now on, has free and unlimited access to God. All you have to do is have faith. All you have to do is believe in God 100 percent. For Jesus, faith means belief not in the false gods of empire, the nation/state, the temple state, the power of weapons or money, but in the living God, whose reign is characterized by love, justice, and peace. If you believe 100 percent in this living God, you will be led, guided, and protected; and you will be given everything you need. So just have faith, and all will be well.

If we believe in our hearts that God can do what we ask, then it will be done for us. This is the mystery of faith and intercessory prayer. Often Jesus could not perform miracles because people did not believe in him. The same continues today. God cannot help us, the way God has arranged reality, without our cooperation, without our belief in God, without our active participation. So do not doubt but believe, Mark instructs, and it shall be done for you. When we pray, we must believe that we will receive what we ask for, and we will receive it. Jesus teaches the requirement of faith as the one necessary ingredient of prayer, as a law of nature, and it is worth exploring and experimenting with. It can be applied to any request of goodwill that fits into the kingdom of God. So, for example, the Quakers in Britain prayed for the peaceful abolition of slavery; they believed in the power of their prayer, and it mobilized them, a group of powerless people, to build a movement that led to the peaceful abolition of slavery in Britain. We too can apply this teaching to, say, the abolition of nuclear weapons. If we all start asking the God of peace daily for the abolition of nuclear weapons, and believe that the day of nuclear abolition is coming, then we will be inspired to pitch in and make it happen, just as God does what God can to make it come true. With all this spiritual energy being mobilized, nuclear disarmament will become inevitable.

From this perspective, we see that things that seem impossible—such as moving a mountain, abolishing slavery, or nuclear disarmament—are possible and achievable. But the seemingly impossible requires faith, steadfast intercession, and the accompanying action. Myers puts it this way:

> Faith in the God-who-is-not-in-the-temple, then, means that the disciples must also repudiate the temple state. Mark insists that the overwhelming power and legitimacy of both the Roman "legion" [the pigs who ran into the sea after the healing of the Gerasene demoniac] and the Jewish "mountain" will meet their end—if the disciples truly believe in the possibility of a new order. That is to say, faith entails political imagination, the ability to envision a world that is not dominated by the powers. (*BSM*, 305)

If the teaching shocks us, or if we do not see any mountains moving, then perhaps that's a sign of our lack of faith, our lack of imagination, our inability to believe in and ask for the impossible. We believe in our weapons, we believe in the country, the flag, the police, and the military. We might believe our doctor, our lawyer, even our accountant. But we barely believe our priest or minister, and we barely believe in God, even if we think we believe. Faith in God requires complete and total surrender to God, and complete and total trust in God, and since we are living in relationship with the living God, we defer all things to God, but we also plead for global miracles of justice and peace. From that life of faith and intercession, we go forward and start moving mountains to the amazement of everyone. This was the normal experience of the saints and can be our experience too, if we start experimenting with sincere firm belief and bold intercessory prayer for justice and peace.

Here's the catch: every time you pray—and that means literally, every single day, every single moment of prayer—you must also forgive all those who ever hurt you. We are people who go through life day after day saying to God, "I forgive everyone who ever hurt me, all the people who have hurt me throughout my life, in big and small ways. Please forgive me as I forgive everyone." This is the key to nonviolence, the doorway to inner peace, and the path to endurance in the lifelong nonviolent struggle for justice and disarmament given all its obstacles, setbacks, betrayals, and hurts. Forgiving everyone over and over again enables us to let go of all the harmful influences we cling to—the hurts, resentments, grudges, anger, and bitterness. We let it all go. We forgive everyone, because we know we have hurt many people, too, and we too need to be forgiven. This is how Jesus was able to maintain his nonviolence throughout his life. He forgave everyone who hurt and attacked him every step of the way. By the time he was being nailed to a cross, he could forgive his killers because it had become second nature to him. It was his mantra. It needs to be ours as well.

Forgiveness is now the sole condition for prayer, as Myers sums up:

> Jesus' attack upon the temple thus appropriately concludes with a new "site" for prayer now that the "house of prayer" has been abandoned. This new site is neither geographical nor institutional but ethical: the difficult but imperative practice of mutual forgiveness within the community. As the discipleship catechism stressed, inequality can be prevented only by a living practice of reconciliation and the renunciation of power and privilege. The community's practice of forgiveness becomes the replacement of the redemptive/symbolic system of debt represented in the temple. The community becomes . . . the place of prayer "for all peoples." (*BSM*, 306)

"Why Are You Testing Me?" (11:27–13:2)

Jesus returns to the scene of the crime and is immediately accosted by the chief priests, the scribes, and the elders: "By what authority are you doing these things? Who gave you this authority to do them?" they demand to know. As in Matthew, Jesus asks about the origin of John's baptism, they refuse to answer, so he refuses to answer them either. He is not a pushover. He's not mean or violent, but he is not passive. He nonviolently turns the table back on his attackers and questions them about God's action through the famous prophet, his predecessor, John the Baptist, and in doing so, he puts them on the spot and exposes their hypocrisy. This will become the pattern until they eventually arrest and kill him.

In response to this political confrontation, Jesus launches into a story—the parable of the man with the vineyard, who leased it to tenant farmers, and left on a journey. Sometimes called, "the parable of the tenants," we have already heard Matthew's version (Mt. 21:33–46), where I proposed a post-supersessionist reading, and we will later hear Luke's version (Lk. 20:9–19). Mark's vineyard owner sent a servant to get some produce, and so they beat him. So he sent another servant, and many others, all of whom were beaten or killed. So he sent his son, "his beloved son," whom they killed and threw the body out of the vineyard.

"What will the owner of the vineyard do?" Jesus asks. That's the question Mark asks the reader as well. The question is the key. He's trying to impress upon us the serious consequences of systemic violence and injustice against the poor, the prophets, and the earth itself (the vineyard) by the ruling class, then and now. All through history, the prophets have been killed, right up to Gandhi, Dr. King, and Oscar Romero in our own time. Each year now, hundreds of environmental activists are brutally killed around the world for defending Mother Earth. Most horrifically, we killed the Beloved Son of God. What will the owner of the vineyard do? What will happen to us for killing the prophets, killing hundreds of millions of people through warfare, and preparing right now to destroy the planet itself through our nuclear arsenal and destruction of the earth and her creatures? The question should prick our conscience.

This parable reminds me once again of Archbishop Oscar Romero's urgent pleas to the death squads and Salvadoran government in the months before his assassination to repent; stop stealing, torturing, and killing; and join him in caring for the people and "vineyard" land of El Salvador, "the land of the Savior." It reminds me of Rev. Paul Schneider, the first Protestant minister executed by the Nazis. From his cell in Buchenwald, he spoke out non-stop with urgent, loving pleas and warnings to his brutal Nazi captors who responded with relentless beatings, tortures, and humiliations. He continued to beg them in the name of Christ to repent and be converted, until they finally murdered him.

The parable is an attempt to wake up the religious and ruling authorities who challenge Jesus and want to kill him. It's a roundabout way of calling us all to God's will and life of total nonviolence. Do not kill the prophets of justice, peace, and creation; do not destroy the earth and her creatures. Do not kill anyone anywhere ever again. Learn to share everything on earth equally, to include everyone and create a sustainable, just culture of peace. That's the message.

Mark's version says the tenants will be killed and the vineyard given "to others." We find here again the possible seeds of supersessionism, which might refer to Mark's eager use of replacement theology of the Jewish people and leadership with the Gentile Christian church and leadership. But in the context of Mark's Gospel, rather, we can read it not as replacement theology or supersessionism, but as a universal call for transformation of everyone everywhere to God's will and new life in the promised land of peace and nonviolence. It is important to note that this parable directly refers back to Isaiah's image of the earth as God's vineyard (Isa. 5:1–7). Unlike Isaiah's image, in this case the vineyard is not destroyed. When God comes to visit his vineyard, the paradise he created for humanity, and finds bloodshed committed by those entrusted to care for humanity and the earth, we are being told time and time again, there will be consequences. God will not so much punish us as allow our violence to come crashing back down upon us. The teaching, once again, is about consequentialism, or the law of karma: the violence that you do to others will in turn be done to you. All those who live by the sword will die by the sword. Today, the earth is being destroyed by unimaginable corporate greed, the digging up of fossil fuels, and our refusal to use alternative sources of energy. This in turn will lead to greater poverty, more wars, and perhaps the use of nuclear weapons. If Jesus says God was upset with the religious and ruling authorities of his day, what would he say about what we humans are doing today? To put it another way, Who owns the earth? Do we, do the nations, do the corporations and their military might? Or does the Creator?

Jesus quotes Psalm 118:22 to explain himself. He is the stone that the builders rejected; he will become the cornerstone. Mark could be interpreted as saying that the Jewish leaders (the caretakers of the vineyard) have indicted and condemned themselves by rejecting the leadership of the nonviolent Christ, the real cornerstone. But we note, too, that Mark is also drawing upon the story of Jeremiah the prophet, who infuriated the religious authorities with his radical call for justice and judged them for doing evil and not caring for the earth and the poor (Jer. 26:1–2, 6–16). What's noteworthy is that, in my opinion, Jeremiah speaks not so much of rejection and destruction as of transformation, restoration, and a return to God's good grace (26:13)

Here in Mark, the authorities are furious and, for the third time, they want to arrest him but they fear the crowd so they leave him alone. Jesus faces the same treatment for his prophetic parables as Jeremiah did for his prophetic truth-telling (Jer. 26:1–16). Notice how Jesus fearlessly and sometimes poetically speaks truth to power, with a total disregard of the consequences to himself. He calls for a complete break with institutionalized religious injustice as well as with the empire itself, in his strict obedience to the God of peace and allegiance to God's reign of peace. His daring prophetic speech, combined with his nonviolent civil disobedience, will inevitably lead to his arrest. Mark is trying to impress upon us the reader as well as the disciples the kind of life we are called to live: to take bold nonviolent action for justice and to speak that same bold, daring, prophetic truth to power regardless of the consequences to ourselves. I suggest, then, that in keeping with the entire context of Mark's Gospel and its urgent call for conversion to God's reign of nonviolence, we cannot conclude from this story that God is violent. Rather, we conclude that our violence has profound consequences not only for those we hurt and kill and for all of creation, but also for ourselves. We will not live in peace and enjoy the promised land, much less do our part to care for it.

The confrontations continue. The authorities return, try to flatter Jesus, then try to trap him with a question. "Is it lawful to pay the census tax to Caesar or not? Should we pay or should we not pay?" "Why are you testing me?" he asks them. They are desperate to catch him, trap him, and stop his truth-telling. They think they are doing good, but they are actually servants of the culture of injustice and death.

Jesus does not carry coins. If he had carried Roman coins, it would have been idolatrous, because Caesar's image was on the coin, and Caesar claimed to be God. So, he asks to see a coin, and when they pull one from their pockets, they reveal that they, the religious authorities, carry Caesar's image, which means they are idolators. A denarius would have an image of Caesar with the inscription: "August and Divine Son."

"Repay to Caesar what belongs to Caesar and to God what belongs to God," he tells them. The best meaning of the phrase, according to Myers, would be, "Repay the one to whom you are indebted." It remains one of the most political teachings in the Bible, and also the most misunderstood. Myers unpacks it as follows:

There are simply no grounds for assuming (as so many bourgeois exegetes do) that Jesus was exhorting his opponents to pay the tax. He is inviting them to act according to their allegiances, stated clearly as opposites. Jesus has turned the challenge back upon his antagonists: What position do they take on the issue? This is what provokes the strong reaction of incredulity from his opponents—something no neat doctrine of "obedient citizenship" could possibly have done. . . . Mark's own allegiance is made clear by the entire narrative of the last three episodes taken together. Mark in no uncertain terms rejects the option of political cooperation with Rome and repudiates the authority of Caesar and his "coin." (*BSM*, 312)

Myers concludes that, just as Jesus was hunted down, trapped, and interrogated by the ruling authorities about allegiance to the empire and to the violent revolutionaries, so was Mark's community. These passages point to their rejection of both the Roman colonial presence and the violent revolt against it.

Having been challenged by the Pharisees and the Herodians, a third contingent of the ruling class, the Sadducees, made up of rich landowning patrician families, now takes its turn attacking Jesus. They make up a long, convoluted story about a man who dies leaving a wife, how his brother marries the widow but then he dies, and eventually five more brothers in turn marry the woman, and all die, leaving no descendants. "At the resurrection whose wife will she be?" they ask him. Elisabeth Schüssler Fiorenza has taught that this passage is not so much about resurrection but is "another way in which the kingdom subverts the dominant social order, in this case the patriarchal objectification of women" (*In Memory of Her*, 144). Their question concerns maintaining their socioeconomic status through the posteriority of the seven sons, as Myers explains. They are certainly not concerned with the poor woman or whom she would "belong to" in the afterlife. Patriarchal marriage does not exist in God's reign, Jesus announces. There will be no more patriarchy, sexism, ownership, privilege, or elitism in God's reign (*BSM*, 315).

"Are you not misled because you do not know the scriptures or the power of God?" Jesus asks them—and all of us. Do we understand the scriptures or the power of God as the nonviolent Jesus does? If we want to do that, we have to read them, study them, and preach them from the perspective of creative nonviolence, so that we might understand universal love, compassion, and peace, and work for a new culture of God's reign. Jesus goes on to explain how those who are raised in God's reign are like the angels, and God is the God of the living, not of the dead. "You are greatly misled," he tells them.

The Sadducees have a vested interest in denying any other "world" except the present one, which they control. Myers comments, "Jesus conceives of resurrection not as a static doctrine but a living hope for the transformation of the world." He speaks of the dead "rising to life" and "being raised." So he is speaking about "an eschatological vision of world transformation" (*BSM*, 316).

In the last confrontation, a scribe questions Jesus about "the greatest commandment," and in response, Jesus "silences them once and for all" (*BSM*, 317). "The first is this," Jesus says, quoting Deuteronomy: "'Hear, O Israel! The Lord our God is Lord alone! You shall love the Lord your God with all your heart, with all your soul, with all your mind, and with all your strength.'" Then, Mark's Jesus adds a close second commandment from Leviticus 19:18, which comes after a list of teachings insisting that people serve the poor, work for justice, liberate the oppressed, and do everything to improve life for everyone. "'You shall love your neighbor as yourself.' There is no other commandment greater than these." Here in a nutshell is the gospel: we practice *agapē*/unconditional love for God with heart, soul, mind, and strength, and the same *agapē*/unconditional love for our neighbor, for every other person. Jesus's strict nonviolence creates the boundary and possibility for such unconditional love. Without the boundary and vision of nonviolence, we cannot love our neighbors, much less ourselves, and still more, the God of universal love.

The scribe affirms his response, and Jesus appears to affirm him, saying, "You are not far from the kingdom of God." But, alas, the scribe does not enter the kingdom of God, or show interest in entering, because he remains a scribe and therefore still supports the social order of oppression, classism, and empire. Notice that Jesus does not call him to be a disciple. Myers suggests that Mark's community did not believe one could be both a scribe and a disciple.

Jesus goes on to speak of the scribes and their claim that the Messiah is the son of David. He thoroughly denies that and, in doing so, renounces the old vision of David's messianic kingdom. His messiahship and kingdom are entirely new, different from the dominant world order, for it is based on universal love and justice for the poor and oppressed. With this revolutionary teaching, we're told, the crowd was delighted.

He then launches into a full-on attack of the scribal class. They "like to go around in long robes and accept greetings in the marketplaces, seats of honor in synagogues, and places of honor at banquets. They devour the houses of widows and, as a pretext, recite lengthy prayers. They will receive a very severe condemnation," Jesus says. They seek to enjoy and maintain privilege and status in the name of God and at the expense of the poor, whereas Jesus calls his followers to renounce privilege and status and become the last of all and servant of all, like him. The fact that the scribes live comfortably off the money of the poor, oppress the poor, especially widows, and do so in the name of God is what disturbs Jesus the most. Their work maintains the dominant social order, so their entire elitist class has to go.

Myers's explanation that Jesus's condemnation of the rich who put large sums into the temple treasury is especially shocking. Mark reports that Jesus "sat down opposite the treasury and observed how the crowd put money into the treasury":

> Many rich people put in large sums. A poor widow also came and put in two small coins worth a few cents. Calling his disciples to himself, he said to them, "Amen, I say to you, this poor widow put in more than all the other contributors to the treasury. For they have all contributed from their surplus wealth, but she, from her poverty, has contributed all she had, her whole livelihood."

For two thousand years, priests, ministers, and scholars have told us that Jesus praises the piety and devotion of the poor widow. This is a misreading of Mark. Jesus laments that she gives her wealth to the temple treasury! She is a poor widow, and therefore extremely close to God, but the temple system conditions her to give her money to the wealthy elites. They should give their money to her, lift her out of poverty, and help her live with dignity and justice, as Myers writes:

> Bourgeois scholarship, oblivious to Mark's critique of the political economy of the temple, portrays the common theme as the contrast between the religious hypocrisy

of the scribes and the genuine piety of the poor woman. . . . The temple has robbed this woman of her very means of livelihood. Like the scribal class, it no longer protects widows, but exploits them. As if in disgust, Jesus "exits" the temple—for the final time (13:1). (*BSM*, 320–22)

Jesus leaves the temple, and, once again, we hear from the clueless male disciples. They try to get Jesus to notice the magnificent temple buildings and its stones. It's as if they have heard nothing he said, as if they have ears but do not hear. "Do you see these great buildings? There will not be one stone left upon another that will not be thrown down," he tells them. Myers points out that the temple was destroyed by fire in the year 70 by the Roman soldiers, so this is a clue that Mark was written shortly before that. I suggest that it points to the inevitable consequence of systemic injustice, warfare, and empire. Those who live by systemic violence will suffer the consequences of violence. This is the way violence works. The temple state system needed to fall away because it oppressed the poor in the name of God and served only the elite religious and ruling authorities. Likewise, the institutions of imperial power today, whether in Moscow, London or, yes, even Washington, D.C., will one day all be destroyed because they are rooted in global domination of the poor, permanent warfare, and the destruction of creation. They are all doomed, starting with the magnificent five-sided building of the Pentagon. It is inevitable that after having brought death and destruction over the past century to millions that the forces of death and destruction will turn on it and those who manage it. The September 11 attacks were merely a sign of the greater violence to come, given the death and destruction the United States has wrought upon the world.

"Be Watchful!" Jesus's Visionary Sermon on Eschatological Nonviolence (13:3–37)

Jesus has completely repudiated the temple state and thus the socio-symbolic order of Judaism based on their exploitation of the poor. As Myers points out, for any Jew of the time, this repudiation of the temple system would have been the end of the world (*BSM*, 323–24). Jesus takes a seat on the Mount of Olives, which looks out at the temple and the holy city. He begins to teach his disciples about how to endure the end of the world as they know it. He warns them not to join a messianic war in defense of the temple but rather to witness to the coming of a new world where the entire order, from the temple state to the Roman Empire, is overturned and God's reign of peace breaks through. Remember, the world of the late 60s was at war: Nero was dead, Rome was in civil war, Palestinian violent rebels had reclaimed much of the territory—even for a while, Jerusalem—and everyone probably lived in fear and terror. We know that finally in the year 70, the Roman army attacked and destroyed Jerusalem after five months of fighting and burned the temple to the ground. If Mark is written a few years before this, then the apocalyptic reflections that follow make sense. So, after all his courageous civil disobedience and prophetic truth-telling in the temple, Mark's Jesus offers one last sermon on revolutionary, eschatological nonviolence.

"See that no one deceives you," Jesus begins. "Many will come in my name saying, 'I am he,' and they will deceive many." The first warning is not to be deceived by false messiahs but instead to stay faithful to Jesus, to trust in him, and to follow him on the way of non-violence. This will get even harder as the world erupts into ever greater violence. He lists wars, earthquakes, and famines as inevitable events, all the products of the world's systemic violence. The commandment: Do not be alarmed. That is to say, stay centered in faith in the God of peace.

For Mark, the commandment "Do not be alarmed" means—remain steadfast in your nonviolence. Do not rush off and join the rebels to protect Jerusalem or take over Jerusalem or fight Rome. As in every war, people start to panic, especially if they are being invaded, and they throw their peaceableness out the window and join the violent resistance, as people of goodwill have done in Ukraine, as opposed to the nonviolent resistance demonstrated in Denmark, Norway, and Bulgaria against Nazi invaders. Do not resort to violence or warfare, no matter what, no matter how noble the cause. Remain faithful to the way of nonviolence. This is as challenging today as it was back then, perhaps harder, because we are inundated with media propaganda telling us how God blesses our troops and, essentially, approves our warmaking causes. This is not the way of the nonviolent Jesus.

"Watch out for yourselves," he tells them next. You are going to be attacked, persecuted, hauled into court, beaten by devout religious fundamentalists, and forced to stand before governors and kings. Stay peaceful and nonviolent throughout, and you will be able to give witness to the nonviolent Jesus, he says. Continue to preach the gospel of peace. Even when you are handed over, do not falter but speak out when your time comes, and trust that his Holy Spirit will speak through you. At some point, the violence will overtake everyone like a plague. Everyone will take sides—with the Jewish violent rebels or the Roman soldiers. Even your own relatives will be infected with the contagion of war, turn against you, and have you put to death. "You will be hated by all because of my name," he states. "But the one who perseveres to the end will be saved."

Why are they/we going to be persecuted and universally hated? Because we are following the nonviolent Jesus and engaging in nonviolent direct action and public prophetic truth-telling against the culture of violence and war, the entire dominant social order—and it is not going to be well received. We will not align ourselves with any side of violence in any war or at any time. That means that we will be hated more than loved.

Next, Jesus warns them to flee to the mountains when they see "the desolating abomination," that is, the Roman imperial sign standing in the temple, as well as the Roman military siege of Jerusalem. That is a sure sign that the house of God and the holy city have been completely taken over by the empire and the emperor who claims to be God. Notice Mark's strange comment addressed directly to his readers: "Let the reader understand." This is the only time Mark ever addresses the reader directly, and it offers a clue to the life-threatening danger that the evangelist and his community face during this time of rebellion, invasion, and war. Mark's community is nonviolent and nonaligned, so like the nonviolent Jesus they are underground, in hiding, probably being hunted down by all sides. Mark cannot write blatantly about "the Roman Empire invading the temple and the holy city," because they might be caught, captured, and immediately executed, which is what both the Romans and the Zealots did. If we are to understand what Mark is actually saying, as he asks us to, then we have to imagine this text as if it were telling us about the nonviolence of Jesus placed in the middle of the Rwandan genocide or the Nazi invasion of Poland or the U.S. bombing of North Vietnam or El Salvador's civil war with its countless death squads, or the Russian war on Ukraine. These teachings are politically dangerous, literally revolutionary and treasonous, and so this Gospel he is writing is a matter of life and death for his community.

We can apply Mark's warning to the horrors of the past century right up to today. Just as the Roman Empire took over the temple and the city, so did the Nazis take over the German churches and church leaders, and so has the same spirit of nationalism taken over the U.S. churches, which proudly place American flags in their sanctuaries, showing everyone where their real allegiance lies. The effect of patriotism and nationalism taking over houses of worship and prayer will be devastating, as Jesus describes, because the violence these nations and empires unleash will be done then in the name of God and will be claimed to be the best way to serve God, as the insane Nazi leaders claimed, and as American leaders have done, whether dropping firebombs on Tokyo or nuclear weapons on Hiroshima or carpet-bombing Vietnam or Iraq.

Jesus speaks of "tribulation" the likes of which has never been seen before. Alas, we have seen these tribulations up close, from Hiroshima and Nagasaki to the present day when we stand on the verge of a global nuclear holocaust and in the throes of catastrophic climate change. Jesus is not exactly predicting the future; he is pointing out that, if humanity's addiction to violence, war, and empire is not stopped, it will destroy the world. Because we have so thoroughly rejected Jesus's way of peace, everything he warned against is coming true right now, two thousand years later.

Again, Jesus warns against false messiahs and false prophets who will mislead us into their campaigns of violence, nationalism, and messianic warfare in one form of another. "Be watchful!" he insists. "I have told it all to you beforehand." His way of nonviolence is like walking a tightrope. One can easily be misled and fall off the way. Jesus's call to be watchful is like Thich Nhat Hanh's teaching on practicing mindfulness. We try to live in the present moment, to be fully conscious, to be aware of ourselves, what's happening inside us, what disturbs us and threatens us, and to keep returning to our breath that we might be centered in the spirit of peace and nonviolence every day, every hour, every moment. We never give in to violence, we remain nonaligned, against violence on all sides, and we side ultimately with humanity and creation itself.

The warnings get worse. In this apocalyptic vision of the end of the world, the sky will literally fall upon us. The sun and moon will be darkened and the world will fall into darkness. The powers in the heavens will be shaken. All of this hints at the effect of Jesus's execution to come but also points to the effects of global violence to come, from the destruction of Jerusalem to our own wars, and the effects of catastrophic climate change, with its permanent wildfires, droughts, floods, tornadoes, massive hurricanes, rising oceans, and record heat. If we kill the light of the world and reject his way of nonviolence, over and over again, we will fall together into ever deepening darkness and catastrophe. The solution is to stay faithful to Jesus's way and to remain watchful.

But a day is coming when the Son of Humanity will return "in the clouds with great power and glory" and send out his angels to gather his elect from all over the earth. It's fantastic language used to urge the disciples—and the reader—to stay faithful to Jesus's way and to trust that he will guide us, lead us, and ultimately take care of us—that one day, all will be well.

"Learn a lesson from the fig tree," he teaches them. Earlier the four disciples had asked Jesus for a sign when these things will take place. Instead, as Myers comments, Jesus tells them to read the signs of the times, to use political discernment in the historical moment to understand what is happening in the world and the coming of the God of peace (*BSM*, 330). Just as you can tell by the fig tree's leaves that summer is near, when these things begin to happen, know that "he is near, at the gates." Because we know the meaning of the cursed fig tree earlier, we know that Mark is emphasizing that the entire social order, not just the Roman Empire but even the temple system itself, has to be done away with, and we need to prepare for the coming of an entirely new order led by the Son of Humanity. This will begin with the crucifixion and resurrection of Jesus, when the way of nonviolence is revealed as the way toward new life, toward a new culture of peace. That's why Mark adds that this generation will witness this, and his words will never pass away. The turning point of nonviolence is at hand, and the teachings of nonviolence will always be with you.

The sermon ends with the declaration that no one knows when these things will happen except God. So Jesus commands again: "Be watchful! Be alert! Watch! Watch!" It is an urgent appeal: be on alert at all times, for the rest of your life, on the lookout for the God of peace, the Son of Humanity, the coming of God's reign. Mark concludes with a short parable about servants and a gatekeeper who have to be on alert at all times because the owner can return at any minute. "Watch, therefore, because you do not know when the lord of the house is coming, whether in the evening, or at midnight, or at cockcrow, or in the morning. May he not come suddenly and find you sleeping. What I say to you, I say to all: 'Watch!'"

For me, this commandment to "watch" is the commandment to remain nonviolent no matter what, especially as war erupts and all hell breaks loose. We do not kill, no matter what anyone on any side says, including the Roman emperor or the American president or the false prophets of our times—that is, various priests, bishops, ministers, and rabbis who support our wars and bless our troops and weapons. For the nonviolent Jesus, there is no cause, no holiness, no crusade, however apparently noble, worth taking a single human life. We are on permanent watch for the coming of the new day of peace, a new world without war.

Few Christians understand this. Mark's Jesus demands nonviolence from his followers. Few today can even conceive of this, and so we remain far from the nonviolent Jesus. We do not want to keep watch; we want to take up the gun. Here's how Myers sums it up:

> The second half of the sermon employs apocalyptic myth in order to compel the disciples/reader to enter into the "historical moment," to choose between the old and new order, both of which stand at the edge of history. It is, to be sure, the moment of the war; but that very historical crisis drives Mark to look deeper still. Why not aid and abet the rebel cause? Because it was mere rebellion, the recycling of oppressive power into new hands. To journey deeply into history, to experiment with a political practice that will break, not perpetuate, the reign of domination in the world—that is the meaning of Mark's final call to "Watch!" It is a call to nonviolent resistance to the powers. (*BSM,* 343)

There is, finally, an even deeper meaning to the command to watch: we are being prepared to keep watch as the nonviolent Jesus takes up the cross, undergoes suffering and execution, and rises to new life. As we his disciples watch the unfolding action of nonviolence, we see the fall of the culture of violence, war, empire, and death. Through the cross of nonviolent suffering love, the powers and principalities have fallen and God's reign of peace is breaking through. We are on alert to watch as this happens and then, ultimately, to join his campaign of disarming, transforming nonviolence.

The Arrest and Execution of the Nonviolent Jesus:
The End of the Beginning of Total Nonviolence (14:1–15:47)

We've come to the end of the world—and the beginning of a new one. With the arrest, torture, and execution of the nonviolent Jesus, and then his resurrection, the old order, the culture of violence, war, empire, and death itself, has fallen. With his resurrection, with God's affirmation of Jesus's life and his grassroots movement of nonviolence, a new world has begun—a world of social, economic, racial, and environmental justice, universal love, and infinite peace, the reign of God in our midst. This is what Mark declares in the final chapters of his Gospel.

The story is familiar, and it's hard to take because it feels like the end of the world, especially with Mark's urgency. We're told at the beginning that "the chief priest and the scribes were seeking a way to arrest him by treachery and put him to death." The worst of organized religion for all to see—its corrupt leaders planning an assassination to protect their privileged status and even the evil empire. Jesus is in Bethany, having dinner at the house of "Simon the leper," which is striking because no leper has ever been named before, much less hosted a dinner party for Jesus. He was probably cured by Jesus. Just then, a woman pours expensive perfumed oil on Jesus's head—and all hell breaks loose. Some were indignant, saying, "That money should have been spent on the poor." They were infuriated with her.

"Let her alone," Jesus tells them. "Why do you make trouble for her?" he asks. "She has done a good thing for me. The poor you will always have with you, and whenever you wish you can do good to them, but you will not always have me. She has done what she could. She has anticipated anointing my body for burial. Amen, I say to you, wherever the gospel is proclaimed to the whole world, what she has done will be told in memory of her."

Here we have the quintessential nonviolent Jesus, a man of God's authority on the side of women, standing up for women, defending women, and protecting women from male harassment. This crucial aspect of Jesus's nonviolence has been lost to history, thanks to men who have put themselves in charge of the story. Just as his movement became co-opted by empire and warmaking, its institutional churches became embedded in male domination and patriarchy. Jesus would want us to continue to denounce sexual harassment, patriarchy, and every form of gender inequality, violence, and sexism, because his visionary nonviolence sees humanity as complete equality between men and women and all people. As far as the men of his time were concerned, this was not just outrageous or revolutionary—it was treasonous. In many quarters today among churchmen, not much has changed.

That is why Mark's Jesus makes a point of saying that this woman must be remembered throughout history. For the first time, someone in the story honors Jesus's journey to the cross and supports and affirms him. The male disciples, those early churchmen, could not hear—or refused to hear—this part of Jesus's message, the part about his death. They fought this part of Jesus's journey every step of the way. But this woman heard Jesus and understood him and received his message in full. By pouring oil on him, the woman anoints him and blesses him to face his suffering and death in grace, strength, and faith. In her, he finds a true follower who encourages him on his difficult journey to martyrdom. He wants her to be remembered because she has become the model disciple. Notice that her name has not been remembered; none of the men could remember her name. But her act was remembered, because it stood out, because they could never forget it, and because Jesus wanted it to be remembered.

I always presumed it was Judas who denounced the woman for anointing Jesus. John will later tell us that Judas carried the money bag and stole from it. If it was Judas, then Jesus's strong reaction—"Let her alone!"—might have enraged him and led him to leave Jesus. He'd had enough; he was looking for money. So, Mark tells us how Judas went to the chief priests, offered to hand Jesus over for a fee, and plotted his betrayal.

The Blood of the New Covenant of Nonviolence (14:12–31)

We now have an underground movement in hiding that is being hunted down by the authorities and about to split up because one of them is deliberately going to destroy the leader and the whole community. When it comes time for the Passover meal, Jesus sends the disciples into the city where he knows someone secretly who can lend them a room. "Go into the city and a man will meet you, carrying a jar of water. Follow him. Wherever he enters, say to the master of the house, 'The Teacher says, "Where is my guest room where I may eat the Passover with my disciples?"' Then he will show you a large upper room furnished and ready. Make the preparations for us there." Remember: men did not carry jars of water. Only women and slaves did. That was the signal for their underground movement. Like other movement leaders, Jesus had connections with people who secretly wanted to help, and would. Simon the leper and Joseph of Arimathea are just two examples who are named.

The Last Supper then is not a happy occasion: it is filled with tension, fear, stress, and, worse, betrayal and argument. Yet, on Jesus's part, it is the moment of his greatest intimacy, unconditional love, and invitation. It is the night before Jesus is tortured and executed. The women followers would certainly have been there, probably cooking and preparing the meal. When it gets dark, Jesus and the Twelve arrive in the upper room. It is then, as they are eating, reclining at the table, that Jesus can see the end even more clearly. "Amen, I say to you, one of you will betray me, one who is eating with me." They are shocked and upset and, one by one, deny it. Then Mark tells us:

> He took bread, said the blessing, broke it, and gave it to them, and said, "Take it; this is my body." Then he took a cup, gave thanks, and gave it to them, and they all drank from it. He said to them, "This is my blood of the covenant, which will be shed for many. Amen, I say to you, I shall not drink again the fruit of the vine until the day when I drink it new in the kingdom of God."

Jesus takes the Passover meal, the central ritual of Judaism, and transforms it into a new, living spiritual encounter with him rooted in the way of the cross, into his way of offering his life for us, and into an invitation for us to do the same for others. One of them is about to betray him, destroy the community, and make it possible for the ruling authorities to execute him, but he moves closer and deeper to the disciples, and to humanity, with this invitation to share in his Passover meal. The scene is fraught with tension because at any moment the authorities could burst through the door. Jesus can tell that they will all leave him when he is arrested. "All of you will have your faith shaken," he announces. This disturbs each of them, but then he offers a strange promise of redemption and renewal, which becomes a key sentence for Mark: "But after I have been raised up, I shall go before you to Galilee." That one verse will change everything. Myers writes:

> It is important for Christian readers to recognize that in Mark this "eucharist" is not described as a "memorial"; it is not backward-looking but forward-looking. Through the symbolic action of table fellowship, Jesus invites the disciples/reader to solidarity with his impending arrest, torture, and execution. In this episode, Mark articulates his new symbolic center, and overturns the last stronghold of symbolic authority in the dominant order, the high holy feast of Passover. In place of the temple liturgy Jesus offers his "body"—that is, his messianic practice in life and death. It is this very "sanctuary/body" opposition that will shape Mark's narrative of Jesus' execution. (*BSM*, 364)

As we ponder Jesus's offering of the bread and the cup, we begin to understand the depths of his messianic salvific nonviolence through his way of the cross. He takes the bread and says, "Take it; this is my body." Then, he takes a cup, and says, "This is my blood of the covenant, which will be shed for many." He refers to the covenant, but what he is doing, as the other Gospels state, is offering a *new* covenant—a covenant of nonviolence. Here, at this final hour, he offers a new covenant between God and humanity that is based in the nonviolence of his paschal mystery, which he invites us to share.

There is no mention of a slaughtered lamb at this Passover meal because he is the lamb being slaughtered for resistance to the empire. His perfect nonviolent suffering love will become a spiritual explosion that will touch, disarm, and redeem people down through history. He wants us to participate in his redemptive nonviolence, his steadfast resistance, and his self-giving love, so he institutes his own Passover meal that we can partake of daily to renew our own participation in his disarming, nonviolent love. The great mythic stories of divine violence told in the Hebrew Scriptures have come to an end: Abraham being asked to kill his son; Moses being told to liberate the Egyptian slaves and killing Pharaoh's army in the process; Elijah calling down hellfire on his enemies; King David and any other biblical heroes killing their enemies. From now on, God is fully revealed as a nonviolent God of universal love and universal peace, and so God's people are people of universal love and universal peace. God grants us complete free will, and from now on, in agreement with this new covenant, we live and act as God desires, within the boundaries of nonviolence, so that we might practice universal love and peace.

As we his followers share in Christ's body and blood, we pledge to give our bodies and blood in nonviolent resistance to the structures of violence as Jesus did. We follow him on the way of the cross so that his global campaign of active nonviolence will spread and disarm cultures of violence and empires everywhere. The catch is that, like Jesus, we are not allowed to break other people's bodies or shed other people's blood. If we participate in Jesus's Passover meal, his new covenant of nonviolence, we commit to his way of meticulous nonviolence. Our preference is now with Jesus, to give our lives for suffering humanity even unto our own suffering and death without any desire for retaliation, and to refuse to harm or kill anyone else along the way. This covenant of nonviolence, the invitation to share in the way of the cross, becomes the hallmark of Jesus's religion and the doorway to universal love.

Few Christians in history have understood this, however, because it has rarely been taught. Even fewer have chosen to live within Jesus's new covenant of nonviolence. We much prefer our old way of warfare and domination. Ever since Constantine the emperor supposedly converted to Christianity, legalized Christianity, and invited Christians to join his army and kill for him, Christians have rejected Jesus's new covenant, his way of peace and not harm. They have justified war, waged war, led crusades against non-Christians, enslaved other human beings, built and used nuclear weapons, and killed hundreds of millions of people. Yet, even as we violate and reject his new covenant, we partake of the Christian Eucharist as if we are sharing in the life of Jesus, as if we can have it both ways. Actually, we mock him and his new covenant. Still, his covenant of nonviolence remains for anyone who dares accept it and experiment with his radical form of resistance and revolution.

"Watch and Pray" (14:32–42)

Next, Jesus leads the disciples back to their garden hideaway, a place called Gethsemane, and he tells them, "Sit here while I pray." Notice, this is only the third time in Mark that Jesus prays.

> He took with him Peter, James, and John, and began to be troubled and distressed. Then he said to them, "My soul is sorrowful even to death. Remain here and keep watch." He advanced a little and fell to the ground and prayed that if it were possible the hour might pass by him; he said, "Abba, Father, all things are possible to you. Take this cup away from me, but not what I will but what you will." When he returned, he found them asleep. He said to Peter, "Simon, are you asleep? Could you not keep watch for one hour? Watch and pray that you may not undergo the test. The spirit is willing but the flesh is weak." Withdrawing again, he prayed, saying the same thing. Then he returned once more and found them asleep, for they could not keep their eyes open and did not know what to answer him. He returned a third time and said to them, "Are you still sleeping and taking your rest? It is enough. The hour has come. Behold, the Son of Humanity is to be handed over to sinners. Get up, let us go. See, my betrayer is at hand."

He confides in Peter, James, and John that he is "sorrowful unto death" and tells them to remain and keep watch. Here, in this moment of distress, Jesus calls out to God, and for the first time, Mark specifically includes the Aramaic word "Abba," meaning, "Daddy." Jesus calls out with great intimacy to God, asking his Daddy to take this cup of suffering away from him but then prays that he does God's will, not his own. When he returns, he finds the disciples sound asleep. He questions them and orders them, "Watch and pray." Twice more he goes off to pray, returns, and finds them asleep. He questions them, but it is too late. "Get up, go, see," he tells them in a series of commands. "My betrayer is at hand."

Why is he "sorrowful unto death"? Because he's about to be tortured and executed, but also because his disciples do not understand a word he is saying, and they will betray him, deny him, and abandon him, every last one of them. He's "sorrowful unto death" because no one accepts his way except for the woman who anointed him, whom the male disciples harassed. He's "sorrowful unto death" because he wants everyone to join his public campaign of nonviolent resistance to empire and the culture of injustice, and apparently no one has made a serious commitment to this campaign. He's "sorrowful unto death" because humanity prefers empire, injustice, war, greed, and violence of every kind. Worse, he's "sorrowful unto death" because they do not want a God of peace; humanity prefers a god we can understand—the false gods of war and empire. Jesus is thoroughly rejected by one and all.

Why does he pray for the strength to do God's will? Because God's will is that he practice and embody revolutionary nonviolence and accept the consequences, which can only be, in such a violent world, retaliation against him, crushing him to death and exterminating his movement. The powerful do not freely relinquish power; they cling to every drop of their dominating power and use the infliction of violence and death on anyone, beginning with movement leaders, without batting an eyelash. To do God's will means to accept the consequences of revolutionary nonviolence: rejection, betrayal, arrest, jailing, torture, and execution by the system. God's will also means that Jesus has to undergo this torture and execution with steadfast nonviolence through to the very end, even to the point of praying that God forgive his killers. He is sent to be the one person in human history who embodied total nonviolence every step, every moment of his life until his last breath. He undergoes violence and death knowing that in his resurrection he will take away the ultimate power of the state, the power of death. Death will no longer have power over him or anyone who follows him on his campaign of revolutionary peace. If he can practice perfect nonviolence unto death, he will overcome death and death will lose its sting. Death will no longer have the last word. Life will win out.

It's not that God is an evil, violent being who wants Jesus to be tortured and killed. Nor does God *need* Jesus to be tortured and killed to satisfy some theological formula of sin and justice. It's that God wants Jesus to live the way of peace and lead a campaign of peace and unconditional love that will inspire humanity, disarm humanity, and transform the world. God wants humanity to freely choose to follow Jesus's way, to live as he lived; God wants Jesus to model what it means to be human, truly human in the image of God, living out God's peace, compassion, and justice. We can reject God's way, and God hopes that through Jesus's steadfast nonviolence and universal love, even to the point of his suffering and death, humanity will wake up and welcome God's reign of peace and participate in it joyfully. It's a great risk God is asking Jesus to take—to model nonviolence so that we can learn how to put away our weapons, trust God's love, and help bring God's reign to life here and now. Alas, God's plan and the nonviolent Jesus are rejected, not just by the religious and ruling authorities but by his closest friends, disciples, and relatives. We reject his way still, even as we sing hymns to him but go right on supporting the systems of violence and war. So, Jesus is "sorrowful unto death," then and now.

"Have You Come Out as against a Robber, with Swords and Clubs, to Seize Me?" (14:43–72)

After offering his life and new covenant during the Passover meal, Jesus prays in agony late into the night while his hapless disciples sleep. They cannot and do not support him. One of them betrays him. Next they will all abandon him. Then the group leader, Simon, who was once called Peter but has since been relegated to his pre-discipleship name, denies even knowing Jesus. The breakdown of the Jesus community is shocking and is one of the main reasons he is sorrowful unto death. He could not keep his community together. They simply cannot comprehend what he is talking about, nor the meaning of his impending death, nor why he won't defend himself with violence. We can imagine them thinking about all the signs and wonders he has performed, the power they know he has at his disposal, and yet he allows this horrible sequence of events to unfold. Why won't he fight? Why doesn't he perform a great miracle now? Why not destroy all his enemies and establish God's reign? What is he waiting for?

Judas arrives with an armed crowd of soldiers and guards carrying swords and clubs, accompanied by the chief priests, the scribes, and the elders. It is a full-on organized military assault done under the cover of night. Jesus has no recognizable features, so Judas kisses Jesus to identify him to the soldiers, who grab him and arrest him, but not without one last final betrayal by the disciples. "Have you come out as against a robber, with swords and clubs, to seize me?" Jesus asks. Robbers were members of the armed rural resistance, the violent revolutionaries with whom Jesus will be executed in a few hours. "Day after day I was with you teaching in the temple area, yet you did not arrest me," he says. They know Jesus teaches nonviolence and practices it, but they cannot fathom what this nonviolence means or how he has used it to shape a new community. They come expecting violence and are ready to kill him and his community on the spot if necessary.

All of this is to be expected in the world of violence. The worst, however, is the response of Jesus's disciples. One of the bystanders draws his sword, strikes the high priest's servant, and cuts off his ear. John's Gospel will later identify the violent defender of Jesus as none other than Peter himself. After years of daily instructions on nonviolence, what does Peter do? He tries to kill to protect the nonviolent Jesus. Because Mark does not name the person, we know it could have been any of the disciples. So, we realize that every one of them has rejected Jesus's offer, just a few hours earlier, of a new covenant of nonviolence. When Jesus refuses to fight back to defend himself, they finally realize how deadly serious he is about his nonviolence. Now, all as one, they suddenly understand—he's not going to defend himself with violence! Which means, he is not going to allow us to defend ourselves with violence either. Which means, let's get out of here! So, they run away and leave him to his fate.

We have to go slow with the disciples, because most people in that situation would have done the same thing. Few people accept the way of nonviolence unto death. Gandhi knew he was going to be killed, and he even knew his assassins. He was depressed in the last few years of his life because of it, and he begged God for the grace to be as nonviolent and forgiving as Jesus. Dr. King knew in the last year of his life that he would soon be killed by the system. He was depressed and anxious and developed a serious tic. Only in the last few weeks of his life, according to Harry Belafonte, had he made peace with his impending death. With that, his tic went away. It was the same with the martyred archbishop Oscar Romero. He spent a lot of time praying for the grace to be faithful and peaceful as he faced his assassins. He was assassinated while saying Mass, in front of a congregation of nuns. Sr. Dorothy Stang knew she would be killed for speaking out publicly against the landowners in the Brazilian jungle who were tearing down the Amazon. As they approached to kill her, she pulled out her Bible and started reading the Beatitudes out loud. She died reading the Beatitudes, according to eyewitnesses. These are the true holy disciples of the nonviolent Jesus who accepted and lived in his new covenant. Their heroic nonviolent lives have affected billions of people in a positive way. But what they did is not easy to do. It wasn't easy for them, and it's little wonder that so many of us fail to follow their and Jesus's example.

Mark refers in passing to a young man who was present in Gethsemane. He wore only a linen cloth. He was seized by the authorities but slipped out of the cloth and ran off naked. Why this strange detail? Many speculate about its symbolism, but I think it's simpler. Paul refers in his letters to Peter's son John Mark. How is it that Mark's Gospel emphasizes so many specific details about Peter's misunderstandings and failings, even his terrible three denials that come next? I presume that Peter told his son Mark all about them and, further, that Mark may have witnessed them himself, because he grew up with Jesus and was part of Jesus's community. As he grew older, he formed a community around him, told them all the stories of his father and the Holy One, and eventually he and his community wrote them down for posterity. I think Mark himself was the young man in the white cloth who ran off into the night.

So, Jesus is led away to be interrogated in the house of the high priest with all the chief priests, the elders, and the scribes present. Peter "follows" at a distance. He takes a seat next to the guards in the high priest's courtyard and warms himself by the fire. Jesus is being denounced by false witnesses who state all kinds of lies against him—while Peter sits a few yards away, warming his hands with the armed guards. Jesus remains silent throughout, until finally, the high priest asks him directly, "Are you the Messiah, the son of the Blessed One?" Jesus answers, "I am, and you will see the Son of Humanity seated at the right hand of the Power and coming with the clouds of heaven.'" At that the high priest tears his garments and says, "What further need have we of witnesses? You have heard the blasphemy." With that, they condemn him to death and begin to spit on him, blindfold him, mock him, and strike him repeatedly.

Earlier, Peter had said to Jesus, "Even though all should have their faith shaken, mine will not be." Jesus said, this very night before the cock crows twice you will deny three times that you even know me. "Even though I should have to die with you, I will not deny you," Peter promised. And so, while Jesus is being struck and mocked, someone identifies Peter, who is warming his hands by the fire in the courtyard, as an associate of Jesus. He denies it. He walks to the outer courtyard, as a cock crows in the distance. Another woman identifies him, and he denies it again. Finally, a group of bystanders recognize him as a follower of Jesus; they recognize his Galilean accent. With that, Peter begins "to curse and to swear," saying, "I do not know this man about whom you are talking." As the cock crows a second time, Peter remembers Jesus's prediction and breaks down sobbing. The betrayal, abandonment, denial, and rejection are complete. The nonviolent Jesus is on his own to face the hounds of hell.

Fifty years later, John's Gospel will fill in the details and bring the denials of Peter to closure. With an eye for detail, John will note how Simon warms his hands on a *charcoal* fire in the courtyard of the Roman Empire, while Jesus is being tortured and interrogated. Later, by the Sea of Galilee, John will tell of the risen Jesus who gathers his broken community back together around his own *charcoal* fire in his new courtyard of resurrection peace. There he will ask Simon Peter three times if he loves him, and offer him the gift of forgiveness and redemption.

"Jesus Gave a Loud Cry and Breathed His Last" (15:1–47)

Morning comes, the whole Sanhedrin gathers in council and leads Jesus to Pilate, who questions him. Jesus remains silent, much to Pilate's amazement. Mark portrays Jesus as the judge over the charade, the whole system. Pilate asks the crowd what they want him to do. They call for the release of the violent rebel and murderer Barabbas, and for the crucifixion of Jesus. Why, what evil has he done? Pilate asks the crowd, which only calls out even more loudly for crucifixion. "Wishing to satisfy the crowd," Mark writes, Pilate "released Barabbas to them and, after he had Jesus scourged, handed him over to be crucified." "Mark's Pilate fully understands the political character of Jesus' practice as a threat," Myers concludes, "approves of his elimination and is willing to exchange a known political terrorist (Barabbas) in order to secure it" (*BSM*, 373).

Jesus is legally tried and condemned to capital punishment for the capital crime of leading a movement of resistance against the temple state system and the Roman Empire. He has been trying to build a grassroots movement of nonviolent resistance, and he is succeeding to the extent that people all over the city know about him. So, the Roman governor sees him as a threat and eliminates him immediately. To stop a grassroots movement, the culture of violence always decapitates it; it kills the movement's charismatic leader, from Jesus to Dr. King.

Jesus is dragged inside the Roman procurator's headquarters where the whole cohort is sitting around with nothing to do, except probably drink. These six hundred bored, perhaps drunken, Roman soldiers assigned to protect the Roman governor during the Jewish Holy Days now have something to do. This hapless, skinny hick from the outback claims to be a king, so they have fun with him in an orgy of violence. They mock him by clothing him in purple, putting a crown of thorns on him, saluting him, striking him on the head, spitting at him, and kneeling before him. Jesus is silent and passive. If he had said anything at all, he would only have been beaten further. His hour has come and he knows it.

They lead him through the streets to an abandoned quarry outside the city walls where they execute rebels on wooden crosses and then toss their bodies into a pit for the vultures. Mark notes that they make a passerby, Simon a Cyrenian, carry the cross of Jesus, because he would have been too weak from being tortured to carry it on his own. They strip Jesus naked, nail him to a cross, and raise it high for people who are coming and going to see. Crucifixion was deterrence. It said to the population: if you dare challenge the ruling authorities or the Roman Empire, this is what will happen to you. They place an inscription over his head calling him "The King of the Jews." They crucify violent revolutionaries on either side of him who join in mocking him. The crowds walk by him "shaking their heads," we're told, as they mock him saying, "Save yourself by coming down from the cross." The chief priests and scribes, who had harassed and interrogated Jesus, now mock him further, saying, "Let the Messiah, the King of the Jews, come down from the cross that we may see and believe." The cross, to put it mildly, is the stumbling block. No one can believe that this way of resistance can be part of God's plan. They state what everyone thinks: if there's another way to God's reign than the cross, then we will believe in your vision, but we cannot believe in you or your way of nonviolence if it involves the cross.

Jesus hangs on the cross for six hours, from nine in the morning until three in the afternoon, when he cries out, "My God, my God, why have you forsaken me?" citing the opening line of Psalm 22, which starts in total despair and abandonment but moves into exultation and rejoicing at God's fidelity. Darkness comes upon the whole land, as if the sun no longer works, like a total eclipse, as if the end of the world has come. "Jesus gave a loud cry and breathed his last," Mark writes. At the moment of his death, "the veil of the sanctuary was torn in two from top to bottom." With that tearing, the temple state system, the dominant world order, according to Mark, breaks in two and dies. The world as we know it comes to an end.

Mark's denouement features three characters or groups. First, the Roman centurion who killed Jesus, says, "Truly this man was the Son of God!" Many incorrectly conclude that this means the Roman official who presided over the execution of Jesus has converted, that the Gospel must then allow support for the nation/state system, the empire, and the military. Not at all. It does not mean he converted or that the Roman Empire was not behind the death of Jesus. The empire and its military killed the nonviolent Jesus, and this person ran the whole execution. If he believed that Jesus was the Son of God, for Mark, then he would become a follower of Jesus and be bound by the strict rules of nonviolence. He would have nothing to do with the Roman military; he would quit and probably be immediately crucified himself. But that is not what happens. Four sentences later, we read that Pilate summoned this centurion to learn if Jesus was dead, and the centurion reported to Pilate that, yes, Jesus was dead. He does not tell Pilate that the crucified one was the Son of God; he does not change his life and become a disciple. If anything, in saying, "This man was a son of God" (perhaps a better translation), this official representative of the Roman Empire might well have been echoing the many demons who called Jesus the son of God; they recognize him but have no intention of following him.

Mark also writes of Joseph of Arimathea, a prominent member of the council, the Sanhedrin, who got Pilate's permission to claim the body, had it taken down from the cross, and laid it in a new tomb. We have long presumed that Joseph was a good man, perhaps a secret follower of Jesus, who did a good thing in burying Jesus. Not necessarily. We're told he was "expecting the kingdom of God," but that is not high praise in Mark's book. As Myers suggests, the Jewish leadership was "anxious to hastily dispose of the whole matter before any protest could be made" (*BSM*, 395). So another way of considering Joseph's involvement is to see him in his official capacity as helping to bury the evidence, literally the body, and with it, the whole threat to the Jewish authorities' power and domination. Case closed. Joseph took care of everything before the sabbath began, however fast and improperly. Jesus was now a disappeared person.

Then there are the women. Here at the end, Mark finally tells us that there were several faithful disciples of the nonviolent Jesus: a group of Galilean women who followed him from Galilee to Jerusalem, who also served him, and who stayed with him even after the male disciples betrayed, denied, and abandoned him. Once again, Mark turns the discipleship story upside down; the male disciples fail Jesus, but the women remain faithful the entire time. Mark names three: Mary Magdalene; Mary the mother of the younger James and Joses; and Salome. Myers notes that this second Mary has children with the same names mentioned earlier in reference to Mary of Nazareth, Jesus's mother (6:3). Perhaps Mark now identifies Mary not as the mother of Jesus, but in his eyes, more importantly, as a faithful disciple of Jesus. "This is the last—and given the highly structured gender roles of the time, surely the most radical—example of Mark's narrative subversion of the canons of social orthodoxy," Myers concludes. "The world order is being overturned, from the highest political power to the deepest cultural patterns, and it begins within the new community. It will be these women, the 'last' become 'first,' who will be entrusted with the resurrection message" (*BSM*, 396–97).

The women watch Joseph roll a stone against the entrance of the tomb. They are faithful to the end, but, even so, they walk back into the city at sunset, devastated. The story is over. Jesus has completely failed. The system of war and empire has won. The religious authorities were right; the empire is all powerful, there is nothing that can be done. Death does, in fact, get the last word.

"Go Back to Galilee and Start His Campaign of Nonviolence All Over": The Never-Ending Story of Gospel Nonviolence (16:1–8)

On Sunday morning as the sabbath ends and the sun rises, the three women return to the tomb with spices to properly anoint the dead body. Mark says they arrive to find the stone rolled back from the entrance to the tomb. They enter and see a young man sitting in a white robe (symbolizing martyrdom, reminding us of the transfiguration). "They were utterly amazed," Mark states. The young man says, "Do not be amazed! You seek Jesus of Nazareth, the crucified. He has been raised; he is not here. Behold, the place where they laid him. But go and tell his disciples and Peter, 'He is going before you to Galilee; there you will see him, as he told you.'" With that, the three women "fled from the tomb, seized with trembling and bewilderment. They said nothing to anyone, for they were afraid." With verse 8, Mark's Gospel ends.

That sentence is the end of Mark, but few realize it. One or two hundred years later, eleven verses were added to wrap it up and make it sound like the others. This addition was approved and added to Mark by the Council of Trent. In the seventh to ninth centuries, a further sentence was added to subvert Mark's revolutionary text and make it more officially "religious." I believe that neither of those false endings is authentic or worthy of Mark. Mark's Gospel, even with its sudden ending—especially with it!—is a work of genius, the first of its kind.

Ched Myers argues that Mark knows what he is doing, that his abrupt ending is deliberate. There is deliberately no appearance of the risen Jesus in Mark's account. Think of it: this is the earliest version of the resurrection story, yet we do not meet the risen Jesus. His body is not in the tomb. Instead, a mysterious young man dressed in white sits there and tells the women that the Crucified One has been raised and is going before them to Galilee where they will see him. The women run away terrified.

If we take Mark's version as intentional, then Mark's chapter 16 is not an ending but a continuing, a new beginning. The disciples and Peter—as well as us, the readers—are told to return to Galilee, the place where the journey began, where we will meet the risen Jesus. That can only mean that once there, where the story began, they will be called all over again to take up radical discipleship and undertake their own campaign of nonviolence toward Jerusalem. In other words, the story ends with a command that it is our turn to take up the way of the cross as nonviolent resistance to empire, just as Jesus did, and march to Jerusalem, where we will take our turn engaging in direct action and face the consequences. Along the way, they are told, they will meet Jesus because he is risen. So a risen martyr is going to call them to step up to the plate and risk becoming martyrs of nonviolence and resistance. No wonder the women are terrified and take off running! Myers writes:

> Mark does not narrate the appearance of the risen Christ. I would contend that Mark is not pointing "beyond" his narrative world at all. This "future" point of reference is the same as the "past" one: Galilee. And where is that? It is where "the disciples and Peter" were first called, named, sent on mission and taught by Jesus. In other words, the disciple/reader is being told that that narrative, which appeared to have ended is beginning again. The story is circular! The full revelation of the Human One has resulted in neither triumphal victory for the community (as the disciples had hoped), nor the restored Davidic kingdom (as the rebels had hoped), nor tragic failure and defeat (as the reader had feared). It has resulted in nothing more and nothing less than the regeneration of the messianic mission. . . . Here both the realism and genius of Mark are fully revealed, for the final narrative signal is fraught with ambiguity. . . . We do not entirely understand what "resurrection" means, but if we have understood the story, we should be "holding fast" to what we do know: that Jesus still goes before us, summoning us to the way of the cross. And that is the hardest ending of all: not tragedy, not victory, but an unending challenge to follow anew. Because that means we must respond. (*BSM*, 398–99, 401)

Myers concludes that the best way to understand Mark is to enter his Gospel story right now in our own historical moment in "militant nonviolent struggle," what Gandhi called "satyagraha," or truth force, by participating in the ongoing campaign of nonviolent civil disobedience against all oppression, domination, violence, warmaking, and empire. Mark insists we bring the story to life, even as we fail in our resistance and get crushed by the state, knowing that we will share in the life of the nonviolent Jesus. We will fail, but with faith, courage, and perseverance, as we suffer through this failure unto our own deaths, we will sow seeds of nonviolence. They will grow and inspire others to take new risks in the nonviolent struggle for justice and one day will reap a harvest of justice for the coming of a new culture of nonviolence and peace here on earth.

Mark tells us that Jesus is risen, that in the end, death does not get the last word, that life is stronger than death, that active nonviolence is stronger that systemic violence, that organized steadfast resistance to structured violence and empire eventually works and wears down the system. With Mark's apparently ambiguous version of resurrection, the days of empire, war, and the whole culture of death are coming to an end because the followers of this martyr are returning to the place of origin where his grassroots movement started and starting it all over again, with the same determination and persistence he demonstrated, even though they know the brutal outcome. His message and life have become contagious, and will bring down the walls of injustice and empire.

So, the eleven men disciples and the women disciples apparently return home, regroup, form new small communities, and start anew walking the way of Jesus. This time they are not afraid. Somewhere along the way, they meet the risen Jesus and find him to be as gentle and peaceful as ever, and they see that God is with him, that the finger of God is upon him and them. So they set off in the footsteps of the revolutionary Jesus, this time on their own campaign of nonviolent resistance to Jerusalem, Rome, and their own crucifixions, because they know now that death is only temporary. They proclaim God's reign fearlessly and call for the fall of the culture of death, even if it means their own deaths. They willingly head toward their own tombs and, like Jesus, know they will occupy them only briefly.

This movement of resurrection nonviolence will become more and more contagious over time. The poor and marginalized throughout the empire will hear the good news of liberation from slavery to the culture of violence, and will come forward to join "The Way" and take up the public campaign of Gospel nonviolence. It will be the undoing of empire. Two thousand years later, with a long history of failure and defeats, nonetheless, the global grassroots movement of active nonviolence is spreading to every corner of the world. It will never end until every human being is disarmed, until the system of injustice and empire is dismantled, and until God's reign of peace is welcomed by every human being on earth. That's the message of the young man dressed in white, of the holy women, and of Mark's community.

A s we conclude our journey with Mark, I invite us once again to pause, take a deep breath, and turn in prayer to God. We have tried to walk with Mark's Jesus from Galilee to Jerusalem, to keep up with his permanent campaign of nonviolent resistance and non-stop civil disobedience to the culture of violence, domination, and empire, to follow him even through the collapse of his community, his arrest, torture, and execution. We leave Mark with the tale of a mysterious figure in white pointing us back to Galilee, to take up the journey where he left off, and to look for the risen, nonviolent Jesus along the way.

The only way, then, to understand Mark and to encounter the risen Jesus is if we ourselves—that is, you and I, dear reader—step into the Gospel, take up the story in our own present-day Galilees, and march toward our own present-day Jerusalems in our own public campaign of active nonviolence and steadfast resistance—that is, if we take up the cross and dare risk resurrection. In a world on the brink of nuclear warfare, the unfolding, unimaginable catastrophes of climate chaos, and extreme global poverty and oppression, the only way Jesus makes sense, according to Mark's story, is through the actual practice of our own radical discipleship to his revolutionary nonviolence lived out right now in this present moment.

If you want to meet the risen nonviolent Jesus, you can, he says. Take to the streets in permanent nonviolent protest of systemic violence and injustice. Give your life in steadfast resistance to every structure of violence, to war, racism, poverty, nuclear weapons, and environmental destruction. Invite everyone everywhere to drop everything in their lives and join this holy, global, grassroots movement of active nonviolence for disarmament, justice, and creation. Engage in public truth-telling and nonviolent civil disobedience as a way of life and testify in court about your Gospel vision of a new culture of peace and justice. Get arrested, go to jail, risk your life in the nonviolent struggle for justice. Be Gandhi, be Dr. King, be Dorothy Day, be Oscar Romero. Practice eschatological nonviolence and step into resurrection, that new realm where death has no power. Along "The Way," you will become part of the story, you will know the risen Jesus personally, and you will enter the kingdom of God. Amen!

LUKE

The Grassroots Campaign
of Peace, Nonviolence, and Compassion

Go on your way. Behold I am sending you like lambs among wolves. . . . Into whatever house you enter, first say, "Peace to this household." If a peaceful person lives there, your peace will rest on him; but if not, it will return to you. . . . Whatever town you enter and they welcome you, eat what is set before you, cure the sick in it and say to them, "The kingdom of God is at hand for you." (Lk. 10:3, 5–6, 8–9)

As he drew near, he saw the city and wept over it, saying, "If this day you only knew the things that make for peace. . . ." (Lk. 19:41–42)

One of them struck the high priest's servant and cut off his right ear. But Jesus said in reply, "Stop, no more of this!" Then he touched the servant's ear and healed him. (Lk. 23:50–51)

*   *   *

Since many have undertaken to compile a narrative of the events that have been fulfilled among us, just as those who were eyewitnesses from the beginning and ministers of the word have handed them down to us, I too have decided, after investigating everything accurately anew, to write it down in an orderly sequence for you, most excellent Theophilus, so that you may realize the certainty of the teachings you have received. (Lk. 1:1–4)

*   *   *

With this opening sentence, the Gospel of Luke sets a different tone and mission from Matthew and Mark. Right away, we notice a prologue that resembles Greek and Roman literature. It was probably written between 72 and 90, five years or so after Mark, a few years after the Roman military's destruction of Jerusalem, perhaps around the same time as Matthew. We know Luke's name as a comrade of Paul (Phlm. 1:24), who supported Paul while he was in prison (2 Tim. 4:11). He is considered to be a Gentile, perhaps a doctor, and possibly even from the Greek city of Antioch. His Gospel seems intended for a wide, even global, audience of both Jews and Gentiles.

Unlike the other Gospels, Luke's Gospel is addressed to a specific individual named "Theophilus" (or "Friend of God"). Some speculate that this "most excellent Theophilus" is an official *in Rome who has begun to study the faith and is considering conversion to Christianity. A question has been raised that perhaps Luke was hoping to spread the gospel throughout the Roman Empire, maybe even help legalize Christianity, by writing this book for such an important, though anonymous, political leader, perhaps a Roman senator. Further, Luke's Gospel is only part 1. Luke continues the saga with part 2, the story of the early church, the Acts of the Apostles, which also begins with a dedication to Theophilus.*

Luke draws on Mark, Matthew, and the unknown source "Q," consisting of sayings of Jesus, that he shares with Matthew, but he adds many original teachings, stories, people, and parables. Luke's Jesus teaches and models universal compassion and, in that way, fulfills his calling to be the universal Savior of humanity. He practices total nonviolence and insists from day one that we side with the poor and the marginalized if we want to follow him. He is portrayed as someone who deliberately goes into the wilderness to commune in nature with his beloved God and, at the same time, mobilizes a grassroots movement of creative nonviolence whereby his followers are sent out in pairs to do his work and to proclaim the coming of God's reign of peace—and thus to bring down the empire.

In particular, Luke's Gospel is filled with women, from Elizabeth and Mary to Martha and Mary of Bethany to the many faithful women at the cross and the empty tomb. Luke refers to women forty-five times in his Gospel. Luke's genealogy traces backwards from Joseph to David all the way to Adam himself and has only two names in common with Matthew (Shealtiel and Zerubbabel), but what's even more unusual is that it seems to be Jesus's genealogy traced backwards from his mother's side. It's the lineage of Mary! Luke's account of Mary's journey from the Annunciation to the Visitation to the Magnificat foreshadows the Gospel journey of contemplative to active to prophetic nonviolence. At the birth of the nonviolent Jesus, a host of angels appear in the sky praising God and singing to the shepherds of Bethlehem, the poorest of the poor, about the coming of peace on earth. Women support Jesus and the community financially, follow him even as he carries the cross, and then witness his resurrection.

Luke launches Jesus from his hometown of Nazareth, in a dramatic opening scene in the synagogue, where he reads from Isaiah's call to bring good news to the poor and then announces that he has fulfilled the scriptures. After a fierce exchange, the congregation tries to kill Jesus by throwing him off a cliff! With this cliff-hanger beginning, the story of Jesus is set: Jesus brings good news to the poor, he builds a grassroots movement for this purpose, the authorities threaten to and eventually kill Jesus, and the story is repeated by his followers up through today.

Luke paints the call of the first disciples through the miracle of catching hundreds of fish and then inviting the fishermen to become fishers of men and women. He shortens Matthew's great Sermon on the Mount, sets it on a plain so that Jesus is portrayed as accessible to everyone, and makes it sharper and more pungent. Luke's Beatitudes, for instance, include a series of "woes" to those who are rich, well fed, laughing, and praised and honored, instead of persecuted for working for justice. Luke's Jesus repeats the command to love one's enemies and concludes with a call to be as universally compassionate as God. His Sermon on the Plain sums up all his teachings and becomes the center from which the rest of the Gospel flows.

In the transfiguration, Luke adds a conversation with Moses and Elijah, who encourage Jesus to carry the cross all the way and to complete his exodus. Luke's Gospel stresses the call to repentance using stories of a recent massacre that Pilate ordered and the tragedy of a tower's collapse, as well as references to Noah and Lot. He relentlessly calls out the hypocrisy of the religious authorities.

In Luke, we do not hear Mark's urgent call to resistance or Matthew's urgent appeal to faithful Jews that Jesus is their Messiah. We find many public acts of compassion toward the poor, the marginalized, the lame, the blind, the mute, the deaf, the enemy, even the dead. For example, Luke tells of Jesus coming upon a funeral procession in Nain, where he sees the grief of the mother and raises the boy from the dead. We hear how he heals ten lepers, but only one, a Samaritan, returns to thank him. In Jericho, he invites the tax collector Zacchaeus to host him for dinner, much to the scandal of the religious authorities. Time and again, Jesus mixes with the wrong people and does the wrong thing only to face the threats of the religious authorities.

Luke includes eighteen parables found only in his Gospel, four of which become cornerstones of Jesus's seminal call for compassion toward the poor—the Good Samaritan, the prodigal son, the rich man and the poor beggar Lazarus, and a dishonest judge and a persistent widow. Others include stories about a friend who knocks on one's door at midnight, a barren fig tree, a lost coin, an unjust steward, a Pharisee and a tax collector, and ten gold coins. Many parables feature feasts, and there are many meals in Luke's Gospel, as if to emphasize how Jesus used the intimacy of sharing a meal as the best time to teach and model compassion and peacemaking.

As Jesus approaches Jerusalem, Luke shows him breaking down and weeping over the city, lamenting, "If this day you only knew the things that make for peace," one of the key Gospel moments in the life of the nonviolent Jesus. Luke names three specific criminal charges brought against Jesus—he misleads the people; opposes payment of taxes to Caesar; and claims to be a king. In Jesus's last hours, Luke tests the disciples and us readers by having Jesus tell the disciples to go buy swords, only to discover how happily they—and we—are willing to resort to violence, to which he responds, "Oh forget it!" Only Luke portrays Jesus before Herod, whom earlier he called "that fox." As he carries the cross, Jesus meets a group of weeping women whom he tells not to weep for him. One of the two violent revolutionaries crucified with him asks Jesus to remember him when he comes into his kingdom. Finally, as Jesus dies on the cross, Luke's Jesus surrenders completely to God, saying, "Father into your hands I commit my spirit."

After Jesus's resurrection, Luke offers a long unique account of Jesus's appearance to two downcast disciples on the road to Emmaus. Along the way, he engages them, in effect, in a Bible study, and then reveals himself to them in the breaking of the bread. We can easily speculate that this story of the road to Emmaus is intended for Luke's own community struggling to find Jesus, feeling his spirit as they tell his story, and experiencing him in the breaking of the bread. This sweeping resurrection account continues to encourage Christians and communities everywhere by stirring the fires within our hearts. In the upper-room appearance to the eleven disciples, Jesus says, "Peace be with you," questions their doubts, eats some fish, explains all the scriptures to them, and then names them as "witnesses." Luke ends with Jesus blessing his disciples and being taken up to heaven, which fills them with great joy and sends them back to the temple, the scene of the crime, to praise God continually.

At the center of Luke's Gospel stands a unique turning point in chapter 9, verse 51. One day, "Jesus resolutely determined to journey to Jerusalem and sent messengers ahead of him." With that, Luke clearly portrays Jesus as organizing and leading a long grassroots movement that would culminate in nonviolent civil disobedience in Jerusalem. Only Luke tells in detail about seventy-two disciples sent out ahead of Jesus on the mission of nonviolence—to expel the demons of violence, to heal everyone from the culture of violence, and to announce the coming of God's reign of peace. Luke's Jesus resembles Gandhi and King as the ultimate movement leader, grassroots organizer, and nonviolent resister. Jesus is a revolutionary, but a nonviolent one, something the world has never seen before, something we rarely see today. Luke makes it clear that his disciples practice grassroots, active, movement-building nonviolence in order to spread peace to everyone everywhere, near and far.

Luke will take up the story of Jesus's grassroots movement of creative nonviolence in the Acts of the Apostles, where we will hear how the disciples start to preach in Jerusalem, and begin their own discipleship rhythm of arrest, imprisonment, and martyrdom. The formerly hapless disciples rise to the occasion and become the public peacemakers Jesus had formed them to be.

As we will see, Luke's Gospel calls us to follow the nonviolent Jesus on his public campaign of peace and compassion. It feels like a softer version of Mark and Matthew, but don't be fooled: it holds the same dynamite, the same challenge, the same urgent call to seek God's reign of peace in our midst. Luke's Jesus practices nonviolence and universal compassion, and he insists that, if we dare to follow him, we do the same and join his global movement of disarming nonviolence to welcome God's reign of peace.

The nonviolence that Luke's Jesus portrays is what Gandhi called "the nonviolence of the strong" and what Dr. King called "militant nonviolence." There is nothing passive, quiet, or complacent about it. Luke's Jesus breaks through "negative peace," what Dr. King described as a fake veneer of peace with the way things are, while underneath systemic, institutionalized injustice crushes and kills people. Luke's Jesus engages nonviolence as a power more potent than the Roman military or the empire itself, the power of God available even to the poorest of the poor, to transform any situation and culture to welcome God's reign and bring about justice and equality.

Further, Luke's Jesus practices what Gandhi called "the constructive program" as he organizes and builds a movement of nonviolent resistance to the culture of violence and points us to God's reign of peace. He heals everyone who is sick, expels every demonic power of violence and nationalism that possesses people, and restores everyone into the Beloved Community of universal love. He does what Peter Maurin and Dorothy Day outlined as the mission of the Catholic Worker: "to build a new society within the shell of the old," to start the process of creating a new culture of justice, equality, and nonviolence even as we resist and turn away from the culture of injustice, inequality, and violence.

For Luke, Jesus's revolutionary nonviolence is a spiritual path, a way of life, and a political methodology of organizing goodness, compassion, and love to transform the culture for God's peace. The nonviolence of Jesus in Luke requires steadfast, fearless bravery and courage, boundless compassion to the poor and disenfranchised, relentless prophetic truth-telling, willingness to grieve over humanity's rejection of God's reign in our midst, and a resolute determination to go forward come what may, resisting empire and violence with the good news of justice and peace. As Luke's risen Jesus explains to the discouraged and hopeless disciples on the road to Emmaus, God works through human history from Moses to the prophets and now through the early community, and we are summoned to join that lineage and continue that movement as Gandhi and Dr. King did to end poverty, war, racism, killing, nuclear weapons, and environmental destruction, and to welcome God's reign of nonviolence and compassion in every corner of the world. That is our mission. We are witnesses of these things, and, like the Galilee 72, we are sent forth as fishers of men and women, as lambs into the midst of wolves, to call everyone to drop what they are doing, turn away from the culture of violence and war, and welcome God's reign of universal love and peace here on earth, right now.

Please note: much of what follows you have heard before in Matthew and Mark, and it may feel repetitious. If you read it slowly over time, however, you will make new discoveries of God's way of nonviolence that go beyond Matthew and Mark, so I urge patience, peace, and prayer as you proceed into Luke.

"Guide Our Feet into the Path of Peace" (1:1–3:20; 3:23–38)

Luke starts off with the two mythical tales of the birth of John the Baptist and the birth of Jesus. Mark and John have no infancy narratives, and this narrative is far more elaborate than Matthew's. Each account emphasizes the mission of peace and nonviolence that John and Jesus would fulfill for God. First, we're told how the angel Gabriel appeared to John's father, Zechariah, to announce John's birth, and how Zechariah doubted. Then we're told how the angel appeared to Mary, who raised questions but accepted the news, then ran to visit Elizabeth, John's mother. Finally, we hear of the two births. The two parallel stories complement each other and point to the trajectory of God's plan for the coming of peace on earth. First, the birth of John the Baptist.

Zechariah, a priest, and his wife, Elizabeth, were righteous, faithful, and blameless before God, Luke begins, but they had no children. Then one day while Zechariah was in the sanctuary lighting the incense on the altar, the angel Gabriel appeared to him. He was "troubled" and "afraid." But Gabriel said, "Do not be afraid. Your prayer has been heard. Your wife Elizabeth will bear a son and you shall name him John. He will be great in the sight of the God of peace, be filled with the Holy Spirit, and will turn many of the children of Israel to the God of peace," the angel said. "He will prepare a loving, nonviolent people fit for the God of peace."

Zechariah didn't believe a word of it. "Are you kidding?" he says in effect. "I am an old man, and my wife is advanced in years." His doubts were not well received. "I am Gabriel, who stands before God," the angel responds. "I was sent to speak to you and to announce to you this good news. But now you will be speechless and unable to talk until the day these things take place, because you did not believe my words, which will be fulfilled at their proper time." And so, Zechariah paid the price for his lack of faith.

With that, Luke gets to the heart of the matter: there are consequences for our lack of faith in the God of peace and God's actions among us. Therefore: Do not disbelieve. Do not doubt. Do not let your skepticism and cynicism control you. Instead, take a leap of faith, and say yes to any movement of the God of peace. Say, "Okay, God, I believe in you. Whatever you say to me, whatever you think of me, whatever you want of me is fine with me because whatever you say or think of me will be infinitely better than my tiny, warped ideas and disbeliefs."

Most of us go through life mumbling and grumbling, refusing to believe in God whole-heartedly until we have proof. I never understood how people preferred to believe in their own limited judgments instead of in God, as millions of saints and peacemakers throughout history have done. Since I was young, I never trusted my own judgments. What do I know? When I look to the saints and peacemakers of history, and see what they believed and how they acted, that has always been good enough for me. I do not believe my doubts; they're not trustworthy. Zechariah was a holy, righteous, and faithful person, but deep down, he so trusted himself, including his doubts, that when Gabriel stood right before him, he didn't believe his eyes and ears. Later, of course, when Elizabeth gave birth to John, and when people disapproved of her choice of his name, his father wrote it on a tablet, instantly began to speak and praised God for God's loving action and presence among us. People were amazed and overjoyed.

So Luke tells us how God is coming into history and preparing a way of peace among us by sending us a great prophet of peace and justice. What I take from the story is that God continues to act throughout history, right up until today, even among the least of us, and therefore, we do not need to doubt God as Zechariah did. Instead, we can believe and accept the good news of God, as Mary will, and do whatever the God of peace wants us to do. Nothing else is working in the world. We might as well place all our chips on the God of peace and any act of God's creative nonviolence in our lives.

Luke pivots from the great Zechariah's disbelief to his astonishing hymn of praise, a brilliant text original to Luke:

Blessed be the God of peace, the God of Israel,
> for the God of peace has visited and brought redemption to God's people.
God has raised up a horn for our salvation
> within the house of David God's servant,
even as God promised through the mouth of God's holy prophets from of old
> salvation from our enemies and from the hand of all who hate us,
to show mercy to our ancestors
> and to be mindful of God's holy covenant
and of the oath God swore to Abraham our father,
> and to grant us that, rescued from the hand of enemies,
without fear we might worship the God of peace in holiness and righteousness
> all our days.
And you, child, will be called prophet of the Most High,
> for you will go before the God of peace to prepare God's ways,
to give God's people knowledge of salvation
> through the forgiveness of their sins,
because of the tender mercy of our God
> by which the daybreak from on high will visit us
to shine on those who sit in darkness and death's shadow,
> to guide our feet into the path of peace. (Lk. 1:67–79)

Zechariah's canticle focuses on how God is trustworthy and faithful; how God keeps God's part of the covenant with the people of God; how God has consistently shown mercy to God's people; and how God invites us to worship in holiness without fear; how God's tender mercy will light our way into the path of peace. With this explanation, Luke sets the stage for God's visitation among us. God is faithful and trustworthy. The God of peace has not abandoned us but will shine God's light into the darkness of the culture of death and lead us on the way of peace. John the Baptist and Jesus will announce this and embody it, and will call humanity to join God's guiding light on the path of peace. Unlike Zechariah, we need not doubt God's faithfulness. We have heard Zechariah's canticle and can embark on the path of peace, following John the Baptist as he prepares a way for the God of peace.

Notice that Zechariah addresses the child John, giving him his mission: to prepare God's ways, to give God's people knowledge of salvation, to announce that their sins are forgiven, to explain the tender mercy of God, to lead all those stuck in darkness and death's shadow at daybreak in the light of a new day, and to guide everyone onto the path of peace. As we join Zechariah in praising God for the divine work of peace among us, Luke invites us to take this mission to heart as well, to claim it as our personal mission. Just as John is a disciple of the nonviolent Jesus sent to lead everyone into God's path of peace, so too each of us has been sent to prepare God's way, to give people knowledge of salvation and the forgiveness of sins, to help everyone welcome the tender mercy of God and the light of Christ that all humanity might now turn away from darkness and death and live in the light of Christ's peace.

When we reflect on the birth of John the Baptist, we hear several invitations that make for good news. First, "Do not be afraid." This is one of Luke's major themes. There is no reason to be afraid anymore. Later, we will begin to understand that total nonviolence and discipleship to the nonviolent Jesus require steadfast fearlessness. For now, we can just put aside our fears. Next, we're told that God answers prayers, that God has done the impossible for beloved Zechariah and Elizabeth. As we try to be as holy, righteous, and faithful as them, we too can trust that God hears our prayers for new life, light, and peace, however impossible they might be. Next, we're invited to believe, even if we do not fully understand what God is saying. We take it to heart and trust whatever the good God is saying to us, knowing that it is good for us, for our own good. Moreover, like Zechariah, Elizabeth, and everyone in the story, we too can rejoice. For us, that means that we rejoice from now on at any and every sign of God's loving presence and peacemaking action in the world. Finally, the story invites us to take up the path of peace, and so, as we embark on Luke's story, we agree to start living in the light and walking the path of peace. That journey becomes the goal and mission of our lives. As we embark on this journey, foretold by Zechariah, we too prepare for the nonviolent Jesus who walks the path of peace, shows us the path of peace, teaches us the things that make for peace, and ultimately embodies peace as the way itself.

Jesus's Teacher of Nonviolence: Mary and the Three Movements of Gospel Nonviolence (1:26–56)

Luke presents Jesus as the God of peace who comes among us in total poverty into our impoverished world of war and empire, who brings with him God's reign of peace and nonviolence, and who invites us to follow him on the path of love, compassion, and justice. With his birth, we hear the angels announce the coming of peace on earth. Luke will honor Jesus's birth because he is the greatest peacemaker in history. He marked the path of peace toward Jerusalem, where he will confront imperial injustice and call us to learn the things that make for peace; he endured rejection, betrayal, torture, and execution in the holy spirit of nonviolence, and rose to offer his gift of peace and send us out all over again on his path of peace.

How did Jesus learn all this? Luke offers an amazing answer. He presents Mary, Jesus's holy Jewish mother, as his teacher of nonviolence. Here in chapter 1, Luke tells the story of Mary's journey as three movements of creative nonviolence: the first, the Annunciation as a story of contemplative nonviolence, which leads to the second, the Visitation as the story of active nonviolence, which leads to the third, the Magnificat as the vision of prophetic nonviolence.

Mary's journey begins with contemplative prayer, so Luke teaches that the spiritual journey of peace and nonviolence begins with contemplative peace and nonviolence. Later, he will tell how Jesus periodically slips away into the solitude of nature to commune alone with God in peace. Jesus, too, practices contemplative peace and nonviolence. The Annunciation is a scene of contemplative prayer by which Mary communes with the God of peace. Mary is a nonviolent person and therefore a contemplative. She sits listening attentively to God, and in that silence and stillness, she encounters God and is ready for God. This is what Jesus learned from his mother, and what we have to learn from her, too. We will see this in Jesus's first public appearance when he sits by the Jordan River after his baptism and, in that contemplative peace, hears the God of peace call him "My beloved," which sets him on his journey.

So, the first lesson of Lucan nonviolence is to sit in silence and solitude, in contemplative prayer, to open ourselves to God, to listen for God, and to be available if the God of peace chooses to speak. As Mary would have known, the first step in a peaceful life is to spend time in peace with the God of peace, to prepare a peaceful place in our hearts for the God of peace, to let the God of peace speak to us, to be ready if the God of peace sends us forth as peacemakers into the world of war.

Even though Mary is a person of prayer, like Zechariah, when the angel comes and greets her, she's scared. Mary's first reaction is fear. She is deeply disturbed. This is also instructive. When God enters our lives, we are afraid and disturbed. The first thing the angel says, once again, is "Do not be afraid." So Lucan nonviolence also begins with a commandment, "Do not be afraid." If we are going to proceed with Mary's journey and read Luke's Gospel and ultimately take up Jesus's way of nonviolence, we have to examine our fears right from the start, let them go, and embark on a new spirit of fearlessness, as Mary and Jesus did.

Mary speaks with the angel, asks questions, and moves from fear to confusion. The angel tells us, "The God of peace is doing this in you; a child will be born; he will be the savior of the world."

What? "Savior of the world"? Isn't that a title reserved for the emperor? Isn't the Roman emperor the Savior of the world? Isn't he divine, as his armies and procurators tell us? "You shall name him Jesus," the angel continues. "He will be great and will be called Son of the

Most High, and the Lord God will give him the throne of David his father, and he will rule over the house of Jacob forever, and of his kingdom there will be no end."

Wait—his kingdom will have no end? We are so used to this, it's hard to fathom the terrifying, unfathomable, political, revolutionary nature of this announcement. Right from the get-go, we are talking about an illegal vision, an illegal hope, an illegal plan—to welcome some kingdom other than the Roman Empire. We think of this scene as some pious, spiritual experience, but it could not be more political or dangerous or revolutionary. This child will be greater than the empire; his kingdom will be far greater than the Roman Empire; and his kingdom will have no end. As we will soon learn, his kingdom is a reign of universal love, universal compassion, universal peace, and total nonviolence. Do we want that? Is Mary willing to risk political trouble with the current kingdoms of the world to welcome this never-ending kingdom of peace, love, and nonviolence? Are we?

Mary asks how this will happen. "The Holy Spirit will come upon you, and the power of the Most High will overshadow you. Therefore, the child to be born will be called holy, the Son of God." The angel continues, telling her about Elizabeth, and thus gives Mary some support and encouragement in this divine adventure. Mary is not alone. "Behold, Elizabeth, your relative, has also conceived a son in her old age, and this is the sixth month for her who was called barren, for nothing will be impossible for God." Notice, the angel testifies about the power of God: God can do anything.

"Behold," Mary replies, "I am the servant of God. May it be done to me according to your word." With that, the angel left her.

How is Mary able to accept the angel's revolutionary message? How could she say yes? This political announcement can only mean trouble for the child, and therefore for her, but she says yes without batting an eye. The answer lies in the way she speaks about herself. She knows who she is; she calls herself "the servant of God." This is one of the most important teachings Mary will give to Jesus and the rest of us. The journey of peace and nonviolence comes down to our identity. This is how the spiritual journey of peace begins. Mary knows that, first and foremost, she is the servant of the God of peace, so to speak, so if the God of peace wants her to do something, the answer is yes, no matter what, because her sole purpose and mission in life are to serve the God of peace. Mary is not a self-centered narcissist or egomaniac. Her focus is on God; she has surrendered her life to God. She is not in control of her life; God is. She had let go of her life long before, so when the angel appeared and explained everything to her, it was easy to say, "Behold God's servant," because she knew who she was.

Mary's yes raises deep questions for us. Who are we? How do we see ourselves? What is our fundamental, bottom-line identity? The culture of war is always telling us who we are. Mary, by contrast, is a peacemaker. Luke is teaching us that if we want to be peacemakers like Mary, we have to identify ourselves first and foremost as servants of the God of peace. If you call yourself a servant of the God of peace, you will try to do the will of the God of peace and thus become a peacemaker. You will not be in control of your own life; you will hand over control of your life to the God of peace to use to make peace in the world of war.

This is the best way to understand ourselves and life, and a holy spiritual practice. According to Luke, Jesus clearly learns this lesson from his mother. There by the Jordan River, he learned that he was the beloved Son of the God of peace. During his forty days of fasting in the wilderness, his greatest temptation was to renounce this fundamental identity. As Luke will write, the tempter kept challenging him, "If you are the Son of God, prove it. . . ." Jesus doesn't need to prove it, and he doesn't doubt it or reject his true identity. Notice, too, that in the Garden of Gethsemane, Jesus repeats the prayer he learned from his mother: "Let it be done to me according to your will." Long ago, Jesus learned from his mother to surrender his life, his control, and his will to the God of peace, so when his final hour came, he was ready to stay the course and do what he had always done—surrender completely to God, just as his mother taught him.

As we ponder the story of the Annunciation, it is important to reflect that the God of peace does not send the holy angel to the emperor, or the Roman procurator, or a military leader, or some arrogant, self-righteous religious authority. The angel is sent to a poor, unwed woman on the outskirts of the empire in the middle of nowhere. This is one of the key teachings of Luke: women are equal to men; God calls women just as God calls men; and, therefore, patriarchy and sexism have to end. They have no part in the reign of the God of peace. More, God is at work not at the center of the culture of violence and war but at the margins, among the poor, where no one would expect God to dwell, because those are the places where God's reign can break through.

Mary's experience of contemplative peace and nonviolence leads to a second movement, to active peace and nonviolence. Her experience of God pushes her out of herself and leads her to "love her neighbor" and "show compassion to someone in need." These public actions would become bedrock teachings of Luke's Jesus.

We're told that Mary immediately set off in haste to the hill country to visit Elizabeth. In this second movement, Luke tells the story of two women sharing their experiences of God, serving one another, and in this way, living Gospel nonviolence and welcoming God's reign of peace:

> When Elizabeth heard Mary's greeting, the infant leaped in her womb, and Elizabeth, filled with the Holy Spirit, cried out in a loud voice and said, "Blessed are you among women and blessed is the fruit of your womb. How does this happen to me that the mother of my Lord should come to me? For at the moment the sound of your greeting reached my ears, the infant in my womb leaped for joy. Blessed are you who believed that what was spoken to you by the Lord would be fulfilled."

With this movement, Luke teaches that the contemplative prayer and heartfelt surrender to God in the life of the nonviolent Mary leads her to get up, go out, and reach out in love to her neighbor in need, and it will do the same with us. Contemplative nonviolence pushes us out of ourselves. Just as we are focused on God and doing God's will, our encounter with God in our contemplative prayer stirs us to take action on behalf of those in need, starting with those around us, like the elderly, needy Elizabeth.

Notice, too, their conversation. What is the first thing Mary says when she reaches Elizabeth? She would have said the word, "Shalom!" meaning, "Peace be with you." Jesus will later make this greeting the basis for the mission on which he sends his seventy-two disciples. Whatever house you enter, he will teach them, say, "Peace be with you." When he rises from the dead, this will be his repeated greeting to the stunned disciples. Luke teaches here that active nonviolence and love for those in need uses the language of nonviolence. After our contemplative experience of peace and nonviolence, we speak a new language. We need never say mean, bullying, hurtful, or violent words to anyone ever again.

When Elizabeth hears Mary's greeting of peace, she rejoices, and even the child in her womb jumps for joy. Luke is teaching us here that the words of peace lead to joy, consolation, and, ultimately, blessing. If we speak words of peace to one another, we will console and give joy to one another. If we speak words that hurt, insult, belittle, and humiliate, if we speak words of violence and war, we will not console anyone or give anyone joy. This is obvious but it needs to be underlined. As we engage in nonviolent, loving action, we practice nonviolent communication and speak words of peace.

The story of the Visitation is the story of two pregnant women who have dramatic experiences of God and share these experiences with one another and in the process give each other great joy and consolation. Another lesson from this second movement of nonviolence, the story of the Visitation, is that when we reach out in love to serve someone in need, we transform our relationships, friendships, family, and community and bring them peace and joy. This is part of the mission of nonviolence: to bring others peace, joy, and consolation. To do that, we learn from the nonviolent Mary to speak the words of peace with one another and share our experience of the God of peace with one another. In every conversation we should ask one another about our experience of God, where God is coming to us, where we are finding God in daily life, and what God is saying to us. As we share our experience of God with one another, we will receive the gift of peace and rejoice. That will lead to all new blessings.

Notice how Elizabeth responds to Mary's word of peace with two beatitudes: Blessed are you, and blessed is your child. She blesses Mary and her unborn child. Luke shows us here that this is how holy peacemaking women, the teachers of John the Baptist and Jesus, speak to one another. They speak the language of beatitudes. They bless one another, and in doing so they bless God. So Luke asks us, How do we bless one another? What beatitudes do we speak? Have we ever spoken a beatitude to another? Notice, too, that even the unborn John the Baptist rejoices at the greeting of peace, at the news of Jesus. He is so attentive and alert that he recognizes the God of peace even before he is born! Luke asks us: How do you rejoice at the visitation of Jesus in your life? When have we recognized the God of peace, the nonviolent Jesus, coming into our lives? How can we help one another celebrate the coming of the God of peace?

Then Elizabeth asks a question: "Who am I that the mother of my Lord should come to me?" Once again, Luke raises the importance of identity. Mary knew who she was. She called herself the servant of the God of peace. Elizabeth isn't sure. "Who am I?" she asks Mary. Like Mary, we have to claim our identities as servants of the God of peace and know who we are. Like Elizabeth, we can learn from Mary that we too are servants of the God of peace.

Finally, Elizabeth gives a third beatitude: "Blessed is she who trusted that the Lord's words would be fulfilled!" With this beatitude, Luke's Elizabeth invites us to trust the God of peace, to say yes to God and let God's word of peace be fulfilled in us. Like Mary, we will be blessed if we do our part to serve the God of peace, to welcome God and God's reign of peace, even if we do not fully understand it.

From Luke's Visitation story, we learn to become activists of God's reign, to reach out to those in need, to love our neighbors. Contemplative nonviolence pushes us to action—not vertical action, so that we focus solely on God and me alone—but horizontal action, to serve those in need around us, to offer concrete love in action. If we follow the example of Mary, Jesus's teacher, we reach out to the poor, especially to women and children, to serve the poor, accompany the poor, walk with the poor, befriend the poor, stand with the poor, and ultimately defend the poor, give our lives for the poor, and become, like Mary and Jesus, one with the poor. Along the way, with Mary and Jesus, we put into practice concrete love for those in need so that we live in solidarity with all those in need, as Gandhi and Dorothy Day did. This global solidarity of peace and love toward all those in need will inevitably lead us to work and speak out for justice and peace. That becomes the third movement of Mary's journey of peace and nonviolence: the Magnificat.

The third movement of Mary's progression is prophetic nonviolence. Mary has journeyed from contemplative nonviolence to active nonviolence and now to prophetic nonviolence. Her acceptance of God's will and her reaching out to Elizabeth fill her with joy and consolation, which leads her to proclaim a bold prophetic statement that is both a political denunciation of the empire and its culture of greed, war, and injustice and a proclamation about the God of peace and all that the God of peace is already doing and will do for justice and peace throughout human history.

Remember: Mary is a nobody. She is a poor and pregnant and about to be homeless refugee. Yet God has chosen her, and Luke portrays her here as a prophet of peace, directly in the tradition of Isaiah and Jeremiah. Luke's Gospel is showing us, as Jesus eventually learned, that the spiritual journey of peace leads us to speak out publicly against systemic injustice and for the coming of God's reign of justice and peace. This means that, like Mary and Jesus, we too will have to become prophetic peacemakers who proclaim a new Magnificat to the world of injustice and war.

The only characters in the story are Mary, Elizabeth, their unborn sons, and the angels—and yet Mary is confident and filled with joy, and she sees the whole outcome. She believes her Magnificat. She demonstrates unbridled faith and hope in the God of peace, the coming of God's reign of peace, and God's loving action throughout history.

"My soul proclaims the greatness of God; my spirit rejoices in God my savior." These are words of great consolation, focused on God, God's greatness, and God's saving action. It is also a public proclamation. With this proclamation, Luke demonstrates how Mary taught Jesus, who will in turn teach his disciples and the rest of us to speak out publicly about God's greatness and saving action. From the start, Mary's example invites all of us to be public peacemakers who serve, praise, and proclaim the God of peace.

"For God has looked upon God's servant's lowliness; from now on all generations will call me blessed. The Mighty One has done great things for me." She says that God has been active in her life. She knows that she is blessed and can see the future, that everyone will be touched by this blessing. In other words, for Mary, and later, for Jesus, life and the journey of peace are not about results and success but about being blessed by God and sharing that blessing.

Notice too that she says God's eyes are on God's servants, the poor, the lowly, the peace-makers.

"Holy is God's name. God's mercy is from age to age to those who fear God." Mary describes God's very name as holy precisely because God is a God of mercy, a God of nonviolence, a God of love. Mary knows who God is and what God is like, and she tells us this because she has encountered God. Through this proclamation, Luke invites us to announce that, contrary to what the culture of war and greed says, God is a God of mercy and peace. Also, that God's peace, mercy, and nonviolence are permanent, upon everyone throughout history. I translate that also to mean that God is at work from generation to generation through movements of nonviolence. Even though we won't read it in the daily papers, we can take heart that, as people encounter God and follow the nonviolent Jesus, as they join God's peace movement and help disarm the world in preparation for the coming of peace on earth, they are doing God's work, and God is working through them.

Mary then lists all the revolutionary actions God has done and is doing. She does not offer pious platitudes. She speaks radical, political words about social and economic justice for the poor and marginalized. In many places around the world, resisters could be killed for saying such things. During the Dirty War in Argentina in the 1970s, for example, the Mothers of the Disappeared stood in the streets of Buenos Aires with the Magnificat written on their placards. The publicity was too much for the evil junta, so they banned the Magnificat! You could be arrested for reciting Mary's word in public.

Luke's Mary announces to Elizabeth and the rest of us that the living God of justice and peace is leading a global, nonviolent revolution on behalf of the poor and oppressed:

God has shown the strength of his arm; God has scattered the arrogant of mind and heart. God has thrown down the rulers from their thrones; God has lifted up the lowly.

God has filled the hungry with good things; God has sent the rich away empty.

God has helped Israel God's servant; God has remembered God's mercy, according to God's promise to our ancestors, to Abraham and Sarah and their descendants forever.

Mary declares that all these events have already happened and are happening; that God shows a preferential option for the poor; that God liberates the oppressed; that God topples rulers, emperors, and presidents; that God lifts up the lowly and feeds the hungry; that God sends the rich away empty; that God has helped God's servants; that God has remembered mercy; that God is faithful; in short, that God has done and is doing great things for humanity, for justice, for peace, and therefore we should all rejoice.

With this dramatic prophetic climax, we readers are stunned. These words reveal the true nature of Mary of Nazareth. She is a brilliant, holy prophet, perhaps the greatest in history, and we are left to ponder who this child of hers will become. With her for a mother, we are not surprised at the wisdom, radical vision, and bold public prophetic words and deeds of Jesus. He surely learned from his mother how to speak publicly, boldly, and prophetically. He knew to keep the focus on God's nonviolent action among us, as she did. He could teach his followers these things because he learned them firsthand from one of the greatest prophets in history. As we study the Magnificat and learn to proclaim our own magnificats throughout our lives, we boldly denounce injustice, war, greed, and violence of every kind; but, like Mary, we also boldly announce the coming of a new age of justice, equality, liberation, and peace. Moreover, we explain that this is the work of God, that this is what holiness looks like, that God has remembered mercy and nonviolence and we should too. We know from Luke's Mary that the spiritual journey, the meaning of life, the movements of nonviolence are about cooperating with God's peace and justice movement, and about letting God use us to spread God's mercy and peace far and wide.

"Glory to God in the Highest and on Earth Peace":
The Birth of the Nonviolent Jesus (2:1–40)

Scholars now think that the Roman calendar is off by a few years, that Jesus would have been born in the year 6 BCE. Luke sets his birth during the reign of Roman emperor Augustus, who ordered the population to address him as "God and Savior" because he established "peace on earth," otherwise known as the Pax Romana, the Roman Empire's reign of peace. Of course, this forced peace came about through genocide, enslavement, occupation, oppression, enforced poverty, and violence of every kind, so that the Roman Empire and its divine emperor could rule the earth. It had nothing to do with true peace. If anyone disobeyed the emperor or resisted the empire, they were immediately arrested and executed. To continue its propaganda machine about its greatness and to assess its control, the empire held a census. During the census year, every man had to pack up his family and return to his place of birth to be enrolled in the empire. Women did not count—literally. They were not considered fully human. And so, Luke sets the birth of Jesus at the time of the Roman census and sends Joseph and Mary to Bethlehem, the land of Jesus's storied birth. The sole purpose of the census is to collect money through taxation for the empire and the ongoing maintenance of the Roman military and its recruits. It is in this context of imperial domination, power, greed, disruption, and militarism that the powerless child of peace comes.

Joseph takes Mary, leaves Nazareth, and journeys to Bethlehem because he is a descendant of David. Luke places Jesus in a direct lineage from King David himself. There, in the rural village of Bethlehem, not far from the holy city of Jerusalem, Jesus is born—not in a palace or religious setting, but in a manger, a shelter and feeding trough for animals. Every inn was filled, and the young couple were so poor that Jesus was born literally in a barn. We can imagine that Joseph took Mary to a relative's house, which would have been all of one room and probably already crowded with other guests, so they were put up in the shed where the animals stayed.

But the angel Gabriel has already told us that this poor child is the true God and Savior of the world, that unlike the false god whose reign comes through killing and imperial domination, Jesus's reign will spread through universal love to become a reign of peace that uses only peaceful means to grow and spread. Luke emphasizes this political message of an alternative reign by having angels appear to the poorest of the poor—the shepherds living in the nearby fields, keeping the night watch over their flocks. An angel appears to them and "the glory of the Lord shone around them," and like Zechariah and Mary, they were terrified. So, as before, the first word of the angel is "Do not be afraid." Every message of the Roman Empire instills fear. That was the message of the culture of war and the emperor throughout Jesus's lifetime, and it's the message broadcast today by nations and leaders who posture and threaten and jockey for power: "Be afraid. Be very afraid." By contrast, the Gospel of peace begins with a different message. Every message of the God of peace and the peacemaking Jesus begins with "Do not be afraid." The days of fear are over, Luke announces. "You have nothing to fear. Real peace is at hand. A nonviolent savior is coming to the rescue with a way out of this empire of violence and a way into a new life of eternal peace."

"Behold, I proclaim to you good news of great joy that will be for all the people," the angel declares. "Today in the city of David a savior has been born for you who is Messiah and Lord. And this will be a sign for you: you will find an infant wrapped in swaddling clothes and lying in a manger." Luke is the only one to name Jesus as "savior." With this title, first-century Jews would have looked for an heir of David to restore Israel to power; here, Luke adds "Messiah" and "Lord" to announce that Jesus will save everyone, Jew and Gentile, the entire human race. The nonviolent Jesus has come to save everyone, and not just everyone alive in that place and time but everywhere throughout history.

The angel, indeed, all of heaven, is so excited that they cannot contain themselves. Suddenly, the angel is surrounded by "the heavenly host," which begins to praise God and announce the coming of peace on earth. "Glory to God in the highest and peace on earth to those on whom his favor rests," they say. Other translations render the phrase this way: "Glory to God in the highest and on earth peace, good will toward people."

With this statement, Luke offers not only a summary of his Gospel but a summary of the life and message of Jesus. God is glorified for coming among the poor, saving the poor and all humanity, and bringing this good news to the poor. Therefore, at the same time, peace is coming upon all on whom God's favor rests. Because Jesus is Savior, Messiah, and Lord of all, because God is glorified for saving all humanity through Jesus the Savior, in effect, Luke is saying, God's favor is now upon every human being, Jew and Gentile, including the poorest, most outcast, most excluded, the most marginalized. Every human being now has access to God's peace. Everyone is welcome into God's eternal reign of peace, and that peace is coming on earth right now.

Peace on earth. This is the opposite of everything the Roman Empire stands for, despite its Pax Romana propaganda. The Roman Empire, like every empire and culture of greed and war, is here for one purpose: to bring "war on earth" so that it can maintain its total domination and steal all natural resources for the ruling class. From Caesar to the present, every ruler maintains power by military might, warmaking, and the infliction of death on human beings. There has never been peace on earth. But here, God's angel announces the coming of peace on earth. If every human being turns to Jesus the Savior, listens to him, obeys his teachings, and welcomes his reign of peace, there will be peace on earth, and the God of peace will be glorified. This is the reason for the ecstasy of the heavenly host.

The astonished shepherds set off to find this sign and eventually discover Mary and Joseph and the infant lying in the trough. They tell the parents about the heavenly vision and announcement, and the parents are amazed. "Mary kept all these things, reflecting on them in her heart." The shepherds leave, "glorifying and praising God for all they had seen and heard." With these details, we see the firstfruits of the birth of Jesus and the angel's proclamation: the parents and the shepherds feel peace and glorify and praise God. Likewise, from now on, all followers of Jesus will reflect on these things in their hearts and glorify and praise God for all they have seen and heard.

Joseph and Mary are presented as devout, faithful Jews who follow the law. Jesus is circumcised, named, and brought to the temple in Jerusalem, where Mary is required to offer a one-year-old lamb as a burnt offering and a turtle dove or young pigeon as a sacrifice for her sin, for the uncleanness of giving birth. Because she is poor, Mary is allowed to offer two turtledoves or two young pigeons instead. This is precisely the systemic theft of the poor in the name of God that Jesus will witness at the age of twelve when he visits the temple again and that he will directly act against shortly before his death, when he clears the temple of its moneychangers.

Luke introduces two holy Jewish elders, who affirm everything the angel and the shepherds have foretold. They announce that this child Jesus is in fact the real Messiah, the fulfillment of the law and the prophets. Simeon is "righteous and devout, awaiting the consolation of Israel, and the Holy Spirit was upon him." He has been told in prayer that he will not die without seeing the Messiah. Luke here writes like Dickens or Dostoevsky, describing how the devout old man takes the baby in his arms and blesses God. "Now, Master," he says, "you may let your servant go in peace, according to your word, for my eyes have seen your salvation, which you prepared in sight of all the peoples, a light for revelation to the Gentiles, and glory for your people Israel." Again, we see the fruits of the birth of Jesus: God is praised and glorified, and a faithful old man is filled with the grace of peace because he knows now that God is faithful, that God will indeed save all people. Once again, the parents are amazed. Luke then focuses again on Mary. Simeon says to her, "Behold, this child is destined for the fall and rise of many in Israel, and to be a sign that will be contradicted and you yourself a sword will pierce so that the thoughts of many hearts may be revealed." In the midst of praise, peace, and amazement, Luke hints at the cross to come. This child will be a sign to the world, and that can only mean that he will be rejected and suffer, which means that you, too, Mary, will have to suffer for love of this child, so that in your nonviolent suffering love, the hearts of many billions of people may be broken open and surrendered to the God of peace in perfect love.

Then Luke introduces an eighty-four-year-old widow named Anna, whom he calls "a prophetess." "She never left the temple, but worshiped night and day with fasting and prayer," Luke writes. She gave thanks to God, we're told, "and spoke about the child to all who were awaiting the redemption of Jerusalem." With these two holy figures, Luke prepares us to understand that this child truly is Savior, Messiah, and Lord, that he will bring peace on earth. With this child comes redemption for all faithful Jews, but also for all Gentiles, Romans, and people everywhere. Mary and Joseph return to Nazareth with the child, and Jesus grows up "filled with wisdom, and the favor of God was upon him."

Luke's account of the birth of Jesus emphasizes that nothing like this has ever happened before, that this child is far greater than the Roman emperor, that his kingdom is far greater than the Roman Empire, that he will save every human being and bring lasting peace on earth. We too are amazed by this announcement and are left to ponder it in our hearts. With these characters—Mary, Joseph, the shepherds, Simeon, and Anna—the ground has been well prepared for the story to unfold. But Luke offers one more tale from Jesus's youth to help us understand who he is.

"Did You Not Know That I Must Be in My Father's House?" (2:41–52)

Every year, Joseph and Mary traveled to Jerusalem for Passover, and when Jesus was twelve, he was accidentally left behind. The caravan had started back, and the parents thought he was somewhere else with the group. Later, they realized he had stayed behind, so they returned to Jerusalem to find him. It took three long days. They were probably at their wits' end. Finally, they discovered him in the temple, "sitting in the midst of the teachers, listening to them and asking them questions." "All who heard him were astounded at his understanding and his answers," Luke writes. With this scene, we see Jesus already as a great teacher who possesses profound wisdom and spiritual understanding. We know that, though born in total poverty, he is a natural-born genius.

None of this appeases his desperate parents. "Why have you done this to us?" Mary asks him. "Your father and I have been looking for you with great anxiety."

"Why were you looking for me?" Jesus asks them. "Did you not know that I must be in my Father's house?"

Jesus's answer is simple, pure, and true—and no one knows what he is talking about. Luke describes the boy as already knowing God as his Father, as aware of himself as God's Son, as an equal to the religious authorities. His home is in the temple, serving God his Father. At this point, Jesus detaches from Mary and Joseph, as he understands more clearly his relationship with his heavenly Father. Mary and Joseph are probably mystified but remain gentle and nonviolent toward him, as he is toward them. So they tell him that they have to return to Nazareth, and he agrees, and grows up being obedient to his parents.

One could conclude, given the hostility and lack of understanding the religious authorities would later show, that Jesus realized even at that young age that he could not reason with them. They were stuck in the big business of temple commerce and power and had no real interest in fully understanding the living God, much less the scriptures. Young Jesus probably realized it was futile trying to teach them, so he might as well return home to Nazareth and live with his holy, faithful, gentle parents. By choosing to return to the rural outback of Nazareth, Jesus chooses once again to go to the margins far from power. He has learned that God and God's love, compassion, peace, and nonviolence are not found in the center of power among the elite and ruling class. He would have a lifetime to think on his experience in the house of God, the Jerusalem temple, which the religious authorities had turned into a money-making religious machine. One day, he would return to Jerusalem and have something to say to the religious authorities about God's house and how to worship the God of peace.

"A Voice of One Crying Out in the Desert" (3:1–20, 23–38)

Fast forward a few years. There, out on the margins of the empire, John the Baptist appears. He's like a wild, holy prophet who becomes an instant sensation for his prophetic denunciations of the empire and call to repentance and return to God. Luke gives us the specific time and place, as if he was saying, "In 1984, when Ronald Reagan was president and waging war upon the poor people of Nicaragua . . . ," or "In 2003, when George W. Bush was president and bombing the children of Baghdad, in faraway Iraq. . . ." Tiberius Caesar has been ruling the world as emperor for fifteen years; Pontius Pilate is governor of Judea; and Herod is the tetrarch of rural Galilee. Into this world of empire, power, and violent domination, Luke writes, "the word of God came to John, son of Zechariah, in the desert."

This is significant, first of all, because it means that the word of God did not come to Tiberius, Pilate, or Herod. It touched someone on the far margins of the empire. The desert was considered a wasteland where God did not dwell. Nothing good came from the wilderness. Yet Luke places the word of God in the desert, in the wilderness, not in Jerusalem, not in the center of power but at its farthest margin. This word of God came to John there in that remote no-man's land, and from there this holy sage proceeded to proclaim God's word far and wide.

John walks everywhere, "proclaiming a baptism of repentance for the forgiveness of sins." He calls everyone on the outskirts of the empire to turn away from the empire, to be converted from the culture of violence, that they may be forgiven and prepared to welcome God and God's reign of justice. Like Matthew, Luke presents John as the fulfillment of Isaiah's vision. He is the one who cries out in the desert, "Prepare the way of the Lord, make straight his paths." His message to the poor and marginalized is: Get ready. The Messiah is coming, so change your lives, renounce your participation in the empire, and join me in transforming the culture so that we might be ready for him.

But Luke quotes more of Isaiah to describe the total transformation that is about to happen: "Every valley shall be filled and every mountain and hill shall be made low. The winding roads shall be made straight, and the rough ways made smooth, and all flesh shall see the salvation of God." Everything is about to change; everything will be turned upside-down. All humanity, which is blind, will now be given vision to see God. Not only will the Messiah heal humanity so that it can see, but, in the presence of this Messiah, humanity will see God.

Luke's John resembles Matthew's fierce prophet. While Matthew's John criticizes the religious authorities, Luke's John criticizes everyone. "You brood of vipers!" he names the crowd. "Produce good fruits as evidence of your repentance." This teaching becomes a critical text for Luke, who insists that every human being should produce the good fruit of justice and peace with their lives, and not the evil fruit of injustice and violence. Vipers attack, bite, and kill people; a brood would be a whole collection of vipers, ready to kill. I suggest that Luke's John is condemning the people for their support of systemic violence and challenging them instead to do something useful and good with their lives.

What's fascinating about Luke's version is that the crowd responds positively to this fierce challenge. Crowds rarely convert to the call to repentance in any of the Gospels: "What should we do?" they ask John. This is the first question that anyone who is open to God and to God's call to change should ask. It remains the question we should all be asking today in our prayer, in our communities, and in the world. "What should we do, John the Baptist? What should we do, Jesus of Nazareth? What should we do, God of Peace?" As we read the Gospel of peace and look out at the world of permanent war, nuclear weapons, environmental destruction, and global suffering, it becomes the question of our lives. "What should we do?" If we are sincere, we will sit with this question, like the people in the desert, and wait for an answer. As we proceed with Luke, we will take up the challenge and make the changes named so that the Gospel transformation of peace can begin here on earth, beginning with ourselves.

Luke's John has answers, and they are specific and radical. "Whoever has two tunics should share with the person who has none. And whoever has food should do likewise." The focus, for Luke, is service to the poor and hungry. That's the first response and sign of our conversion to God. If we are truly repenting for our complicity in the culture of violence, then we start giving our extra possessions to the poor and feeding those who are hungry. This teaching holds today. All First World people should give away their extra clothes and possessions to the poor and help feed the hungry, whether through service at their local soup kitchen or financial contributions to organizations that feed the hungry. When we encounter hungry homeless people, we should feed them and care for them. Period.

Luke then notes that some tax collectors and soldiers were responding to John's call and asked what they should do too. "Stop collecting more than what is prescribed," he tells the tax collectors. That requires a radical change in behavior, because tax collectors charged more for themselves. To the soldiers, he said, "Do not practice extortion, do not falsely accuse anyone, and be satisfied with your wages." Again, this meant a radical change of behavior. They were to be just and honest. If the tax collectors and soldiers followed John's teachings then and now, it would erode the power of the empire and the culture of greed and violence.

"I am baptizing you with water, but one mightier than I is coming," John tells the crowd. Luke then uses the same words that appear in all four Gospels: "I am not worthy to loosen the thongs of his sandals." He has been telling the crowd to convert and change their lives through the act of his baptism; then he turns the attention away from himself toward the one who is coming. As in Matthew, Luke uses dramatic imagery to describe the coming Messiah. "He will baptize you with the Holy Spirit and fire." Luke will bring this promise to life at the end of his Gospel and the beginning of volume 2, the Acts of the Apostles, when the Holy Spirit will descend on his apostles as fire. "His winnowing fan is in his hand to clear his threshing floor and to gather the wheat into his barn, but the chaff he will burn with unquenchable fire." This, Luke concludes, is good news to the people. Why? Because the entire empire will one day fall. The culture of violence, greed, and war is going to be swept away, and justice and peace will become the new standard. Through the spreading of Gospel nonviolence, people will claim their power in grassroots movements, and, when that happens, it becomes contagious, catches fire, and undercuts any injustice from the Roman Empire to apartheid.

Luke cuts to the chase to report that Herod responded to reports about John's growing grassroots movement against the empire by arresting him and putting him in prison. With this immediate, shocking turn of events, we realize once again what a threat John the Baptist is to Herod, Pilate, Caesar, and the empire. We are so used to John that we can easily dismiss him or, at best, find him a curious character. But he wasn't that at all. John the Baptist called for resistance against the empire and set in motion a grassroots movement of revolution against the ruling class. The empire responded as empires always respond to those who threaten its power: by silencing the leader and eventually killing him. A more interesting question might be, Why didn't Herod act sooner, or even, why did he keep John in prison for a time instead of killing him quickly? Because John enjoyed widespread popular support and Herod feared that. Even autocrats have to measure the power of popular grassroots movements if they want to stay in power.

What does that mean for us readers? As we hear John's call for repentance and conversion, and start to change ourselves as the crowd does, we too join the grassroots movement of nonviolent revolution against the culture of war, violence, greed, and injustice today, to help prepare for the coming of God's reign of peace. That means that we too are willing to risk the same fate as the great Baptist, because we too side with God and the prophets against empire. We too are willing to give our lives for this grassroots campaign to convert humanity and welcome God here on earth. As we ponder our response to John and his call to conversion, we note that this is exactly what the Messiah will do.

Luke writes two sentences to describe the baptism of Jesus and then presents the genealogy of Jesus. As we conclude Luke's infancy narrative and his introduction of John, let's look first at the genealogy of Jesus before we turn to Jesus's baptism. What is important to note is that, whereas Matthew's genealogy emphasized Jesus's Jewish roots by starting with Abraham and going forward to David and Joseph, Luke emphasizes Jesus's universal roots, by going backwards all the way to Adam, "the son of God."

Jesus is presented here as a universal figure, a Messiah connected to everyone, like everyone, available to everyone who ever lived. He is a direct descendent of David, Abraham, and Noah, possibly even the prophet Nathan, rather than through King Solomon, showing how Jesus fits in with the lineage of the ancient prophets. But all of us can trace our roots back to Adam, so to speak. All of us, ultimately, are sons and daughters of God. Luke's Jesus is the ultimate human being, the ultimate everyman, full of wisdom, peace, and love.

With that, the stage is set for the nonviolent revolution to begin.

"You Are My Beloved Son: With You, I Am Well Pleased" (3:21–22; 4:1–13)

One of the distinctions of Luke's Gospel is how Jesus prays before every major turning point in his public life. Luke notes that Jesus prays at his baptism, when he hears the voice of God; when he chooses the twelve apostles; when he is transfigured; when he is alone with the disciples (leading them to ask him to teach them how to pray); at the Last Supper; in the Garden of Gethsemane; and on the cross, in his last breath. In the first public event of Jesus's life after he is baptized by John in the Jordan River, Luke observes that Jesus then sat in prayer. While he was praying, we're told, "heaven was opened, the Holy Spirit descended upon him in bodily form like a dove, and a voice came from heaven." These three actions would be life-changing for anyone, but it was the message from heaven that set Jesus in motion. "You are my beloved Son; with you I am well pleased."

Jesus was able to embody total nonviolence and universal love because he understood and accepted his true identity as the beloved Son of God, which was revealed to him at this very moment while praying after his baptism. Because he accepted his true identity and decided to be faithful to it, nothing stood in his way. He did not give in to fear, worry, anger, anxiety, doubt, despair, or violence; in the end, even death did not have power over him. He was fully human precisely because he claimed that identity as God's beloved. Since he knew that God was peaceful, loving, and nonviolent, because he heard the voice of God and knew that voice, he knew then that to be the beloved Son of God was to be peaceful, loving, and nonviolent. In that spirit, he walked forth into the culture and announced that everyone was invited to claim their true identity as God's beloved sons and daughters and become peacemakers who practice universal love and total nonviolence.

Luke offers a helpful detail. All this happened while Jesus was praying. That's a clue for the rest of us who would dare follow Jesus. Like Jesus, we have to become people of prayer. Like Jesus, we too sit in meditation every day. I suggest thirty minutes of quiet, silent time alone, when we close our eyes, breathe naturally, settle our minds on our breath, surrender ourselves to the God of peace, place ourselves in the presence of the nonviolent Jesus, and listen. Through this daily practice of meditation, we open ourselves to the moment when the God of peace chooses to call us God's beloved, to say, "You too are my beloved." But we cannot hear God if we are running around busy. Like Jesus, we have to make it a priority to put ourselves at the disposal of God, to sit and wait in peace for God to speak.

If we want to live in intimate relationship with God as Jesus did, we have to dedicate some quality time each day for a check-in with God. Most people say they're too busy to take time for meditation, but that's just an excuse. Mahatma Gandhi was a busy person—he was running a revolution!—yet he spent one hour every morning in meditation, and one hour every afternoon in meditation for some thirty years. Because he was so busy, he argued, he had all the more reason to make his meditation time a priority. As other saints discovered, if you make time for God, more time opens itself to you because you don't feel as stressed and harried. You can go through your day living in your best spirit because you began your day centered in God, in the truth of your relationship with your God. As you learn to accept your true identity as God's beloved son or daughter, you learn to realize that God is your beloved Father or Mother, and so you go through life centered in this intimate relationship of unconditional love. If you do that, over time you will develop the capacity to live as Jesus did and to go about your days with his spirit guiding you.

The practice of daily prayer leads to mystical nonviolence. As we see in the life of Jesus, we center ourselves in peace and live within the boundaries of nonviolence because we are disarmed daily by our loving God. We have no need of violence in any form, nor do we fall prey to the trappings of the culture that can consume us and mislead us into various false identities. We know ourselves and we know God. We learn through our contemplation that God is the living God of peace and universal love, and that begins to rub off on us. We begin to act as if we really are sons and daughters of God. Peace, love, and the daily disciplines of a nonviolent lifestyle become second nature to us. Mystical nonviolence becomes our ordinary life, our new normal, our daily routine.

As in Matthew, Luke describes how Jesus heads off into the desert for forty days of prayer and fasting to explore the meaning of his calling. Because the Holy Spirit descended upon him, he was filled with the Holy Spirit, Luke writes. If we try to imagine what it would be like to dwell in the desert for forty days, eating nothing, seeing no one, being completely on our own, we realize that we might be tempted to give up. Jesus is tempted to reject his true identity as the beloved Son of God, and if he rejected that temptation, he would eventually give in to all forms of resistance to God, including violence.

Luke describes three temptations that centered on the demonic temptation to reject Jesus's core identity as God's beloved. Each temptation begins with, "If you are the Son of God . . ." In other words, prove it! This is the voice of the culture of violence, empire, and evil. "Who do you think you are? There is no way you, of all people, a total loser, could be the beloved son of God." Just as Jesus heard and claimed his identity as God's beloved and was subsequently tempted to reject that identity and go along with the ways of violence, we his followers are tempted to reject our own identities as God's beloved sons and daughters and to go along like everyone else, supporting a culture set against God's ways.

Many temptations challenge our belief in nonviolence and the God of nonviolence. They say, "How can God be nonviolent when the world is so violent? You don't believe nonviolence actually works, do you? Do you really think God is going to protect you in the face of a violent person, a warmaking nation, or even nuclear weapons? God can't protect you. God won't protect you. You are delusional. There is no God. Violence is the way of the world, and violent self-defense is the basis for human relations. It's okay to kill to defend yourself or to get what you need—that's just the way of the world!"

In Luke, as in Matthew, these temptations to violence come in the form of despair, domination, and doubt. First, the tempter says, "If you are the Son of God, command this stone to become bread." Jesus is hungry, and the temptation to despair says, "Do something now so you can have food and not be hungry anymore!" It's a temptation to stop all this self-denial, humility, introspection, emptiness, and spiritual searching for God. It's saying, "If you really are the Son of God, then be as powerful as God, play God, turn stones to bread, feed yourself, and for that matter, feed the entire human race. End world hunger. Everyone will love you." It's a temptation to inhuman, magic solutions, to get immediate results, to control the outcome of his journey.

But that's not the way of nonviolence. Nonviolence doesn't give in to despair or even try to control the results, the outcome, of our lives and peace work. It trusts totally in God, places our hope in God, even leaves the results, the outcome, to God. In nonviolence, we surrender our will entirely to God, as Jesus does here. He refuses to be in charge; God is completely in charge of his life. Like Jesus, we try to surrender ourselves entirely to God, God's will, and God's word; to sit in the groundlessness of peace, the emptiness of inner nonviolence; and to feel the insecurity and vast openness there—and trust in God moment by moment. If Jesus turns stones into bread, he'll be saying that he doesn't need God. In effect, he would be rejecting God, saying, "I'm in charge, not God." In doing so, he would be doing his will, not God's will.

The same is true with us. If we try to play God, to be in total control, to take charge of despair by determining the outcome and results of our actions, then we are saying that we do not need God. In that choice, we move away from the humility of nonviolence that relies on God and choose arrogance, pride, and power. We would continue to do our own will and not rely on God and God's will. Jesus refuses to give in to despair but instead humbly trusts in God. He knows that reliance on God, even for food, is everything. That is why he quotes the scripture: "It is written, 'One does not live by bread alone.'" Jesus is saying, "We live by the word of God. We need God. We are human. God is God. So we rely completely on God and God's will and word." By rejecting the temptation to play God, to take control of the situation, and to get some immediate results, Jesus maintains his human nonviolence and remains centered in his love, trust, and dependence on God. In this way, he humbles himself and enters the fullness of nonviolence, which requires 100 percent surrender to God and reliance on God. He chooses to remain who he is—God's humble beloved Son— and not try to outdo God.

Next the tempter shows him all the kingdoms of the world in a single instant. "I shall give to you all this power and their glory; for it has been handed over to me, and I may give it to whomever I wish," the tempter said. "All this will be yours." Imagine that! Think of all the good Jesus could do, disarming all the nations of the world and bringing about justice. But there's a catch: "All this will be yours, if you worship me." Jesus has to renounce being the beloved of God and serve evil; in doing so, that would be the end of any good that he might have done as ruler of the world, because he would be in the service of violence and death itself. He would have to worship a false god and, in doing so, not only reject his identity but lose his soul.

This is the temptation to domination, which requires the rejection of God as Lord of the world and the pursuit of our own ego power over the world. It takes our focus away from God and turns our being toward the world, and the evils of the world, which will eventually consume us with the nothingness of evil. Nonviolence requires the acceptance of a certain level of powerlessness and groundlessness so that God is in control of our lives and the world, not the other way around. By pursuing global domination, Jesus would reject the prerequisites of nonviolence, renounce God, and end up consumed by power, corruption, arrogance, hatred, and evil. There would be no love in him, much less universal love, compassion, and peace.

"It is written," Jesus responded, "'You shall worship the Lord, your God, and God alone shall you serve.'" Jesus stood his ground: he would worship and serve God, and God alone. He would not worship or serve any false gods, any pretenders to the thrones, and that included every nation/state and empire that demands allegiance. Jesus would try to speak to, convert, and disarm all the nations, kingdoms, and empires of the world—but he would not use their means of violence, domination, or coercion to impose his will. He would risk being ignored or, worse, resisted and crushed to death, but he would worship and be faithful to his beloved God of peace.

Finally, the tempter leads him to Jerusalem, makes him stand on the parapet of the temple, and tells him, "If you are the Son of God, throw yourself down from here." Literally, Jesus is tempted to kill himself. The temptation to doubt God is now a temptation to choose the way of death. Because Jesus has twice quoted the scriptures to the devil, this time the devil turns the scriptures against Jesus in his effort to make him doubt God and do violence to himself. The devil quotes two verses to Jesus: "He will command his angels concerning you, to guard you," and "With their hands they will support you, lest you dash your foot against a stone." The devil tempts Jesus, saying, "If you are so convinced that God exists, that God loves you, that God calls you God's son, prove it. Throw yourself off the roof and let's see God come to catch you." Once again, the temptation to doubt requires some kind of magic, inhuman act disguised in spiritual language, which leads to violence and death. The minute we doubt God, do not trust God, and do not rely on God's will and word, we forget who we are, try to control every situation, and end up sliding down the path toward death, like the alcoholic who slowly drinks himself to death, or those caught up in warfare who place their trust in weapons and generals and end up killing each other.

Faith in God leads to quiet faith in God's way of nonviolence so that we live in peace with ourselves and one another and trust in God and do no violence to anyone, including ourselves. Faith demands nonviolence. It requires nonviolence, because God is nonviolent, so we have to be nonviolent like God, but God is also all-powerful, so we can trust in God's power to lead us correctly on the path of life. We can measure the depth of our faith by observing how deeply we go into nonviolence. If we are violent to ourselves or others, we have yet to begin to believe in God. Keep in mind that we treat ourselves and others violently when we speak without love or fail to be respectful of every human's dignity, including our own. If I reject myself and put myself down, rather than showing compassion to myself, I am not believing in God but doing violence. If I judge others rather than see them with God's love and greet them with God's peace, I am not believing in God but continuing the cycle of violence. When we place all our trust in God, however, we simultaneously let go of any inclination to violence and learn how to be steady, calm, and mindful in faith through any situation. So, Jesus quotes the scriptures back at the devil, saying, "It also says, 'You shall not put the Lord, your God, to the test.'" Once again, Jesus trusts God and refuses to test God, and so he remains steadfast in nonviolence, including nonviolence toward himself. This affirmation of faith in God and God's way of nonviolence silences Satan, at least for now.

Mahatma Gandhi models for us a way to resist these temptations of violence, despair, domination, and doubt, all the temptations to reject God, God's way of nonviolence, and God's calling to us to be God's sons and daughters. Gandhi refused all power, most notably, even the chance to become the first prime minister of a free India. He refused to doubt God, give into despair, or play God and be inhuman. He maintained his faith in God and God's nonviolence to the bitter end. He said in the end that we need to seek the truth, to speak the truth, and to trust that the truth is the truth, and just do what is true, right, and good, regardless of the outcome to ourselves, and leave the rest to God. That's why he kept practicing downward mobility, even moving in his sixties to the poorest place in India, into a village of Untouchables in Wardha. He increased his prayer time in the last decades of his life to two one-hour silent meditation periods a day, as well as a strict day of silence every Monday. He wanted to be faithful to God and to God's way of nonviolence first and foremost, so he stood his ground, and in the end, did far more lasting good than he would have had he given in to despair, domination, doubt, or violence.

By standing his ground, Jesus refuses to be spectacular, powerful, dominating, despairing, arrogant, or doubting. He will stay centered in the God of peace and therefore God's way of peace. His steady mindfulness, calm inner strength, and disposition of nonviolence will become the hallmark of his life and will allow him to do far greater things than any inhuman act of turning stones to bread, dominating the world, or throwing himself off the temple. Jesus instead will embody peace and love, so that in the end, he will disarm everyone and win everyone over to the ways of love, faith, and peace. His refusal to reject God and God's invitation to be God's beloved is a choice each of us can make as well. When he calls us to follow him, he calls us to reject all these temptations and to claim our fundamental identities as God's beloved, and to go forth in that same spirit. We can do this because he has shown us how and called us to follow him on that path.

"Today, This Scripture Passage Is Fulfilled in Your Hearing": The Nonviolent Revolution Begins (4:14–6:11)

"Jesus returned to Galilee in the power of the Spirit," Luke writes. He began teaching, preaching, and speaking out everywhere, and news of him spread like wildfire. Everyone spoke well of him—until he returned to his hometown of Nazareth.

In one of the most remarkable, shocking, and important passages of the four Gospels, unique to Luke, Jesus entered the synagogue of Nazareth on the sabbath, stood up to read, was handed a scroll of the prophet Isaiah, and picked out the conclusion, chapter 61, of all chapters. According to Luke, he read this passage out loud to his hometown neighbors:

> The Spirit of God is upon me, because God has anointed me to bring glad tidings to the poor. God has sent me to proclaim liberty to captives and recovery of sight to the blind, to let the oppressed go free, and to proclaim a year acceptable to God. (Isa. 61:1–2)

"Rolling up the scroll, he handed it back to the attendant and sat down," Luke writes, "and the eyes of all in the synagogue looked intently at him." The detail in this sentence creates the suspense and tension of a thriller and sets the stage for the bombshell announcement to follow. "Today this scripture passage is fulfilled in your hearing," Jesus says. "All spoke highly of him and were amazed at the gracious words that came from his mouth."

Of all the texts in the Hebrew Scriptures that Luke could use in this scene, he has Jesus choosing Isaiah 61, the culmination of the writings of Isaiah as a call to justice and liberation, the vocation of the Messiah and all those who would follow the Messiah. The declaration by Jesus that he is fulfilling this text on that sabbath day in Nazareth is stunning and awesome, and truly good news. Who in all of human history would dare say, "Today, I am fulfilling this ancient oracle, this biblical call to justice and liberation"? By daring to say that he is fulfilling the scriptures, we see how he is being faithful to his calling by the Jordan River, his mission to be the beloved of the God of peace. The verses of Isaiah outline the job description of this new Messiah, and therefore, the job description of everyone who would ever dare follow him, and so they are worthy of serious reflection. Not only do they describe the Messiah's mission in social terms, but they portend the coming of the Jubilee Year (based on Leviticus 25), when all debts in society will be wiped away and a new, more just and equal society will begin.

First, Isaiah writes that "the Holy Spirit of God is upon me." We already know that the Holy Spirit of God is upon Jesus because Luke told us how it came down upon Jesus in bodily form while he was praying by the river after his baptism. That experience filled him with the fire of divine love, led him into the desert to fast and pray, and inspired him to reject every temptation to violence, despair, domination, and doubt. Later in the Gospels and in Acts, the Holy Spirit will come upon Jesus's disciples, and it continues to come upon us today. We too are meant to be on fire with universal love, to go forth like Jesus and speak out for justice, liberation, and peace.

"God has anointed me to bring good news to the poor." This is the mission of the Messiah, and therefore our mission too. Everything we do and say is for the poor, not for the rich, and it is intended to be good news for the poor. What would be good news for the poor? The end of their poverty! Jesus will serve the poor morning, noon, and night, by healing them, feeding them, and liberating them from poverty and oppression. And just as his presence, actions, and teachings are good news for the poor, it must be noted that Jesus does not bring good news to the rich. Jesus brings bad news to the rich. His message to the rich, as we will see, is, sell your possessions and give all that money to the poor and then join my campaign for global social and economic justice.

"God has sent me to bring liberty to captives." Sometimes this is translated as "release to prisoners." Jesus claims this mission as his own: he has been sent by God into the world to release all those who are held captive and imprisoned. Then and now, it is a call to find ways to release and liberate everyone being held, whether literally in bondage, or in any other way. Jesus would liberate people from captivity to the Roman Empire, as well as the unjust fundamentalism and nationalism that trap people in small thinking. He would release all those enslaved, whether literally or to poverty, oppression, imperial occupation, and the demonic spirits of violence. He wants everyone to be free, and that newfound freedom, he will insist, comes within the boundaries of his way, which uses no shaming, coercion, or harm.

Today, this mission to liberate all those held captive is needed more than ever, as billions of people are held in poverty, racism, war, nationalism, and empire, stuck in violent systems with no way out. Anyone who wishes to follow the Jesus of Luke 4 will likewise be sent to bring liberty to all those held captive, release to all those imprisoned, and freedom to the world's poor, hungry, and oppressed. As we try to enact this mission, we realize with Jesus that every person is un-free in some way, and much of that captivity issues directly from unjust and inhumane systems. With this mission, we work for restorative justice, an end to the prison systems of violence and punishment, for the healing of all those stuck in every addiction, for the abolition of the death penalty and prisons themselves, for a new age in which people can be healed and trained to live in freedom and to extend freedom to others. As Abraham Lincoln once said, the pursuit of freedom will open up the possibilities of new freedoms we had not imagined.

"God has sent me to bring recovery of sight to the blind," Jesus tells the congregation in Nazareth. He will go forth from Nazareth to touch blind people and give them new sight. He will give them the privilege of seeing him and discovering the fullness of life. But more, Jesus sees that we are blind, that we lack vision and fail to see God or God's reign in our midst. He knows that no one can see a way out of our predicament. The nonviolent Jesus is the only person with the vision to see God, to see God's reign of peace at hand, to see what it means to be human, and to see what humanity could be like if we returned to God's way of peace. Jesus announces then that he has come to give sight—that is, vision—to every human being. He will heal the blind and touch their eyes, even if it is illegal to do so. We will begin to see these healings as parables of the healing that God is offering to blind humanity in the visionary Jesus. He will offer to touch each one of us and gift us with vision so that we can see ourselves as God's beloved sons and daughters, so that we can recognize God's reign of peace and understand life as a journey of peace into God's reign. As his disciples begin to accept his vision, they will join him in proclaiming God's reign of peace at hand, which means that they will help everyone reclaim their vision, their sight, their imaginations, to see a way forward, the possibilities of a new kind of world based in justice, nonviolence, and equality for every human being and creature. As more and more people begin to see life through the eyes of the nonviolent Jesus, they begin to see every other human being as a beloved sister and brother and how we might learn to live in peace with one another. Luke invites us to accept Jesus's vision and to join his missionary campaign to bring this vision to everyone else.

"God has sent me to let the oppressed go free." Jesus's mission to liberate captives is taken one step further by this mission to free the oppressed. This refers to the systemic, institutionalized violence that oppresses and crushes billions of people around the world. Jesus has come to confront, challenge, resist, and end every form of systemic oppression and to free the oppressed to live in peace and dignity. In doing so, Jesus will also free the oppressors so that they no longer hurt other people, so that they too can discover a new dignity in the freedom of nonviolence. In this work of global political, social, and spiritual liberation, Jesus frees everyone so that no one is a victim or a victimizer.

"God has sent me to proclaim a year acceptable to the Lord," Jesus concludes. This, we now know, was the Jubilee Year announced by God to Moses on Mount Sinai in the book of Leviticus (chapter 25). Every seventh year, all fields were to lie fallow and all produce were to be shared, and then, every forty-nine years, all money and all land were to be redistributed equally. (For further study, see Trocmé, *Jesus and the Nonviolent Revolution*, 27–52). In this Jubilee year, the rich relinquished their money and land and gave it to the poor so that now everyone shared everything equally. No one practiced the Jubilee in Jesus's time, certainly not the people of Nazareth, but Jesus steps up to the podium on this day and announces, to the shock of everyone, that today the Jubilee has begun.

Imagine if that were to happen in the United States. All the rich on Wall Street, all the CEOs, all the billionaires and millionaires, all the politicians, generals, weapons manufacturers, and oil company executives would relinquish their money, their mansions, and their lands so that everything would be shared equally with every other person in the nation, including the homeless, the farmworker, the day laborer, the janitor, the fast-food worker, the teacher, the nurse, and every low-income person. But you might say, that would be the end of capitalism as we know it! That would mean socialism! That's communism! No, the nonviolent Jesus would say, that's the biblical year of Jubilee being practiced as Moses taught, as Isaiah outlined, and as I have announced.

Imagine if the entire planet underwent a Jubilee Year! Imagine if super billionaires and all the oil barons and sheiks gave up all their money and it was redistributed among the poorest of the poor, starting with the impoverished millions in Malawi, Haiti, Bangladesh, Congo, Sudan, and Honduras. Imagine all those people having good food, clean water, housing, land, decent work, good education, free healthcare, and dignity, where everyone could enjoy the land, the mountains, the coastlines, and the oceans. This is what Jesus proclaims in the synagogue in Nazareth at the start of his public life! This is his message and mission. This is the work of Jesus for the rest of Luke's Gospel, and for the rest of time, and this must become the mission of everyone who dares to follow Jesus today.

The Jubilee Year insists that all land and all natural resources belong to God, that people are just tenants leasing the land and its resources. The owner can do what he wants with them, and he wants them periodically redistributed so that everyone can share in the land and resources equally. There would be no more accumulation of land, resources, or money in the hands of a few while billions starved, suffered, and died in poverty. That is not the will of God. Jesus has come to announce a permanent never-ending Jubilee Year. This redistribution of land and wealth would be healing to the creatures and to creation itself. We would all finally embrace the wisdom that indigenous peoples learned long ago.

Is such a Jubilee possible in today's unjust world? Yes. Through tremendous grassroots organizing, the Jubilee 2000 Campaign in the late 1990s gathered some twenty-four million signatures on a petition that led to the G7 Finance Ministers in 2005 canceling some $130 billion in debt to the world's thirty-six poorest nations. This had never happened before, and it was a breakthrough of global justice and hope. Money spent on paying off massive debt to the rich nations could now go to real human needs in these impoverished places. Today, the debt cycle continues, and the world's poorest nations continue to pay sometimes 20 percent of their budget for loans from the rich nations on behalf of their debts. It's a never-ending downward spiral that needs to be broken once and for all so that the world's poorest nations can be permanently lifted out of crushing poverty. Today, we need a permanent Jubilee Year.

Jesus announced the Jubilee Year as a way to welcome God's reign of justice and peace on earth, and his visionary revolution summons us to make that revolution come true. One of the most significant books about Jesus in the twentieth century, in my opinion, is *Jesus and the Nonviolent Revolution*, written by the legendary French peace activist André Trocmé and published in 1961. Trocmé's book was the first to apply the way of nonviolence to the Gospel stories of Jesus, and he puts the proclamation of the Jubilee Year front and center in the story of Jesus. His book paved the way for the research of John Howard Yoder (*The Politics of Jesus*), James Douglass (*The Nonviolent Cross*), Walter Wink (*Engaging the Powers*), Ched Myers (*Binding the Strong Man*), and others. Trocmé understood Jesus's nonviolence not as a tactic or a strategy but as a matter of obedience to God. In particular, he begins his study and bases his thesis on the revolutionary nonviolence of Jesus described in Luke 4, especially the proclamation of the Jubilee Year. It is hard for us to understand the revolutionary politics of nonviolence outlined by Isaiah and announced by Jesus in Nazareth, Trocmé suggests. If this really is the mission of Jesus, then those in power would never allow him to complete his mission. They would eventually have to arrest him and kill him, as they did, because his movement meant the end of every form of oppression and domination. Trocmé writes:

> I use the term "revolution" intentionally because the social readjustments commanded by Moses were far more radical than the efforts of modern revolutionaries. Contemporary revolutions grow primarily out of economic disparities caused by technological developments. Jesus' revolution, on the contrary, drew its strength from God's liberating justice. By proclaiming the Jubilee, Jesus wanted to bring about a total social

transformation, with an eye to the future, yet based on the vision of justice God had already set forth in the past. The Jubilee demanded, among other things, expropriating the lands of the wealthy and liquidating the usurious system by which the ruling class prospered. . . .

When Jesus proclaimed good news to the poor, liberty to the captives, and sight to the blind, his audience knew very well what he meant: now is the time to put into effect the year of Jubilee. Jesus' speech in Nazareth was no sermon of religious platitudes. He was announcing that a social revolution was underway—the messianic reign had begun. For the poor, this was good news. All things would be made right again. For those whose interests were vested in the establishment, however, such news was a threat. (Trocmé, *Jesus and the Nonviolent Revolution*, 16–17, 27)

Trocmé lists four essential ingredients for Jesus's Jubilee Year as originally outlined in Leviticus 25: everyone lets the land lie fallow for a year; we cancel every debt from every person who owes us money (which Trocmé insists is at the heart of the Lord's Prayer); we liberate all slaves (which includes liberating all those stuck in chronic indentured servitude to pay back debts); and the redistribution of all capital, wealth, and property equally, so that the poor and the marginalized have an equal share of money, land, and wealth along with everyone else. Jesus says that he has come to fulfill Moses's vision and law; he has come to turn the social order upside-down.

With the reading of this text, the proclamation of the Jubilee Year, and the announcement of its fulfillment in the person of Jesus, today, here in the synagogue in Nazareth, the people are astonished and amazed. All speak well of Jesus, But then some voices start to mumble. As they begin to understand the radical politics Jesus espouses, based on the law and the prophets, and apply them to their own life in Nazareth, they begin to object. Jesus's announcement is bad news for those in power, those with money, those who own land, even in the little village of Nazareth.

So they turn against him. "Isn't this the son of Joseph?" they ask one another. "Who do you think you are?" they say in effect, much like the tempter in the desert. "Surely, you will quote me the proverb, 'Physician, cure yourself,'" he responds. "Amen, I say to you, no prophet is accepted in his own native place," he tells them. With that, he acknowledges that no one in the congregation really accepts what he is teaching. How could he be the fulfillment of the great prophet Isaiah when we've all known him since he was a little kid running around town? So Jesus ups the ante and becomes quite blunt:

"Indeed, I tell you, there were many widows in Israel in the days of Elijah when the sky was closed for three and a half years and a severe famine spread over the entire land. It was to none of these that Elijah was sent, but only to a widow in Zarephath in the land of Sidon. Again, there were many lepers in Israel during the time of Elisha the prophet; yet not one of them was cleansed, but only Naaman the Syrian."

In response to these three sentences, the crowd tries to kill Jesus. They are furious at him. They drive him out of the town, lead him to the brow of the hill, and intend to throw him headlong over the cliff. "But he passed through the midst of them and went away."

What did he say that so infuriated the pious faithful of Nazareth? This is important to understand. By choosing Isaiah 61 and announcing that the Jubilee had begun today in their hearing, he was announcing the beginning of revolution. As they started to murmur and question him, then doubt him and attack him, he told two stories, saying in effect, God did not send the holy prophet to the righteous faithful, but to the person the righteous faithful hated the most—a distant enemy, first, the widow in Zarephath, Sidon, and next, Naaman the Syrian (a non-Israelite). It would be like this: imagine a right-wing, Christian fundamentalist church, where the fervent faithful wave the flag, wear MAGA hats, own guns, and espouse a new kind of American fascism in the name of God. If Jesus appeared to them, he would announce that God would not send a holy prophet to them but to a Muslim widow in Baghdad, whose husband was killed by U.S. bombs during the Iraq War. Or the holy prophet would be sent to a Muslim leader in Kabul, Afghanistan, where the United States waged its longest war, destroyed the country, stole its money and resources, and then left it to die. The congregation would feel insulted because their self-righteousness would have so blinded them that they would consider themselves the only holy people on the planet, and far greater than any Muslim women and men in Iraq and Afghanistan. But Jesus is not afraid to proclaim the revolution and let the chips fall where they may. By making his pointed statement about the widow in Zarephath and Naaman the Syrian, he challenges the self-righteousness of the Nazarene community. They should have rejoiced with him that God is so generous and universally loving that God would send the holy prophet to the widow in Zarephath and Naaman the Syrian. They should have praised Jesus for pointing this out and should have begged God for the grace to be like the widow in Zarephath and Naaman the Syrian. Instead, they tried to kill Jesus in response. His truth-telling exposed their latent violence, which underlies all religious fundamentalism, self-righteousness, and pietistic nationalism. What the congregation did not realize was that they had the greatest prophet in history in their midst—indeed, someone greater than a prophet.

What is equally powerful about this story is how Jesus avoids assassination and escapes unharmed. Jesus is nonviolent and understands the methodology of nonviolence, and, like many who were attacked by violent mobs, such as John Wesley and Gandhi, Jesus knew how to maintain his peace and calm and walk away right through their midst. It would seem like magic to us, as if he put a spell on the crowd, but it is not magic at all. When everyone is insane with violence, and you practice and maintain steadfast nonviolence, you have a power and an aura of sanity that no one understands, that others might even fear or want to steer clear of. Jesus knew how to respond nonviolently in the face of violence when he was threatened, and every follower of Jesus needs to learn this skill as well. These days, we could all attend nonviolence training workshops, like the ones held during the heyday of the civil rights movement, and learn through role playing how to respond nonviolently when faced with the threat of violence. Perhaps that will help us all learn to act more like Jesus, instead of the devout, faithful, and violent townsfolk of Nazareth.

"Put Out into Deep Water and Lower Your Nets for a Catch" (4:31–5:11)

Jesus moved on to Capernaum, where he taught in their synagogue and astonished them with his teachings "because he spoke with authority." A man shouted out to him, "Have you come to destroy us? I know who you are—the Holy One of God!" "Be quiet!" Jesus told him. "Come out of him." The man was possessed by a demon, who threw the man down and came out of him without doing him any harm. All were amazed and asked, "What is there about his word?" Jesus spoke with authority, as John will tell us later, because he *was* the Word, the Word of God, and the Word of God has power. Later, too, he will give this power to the apostles to expel all demons and cure all illnesses. That power is available to each of us who chooses to embrace Jesus's way of love and liberation.

In a world of violence, most of us are possessed by the demons of violence. It has become so normal that we do not think it out of the ordinary. We hardly notice it; we don't realize we have become zombies. What is noticeable, strange, and out of the ordinary is someone who is not possessed, such as Gandhi, King, Dorothy Day, or Thich Nhat Hanh. Any of us can practice the peace and nonviolence they manifested and, in doing so, expel the demons of violence from others and invite them into the freedom of peace and nonviolence. Our nonviolent presence, combined with the word, authority, and power of the God of peace, can expel the demons of hate and violence that entrap so many and liberate them into the sanity of mindfulness and peace.

For example, many people in the United States are possessed by the spirit of guns, by the power, sense of security and protection, and authority and control they give. A demonic spirit is anything that brings violence and death. Through the organizing and propaganda of the National Rifle Association, as I have experienced, NRA members are so possessed that it's almost as if the gun were part of their body and any effort toward gun control or the abolition of military weapons among civilians is a threat to their very selves. To act like the nonviolent Jesus among those possessed by gun violence would be like saying to a member of the NRA, "You don't have to be possessed by guns anymore. You can be free of guns. You can live in peace without guns or slavery to the NRA. There's a whole other, better life out there, a new life of peace and freedom." Daniel Berrigan called it "gunlessness." If they would open to the grace of the moment, they would be liberated. We see this happen in so many miraculous ways in the various Twelve Step movements, where people receive the grace, humility, courage, and strength to be freed from their demonic addictions such as alcohol or drugs.

I once led a day-long retreat for hundreds of people in Phoenix about Jesus, St. Francis, and nonviolence. After the closing Mass, someone came up to me and asked, "Are you really saying you are against violence, guns, war, and nuclear weapons?" "Yes," I said with a smile. He said, "My whole life is based on violence, guns, war, even nuclear war. I collect guns and have dozens in my living room. But if you tell me to, I will get rid of them." So, I said, "In the name of the nonviolent Jesus, I order you to get rid of all your guns." I asked him to contact me when he had done it. Two days later he sent an email. His family helped him dig a big hole in his backyard, where he dumped his guns, poured concrete over them, and buried them. "They're all gone," he wrote, and he felt better already, he said. He was a new man, freed from slavery to violence and guns, freed to be nonviolent and to follow the nonviolent Jesus. Any one of us can do this, if we dare. Anyone can help liberate another into the sanity and freedom of nonviolence, and anyone can take new steps forward into the sanity and freedom of nonviolence.

This liberating, healing work becomes the work of Jesus and the mission he will send his followers to live out. Luke next describes a typical Galilean day for the nonviolent Jesus: He left the synagogue, entered the house of Simon, and healed Simon's mother-in-law, who was afflicted with a severe fever. Everyone in town brought their sick ones to him; he laid hands on each of them and cured them all. As people gathered near him and experienced his disarming love, literally the demons came running out of them and they too began to radiate God's disarming love. People became sane in the presence of Jesus's breathtaking sanity.

Early the next morning, Jesus walks off by himself "to a deserted place." Jesus wants to pray and meditate alone, in the solitude of nature. Luke sprinkles these little vignettes throughout his Gospel to emphasize how Jesus seeks to maintain his intimate relationship with the God who called him "My beloved." In doing so, Jesus realizes his mission again and again. When the crowds catch up to him and plead for him to stay, he tells them that he comes to announce God's reign far and wide, and so he must move on. "I must go to the other towns to proclaim the good news of the kingdom of God, because for this purpose I have been sent." With that, he heads off to speak in synagogues throughout the region. Jesus is, in effect, on a permanent speaking tour, building a grassroots campaign of social transformation to welcome God's reign.

To do that, he needs workers and organizers, so he starts recruiting people to join his movement. But he doesn't just hire people to be his administrative staff and public relations agents. He calls people to become *disciples*. This is unique. Who calls people to be disciples? This act alone shows great confidence and faith in God and in Jesus's mission to proclaim God's reign. Luke begins chapter 5 with the dramatic account of the call of two sets of brothers who are fishermen. Jesus is teaching by the Sea of Galilee, but because the crowd is so large, he gets into one of the boats and sits in the boat and teaches the crowd from there. When he finishes, he turns to Simon, owner of the boat, and says, "Put out into deep water and lower your nets for a catch." This is one of the great sayings of Jesus, which he would say to each of us if he could. Simon and his crew have been fishing all night, they have caught nothing, and they are exhausted, and now this religious guru, who knows nothing about fishing, is telling them to head out to sea for a catch? "Master, we have worked hard all night and have caught nothing, but at your command I will lower the nets," he tells Jesus. Of course, as the story goes, they catch so many fish that the boat almost sinks! A second boat comes and almost sinks too, because of the massive catch. Luke writes:

> When Simon Peter saw this, he fell at the knees of Jesus and said, "Depart from me, Lord, for I am a sinful man." For astonishment at the catch of fish they had made seized him and all those with him, and likewise James and John, the sons of Zebedee, who were partners of Simon. Jesus said to Simon, "Do not be afraid; from now on you will be catching men and women." When they brought their boats to the shore, they left everything and followed him.

Why would Simon feel so unworthy before Jesus that he tells Jesus to leave him because he is a sinner? How could a pile of fish spark such profound inner awareness of one's faults and failings? Luke is telling us something about the presence of Jesus. He is an amazing teacher who holds the crowd spellbound with his talk of God's reign of justice and peace, a miracle worker who heals the sick with the touch of his hand, but also a spiritual presence of peace the likes of which no one has ever experienced. In his presence of infinite peace, nonviolence, and universal love, we realize how far short we fall, how filled with conflict, violence, and hate we are, how broken and weak and selfish we are. The presence of the nonviolent Jesus shines a bright light on our weaknesses and brokenness, but because he is so solidly peaceful, gentle, loving, and mindful, we do not collapse from this self-revelation; instead, we jump at the possibility of becoming as bright and clear as he is.

Because Jesus is infinitely compassionate, he doesn't let Simon's protest stop him. On the contrary, he has come to call broken people, and because Simon acknowledges his brokenness, Jesus wants him. This is a person he can use to call others. First, he tells Simon, "Do not be afraid." Simon and the others were terrified by this miracle. Jesus remains calm and peaceful. Then, he tells them about their lives to come: "From now on, you will be fishers of men and women." With that turn of phrase, that peacefulness, that invitation into fearlessness, they drop everything they have ever known, including their livelihood, and walk off with Jesus to be his disciples forever.

Ched Myers notes that Galilee was "ground zero for Rome's efforts to exploit and extract resources in the occupied territory of Palestine." Herod Antipas was building a city by the Sea named "Tiberias," after the emperor, where the empire could regulate the prosperous fishing industry. Now Rome controlled the fishing industry and disenfranchised peasant boatmen.

> Native fishermen, who had traditionally harvested these waters in a sustainable fashion for local consumption, were now required to buy fishing leases from the regime. The Herodians taxed them and controlled their markets in order to fund roads, harbors and factories. Processing plants (such as one in Magdala, where Mary was from) turned fish into salt preserve or sauce for export. Elites looked down on fishermen even as they depended upon their labor. One ancient papyrus called them "the most miserable of professions." So, when Jesus of Nazareth showed up at the sea, he was walking right into a distressed economic landscape. The ancient fishing village of Capernaum, just up the coast from Magdala and Tiberias, was profoundly impacted by Herodian policies. This made it a logical place for Jesus to commence building a movement of dissent, beginning with restless peasant fishermen who had little to lose and everything to gain by overturning the status quo. (Ched Myers and Elaine Enns, "A Vision of Restored Abundance," in the journal *Hospitality* [June 2022], 6)

When Simon complains that they have caught nothing after being out all night long, that's because the Herodian takeover is depleting the sea of its fish, Myers argues. Further, he suggests that Simon's response is one of shame: it's the sinful Herodian system that he serves that led to the depletion of fish and destruction of Creation as it was intended. Myers also suggests that Simon and the gang are paranoid, and rightly so, because they could be arrested for catching all these fish inspired by an itinerant preacher who does not have a fishing license. In other words, this windfall was illegal!

When Jesus calls them to join his campaign to catch people, he's inviting them to take on the system that enslaves them and destroys creation, as Myers observes:

Jesus is remembering the promises of his people's prophets that the Creator demands justice from those who oppress the poor. Such as Jeremiah who envisions the Creator "sending for many fishermen" in order to catch the leaders of Israel "who have polluted the land" (Jer. 16:18). Or Amos, who warns the elites of Israel that the Creator will "take them away with fishhooks" to justice (Amos 4:2). Or Ezekiel's rant against Egypt's Pharaoh, that the Creator "will put hooks in your jaws and pull you up from your rivers," along with the fish to which you claimed exclusive rights (Ez. 29:3–4). For Jesus, who not only knew the prophetic literature but sought to embody it anew in his context, this "fishers of people" idiom was a divine invitation to poor folks to join him in overturning structures of power and privilege in order to restore both Creation and justice. (Myers and Enns, "Vision of Restored Abundance," 6)

For Myers, the call to follow Jesus is a call to join his nonviolent grassroots campaign to resist the empire and all its oppression of the poor and destruction of creation, and to restore God's justice for the poor and creation. These poor fishermen are ripe for a campaign of justice, so they drop everything to follow the teacher and organizer. Discipleship to the nonviolent Jesus, we are realizing, means joining his ongoing grassroots campaign of justice, disarmament, and nonviolence to resist empire, systemic injustice, oppression of the poor, and the destruction of creation, and to restore God's justice for the poor and creation. The call to discipleship is not a campaign to save souls and let Jesus be your personal savior as much as a call to bring down every empire, end all injustice and oppression, and welcome God's reign of justice and peace for all humanity, starting with the world's poor and creation itself.

"I Have Not Come to Call the Righteous to Repentance but Sinners" (5:12–6:11)

Jesus moves on to another town where he's met by a leper who falls to the ground before him, pleads with him, and says, "Lord, if you wish, you can make me clean." Jesus touches him and says, "I do will it. Be made clean." And the leper is immediately healed. Luke presents Jesus as a Messiah full of compassion and totally at the service of the poor and ostracized. In those days, you couldn't get any poorer than being a leper, which meant you were completely ostracized from society and shunned. The stigma of shame attached to leprosy was so horrific that it was illegal to associate with a leper, much less to touch one. When Jesus reaches out and touches the leper, he commits civil disobedience. He could be rejected by the local Jewish community and leaders for this illegal activity. But he wants the poor and the sick to be made whole and healthy right now, no matter the cost to himself. More, he wants them restored to society, to be welcomed back into the community with open arms. For Jesus, every culture and community should be all-inclusive, multiracial, and all-encompassing. No one would be excluded, no one shunned, no one ostracized. These are signs of God's reign at hand.

To emphasize the point, Jesus orders the healed man not to tell anyone but to show himself to the priest and offer the ritual that Moses prescribed (Lev. 14:2–9) so that he will be fully restored to the community. He wants the man's shame erased. He knows that full healing requires total acceptance by the human family. He also wants the local religious official to begin his own conversion journey of welcoming lepers back into the community. We don't know what happened to the man, but Luke reports that news spread fast about Jesus and even greater crowds appeared to listen to his teachings and be healed. Then Luke adds, "He would withdraw to deserted places to pray." Luke emphasizes that Jesus stays centered in God by returning daily to his private communion with God in meditation where he knows himself as beloved and is affirmed to continue his mission of peace, compassion, love, and justice.

Luke then tells the story from Mark about the healing of the paralyzed man. Jesus was teaching the crowd in the community house, when some men lowered a paralyzed man on a stretcher down through the roof in front of Jesus. When he saw their faith, he said, "As for you, your sins are forgiven." The scribes and Pharisees are appalled and murmur about "blasphemy," so Jesus asks, "What are you thinking in your hearts? Which is easier to say, 'Your sins are forgiven,' or 'Rise and walk'? But that you may know that the Son of Humanity has authority on earth to forgive sins," he said to the paralyzed man, "I say to you, rise, pick up your stretcher and go home." The man stood up, picked up his mat, and went home glorifying God. Luke says that everyone was astonished and struck with awe and glorified God.

The famous episode touches on many themes, but the key one for Jesus is forgiveness. We're being taught that Jesus, the Son of Humanity, is the one who can forgive us. In those days, people would have judged that the man was paralyzed because of his sins. Jesus wipes away that judgment and considers this more important than the actual healing of the man. Such talk offends the religious officials, who consider him a blasphemer, but they are left speechless when he heals the man. Notice how he commands the sick man to "rise and walk." In effect, we can conclude that Jesus says that to every needy person who comes to him: You are forgiven, so rise and walk. The word "rise" alludes to resurrection; the man was considered dead, but Jesus raises him from the dead. The word "walk" alludes to discipleship; the man can now follow the nonviolent Jesus on the path of peace, love, and compassion. He too has a mission.

But Jesus's question hangs in the air: "What are you thinking in your hearts?" The Gospel asks us, Are we hard-hearted, self-righteous, judgmental people, like the religious authorities, who support the culture of condemnation, oppression, exclusion, and violence, or are we open to forgiveness, healing, compassion, mercy—even resurrection? It is a question that confronts every one of us.

Next, Jesus calls Levi the tax collector. "Follow me," he says to him, and Levi gets up from the customs post, leaves everything, follows Jesus, and that night gives a great feast in Jesus's honor. The religious authorities who are watching Jesus see him at the feast, eating and drinking with tax collectors and other unsavory people. For them, Jesus appears to be flagrantly violating every law in the holy book about cleanliness and who is worthy of association. Jesus will have none of it. He has come to bring good news to the poor and liberate the oppressed; that means he is on the side of the poor, the oppressed, the marginalized, and the excluded. We already know that from his mission statement in Nazareth. So, we are ready to hear Jesus's famous retort: "Those who are healthy do not need a physician, but the sick do. I have not come to call the righteous to repentance but sinners." Jesus has come to call us to live free from now on in God's reign. He's inviting them through the intimacy of sharing a meal into the visionary reign of God's peace, but also, here and now, in his reign-of-God, grassroots, all-inclusive, nonviolent movement and showing them what it's like. The religious authorities cannot begin to imagine such freedom because they are completely stuck in their self-righteous fanaticism, in their obsession with the culture and the empire, and therefore in their power, control, rules, and laws. Jesus stands completely outside their power and control, outside the rules, and seeks to welcome anyone into God's reign who wishes to come, beginning with all those who are currently excluded by the culture.

Jesus's answer could have silenced the scribes and Pharisees once and for all. Moreover, they could have rejoiced and said, "That is so beautiful! You want to welcome everyone in need into God's reign! We too are sinners, broken, complicit with the culture of violence and exclusion. We too want to turn away from the culture and enter God's all-inclusive reign of compassionate love!" Instead, they dig in deeper with their resentment and attacks.

"The disciples of John fast often and offer prayers," they say to him, "and the disciples of the Pharisees do the same; but yours eat and drink." "Can you make the wedding guests fast while the bridegroom is with them?" Jesus asks the authorities. With this parable, he offers himself as the bridegroom come to be with humanity; his presence is a time of celebration. Everyone is welcome to the eternal wedding party of God's reign. "But the days will come, and when the bridegroom is taken away from them, then they will fast in those days," he explains.

Then he offers three parables: "No one tears a piece from a new cloak to patch an old one. Otherwise, he will tear the new and the piece from it will not match the old cloak. Likewise, no one pours new wine into old wineskins. Otherwise, the new wine will burst the skins, and it will be spilled, and the skins will be ruined. Rather, new wine must be poured into fresh wineskins. And no one who has been drinking old wine desires new, for he says, 'The old is good.'" I hear Luke trying to tell us that Jesus makes everything new. He brings a new cloak and new wine. But some people, namely, the religious establishment and imperial rulers, want things to stay the same, so they reject his new wine. They want the old wine; they like the way things are because they do well under the current system. They profit from it. They are rich and powerful, and the rich and powerful never want change. Perhaps they were sincere originally, thinking their position was best for all in Israel, but power and possessions have warped and closed their minds to the fullness of truth that Jesus offers.

The nonviolent revolution that Jesus announced in Nazareth is under way, and he is determined to bring it about, whether those in power accept it or not. He knows that his revolution will be resisted and that, in the end, those in power will do away with him. He can read the writing on the wall; he saw the signs that first day when he announced the revolution in Nazareth. That is why he says that one day the bridegroom will be taken away and his followers will grieve and fast. That day has come. We are living that reality these days, and so we grieve and fast—and do our part to proclaim and welcome Jesus's nonviolent revolution for the coming of God's reign of peace.

And so, the public attacks continue. He was walking through a field of grain on a sabbath. The Pharisees were tracking him, following him, watching him, like paparazzi, or more like armed police, ready to strike at any opportunity. They wanted to catch him breaking the law so they could stop him and bring him down. His disciples were eating the grain, so they questioned him, "Why are you doing what is unlawful on the sabbath?" "Have you not read what David did when he and those who were with him were hungry?" he asked them, using genuine nonviolent communication. Notice, he simply questions them. "Haven't you read the scriptures? How David went into the house of God, took the bread of offering, which only the priests could lawfully eat, ate of it, and shared it with his companions?" This reference to David's illegal eating of bread silences the religious authorities. Then he delivers the punch line: "The Son of Humanity is lord of the sabbath." Once again, he identifies himself as the Son of Humanity and announces that he reigns over even the sabbath. This must have infuriated them. They cannot allow anyone to claim that they are above the sabbath and its laws. If Jesus is lord over the sabbath, then he is lord over them, and everything they stand for needs to fall away. The only logical response is to become his disciples.

Luke reports then another illegal act on the sabbath: the healing of the man with the withered right hand. As we heard in Mark, Jesus is teaching in the synagogue when he sees the poor man. The authorities are watching him closely to catch Jesus if he breaks the law. He calls the man forward and makes him stand before everyone. Then he directs a pointed question not to the man but to the crowd, which means, the religious authorities: "I ask you, is it lawful to do good on the sabbath rather than to do evil, to save life rather than to destroy it?" They do not answer him. "Stretch out your hand," he tells the man, and his hand is fully restored. Then, Luke reports, "They became enraged and discussed together what they might do to Jesus."

Why? Because he broke the law. They idolize the law and use it to maintain their power, control, and wealth, which means they have to put a stop to anyone who threatens their power. Notice, again, that Jesus does not violate the sabbath law in secret: he makes sure everyone can see what he is about to do. He acts publicly. It's as if he dares them to challenge his authority. He calls the man forward but makes him wait, instead of healing him, so he can question the authorities. He's trying to prick their consciences. "What is the purpose of the law?" he asks in effect. "What is the purpose of religion? Why are we here? Isn't it to do good rather than evil, to save life rather than destroy it?" They should have answered yes and cheered him when he healed the man. But they are attached to their power and to the system that dominates and oppresses the needy. Jesus will have none of it and turns it all upside-down.

We might easily dismiss the religious authorities in the synagogue as being ignorant, but most Christians today act like them rather than like the daring but nonviolent Jesus. We too are stuck in the culture of domination. In particular, fundamentalism and nationalism blind us to the life Jesus offers us. The nonviolent Jesus still asks us, "What is the purpose of faith and life? Isn't it to do good, not evil? To save life, not destroy it?" With this story, Luke pushes us to be as loving and compassionate as Jesus, so that we no longer do anything that is evil or destroys life, and that we do only what is good and saves life.

Blessings and Woes: The Sermon on Peace, Love, and Nonviolence (6:12–49)

In chapter 4, Jesus announced the start of his nonviolent revolution, with a mission of good news for the poor, liberation of the oppressed, and a Jubilee Year of debt forgiveness.

If we understand Luke's story of Jesus within that launching point, then we can understand Luke's emphasis on good news and justice for the poor and the path of faith, peace, and compassion required to bring that about. In chapter 5, Luke's Jesus begins to call followers to join his revolution and goes throughout the land proclaiming it and embodying it by healing and welcoming the sick, the poor, and the outcast. Now in chapter 6, Jesus picks twelve apostles to lead his permanent revolution of nonviolence, and then, as in Matthew, he lays out his teachings in simple, clear terms as a new way of life, a new way of being human in an inhuman world.

Scholars agree that Luke and Matthew shared the same unknown source, traditionally called "Q," which would have included a series of sayings and teachings that Matthew gathered together to form his Sermon on the Mount. Matthew presents Jesus as the new Moses offering the new commandments of nonviolence, outlined in the eight Beatitudes, the six antitheses, and two more chapters full of teachings on every aspect of the life of peace.

Luke takes those sayings and teachings and cuts them down, sharpens them, and brings them together in a shorter, more compact, and even more powerful way. Instead of a new Moses on the mountaintop, Luke's Jesus speaks on a flat plain; he is equal to everyone, teaching everyone, and available to everyone, Gentiles included. The Beatitudes are cut in half, and Luke adds a series of woes. There are no antitheses, just a long to-do list that makes up the ingredients of a life of universal love, universal compassion, and active nonviolence. In many ways, it's more to the point but just as shocking, overwhelming, and definitive as Matthew's.

To begin this key section, Luke tells us that Jesus spent the entire night on the mountain praying to God. It is the clearest description of Jesus at prayer. To put it mildly, Jesus does not live a kindergarten-level spirituality. He is alone, outdoors, probably cold, and determined to commune with God all night long, regardless of how tired he is. We know from Luke that Jesus regularly slips away to meditate alone with God. But here, Luke specifically presents Jesus praying all night because he is facing a decision about how to proceed and he's preparing to give his teachings to the world. When he comes down the mountain, he knows what to do and what to say. He will name twelve men as apostles, that is, those "sent forth," who will be his front line, advance men for his nonviolent revolution. Once he has his team in place, he will give his great sermon as he heard it from God.

Luke says that Jesus calls all his disciples to him—there are probably hundreds—and from this large pool, he picks twelve to be his special advance team. Unlike Matthew, who simply lists them as apostles, Luke writes that Jesus himself uses the word "apostles" to describe the Twelve. They are "those sent on mission." In the whole New Testament, only Paul and Barnabas, later in Luke's Acts (4:4, 14), are also named apostles, with perhaps Andronicus and Junia (Rom. 16:7). We notice that, among the Twelve, Luke describes Simon (listed in Matthew and Mark as a Canaanite) as a member of the violent revolutionary group, the Zealots, who led a revolt against Rome between 66 and 70 CE. Given Jesus's clear call for a nonviolent revolution in the Nazareth synagogue, Luke implies that Simon the Zealot renounced his violence to join the Jesus community because he saw that Jesus believed in the vision of justice and resistance to empire but that he had a more powerful methodology of resistance through his way of active nonviolence.

Readers note as well that no women are named as apostles. Women clearly were part of the discipleship community and are listed as faithful disciples who followed Jesus to his death and beyond, but they were not named as apostles according to these texts. We might wonder if there might indeed have been women named as apostles, but the male writers forgot them or erased them from history. One feminist scholar suggests that Jesus would have named only men because he was trying to convert primarily men, who are stuck in patriarchy, war, and empire, to his way of peace, love, and nonviolence. Women, she writes, would easily have grasped the gospel message because by and large they were living it as the most oppressed class of people. Today, we realize that Jesus was a radical feminist who welcomed women, defended women, and liberated women. In his vision of nonviolence, we understand that women are equal to men in every aspect of the life of Christ and therefore that they should have equal access to every ministry of discipleship.

Luke writes that Jesus walked down to "a stretch of level ground," where a huge crowd of people had gathered to hear him and be cured. He cured them all and expelled all their demons. "Everyone sought to touch him," Luke reports, "because power came forth from him and healed them all." After these three actions—naming his twelve apostles, healing the sick, and expelling demons—Luke writes that Jesus "raised his eyes toward his disciples" and taught them his Beatitudes and great sermon. If he raised his eyes, that meant he was probably sitting down on the ground, and the crowd was seated before him on the ground. It could also mean, according to one commentator, that he was kneeling.

Luke cuts the blessings in half to focus on the suffering poor and oppressed, and those who speak out for their liberation and for justice and pay the price:

Blessed are you who are poor,
    for the kingdom of God is yours.
Blessed are you who are now hungry,
    for you will be satisfied.
Blessed are you who are now weeping,
    for you will laugh.
Blessed are you when people hate you, and when they exclude and insult you,
    and denounce your name as evil on account of the Son of Humanity.
Rejoice and leap for joy on that day! Behold, your reward will be great in heaven. For their ancestors treated the prophets in the same way.

Luke's Jesus blesses and affirms the poor first of all, and announces that the kingdom of God belongs to them here and now. Notice, Luke drops Matthew's qualification "poor in spirit." Luke's Jesus is talking about the materially poor, those who struggle to survive each day. Nearly five billion people around the planet fit into that category at the moment. They suffer without adequate food, clean water, plumbing, housing, healthcare, education, jobs, or dignity. Jesus is saying that God is on their side, is with them, and is giving them God's kingdom. This means that, for Jesus, God is doing everything God can to get them out of poverty, and the rest of us must do the same. As disciples of Jesus, then, our focus must remain, first and foremost, like his, on the poor.

Next, Luke's Jesus blesses and affirms those who are hungry now. Notice Luke's change: he does not talk about those who hunger and thirst for justice. Instead, he focuses on those who are literally hungry—the starving poor. Today, there are hundreds of millions of them. He promises that they will be satisfied, which means that God is doing everything God can to feed them, and that we should too. In other words, the spiritual life, the way of universal love, begins with feeding the hungry.

Then, Luke's Jesus blesses and affirms those who weep, which is slightly different from those who mourn. If one is weeping, one is in the deep throes of grief, pain, sorrow, and loss. Jesus promises them that one day they will laugh. "Laughter" is not a word one associates with the Gospels. Luke's Jesus brings laughter to the poor and weeping because he will end their weeping, sorrow, and grief. Laughter means contentment, happiness, and joy. It is one of the signs of life and resurrection.

Finally, Luke's Jesus blesses and affirms those who continue the lineage of the prophets of old, such as Jeremiah, Jonah, Ezekiel, Isaiah, and Micah, those who speak out for justice and peace and are persecuted for their prophetic speech. Here Luke seems to combine Matthew's list of those who hunger and thirst for justice and make peace, and then are persecuted for it like the prophets. In particular, Luke names those who are "hated," "excluded," "insulted," and "denounced" because they speak out for the nonviolent Jesus and carry out his campaign of justice and peace. If you speak out and act like the nonviolent Jesus, if you announce his nonviolent revolution as he did in the Nazareth synagogue and travel through the land promoting justice, liberation, and peace, you will be attacked just as he was—and this means you are greatly blessed, the most blessed of all! You are living the legacy of the prophets of justice and peace. You manifest an authentic discipleship to the revolutionary, nonviolent Jesus, the greatest of the prophets.

All those who are denounced and persecuted should "rejoice and leap for joy." This is an astonishing statement. If you are denounced and hated for speaking out for justice and peace, instead of feeling down, dejected, or sorry for yourself, you should start dancing for joy! You will be greatly honored in heaven because God is on the side of the struggle for justice and peace; God is looking for people to carry on the prophetic tradition of speaking out for justice, peace, and creation.

This fourth Beatitude asks us: Which side are we on? In a world of violence, systemic injustice, the nuclear threat, and environmental destruction, where there is so much work to be done, it asks, Do people hate you, exclude you, insult you, and denounce you because you speak out for justice and a global nonviolent revolution as Jesus did? How much trouble are you causing for justice and disarmament? To fulfill this Beatitude, we have to rock the boat and disrupt the false peace of the culture of war. The blessing is to become a lifelong, public agitator for justice, disarmament, and creation, to keep at it despite the setbacks, roadblocks, obstacles, and denunciations we face. It's not that we seek rejection and alienation, but we know now to expect it. In a world of total violence, injustice, and war, everyone who speaks out and organizes for justice and disarmament will be hated and denounced. This comes with the job description. The trick is to discover the blessing within the public cursing.

As if to emphasize this prophetic calling and to demonstrate it, Luke adds what no other evangelist does: a list of woes which Jesus proclaims. The role of the prophet, according to the scriptures, is to *listen* to the God of peace and justice, and then *announce* to the culture of war and injustice the message that the God of peace and justice wants to say. That message usually takes two forms: announcing and denouncing. On the one hand, the prophet announces the good news that God's reign of peace and justice is at hand, that God sides with the poor and is at work liberating the oppressed, and that we are all invited to practice universal nonviolent love as a new way of life. On the other hand, the message requires that we denounce that anti-reign of war and injustice that is consuming us and destroying us like a plague. We can no longer simply try to be good and do good; we also have to denounce evil and resist systemic evil. The prophets of old spent most of their time denouncing greed, war, oppression of the poor, and all the violence of empire while announcing God's justice and mercy. They would fearlessly say, "Woe unto you who oppress the poor, turn your back on the needy, and hurt any person or creature, and kill the enemy." They were persecuted for their truth-telling. In this spirit and tradition, Luke's Jesus drops his bombshells:

> But woe to you who are rich,
>   for you have received your consolation.
> Woe to you who are filled now,
>   for you will be hungry.
> Woe to you who laugh now,
>   for you will grieve and weep.
> Woe to you when all speak well of you,
>   for their ancestors treated the false prophets in this way.

With these woes, Luke's Jesus has officially turned the world upside-down. He declares that those who are rich, full, and laughing have in effect received all they will ever receive; it's downhill from there. Those who are rich in a world of poverty, full of good food in a world where millions starve, and laughing while so many grieve and weep from the violence of the world's war and injustices will never get any farther. The poor, the hungry, the weeping, and the persecuted will not only receive riches, food, laughter, and justice—but eternal life with the God of peace and justice.

The words are hard, shocking, and revolutionary, then and now. They go against everything we presume—that we should try to make money, save money, get rich, eat well, never grieve, and be merry and—most shocking of all—try to live in such a way that everyone speaks well of us. This last woe delivers a powerful knockout punch. The sign of a false prophet, or anyone who is not speaking for the true God of peace and justice, in a world of permanent warfare and systemic injustice, is that everyone speaks well of you. If everyone speaks well of you, you have a serious spiritual problem, and you don't even know it. That's a clear sign that you are not fully following the troublemaking, nonviolent Jesus and his Beatitudes, that you are not speaking out for justice, disarmament, and creation the way he and the prophets did, from Jeremiah to Martin Luther King Jr. Yes, you can have some people speak well of you for your work for justice and peace, but not all. If you are truly working for justice and peace, which means publicly resisting the culture of violence, war, and injustice, the ruling authorities and their spokespeople will have to put you down and publicly discredit you in every possible way.

We can understand Jesus's woes better as we study the lives of the prophets in our own time, such as Gandhi, Dr. King, Dorothy Day, Desmond Tutu, and Oscar Romero. Each of them publicly denounced injustice, racism, poverty, and war, and they paid a heavy price for it, even to the point of being assassinated. While it might seem that they led glamorous lives as famous spiritual, moral leaders admired by millions, the reality for them was different. Yes, some people held them in high esteem, beginning with the poor and oppressed; but the powers that be attacked them whenever they posed a threat to the status quo. Most were ridiculed in the media; all were arrested, prosecuted, and jailed; some were assassinated. My friend Archbishop Tutu, for example, was under the nearly constant threat of death throughout his life, first for speaking out against apartheid and, later, for criticizing the corruption of the African National Congress. He felt the sting of his prophetic work, but he kept his heart and mind focused on the God of peace and justice, studied the Gospels daily, and learned to rejoice. He didn't mind having people mock him and condemn him for justice and peace. He was often too busy laughing and dancing.

One way to understand these woes is to see them as explanations of the limited consequences of our complicity with the culture of violence and injustice. If we seek only to make money and get rich, eat and drink well, laugh and have a good time, and make sure everyone likes us by never rocking the boat, then we have failed at life. We will not enter God's reign of universal love because we are focused on ourselves and on serving our selfish desires, not on God and suffering humanity. To put it bluntly, we do not care about others. Our lack of action on behalf of the poor, the hungry, the grieving, and the oppressed reveals the true nature of our cold, self-centered, hard hearts. We have no empathy, no compassion, no concern for justice or mercy or peace.

If we never speak out against unpleasant issues such as the nuclear weapons industry, white racism, corporate greed, the NRA, or the fossil fuel industry, then we will remain silent accomplices of the culture of violence and injustice and will stand against God's reign. If we stay on this path, we are doomed to the consequences of selfishness. We might think that we live a sophisticated spiritual practice and routine, but if our private prayer does not lead to public work for justice and disarmament, and the public consequences for our stand, then we are not yet living radical Gospel discipleship to the nonviolent Jesus. We do not so much "seek to be consoled as to console, to be loved as to love, to be served as to serve." We want to follow Jesus into the heights of nonviolence, including the public work that brings public opprobrium, to help break new ground in the proclamation of God's reign of peace on earth.

With his woes, Jesus shakes us, wakes us, and tries to take us out of the daze the world has put us in. He does not want us to waste our precious life going along quietly with the world's selfishness but to stand against it, to live against it, and to witness to God's reign against it. He wants us to get out of ourselves and publicly side with the poor, the hungry, and the grieving and to speak out against every form of injustice and harm. This is the spiritual life in a nutshell.

After these blessings and woes, Luke's Jesus shares his revolutionary vision of love lived out in a radical, transformative way. The love that Luke's Jesus teaches is both personal and interpersonal, but also universal and global, encompassing and including every human being alive during his time, and every human being before or since.

263

Luke takes Matthew's Sermon on the Mount and compresses it down to the bare essentials; and to emphasize the point, he begins and ends his to-do list with the commandment of universal, nonviolent love: love your enemies. "But to you who hear I say, love your enemies." Note that he's speaking to his disciples and to anyone who hears him, including us today. Note, too, that Luke has removed the qualification of the antitheses, "You have heard it said . . . , but I say to you. . . ." With that qualification, we know that Jesus was speaking in nation/state terms, that the "enemy" was not someone across town with whom we have conflict but any nation being targeted by our own nation. For people living in the United States, that we would mean that we would somehow try to actively love the people our country has bombed and killed and continues to threaten.

To love our nation's enemies means that we must, first of all, work to stop our country from killing them. To love them, we try to get to know them, listen to their stories, and befriend them. That would include traveling to their land and meeting them face to face. Many thousands of Christian peacemakers in the United States have done just that over the past fifty years and have traveled at great risk to Vietnam, Nicaragua, El Salvador, Palestine, Iraq, and Afghanistan. Millions more have worked to end U.S. wars. These efforts, however small they seem, manifest the commandment of Jesus to "love your enemy." They demonstrate universal *agapē* in action.

Surely Luke's commandment to "love your enemies" includes this same nation/state language. Luke's Jesus calls for active love that crosses borders, and we see Luke emphasize this in Jesus's association with Samaritans and in his parable of the Good Samaritan, in which he uses "the enemy" of the Jewish people as an example of perfect compassionate love for one's neighbor. But Luke widens the command to love our enemies to include all those despised and hated by one's group, culture, or nation. So for African Americans, it means loving members of the Ku Klux Klan—a love that requires public nonviolent resistance. For North Americans, it means loving immigrants who illegally cross the border; instead of hating them and blocking them, we are to welcome them as long-lost brothers and sisters. For Hindus and Muslims divided along religious lines in India, Pakistan, and elsewhere, it means active love that welcomes the other as a brother or sister, as Gandhi exemplified.

Love of enemy invites us to break down the ordinary restrictions, borders, and boundaries of love, and to widen our love as far as possible to include every person as a beloved brother or sister. It commands us to disobey the whims of dictators, presidents, and rulers who order military invasions, occupations, bombing raids, and imperial rule and inflict death on sisters and brothers across the planet. Jesus tells us not to obey their universal hatred and violence but to obey God's universal love and nonviolence. If we put this commandment to love our enemy into practice, we not only help bring down all divisions but perhaps help the nation/state system transform so that God's reign might manifest itself in a new global culture of peace and cooperation.

"Do good to those who hate you," he says next. This line is unique to Luke, and it goes against every grain in the culture. If someone hates you, the world teaches us to hate them back. If we do that, Jesus points out, then we are no different from them. We now are filled with the same poison of hatred that will eat away at us from within and eventually destroy us. Note that Jesus's command to do good to those who hate us comes in the context of his teaching about love for the enemy. If we respond with active goodness to those who hate us, we will disarm them. If they are caught up in hatred, they will only know how to respond to further hatred. So he commands that we respond with goodness and love instead, and let the cognitive dissonance that follows lead to their conversion, the end of the hatred, and the rebirth of love in those previously filled with hatred.

This methodology of goodness was at the heart of Martin Luther King Jr.'s efforts. He tried to "organize goodness" against systemic racism and hatred, as manifested, for example, in the strict evil segregation practices of Birmingham. In his campaigns, he led people to nonviolently resist organized hatred and evil and, in certain instances, to respond with goodness through active nonviolence to those filled with hatred, such as white politicians, policemen, and Klansmen. This response of steadfast goodness, which he called "creative nonviolence," led to many social miracles, most especially the end of legalized segregation. He taught that "hatred cannot drive out hatred; only love can drive out hatred." His was a shining example of Jesus's teachings. Jesus expects every one of his disciples to practice this way of steadfast goodness and creative nonviolence. As Luke insists, it is a requirement of discipleship.

"Bless those who curse you," Jesus continues. To bless someone is to call down every grace of peace, love, and healing from God upon those filled with hate who curse you. Anyone can do this. Blessing people is not just the preserve of priests and ministers. Blessing others is a simple tool that we can all use every day. It holds great power to heal and turn people to God. Couples should bless each other, parents should bless their children, church members should bless each other. One can do it with a silent whisper, saying, "I bless you, God bless you, may God heal you and keep you." One can ask the other to bow their head and one can extend one's hands over them or place their hands on the head of the other and articulate a prayer of blessing like, "May the God of peace bless you abundantly and give you every good grace of peace, love, healing, and joy, that you might always follow Jesus." This should be the normal practice of Christians. If every Christian started blessing one another, beginning within the family, our violence would decrease and our love, indeed our very sanity, would increase.

Luke's Jesus commands us to take this simple practice and extend it to those who curse us. Instead of cursing back, which is what the culture of violence teaches, he demands that we respond with a blessing. This should be the normative behavior of every Christian. We curse no one but bless everyone, especially those who curse us. We can use the small moments of our day to practice blessing those who irritate us or rub us the wrong way, so that in those harsh encounters, if someone should curse us, we can respond instinctively with a blessing. As with everything Jesus teaches, this teaching requires training and practice.

Those who side with injustices of all sorts will curse us for standing in their way, for speaking against injustice. When we encounter them at peace vigils and demonstrations, we will have the chance to put Jesus's teaching into practice and bless them. This was the ordinary practice of the early church. We need to reclaim this method of non-retaliation and positive blessing, while making sure we Christians refrain always from cursing others.

"Pray for those who mistreat you," Jesus commands. This is the first time Jesus has mentioned prayer in Luke's Sermon on the Plain. Notice he doesn't command us to pray for ourselves or our families. He doesn't tell us to pray that we might be safe and sound. He continues to prepare us to "lose" our lives for his sake—that is, to follow his way without worrying about our safety and prosperity. Whoever mistreats us and persecutes us should become the focus of our daily, intense prayer. We love them, and we want them converted to the Way of Jesus, to be healed and whole and full participants in God's reign of peace. This is how Jesus himself must have responded to those who mistreated him, even to those who tortured and executed him. He prays for everyone, especially those who hurt or mistreat him. As we reflect on the word "mistreat," we can conclude that it means harm, and because many people harm us throughout our lives, we end up, like Jesus, praying for everyone.

"To the person who strikes you on one cheek, offer the other one as well," he says, "and from the person who takes your cloak, do not withhold even your tunic." Luke's Jesus commands nonviolent resistance to evil through the example of turning the other cheek if struck and giving your inner garment if someone takes your outer garment. Gandhi called this "non-cooperation" with violence. We simply refuse to cooperate with the cycle of violence. We stop the cycle by not retaliating with further violence, even to the point of accepting suffering without retaliating as we struggle for justice and peace. Jesus is preparing his disciples whom he will send to lead his campaign of active nonviolence to Jerusalem and the world. They will encounter brutal soldiers and authorities who will strike them and take their cloaks—as these authorities will eventually do to Jesus himself. The disciples are not to retaliate with further violence. He wants to disarm the offenders through the nonviolence of his followers. In effect, Jesus is leading a classic nonviolence training session there on the plain, just as Gandhi and Dr. King did with their followers before every public campaign, march, and civil disobedience action. We too need to teach one another how to respond nonviolently to the police or attackers before we undertake public demonstrations so that our public witness is meticulously nonviolent, peaceful, and prayerful.

"Give to everyone who asks of you, and from the one who takes what is yours, do not demand it back," Jesus teaches. He's trying to break us from our deeply rooted selfishness and lead us into the freedom of selflessness. He wants us to live like him, to spend our days giving everything we have to others. In this way of life, we give to everyone who asks of us, and we do so happily. We do not cling to or hoard possessions. We share what we have with others, especially with those in need and those who cannot repay us. We give our food, money, hospitality, and help. We give our attention, our patience, our kindness, and our respect. We give our time, even our lives. We don't even mind if someone takes what is ours. We want to be like St. Francis and Dorothy Day and spend our time on earth serving the poor and bringing them comfort. We are on the Gospel journey of downward mobility and do not desire to collect possessions, save money, and have much. From this upside-down perspective, we are grateful to those who ask of us, because they help us simplify our lives, remind us of our dependence on God, and better follow Jesus, who gave everything he had, even to the point of giving his life for humanity.

"Do to others as you would have them do to you," Jesus says. The Golden Rule is found in every major religion, yet it continues to be ignored and dismissed as a social rule of life. If it were collectively practiced, our personal lives would be more peaceful and the world would be safer, more just, and more nonviolent. We've heard this teaching many times, but it still stands as true and right. Luke invites us to take up this rule all over again and put it into practice in the small ordinary moments of daily life and, if possible, to promote it in the culture and the world. We would not want anyone to hurt us, rob us, oppress us, bomb us, or kill us, and so we do not do these evil things, and we do our best to stop them from happening to others. If they are being done to others, we want people to stand up and help stop the violence, so that's what we do too. To get to the root of the problem, we teach and promote Jesus's nonviolence as a way of life so that everyone can live out the Golden Rule more easily.

"For if you love those who love you, what credit is that to you?" Jesus asks. "Even sinners love those who love them. And if you do good to those who do good to you, what credit is that to you? Even sinners do the same. If you lend money to those from whom you expect repayment, what credit is that to you? Even sinners lend to sinners and get back the same amount." With these three questions, Jesus urges us to go beyond the limits of worldly, selfish expectations, into the practice of selfless, limitless love, goodness, and generosity. He points out that there's a greater reward if we practice this kind of generous, selfless love. He wants us to enter the limitless love, goodness, and generosity of God and to lavish everyone everywhere, especially the poor and the enemy, in the same way God does. If we do this, we will experience here and now an inner reward—a deep satisfaction and consolation—that the world can never give. He wants us to be universal people like him.

If we all practiced this teaching, then our common conditional, selfish, and limited love would dissipate. We would begin to understand and see God's reign of love all around us. We would discover entirely new vistas of love and life that we never dreamed of because the culture blinds us to that big imagined vista. With this teaching, Jesus calls us to be ordinary saints who practice the love and goodness that the saints practiced. We see this kind of unconditional love in the life of Dorothy Day, for example, the founder of the Catholic Worker. She spent her long life living with the homeless, protesting war and nuclear weapons, owning no money or possessions, publishing a newspaper about Gospel living, and traveling across the country and into the land of the "enemy" (Cuba, Russia, Tanzania) to share her vision of peace. She came to embody selfless love, goodness, and generosity. As Thomas Merton once said in a letter to her, "You are the richest person in America."

To emphasize his point, Luke's Jesus repeats the central commandment: "Rather, love your enemies and do good to them, and lend expecting nothing back; then your reward will be great, and you will be children of the Most High, for God himself is kind to the ungrateful and the wicked." This is the bottom-line work of the disciple of the nonviolent Jesus. We are people who practice limitless, selfless, universal love and generosity. We love all enemies of our culture and nation; we do good to them even as others do evil to them. We love them so much that we try to stop all the evils done to them, including the waging of war and death upon them. We lend and give to those in need without any desire of reciprocation. We do this as disciples of the nonviolent Jesus, who practiced this very same limitless, selfless, love morning, noon, and night. This becomes for us a normal way of life, as it was for him.

Some get turned off by the word "reward," but it's important to note that Jesus is not just referring to life after death in the reign of God. He's referring to life here and now. If we practice this love for enemy, goodness-toward-those-who-do-evil, and generosity-toward-those-who-cannot-repay-us, we will discover a new kind of consolation found in the truth, rightness, and goodness of the act itself. This is an ancient spiritual teaching much neglected in our time. We do the good, even to those who do not do good, *because of the rightness and goodness of the act itself.* We show love for the enemies of our culture and nation because it's the right thing to do, because this is the truth of our common humanity—that we are all children of God and called to live in God's love. We give to those in need without expectation of a return because this is the right thing to do, this is what it means to be human, this is how members of the human family treat one another. We give to those in need. Who cares about getting something in return? Not us. We no longer live according to an outlook of scarcity and fear. Instead, we plumb the depths of an inner freedom that the world cannot give. It's a new kind of mystical freedom within the life of love whereby we know who we are and where we live as our true selves. In this way, we begin to radiate the God of universal love. Jesus tells us in the midst of this instruction that God is loving, good, and kind to the ungrateful and wicked, that by God's very nature God is universally, unconditionally loving. This is what God is like. God cannot do otherwise.

As with Matthew's Sermon on the Mount, these commandments are rooted in the revelation of the nature of God. Jesus shatters the old images of God as violent, hateful, mean, vengeful, angry, or warlike. That is not the way God is, he insists. God practices love for all of creation, including us; that is the nature and way of God. Jesus wants us to be like the living God, to act and love widely as God does. Jesus commands us to reject all the false notions of God, to dismiss our own doubts about God's love, and to ban all false theologies that justify violence and vengeance in the name of God. With this image of God, we can follow Jesus on the path of nonviolence and even give our lives in his nonviolent revolution knowing that we are serving a wonderful God who stands by us.

With this repeated instruction comes a new commandment: "Be merciful, just as your Father is merciful." Matthew's version says, "Be perfect," but Luke's adaptation means, "Be infinitely, universally compassionate as God is infinitely, universally compassionate." God has compassion on every human being and on all sentient beings; Jesus commands us to do the same. If we try to be as merciful and compassionate as God, our lives will change for the better, and so will the world. We will start loving and serving everyone unconditionally, but most importantly all those that the culture deems unworthy of our compassion.

"Stop judging and you will not be judged," Jesus instructs. "Stop condemning and you will not be condemned. Forgive and you will be forgiven." With these instructions, he calls us to a new kind of life in which our love, mercy, and compassion for everyone are purified. We stay focused on the God of mercy and compassion and in the process stay centered in the peace of the present moment so that we no longer judge or condemn others or hold grudges or resentments. We let all of that go, every day, every hour, and stay focused on God and our practice of universal love. We are freed from judging and condemning and grudges. We don't need to do that anymore. We see through the eyes of mercy and compassion, through Jesus's eyes. Along the way, we discover how the nonviolent Jesus looks at us with infinite mercy and compassion—without a trace of judgment or condemnation. We start to want to live and see as he does.

This practice of no-judging, no-condemning, and total forgiveness may seem impossible, but deep down we know how to do it. We each have at least one person we have felt unconditional love for, such as a parent, a grandparent, or a child. If we have unconditional love for a child, for example, we find ourselves infinitely patient with that child. We don't judge or condemn the child but instead offer help and affirmation. God is like that to us, toward every human being, and Jesus is trying to get us to be like that toward all others. He's calling us to a new kind of love whereby we are patient and kind with strangers, always affirming, never judging, never condemning, quick to forgive, and ready to help. He wants us to move out of ourselves, to stop our self-obsession and narcissism and become totally other-oriented so that we outdo one another in loving-kindness. In this way, we become more and more like God, who acts this way toward us, and we fulfill our vocations to be God's beloved sons and daughters.

Another way to look at this teaching is to understand it in terms of other human beings. We do not judge or condemn any other human being; but we do judge and condemn evil—such as gas chambers, cremation ovens, electric chairs, and nuclear weapons. If we practice these teachings, we will learn the loving nonviolence that condemns the evil but not the people who do the evil. For instance, when my friends and I keep vigil at Los Alamos Nuclear Weapons Laboratories in New Mexico, we are careful not to judge or condemn anyone, but we do publicly and gently denounce the development of nuclear weapons and call for their abolition. We can't judge the nuclear weapons makers because we are called to love them. Besides, they are the ones who know how to dismantle them! We need them. We have to win them over with friendship and love. This is the non-judgmental methodology of Jesus's nonviolence.

"Give and gifts will be given to you—a good measure, packed together, shaken down, and overflowing, will be poured into your lap, for the measure with which you measure will in return be measured out to you." In this phrase, unique to Luke, Jesus tells us that, since the law of reality is "what goes around comes around," give to others with wild generosity in a spirit of love and compassion and you will receive far more love, kindness, and compassion. He invites us to outdo one another in love, generosity, compassion, and service, not to outdo one another in hatred, violence, condemnation, or punishment. He calls us to a great, big, wild generous love toward everyone, a heartfelt love as wide as the world, as big as God's.

One way to approach these teachings is to start experimenting with them to see if they are true and doable. We can try taking small steps of unconditional love and generous compassion and see what happens. We can work with them and experiment with them in the small, ordinary moments of the day when we are about to be impatient, judgmental, condemnatory, rude, critical, or unforgiving. If we take a deep breath, think before speaking, ask God for the grace, and respond with this kind of unconditional love and compassion, we may find life easier for ourselves and make life easier for others. Not only will we help others and make their day more pleasant, but we help ourselves. If we apply these teachings socially to our church community, school, institution, or neighborhood, we may find that life becomes more peaceful for everyone involved. If we could apply these teachings socially, nationally, politically as a nation to the world, we would begin to let go of fear, celebrate life, dismantle our arsenals, share our resources, and protect our common home. These teachings hold the key to humanity's survival, good gifts beyond our wildest dreams.

With that, Luke moves on to a series of short sayings and teachings to help us better understand the Jesus way. First, Luke points out that this new life requires vision. We are called to see life and one another from a whole new perspective. We see every human being as a brother or sister to be loved and served. If we exclude one person or group of people from this vision, we are still blind and unable to see as God sees. And so, Jesus asks, "Can a blind person guide a blind person? Will not both fall into a pit?" The answer is, "No, a blind person cannot guide a blind person. They will both fall into a pit. Only a seeing person can guide a blind person." Jesus wants us to see, and then to lead one another on the path of life, to help each other so that none of us falls into a pit. And yet, that is precisely what we tend to do: in our blindness, we lead one another into a pit and spend our lives in the pits. If the whole human race is blind, as John's Gospel will later assert, then the whole human race is falling into a pit, and today that pit is the bottomless abyss of permanent warfare, nuclear threat, and climate catastrophe. We need to beg for the gift of vision to see with Jesus's eyes so that we can all climb out of the pit of destruction and return to the path of life.

"No disciple is superior to the teacher," he says, "but when fully trained, every disciple will be like his teacher." With this saying, Luke explains what Jesus is doing with his disciples on the great plain: he is training them for radical discipleship. As with anything in life, if you want to learn something new, you have to be trained. Jesus is training them to live an entirely new way of life in keeping with God's nature of love and justice. This should be the program of every Christian church, community, school, and mission—to train everyone in the Gospel methodology of Jesus's way.

Back to the question of vision and our own blindness. "Why do you notice the splinter in your brother's eye, but do not perceive the wooden beam in your own?" Jesus asks in one of his most provocative questions. "How can you say to your brother, 'Brother, let me remove that splinter in your eye,' when you do not even notice the wooden beam in your own eye? You hypocrite! Remove the wooden beam from your eye first; then you will see clearly to remove the splinter in your brother's eye." With this important teaching, Jesus points out that each of us has a wooden beam in our eye, blinding us and preventing us from seeing and living—much less helping someone else. We have to keep reminding ourselves this truth about our blindness. We tend to forget it. We go around trying to take the painful splinter out of someone else's eye, telling them how to improve their lives, when all along we are unaware of our own predicament and inability to see clearly. We cannot see anything, nor can we help anyone. If we want to see, if we want to help others, he teaches, we have to remove the wooden beam from our own eye first.

How do we remove the wooden beam from our eyes? This is the task at hand. Each of us is blind, yet we think we see. Luke tells us in no uncertain terms how to remove the wooden beam from our eyes: love everyone everywhere unconditionally and universally; show compassion and mercy to everyone everywhere; renounce judging, condemnation, resentment, violence, and hostility; forgive everyone who ever hurt you; share your resources with the needy; give what you have to others, especially those in need, without any desire for reciprocation; humbly turn your lives over to the God of peace and God's reign; and, along the way, turn away from the culture of violence, injustice, and war and join Jesus's campaign to proclaim God's reign of peace and justice. If we do these things, we will begin to remove the wooden beam from our eyes and to see through the eyes of the nonviolent Jesus.

"A good tree does not bear rotten fruit, nor does a rotten tree bear good fruit," he says. "Every tree is known by its own fruit. People do not pick figs from thornbushes, nor do they gather grapes from brambles. A good person out of the store of goodness in his heart produces good, but an evil person out of a store of evil produces evil; from the fullness of the heart the mouth speaks." With this saying, as in Matthew's version, Jesus invites us to have hearts full of goodness, love, compassion, mercy, and peace. He wants us to speak from deep, heartfelt love and compassion. He's trying to disarm our hearts and form new nonviolent hearts within us that we might be full of goodness and bear good fruit for God and humanity. It's not that we were born bad or rotten; on the contrary, each of us was born intrinsically good, full of goodness. But through the violence of the world, we have been saturated with violence, hurt by violence, and trained to be violent. Jesus is training us to be nonviolent like him, to have sacred, nonviolent hearts like his, to love everyone everywhere unconditionally and compassionately as he does, and thus to bear good fruit for God and humanity. This is the purpose of life, according to Luke's Jesus. He wants us to bear good fruit.

Perhaps we can reflect on what kind of fruit our lives are bearing. As we look back on our lives, we ask ourselves, Have we helped others, especially the poor and needy? Have we tried to bring justice and peace to the world? Have we brought love, healing, liberation, clemency, and new life to others? Or have we made life harder for others? Have we brought pain, misery, and sadness to others? Have we spent our days in selfish pursuit of money, pleasure, possessions, and honors? Have we inflicted violence on others or supported the culture's many versions of harm? If so, how can we change ourselves so that for the rest of our lives we bear good fruit?

If we want to be disciples of the nonviolent Jesus, we need to let these great teachings form us, change us, and transform us, as Gandhi did. We need to apply them concretely to daily life so that we might bear the good fruit Jesus is looking for. We can always turn over our lives to the nonviolent Jesus and the God of peace and start down a new path of service, kindness, and unconditional love toward others. Turning over a new leaf in itself will bear good fruit. Every effort of love bears good fruit. We can take heart, knowing that if we are trying, then we are on the way. Through daily, prayerful meditation, we can give our lives over to the God of peace and let God form us and guide us that we will bear good fruit, even if we do not know it.

Luke ends his great Sermon on the Plain with the same question and parable as Matthew: "Why do you call me, 'Lord, Lord,' but not do what I command?" It is useless to proclaim Jesus as Lord and to tell folks he is our personal savior if we do not do what he commands. He is not our Lord if we do not live as he lived. If we hurt people and hate people, then we are hypocrites who mock Jesus. If we want to know what God's will for us is, all we need do is read and obey Matthew's Sermon on the Mount and Luke's Sermon on the Plain. Luke repeats Matthew's closing parable to make the point:

"I will show you what someone is like who comes to me, listens to my words, and acts on them. That one is like a person building a house, who dug deeply and laid the foundation on rock; when the flood came, the river burst against that house but could not shake it because it had been well built. But the one who listens and does not act is like a person who built a house on the ground without a foundation. When the river burst against it, it collapsed at once and was completely destroyed."

Luke ends with a warning: act on these teachings. Time is short, the flood is coming, disaster is just down the road. If you live according to Jesus's teachings, you will be fine. If you do not, you will be wiped out.

Be smart. Take these teachings to heart. Set out on a new path in the footsteps of the nonviolent Jesus. What have you got to lose? Nothing that actually matters. This is the way to the fullness of life. Live out his teachings and discover new vistas of love, new horizons of peace, and new depths of life.

"I Tell You, Arise!" (7:1–9:50)

Jesus teaches his disciples to follow him, then embarks on his journey to proclaim God's reign, heal the sick, and model his teachings. In Capernaum, some elders approach Jesus on behalf of the Roman centurion, the head of a Roman military unit, and ask him to come and save his slave who is sick. He built the synagogue for us, they tell Jesus. So, Jesus heads off to the centurion's house, but as he approaches it, the centurion sends a message: he's not worthy to have Jesus enter his house. "Say the word and let my servant be healed," the message reads. Jesus is amazed and tells the crowd, "Not even in Israel have I found such faith." With that the servant is healed.

There is no sign that Jesus approves of the centurion's military occupation of Galilee. On the contrary, we assume Jesus remains vehemently opposed to systemic violence and empire. But Jesus practices universal, nonviolent love, even toward his enemy, even toward a Roman centurion, even as Jesus stands against Roman occupation and violence. He is there to heal the slave, the poorest person in society. And, while Matthew's version will include Jesus's speech about the all-inclusive nature of God's reign, where many will come from east and west, Luke moves that speech to chapter 13, to a section of teachings on God's reign, where he will add that many from all over the world will enter God's reign and get to sit at table with the prophets in heaven; that the last will be first and the first will be last.

Jesus's encounter with the funeral procession near the village of Nain appears only in Luke. I consider this one of the most touching, beautiful, and inspiring stories in the four Gospels. As Jesus, his disciples, and the crowd approach the city gate, a dead man is being carried out in an open coffin to the village cemetery. His mother, a widow, follows, weeping. A large crowd from the city follows her. Jesus sees her weeping and, Luke reports, "was moved with compassion for her." He said to her, "Do not weep." Then Luke offers the details. "Jesus stepped forward and touched the coffin." (Note: that would have made him ritually unclean, but he won't do the proper ritual to be clean again.) When he did this, the funeral procession stopped. "Young man," he said to the dead man, "I tell you, arise!" The dead man sat up, fully alive, and began to speak, and Luke adds, "Jesus gave him to his mother." The entire crowd was suddenly terrified, "seized with fear," and at the same time, "glorified

God," saying, "A great prophet has arisen in our midst." These words remind the reader of the prophet Elijah's resurrection of the only son of a widow of Zarephath (1 Kgs. 17:17–24). "God has visited his people," they said.

With this story, Luke presents Jesus's authority not only over illness and division (the centurion and his sick slave) but over death itself. Jesus literally can stop a funeral procession in its tracks. He is not afraid to face death and touch it, as he does when he touches the coffin. In Jesus, the forces of death itself are brought to a halt. He has come, as John will later say, to bring "life and life to the full" for everyone. He wants to end the reign of death, literally. The reason for this, Luke writes, is that Jesus's heart is full of compassion. He has preached earlier in the week that we should all be as merciful and compassionate as God in heaven, and now he demonstrates what the fullness of compassion looks like. If we widen our hearts to be as merciful and compassionate as Jesus, we too can stop the forces of death in their tracks and raise the dead. In our time, that would translate in very clear terms into the politics of compassion and nonviolence. If we exercise the compassion of Jesus in our own lives and spread it far and wide, we can abolish the death penalty and nuclear weapons and end gun violence, racism, hunger, and war itself. We simply would have nothing to do with death anymore because we are people of compassion, and compassion leads to resurrection.

This unique Gospel story calls us to expand our imaginations individually, collectively, and globally and see how we can transform the culture of death into one of life. Luke's Jesus calls us to be people who raise the dead, who stop the forces of death in their tracks, who try to end weeping and grief and spread resurrection and joy. We can do this by practicing a new kind of social, global compassion toward those who weep and suffer as we try to ease their pain and relieve their suffering and institutionalize compassion and nonviolence. As followers of the nonviolent, compassionate Jesus, we can say to one another, "I tell you, arise!" We can help each other live life to the full and stop giving in to the forces of death.

One person who exemplified this Christian vocation of resurrection was my friend Dr. Paul Farmer, founder of Partners in Health, the world-famous doctor who helped bring free healthcare to the poorest of the poor around the world, from Haiti to Rwanda. His story is described in the best-selling book *Mountains beyond Mountains* by Tracy Kidder. When he moved into Rwanda to set up its healthcare system, Paul was able within a few years to cut the death rate for the entire nation by an unprecedented 80 percent. In the Netflix movie about him, *Bending toward Justice*, there is a scene where he is treating a dying Rwandan woman, who is describing how her father is at home building her coffin. He says to her, "Tell your father to stop building your coffin. You're going to live." By bringing First World healthcare and compassion to the Third World poor, Paul Farmer brought resurrection to people stuck in the throes of death. He modeled the Christian vocation to offer compassion, raise the dead, and make peace.

Luke uses this great story as a set-up for a conversation between Jesus and John the Baptist's disciples. Two of John's disciples are sent to ask Jesus, "Are you the one who is to come, or should we look for another?" His answer sums up the Gospel of Luke: "Go and tell John what you have seen and heard: the blind regain their sight, the lame walk, lepers are cleansed, the deaf hear, the dead are raised, the poor have the good news proclaimed to them. And blessed is the one who takes no offense at me." With this answer, Jesus shows how he is making the revolutionary vision of Isaiah come true. He is a revolutionary not in theory or rhetoric but in actual practice. His revolution is nonviolent and is aimed at the people who need it most: the poor, the blind, the lame, the lepers, the deaf—even the dead! With this answer, too, he lists the job description for everyone who would follow him.

But it's Jesus's final beatitude that is most revealing. Blessed is the one who takes no offense at Jesus. Why does Luke include that? Perhaps John and his followers might be offended because Jesus does not measure up to their idea of what a messiah should be. Everyone was still enthralled with the vision of a violent messiah who would bring justice and wipe away the Romans and the ruling class. Jesus might not live up to John's expectations for an angry activist, even a violent, domineering messiah. Perhaps John is tempted to dismiss Jesus as too spiritual, too nonviolent, too focused on works of healing. Jesus is trying to encourage John and his followers to trust him, to see his good works, and to believe in him. Perhaps Luke is referring to the Pharisees and scholars of the law who hate and reject Jesus as a lawbreaker and a troublemaker. Likewise today, many are offended by Jesus for a variety of reasons, most of which have little to do with him. They blame him for all the failings of the church, its priests and ministers, schools, and institutions. They dismiss him because the world has improved so little and continues to spiral down in destruction. They reject him because they do not get what they want—riches, honor, possessions, or power, as if Jesus would wish these burdens on anyone. The blessing, Luke writes, comes from trusting Jesus, his vision, and his good works, and staying with him come what may.

Later, Jesus asks a series of questions about John the Baptist:

"What did you go out to the desert to see—a reed swayed by the wind? Then what did you go out to see? Someone dressed in fine garments? Those who dress luxuriously and live sumptuously are found in royal palaces. Then what did you go out to see? A prophet? Yes, I tell you, and more than a prophet. This is the one about whom scripture says: 'Behold, I am sending my messenger ahead of you, he will prepare your way before you.' I tell you, among those born of women, no one is greater than John; yet the least in the kingdom of God is greater than he."

Notice how he pushes the crowd to reflect on the meaning of John's presence among them. They know he is special, but what is it about him that is so special? Jesus answers: he is a prophet, but more than a prophet, a messenger of the One who is to come, the greatest person who ever lived. High praise indeed! And yet, Jesus adds, everyone who enters God's reign will be greater than John the Baptist. Therein lies the hope for everyone. If we share in the work of the prophet, proclaiming the coming of God's reign and preparing a way for the nonviolent Jesus, then we too will be great in God's reign.

The Pharisees and scholars of the law, Luke notes, rejected John, and that is why Jesus continues with his questions:

"To what shall I compare the people of this generation? What are they like? They are like children who sit in the marketplace and call to one another, 'We played the flute for you, but you did not dance. We sang a dirge, but you did not weep.' For John the Baptist came neither eating food nor drinking wine, and you said, 'He is possessed by a demon.' The Son of Humanity came eating and drinking and you said, 'Look, he is a glutton and a drunkard, a friend of tax collectors and sinners.' But wisdom is vindicated by all her children."

Here Jesus explains how God sent John the Baptist to convert people to God, but the religious authorities rejected him, and how God sent a nonviolent messiah who will likewise be rejected. Luke laments, "What more could God do to wake us up?" God gives us free will, but many of us, especially self-righteous religious leaders and wealthy people, refuse. Today we could say, God sent us Gandhi, Dr. King, Dorothy Day, Archbishop Romero, the Berrigans, Fannie Lou Hamer, and Rosa Parks, but we still refuse to wake up. But Wisdom, a.k.a. *Hagia Sophia*, the feminine side of God, the Holy Spirit, knows what she is doing and will be proved right in the end, in God's reign.

"The One to Whom Little Is Forgiven Loves Little" (7:36–8:21)

This lament over the rejection by the Pharisees and scholars of the law leads to Luke's tale about the Pharisee who held a dinner for Jesus. Here, Luke rewrites a story told in the other three Gospels about a woman who enters a dinner party in Jesus's honor and proceeds to anoint his feet. The other Gospels use the story to show how she affirmed Jesus's journey to the cross; John will take it even further and use it to teach the disciples how they should anoint one another to go to martyrdom. Luke, instead, uses the episode to emphasize Jesus's call for unconditional mercy, compassion, and love, and how this compassionate love and forgiveness will elicit great love.

During the meal, "a sinful woman" brought an alabaster flask of ointment, stood behind Jesus, wept at his feet, bathed them with her tears, kissed them, and anointed them. Jesus could tell how uncomfortable the Pharisee was with this spectacle. He sensed the tension in the air, and the judgment against this woman. So Jesus told a story and asked a question.

> "Two people were in debt to a certain creditor; one owed five hundred days' wages and the other owed fifty. Since they were unable to repay the debt, he forgave it for both. Which of them will love him more?" Simon said in reply, "The one, I suppose, whose larger debt was forgiven." He said to him, "You have judged rightly." Then he turned to the woman and said to Simon, "Do you see this woman? When I entered your house, you did not give me water for my feet, but she has bathed them with her tears and wiped them with her hair. You did not give me a kiss, but she has not ceased kissing my feet since the time I entered. You did not anoint my head with oil, but she anointed my feet with ointment. So, I tell you, her many sins have been forgiven; hence, she has shown great love. But the one to whom little is forgiven, loves little." He said to her, "Your sins are forgiven." The others at table said to themselves, "Who is this who even forgives sins?" But he said to the woman, "Your faith has saved you; go in peace."

Luke offers two characters for our reflection. The woman has been forgiven and so she lavishes loving-kindness on Jesus, who affirms her and sends her on her way in peace. She is the model disciple. The Pharisee, by contrast, is a law-abiding, upstanding member of the community, probably faultless, decent, and respected. He does a good thing by hosting Jesus for dinner. But when the woman starts crying at the feet of Jesus, he looks down upon her with judgment. Luke zeroes in on this judgment and self-righteousness. Luke's Jesus wants us to break free from judgment and self-righteousness and understand that each of us has been forgiven by God, and that we should fall at the feet of God and weep tears of gratitude. Notice that the nonviolent Jesus has not a trace of judgment or self-righteousness toward the woman, who is known as a public sinner. He has only infinite mercy and compassion for her, and she knows this. He is passionate about liberating every single human being, one person at a time, out of the traps of self-will and the culture of death into God's will and the fullness of life here and now.

Notice how brave the woman is! She has done a courageous act of public nonviolence. She already practices what he has been teaching his male disciples to do—to show love, mercy, and humility. She would have been very unwelcome in that house by everyone but Jesus. She disregards the consequences to herself in this nonviolent action by offering thanks, love, and hospitality to Jesus, hospitality that no one else showed to him. With one creative act, she encourages Jesus and offers him tender, unconditional love, when no one else does, when few in his whole life ever do. In doing so, she takes a stand in public protest against the cold, egocentric religious men who show little love.

Notice, too, that Jesus, who instructed his disciples not to judge or condemn others but to be as merciful as God, practices this rule of life. He does not judge or condemn others, which we do. Notice how nonjudgmental and kind he is to the Pharisee who is so judgmental. He simply tells a story and asks a gentle question. He is a master of nonviolent communication. That's the way he treats all of us who are judgmental and self-righteous. He asks us questions. He wants to break us from judgment and condemnation and lead us to practice the unconditional mercy and compassion of God. He's trying to break open our hearts to widen them into universal, unconditional compassion toward everyone. As we do this, we enter God's reign, in which we encounter not judgment but God's welcoming arms.

This focus on unconditional mercy and compassion is the heart of Luke's Gospel. It marks his narrative of nonviolence. We are called to mirror the mercy, compassion, and love of Jesus, to renounce judgment and self-righteousness, and to offer forgiveness toward everyone. The way to do this is to examine our own resentments, judgments, and self-righteousness and surrender them to God. Then, we forgive those who hurt us and make amends to those we have hurt. We show mercy to all, beginning with those the culture tells us are unworthy of mercy or compassion. Finally, we too need to fall at the feet of Jesus with gratitude that we have been forgiven, that we have been given a second chance, that God continues to love us and show us mercy and compassion.

Luke next reports that Jesus traveled everywhere, "preaching and proclaiming the good news of God's reign." To emphasize his inclusion of women into his community, Luke specifically notes that accompanying Jesus were the Twelve and a group of women—Mary Magdalene, Joanna, the wife of Herod's steward, Susanna, "and many others who provided for them out of their resources." Jesus had formed an all-inclusive, egalitarian community in which women were treated as equal to men. We can safely conclude this because, had he followed the norms of patriarchy, he never would have allowed women near him, much less have included them as part of his inner circle, and Luke never would have made this observation. Jesus was breaking down patriarchy and gender barriers at every chance, starting with his own community. He models what the Christian churches should look like today: all-inclusive, egalitarian, and non-patriarchal.

Next Luke includes the parable of the sower, who sows seed that falls, some on the path, some on rocky ground, some among thorns, and some on good soil where it grows and produces "fruit a hundredfold." "Whoever has ears to hear ought to hear," Jesus says. As in Matthew and Mark, Luke's Jesus is questioned about its meaning. "Knowledge of the mysteries of God's reign of universal love and peace has been granted to you," Jesus tells them, "but to the rest, they are made known through parables so that 'they may look but not see, and hear but not understand.'" If we sit with this teaching, we realize that knowledge of God's reign of universal love and peace has been granted to every human being since the Gospels were written. Jesus explained all the fine details of living in God's reign in his Sermon on the Plain. The question is not who has access to this knowledge but whether we will see, hear, understand—and act on these teachings. He wants us to enter God's reign and live in it here and now as he does by practicing love, compassion, and total nonviolence. The choice is ours.

With the explanation of the parable of the sower, Luke urges us to hear the word of God, take it to heart, and let it form our lives, guide our decisions, and bear good fruit for the God of peace and love. He notes that those who receive it like "rich soil" embrace the word of God with "a generous and good heart" and bear fruit "through perseverance." The word "perseverance" is important. Luke is telling us that the word of God grows within us slowly and bears fruit slowly, over time, just as any plant grows slowly and takes years to grow and bear fruit. He urges the faithful to persevere, stay the course, be faithful to the way of Jesus, and trust that only through a long fidelity will our lives bear good fruit. This is actually quite encouraging; it is a promise that our lives will bear good fruit if we stay the course. All we have to do is live out Jesus's teachings in the Sermon on the Plain and be faithful to them over time. We see that long-term fruitfulness in the lifelong fidelity of recent elders such as Dorothy Day, John Lewis, Ita Ford, Rutilio Grande, Franz Jägerstätter, Sophie Scholl, and Daniel Berrigan. They never gave up, even though they did not live to see the massive societal changes they prayed for. Yet their lives have borne good fruit for countless people. They have inspired millions.

Jesus encourages us to be faithful to the lifelong task of sowing good seeds of peace and justice, to maintain generous and good hearts as we carry on our work, and to trust that our perseverance will bear good fruit. He's talking about being faithful, nonviolent public advocates for God's reign, whether we see the changes we want to see or not. That's why he reminds us that, when we light a lamp, we don't hide it; we place it so that everyone can see the light. We are public people who let our light shine over the entire course of our lives with generous and good hearts, so that sooner or later everyone around us, even those far away, will "come to the light." He concludes his parable of the sower, advising us to "take care how we hear." Those who hear the word of God and act on it, who let their light shine, to them "more will be given."

God is looking for people who will hear the divine word, act on it, and let it bear the good fruit of justice, mercy, love, and peace. That is how God acts. God does not force us to take the divine word to heart and live according to it, but that's what God wants. If we stop and think about it, doing that would be the wisest step we could take with our lives, and yet we hesitate. Instead, we ignore the word of God or, at best, hear it as nice poetry; we do not change our lives so that they reflect God's word acting in us. Just then, Jesus is told that his mother and brothers are standing outside and want to see him but cannot get in because of the crowd, and he responds, "My mother and my brothers are those who hear the word of God and act on it." If we want to follow Jesus, that is what we are supposed to do. If we hear the word of God, act on it, and work to let it bear good fruit in our lives, then we will be brothers, sisters, and mothers of Jesus. That is our calling.

"Do Not Weep Any Longer for She Is Not Dead but Sleeping" (8:22–9:17)

Next Luke includes the story of Jesus in the boat with the disciples, crossing to the other side of the lake. He sleeps soundly as a storm breaks out and the boat takes on water. They wake him, thinking they are about to die. He rebukes the wind and waves, which immediately calm down, then questions the disciples. "Where is your faith?" They then ask one another, "Who then is this, who commands even the winds and the sea, and they obey him?" While Mark emphasizes the boat-crossing stories as lessons in love of enemy, Luke uses them to expose the disciples' lack of faith and to raise the question of Jesus's identity. Both questions are aimed at the reader as well: at this point in the journey, where is our faith in Jesus? Who is this Jesus anyway? Both Jesus and the disciples await our answer. Luke also demonstrates how easy it is for Jesus to cross to the other side, to love the enemies of his people. For him, it means he can take a nap! The male disciples are freaking out, thinking they are about to die, whereas Jesus is catching up on some much needed rest so he will be fully alert and ready to serve when he arrives in enemy territory. He is focused on resting so that he will be fully mindful, rested, and ready to offer unconditional, nonviolent love for the enemy when the moment arrives. He continues to model the way of nonviolent love. Even as the storms of our political actions stir around us, we remain calm, peaceful, faithful, trusting in God 100 percent, even to the point that we can sleep soundly.

Luke copies Mark's dramatic account of the healing of the Gerasene demoniac on the other side of the Sea of Galilee. Jesus calls out the demons who possess the homeless, naked man living among the tombs. It is as if he is possessed by death itself. When Jesus asks his name, he replies, "Legion," the name for a contingent of up to six thousand Roman foot soldiers. Jesus sends the demons into the herd of swine, and suddenly they run off the cliff and, in doing so, ruin the economy of this Roman-occupied region. The entire community is "seized with fear" and beg Jesus to leave, once they see the formerly possessed man, now a model disciple, clothed and sitting at the feet of Jesus. (It's almost as if they had long depended on their mutual fear and loathing of the possessed man to unite them and keep them together as a community in the midst of their occupation. Instead of hating the Romans, they took out their resentment on the possessed man. That's how prejudice and racism continue today.) The man begs Jesus to take him with him, but Jesus sends him to proclaim all that God has done for him. So, the healed man goes throughout the territory proclaiming all that Jesus has done for him.

Once again, the Gospel shows us how the nonviolent Jesus liberates us from the forces of death. Everyone in this story is possessed by the evil spirit of the Roman military; the naked, homeless man living among the tombs merely symbolizes their common possession. Jesus frees them all. With the death of the swine, the local people would not be able to feed the Roman military, who would probably move on, leaving them free but poorer. They would rather have the military occupation because then they would have jobs and income. Today there are places around the United States and the world that are "occupied" by the U.S. military or the weapons industry, the people having no clue that they are "possessed" by the demonic spirit of violence. They don't care that they are stuck in death; they prefer the job, the income, the livelihood, even if it's a job rooted in death. We could look at the places where the Trident submarine is docked, in Washington, Georgia, and Connecticut; or the local communities around Lawrence Livermore National Laboratory, the Los Alamos National Laboratory, or the Pantex Plant in Amarillo. Even though the sole purpose of these facilities is to prepare for mass murder, the local people don't mind. If Jesus showed up and expelled the demons of death from their communities, they would ask him to leave too.

We're left with the image of poor Jesus, turned away because he brought healing and new life. They should have applauded him, celebrated him, thrown a party for him and the healed man. But they are controlled by fear and death, just as we are today. So Jesus leaves, and the healed man sets off to tell everyone what happened. He is the model disciple and shows us how to respond if Jesus frees us from the culture of death.

The story of the healed man among the tombs raises many questions: Where are we in the story? How are we possessed by the culture of death? Do we want to be liberated from slavery to this culture? Do we want the freedom and new life that Jesus offers? What are the economics of God's reign, and what would they look like if we applied them here and now? How is Jesus liberating us, and how are we announcing the good news to others?

Back in Capernaum, Luke reports that the crowd welcomes Jesus. We're told the story of Jairus, an official of the synagogue, who begs Jesus to come heal his sick twelve-year-old daughter. As they set off, a woman "afflicted with hemorrhages for twelve years," comes up from behind, touches the tassel of Jesus's cloak, and is cured. He stops and asks who touched him. The woman comes forward trembling, falls at his feet, and confesses that she touched him and has been healed. "Daughter, your faith has saved you," he says. "Go in peace." By calling her "daughter," he names her and recognizes her and gives her dignity. He would not let his healing power go without establishing a personal relationship. He affirms her faith and sends her on her way in peace. We can assume that this is how Jesus treats everyone: he heals us, knows us, names us, affirms our faith, and sends us forth to live in his peace.

When someone tells Jairus that his daughter has died, Jesus says, "Do not be afraid; just have faith and she will be saved." When he sees the crowd in the house weeping and mourning, he says, "Do not weep any longer, for she is not dead, but sleeping." For this, they ridicule him. Inside, Jesus takes her by the hand and calls to her, saying, "Child, arise!" She does, and he tells them to give her something to eat. (Notice the impressive gentleness, thoughtfulness, and kindness of Jesus, his fundamental human compassion, as he makes sure all her needs are met and that she feels good again.) Once again, we witness Jesus's power over sickness and death and hear his basic commands to all of us: "Do not be afraid. Just have faith. Do not weep any longer. Arise!" If we take these words to heart and choose faith over fear, not only will we rise above the culture of death but we will help raise one another to new life. This story within a story invites us to faith beyond understanding, fearlessness beyond comprehension, and resurrection hope even in the face of the ultimate despair. Dare we choose that? Dare we try to raise one another to new life?

In effect, the nonviolent Jesus is calling everyone stuck in the culture of war and empire, everyone living under the weight of empire then and now, to rise. This word "rise" is a call to be empowered with the Holy Spirit of God so that we no longer serve the forces of death or give in to them. As Jesus instructs and trains his apostles and disciples, he's actually empowering them with the spirit of resurrection to walk into the culture of death and dispel all its power and lead everyone into the fullness of life in God's reign.

Jesus then gives the Twelve "power and authority over all demons and to cure diseases" and sends them forth to proclaim God's reign of peace and to heal all the sick. These tasks sum up what he has done so far, and what he has been training them to do. Now he gives them the "power and authority" to do these things just as he does. Just as he sends us out today to extend to others his love and liberation. He wants each of us today to be fully empowered to resist the forces of death, to free one another from all forms of slavery and death, and to live in the peace of God's reign.

It's hard to imagine the scene that Jesus and the Twelve are facing. Imagine Rwanda, El Salvador, Bangladesh, or Haiti. People are suffering disease and death, powerlessness and hopelessness under the crushing weight of the Roman Empire and its religious yes men. It's precisely into this cauldron of fear, despair, poverty, and violence that Jesus sends the Twelve. Their work of healing, expelling, and proclaiming will empower the people and give them new hope in the God of peace. It will free them from the clutches of Rome, just as the Gospel should free us today from the clutches of any country or empire, including our own.

To the Twelve he gave strict instructions: "Take nothing for the journey, neither walking stick, nor sack, nor food, nor money, and let no one take a second tunic. Whatever house you enter, stay there, and leave from there. As for those who do not welcome you, when you leave that town, shake the dust from your feet in testimony against them." Luke reports that the Twelve headed out, walking from village to village, healing the sick, expelling demons, and proclaiming the coming of God's reign. In doing this, they were dismantling the power of empire over the population. People were being healed of fear and powerlessness and empowered to stand in the peace of God. Because this subversive campaign threatened the empire, Jesus sent them out as people in flight, in an underground movement, with an urgent task. They were to stay where they were received and heal those people. As for those who rejected them, they were to shake the dust from their feet so that their rejection might not cling to them. They were free people, filled with peace, hope, and love, sent to minister to the poor and oppressed in the outskirts of the empire. Their message, if people would let them proclaim it, would bring good news to the poor.

Later, the Twelve returned and told Jesus all they had done. Notice his continued kindness and compassion as he leads them off to a quiet place to rest. He teaches them to be compassionate to themselves as they live out his mission, to practice self-care. In this case, the crowds followed him, and so he teaches them about God's reign and heals their sick. It's in this context that Luke tells the first tale of the multiplication of the loaves and fishes.

The disciples want to dismiss the crowd because, they say, people need to eat, though I've always presumed that meant they themselves wanted to get something to eat. Jesus, however, continues to empower them. "Give them some food yourselves," he tells them. They are incredulous. How could they possibly feed thousands of hungry people? For Jesus, anything is possible if it is done in love for the service of the needy and the glory of God. All we have are five loaves and two fish, they say, and there were some five thousand men, not to mention the thousands of women and children. "Have them sit down in groups of fifty," he tells them. By forming the crowd into groups, Jesus breaks down the impersonal nature of the large crowd and makes it possible for people to turn to one another, introduce themselves, and get to know each other. Suddenly, they become neighbors and friends and begin sharing what the Master has been teaching.

In foreshadowing the Passover meal on the night before his execution, Luke's Jesus took the five loaves and the two fish, looked up to heaven, said the blessing, broke them, and gave them to the disciples to set before the crowd. "They all ate and were satisfied," he reports, and twelve baskets were filled with the leftovers. Jesus miraculously feeds the crowd. In this telling, we begin to understand how Jesus inspired everyone to share what they had with one another so that everyone would eat and be filled. It became a foretaste of heaven. They saw him bless the food and place it before the crowd, so then they would have done the same: taken out their few loaves and fish and placed them before the others in their group. The formation of small groups is the key to everything, then and now. Suddenly, the event became a massive potluck, and, as with any church potluck dinner today, there would have been more than enough for everyone and plenty of scraps left over. Women would have brought food for themselves and their children, and they would have passed it around and shared it with those who had no food, just as the Master had done. In this giant picnic, like a big music festival, everyone would have been full, relaxed, and happy in the presence of the Master. Of course, Jesus wants us to live and act like this today, to share our food and resources with those in need so that no one is hungry, homeless, or ill-clad. He wants everyone to have what they need, and the only way that is going to happen is if those of us who have too much share what we have with those who have too little.

As we face the collapse of our economy, catastrophic climate change, and ever-worsening violence, more and more of us are going to have to learn the lessons of African and Latin American Christians who learned the hard way to form small, grassroots base communities of prayer, study, and action, where they shared their resources with one another, encouraged one another in their common struggle for justice, and comforted one another along the way. They understood this Lucan detail of small group formation, and, by organizing tens of thousands of grassroots base communities, they brought about waves and movements of justice, democracy, and peace across their regions. We all need to learn this way, to find human ways of organizing and supporting ourselves as the institutions and cultures collapse, so that we will all have enough food and wisdom to survive in peace, even to thrive.

"The Son of Humanity Must Suffer Greatly and Be Rejected" (9:18–50)

After this big day, Jesus retreats in solitude to pray as his disciples sit nearby. He asks them who the crowds say he is and then turns the question to them: "But who do you say that I am?" Commentators always note that the question includes God's name given to Moses, "I Am." Peter answers, "The Messiah of God," which causes Jesus to rebuke him and tell them not to say this to anyone. Luke's version goes easier on Peter than the other Gospels, but it's still a firm rejection of the title Messiah as they understand it. "The Son of Humanity must suffer greatly and be rejected by the elders, the chief priests, and the scribes, and be killed and on the third day be raised," he tells them. They must have been shocked and confused by this saying, but Jesus is trying to break them of their misconceived notion of the Messiah as a military leader who will overthrow the empire and restore Israel to secular, worldly power. Jesus knows the book of Isaiah, which he read from in Nazareth. He is the Suffering Servant of God, a nonviolent Messiah, who will indeed resist the empire and in the process be crushed to death by it. But he tells the confused disciples that death does not get the last word.

"If anyone wishes to come after me," he tells them all, "he must deny himself and take up his cross daily and follow me." Discipleship to Jesus means renouncing one's will and comfort and following his example. Notice that Luke adds the word "daily." This nonviolent resistance to the culture of empire and death is a daily practice. It marks our life. This is what we do, what we are known for, what gets us into trouble. We are not successful people as far as the world goes because we live in a constant conflict, permanent nonviolent resistance to the world of violence and death.

"Whoever wishes to save his life will lose it," he says, "but whoever loses his life for my sake will save it." As people who carry the cross of nonviolent resistance every day, we give our lives away for Jesus and his campaign to proclaim God's reign. We focus our entire lives on the coming of God's reign of peace and justice. This is our passion and our purpose. We are not trying to achieve money, possessions, or success for ourselves, even though we might like those things. We have no choice. We want to follow Jesus first and foremost, and so that's that.

Think of the noble people who gave their lives nonviolently for an end to slavery—the Abolitionists, such as the Grimké sisters (Sarah and Angelina), William Lloyd Garrison, and Frederick Douglass. Or civil rights activists like Medgar Evers, Fannie Lou Hamer, Viola Liuzzo, Glenn Smiley, Dorothy Cotton, Bayard Rustin, and John Lewis. They carried the cross of nonviolent resistance every day of their lives. Their lives were not their own. Cesar Chavez, leader of the farmworkers, once told me that his life was no longer his own. He had given it away to the farmworkers and the struggle for justice, and he lived full-time at their service and that was how he followed Jesus. It meant carrying the cross daily. In following Jesus to create a new culture of justice and peace, we acknowledge that our lives are no longer our own. They belong to God and God's work to transform humanity.

"What profit is there for one to gain the whole world yet lose or forfeit himself?" Jesus asks. There is no profit in gaining the world yet losing one's soul. Nothing is worse than losing our lives for the wrong purpose—for money, possessions, and success. Luke's Gospel summons us to set our sights on a far nobler purpose: God's reign of justice and peace.

"Whoever is ashamed of me and of my words," Jesus says, "the Son of Humanity will be ashamed of when he comes in his glory and in the glory of the Father and of the holy angels. Truly I say to you, there are some standing here who will not taste death until they see the kingdom of God." If we stand by Jesus and live according to his words and join his campaign, just as we side with him, he will side with us. He promises that his disciples will see God's reign, as they do indeed by the end of the story. Yet even today, if we give our lives as the saints and prophets did in the nonviolent struggle for justice and disarmament, we too will see God's reign at hand.

That's what happened next to Peter, James, and John, when Jesus took them up the mountain with him to pray. There, "while he was praying, his face changed in appearance and his clothing became dazzling white." Moses and Elijah, representing the law and the prophets, appeared next to him and, according to Luke, were talking with him about "his exodus that he was going to accomplish in Jerusalem." Peter, James, and John had been sleeping, Luke also adds, as in the scene in the Garden of Gethsemane. But they woke up and saw the vision of the transfigured Jesus. Then Peter blurted out, "Master, it is good that we are here; let us make three tents, one for you, one for Moses, and one for Elijah." As he spoke, a cloud came over them, cast a shadow over them, and then they entered the cloud and became frightened. Then a voice spoke from the cloud saying, "This is my chosen Son; listen to him." With that, Jesus was there alone.

Luke's version makes clear that the transfiguration not only reveals the glory of the risen Jesus but is also a spiritual experience for Jesus that encouraged him to carry out his campaign of nonviolence to Jerusalem and to death on a cross. People have long spoken about this story as a foretaste of his glory but miss the harsh reality. Peter, James, and John have not encouraged Jesus on his journey to the cross. Elsewhere, Peter rebuked Jesus after he spoke about his inevitable crucifixion. No one in the story so far supports Jesus and his talk of the cross! No one. But here, that's exactly what Moses and Elijah do. They encourage Jesus to complete his journey, which Luke names as the real "exodus" for humanity, whereby Jesus leads the entire human race through loving nonviolence into the promised land of God's reign of peace. They give Jesus strength, consolation, and courage to keep going while the three disciples sleep through the transfiguration. These three symbolize the male-dominated church then and now. Once they wake up, they say all the wrong things. Instead of encouraging Jesus as do Moses and Elijah, they speak of how good it is that *they* are there with Jesus. Their focus is on themselves, not Jesus. They should have said, "How good it is that Moses and Elijah are here to encourage you, Jesus, and we want to encourage you, too." This detail shows us the need to wake up and be attentive to Jesus, to focus on him and his needs, not ours.

Then, as with everyone who has an experience of God, they try to take control of the situation. Peter wants to build tents for Jesus, Moses, and Elijah, so that they can stay there forever, which was exactly the wrong thing to say. They should have remained silent and bowed down and worshiped Jesus. But they want to control God, as we all do. When the cloud comes, they are terrified. They have moved from sleeping through the transfiguration to focusing on themselves to trying to control God, and when they can't control God, they become afraid. This is typical of us humans, isn't it? Instead of serving and worshiping

God and encouraging one another on the way of the cross, we struggle to gain control and become afraid when we can't. Jesus, too, would have been tired from climbing Mount Tabor, but he is fully awake and alive, thinking about his journey to Jerusalem and what awaits him there. He is not afraid but transfigured into white light and peace and is consoled by the presence of Moses and Elijah and their heartfelt encouragement.

With all these details to ponder, the ultimate question is: Dare we encourage Jesus on his journey of the cross? Can we do what Peter and the others were unable to do? Can we support Jesus in his ongoing exodus work to lead humanity out of death and into life?

Then a voice speaks from the cloud and names Jesus "My Beloved," "My Chosen One," just as before by the Jordan River after his baptism. This time, however, the voice is addressed to the terrified disciples and issues a new commandment: "Listen to Jesus!" If we ever wondered what God would say if God just spoke out loud to us from the heavens, this is it: Listen to Jesus. Like Peter, James, and John, it's the one thing we do not do and do not want to do. We remain asleep, and when we wake up, we try to take control of God and get God to do what we want, and then we become afraid when we can't bend God's will to ours. Jesus keeps talking about the way of the cross, and we simply do not want to hear it, do not want to encourage him, even if Moses and Elijah themselves show up and do just that, even if God speaks directly to us from the heavens.

As we sit with the story of the transfiguration, we realize that God is telling each of us to listen to Jesus and then to do what he says. Luke has just outlined everything Jesus would say to us: "Repent and believe the good news of God's reign. Love your enemies, turn the other cheek, bless those who curse you, do good to those who hate you, stop judging, stop condemning, forgive, and be as merciful, as compassionate, as God." To be doers of the word, we first have to be listeners of the word. For the rest of our lives, we want to be people who listen to Jesus, who read his Gospel, sit with his words in quiet meditation, and put his teachings into practice in our daily lives.

They walk down the mountain, where they're met by a large crowd and a man with a sick boy who has an evil spirit that throws him into convulsions and seizures. "I begged your disciples to cast it out but they could not," he said. After his transfiguration and affirmation from Moses and Elijah, this failure on the disciples' part seems to frustrate Jesus and cause him to lament. "O faithless and perverse generation," he says, "how long will I be with you and endure you? Bring your son here." This is one of the few times, perhaps the only time, when we hear Jesus express frustration and grief over his journey, that what he is doing is such a hard and thankless task, that even his best friends remain clueless, that they don't seem at all interested in listening to him and will never be able to understand him. But he quickly regroups. He rebukes the unclean spirit, heals the boy, and gives him to the father, leaving everyone "astounded." Even if he is frustrated with the disciples—no matter. He lets it go and moves on. He keeps on showing compassion for those in need, healing the sick, teaching his disciples, and doing God's will. Once again, he models the life of compassion and nonviolence. Like him, we have to put aside our frustrations and get on with the task of selfless service, healing, and peacemaking. And along the way, we want to learn how not to frustrate Jesus but to get on with the hard task of listening to him, doing what he wants, and becoming his faithful, Beloved Community.

With that, he turns to the disciples and tries to teach them one more time the hard facts of discipleship. "Pay attention to what I am telling you," he says. That right there is a clue. God just told Peter, James, and John to listen to him, and now he tells the whole group to listen to him. Why does he say, "Pay attention"? Because they were *not* paying attention. Not much has changed. We all try to tell Jesus what to do, what needs to be done, what he should do for us. Luke invites us to pay attention to what Jesus says and does, and to do likewise.

"The Son of Humanity is to be handed over to men," he says. This utterly baffles the disciples—as well as us readers. He has a successful thing going on. Huge crowds follow him. Everyone wants to be near him. People want to be healed by him. Why would he wreck it or allow himself to get into some kind of trouble? Like Matthew and Mark, Luke emphasizes the point: "They did not understand this saying; its meaning was hidden from them so that they should not understand it, and they were afraid to ask him about this saying." This trend continues today among Christians; we do not understand the way of the cross and are afraid to talk about it. We would prefer not to risk our lives in nonviolent resistance to the culture of injustice and war, so we don't do that, much less talk about it. We do that to our detriment. Actually, Jesus's way of the cross is the path toward our salvation, toward justice and peace, toward a new world if we want it.

Instead, like the disciples, we start arguing about which one of us is the greatest. Instead of focusing on the way of the cross and accompanying the nonviolent Jesus today in the struggle for justice and disarmament, we're stuck in egotism, narcissism, pride, and arrogance, thinking that we know better, that we deserve honors and attention, that we're better than others. "An argument arose among the disciples about which of them was the greatest," Luke reports. He was trying to tell them that he was to be tortured and executed, and they argue among themselves about who's the greatest. It would be comical if it wasn't so tragic. Throughout churches today, everyone argues about who is greater, and most of us think we are. Meanwhile, Jesus is still talking about the way of the cross and the need for us to follow him there. We need to finally shut up, stop focusing on ourselves, listen to him, and get on with the way of the cross as a life of permanent nonviolent resistance to the culture.

But notice: Jesus has infinite compassion toward them. He does not blow up or chastise them. He was frustrated with them earlier, but he took a deep breath and centered himself in God's mercy once again. He's so nonviolent that he shows infinite patience toward his egotistic male disciples. Luke says he took a child, placed it by his side, and said, "Whoever receives this child in my name receives me, and whoever receives me, receives the One who sent me. For the one who is least among all of you is the one who is the greatest." In this teaching, he actually encourages us to be the greatest, but he turns the definition of the greatest upside down. Instead of being the strongest, most powerful person, the greatest is the smallest and least among us. If you want to be great, then be the last and least, the servant of all. As we go downward into humility, we lose interest in arguing about being great. We become humble and compassionate.

John changes the subject. "Master, we saw someone casting out demons in your name and we tried to prevent him because he does not follow in our company," he says. Notice that for John the focus again is not on Jesus but on himself and the other disciples. John's upset that someone else is doing Jesus's work but is not part of "our company." He wants to control this person, but Jesus is not interested in controlling anybody. He's interested in casting out all demons and liberating everyone into the freedom and new life of God's reign. He's on a mission. "Do not prevent him," Jesus says, "for whoever is not against you is for you." From now on, we presume that everyone is on the side of Jesus, on the journey of peace, nonviolence, compassion, and love. If they are not actively against us and this path of peace, then they are on the journey with Jesus, even if they do not know it. They simply need to be encouraged to follow the nonviolent Jesus more and more.

Jesus's Grassroots Campaign of Peace and Nonviolence Begins (9:51–10:42)

More than any other Gospel, Luke makes clear that Jesus was a grassroots movement organizer and leader like Mahatma Gandhi and Dr. King, and that he launched a determined *satyagraha* campaign of truth and nonviolence from Galilee to Jerusalem, where he confronted systemic injustice in a dramatic, symbolic act of civil disobedience. The turning point is worth noting: Lk. 9:51. This is the moment when the Jesus movement is officially launched: "When the days for his being taken up were fulfilled, he resolutely determined to journey to Jerusalem, and he sent messengers ahead of him."

To understand the profound meaning of this sentence, we need to turn again to Gandhi and King. After one year of preparation and training in nonviolence, Mahatma Gandhi set off on March 12, 1930, with seventy-eight nonviolent resisters on a twenty-four-day, 239-mile march from his ashram to the coastal town of Dandi, where he made salt from the ocean and called for India's independence from Britain. Because Britain held a total monopoly on salt in India, Gandhi's act was illegal. Initially, his friends and followers were dismayed at Gandhi's symbolic choice of salt. But hundreds of millions of oppressed Indians were galvanized by his march and action, and they undertook their own local civil disobedience actions, including distributing and selling the illegal salt. Over sixty thousand Indians were jailed for civil disobedience in the months that followed. Gandhi's campaign marked the beginning of the end of British rule in India. Gandhi's march and nonviolent civil disobedience campaign illustrate what Jesus did two thousand years earlier, as he "resolutely" set off for Jerusalem, where he would break the law and confront imperial rule with the power of truth and nonviolence.

We see Jesus's campaign as well in the historic civil rights march from Selma to Montgomery, Alabama, which began on March 7, 1965, when John Lewis and Hosea Williams led some six hundred people out of Selma to protest the many racist restrictions that prevented African Americans from voting. When they reached the Edmund Pettus Bridge, they were attacked and severely beaten by hundreds of white Alabama police officers. Two days later, Dr. King led twenty-five hundred African Americans on a second march but stopped it after they crossed the bridge so as not to violate the federal court injunction. On March 21, a third march to the state capitol began. By the time they arrived in Montgomery on March 25, more than twenty-five thousand people had joined them, including religious leaders from around the nation such as Rev. Daniel Berrigan, Rev. Henri Nouwen, and Rabbi Abraham Heschel. There, Dr. King gave a dramatic speech, saying,

We are on the move now and no wave of racism can stop us. We are on the move now. The burning of our churches will not deter us. The bombing of our homes will not dissuade us. We are on the move now. The beating and killing of our clergymen and young people will not divert us. We are on the move now. The wanton release of their known murderers will not discourage us. We are on the move now. Like an idea who time has come, not even the marching of mighty armies can halt us. We are moving to the land of freedom! (*A Testament of Hope,* ed. Washington, 228–29)

After repeating the phrase "How long? Not long!" he ended by quoting the famous hymn, saying, "Our God is marching on! Glory, hallelujah. Glory, hallelujah. His truth is marching on!" A few months later, their efforts produced the Voting Rights Act, securing the right to vote for all Americans.

Like Gandhi and Dr. King, Jesus sent organizers ahead of him preparing people for his arrival, energizing the population, and calling people to welcome God's reign of peace. All of this was dangerous and illegal in that occupied landscape. Though his actions would lead to his arrest and execution, as we know now, the movement continued for three centuries as the early Christians refused to fight for the Roman Empire or to idolize Caesar even at the cost of their own lives, and in doing so, they helped hasten the fall of empire.

The first test of their nonviolence came as James and John entered a Samaritan village to prepare for Jesus's arrival only to be told that Jesus was not welcome because he was headed to Jerusalem, where their hated enemies, the Judeans, lived. Clearly, James and John were not prepared for rejection. But Jesus was. He had survived the assassination attempt in his hometown of Nazareth and the ongoing hostility of the religious authorities. He expected rejection.

So, what do James and John do? How do they respond to this rejection? They ask Jesus, "Lord, do you want us to call down fire from heaven to consume them?" They had just heard the Sermon on the Plain and been commanded to practice universal love and creative nonviolence, and how do they respond? "Do you want us to call down fire from heaven to consume them?" Luke writes simply that Jesus turned around and rebuked them.

This is one of the most telling episodes in the Gospels and, unfortunately, even more relevant today. Two thousand years later, we still want to call down hellfire on those who threaten or anger us. In fact, we have actually built the most destructive weapons in history to do it, and then we did it. We called down nuclear hellfire and killed hundreds of thousands of sisters and brothers in Hiroshima and Nagasaki, and since then, we have built tens of thousands more nuclear weapons and are closer than ever to using them, even at the risk of killing the human race and destroying the planet. We have far surpassed the ignorance, the violence, and the will to kill and destroy demonstrated by Jesus's closest friends, the brothers James and John.

For the past century, Christians have been calling down hellfire non-stop. During World War II, the fire bombings of Dresden and Tokyo were beyond comprehension. During the Vietnam War, the United States carpet-bombed Indochina and killed millions. The U.S. bombings of Iraq were actually far greater. With drone technology, we have now called down hellfire upon the people of Afghanistan and elsewhere with unmanned aircraft. By doing this, we are ensuring that someday, in this downward spiral of hellfire, we ourselves will be bombed with hellfire from the sky. What goes around comes around.

We, too, have heard Jesus's call to practice universal love and total nonviolence, but we still ask, "Lord, do you want us to kill them? Lord, do you want us to shoot them? Lord, do you want us to electrocute them? Lord, do you want us to use drones against them? Lord, do you want us to drop nuclear bombs on them?" Worse, we've gotten beyond the point of asking him. We just do it. It's as if we presume Jesus would support any violence or warmaking that we feel is necessary. Actually, we don't care what he thinks. We have totally rejected his way of nonviolence. We don't even give him lip service anymore.

What we do not realize is that we are addicted to violence and war and are out of control. Jesus's rebuke to the disciples and to us is a blessing! We should rejoice that he rebukes us because he's calling us back to sanity, trying to knock some sense into us, to do an intervention among us, to sober us up and return us to our Higher Power, the God of peace and the boundaries of nonviolence. If we support violence and war, then we have turned against the God of peace. Jesus wants us to love and serve the God of peace at all times, every moment, which means surrendering our will and doing God's will of peace and compassion. We should rejoice that Jesus is nonviolent because, in the end, after everyone in history rejects Jesus and his invitation to peace, he still has mercy on us, rebukes us, and invites us into the sanity of nonviolence.

Our wars, weapons, and bombing raids have not made us safe or secure; they have only worsened the violence in the world and bankrupted us. We might as well try Jesus's way. He wants us to stop our ongoing preparations to call down hellfire and instead to call down blessings of peace from heaven upon everyone, the holy fire of Pentecostal nonviolence upon our poor world, so that we might all live in peace with one another. Luke pleads with us to do the right thing and choose peace.

Luke then adds several short teachings about discipleship. He's trying to teach us readers what it means to follow Jesus: we have to completely surrender our lives to him and actually embark on his path. Someone says to him, "I will follow you wherever you go." Jesus answers, "Foxes have dens and birds of the sky have nests, but the Son of Humanity has nowhere to rest his head." If you want to follow Jesus, you have to let go of all worldly security as he did, enter into the groundlessness and emptiness of reality, trust completely in the God of peace, and walk forward in faith. We no longer rely on money or weapons but on God and God's transforming grace and peace.

Jesus says to someone, "Follow me," and the person responds, "Lord, let me go first and bury my father." Think for a moment: in those days, the number-one duty of a Jewish son was to care for his father and be with him until his death. In other words, this person's father is still very much alive. He's saying to Jesus, "When my father dies, when I finished my duty to attend to him, then I will come and follow you." It's a good answer, and it shows that he is a faithful, obedient son of his father. But Jesus is way beyond all that. "Let the dead bury their dead," he tells him. "You, go and proclaim the kingdom of God." Jesus wants the man to join his campaign now and not wait one more minute, no matter how noble the excuse. "Go forth and proclaim God's reign of peace and justice," he orders the man. That's what Jesus tells each of us.

Another person tells him, "I will follow you, Lord, but first let me say farewell to my family at home." This is a problem for many: we place family before discipleship to Jesus, when in fact if we placed Jesus and his work first, our families would be much better off. Jesus responds, "No one who sets a hand to the plow and looks to what was left behind is fit for the kingdom of God." The key word is "fit," as in "fitness." If we want to run a marathon, we need to go to the gym, work out, and get fit. We need to train so that we are ready for the marathon. It's the same with discipleship to Jesus. Once we put a hand to the plow, to the work of sowing seeds for a harvest of peace for the God of peace, if we turn around to see what was left behind, we lose control of the plow. It will veer off course and ruin the whole field. The desire to turn back and think of what we left behind shows that we are not fit to do the work, to plow a field for God's reign. We have not yet surrendered our lives to Jesus, God's reign, and the work at hand. That's what Jesus wants and needs—total dedication to steering the plow and planting a new field for a new harvest of peace for the God of peace.

"Go on Your Way; Behold I Am Sending You like Lambs among Wolves" (10:1–24)

With that, the campaign begins. Jesus creates thirty-six teams of nonviolence trainers and sends them out in all directions into the war-torn countryside to invite people out of war, poverty, racism, and empire into the new life of loving nonviolence. He's not just a community organizer or a movement builder; he's a nonviolent general who commands a nonviolent army. But instead of waging war, he wages peace. He sends them out to disarm everyone, dismantle the empire, and lead humanity into the peace of God's reign. He mobilizes an astonishing campaign of active nonviolence, an authentic peace movement—right there on the edge of the brutal empire, and it will continue until he gets to Jerusalem, and after that, too.

"Go on your way!" he begins. Note the imperative tense: *Get going! Go forth and make peace!* In Matthew, he says, "Be wise as serpents and innocent as doves"—which means there are times when we get to "coo," but times when we need to "hiss." That's what people of nonviolence do: we coo and hiss, but we don't hurt anyone. Here in Luke, he says simply: "Behold, I am sending you like lambs among wolves." What an image! Jesus sends us into the world of war, greed, and violence as peaceful, gentle, unarmed people. We are to be as vulnerable and harmless as lambs.

Now let's take a moment and imagine a little lamb surrounded by a pack of wolves. That's Jesus's description of the life of the disciple, the life of nonviolence in a culture of violence, the peacemaker in a world of permanent war. What can we expect when we go forth to make peace? To be eaten alive! This has been my experience. Yes, I've met many nonviolent peacemakers, and sometimes I've been well received, but I have more often found myself surrounded by a pack of wolves that growl, show their teeth, and seem ready to pounce. Occasionally, they do. This is the normal life of the authentic peacemaker. If you are really speaking out for peace, you will encounter the wolves. I can testify to that after a lifetime of arrests, jailings, rejections, courtroom hearings, guilty verdicts, death threats, church condemnations, insults, hate mail, and so forth. This is the life of nonviolence if you dare to go deep. We get to practice nonviolence and see how real, how true, how authentic our commitment to Jesus's way really is!

The problem for me and for most of us is that we forget our "lamb" nature and think we have to become wolves in order to transform the other wolves. But that is not the way of the Good Shepherd, the Lamb of God, our gentle Jesus. He insists that nonviolence is not only the best way to change things but is also our true nature as the sons and daughters of the God of peace.

Beware of wolves in sheep's clothing, he says elsewhere. If we undertake this painful mission of peacemaking in a culture of war, we need to be lambs in lamb's clothing, not wolves in sheep's clothing. We need to get rid of the violence within, the roots of war and empire that lurk inside us. Given that we are all addicted to violence, perhaps it's better to say, we need to befriend our inner "wolf" and disarm him. We need to participate in our own inner disarmament and cultivate our true nonviolent nature if we are going to enter the culture of violence, meanness, and militarism and offer a real gift of peace. The goal, we remember from Isaiah, is that the lion—and the wolf—will lie down with the lamb. Neither kills nor is killed.

The details of the mission are clear: take nothing for the journey—no money, no sack, no sandals—and greet no one on the way. When we remember that Jesus is sending his followers into the Galilean countryside where the Roman death squads roam around, on alert to kill anyone who stirs up the public with talk of revolution, then his admonition makes perfect sense. He's organizing an underground movement. His advice is practical. Be on alert, ready to go. There's nothing idealistic about this; it's serious and practical.

The disciples' mission is to proclaim peace, bring peace, make peace, and welcome God's peace. Jesus instructs:

"Into whatever house you enter, first say: 'Peace to this household.' If a peaceful person lives there, your peace will rest on him; but if not, it will return to you. Stay in the same house and eat and drink what is offered to you, for the laborer deserves his payment. Do not move about from one house to another. Whatever town you enter and they welcome you, eat what is set before you, cure the sick in it and say to them, 'The reign of God is at hand for you.' Whatever town you enter and they do not receive you, go out into the streets and say, 'The dust of your town that clings to our feet, even that we shake off against you.' Yet know this: 'The reign of God is at hand.' I tell you, it will be more tolerable for Sodom on that day than for that town."

If we try to apply this mission to our lives today, the first step would be to learn the language of peace. From now on, every word we speak is a word of peace. We try to make people feel at peace, to be a peaceful presence in their midst, to affirm their peace, and to lead people deeper into God's peace in their own lives, even in their own homes. By being calm and peaceful, he suggests, we offer a healing gift. My friend and teacher Thich Nhat Hanh put it this way: If you are a rock of peace, if you attend to that first and foremost, you will bring peace to everyone around you. You will be mindful of every word you say so that you practice nonviolent communication, so that your presence and your words serve, disarm, and heal others, so that you truly are an instrument of God's peace. In the end, all our words "make for peace" and we spend our lives in one long spiritual conversation of peace and nonviolence.

This mission and work of peace are really needed today. We seem to speak only the language of war and violence, even in our day-to-day relationships and encounters. We yell at one another as we drive, we fight with relatives and coworkers, and we add to the general maelstrom of anger and hatred that fills the airwaves and the internet. Worse, we Christians seem to be leading the way. We seem full of hate, hell-bent on the anti-Christ mission and language of violence, anger, hatred, condemnation, and war.

Each one of us can do our part to change this direction by taking up Jesus's campaign of nonviolence, adopting his language of peace and nonviolence, and practicing his peace so that our very presence is disarming and healing. Wherever we go, we can talk about God's reign of peace, help people step into God's reign of nonviolence, and work for a new culture without war, poverty, racism, or violence. We can spend our lives living his mission.

Notice that Luke's Jesus issues blessings to those who welcome people of peace and warnings to those who reject peace. To his disciples, he advises them to shake off the dust from the places that reject them so they are not tainted by rejection, so they hold no grudges, hurts, or resentments. He tells them to keep their focus on God's reign and on proclaiming God's reign, not on being rejected. Notice that his warnings to those who reject the peacemaking disciples are addressed socially, not just to individuals but to communities, towns, and cities. Those villages which reject his peacemaking disciples will suffer worse consequences than the mythically sinful and unjust city of Sodom.

In particular, Luke's Jesus offers two woes. "Woe to you, Chorazin! Woe to you, Bethsaida! For if the mighty deeds done in your midst had been done in Tyre and Sidon, they would long ago have repented, sitting in sackcloth and ashes. But it will be more tolerable for Tyre and Sidon at the judgment than for you." These two Galilean villages where Jesus preached could have repented and transformed themselves into communities of peace. He compares their failure to repent to the Gentile villages of Tyre and Sidon, where he must have been well received. They would have responded like the people of Nineveh, by sitting in sackcloth and ashes.

If Jesus issues such dire warnings to Chorazin and Bethsaida, what would he say to Washington, D.C., and New York City, where so much imperial military power, systemic violence, and corporate greed threaten to destroy the planet? One can conclude that the major cities of the Global North, especially in the United States, will suffer far worse spiritual consequences than Chorazin and Bethsaida because of their divisions, injustice, and violence. We asked this question every year in the small desert town of Los Alamos, New Mexico, where all U.S. nuclear weapons are built. Each year on the anniversary of the U.S. atomic bombing of Hiroshima, hundreds of us walk through Los Alamos, put on sackcloth, pour ashes on the streets, and sit in contemplative prayer and silence "to repent for the mortal sin of war and nuclear weapons and beg the God of peace for the gift of nuclear disarmament," as I have instructed the crowd every year. We are trying to do what Chorazin and Bethsaida did not do, what the people of Nineveh did. This public act of repentance is the kind of response Luke's Jesus expects at a minimum if we want to enter God's reign of peace. If we are in a far worse predicament today than the people of Chorazin and Bethsaida, then we need to get busy repenting together, as cities and nations, and begin re-forming ourselves into communities of peace.

"As for you, Capernaum, will you be exalted to heaven? You will go down to the nether-world," he continues. Capernaum was the hometown of Peter, where the community house was located. After all the miracles and teachings Jesus offered there, they too should have repented and transformed, he explains, but they did not. They went on with business as usual, and together they will suffer the spiritual consequences of not repenting. Because they did not convert to nonviolence and resist imperial violence, they would be destroyed by the empire.

"Whoever listens to you, listens to me," Jesus concludes. "Whoever rejects you, rejects me. And whoever rejects me, rejects the one who sent me." These teachings promise that, if we sincerely, honestly, prayerfully, and nonviolently speak the Gospel message of peace in Jesus's name, then we speak for him. If we hear someone speaking this Gospel message in his name, we should listen and take the message to heart, because Jesus himself is speaking to us, and so is the God of peace. One lesson to take from these teachings is that we should listen only to and for the voices that speak the words of peace and nonviolence. We should not take any other voices to heart. From now on, we are on alert to hear the words of the nonviolent Jesus and the God of peace as spoken by the peacemakers in our midst.

What's so shocking about Luke 10 is that the Galilee 72 apparently fulfilled their mission! "The seventy-two returned rejoicing," Luke writes, "and said, 'Lord, even the demons are subject to us because of your name.'" They had indeed gone into villages, spoken the words of peace, offered themselves as peaceful people, healed people by their peaceful presence and message, and taught everyone about God's reign, inviting everyone to this new way of life. They were welcomed, and their message was taken to heart. The disciples were surprised and amazed to find that people were open and hungry for the good news of peace. The seventy-two were profoundly consoled and filled with joy. They had served God and made a positive difference in the lives of many people.

Luke is teaching us about the positive spiritual consequences of joining Jesus's mission of peace and campaign of nonviolence. If we take up his mission, go forth and proclaim peace and God's reign, and heal others through our peaceful presence, we ourselves will be greatly blessed, consoled, and filled with joy. Because this is the work of God and the Holy Spirit, we will receive spiritual consolation. This is the most important work we can do with our lives from God's perspective, and God will bless us here and now if we do this. We will feel the positive effects in our lives. This rings true for me and all my friends who engage in public peacework. Despite the periodic rejection and persecution we experience, deep down we know an inner joy and spiritual consolation that cannot be found anywhere else. Our lives have deep meaning because we are doing the work of the God of peace in a world of war.

But the story doesn't end there. Luke goes on to tell us for the first time how Jesus reacts, in particular, how Jesus feels. "I observed Satan fall like lightning from the sky," he tells them. Once again, we're hearing a code word for the Roman Empire. By organizing and launching his grassroots campaign of peace and nonviolence, Jesus could see the beginning of the end of the empire. It was falling like lightning from the sky. This is what Gandhi experienced in his famous 1930 Salt March. Once he arrived at the sea and made his illegal salt, breaking the British monopoly, he set off a grassroots movement that ensured the end of British rule over India. Gandhi could see the end of British rule that day, even though the leaders of the British Empire could not, and other movement leaders could not. Gandhi lit a fire that ignited among the populace and empowered everyone to shake off tyranny. Likewise, Jesus could see the end of the Roman Empire the day the seventy-two disciples returned rejoicing. Grassroots movements of peace and nonviolence, which announce the end of war, injustice, greed, and oppression, always work. They begin to erode the prevailing anti-God culture, and eventually the culture of violence collapses, giving birth to a new world, if people want it.

"Behold, I have given you power," Jesus tells his disciples, "power 'to tread upon serpents' and scorpions and upon the full force of the enemy and nothing will harm you." What a promise! We have been given power—power over all the forces of death. We have a way to resist every form of violence and transform it without being destroyed in the process.

This is how Dr. King defined nonviolence. "Nonviolence is power," he said. We are not powerless, he insisted. The empire, the war machine, the media, the culture of violence want us to feel powerless, inadequate, and helpless, but that is not God's will. God gives us the power of love and truth through the grassroots methodology of fearless, courageous nonviolence to bring down the structures of violence and injustice—in Dr. King's case, to take on segregation, racism, and war. Gandhi, too, told the people of India that, even though they were poor, they had far more power than the British Empire in all its pomp and glory. He was speaking of "people power." If we come together, organize ourselves, and stand firm in nonviolent opposition, we can get the British to leave India peacefully, he said. He described active nonviolence as "a force more powerful than all the weapons of the world combined"—if only we dared to use it. If we claim it, practice it, and live it, we can trust that our survival is already guaranteed. This is the promise of Jesus: if you practice and teach nonviolence, no harm will come to you. Nothing can truly hurt you. Instead, you will wield the power of God to disarm and transform the world.

The best way to respond to this teaching is to experiment with it. I have done so over the course of forty years and have experienced its truth while under arrest, in jail, in war zones, and in public confrontations, even when I've been threatened personally with violence and death. I always felt the God of peace protecting me. I believe Gandhi and Dr. King would say the same thing, that they were protected throughout their lives. Like Jesus, they were willing to give their lives for the cause of nonviolence, justice, and disarmament, if it would help, and they would know that, no matter what, they would be held safely in God's hands.

"Do not rejoice because the spirits are subject to you," Jesus tells the seventy-two. "Rejoice because your names are written in heaven." Here again is a surprising and happy teaching: he wants us to rejoice! The only suggestion he makes is that we do not focus on ourselves. In effect, he's saying, do not claim any credit for expelling demons or working miracles; only God can do that. God is working through us; we are simply channels. All the credit goes to God, who chooses to work through us if we allow it. Focus instead on God and God's reign, even in your joy. Rejoice because your names are written in heaven. God knows well what we have done because God has worked through us and God will remember this. God has written our names in God's book. We can rejoice at what God is doing in our lives, and that we are of service to the God of peace.

I suggest that this is something worth aspiring to, that we should live so that our names are written in God's book. Anyone who participates in God's peace movement and Jesus's campaign will make the heavenly ledger. If we participate in Jesus's peace and nonviolence movement today, then deep down, no matter what, we are people of joy. I have experienced that in the great peacemakers that I have personally known, such as Daniel Berrigan, Desmond Tutu, Coretta Scott King, Mother Teresa, Dom Helder Camara, Cesar Chavez, John Lewis, Franziska Jägerstätter, Paul Farmer, and Thich Nhat Hanh.

"At that moment, Jesus rejoiced in the Holy Spirit," Luke writes. This is momentous! *This is the only occasion in the four Gospels where Jesus is filled with joy!* Why does Jesus rejoice? Because his followers did what he said, went forth as missionaries, and proclaimed peace and brought peace to those they encountered. For those who wish to follow Jesus, this outcome should be our goal. We want to make Jesus rejoice because we are doing his work and bringing God's "kingdom" into reality here and now. We do not want to make Jesus sad, to hurt Jesus, to betray Jesus, or to crucify him all over again. To make Jesus rejoice today requires that each of us carry on his public campaign of peace. We try to go forth as the seventy-two did and speak words of peace to the culture of war, heal all victims of violence, and proclaim the coming of God's reign as a new culture of justice, compassion, and peace. We try to fulfill our own mission of peacemaking and experience the joy and consolation of proclaiming God's reign publicly and, in the promise, make Jesus rejoice. As his followers, we want to bring Jesus only joy, not grief.

"I give you praise, Father, Lord of heaven and earth, for although you have hidden these things from the wise and the learned you have revealed them to the childlike," Jesus says rejoicing. "Yes, Father, such has been your gracious will." Whereas we might expect intellectuals, lawyers, politicians, religious authorities, the rich, and the powerful to fulfill Jesus's mission of nonviolence, that does not happen. Only those who open themselves freely to the vision and will of Jesus can accept his mission and fulfill it. Moreover, Jesus names this precisely as the "gracious will" of God, that the childlike, not the wise and learned, embrace and fulfill his mission of peace. With this profound revelation, we might examine ourselves to see which category we fall into—the wise and the learned who reject Jesus's way of nonviolence, or the childlike who embrace it and fulfill it.

I would like to pause for a moment over these two words: *gracious will*. If you asked me, "What has been the most difficult passage, the greatest breakthrough you have had studying these Gospels?" I would point to these two words. How could it be God's will that God has revealed the wisdom, way, hope, and vision of Gospel nonviolence to so few people, to the childlike, and not to everyone? Why have so few Christians in the last two thousand years understood Jesus's message and campaign of peace and nonviolence? How could this be God's will? Why is it God's *gracious* will?

This is one of the rare occasions in the Gospels where Jesus refers to God's will, and, in order to understand Jesus's way of nonviolence, we have to understand God's will. We heard his mother in the story of the Annunciation say to Gabriel, in effect, "Behold, I am the servant of God. I only want to do God's will, so yes let it be done according to your word." We hear Jesus teach his disciples to pray in the "Our Father," by begging, "Your kingdom come, your will be done on earth as it is in heaven." We will hear Jesus later, the night before he is executed, pray for the same grace, "Not my will, but your will be done."

If we apply the vision and methodology of Gandhian/Kingian nonviolence to the life of

Jesus, eventually we also have to apply it to our understanding of God, to all spirituality and theology. We heard Jesus announce in the Sermon on the Mount that God is a peacemaker and the God of universal love, which means God is nonviolent. Jesus then calls all of us to be sons and daughters of this God of peace, nonviolence, and universal love.

But if God is truly, totally nonviolent—then God *has* to give humanity complete and total free will! There can't be, in our God, one drop of violence or coercion toward any single human being. God cannot appear to us in all God's glory in Times Square, because humanity would all repent, fall down in worship and awe, and focus on God. Instead, God treats us like any loving, nonviolent parent. God lets us grow and fail and fall until we mature into peaceful adult sons and daughters. He invites us over the centuries through his saints and prophets to the wisdom of peace, nonviolence, and compassion—and finally he sends us the nonviolent Jesus, the clearest revelation of the nature of God in all of human history. So God does not force us to love one another, to make peace, to work for justice, to be nonviolent. Instead, God invites us, calls us, and guides us to his way and wisdom of nonviolence until that day when the scales fall from our eyes and hearts and we see and know what it means to be human—to be loving, peaceful, and nonviolent. We're all like Helen Keller, blind, deaf, and mute, crazy in our violence, until that day when we finally make the connection that the Teacher has patiently tried to teach us—that these finger movements in her hand mean water; that God really wants us to drop our weapons, love and serve one another, and live forever in peace and nonviolence here and now as God's sons and daughters. The more one reflects on the mystery of God's great gift of free will, the more we realize how gentle, loving, and kind God is to each and every one of us, how *gracious* God's will is, that even in the desire for us to learn the way of nonviolence, God remains patient, gentle, and nonviolent. We do have a gracious God, whose will is infinitely gracious. For me, in some ways, these are the most profound two words of the Gospels.

If, as followers of Jesus, we want to bring him joy and lead him to praise God for us, for our part in his ongoing grassroots campaign of peace and nonviolence, we have to be childlike, which means, we have to be the people who fulfill God's gracious will. The question becomes, How do we do that? Every word out of the mouth of Jesus teaches us how to do that, especially the Sermon on the Mount and the Sermon on the Plain. But, as I study these words, I think it all comes down to complete surrender of our will to God's will. Like Mary in Nazareth and Jesus at Gethsemane, our prayer becomes over and over again, "Your will, not mine, be done." Jesus invites us to surrender every part of our lives, our hearts, our minds, and our souls to God, to surrender every single problem, struggle, and crisis we face, every trace of fear, anger, resentment, hostility, hatred, or violence, everything to God—to let it all go and then live in the peace of knowing that God is in control of our lives and we do not have to worry about or fear anything. We are the ones who do God's gracious will, and we now join Jesus in inviting everyone to do God's gracious will of peace and nonviolence through total surrender of our will.

But there's still more that lies within these mysterious words. If it's God's gracious will to give us free will and not force us to do God's will of nonviolence, and if humanity to a person down through history has consistently rejected God's will of nonviolence to the point that now we have permanent warfare and poverty, nuclear weapons, and catastrophic climate change on the brink of global destruction, then this gracious, gentle God must be a God of permanent suffering love who is patiently waiting for every single human being to put down the sword and come back home to God's house of peace and live in God's way of nonviolence. Luke will suggest this image of a patient God who waits for us and is on the lookout for us to turn around and return home in his memorable parable of the prodigal son.

"All things have been handed over to me by my Father," Luke's Jesus says as a kind of coda to the story. "No one knows who the Son is except the Father, and who the Father is except the Son and anyone to whom the Son wishes to reveal him." Here we have a theme that will later be explored by John's Gospel: the relationship between God the Father and God the Son and the revelation of God the Father by the Son to those he chooses. We readers are beginning to realize that Jesus is the beloved Son of God, that he has revealed himself to his disciples, and that the more they follow him and do what he says, the more the empire crumbles and God's reign comes to earth. "Turning to the disciples in private he said, 'Blessed are the eyes that see what you see. For I say to you, many prophets and kings desired to see what you see, but did not see it, and to hear what you hear, but did not hear it.'" With that, we too are let in on the secret, the revelation that only the peacemaking disciples witnessed.

The story of the Galilee 72 invites further reflection and study, and even our own experimentation and implementation. We can ask, Why do we hear so little about the Galilee 72? Who were they? What became of them? Why don't we honor and emulate them? Do we want to fulfill the mission of peace, like them, and have our names written in heaven, and make Jesus rejoice? Dare we go forth and speak the words of peace to the culture of war, heal the victims of violence, expel the demons of destruction, and proclaim God's reign? We might note that the most beloved saint in history, St. Francis of Assisi, took this passage to heart. He saw his life as a long peacemaking mission, and he tried to send his brothers and sisters out on that mission. Like Jesus, he rejoiced when they fulfilled their mission. Like the first disciples and St. Francis himself, we should get on with the work of peace to help make Jesus rejoice.

I think Jesus is still looking to send people out on his mission of peace and nonviolence. Any one of us can experiment with this text and undertake our own mission of peace. We can go forth into the streets with our friends and hold up our signs calling for an end to war, racism, nuclear weapons, and environmental destruction, and the coming of a new land of peace and justice. We can be like lambs in the midst of wolves and model the nonviolence of Jesus. We too can denounce the demons of war and systemic violence and wield the power of nonviolence through public protest and resistance movements, and rejoice to see that power unfold and transform the culture.

Luke 10 asks, "How have we undertaken the Gospel mission of peace today? How is the nonviolent Jesus sending us out as peacemaking lambs into the midst of wolves to announce the good news of peace and practice nonviolence? How do we proclaim God's reign of peace, expel the demons of war, heal the victims of violence, and wield the power of nonviolence even in the face of the culture of death? How have we experienced God's protection and not come to harm as we have taken to the streets publicly in grassroots campaigns of nonviolence, disarmament, and justice? When have we seen the empire of war and injustice fall? What causes us to rejoice in our work for justice and creation? Do we rejoice that our names are written in heaven? Does our discipleship lead Jesus to rejoice?" Luke's story urges us to put aside our fears and set out on the mission like the seventy-two and know that, as we do, the culture of war and violence will start to fall all over again, and one day we too will rejoice that our names are being written in heaven.

"Do This and You Will Live" (10:25–42)

In the Sermon on the Plain, Luke packed together all of Jesus's commandments of universal love, universal compassion, and total nonviolence. Then, he presented a story found only in his Gospel of Jesus sending out seventy-two disciples to go ahead of him in a grassroots movement to live and proclaim these teachings. Now, when confronted by an expert in the law, Luke's Jesus gives us another one-of-a-kind, staggering parable about the meaning and practice of unconditional, nonviolent, compassionate love. Luke begins by telling us that this great "scholar of the law" (probably a scribe) stood up to test Jesus. Right there, we see a problem. We now know that we should never test Jesus, just do what he says. This legal expert doesn't know what we know and puts the question to him: "Teacher, what must I do to inherit eternal life?" Notice once again that the legal expert focuses on himself, not God, as if it's his right to "inherit" eternal life. He is entitled; he does not approach Jesus as a beggar. "What is written in the law?" Jesus asks him. "How do you read it?" Notice that Jesus does not dismiss the expert or get angry but instead meets him where he is—focusing on the Mosaic law itself. "You shall love the Lord, your God, with all your heart, with all your being, with all your strength, and with all your mind, and your neighbor as yourself," the scholar says. "You have answered correctly," Jesus tells him. "Do this and you will live."

Astute readers will notice how Luke has reversed Mark and Matthew's telling. In this case, Jesus questions the questioner, draws out the answer from the legal expert, and then affirms his answer. As with Mark and Matthew, the commandment is to love God with all one's heart, being, strength, and mind. But, instead of adding a second commandment, Luke adds Mark's and Matthew's second to the first, to make it one great commandment to practice universal love for God and neighbor. Luke insists that we are created for universal love, and we should spend our days in universal love for God and every human being and all of creation. Luke breaks down the difference between God and neighbor to call us into the practice of Christlike love. In doing so, he describes the way of Jesus, who loved God with all his heart, soul, mind, and strength, morning, noon, and night, and equally loved every human being he met with all his heart, soul, mind, and strength, even if that person did not love him back or threatened him with violence.

"Do this and you will live," Jesus tells the legal expert. He calls the legal expert to go beyond the boundaries of the law into unconditional, universal love for God and all humanity. If you do this, he teaches, you will live, meaning, you will enter eternal life today in the presence of God and live in the fullness of life from now on with the God of life. Because we love universally both God and neighbor, we have no room for anything that opposes that love, anything anti-love. Death cannot come near us. We live, and will live, forever with God.

Luke uses this encounter to increase the tension and offer a unique parable, one of the most famous stories in history, the parable of the Good Samaritan. It is worth several readings and a great deal of reflection. This story is meant to be put into practice. Luke's Jesus wants us to live out the parable, that we all might live in the fullness of life from now on. But living out the parable is probably the last thing the legal expert—or any of us—wants to do!

First, we notice that the legal expert wishes to justify himself before Jesus. Here we find a common human defect: we want the praise, focus, and attention to be on us, not someone else. We want to justify ourselves, to make ourselves look good before others. So the legal expert asks, "And who is my neighbor?" He's trying to catch Jesus, to show off before Jesus, and to trap Jesus in a discussion about the law. But once again, Jesus seizes the opportunity to call the legal expert and all of us beyond the boundaries of the Mosaic law and into the wide horizons of God's limitless, compassionate love.

The story is familiar to most of us, but the longer we sit with it, the more revolutionary it becomes. A man was robbed, stripped, beaten to a pulp, and left for dead along the dangerous desert road from Jerusalem to Jericho. He lay in a ditch, covered with blood, as three people passed. The first two were experts in the Mosaic law—a Levite and a Jewish priest. Both saw him, and both crossed the road to avoid him. He would have been considered unclean, and, according to the law, one does not go near someone who is unclean. The third person saw him and was moved with compassion and pity. He had empathy—he noticed the feelings of others and cared for those who suffered. He too was preoccupied with his journey, but for him compassion toward those in need came first. He stopped his journey in the face of human suffering because he had placed a priority on relieving human suffering. That's what it means to be human—to put first those who are suffering.

Luke uses a long list of active verbs to tell what the man did. He saw the man, he was moved with compassion, he approached him, he poured oil and wine on his wounds, he bandaged them, he lifted him up on his horse, he took him to an inn, and he cared for him. Note this: the next day, Luke says, he gave two silver coins—a fortune—to the innkeeper with instructions to take care of the injured man at any cost, with a promise that he would repay the innkeeper on his return journey. This means that the man spent the whole night in the inn caring for the victim! He interrupted his trip, postponed his journey, and dropped everything to restore the injured man to health.

The traveler's goodness and compassion are unconditional. He puts others before himself, particularly those who are suffering. But the man's identity is the shocker: he's a Samaritan, a hated enemy of the Judeans. Samaritans were beyond unclean; they were evil and should be killed. Jesus names the hero of the story as the hated enemy of the legal expert. It would be like telling a group of fundamentalist Christians that the highest example of human goodness and morality was not among them, but was a Muslim in Kabul or Baghdad, the target of U.S. missiles. They would be appalled. The parable carries a shocking punch line. It's the enemy who shows us how to love, how to be compassionate, how to be human, how to be godly.

"Which of these three, in your opinion, was neighbor to the robbers' victim?" Jesus asks the legal expert. It's a question he asks all of us. Who is my neighbor? How do I love my neighbor? How far am I willing to go to love my neighbor? Notice that Jesus twists the question and turns the noun "neighbor" into an action verb. He wants us to act like neighbors to our neighbors, which means to show unconditional compassion to any human being we ever meet, first and foremost, those who are suffering in any way.

"The one who treated him with mercy," the legal expert answers. "Go and do likewise," Jesus says. Jesus tells the legal expert that the days of religious legalism are over. From now on, we practice compassion, love, and peace toward everyone in need, everyone who suffers, and everyone who is a victim of violence, just as Jesus does.

I like to think that Jesus drew this story from his own experience. Perhaps he found someone in a ditch and spent a day and a night caring for him. Maybe Jesus himself was robbed and thrown into a ditch and someone took care of him. In either case, the story is central to Luke's understanding of Jesus. Matthew, you recall, took the story to its furthest conclusion when he identified the robbers' victim as none other than Jesus himself. "Whatever you did to the least of these, you did to me" (Mt. 25:40). Anyone in pain, anyone in need, anyone who is suffering is our neighbor and demands our immediate attention and compassionate action, regardless of our own plans. We are people who drop everything to serve those in need.

Martin Luther King Jr. took the parable of the Good Samaritan even further, if that's possible. The night before he was assassinated, he told the Memphis crowd that his coming to assist the garbage workers' strike was because of the Good Samaritan story. They were in need, and he had to stop what he was doing to help them. Further, he said, the whole world has become one long, dangerous Jericho Road, filled with robbers and people of violence. There were people beaten and bleeding in ditches everywhere around the world. He not only wanted to relieve the suffering of so many sisters and brothers, particularly its poor and oppressed; he wanted to disarm and transform the Jericho Road so that no one would ever again be robbed, beaten, or killed, there or anywhere! He wanted to eliminate the weapons and roots of violence so that the world would become a culture of nonviolence and the Jericho Road would be a peaceful experience.

The revolution of chapter 10 continues with one final mind-blowing story. Jesus is having dinner at the house of his friends Martha and Mary, and, instead of helping with the meal and the serving, Mary sits at the feet of Jesus listening to him speaking. Martha is upset by this and asks, "Lord, do you not care that my sister has left me by myself to do the serving? Tell her to help me." "Martha, Martha, you are anxious and worried about many things," Jesus answers. "There is need of only one thing. Mary has chosen the better part and it will not be taken from her."

It was a fair complaint, right? Why should Martha have to do all the work? Shouldn't Mary help out? That is not at all what this story is about. Martha is upset because Mary is breaking all the rules, not just of decorum, but of the Mosaic law.

For centuries, this story has been interpreted by privileged, upper-class, European men as symbolic of the tension between the active and contemplative life. To quote Joan Chittister: "Baloney!" This story is pure revolution! It's hard for us twenty-first-century readers to grasp the shocking earthquake in the nature of things here. Women were not allowed in the front room with the men! Women were certainly never allowed to sit near a holy rabbi as he taught. Not only does Mary break through the gender wall of patriarchy, but Jesus encourages it! Martha was right to be upset; this was dangerous, illegal activity that Mary was engaged in. Martha and Mary could get in trouble; even at her best, Martha could be trying to protect Jesus by telling him to tell her sister to return to the kitchen where she belonged, away from the men. But lo and behold, Jesus supports Mary and announces that this is what is needed in life—to listen to him, regardless of the consequences. If Mary was seated at his feet listening to him teach, then she has become a full-fledged disciple of Jesus. This is the true position of a disciple—to sit at the feet of the master teacher and listen to his wisdom.

With this story, Luke's Jesus breaks down the wall of patriarchy and sexism and announces that Jesus has come for everyone, women as well as men, that there are no boundaries to his way and his call to discipleship. We now know that, according to Luke, Jesus had at least one serious disciple who was a woman. In Jesus's circle, everyone is welcome, everyone is equal, everyone is included. No one is ever to be excluded again. Alas, today most Christian churches continue to exclude women, the poor, and outsiders from the fullness of discipleship life. Most prefer the old ways of patriarchy, class, domination, and exclusion. But Luke sets the standard and the measure: the one thing necessary for life is to become a serious disciple of the nonviolent Jesus, to spend our days sitting at his feet, listening to him, and doing what he says. From now on, the churches should do their best to welcome every human being into that circle of discipleship, nonviolence, and community, to help everyone listen to Jesus's teachings, and to encourage everyone to practice them publicly.

"Ask and You Will Receive; Seek and You Will Find; Knock and the Door Will Be Opened" (11:1–12:59)

Luke turns next to the subject of prayer and gathers Jesus's teachings on prayer. He starts by pointing out that Jesus "was praying in a certain place." This is an important detail for all those who would follow him. Jesus was not a mindless activist on the run, nor was he an anxious, stressed-out control freak, nor was he confused or fearful. He was focused entirely on God and his mission to promote God's reign of peace on earth. To keep the focus on God and the mission, according to Luke, Jesus took formal time every day for quiet meditation with God. Luke wants us to know that this daily communion with God in solitude is a characteristic of Jesus and therefore must become a characteristic of our discipleship. If we want to follow him and live out his teachings, we too have to spend formal time with the God of peace every day in quiet meditation. We cannot do this work or live this life or carry on the mission on our own. If Jesus needed quiet daily prayer, then certainly we do too.

We are not told how Jesus prayed or what happened, only that he went apart and quietly sat in prayerful meditation. Actually, that's more than enough to go on. That's what we can do as well. I recommend thirty minutes in the morning as the day begins so we can get our bearings and recenter ourselves, our hearts, and our lives in God. We come before God and Jesus, offer ourselves to God, surrender our will to God, let God love us, and let God speak to us. Our prayer becomes not so much telling God what to do as listening to God. Sometimes, the listening turns into simply being and attending to God's abiding presence. If we are faithful to this meditation time as the most important time of our day, then it quickly becomes a safe place where we can be our true selves and offer all our problems and struggles as well as gratitude and gifts to God. There in that quiet space, we will be healed and will be given a new level of God's peace. We will discover that we are no longer alone. From now on, we will live in a secret, intimate relationship with the God of peace just as Jesus did. We will want to spend time each day with God because there we feel loved, safe, and secure. We enjoy being with God, and living with God, and living for God. That safe place of daily quiet meditation becomes our true home. After that, we can face anything and go forward to speak and live the Gospel of peace because, over time, our lives have been completely surrendered to God and the doing of God's will.

This intimate relationship we share with God, which forms the backbone of our daily lives, becomes contagious, Luke reports. The disciples see Jesus sitting in quiet meditation, and they become curious. Notice that Jesus does not tell them to pray. He goes off quietly to pray, and they notice him doing this every single day. Finally, one of them speaks up and says, "Teach us to pray just as John taught his disciples." Like Jesus's disciples, if we study his life and behavior, we too will want to pray as he does. We will want what he has—an intimate, loving relationship with God that stands at the center of our lives.

Luke's Jesus begins his teachings on prayer with the Lord's Prayer. These teachings appeared in Matthew's Sermon on the Mount, but here, they stand alone in the context of Jesus in his own quiet meditation with God. "When you pray, say: 'Father, hallowed be your name. Your kingdom come. Give us each day our daily bread and forgive us our sins for we ourselves forgive everyone in debt to us, and do not subject us to the final test.'"

Luke deletes the first-person plural pronoun and tells us simply to address God affectionately and intimately as "Father." God is not some fearsome, cruel old man in the sky who can't wait to throw us all into hell. Instead, with this word, we know from Jesus's experience that God is a gentle, loving father who loves us, takes care of us, feeds us, and protects us. This intimate approach becomes the basis of our relationship with God. We are children who call out to our gentle, loving parent. We begin to know and experience God as gentle, loving, and kind. If we watch a really great parent in one of their better moments, we see how they are attentive, helpful, and gentle with children, how they try to make their kids happy, and how they guide their children through the day. According to this prayer, that's what God does with us, if we allow it. We let our beloved God take care of us and guide us through each day. If we turn away from God, throw a temper tantrum, spend our days screaming and yelling and even running away from home, we are lost. We also bring great pain to God. That's basically what every human being does, to varying degrees. The prayer of Jesus calls us back, first and foremost, to the primary relationship in our lives—to our gentle, loving God whom he calls "Father." We start there, before our God, attentive, present, and loving, acknowledging that God's very name is holy, and we sit in the peace and hallowedness of his name. By acknowledging his name as holy, we reject all the idols and false gods of the world, including the emperor Caesar. None of them is holy. None of them is the true, holy, living God.

The first and most important request is for the whole human race: may your reign come here and now on earth, in our hearts and lives, everywhere and for everyone. We seek God's presence, and we long for the whole human race and all of creation to live in that presence from now on.

We don't recognize this as a political prayer, but it is. With this prayer, we pray for the disruption and failure of every system and plan not aligned with the characteristics of God's reign. With this prayer, we renounce our allegiance to our nation/state and pledge our allegiance to the reign of God and all its social, economic, political, climate, and spiritual implications. We are no longer Republicans or Democrats or even Americans. We are full-time children of God and citizens of God's reign. That is why we pray morning, noon, and night: "Your kingdom come." We know that in God's reign there is no racism, no sexism, no exclusion of any kind. Every human being is beloved infinitely and unconditionally by God. That means that our many systems of judgment, coercion, and domination must be dismantled and rendered inoperable. With this prayer, everything about the world must change, starting with ourselves.

Luke has removed Matthew's next request: "Your will be done." Luke knows that if we want God's reign to come to earth, if we strive to live in God's reign every day, one day at a time, we try to do only God's will, not our own or another's. We have seen in the story of the Annunciation how Mary tells the angel that she is the servant of God, and so God's will be done. In the Garden of Gethsemane, we will hear Jesus pray, "Your will be done, not mine." We readers are learning from Mary and Jesus that doing God's will, not our own, is a prerequisite for prayer, discipleship, and the coming of God's reign of peace on earth.

In this context, we ask God for what we need: food, forgiveness, and protection. First, we ask for our daily bread. We know that God provides everything for us, that we can do nothing without God. This request is for God to take care of our bodies, our health, and our basic human needs. It will also become a request for the body of Christ in the breaking of the bread, the Christian Eucharist. It is this "Bread of Life," as John's Gospel calls it, that we are asking for and relying on. We ask for bread for ourselves and for everyone, for every hungry person on the planet. In the asking, we realize that God will use us to do the feeding and send us out to feed the hungry. Because we have asked for daily bread on behalf of the whole human race, we are happy to do our part to feed the hungry.

Next, we ask God to forgive us our debts and sins, and we pledge in the same breath to forgive everyone who ever hurt us. This request asks God to let us off the hook because we have already let everyone else off the hook. We can expect to receive the same mercy and compassion that we give others. This prayer reminds us to practice unconditional mercy, compassion, and forgiveness in the hope that God will show the same to us. Remember, too, André Trocmé's teaching that this line is part of Jesus's mission statement in Luke 4 in Nazareth, part of Isaiah's call for a Jubilee, the forgiveness of all debts owed by the poor to the rich. With this daily prayer, we tell everyone who owes us anything that they do not need to repay us. For First World North Americans, that means we forgive the debts of all poorer countries in Africa, Latin America, and Asia so that they can stand on their own and know the fullness of justice and liberation. This prayer for forgiveness calls for a radical new economics. It means we ourselves are taking up Jesus's mission and doing our part today to advance the Jubilee cancellation of debt and the global redistribution of land and wealth for the good of every person.

Finally, we ask God not to test us but, in effect, to bless us that we might live in faith, hope, love, and peace. It is the ultimate prayer of dependence on God and total surrender to our God. As with forgiveness, we do not put people to the test just as we do not want to be tested. We pledge to live faithfully according to God's will and God's reign so that God will never need to test us.

Luke's Jesus offers next a short parable about persevering in prayer.

"Suppose one of you has a friend to whom he goes at midnight and says, 'Friend, lend me three loaves of bread, for a friend of mine has arrived at my house from a journey and I have nothing to offer him.' He says in reply from within, 'Do not bother me. The door has already been locked and my children and I are already in bed. I cannot get up to give you anything.' I tell you, if he does not get up to give him the loaves because of their friendship, he will get up to give him whatever he needs because of his persistence."

The key word here is *persistence*. If we persist with God, Luke's Jesus teaches, then God will help us. Apparently, God wants to be in relationship with us. That means we are called to do God's will and to love and serve God; likewise, God will love us and help us in emergencies, such as when a friend shows up in the middle of the night and we have no food to offer. We can call on God anytime, and God will hear us and answer us. This kind of persistence in prayer, however, assumes our total surrender to God. It is the disciple who is giving 100 percent of himself or herself to God and to the way of the nonviolent Jesus who can beg God for help and be assured that he or she will be satisfied with an answer. We can trust God because we are trying to do only God's will, not our will, and so ultimately we accept whatever answer we receive. Remember, this tale concerns emergencies. Most of the time, we go through our days living in the present moment, surrendered to God, loving everyone unconditionally, and trying to proclaim and serve God's reign of loving nonviolence. Over time, we realize that we don't need to bug God with our demands. We know God is taking care of us as would an attentive, loving father. We surrender to God all our concerns, problems, struggles, and questions. We surrender control of our own lives to God and let God order our lives. We spend our days giving thanks to God for so many gifts given to us. We smile, laugh, and rejoice with our beloved God. We don't need anything.

With this understanding of prayer as an intimate relationship with our beloved God, Luke encourages us to ask, seek, and knock, and trust that God will help us. "Ask and you will receive; seek and you will find; knock and the door will be opened to you," Jesus teaches us. "For everyone who asks, receives; and the one who seeks, finds; and to the one who knocks, the door will be opened." As with Matthew, Luke's Jesus encourages us to engage God, to seek God, to search for God every day in every possible way. This is what God desires: God wants us to seek God. So, if we ask God for what we need, we will receive what we need. If we do not ask God, if we live as if we are in control of our lives and do not need God's help, we will not get it. God is humble, shy, and modest in this regard. God tries not to intervene unless we ask for help. If we ask God, if we recognize our need for God, then God will come running. If we choose not to rely on God but to rely on ourselves, then God lets us do so—and we will fall on our face every time until we learn the wisdom of surrendering and relying completely on God.

Likewise, if we seek God and God's blessings, we will find them. If we do not seek God and God's blessings, we will not find them. Then, as we age, we will complain about the absence of God in our lives. Why should God come into our lives if we do not want God, if we do not seek God? God has feelings, too, and wants our love. If we search for God, we will find God. As Rabbi Abraham Heschel wrote, it's not that God is hidden; it's that God is hiding. In that subtle difference, God wants us to seek out and find God. That journey for God every day of our lives is the journey of peace, love, and nonviolence in the footsteps of Jesus. More and more, we end up surrendering our lives to God and living like Jesus in the present moment of universal peace and love.

Likewise, if we knock at the door of God's house, it will be opened. If we do not knock at the door of God's house, it will not be opened because no one will know we are there, and so we will remain locked outside in the cold. We cannot complain about not knowing God or seeing God or being with God if we do not seek God and try to enter God's house. But if we take time in prayer every day to surrender our hearts and lives to God, to seek God, and to knock at the door of God's house in God's reign of universal love, we will find God and enter God's house, and begin to live more and more every day as if we are in the presence of God and in God's reality of complete love.

Then Jesus questions his disciples about the nature of the God they are petitioning. If a son asks his father for a fish, will the father give him a snake? If he asks for an egg, will the father give him a scorpion? If a son asks his father for food, would any father give his son something that could kill him instead? No. So Jesus asks, "If you then, who are wicked, know how to give good gifts to your children, how much more will the Father in heaven give the Holy Spirit to those who ask him?" Even in our wickedness, he points out, we give good gifts to our children. Even more so, our heavenly Father, who is pure goodness and unconditional love, will give us very good gifts. God can give only good gifts.

Here Luke makes a change from Matthew and adds that if we ask for the Holy Spirit, God will give us the Holy Spirit, implying that this is the greatest gift we could ask for. Luke's Jesus encourages us to ask for and welcome the Holy Spirit of God, that we might always live in God's very spirit as Jesus does. The slight change emphasizes the focus on the nature of God, what we think God is like, the nature of our requests to God, and what might be the greatest gift we could ask from God. For Luke, as we will see later in the Acts of the Apostles, the greatest gift from God is the Holy Spirit. Then God will live in us as God lived in Jesus, and we will live in God's reign and love as Jesus loves.

"Whoever Is Not with Me Is against Me" (11:14–54)

After driving out a demon that prevented a mute person from speaking, Jesus is accused of being possessed by demons. If Satan is divided against himself, then his kingdom will fall, Jesus says in response to the accusations. Then he puts it to them plainly: "If it is by the finger of God that I drive out demons, then the kingdom of God has come upon you." You be the judge, he tells them.

Luke makes only slight edits to Matthew's and Mark's stories of the attacks on Jesus, and he goes on to present Jesus as the stronger man who overcomes a strong man and his palace and possessions. Likewise, he uses the parable to invite people to join his campaign to transform the world of violence into a new world of compassion and justice. "Whoever is not with me is against me," he says, "and whoever does not gather with me scatters." Luke summons us to be with Jesus and to gather everyone beginning with the poor, the excluded, the marginalized, and the disenfranchised. If we are not welcoming everyone into the human community, into God's reign come to earth, then we oppose Jesus's mission. That is the work of Beelzebul—to scatter, divide, and destroy the human family.

Luke repeats Matthew's explanation of how demons work inside us. The parable of the unclean spirit resembles any present-day diagnosis of addiction. The demon leaves, roams around, returns to find a cleaner soul, and finally goes and gets seven other demons more wicked than itself to move in, so that "the last condition of that person is worse than the first." Here is the story of the alcoholic, the drug addict, the sex and lust addict, and the gambling addict who try to get sober on their own, only to fall off the wagon and end up worse than before. Addictions are progressive and can eventually kill us. We are all wounded sinners. Our hearts are broken. We are damaged. As we grow older, the resentments, egotism, anger, selfishness, lust, greed, and pride become unmanageable and destroy us. To cover the pain, we drink or do drugs and lose control of our lives. The Synoptic Gospels describe humanity as completely broken, stuck in sin, addicted to ego and violence. Jesus is the nonviolent intervention of God who binds the demons and liberates humanity into sobriety. The Gospels offer a kind of Twelve Step program, where we live in a community of love and mutual support, confess our addictions and sins to one another, turn to our Higher Power, make restitution, and live sober, peaceful, holy lives one day at a time through the grace of God and in total reliance on the Holy Spirit at every moment. If the world is addicted to violence and death, Jesus is the liberator who expels the demons of addiction and leads us to a new global sobriety of nonviolence whereby we can live sanely and soberly in God's reign of peace. This is the only path to sanity and life, Luke tells us; otherwise, the demons of violence and death will eventually consume us and destroy us, and we don't want that.

Jesus wants to free us—as individuals and as a society—from every demon of violence, selfishness, and death, and to give us the Holy Spirit within us so we can live in the total freedom of God's love, compassion, and wisdom. The only way out of our collective insanity is the Gospel path of repentance and the sobriety of depending on God to liberate and heal us.

When a woman in the crowd calls out and blesses Jesus's mother for raising him, Jesus answers, "Blessed are those who hear the word of God and observe it." This beatitude brings the crowd back to the reality of what God truly wants in us: cooperation with the ways of God's reign. Family ties don't matter; pedigree doesn't matter. Working with God rather than against God is what counts.

"No sign will be given to this generation, except the sign of Jonah," Jesus tells the crowd, in words we have heard before in Matthew and Mark. He speaks of the Queen of the South who traveled far to hear the wisdom of Solomon, and the people of Nineveh who repented at the preaching of Jonah; they will condemn this generation "because there is something greater than" Solomon and Jonah here. As we saw in Matthew's account (see 12:38), we know that Luke is referring to Jesus's spectacular nonviolence, compassion, and universal love, and his grassroots campaign of peace and nonviolence, and we will learn it for sure in his meticulous nonviolence unto death and see it in his resurrection. Luke says that the people of Nineveh repented at the preaching of Jonah, which was rooted in the threat of God's violence, punishment, and destruction, and that "there is something greater than Jonah here." What is Luke's Jesus referring to? Simply, the preaching of Jesus that is rooted and modeled in total nonviolence and his announcement that God is a God of peace, universal love, and total nonviolence. Even Jesus's disciples have begun preaching this shocking good news about the God of peace and God's coming reign of peace. Therefore, according to Luke's Jesus, everyone everywhere ought to repent of the culture of violence, war, and empire, and embrace Jesus's vision of God's reign of peace, which is at hand right now.

Jesus wants us to live and walk in the light rather than fall and die in the darkness, Luke continues. He first offers the image of a lamp that offers light for everyone to see, then changes the image and speaks of the eye as "the lamp of the body." The eye can fill the whole body with light so that we can live in the light and peace of God; but if it is unhealthy, we'll be left in utter darkness to die. "Take care that the light in you not become darkness," he warns. "If your whole body is full of light, and no part of it is in darkness, then it will be as full of light as a lamp illuminating you with its brightness."

If we live in darkness, then we walk in darkness; we stumble and fall and eventually die. We cannot survive in the darkness of this violent world, and in the many forms of personal darkness. Take care to protect your eyes that you only let in the light, Luke's Jesus teaches. He wants us to be full of light, to be bright and illuminating. How do we take care to live in the light? By following his teachings of daily prayer, surrendering to God's will, and living in God's reign. If we see through Jesus's eyes, if we take up his vision, then we will live in the light.

At dinner at the home of a Pharisee, Jesus scandalizes his host by not doing the ritual acts of cleaning before the meal according to Mosaic law. He breaks the law! He engages in civil disobedience in the house of a Pharisee, for all to see. Jesus is trying to teach the religious authorities—and the rest of us—that there is a higher law, the law of God, to be obeyed; that our hearts should be set on God, not on rules, regulations, and appearances that no longer apply or serve in our dark world of violence and empire. He nonviolently creates tension to shake people up, wake them up, and create the space for them to hear him.

"Oh, you Pharisees!" he says. "Although you cleanse the outside of the cup and the dish, inside you are filled with plunder and evil. You fools! Did not the maker of the outside also make the inside? But as to what is within, give alms, and behold, everything will be clean for you." For Jesus, what goes on inside of us is most important. He knows we're all filled with "plunder and evil," and that's what we need to be cleansed of. As Matthew's Beatitude says, he wants us to clean our hearts, to have nonviolent hearts that radiate universal love and compassion. In this critically important verse, he announces that, if we give alms to the poor, "everything inside us will be cleansed." Here's the way out! If we surrender our hearts to God and give money to the poor and needy and to those who struggle for justice, our insides will be purified.

With this teaching, Jesus points a way forward for the Pharisees to break free from legalism and self-righteousness into justice and compassion. But Jesus doesn't leave it at that. He goes on to warn them sternly with three woes. "Woe to you Pharisees," Jesus says three times. He states these woes at a dinner given in his honor (unlike Matthew 23). If we ponder the context of this story, Jesus appears to be rude. But if we understand the power of the

Pharisees and the harm they have done, and Jesus's perspective of compassion and nonviolence, and if we hear them as a lament offered from the depths of love, we realize that Jesus is not angry but grieving and pleading with his host and the other Pharisees. More, according to Luke, he has spent a lifetime compassionately listening to the Pharisees, starting at age twelve. He loves them and tries with all his nonviolence to reason with them, to wake them up, and to lead them to his wisdom. "You pay tithes of mint and of rue and of every garden herb, but you pay no attention to judgment and to love for God. These you should have done, without overlooking the others." He's telling them to focus on God, God's love, and God's judgment, rather than on their own judgment of others and the minutiae of legalism. "You love the seat of honor in synagogues and greetings in marketplaces," he continues. He points out their hunger for honor and control; perhaps he hopes their eyes will be opened to their self-preoccupation and they will respond by seeking humility and selflessness.

Finally, Jesus offers one of his strongest statements to this group: "You are like unseen graves over which people unknowingly walk." To understand how strong this language is, we must remember that, according to their religious law, nothing was more unclean than a grave full of rotting bones. They have missed the whole point of the Mosaic law, Jesus says. You worry about cleaning your hands solely for appearances so that you can be seen to be law-abiding religious leaders, when in fact, you are filled with impurity, violence, evil, and death itself. When he says they are like tombs filled with dead bones, he is telling them they are already dead! Jesus wants to root out every trace of uncleanliness inside us, which means every trace of death inside of us so that we can be clean in the sight of God. This warning is addressed to everyone who undertakes religious obligations simply to appear as a good person or a law-abiding citizen. Forget that, he says. Clean your hearts, humble yourselves before God, practice nonviolence and compassion, give money to the poor, and follow Jesus on the path of surrender to God and God's reign. That is the path to God and the fullness of life.

"Teacher, by saying this you are insulting us too," a lawyer says to him. They hear his words as judgmental and mean, as many read them today. They cannot imagine the depth of love and compassion within him. These warnings were a profound grace and blessing to these religious and legal authorities, and to us—if we have the humility to take them to heart and to trust the One who speaks them. They are like the loving words of someone doing an intervention with an addict, a kind of last-ditch attempt to save them. They are like the thousands of words that activists say in their peace vigils at nuclear weapons plants: "Stop preparing for nuclear war. Stop serving the powers of Death. Work for peace and start living!"

"Woe also to you scholars of the law!" he says to them three times. "You impose on people burdens hard to carry, but you yourselves do not lift one finger to touch them." This first critique challenges all of us to spend our days liberating others, not imposing burdens on them. He wants us to lift the burdens off those who are oppressed, poor, and marginalized. His invitation should cause us to ask ourselves, "What do I need to do to ensure that my life does not impose a burden on anyone? How can I help lift the burdens off those who suffer?"

"You build the memorials of the prophets whom your ancestors killed," Jesus continues. "Consequently, you bear witness and give consent to the deeds of your ancestors, for they killed them and you do the building." Here he challenges the authorities for not hearing and following God's prophets of truth and justice. He wants us to listen and heed the words of God's prophets and to become holy prophets of justice and peace as well. He looks for followers who will risk their lives and speak truth to power as the prophets did, not spend our lives punishing, ostracizing, and killing the prophets or even memorializing them once they are safely dead. We see this today in India as people memorialize Gandhi with statues and images on their money, but actually they continue to support the warped politics of his assassins by encouraging hatred, racism, greed, and war. Likewise, today, in the United States, we pay lip service to Dr. King with a national holiday but do not commit ourselves to his work of ending poverty, racism, and militarism. "The wisdom of God said, 'I will send to them prophets and apostles; some of them they will kill and persecute' in order that this generation might be charged with the blood of all the prophets shed since the foundation of the world, from the blood of Abel to the blood of Zechariah, who died between the altar and the temple building," Jesus continues. "Yes, I tell you, this generation will be charged with their blood!" With that, he warns his powerful listeners of the spiritual consequences of killing the prophets and memorializing them instead of joining their ongoing work of justice, compassion, and peace. This warning remains today. We will suffer the long-term spiritual consequences, the bad karma, of our silent refusal to join the prophetic work for justice and peace.

"You have taken away the key of knowledge," he tells them in conclusion. "You yourselves did not enter and you stopped those trying to enter." With these words Jesus pointedly tells the religious authorities that they have utterly failed to lead their people to knowledge, wisdom, or indeed, God. If they were interested in entering holy knowledge or the wisdom of God, they would have joined Jesus's way of compassion and peace. Instead, they have not entered the wisdom of God, and they have prevented others from entering. In response to this truth-telling, Luke reports, "the scribes and Pharisees began to act with hostility toward him and to interrogate him about many things, for they were plotting to catch him at something he might say." He tries to reason with them, to teach them, and to be honest with them. For that last-ditch effort, his days are numbered.

The charges against ruling, powerful authorities have only worsened over the centuries. Today, many authorities, rulers, and politicians seek their own acclaim, glory, power, and domination rather than seek the wisdom of God. In doing so, they not only fail to enter God's wisdom, but they also prevent thousands, millions, of others from entering. We see this in the way Congressional leaders, FOX News broadcasters, and even some church leaders support war, bless guns and nuclear weapons, remain silent in the face of racism and corporate greed, maintain patriarchal and class structures, and ignore the prophetic call for justice and nonviolence from the likes of Archbishop Romero, Dorothy Day, and the Berrigans. Luke cries out across the centuries not to waste one's life in self-seeking power and domination, not to block God's work for justice and peacemaking, but rather to join the lineage of the prophets by supporting the movement toward justice and love. Luke's Jesus wants us all to live out the wisdom of God and to enter God's reign of peace.

"The Hairs of Your Head Have All Been Counted" (12:1–15)

As we begin chapter 12, Luke reports that people were crowding in so tightly to see him that "they were trampling one another underfoot." Jesus is like a rock star, mobbed by the crowds. (This widespread popular support is a key reason why the authorities did not arrest and kill Jesus immediately. They would have to wait for the perfect opportunity.) Everyone wants to hear him, meet him, touch him—everyone, that is, who is poor, oppressed, excluded, ostracized, sick, or marginalized in any way. In Jesus, the poor have heard good news and found liberation, just as he promised when he set out on his campaign of nonviolence from the synagogue in Nazareth.

"Beware of the leaven—that is, the hypocrisy—of the Pharisees," Jesus tells his disciples. "There is nothing concealed that will not be revealed, nor secret that will not be known," he continues. "Therefore, whatever you have said in the darkness will be heard in the light, and what you have whispered behind closed doors will be proclaimed on the housetops." Here, Jesus instructs his disciples not to be hypocrites like the religious authorities, but instead to be honest, sincere, humble, and authentic, people of integrity through and through. He wants them to be rooted in the love and compassion of God deep within their own hearts so that everything they do flows out of the actual love of God. He's not looking for impostors, people of violence pretending to be pious and peaceful, but rather real spiritual seekers, people who really work at their inner disarmament and practice universal love and compassion for all. He promises that, in the end, everything about us will be revealed, every secret will be known, and everything said in the dark will be brought to the light of day. So he encourages us to be as authentic as possible, to humbly confess our brokenness and darkness, to surrender everything to the light of God, and to do only God's will. This teaching is another perspective on Jesus's call to repentance and humble submission to the will of God, so that we become true servants of the living God, and not servants of money, power, the empire, or our own dominating egos.

"I tell you, my friends, do not be afraid of those who kill the body but after that can do no more," Jesus continues. "I shall show you whom to fear. Be afraid of the one who after killing has the power to cast into Gehenna; yes, I tell you, be afraid of that one." He calls his followers "my friends." We can claim that title for ourselves and aspire to be friends of the nonviolent Jesus, if we live according to his word. Next, he tells us, "Do not be afraid." Do not be afraid of anyone in this world who can hurt you or kill you. He fearlessly walks through life and wants us to do the same. We have nothing to be afraid of in this world. His warning about fearing the One who can cast us into Gehenna may disturb us, but it is a blessing. He calls us to believe in God, to have respect for God, and to maintain the ancient "fear of God," which is best translated as "awe of God." Again, our lives are meant to be lived in humble submission to an all-powerful, loving, nonviolent God. God is God, and we're not, so this is an appropriate, reasonable, helpful teaching if we understand it within the framework of wisdom, compassion, and peace. God does not want to throw us into Gehenna; God wants us to be God's beloved sons and daughters and share eternal life in God's loving presence. That's where we are headed as we offer ourselves to God in loving humility, respect, awe, and worship.

"Are not five sparrows sold for two small coins?" Jesus asks. "Yet not one of them has escaped the notice of God. Even the hairs of your head have all been counted. Do not be afraid. You are worth more than many sparrows." Here Jesus goes further and insists that we have nothing to fear precisely because God loves us so completely and gently. God is so wildly in love with every single human being that God knows everything about us, every cell in our bodies, and has even numbered the hairs on our heads. God loves us unconditionally, dotes on us, looks after us, and wants only to help us. Like a parent who knows and cares for their baby's body, God knows and cares for us and has from the moment God first thought of us to our births to the present day. We do not need to fear God. We can trust this God, and seek this God, who is so wildly in love with us. It's good to be with someone who loves us that much! These sentences are some of the most beautiful in the Gospel—if they are understood in the context of wisdom, compassion, and peace.

In the short sayings that follow, Luke's Jesus instructs us to trust God, the Son of Humanity, and their Holy Spirit. "I tell you, everyone who acknowledges me before others the Son of Humanity will acknowledge before the angels of God," he says. "But whoever denies me before others will be denied before the angels of God." If we side with God, and side with the nonviolent Jesus, the angels will learn all about it and be filled with awe. Jesus will forgive us, we're told. "The one who blasphemes against the Holy Spirit," he adds, however, "will not be forgiven." This unforgivable sin refers to twisting the spirit of God to support war, killing, idolatry, money, and any violence done to God's people. When religious leaders supported Nazi rule and genocidal practices, they committed blasphemy against the Holy Spirit, as if the Spirit of the nonviolent Jesus could ever support such insanity and systemic violence. The same is true today, when we equate the Holy Spirit of God or Jesus with the United States, its wars, its military, its allegiance, or its power. That blasphemy is an unforgivable sin because it mocks God.

As if to forewarn his disciples that this will, of course, happen, Jesus encourages them to trust in the Holy Spirit in such times of widespread nationalistic blasphemy. "When they take you before synagogues and before rulers and authorities, do not worry about how or what your defense will be or about what you are to say for the Holy Spirit will teach you at that moment what you should say." As we nonviolently resist the structures of violence, war, and blasphemy, Jesus instructs, know that the Spirit of God is with us and will guide us and speak through us. On many occasions, as my friends and I have stood in court before judges or been asked to speak to government or religious authorities, we have trusted that the Holy Spirit will give us the words of truth, peace, and nonviolence to say, in the spirit of love, what might help disarm them and lead them to truth and peace. I find that this instruction works for those who publicly resist the culture and find themselves brought before judges, politicians, or other ruling authorities. God always sides with those who speak the truth, practice nonviolence, advocate for justice, and promote universal love.

When someone asked Jesus to tell his brother to share the inheritance with him, he asks, "Friend, who appointed me as your judge and arbitrator?" For many people, claiming that their inheritance is a primary goal in life, so much so that families squabble and fight over every penny. Here someone asks Jesus to help him convince his brother to give him his equal share. Jesus calls the person "Friend." That's his basic attitude toward everyone. And his question to the man is reasonable: Why appoint Jesus as your judge and arbitrator? Is Jesus the judge and arbitrator of our finances and family inheritance? Does that concern him? Actually, no. All along he has called his disciples and anyone who would listen to give away their money and possessions, seek treasure that will never wear out, and follow him.

So, once again, he tells the crowd, "Take care to guard against all greed, for though one may be rich, one's life does not consist of possessions." I hear him saying to the man, "Forget your inheritance. Life is much more than money or possessions. Come, follow me. Seek first God's reign of peace, and everything will be provided for you." It's a hard teaching at first, but if one opens one's heart in prayer, lets go of fear and control, and trusts in God, one will discover true freedom and peace as one goes through life serving others and following Jesus. Moreover, we will discover that Jesus is our judge and arbitrator but much more—our savior, Lord, and yes, our friend.

"Your Father Is Pleased to Give You the Kingdom" (12:16–48)

With that, Jesus tells the crowd the parable of the rich man, with a full harvest, who builds massive barns to store his harvest so that for years to come he can "rest, eat, drink, be merry." Sounds good, right? Wrong. This is the wrong approach to life, Jesus warns. Forget investments, hoarding, greed, and the life of leisure. Life is short; use your time wisely to serve God and humanity. Invest in the poor, as Dorothy Day once said; there you can expect a lasting return. Give everything you have and your very self to those in need, to the struggle for justice and peace, to Jesus's campaign for a more nonviolent, more just world, and your savings will be your salvation.

The parable continues. God enters, stage left, out of nowhere. "You fool," he says to the rich man. "This night your life will be demanded of you; and the things you have prepared, to whom will they belong?' Thus will it be for the one who stores up treasure for himself but is not rich in what matters to God." The punch line of the parable is that the rich man, who is actually a fool, will die that night, and all his investing, hoarding, and greed will be recognized at once as a sheer waste of time. Money and possessions mean nothing to the living God; the only thing that matters is selfless love, selfless service, selfless discipleship to the nonviolent Jesus in pursuit of God's reign of peace and nonviolence here on earth. If we give our lives for these treasures, we will be "rich in what matters to God" and that is all that matters.

This phrase is classic Luke: to be "rich in what matters to God." This should be the primary goal of our short lives. Instead, the world of violence, greed, and war tells us to get ahead, invest and make more money, emulate the rich and powerful, greedily store up our possessions, and ensure our own security. This world deludes us into thinking that we are in control of our lives, that we will never die, that life is meant for "eating, drinking, and making merry." If you are rich, you don't need God; you forget your dependence on God. If you are poor, you need God and depend on God and live in alignment with God. How wrong the world is, how wrong we are to go along with the mad thinking of the world. Life is short, death is imminent, we must live every day wisely, trusting in God for our security and spending our days growing rich in what matters most to God. Luke cries out across the centuries, inviting us to focus on these words and decide for ourselves what we might do to make ourselves "rich in what matters to God," or an even better translation, "rich for God."

In the spirit of this great parable, Jesus commands us not to worry but instead to seek God's reign and let God provide for our every need. Then we will be rich in what matters to God. Using Matthew's text from the Sermon on the Mount, Luke inserts at this moment Jesus's instructions to the disciples about dependence on God. Someone wants Jesus to help him claim his inheritance from his brother, but Jesus uses that foolishness to teach his disciples to renounce money, possessions, and concerns for food and clothing so that they focus solely on God and doing God's will and seeking God's reign. "Do not worry about your life and what you will eat, or about your body and what you will wear," he tells them, "for life is more than food and the body more than clothing." What is life about then? we might ask. Life is a pilgrimage to God and into God's reign. Life is the fullness of love, compassion, and peace with God, humanity, and creation.

"Notice the ravens," Jesus tells the disciples to make his point. Like every wise, indigenous elder, Jesus encourages us to learn the ways of God from creation and its creatures. "They do not sow or reap; they have neither storehouse nor barn, yet God feeds them." Perhaps we think, "So what?" "How much more important are you than birds!" Jesus exclaims. God takes care of the ravens and all the creatures of the earth, but we human beings are God's beloved children, so God will care for us infinitely more and do everything God can to provide for us, if we align ourselves with God's will and God's way.

"Can any of you by worrying add a moment to your lifespan? If even the smallest things are beyond your control, why are you anxious about the rest?" These two questions are so basic as to be obvious. We have no control over the smallest things and cannot add one moment to our lifespan, and yet we spend our lives trying to control everything and worrying because we can't control anything. This is a foolish waste of time, Jesus suggests with his questions. Wisdom teaches us to let go of all worry, but more, of all control. He wants us to surrender our lives into God's hands, live one day at a time in the present moment, and enjoy our lives in God's love and peace. Worrying gets us nowhere. Controlling ourselves or others doesn't work. In the end, surrendering completely to God and God's way is the only way to live in the ultimate reality of God's love and peace.

"Notice how the flowers grow," Jesus teaches. Here he sounds like the Zen Buddhist master Thich Nhat Hanh. If we study the flowers, if we ponder nature, we can discover the secret of living in peace. "They do not toil or spin," he points out. The flowers do not worry; they do not try to control others. They do not try to add a day to their life spans. Nor do the trees, our dogs and cats, the animals, the dolphins, the whales, or the birds. They all live happily in the present moment and give no thought for the morrow. If we actually did what he says, and took time to notice how the flowers grow, we'd have to stop our running around and sit outdoors under a tree and spend time contemplating nature. If we did that, we would begin to let go of stress, worry, anger, resentments, violence, narcissism, and selfish pursuits of riches and honors. We would learn to concentrate on the beauty of nature, become one with nature, and find God in the creation. That experience alone would transform us into people of Jesus's way. It would also make us fall in love with God's creation and rise to do our part to stop environmental destruction.

"But I tell you, not even Solomon in all his splendor was dressed like one of them," Jesus says, probably pointing to a field of beautiful, colorful wildflowers. "If God so clothes the grass in the field that grows today and is thrown into the oven tomorrow, will God not much more provide for you, O you of little faith?" This is a question to sit with, a Zen koan to ponder. Do not rush into the answer. Ponder it, explore it, experiment with it. Will God provide for you? Does God provide for you? When has God provided for you? What would it look like to live one day at a time as if you relied completely on a gentle, loving God? And so, the teaching concludes:

> "As for you, do not seek what you are to eat and what you are to drink, and do not worry anymore. All the nations of the world seek for these things, and your Father knows that you need them. Instead, seek God's kingdom, and these other things will be given you besides. Do not be afraid any longer, little flock, for your Father is pleased to give you the kingdom. Sell your belongings and give alms. Provide money bags for yourselves that do not wear out, an inexhaustible treasure in heaven that no thief can reach nor moth destroy. For where your treasure is, there also will your heart be."

Here Jesus offers clear guidelines to all would-be disciples: "Do not follow the way of the world; do not act like everyone else; do not waste time in pursuit of money, possessions, land, and honors; do not worry about what you are to eat or drink; in fact, do not worry or have any fear ever again. Those days are over. God knows what you need, God will provide for you, God will take care of everything. Instead, surrender everything to God, give away everything to the poor, become one with creation, breathe in the peace of God, live free in God's spirit of peace, and set your heart on God's reign of universal love. Then you will receive a peace not of this world, and know that all will be well."

Our only treasure is the reign of God. That's what we seek, that's the focus of our attention, that's where we set our hearts. That means that we try to act as if we are already living in God's reign; we try to practice God's love, compassion, and peace. We surrender our wills, our hearts, our actions, and our lives to God over and over again so that we are living with and for God at all times. We try to become God-conscious, God-centered, God-focused. Because we know that God loves us and calls us, we no longer worry, we are no longer afraid. We go forward in complete fearless trust, doing our part in God's reign. We are no longer self-centered. We give what we have to the poor, give our lives away to those in need, become other-centered, and try to share God's reign of peace with everyone.

The good news Jesus announces is that God is pleased to give us God's reign. God does not grudgingly give us God's reign. God does not hold back. We make God happy by focusing on God's reign and welcoming it in our hearts and lives. God rejoices to give God's reign to those who seek it. And so, Luke writes, be on alert for God's reign from now on. "Gird your loins and light your lamps," Jesus continues.

> "Be like servants who await their master's return from a wedding, ready to open immediately when he comes and knocks. Blessed are those servants whom the master finds vigilant on his arrival. Amen, I say to you, he will gird himself, have them recline at table, and proceed to wait on them. And should he come in the second or third watch and find them prepared in this way, blessed are those servants. Be sure of this: if the master of the house had known the hour when the thief was coming, he would not have let his house be broken into. You also must be prepared, for at an hour you do not expect, the Son of Humanity will come."

With these two new beatitudes, Luke's Jesus urges us to be vigilant for the coming of God, to be prepared at all times, even in the darkest moments, and to trust that if God finds us ready, God will wait on us! "Be prepared for God," he tells us. Notice, too, that it is not a question of *if* God might come, but *when*. God is definitely coming for each of us, so wake up and get ready!

"Huh?" Peter asks. "Lord, is this parable meant for us or for everyone?" Jesus simply repeats the instruction and the parable for Peter and for us the readers, in case we still do not grasp the urgency of his message: be prepared, stay awake, be vigilant, God is coming into your life, probably when you least expect it. "Who, then, is the faithful and prudent steward whom the master will put in charge of his servants to distribute the food allowance at the proper time?" Jesus asks Peter. "Blessed is that servant whom his master on arrival finds doing so. Truly, I say to you, he will put him in charge of all his property." With this new beatitude, Jesus blesses the servant who is faithful, prudent, and trustworthy, the one who does what God wants regardless of the outcome for himself, the one who is always on call, ready and waiting for God at every moment. That is the invitation of Luke's Jesus.

For Luke, every blessing is mirrored by a woe, and so he adds a warning to Matthew's version. If that servant is not ready, if he spends his time eating and drinking, if he does violence to anyone, the master will return and punish the unfaithful servant. We are supposed to be nonviolent servants who do not hurt anyone, who do not think of our own comfort, who wait in permanent anticipation for the coming of the God of peace. I do not interpret this parable to mean that God is violent; I interpret it to mean that, if we are violent toward others, we will have to live with the inevitable spiritual consequences toward ourselves, that our violence will come back upon us. The karma of nonviolence insists that the means are the ends, that you reap what you sow, that you get what you give, that what goes around comes around. Spend your life in unconditional love, boundless compassion, active mercy, and steadfast nonviolence, and you will reap the fruits of God's reign.

"Much will be required of the person entrusted with much," Luke adds, "and still more will be demanded of the person entrusted with more." God gives each of us all the graces of peace, love, compassion, and nonviolence for the unique mission that God gives us. Some of us have a lifetime of responsibilities to those around us while others have even more responsibilities to many, many people. In either case, whatever our situation and opportunity, Luke urges us to wake up, be alert, and stay faithful to the way of peace, love, compassion, and nonviolence, to be alert to the coming of the God of peace, to seek God's reign of peace morning, noon, and night—and to trust that we will not only fulfill our mission but be greatly blessed.

"Do You Think That I Have Come to Establish Peace on the Earth?" (12:49–59)

At the climax of chapter 12, we hear Jesus announce that he has come "to set the earth on fire." "How I wish it were already blazing!" he says. From the moment he stood in the synagogue at Nazareth to read the passage from Isaiah about his mission to bring good news to the poor, Jesus has been on fire with his mission. He wants to change the world, to unleash the fires of Pentecost upon everyone on earth so that God's reign of peace might be realized on earth as it is in heaven. He knows that this mission to disarm everyone and welcome God's reign of nonviolence goes against the religious legal system and the Roman Empire, and that he will pay a heavy price for his mission. He's ready to get on with it.

"There is a baptism with which I must be baptized, and how great is my anguish until it is accomplished!" he says. We the readers have heard him warn us about his impending arrest and execution, and we know that he has been on his walking campaign for months. Jerusalem is getting closer. He has been baptized with water and with the Holy Spirit, but he will face another baptism in blood for his public campaign of nonviolence against the culture and empire. As people who care for him, we notice this rare glimpse into his inner life. If we look carefully, we see Jesus reveal what is going on deep within himself. Jesus does not dwell in glorious peace like a Buddha under a tree. He is in "anguish"—permanent anguish until his mission of active nonviolence has reached its climax, and that can happen only at the hands of Roman soldiers.

As those who seek to follow the nonviolent Jesus, to welcome and proclaim God's reign of peace, we too must suffer a kind of permanent anguish that the transformation Jesus longed for has still not occurred and that we have not yet done all we could to proclaim God's reign and resist the structures and forces of death. Jesus's way of peace is marked by anguish. His nonviolence, as Gandhi explained, is the nonviolence of the brave, the nonviolence of the strong. It faces the world with eyes wide open and goes forth to take public action to disarm it, end injustice, and turn everyone onto the path of peace.

So, Luke's Jesus poses a question: "Do you think that I have come to establish peace on the earth?" Matthew's Jesus issues a declarative statement and speaks of a sword, but Luke puts a question to us. Where are we in the story? What do we expect of Jesus? What do his mission, his fiery passion, and his inner anguish mean for us? We want to answer "Yes!" to the question. We know that when he was born the angels told the shepherds of the coming of peace on earth. We have seen him rebuke James and John for wanting to call down hellfire; we've watched him send the seventy-two as lambs into the midst of wolves. Yes, he has come to bring peace on the earth, we answer. And as usual we are wrong.

"No, I tell you, but rather division," Jesus explains. Everyone is united under the spell of empire and the way of violence. He has come to break us from the spell, to liberate us from being brainwashed by the insanity of systemic violence into the sanity of peace. The new life of nonviolence will be misunderstood as insanity by those still trapped in the culture of violence. People will be threatened by our resistance and reject us. As his public campaign and grassroots movement of nonviolence spread, so will division. No one can be neutral about his prophetic word, his fiery mission, his insistent call, and his political denunciation of the culture of empire. It's dangerous because Jesus is rocking the boat, disrupting the status quo, disturbing the so-called peace that comes with acquiescence to empire. If we truly are his followers, then our own lives should follow the same trajectories. Like the nonviolent peacemakers Gandhi and Dr. King, our public lives will bring division to the culture of violence, and we must learn to find a certain peace in this outcome.

What's most shocking about his explanation is that his campaign of nonviolence does not set us against the Roman emperor or his procurator or his centurion—it sets us against our own relatives! We might think that our participation in his campaign will make a difference in the big picture, but much to our chagrin, the first reaction comes from within our closest circle—our own family. As soon as we take up Jesus's public campaign of nonviolence and start working for the abolition of violence, poverty, injustice, war, and empire, those closest to us will turn against us. Families will be divided over the nonviolent Jesus because he demands complete obedience to his campaign and way of life, and people will feel challenged and threatened. They will not want to be disturbed, they do not want to face the world, they do not want to try to make a difference. In Jesus's day, one could be killed for joining this underground movement or for being an accomplice in any campaign against the empire. Roman soldiers regularly hunted down and crucified violent revolutionaries, such as the Zealots. If one's relative started to speak and act like a Zealot, even if he was nonviolent, he might be arrested like a Zealot, and that might taint any close relative as well. Who wants that? Certainly not your relatives! They will think you are crazy and come to take you away.

It's hard to imagine how dangerous it was for Jesus and his community to proclaim God's reign under the permanent watch of the lethal Roman military. If Jesus and his community called for allegiance to the God of peace and refusal to support the culture of killing and injustice, then the empire itself was threatened and would strike back with violence by rounding up and executing its opponents. There was nothing more frightening. No wonder, Jesus says, your own relatives will reject you, renounce you, disown you, and have nothing to do with you because of my campaign. Be prepared for this rejection, he's telling them. This must happen if we are to resist and bring down the culture of violence and death and welcome God's reign of nonviolence and life.

Rejection and division are the natural first consequences of authentic creative nonviolent action in a culture of violence. If we engage in public work, demonstrations, campaigns, and civil disobedience actions as the nonviolent Jesus did, people will be upset with us, starting with our parents, siblings, children, and other relatives. No one likes to be shaken out of their comfort zone, and our very presence will be divisive. We won't have to say anything; whenever we enter a room, people will turn against us, walk away from us, or tell us off to our faces. Many people stuck in the culture of violence do not want to be around someone who works full-time against the culture, the nation, and its war preparations, as the Jesus movement did. People will not want to hear us talk about executions, war, racism, poverty, nuclear weapons, or climate injustice, much less join our projects and campaigns. With this teaching, we know what to expect: rejection even from those closest to us. But we have been trained in nonviolence, forgiveness, and love by the Master himself, so we know how to respond to rejection: with further nonviolence, compassion, love, and forgiveness, as well as carrying on our public work for the coming of God's reign of justice and peace. Once again, we get to practice nonviolence up close and personal, starting with those closest to us, our own relatives.

Jesus ends these shocking teachings by urging us to read the signs of the times. He points out that we can read the weather and know when it is going to rain or turn hot. "You hypocrites," Luke writes, emphasizing our hypocrisy and refusal to wake up to the political reality of the world. "You know how to interpret the appearance of the earth and the sky; why do you not know how to interpret the present time?" Jesus wants us to join his grassroots campaign of disarming nonviolence while there is still time, to wake everyone up to God's way of nonviolence so that God's reign of peace can break through.

We can read the signs of the times. It's on every front page. Are we going to continue to reject Jesus's call to nonviolence? Might we go forward with his campaign, even if those around us reject us, and do what we can to spread it, to stop the killings and the destruction of creation? This requires steadfast faith, persistent nonviolence, and fearless dedication to God. We can do it.

"Why do you not judge for yourselves what is right?" Luke's Jesus asks. This question is original to Luke and seems obvious on its face value. Why don't we judge for ourselves what is right? Why do we wait for others to tell us what is wrong? Why do we do the wrong and believe the lies simply because we are told to do so, even told that they are right? Read the signs of the times, understand the difference between right and wrong, between truth and lies, between life and death, Jesus pleads. Choose what is right, what is good, what is holy, what is wise, what is truthful, what leads to a world of peace for all that will endure and flourish, he cries out from his inner anguish.

Luke ends this heart-breaking revelation of Jesus with a short parable about settling with our opponent before we land in court and get thrown in prison. Do the right thing before silence and complicity with the culture of violence send us all to our doom. Don't go down without a fight, albeit a nonviolent one. His message is one long wake-up alarm: get up, be prepared, be vigilant, take up the cross, join the movement, and welcome God's reign. Don't consign yourself like everyone else to the inevitable woes of the culture of violence. Choose the blessing of peace. Wake up! The alarm clock is ringing!

"What Is the Kingdom of God Like?" (13:1–15:32)

As the nonviolent Jesus gets closer to Jerusalem, his message becomes more urgent. He knows what lies ahead, even though the disciples do not. He has taught them to turn away from the culture of violence and empire and live here and now in God's reign of peace, only to see them time and again misunderstand his call. He has reached out and healed anyone who wanted healing and expelled the demons of violence and death from anyone who needed spiritual liberation, only to be harassed and attacked by the religious authorities, the ones who should have been the first to support his healing, peacemaking work. Soon he will begin to teach primarily in parables as still another way to wake up his listeners. He will tell stories to break us free from the lock-step mindset of empire and religious legalism.

Chapter 13 begins with a dire call for repentance. Some people tell Jesus how the Romans had recently tortured some Galileans and that the Roman procurator Pontius Pilate himself had mingled some of their blood with the blood of their sacrifices to God, in the most horrific mockery of their suffering and worship. We know from the writings of the Jewish historian Josephus that Pilate was a mass murderer. He writes that Pilate had disrupted a religious gathering of Samaritans on Mount Gerizim and massacred everyone (*Antiquities* 18.86–87) and that once, after Pilate stole money from the temple treasury bank to build an aqueduct in Jerusalem, he killed everyone who objected and protested against him (*Jewish War* 2.175–77;

Antiquities 18.60–62; NAB, note on Lk. 13:1). With this reference to the bloodthirsty Pilate and his torture and execution of faithful Jews in Galilee, we remember the context of the Gospel. Think Nazi Germany or Stalin's purges or apartheid in South Africa or the genocide in Rwanda or Mississippi under the Ku Klux Klan or El Salvador under the U.S.-backed death squads. This is the world in which Jesus is leading a public, grassroots campaign. In fact, he is headed directly to the temple, where he will lead a nonviolent raid on the treasury, an act for which we know that Pilate would retaliate with execution.

But notice how Jesus responds to the report of the torture and massacre of the faithful Galilean Jews. He does not weep, he does not cry out, he does not burst out in anger, nor does he lament their suffering or deaths. He uses this frightening account of state terror to try to get people's attention. Jesus is well aware of the Roman Empire and its use of death as a way to resolve its problems. His nonviolent life resists the culture of death, and he invites everyone to join this movement; otherwise, they will always live in oppression, and occupation, and fear that they will be next.

"Do you think that because these Galileans suffered in this way," he asks, "they were greater sinners than all other Galileans? By no means! But I tell you, if you do not repent, you will all perish as they did!" The common misunderstanding and bad theology of the time was that people suffered illness, disability, accidents, or torture and death at the hands of Roman soldiers because they were sinners. In other words, they deserved what they got. God was punishing them for their sins. Not at all, Jesus says. They were not greater sinners; they were victims of the Roman occupation and its rampant militarism, and if we do not resist it, and work to transform it into a culture of nonviolence, we will all suffer the same fate, he says.

"If you do not repent, you will all perish as they did!" This is a crucial teaching, exclusive to Luke's Jesus. He does not want us to go to our deaths as these victims of Roman violence did. Why not? If they were faithful Jews, perhaps even fulfilling the Torah by offering sacrifice in the synagogue, and were tortured and murdered right there—why would he not call us to that same devotion, even if it costs us our lives? This requires deep reflection and concentration on the Lucan mission and campaign of Jesus. The days of ritual sacrifice in worship are over; the days of active nonviolence and universal love as our practice of faith and worship of God have arrived in the presence of Jesus of Nazareth. That means that the ultimate religious practice of devotion and worship of God is to follow Jesus on this new path of faith and activism. Jesus is campaigning for the end of all bloodletting, animal or human, and he will give his life, and have his own blood shed, for the end of killing.

Even if we are arrested, tortured, and killed by the Romans, he says in effect, we do not want to perish as everyone else, as slaves to the culture of death. Jesus is calling us to be fully alive in God's reign of peace. He wants us not to be passive victims but proactive martyrs of the way of peace.

To emphasize his point, he doesn't leave it there. In the only instance in the four Gospels, Jesus refers to a tragic accident, and its meaning and implications. "Or those eighteen people who were killed when the tower at Siloam fell on them—do you think they were guiltier than everyone else who lived in Jerusalem? By no means! But I tell you, if you do not repent, you will all perish as they did!" Here Jesus refers to some unknown incident when a tower fell and killed eighteen people. He shatters the bad theology that they died because they were sinners, guiltier than everyone else who lived in Jerusalem. No, they were not guiltier; they were the same as everyone. But that's precisely the point, he says. Those people were going along, business as usual, and business as usual in a world of violence and death does not lead to a life of true abundance and peace. All of us will die to this physical life at some point, but what matters is, how did we live? If the people who died from the falling tower were following Jesus's way of faith, peace, and transformation, then even their deaths would not be a tragedy.

As Daniel Berrigan would say, these are deep waters.

Let me offer an illustration. In the days after September 11, 2001, I served full-time with the Red Cross as a coordinator of all the chaplains at the Family Assistance Center, coordinating nearly six hundred chaplains ministering to some fifty thousand direct relatives of the victims of the World Trade Center attacks. I also worked several times a week at Ground Zero, wearing my priestly clothes and a yellow fire helmet, counseling hundreds of fire fighters and rescue workers there in the midst of the seven-story pile of wreckage and death. On the day itself, my parents and I had reservations for the Windows on the World restaurant on the top of the World Trade Towers, but my parents canceled the reservation at the last minute, and we had breakfast in their hotel instead. When we heard of the attacks, they left town, and I went downtown to help out and waited with others at St. Vincent's Hospital for the sick and injured to arrive; they never did. When I returned home that evening, I was distraught and confused like many, so I opened the Gospel of Luke to find some teaching to help me understand what Jesus would have to say about the attacks and collapse of the two towers that killed 2,753 people that day in New York City. As I thumbed through my Bible, I came to this passage in Luke 13. I was looking for a word of comfort to say to New Yorkers, and I found Jesus's word to people after the collapse of the tower at Siloam in Jerusalem, where eighteen people died.

"If you do not repent, you will all perish as they did!"

I was shocked and scandalized by these words as I read them alone in my room on the evening of September 11, 2001. Imagine what people would have said if I went out into the streets of New York City that day and said those words! And yet, those words may have been what we all most needed to hear.

It is critically important for each reader of Luke to feel the power and shock of these words today, to begin to understand the scandalous call of Jesus to us at this moment in history as the world stands on the brink of nuclear warfare and catastrophic climate change. As we sit with these words, at first we may find them cold, insensitive, and mean. But we know that Jesus is universally loving and infinitely compassionate, so these words must somehow be a blessing as well as a warning.

Instead of turning away from these words, we need to sit with them. That's what I did—for days and weeks after September 11, as I ministered to thousands of people, even as I stood in the burning ruins of the World Trade Towers. Slowly, the teachings began to make sense, and I understood them as the greatest gift Jesus could offer. If we do not change our lives, quit our jobs, stop our mindless pursuit of money, non-cooperate with American capitalism, consumerism, and corporate greed, if we do not resist militarism and the nuclear industry, then we will all go to our deaths as these poor people did on September

11. Jesus does not want us to participate in business as usual. Those days are over for us. "All our problems stem from our acceptance of this filthy, rotten system," Dorothy Day once said. That could be a modern translation of Jesus's diagnosis of our predicament. He calls us to reject the systems of the world and to embark on an entirely new way in pursuit of God's reign of justice and peace for all. He wants us not to perish stuck in the culture of violence and greed, but to enter the fullness of life here and now and to get ready for resurrection.

Luke does not report how the crowd reacted to Jesus's words. We can only imagine that some walked away, and the male disciples were more perplexed than ever. For everybody, his words felt like a bucket of cold water. They are a rude wake-up call designed to get us to stop sleepwalking through life, to hear the urgent siren to turn toward life while we still can.

In that moment, Jesus offered the parable of the fig tree:

"There once was a person who had a fig tree planted in his orchard, and when he came in search of fruit on it but found none, he said to the gardener, 'For three years now I have come in search of fruit on this fig tree but have found none. So cut it down. Why should it exhaust the soil?' He said to him in reply, 'Sir, leave it for this year also, and I shall cultivate the ground around it and fertilize it; it may bear fruit in the future. If not, you can cut it down.'"

The fig tree of course represents a form of institutionalized religion, with all its laws and rules, which did not bear the good fruit of peace or justice according to Luke's Jesus. Because it cooperated with the culture of injustice and empire, it bore no fruit. It was useless and should have been cut down, according to the parable. Jesus is the gardener who tells the orchard owner, God the Creator, to let him try to care for Judaism in the hope that it still might bear the good fruit of peace and justice.

This parable applies to all world religions today, but especially to Christianity. To the extent that the Christian churches do not bear the good fruit of peace and justice, they are practically dead and should just collapse. This is what we see happening around the world wherever the churches have been co-opted by nationalism, militarism, racism, and greed, where they have not pursued Gospel nonviolence, resistance, peacemaking, and all-encompassing love. Churches flourished when they most fulfilled the Gospel mandate of justice and peace. Usually the churches bore good fruit, even when they were a tiny remnant, as with the Quakers who led the Abolitionist struggle; the Black churches of the South who led the civil rights movement; and the Catholic Worker communities who offered hospitality to the homeless and the first resistance to the Vietnam War. With this parable, Luke calls upon the early Christian community to focus on bearing the good fruit of justice, peace, and love if they want to live. The message holds true now more than ever.

"Woman, You Are Set Free" (13:10–17)

We find Jesus next in a synagogue teaching on the sabbath. He notices a woman who is completely bent over, incapable of standing up, who has suffered like this for eighteen years. Jesus says to her, "Woman, you are set free of your infirmity." He lays his hands on her, and all at once she stands up straight and starts praising God.

Here again we have a story unique to Luke. In this case, Luke demonstrates that Jesus associated with, served, and healed women. This is a scandal, and is even illegal. A holy rabbi simply did not go near an unclean person, much less a woman, much less a woman cursed with a broken back. And a holy rabbi would never touch that unclean woman, not even for the noblest cause. Jesus breaks every rule to heal this woman. Notice that she doesn't ask for healing; she probably cannot even imagine being healed. Jesus takes the initiative and announces that the woman is set free, then heals her by laying his hands on her head. This story does not appear in any other Gospel. Luke deliberately includes it to show that Jesus includes women in his ministry of healing and liberation, that, for Jesus, all are equal, all are children of God. The legacy of patriarchy that this Gospel passage addresses continues to this day; this passage never appears in Sunday readings in most churches. It is not deemed important or noteworthy, but in fact it's critically important to understand the real, all-inclusive, welcoming, and civilly disobedient Jesus.

Luke describes the fallout from Jesus's political act of healing. The synagogue leader and others are furious with Jesus and accuse him of breaking the law by healing someone on the sabbath. "Hypocrites!" Jesus responds. "Does not each one of you on the sabbath untie his ox or his ass from the manger and lead it out for watering? This daughter of Abraham, whom Satan has bound for eighteen years now, ought she not to have been set free on the sabbath day from this bondage?" Notice how Jesus challenges them nonviolently by pointing out how they do not apply the law legalistically when they take care of their animals on the sabbath, and how much more important this human being is than a farm animal. Further, he goes so far as to call this woman "a Daughter of Abraham," the only time in the Bible where such an exalted name is given to a woman, and to a sick and therefore unclean woman at that. By naming her as a Daughter of Abraham, Jesus breaks through sexism and patriarchy to insist on the total equality of women with men, especially in the sight of God and in the eyes of the great Abraham. Jesus even implies that the sabbath, as God's day, is the perfect day to "set free" anyone who has been "bound" by Satan. This is the work of God, to unbind those who have been bound by Satan. Luke reports that his adversaries were "humiliated," and "the whole crowd rejoiced at all the splendid deeds done by him." Jesus spoke the truth with love and compassion and probably did not care about the adulation of the crowd; his sole concern was for this daughter of Abraham, and he was probably very consoled that she was set free, healed and praising God.

"Strive to Enter through the Narrow Door" (13:18–35)

"What is the kingdom of God like?" Jesus asks next. "To what can I compare it?" This is the question Jesus asks the most frequently, and Luke repeats Matthew's insistent focus on God's reign. With this question, we enter the mind of the nonviolent Jesus and learn what should be most on our minds too. He spends his days imagining what God's reign is like, trying to describe it to everyone, comparing it to various things in order to teach us. He knows what it is like, but he barely has the words to tell us. He's trying to describe an entirely new way of life, a new realm in which we dwell in peace with one another and with God. It is the opposite of the Roman Empire and its corruption, but that doesn't begin to describe it.

"It is like a mustard seed that a person took and planted in the garden," Jesus says. "When it was fully grown, it became a large bush and 'the birds of the sky dwelt in its branches.'" The mustard seed is the tiniest seed but eventually grows into a large bush that welcomes all kinds of birds. I think he's telling us that he is the mustard seed, or his very proclamation of God's reign is the tiny mustard seed, which will grow to draw people of every race, language, and way of life to it, like the birds of the sky.

He repeats his question: "To what shall I compare the kingdom of God? It is like yeast that a woman took and mixed in with three measures of wheat flour until the whole batch of dough was leavened." Again, the point is the tiny ingredient of yeast that transforms the whole dough. Jesus sees his proclamation of God's reign as eventually going forth through history and disarming people and nations until the entire world is transformed into a culture of nonviolence, until God's reign comes on earth as it is in heaven.

Luke's parables invite us to ponder God's reign, to seek it, proclaim it, talk about it, and act as if we are already living in it. That requires taking Jesus's teachings to heart, surrendering ourselves to God, and living by them day after day. As we proclaim God's reign, we do our part in the movement so that everyone can live with justice and their basic rights. Others will dismiss your talk as a daydream, and that's when you will discover why it's so hard to talk about the reign of God. We can barely imagine a just or nonviolent world, let alone the reign of God as a new realm of infinite love and peace. This, however, is precisely the task of the Christian, to use their imagination to help others reclaim the vision of a new world of peace.

Someone asks Jesus, "Lord, will only a few people be saved?" He uses the opportunity to urge people once again. "Strive to enter through the narrow door," he says, "for many, I tell you, will attempt to enter but will not be strong enough." The image continues with a serious warning:

> "After the master of the house has arisen and locked the door, then will you stand outside knocking and saying, 'Lord, open the door for us.' He will say to you in reply, 'I do not know where you are from.' And you will say, 'We ate and drank in your company and you taught in our streets.' Then he will say to you, 'I do not know where you are from. Depart from me, all you evildoers!' And there will be wailing and grinding of teeth when you see Abraham, Isaac, and Jacob and all the prophets in the kingdom of God and you yourselves cast out. And people will come from the east and the west and from the north and the south and will recline at table in the kingdom of God. For behold, some are last who will be first, and some are first who will be last."

Luke usually reserves words such as "master" and "arisen" to speak of the risen Jesus in God's reign. People who will not be allowed into God's reign of love and peace will be told by the master, "I do not know where you are from," and will be called "evildoers." There are no evildoers in God's house, only good-doers. Anyone who does good is recognized by Jesus as being a member of his Father's house. It will not matter to Jesus whether we knew him in the flesh during his lifetime; what matters to him is if he knows where we are from— that we come from the same house that he comes from, the house where God lives, where we are from and where we will return.

Then, Luke's Jesus paints a scene of heaven as an eternal banquet where Abraham, Isaac, and Jacob and all the prophets recline at table with Jesus and people from every time and corner of the world—not the chosen ones, the elites, the rich, the powerful, the billionaires, and the self-righteous, but the last and the least, the poor and the lowly, the marginalized and the excluded, and everyone who carried on the prophetic movement for justice and peace. God's reign of peace and love will be the exact opposite of the world. It's going to be very different from what we might expect.

Some Pharisees warn Jesus that Herod wants to kill him, that death squads are on the lookout for him. Jesus calls Herod "that fox." Throughout the scriptures, we have imagery about the sheep, the flock, the Good Shepherd, the greener pastures, as well as the bad shepherds and hirelings. This is the only reference to a fox, and Jesus uses the image to describe the political ruler of Galilee. In this long-running image, the fox is the one who enters the peaceful pasture, kills the sheep, and eats the lamb. Not long ago Jesus sent his disciples out to be as innocent and nonviolent as lambs; now we know there is a fox on the prowl.

"Go and tell that fox," Jesus says, "'Behold, I cast out demons and I perform healings today and tomorrow, and on the third day I accomplish my purpose. Yet I must continue on my way today, tomorrow, and the following day, for it is impossible that a prophet should die outside of Jerusalem.'" Luke alludes to resurrection here, saying that Jesus has come to heal the sick and expel the demons of death, and will accomplish his purpose with his resurrection. Some commentators argue that Luke is saying that Jesus's mission will one day be fulfilled. But I think the reference to his journey, his walking campaign to Jerusalem, and his inevitable death for his prophetic word, allude to his resurrection as the realization of his purpose. In his rising, he shows his power over death itself, including the local political ruler who hunts down and kills people.

As we saw in Matthew, Luke's Jesus laments the state of Jerusalem, where prophets have long been arrested and killed. "Jerusalem, Jerusalem, you who kill the prophets and stone those sent to you," he cries, "how many times I yearned to gather your children together as a hen gathers her brood under her wings, but you were unwilling! Behold, your house will be abandoned. But I tell you, you will not see me until the time comes when you say, 'Blessed is he who comes in the name of the Lord.'" This verse presents a feminine image of God, and not only that, but an animal image of God. Jesus likens himself to a mother hen who gathers her chicks under her wings to protect them as they sleep and grow. Mother hens in fact are fiercely protective and smart and will do anything to guard their broods. Jesus wants to gather all of Jerusalem together so that all there might praise the God of peace together, welcome everyone as sister and brother, and know the fullness of God's reign of peace in the holy city. But they refuse his message and reject him outright. He knows that he will be rejected and killed like the holy prophets of justice and peace who have gone before him. But he warns them: if they reject him, their house—the temple—will be abandoned and destroyed, as it would eventually be by the Romans in the year 70. Even so, some people will welcome him with palm branches and blessings for coming in the name of the Lord.

"Invite the Poor, the Crippled, the Lame, and the Blind" (14:1–35)

The journey continues, and this time we find Jesus dining on the sabbath at the home of one of the leading Pharisees, with everyone observing him carefully. Somehow, a sick man with dropsy (which produces a large swelling of fluid) enters, and Jesus is going to heal that person but decides to use the occasion as an opportunity to call the religious authorities to conversion. "Is it lawful to cure on the sabbath or not?" he asks point blank. He echoes the passage in Mark about the man with the withered hand and other occasions when he broke the sabbath law.

The question cries out for an answer from us today. It can be translated today in a way that confronts our own blindness to those we deem as outsiders. What is God's will regarding how we should treat those different from us: for men, how do we treat women; for white people, how do we treat people of color; for straight people, how do we treat LGBTQ people; for able-bodied people, how do we treat people with disabilities; for rich and powerful people, how do we treat poor and powerless people, and so on. The question opens up a larger question: What does it mean to be human? What does it mean to be Godly? What does God expect of humans? The answer is found in the teachings of the Sermon on the Plain. We are to act and live in a spirit of unconditional love, boundless compassion, selfless service, and total nonviolence at all times. Like Jesus, we are to relieve suffering every chance we get.

By now, we're not surprised by the anger, resentment, and hostility Jesus receives. He puts the religious leaders on the spot, and there was no way they would admit that he might be right, that compassion for the sick takes precedence over the law, or that such compassion precisely fulfills the law, the sabbath, the work of God. Luke writes, "They kept silent; so he took the man and, after he had healed him, dismissed him."

He poses another question: "Who among you, if your son or ox falls into a cistern, would not immediately pull him out on the sabbath day?" Each one of them would immediately rescue their son or ox if it fell into a cistern on the sabbath, of course! "But they were unable to answer his question," Luke concludes.

Remember, Jesus is reclining at table in the house of one of the most powerful, respected individuals of his time, a leading Pharisee, like a seminary rector or bishop. I imagine Jesus to be as gentle as Gandhi or Thich Nhat Hanh. He bears no ill will, no anger, no resentment, no self-righteousness. There is no guile in his question nor any trace of trying to embarrass anyone or assert himself as a wise man. He truly wants to open their minds to the possibilities of boundless compassion, to the love of God, to an open-hearted life that sees every human being as a sister or brother, especially those in need.

Jesus proceeds to teach his host and the other religious leaders with a parable toward "those who had been invited, noticing how they were choosing the places of honor at the table." He invites them to practice humility, to put others before themselves, to choose the lowest place. At a dinner, "take the lowest place so that when the host comes to you he may say, 'My friend, move up to a higher position.' Then you will enjoy the esteem of your companions at the table. Everyone who exalts himself will be humbled, but the one who humbles himself will be exalted." His teaching on humility is central to his Sermon on the Plain and mission for justice. If we let our egos rule our lives, and walk around thinking we're greater than everyone else, as the religious authorities did, one day our lives will come crashing down. On the other hand, if we recognize our lowliness before God, let God rule our lives, and serve those in need, a whole new vista will open before us. People enjoy being around humble people who practice kindness and compassion, who are not self-centered but other-centered. While the world tricks us into inflating our egos, Jesus invites us through the narrow door of humility so that our focus is entirely on God's reign of peace and love.

To the host he says:

"When you hold a lunch or a dinner, do not invite your friends or your brothers or your relatives or your wealthy neighbors, in case they may invite you back and you have repayment. Rather, when you hold a banquet, invite the poor, the crippled, the lame, and the blind. Blessed indeed will you be because of their inability to repay you. For you will be repaid at the resurrection of the righteous."

Here in the house of one of the most powerful people in the region, Jesus talks about the poor and the need to put them at the center of our attention. He issues a new commandment that resonates today: *invite the poor, the crippled, the lame, and the blind.* He follows this commandment with a new beatitude: Blessed will you be, precisely because of their inability to repay you.

Jesus calls us to serve those in need without a trace of desire for reciprocation; our service must be selfless, generous, and loving without a hint of wanting something in return. His teaching goes against the way of the world, which centers on the rich and powerful and on the financial reward they expect for their investments. He puts his focus on the poor and powerless and commands us to do the same. We should put ourselves at their service and hold feasts for them. It is our pleasure to meet their needs, to feed the hungry, to serve those who cannot repay us, to make them happy. Jesus reminds us too of our long-term goal—*the resurrection of the righteous,* a phrase unique to Luke. That's where we are headed. The way into this resurrection is selfless service toward the poor and all those who can never repay us for our service. Only then will we discover the new vistas and surprising rewards of unconditional compassionate love.

How do we "invite the poor"? First, we befriend them, listen to them, accompany them, find out what they need, and then help meet those needs. It can be as simple as distributing food and clothing to the homeless or the local food bank, or volunteering at your local homeless shelter or Catholic Worker house or serving at the local soup kitchen or Meals on Wheels. If we pitch in with others in our local community, it is doable. We can associate with and befriend neighbors or strangers we meet with whom we would not normally socialize. We will find consolation in this holy work and make new friends. We will gain insights to the compassion of Jesus, who threw a feast for the poor when he multiplied the loaves and the fish and fed thousands of hungry people. If we help offer meals and shelter to those in need and care for the poor, the crippled, the lame, and the blind, we will find that we can make a positive difference in the lives of others and that selfless service to those in need brings its own reward.

One of the guests responds to Jesus by offering his own beatitude about sharing in the eternal banquet in heaven. "Blessed is the one who will dine in the kingdom of God," he says to Jesus. Notice that Jesus does not say this beatitude. Why does the guest say this? Is he trying to impress Jesus? The comment exposes the radical nature of Jesus's teaching, which is focused not on life after death but on the needs of the poorest people around us here and now. If we want a place in the kingdom of heaven, he says, we have to serve those near us who can never repay us. That's the ticket into the resurrection of the righteous. The guest's response tries to spiritualize Jesus's teaching and change the topic so that we do not have to address the political reality of systemic injustice and poverty around us. Why bring up such unpleasant matters during a feast anyway? he seems to say. Let's talk about the great party in heaven to come! We are rich in this life, so we are guaranteed a place of honor in the heavenly banquet, he presumes.

Jesus thinks exactly the opposite. He responds with a parable about a great feast (similar to the parable of the wedding banquet we read in Mt. 22:1–10) that points to the truth of the matter—the fact that most of us do *not* want to attend the heavenly feast in the kingdom of God if it involves giving up power, prestige, wealth, and comfort to serve the poor and powerless. We are doing everything we can, Luke insinuates, to ensure that we do not attend God's heavenly banquet. The parable of the great banquet tells of a dinner to which many people are invited, but each of them sends regrets that they are not able to attend. When told this, the owner orders his servant to "go out quickly into the streets and alleys of the town and bring in here the poor and the crippled, the blind and the lame." The last people one would expect at a wealthy man's house are brought in to enjoy the feast. But then, the servant reports to the owner that there is still room, so the owner says, "Go out to the highways and hedgerows and make people come in that my home may be filled. For, I tell you, none of those who were invited will taste my dinner."

Note, first of all, that Luke has removed all the violence and killing we read in Matthew's version and, in particular, the reference to the guest who was not wearing the required garment. Instead, it is a story about how many were invited to the feast but chose not to attend, and how the host instead invited anyone he could find, including bystanders and strangers out on the streets, alleys, and highways. Most commentators say the parable points out how so many of us expect to go to heaven but actually reject Jesus and his invitation to God's reign of peace and love here and now, and how instead God's reign is being given here and now to the poor (as we heard in the Sermon on the Plain), the crippled, the blind, and the lame, to those in need, even to those who do not know God. The party is still on, the heavenly banquet will happen, the invitation to God's reign still stands, the parable declares, but those expected to be there will not be there because they have adamantly rejected God's invitation. The parable warns readers not to reject Jesus and his invitation to God's reign of peace, and instead to seek God's reign with all our hearts by serving the poor, the lame, the crippled, and the blind, and by doing God's will. A post-supersessionist reading makes sense within Luke's overall urgent call to compassion, nonviolence, and universal love as requirements for life in the ongoing celebration that is God's reign and is happening as we speak.

As he walks along followed by the crowds, Luke's Jesus issues another stern requirement of discipleship: if people want to follow him, they have to sever their allegiance to their families and give all their allegiance to him. He is not looking for fans who still obey only their parents or spouses. He wants disciples who do what their master says. "If any one comes to me without hating his father and mother, wife and children, brothers and sisters, and even his own life, he cannot be my disciple," he says. The language is dramatic and harsh. Hate all allegiances, even hate your own ego; surrender everything to Jesus. From the perspective of nonviolence, we know that he wants us to surrender ourselves to him and his way of life and not turn to someone else, such as our parents, to tell us what to do or, worse, to rely on our own egos and desires. Discipleship requires total surrender to Jesus, even the surrender of our lives along the path of nonviolence, even to the point of a deep-down willingness to be martyrs for Jesus's way. Carrying the cross of nonviolent resistance is a requirement of discipleship to Jesus. It means we consciously, humbly, go against our own egos, desires, even members of our families in pursuit of God's reign here on earth. God and God's reign come first, before anything else. As followers of Jesus, we know that our survival is already guaranteed in "the resurrection of the righteous," so we can follow our master all the way to the cross and beyond into the new life of resurrection.

Discipleship to the nonviolent Jesus also requires renunciation of possessions, money, and greed itself. In his parables about building a tower or a king marching into battle, Jesus urges us to prepare to pay the cost of discipleship, which may include our very lives.

"Which of you wishing to construct a tower does not first sit down and calculate the cost to see if there is enough for its completion? Otherwise, after laying the foundation and finding himself unable to finish the work the onlookers should laugh at him and say, 'This one began to build but did not have the resources to finish.' Or what king marching into battle would not first sit down and decide whether with ten thousand troops he can successfully oppose another king advancing upon him with twenty thousand troops? But if not, while he is still far away, he will send a delegation to ask for peace terms. In the same way, every one of you who does not renounce all his possessions cannot be my disciple."

If you do not interiorly renounce your family, your ego, your status, and your possessions, you cannot follow me, Jesus says. At some point, these ties will hold you back and prevent you from going the distance in your discipleship. "Salt is good," Luke comments, "but if salt itself loses its taste, with what can its flavor be restored? It is fit neither for the soil nor for the manure pile; it is thrown out. Whoever has ears to hear ought to hear."

In other words, Luke says, if you get trapped in the ties of family, possessions, power, or self-seeking, you will lose your discipleship and not serve Jesus or God's reign. You will be as useless as tasteless salt, even manure for that matter. Our commitment to the nonviolent Jesus has to be total. If our spouses and families share that commitment, then they would encourage us to risk ourselves in discipleship to Jesus for the coming of a new culture of nonviolence. Indeed, they will take up the cross, too, and join the discipleship journey with Jesus.

"We Must Celebrate and Rejoice, Because Your Brother Was Dead and Has Come to Life" (15:1–32)

Luke offers several more parables that occur nowhere else. He reports that the crowds that followed Jesus included tax collectors and well-known sinners, and so the Pharisees and scribes put Jesus down and criticized him for his association with the unclean, the marginalized, and the unholy. "This man welcomes sinners and eats with them," they charged.

Notice how nonviolent Jesus is as he responds to these accusations. He does not yell or point a finger but instead uses a story to try to awaken their consciences.

"What man among you having a hundred sheep and losing one of them would not leave the ninety-nine in the desert and go after the lost one until he finds it?" Jesus asks. "And when he does find it, he sets it on his shoulders with great joy and, upon his arrival home, he calls together his friends and neighbors and says to them, 'Rejoice with me because I have found my lost sheep.' I tell you, in just the same way there will be more joy in heaven over one sinner who repents than over ninety-nine righteous people who have no need of repentance." The parable of the lost sheep, with its party to celebrate its finding, is pure genius. Jesus uses an ordinary scene in the life of the rural poor to demonstrate God's attitude toward humanity, especially how God rejoices over those who repent, not those who believe they have no need of repentance. While Luke's Jesus focuses on his call of repentance to sinners, and the joy there is when sinners repent and return to God, he also subtly indicts those who believe they have no need of repentance.

As we sit with the parable of the lost sheep, we realize that every human being is a sinner, lost in falsehood and confusion, trapped in a culture set against the ways of God, yet called to repent and come back to God. Further, God is actively searching for every person and calling them back and rejoicing when they return. Instead of believing, as the religious authorities do, that we have no need of repentance because we are not sinners, Luke invites us to recognize the part of ourselves that is lost, even though we pretend we're not. If Luke presumes that everyone is lost in the eyes of God, and most of us do not consider ourselves lost, then we need to discover where we are blind, perhaps through our nationalism, sexism, racism, militarism, or classism. Once we place ourselves within our sinful culture of violence and realize that each of us is complicit in systemic, social sin, then we acknowledge that some part of us is lost. The disciple of Jesus seeks to be humble before God, so we are eager to cry out for help to God, and hope God will rescue us, carry us home, and celebrate us with a party in God's reign of peace.

Luke took this parable from the same source as Matthew, but its theme is so central for him that he adds two more original parables on the theme of saving those who are lost and God's wild compassionate love for those who repent. "What woman having ten coins and losing one would not light a lamp and sweep the house, searching carefully until she finds it? And when she does find it, she calls together her friends and neighbors and says to them, 'Rejoice with me because I have found the coin that I lost.' In just the same way, I tell you, there will be rejoicing among the angels of God over one sinner who repents." Here Luke's Jesus emphasizes God's joy, the joy throughout heaven, when we repent, and the need to turn back to God, to stop being lost, and to bring joy to God through authentic repentance.

The focus is not on the sinner but on God, who searches for us day and night. Every human being is lost, which means God is eternally searching for us. We wonder why God doesn't help us or appear to us, but it's because we are the ones who have strayed from God and given up returning to God. All the while, God spends all his time searching for us. Luke emphasizes the joy that God and God's angels feel when anyone turns back to God. This should be reason alone for our repentance: we want to bring joy to God. The image of the woman calling together friends and neighbors for a celebration is a beautiful image: God as a woman who brings everyone together to rejoice over someone who has returned to God's love. For Luke, the parable urges us to realize that God is looking for each of us and to return to God at once, so that God will rejoice, and we can all get on with the party.

Luke takes this theme to another level with the famous story of the prodigal son. There are so many ways to reflect on the life of Jesus—as servant of the poor, healer, teacher, wisdom figure, spiritual guide, peacemaker, justice advocate, resister, community builder, prophet, and martyr. We could certainly add poet and storyteller to the list. The story of the prodigal son I consider one of the greatest stories in human history. The best commentary on it is by Henri Nouwen in his masterpiece, *Return of the Prodigal Son*, based on Nouwen's seeing Rembrandt's painting of the same name while visiting the Hermitage Museum in St. Petersburg. Nouwen lays out an approach for us to engage with the parable in a way that is disarming, healing, and transforming. Through his own story, he invites us to reflect on how we are like the prodigal son, then how we are like the resentful older brother, but ultimately how we are called to be like the gentle, compassionate, unconditionally loving father.

"A man had two sons," Luke's Jesus begins. "The younger son said to his father, 'Father, give me the share of your estate that should come to me.'" So the father divided the property and gave his son his share. The son traveled far off and "squandered his inheritance on a life of dissipation." We're left to imagine just how recklessly he lived. Just then, famine struck the country. The younger son was left homeless and penniless, and found work tending pigs on a farm. The job paid hardly anything, and he was hungry. He became envious of the corn that the pigs ate. "Coming to his senses," Luke writes, the young man realizes that his father's servants have it far better, so he decides to return home, apologize, and become one of his father's servants. He chooses not to starve to death. In the face of death, he chooses life.

"While he was still a long way off, his father caught sight of him, and was filled with compassion," Luke writes. "He ran to his son, embraced him and kissed him." It's important to note that the father had been waiting for the son this whole time, on a kind of perpetual lookout for him. He'd been sitting on his porch, staring at the horizon all day, looking for his lost son. We note, too, that the father is "filled with compassion." He should have been angry, he should have renounced his son, he should have gotten on with his life. Not this gentle, loving father. There is no anger, judgment, harshness, bitterness, or resentment in the father. There is not a trace of being hurt or wounded, even though he has been hurt and wounded by the younger son. Instead, he feels only unconditional love for his long-lost son, so much so that he runs out to meet his son, embraces him, and kisses him. If this is Jesus's image of God, then we are breaking new ground in our understanding of divine infinite, compassionate love.

"Father, I have sinned against heaven and against you," the son says after the embrace. "I no longer deserve to be called your son." Most of us would agree. We would expect the father to yell at him, denounce him, disown him, and send him away. But this father is full of compassion and understanding. He loves his son wildly. He turns to his servants and orders them, "Quickly bring the finest robe and put it on him. Put a ring on his finger and sandals on his feet. Take the fattened calf and slaughter it. Let us celebrate with a feast, because this son of mine was dead, and has come to life again; he was lost, and has been found." With that, the celebration began.

It is an astonishing image of unconditional love and compassion. The father stops all the work on his property and summons everyone immediately to a party to celebrate the return of his lost son. The clincher is that this son was dead but has come to life, he was lost but has been found. Luke uses language of resurrection to describe the dramatic turn of events. The son had been lost to the power of death, to the culture and all its traps—selfishness, greed, gluttony, alcoholism, lust, and arrogance. But he turned back. He accepted his mistake, his brokenness, his weakness, and headed home, this time with humility. Lo and behold, he discovers that he is still loved, that he was always loved, that he has his life back. Let the party begin!

But the brilliant story doesn't end there. We now hear about the older, faithful son, the good son, the dutiful one. He had been out working in the fields, hears the sound of music and dancing—it's a real party!—asks one of the servants about this commotion. He's told that his brother has returned and his father has killed the fatted calf to celebrate. The dutiful, older brother becomes angry and refuses to enter the house. His deep resentment boils over, so he does what every egotistic, selfish, self-righteous narcissist does: he throws a temper tantrum.

The old man comes out and pleads with the son, but he will have none of it. "All these years I served you," he complains to his father, "and not once did I disobey your orders. Yet you never gave me even a young goat to feast on with my friends. But when your son returns who swallowed up your property with prostitutes, for him you slaughter the fattened calf." Notice the self-centeredness of the dutiful son. Yes, he has obeyed his father, but he's been stewing with resentment because he wants things for himself. Despite his good behavior, on the inside he's not that different from his brother. Why wasn't he given a goat to feast on with his friends? The point: he does not have any compassion or love for his father. He feels only anger and resentment at both his brother and his father. He's actually as selfish as the famous prodigal.

What Henri Nouwen fails to recognize is the context of the story, which is the resentment Jesus witnesses among the Pharisees and teachers of the law: "The tax collectors and sinners were all drawing near to listen to him, but the Pharisees and teachers of the law began to complain saying, 'This man welcomes sinners and eats with them'" (Mt. 15:1–2). The whole story of the prodigal son is really about the resentfulness of the older son, who resents his father's mercy and compassion. This is the key to understanding the work of the nonviolent Jesus: he is calling us to let go of our resentments, anger, ego, and self-will to embrace God's mercy and compassion, and to share that mercy and compassion through lives of loving service and steadfast nonviolence from now on.

How might he have responded to the news that his brother was back, that his father was throwing a party to celebrate? He might have run to embrace his brother and welcome him back. He might have embraced his father and comforted and consoled his poor father who has suffered all these months waiting for the prodigal's return. He might have been the first to lead the dancing and the celebration because his brother who was on the road to death has come back to life. He might have raised a glass and offered a toast to both his father and brother. Instead, the older brother is stuck in self-centeredness as much as his brother was.

330

"My son, you are here with me always," the father tells the older son. "Everything I have is yours. But now we must celebrate and rejoice, because your brother was dead and has come to life again; he was lost and has been found." The father shows unconditional love and compassion to the resentful older son. "You are here with me always" is a statement of total affirmation and loving-kindness. Not only that, but he says that the entire estate—all my wealth, all I own—belongs to you. He invites his son through his loving-kindness to let go of his anger and resentment, to know that he too is well loved, to be at peace, and to celebrate life. The one who was lost and dead is found and alive—that is a cause for celebration and joy. There is no need to cling to past resentments, to remain bitter, to wallow in hate. Step into the fullness of compassion and love, and enjoy the party!

We don't know what happens. The story ends there. Luke moves on. For hundreds of years, people have studied the tale and reflected on the conversion of the prodigal son. Henri Nouwen did that too and spent a year reflecting on his life as the long-lost younger brother. But then one day, while he was sharing his meditation with a friend, the friend pointed out how Henri was more like the resentful older brother. Henri writes that it was a revelation to him. So he spent another year reflecting on the resentment, anger, and bitterness that churned within him. Finally, after he shared his reflections with Sister Sue Mosteller of the L'Arche community, she said, "It doesn't matter whether you're more like the younger son or the older son; we need you to be like the compassionate father!" That was the final break-through for Henri. He realized that he, and all of us, are called to become as compassionate, loving, welcoming, forgiving, and merciful as the Father. This is Jesus's image of God, on the lookout for each of us, waiting for each of us, wanting to welcome us back home, hoping to throw a party for us, and pleading with us to turn back from our selfishness, to drop our anger, resentment, and bitterness, come back home, relax, and join the party.

It's one of the greatest stories ever told, and still, it packs a punch. We can ask ourselves, as Henri Nouwen did, Where are we in the story? Are we like the younger son, wasting our lives, far from God's home, lost and drifting toward death? How can we come to our senses and turn back to God? Are we like the older son—bitter, angry, resentful? How can we become as compassionate, loving, forgiving, and welcoming as the father? How do we celebrate when others come back to life? What keeps us from joining the celebration? What is our image of God, and, based on this story, what is God saying to us these days? How is God on the lookout for us? What keeps us from joining God's party? Why not swallow our pride, thank God, and celebrate? I hope we can all do the right thing and learn to repent, let go of our selfishness and resentments, welcome God's unconditional love and compassion, and rejoice, give thanks, and join God's ongoing celebration of life.

"If They Will Not Listen to Moses and the Prophets, Neither Will They Listen If Someone Rises from the Dead" (16:1–19:27)

Jesus concludes his story of the father with two sons and launches into another story about a rich man whose steward squanders his property. The steward is brought before the rich man and told to "prepare a full account of your stewardship because you can no longer be my steward." The steward realizes he's been caught, wonders what to do, and takes action so that others will still welcome him when he loses his position. So he calls in the rich man's debtors and cuts in half each of their debts for olive oil and wheat. Later, the master commends the dishonest steward for acting prudently. The steward had been charging twice as much for the olive oil and wheat and keeping the extra half for himself, which is why he was dishonest. But now, by cutting down the price for the debtors and charging the actual amount, the steward won the esteem of the debtors. Now, he might be able to get a position elsewhere because people now considered him an honest, just steward.

Luke's Jesus ends this strange story with a mysterious moral: "For the children of this world are more prudent in dealing with their own generation than are the children of light. I tell you, make friends for yourselves with dishonest wealth, so that when it fails, you will be welcomed into eternal dwellings." Jesus is commending the dishonest steward for no longer charging double and stealing the extra for himself, and he teaches us in effect to do the right thing with eternal life: to stop stealing the resources of others and instead act justly toward everyone so that, in the end, God can welcome us into God's reign of justice. The point is to be a child of light, not a child of darkness, and therefore to be honest, just, and fair to others.

Jesus is looking for honest, trustworthy people, as Luke adds in the follow-up teaching. "The person who is trustworthy in very small matters is also trustworthy in great ones; and the person who is dishonest in very small matters is also dishonest in great ones. If, therefore, you are not trustworthy with dishonest wealth, who will trust you with true wealth? If you are not trustworthy with what belongs to another, who will give you what is yours?" He calls us to be honest and trustworthy here on earth in the small day-to-day details with family, work, neighbors, and the world. God will bless us for our honesty. But if we are dishonest, greedy, and not trustworthy in the ordinary matters of life, what would we expect God to think of us? The teaching calls us to transcend the selfishness that comes from greed and dishonesty, and it reaches a climax in the next sentence, which we heard in Matthew's Sermon on the Mount.

"No servant can serve two masters. He will either hate one and love the other, or be devoted to one and despise the other. You cannot serve God and mammon." There it is, he could not be clearer—it's either God or money; you cannot have both. Jesus is not telling us what to do; he's presenting the choice before us. But if we have heard the message of his parables and his call to love, compassion, and service of the poor, we know he summons us to serve God with all our hearts, minds, and strength, and not to waste our one precious life in pursuit of money that will not last. Pursue eternal wealth, the treasure we store up in heaven, an investment that comes through our loving service, compassion, active nonviolence, and doing the will of God. If we seek God's reign, we will find God's reign. If we seek money, then we will never know God's reign.

The religious authorities, Luke reports, who loved money, heard these teachings and sneered at him. Take a moment to notice how Jesus must feel, being sneered at for offering his beautiful wisdom. He is hurt and mocked but does not retaliate or get angry. He must be praying for them, forgiving them, and blessing them, for they know not what they do. They mock him for dismissing their pursuit of money and his call for total faith in God alone. There they stand in front of the nonviolent Jesus, "sneering" at him! How blind they are, how wrong they are. We can see this easily, two thousand years later, but we should go slowly. How do we sneer at Jesus's teachings today? How do we sneer at those who espouse justice, compassion, mercy, and universal love? Who has sneered at *us* for our Gospel stand? Jesus has compassion on them because they do not know what they are doing. How do we show the same compassion when we are rejected by those who do not know what they are doing? Luke warns us to avoid money and greed, and not to end up looking down on the poor and needy, and sneering at those like Jesus who seek an end to poverty and injustice.

"You justify yourselves in the sight of others, but God knows your hearts," Jesus says to them, "for what is of human esteem is an abomination in the sight of God." Think of all the things that we hold in high esteem: the presidency, the military, the generals, the rich, the Oscars, royalty, glamorous celebrities, and rock stars. All riches, worldly honors, possessions, awards, gold, and acclaim are an abomination in the sight of God. What then is of high esteem in God's sight? Loving-kindness to the poor and marginalized; prophetic truth-telling; sincere pursuit of God's reign of universal love and total nonviolence; discipleship to the nonviolent Jesus; being willing to be persecuted, arrested, even killed for speaking out publicly for justice, disarmament, the poor, and creation.

Luke's declaration raises the question, Whose opinion matters most? Those of other people, especially the ones who are rich and powerful, or those of God? Do we want to win the esteem of others by becoming rich and famous in the eyes of the world, or do we want to win the esteem of God, who knows our hearts, sees what we do, and watches as we store up treasure in heaven through our selfless service and pursuit of justice and peace?

"The law and the prophets lasted until John," Luke writes, "but from then on, the kingdom of God is proclaimed, and everyone who enters does so with violence." Up until John, Luke explains, the chosen people lived according to the law and the prophets. But now, since John and Jesus have appeared, people everywhere are hearing about God's reign because they have proclaimed it far and wide. Unfortunately, Luke laments, people try to enter it through violence. They have not understood one word Jesus has taught about God's reign, that it is an entirely new world of nonviolence, that to enter it one has to practice peace, that one must be honest, trustworthy, compassionate, loving, and kind to all. They did not have this word "nonviolence," so they could not quite grasp the call to renounce violence in all its forms. At least we have this Gandhian word to help us now understand Jesus and his Gospel of peace. He does not want us to try to serve God and live public religious lives by bullying others, being greedy and violent, thinking and talking only about ourselves, or supporting the status quo of war and empire. All that has to end.

Luke then adds two sayings found in the other Synoptics. The letter of the law will not become invalid, he says; he is fulfilling it. It is more valid than ever because it guides us to practice universal love, nonviolence, and compassion toward everyone with no exceptions. Also, anyone who divorces his wife and remarries, or marries a divorced woman, commits adultery; what is shocking here is that once again Jesus places women on equal legal terms with men. Men considered only women guilty of adultery. Jesus considers men and women who divorce as equally guilty of adultery.

We come to one of the most powerful, most pointed, most challenging stories in the Bible, a parable unique to Luke that shows the consequences of our failure to offer compassion and justice to the poor. Jesus describes two characters: a rich man, dressed in purple garments and fine linen who dined sumptuously each day, and a poor man named Lazarus covered in sores who lay at his door and who would have gladly eaten the scraps that fell from the rich man's table. Dogs used to come and lick his sores, Jesus says, depicting the poorest, most helpless person imaginable. "When the poor man died, he was carried away by angels to the bosom of Abraham," Jesus says. "The rich man also died and was buried, and from the netherworld, where he was in torment, he raised his eyes and saw Abraham far off and Lazarus at his side." If the parable had ended there, it would have been enough to ponder for the rest of our lives. The implication is clear: the poorest of the poor go straight to heaven, while the rich and comfortable go straight to hell. We do not want to hear this message, and we wonder how it can fit within the perspective of nonviolence.

Luke shocks us with this illustration to jolt us into taking seriously Jesus's teachings: it is hard to enter God's reign if you are wealthy and have many possessions. If you are interested in entering God's reign, go relieve the suffering of every poor Lazarus at your door, and there are millions, perhaps billions of them—suffering, impoverished, homeless, hungry, sick people living and dying on the streets and in alleyways across Africa, Latin America, Asia, and especially India. Spend your lifetime relieving their suffering; be a modern-day Good Samaritan. Don't waste your time while the poor suffer. You will regret your missed opportunity.

But there's more. The rich man in hell calls out to Abraham for help, even to send Lazarus to warn to his five brothers back on earth so they don't end up in the same place of torment. "Father Abraham, have pity on me," he pleads. "'Send Lazarus to dip the tip of his finger in water and cool my tongue, for I am suffering torment in these flames.' Abraham replied, 'My child, remember that you received what was good during your lifetime while Lazarus likewise received what was bad; but now he is comforted here, whereas you are tormented. Moreover, between us and you a great chasm is established to prevent anyone from crossing who might wish to go from our side to yours or from your side to ours.' He said, 'Then I beg you, father, send him to my father's house, for I have five brothers, so that he may warn them, lest they too come to this place of torment.' But Abraham replied, 'They have Moses and the prophets. Let them listen to them.' He said, 'Oh no, father Abraham, but if someone from the dead goes to them, they will repent.' Then Abraham said, 'If they will not listen to Moses and the prophets, neither will they be persuaded if someone should rise from the dead.'"

This ending statement is like an electric jolt every time I hear it. Notice that the rich man in hell addresses Abraham as "father," and Abraham addresses him as "my child." Still, Abraham is not allowed to relieve the rich man's suffering, only to comfort Lazarus who suffered throughout his lifetime. Further, Abraham explains that there is a great divide between heaven and hell so that no one from heaven is allowed to go down and relieve the suffering of those in hell. Those in heaven spent their time on earth relieving human suffering; they would probably still want to do that in heaven. But it's the final plea that gets me: "Send Lazarus to warn my brothers." "Why should I do that?" Abraham asks. "They have Moses and the prophets to listen to." "Yes, but if someone were to rise from the dead, then they will listen," the man in hell says. Then the kicker: "If they did not listen to Moses and the prophets during their lifetime, they will not listen even if someone should rise from the dead."

If people do not listen to the great voices and prophetic visionaries of history—from Moses, Jeremiah, and Isaiah to Gandhi, Dr. King, and Dorothy Day—they will never change. They will never listen to any wisdom. They wouldn't even listen if God spoke from the clouds and said, "Listen!" They wouldn't listen if God appeared in all divine glory with all the angels. They would not listen even if someone should rise from the dead. People refuse to move out of their apathy, complacency, and comfort zones. Yet this is precisely where Luke is taking us and toward which Jesus is pointing: a new life of universal love that is way beyond our comfort zone, that demands we change and undertake public action for justice and service.

Luke's shocking punch line demands serious reflection. How do we respond to it? Do we want to hear this parable, or is it too serious, too depressing, too challenging? What part of us is open to the truth of this extreme parable, this in-your-face punch line? What positive step on behalf of the poor can we take to enact its message in our lives?

If we look at life on earth from God's perspective—not just the mess inside ourselves, but the gun violence, permanent wars, widespread starvation, preparations for nuclear war, and ongoing environmental destruction—and recall God's total nonviolence and therefore God's own boundary of free will, then let's ask ourselves: What more can God do nonviolently to wake us up, enlighten us, and lead us to the wisdom of universal love and peace? God has sent us so many holy men and women, so many prophets of justice and peace, and nearly all have been ignored, rejected, or killed right up to today. We will listen to anyone but them. Millions, billions of people, have preferred to listen to Caesar, Nero, Napoleon, and all the emperors, demagogues, and strong men of history—anyone but a holy prophet of nonviolence who demands we disarm, that everything change. It's as if humanity has been drugged into submission, possessed by the demons of violence, and refuses to throw off empires, dictatorships, fascism, militarism, and capitalism no matter what.

Throughout his parables, Luke alludes to God sending his beloved son in Jesus, and how the ruling authorities set out from day 1 to kill him. Nothing could change the minds of those in power, authority, and wealth—then or now, even if they killed Jesus and he rose from the dead. We can nod our heads and recognize the problem, but that still does not address the challenge of Luke. The Gospel demands our attention and asks, Where are we in the story? What part of us is like the rich man, focused on food, drink, and comfort, while the poor suffer around us? How do we go about daily life in comfort and ignore human suffering, even refuse to lift a finger to relieve it? Who is the Lazarus at our doorstep? What concrete action can we take today to make him or her feel better, to meet their needs? How strongly do we listen to Moses and the prophets, or do we prefer other biblical characters who promise wealth and military victory? How seriously do we listen to the voice of Jesus and his call to radical nonviolence and universal love; how much are we willing to change our lives? What does the resurrection of Jesus mean for us? If we claim to be Christian, and followers of someone who has risen from the dead, how do we rise from our apathy and comfort to carry on Jesus's revolutionary grassroots movement of nonviolence for justice? Dare we join the lineage of the prophets and speak out for an end to war, racism, poverty, nuclear weapons, and environmental destruction? What radical changes in our lives can we make to demonstrate our faith in the nonviolent, risen Jesus?

Luke's parable of the rich man and the suffering Lazarus at his door is the inevitable conclusion of Jesus's earlier dramatic statement in the Nazareth synagogue, where he announced that he had fulfilled the scriptures and had come to bring good news to the world's poor. This parable is good news to the world's poor and bad news for the rich, well fed, and comfortable. Likewise, this parable is the fulfillment of Luke's Sermon on the Plain, with Jesus's blessings upon the poor, the grieving, the hungry, and the persecuted, and his woes upon the rich, the laughing, the well fed, and the oppressors. It sums up the contrasting calls we have seen between Jesus's call to the rich man who walks away sad because he has many possessions and the poor blind beggar who asks for vision, sees Jesus, throws off his cloak, and follows him on the way. The parable of the rich man and Lazarus is the exclamation mark to everything Luke has written and cries out, "Throw off your riches, follow Jesus on the way of total nonviolence, spend your life relieving the suffering of the poor, resist systemic injustice and war, and proclaim the vision of a new culture of justice and peace. Make the resurrection believable through the way you live."

The parable of the rich man and Lazarus is a summons to action, to drop what we are doing and follow Jesus's campaign to fulfill Isaiah's Jubilee vision of good news and justice for the poor. More, it is a precursor to what is to come, for shortly we will realize that the suffering person at our doorstep is none other than the crucified, rejected, suffering Christ in our midst. One day he will rise. Will it make any difference for us?

"Say, 'We Are Useless Servants; We Have Done What We Were Obliged to Do'" (17:1–19)

"Things that cause sin will inevitably occur," Luke continues, "but woe to the person through whom they occur. It would be better for him if a millstone were put around his neck and he be thrown into the sea than for him to cause one of these little ones to sin. Be on your guard! If your brother sins, rebuke him; and if he repents, forgive him. And if he wrongs you seven times in one day and returns to you seven times saying, 'I am sorry,' you should forgive him." With this woe, Luke warns us again not to sin, and especially not to cause "one of these little ones" to sin—that is, one of his disciples, one of the poor and marginalized. When he says, "Be on your guard," he means, "Be mindful, careful, centered. Be aware and conscious of every word and deed you say and do." What do we do when people sin? Reach out to them, love them, help them stop their behavior, forgive them, guide them, coach them in grace. We forgive everyone who says they're sorry and acknowledges their wrongs, no matter how many times. Together, we admit we are sinners still loved by God and called beyond our sins into the new life of discipleship in peace, hope, trust, compassion, and love. We let go of our resentments, practice unconditional compassion, resist injustice, forgive everyone, and stay mindful in peace. This is Luke's prescription for reconciliation. In this way, we practice "the ministry of reconciliation," as St. Paul later called it (2 Cor. 5:18).

Jesus advocates forgiveness, then calls us to practice total faith in God, to know that with God all things are possible. "If you have faith the size of a mustard seed," he tells the disciples, "You would say to this mulberry tree, 'Be uprooted and planted in the sea,' and it would obey you." A small drop of authentic faith is powerful enough to change the world, he says. He wants us to exercise our faith, to believe in God with all our might, which means to do

God's will, not our own. When we surrender totally to God's will and take action through total faith in God, we can do miracles. Faith is the key to our public action for justice and peace. We believe in God and so we go forth and do God's work.

Luke ends this series of short teachings with a parable calling us to see ourselves as "useless servants." "When you have done all you have been commanded, say, 'We are useless servants; we have done what we were obliged to do.'" He is not putting us down but, rather, inviting us to see ourselves humbly as we are before the God of peace. If we do all that we can for God, at best, we can say only, "We are useless servants, just doing what we were obliged to do." God is the one worthy of all the honor and glory, not us. We know that we are broken, selfish sinners, that we are loved and called to follow, and we are happy to do our best, however poorly, for God.

Some translations use "unprofitable servants," but I prefer "useless." It stings because most of us want to be useful. We undertake works and projects, we say things and act certain ways, because we think we are being "useful." Usually, we are wrong. In our self-centeredness, egotism, narcissism, and blindness, we don't realize that we are not being useful at all, just like the male disciples in the Gospels. We get most things wrong and make most things worse. That's why the only prayer, in the end, is one of total surrender to the will of God, to the control of Jesus, saying, "You run my life. Take care of everything. Do with me what you will." Only in complete surrender can we be of any use to Jesus. Only then will we truly do what he commands us to do in the Sermon on the Plain.

At the heart of this discipleship life of faith, love, compassion, and nonviolence is a deep humility before God. We are happy to stand and serve in the presence of God for all eternity as humble servants. What a blessing, what an honor, what an undeserved gift! As we mature and realize our many failings and weaknesses, we become humble, loving servants eager to obey the commandments of the nonviolent Jesus. We are content and happy to do whatever he wants from now on. If we can fulfill his teachings, that is enough, because we know that pleases him, and that's our primary goal, to do his will and please him. Besides, we've tried doing our own will, to be servants of our jobs or money or America, and that doesn't work. It only leads us into selfishness, egotism, delusion, and insecurity and perhaps, without even our knowing it, harms others. Jesus is our Lord and Master, so we happily surrender our lives to him and do the tasks he's given us to do. At the end of the day, we're only too glad to say, "We are merely useless servants, doing what we were obliged to do." Even though we're pretty useless servants, we know we are blessed simply to be in the presence of Universal Love and Peace.

Luke proceeds with another tale we hear only through him. Jesus is walking along the border of Samaria, on the margins between enemy territories, when ten lepers approach and ask to be healed. "Jesus, Master! Have pity on us," they say. He tells them to show themselves to the priest. They walk away, and one of them realizes he's been healed, so he returns, falls at the feet of Jesus, thanks him, and praises God in a loud voice. Then we learn that the one who offered thanks and praise was a Samaritan, the hated enemy of the Judeans. "Ten were cleansed, were they not?" Jesus asks. "Where are the other nine? Has none but this foreigner returned to give thanks to God?" Then he said to him, "Stand up and go; your faith has saved you." The story adds to Luke's insistence that God is welcoming Jew and Gentile into God's reign of universal love, and that we Christians should welcome everyone, too, including foreigners, enemies, anyone, and everyone. We notice that Jesus affirms the Samaritan for having faith in him, saying that this faith made it possible for the leper to be healed.

Besides the political, even the illegal, nature of the healing, we do well to ponder Luke's emphasis on the importance of thanking Jesus and praising God for all that God is doing in us. It is right and just to give God thanks and praise, we say at Mass. But as readers of Luke, we notice the feelings of Jesus. So many people insult him, walk away from him, criticize him, tell him he's possessed, plot to kill him, or try to throw him off a cliff. It's a miracle he's made it this far. Here, after he heals ten people sick with leprosy, only one returns to give thanks. As we ponder where we are in the story and the times we have failed to thank Jesus for the good he does in our lives, we can commit once again to be like this Good Samaritan and spend the rest of our lives thanking Jesus and praising God. Like the gracious Samaritan, gratitude becomes our ordinary, daily practice.

To become truly grateful, we need to be intentional about it. If gratitude is not our habitual routine, a good way to start is to write down at the beginning or end of every day three things we're grateful for. If we feel no gratitude at all, put down the basics: I'm grateful for my eyes, my teeth, my hearing. As we sit with those gifts, we realize we are grateful for other basic gifts: I'm grateful for breathing, for my food, for the ability to walk. Then, we can move out of ourselves and say, I'm grateful for the sky, the mountains, the birds, the ocean, the wind. We get specific: I'm grateful for that robin, that gray squirrel, that brown hawk. Then, we thank God for our relatives and friends, our spouses and children, our lives and our callings. Soon, we move from gratitude to gratitude and find ourselves whispering "Thank you" as our daily, minute-by-minute mantra. We walk through our days giving thanks to God for everything—our health, our food, our families and friends, our work, the creatures, the wonders of creation, the human race, and most of all for Jesus and his way of love, compassion, and peace. There is no limit to things we have to be grateful to God for. Every day becomes a new opportunity for gratitude and praise.

"Behold, the Kingdom of God Is among You" (17:20–37)

In another rare teaching, Jesus responds to a question about the coming of the kingdom of God by saying, "The coming of the kingdom of God cannot be observed, and no one will announce, 'Look, here it is,' or, 'There it is.' For behold, the kingdom of God is among you." It is important to note that the Greek word used here can be translated in two ways, as "among you" and "within you." This teaching is infinitely rich and worthy of our constant reflection. On the one hand, Luke is telling us that the kingdom of God is right there in the middle of this scene in the presence of the nonviolent Jesus. He's also telling his own Christian community and us his readers that the kingdom of God is among us now and within us, as individuals and as a community, to the extent that we listen to Jesus and do what he commands.

As we practice and teach his teachings of universal love, universal compassion, and total nonviolence, we find ourselves in the kingdom of God right now. We can explore how the kingdom of God is within us as individuals in our solitude and out in nature, and we can also notice signs of the kingdom of God among us as a community—in our local church, among our friends and family as we share meals and celebrate life, and among those who participate in the grassroots movement for justice, disarmament, and creation. There especially, as we carry on Jesus's campaign to proclaim God's reign, we will experience God's reign inside us and among us as we press forward in the public work of God's justice and peace.

"The days will come when you will long to see one of the days of the Son of Humanity, but you will not see it," Jesus continues. "There will be those who will say to you, 'Look, there he is,' or 'Look, here he is.' Do not go off, do not run in pursuit. For just as lightning flashes and lights up the sky from one side to the other, so will the Son of Humanity be in his day. But first he must suffer greatly and be rejected by this generation." Just as with his teaching about the kingdom of God in our midst, Jesus tells us that you can't point out the presence of the Son of Humanity. Here he alludes to his disappearance. Like the thousands who have been killed and "disappeared" throughout Latin America, Jesus will be "disappeared." He will soon be arrested, tortured, executed, and hidden away in an unmarked tomb. His disciples will long to see him, but he will be gone. Then, like a flash of lightning, he will appear risen, like lightning east to west, beyond our wildest imagination, and they will know that all is well. We already know that he is the light of the world from his transfiguration, which the disciples witnessed. His resurrection will permanently break through the darkness of the world, and a new day of peace and hope will dawn for those who long to see the Son of Humanity. Now we know that if we follow him in radical discipleship and total nonviolence, the power of his resurrection will light our way like lightning east to west, and we will meet him along the way.

Luke's eschatological teachings address his community's concern that Jesus had not returned as they expected. The trials he promised came crashing down on them, however, as the community members were killed and Jerusalem was crushed. We know that, in the year 64, Nero began to persecute and kill the early Christians. People turned against them; their own families turned them in; they were tortured and killed; every horror that Luke's Jesus foresaw happened. Luke encourages them to stand strong in faith, to trust in Jesus, and to be on the lookout for the flash of lightning.

Luke uses the story of Noah and the flood to urge them to trust that they are being protected in the ark of community. It's a reference that can help us all now as we enter the days of catastrophic climate change. "As it was in the days of Noah, so it will be in the days of the Son of Humanity," we read.

> "They were eating and drinking, marrying and giving in marriage up to the day that Noah entered the ark, and the flood came and destroyed them all. Similarly, as it was in the days of Lot; they were eating, drinking, buying, selling, planting, building. On the day when Lot left Sodom, fire and brimstone rained from the sky to destroy them all. So it will be on the day the Son of Humanity is revealed. On that day, a person who is on the housetop and whose belongings are in the house must not go down to get them, and likewise a person in the field must not return to what was left behind. Remember Lot's wife."

By referring to the stories of Noah and Lot, Luke's Jesus prepares us for the catastrophe that is coming, for death that can catch us all unaware, that we might be ready at any moment to stand before the universal Christ. Don't go with the crowd, Luke warns. Stand against the culture in your nonviolence, be on watch, practice the teachings of Jesus before it's too late!

This is not a message anyone wants to hear. But he digs in further: "Whoever seeks to preserve his life will lose it, but whoever loses it will save it." Luke's Jesus wants us to give our lives away for God, God's reign, the poor, and the marginalized in acts and movements of compassion, nonviolence, and resistance to injustice. If we do, we will find the meaning of life and the fullness of life, for we will find God in the struggle we've entered, which is Jesus's public campaign of global disarmament and transformation. Moreover, Jesus will light our way and one day welcome us.

"I tell you, on that night there will be two people in one bed; one will be taken, the other left," Luke continues. "And there will be two women grinding meal together; one will be taken, the other left." It's interesting to notice how far North American Christians have strayed; many of the "rapture"-teaching Christians think this text means that Jesus is taking someone straight up to heaven, when in fact, the one being taken is being taken by the imperial soldiers to be imprisoned, tortured, and killed. This is what Luke's community was experiencing. The Roman military was destroying Jerusalem and executing Christians. It was the end of the world as we know it. Brothers and sisters in Christ were being brutally killed just as the nonviolent Jesus was killed. Luke urges them to stand strong in faith, to be ready, to trust in God. The end is near, but since we stand strong in faith with God, since we look to the nonviolent Jesus, we can remain nonviolent, fearless, peaceful, mindful, even calm. It's an encouraging message for his persecuted community. It's also an encouraging message two thousand years later to anyone who seeks to reclaim the nonviolence of Jesus, to stand against the global systems of violence, war, and injustice, to resist the forces of death and environmental destruction, and to trust in the God of peace, come what may, no matter what.

Like the early church, no matter what happens, no matter how quickly the end comes, we are ready. We have joined Jesus's campaign of universal love for the coming of peace on earth, so we can rest assured that the nonviolent Jesus will take care of everything. Moreover, we know that one day, if we are faithful to Jesus's way of nonviolence, doing our part in the global grassroots, people-power movement Jesus started long ago for justice, disarmament, and creation, we too will see lightning from east to west across our dark world. Martin Luther King Jr. saw it in all the breakthroughs of the grassroots movement of faithful nonviolence. That's why he told us the night before the government killed him that he had seen the promised land. He experienced a foretaste of resurrection in the civil rights movement—in Montgomery, Birmingham, the 1963 March on Washington, and Selma. He knew that Jesus had risen and was with them and had their back, so Dr. King was no longer afraid. With the lightning fire of resurrection and Pentecost, he could see; he had vision; he became a visionary for all of us who are blind. Likewise, we will all experience lightning east to west—signs of the resurrection—in our own lifelong participation in the grassroots movement of nonviolence and radical discipleship to Jesus. And we need not fear. We know that, however it happens, we step closer to Jesus and God's reign of peace.

"Where, Lord?" they asked him. "Where the body is, there also the vultures will gather." With this mysterious verse, the early community is being assured that the Son of Humanity will definitely come, just as surely as the vultures will come if a dead body is left outside. The vultures will come, and so too, the Son of Humanity will come. We could extrapolate from this strange analogy that the Son of Humanity will surely come for us, so we need not worry or despair.

But the verse is so bizarre. We could ignore it and move on, but, as with everything, it requires time and further reflection. It sounds like some ancient Buddhist teaching on the inevitability of death, as if Luke uses the shocking image of the vultures coming for a dead body as a way to remind the early community that they were all going to die, that even if they weren't being persecuted and killed, they would still die. One day our bodies will rot away, they will be food for the vultures, this is the inevitable future of every human being. We, however, know that we are being invited into God's reign by the nonviolent Jesus, so we take Luke's warning to heart to live intentionally, prayerfully, mindfully, nonviolently, focused on Jesus, trusting in God. As followers of the nonviolent Jesus, we are determined not to serve the culture of death or the idols of death, including any rulers or militaries; instead, we intend to spend every moment serving the God of life. We take heart because, through Jesus, we are right now entering God's reign of peace and universal love.

The key to unlocking these eschatological and apocalyptic writings is to understand them from within the framework of Jesus's nonviolence. Two thousand years after Jesus, we have developed many warped fundamentalist interpretations to justify nationalism, violence, warmaking, and self-righteousness. If there is any justification for violence or warmaking in our interpretation, we know right away that we are reading the text the wrong way, that we are not thinking as God does, that we are not fulfilling Jesus's Luke 4 mission to be good news to the poor or his Luke 6 mission of universal love or the Luke 10 grassroots campaign of creative nonviolence.

As we read these lines, we put on the mind of the nonviolent Jesus. We can measure our interpretation by asking if it allows for the taking of a single human life or if it supports death in any way. Our attitude is that of the poet Edna St. Vincent Millay who wrote a century ago, "I shall die, but that is all I shall do for death." We do not support the killing of anyone because we are sons and daughters of the God of peace and we believe that every human being is summoned to be a beloved son or daughter of the God of peace, and therefore we do not support killing anyone or the methodologies or means of killing in any way, shape, or form. If our spirituality grants that God wants some people—"those people," "them"—to be killed, that their "collateral damage" comes with our salvation, that someone in our vision is expendable, whether they be of a different race, class, ability, religion, nationality, or sexual orientation, we know right away that we have veered from the Gospel of peace and the nonviolent Jesus. Gospel nonviolence is now the boundary within which we live, breathe, pray, think, and act. It is even the boundary within which we read and study the Gospels and worship God in Christian community.

"Pray Always without Becoming Weary" (18:1–17)

It makes sense, then, that Luke next offers a parable to remind us "to pray always without becoming weary." The early community was facing war, empire, persecution, and martyrdom. The end is near, so pray and do not become weary, he tells them. As we struggle to end war, poverty, racism, and environmental destruction through our participation in the grassroots movements for justice and disarmament, we too can lose heart and give in to despair. Pray and do not become weary, Luke's Jesus tells us today. We too need to keep praying, stay strong, and not become weary.

"There was a judge in a certain town who neither feared God nor respected any human being," the parable begins. "A widow in that town used to come to him and say, 'Render a just decision for me against my adversary.' For a long time, the judge was unwilling, but eventually he thought, 'While it is true that I neither fear God nor respect any human being, because this widow keeps bothering me, I shall deliver a just decision for her lest she finally come and strike me.'" It is hard to imagine a powerless widow striking a powerful judge; that would have been unthinkable in those days. But clearly, the point is that her relentless demands have worn him down. Despite being dishonest, he will relent and give her a just decision. If this is a parable about praying continually and not growing weary, then we're called to relentless prayer, like the relentless widow who demands justice. Our prayer is based on total reliance on God, total engagement with God, along with Jesus's strict adherence to nonviolence. So we continually ask God for justice for ourselves and the poor, for disarmament and the coming of God's reign of peace among us and for all creation. God will relent, Jesus promises. God does not want us to give up. If we keep asking and keep doing our part by believing in God and acting properly before God, then God will issue a just decision too.

"Pay attention to what the dishonest judge says," Luke's Jesus teaches. Luke is underlining the story, putting it in yellow highlights. He wants us to study the change of heart that the dishonest judge has, and to learn how to engage God to bring justice. God will hear our non-stop prayers for help that we might faithfully live Jesus's call to justice and nonviolence. "Will not God secure the rights of his chosen ones who call out to him day and night?" Jesus asks. "Will he be slow to answer them?"

We might be tempted to answer, "No, God will not secure the rights of God's chosen ones; God rarely does; God is always slow to answer." Notice the caveat: the question is asked about those who call out to God, day and night. Do we do that? Not if we are comfortable, rich, well fed, and enjoying life. If we don't need God, we're not calling out to God, day and night. We cannot expect for God to hear us, to answer us. But if we are poor, marginalized, struggling to survive, facing harassment for our public work for justice and peace, if we will call out for justice and help with the work of nonviolence and disarmament, we can trust that God will hear us and answer us quickly. That is what Luke's Jesus promises the early community: "I tell you, God will see to it that justice is done for them speedily." This is a promise that we, too, can take to heart. If we keep begging God for justice—and for an end to war, nuclear weapons, racism, gun violence, poverty, fascism, corporate greed, and all the violence that destroys creation—if we pray day and night, we can trust deep down that the God of justice and peace will hear and respond to our requests, and we can rest assured that justice and peace will come soon. So—we do not become weary. We pray always for justice and peace.

But then Luke adds a coda, and it's a bombshell: "But when the Son of Humanity comes, will he find faith on earth?" It's the mother of all questions, addressed to us now in the twenty-first century. We can look at the world in despair and conclude that faith in the God of peace has all but vanished.

A better approach to the question might be to dig deeper into our own faith in the God of peace and Jesus's way of nonviolence, and say to God, "We believe in you, God of peace, nonviolent Jesus, Holy Spirit of universal love, and, come what may, we will continue to believe in you, serve you, and worship you." The question should push us to choose faith in the God of peace and deepen every daily practice of faith, through ongoing self-examination, persistent prayer, unconditional love, service to those in need, as well as determined participation in grassroots movements for disarmament and social, economic, racial, and climate justice. Faith needs to be exercised, just as our bodies need exercise. We need to strengthen our faith, work at it, and put it into practice. We do that by standing up against the widespread faithlessness that leads to all forms of anti-life and anti-God. We can take that stand by claiming our faith and our identities as sons and daughters of the God of peace who live within the boundaries of Gospel nonviolence. We need the God of peace because we are as nonviolent as the saints like Gandhi and King. We can expect hostility, denunciations, harassment, opposition, and even threats for our public stand for justice and disarmament, so we need God to watch over us. We need God to sustain us. As long as we are still breathing, we pledge to believe in the God of peace, surrender ourselves to the God of peace, and trust the God of peace and the divine way of loving nonviolence. God is our Higher Power, and we turn to God over and over again. In this way, the witness of faith spreads along with our nonviolence, and both faith and peace will last longer and grow among people. If we believe, others will believe.

Of course, the danger in all of this is the subtle development of self-righteousness and judgmentalism, which can undermine all our faith and goodwill. Without humility and love, our faith is dead. Thus Luke offers next a parable "for those who were convinced of their own righteousness and despised everyone else." It flows from Jesus's encounters with the humble sick and poor who beg for his help and healing touch as opposed to his confrontations with arrogant religious authorities who presume they know everything, that they are better than Jesus, that they are the true representatives of God and judges of others, and that they deserve their elite status, wealth, power, and privilege. Privilege, power, and possessions can warp even our prayer and spirituality so that we end up even farther from God, trying to control God, feeling superior to God and everyone else. When that happens, we have fallen into the pit of hatred, selfishness, and violence. Instead of loving everyone else, we despise everyone else, including God, Jesus, the prophets, and the saints. We do not want to end up doing that!

"Two people went up to the temple area to pray; one was a Pharisee and the other was a tax collector," Jesus begins. He gives us two extreme examples—the apparently sinless person and the publicly sinful person. Both are in the temple, both are praying, both are turning toward God. One approaches God incorrectly, and one approaches God correctly. "The Pharisee took up his position and spoke this prayer to himself, 'O God, I thank you that I am not like the rest of humanity—greedy, dishonest, adulterous—or even like this tax collector. I fast twice a week, and I pay tithes on my whole income.' But the tax collector stood off at a distance and would not even raise his eyes to heaven but beat his breast and prayed, 'O God, be merciful to me a sinner.' I tell you," Jesus concludes, "the latter went home justified, not the former; for everyone who exalts himself will be humbled, and the one who humbles himself will be exalted."

This original parable sums up much of Luke's teachings about hypocrisy, self-righteousness, and judgmentalism, as well as about humility, mercy, prayer, and the nature of God. It instructs every disciple and every reader to the take the posture of the public sinner, a notorious tax collector, and to repeat every day for the rest of our lives the one-sentence prayer: "O God, be merciful to me, a sinner." This is our basic stance before God. It is not a false humility but a real awareness of our weakness, brokenness, neediness, powerlessness, and sinfulness before the eternal God. We cannot claim any greatness before God or anyone. We dare not instruct God or tell God what to do regarding ourselves or anyone. We come before God as beggars, kneeling with our heads down, our hands outstretched, putting the focus on God: "O God, YOU, be merciful to me." Only then, in true humility before God, will we know healing and wholeness. Jesus and his Holy Spirit, through this Gospel and his saints, continue to call everyone to this position of humility as the necessary prerequisite for the discipleship way of holistic nonviolence, universal love, and heartfelt compassion.

To emphasize the point, Jesus calls the disciples to become as humble and gentle as little children, to welcome the kingdom of God as children, not as learned, arrogant, religious experts. Luke reports that people, probably women, were bringing infants to him for him to bless, but the male disciples were stopping them, rebuking them, and telling them to leave the holy rabbi alone. Typical know-it-all religious men! Trying to control every situation and, in the process, missing the whole point! So, Jesus calls all the children to himself. "Let the children come to me and do not prevent them," he declares, "for the kingdom of God belongs to such as these." What a beautiful teaching, what a good God we have. The kingdom of God belongs to children, to every child ever born, to innocent, helpless, powerless infants in all their wide-eyed love, life, and wonder. God did all of this for them. As sons and daughters of God, we then want to do everything we can to protect, serve, and love infants and children, through nonviolence and boundless compassion, because God created God's kingdom of love and peace for them, because that's how God treats them and welcomes them. With this teaching, every Christian should work to ensure that no child ever again suffers hunger, poverty, disease, homelessness, oppression, abuse, neglect, or war, that every child on earth is loved and raised in a spirit of compassion, gentleness, wisdom, and peace. We aspire to welcome every infant and every child as God does and to make sure they live in peace as God wants them to in God's reign of peace.

"Amen, I say to you, whoever does not accept the kingdom of God like a child will not enter it," Jesus concludes. In light of the previous parable, now we know that we do not follow self-righteous, arrogant religious leaders. We are humble people of nonviolence, compassion, and love. We welcome children and everyone we can in love and peace. We live in awe and wonder before God, and in our childlike wonder, we look at creation and marvel. We see every human being and shower them with extravagant love. We widen our hearts to embrace creation and humanity and, in doing so, we surrender ourselves in love and joy to God and God's reign of love and joy. There are no problems, no anxieties, no worries, no fears, no hatred, no anger, no lust, no selfishness. We are like children going to the circus, filled with hope and anticipation as we enter God's reign of love and peace with each new step, every day of our lives.

To state the obvious, an infant or a little child cannot build a gun, bomb, or nuclear weapon. It cannot drive a Trident submarine or fly an F15 fighter bomber or manage a drone. It cannot dig up fossil fuels, manage ecocide or genocide, or take a single life or manage corporate greed on Wall Street, much less reject someone because of their race, gender, nationality, religion, or orientation. An infant or a little child is utterly dependent on its loving parent. That is the goal for every Christian, every human being—to become as vulnerable, nonviolent, and dependent on our loving God as powerless infants and little children are on their parents. Once we reach that heightened level of consciousness and surrender completely to God, we step into God's reign.

"What Do You Want Me to Do for You?" (18:18–19:27)

With these teachings about letting go of wealth, serving the poor, being humble and child-like, and trusting in God, Luke presents Mark's contrasting stories of the rich official who claims eternal life as his entitled inheritance and the blind beggar who calls out to Jesus for mercy. As Matthew does, Luke only makes minor tweaks to the comparison. "Good teacher, what must I do to inherit eternal life?" the official asks. "Why do you call me good?" Jesus asks back. "No one is good but God alone." "Are you saying that I am the Son of God, the Messiah?" Jesus seems to ask. "You know the commandments," he tells the man. "'You shall not commit adultery; you shall not kill; you shall not steal; you shall not bear false witness; honor your father and your mother.'"

"All of these I have observed from my youth," the official answers. "There is still one thing left for you," Jesus responds. "Sell all that you have and distribute it to the poor, and you will have treasure in heaven; then come, follow me." It is one of the clearest calls to radical discipleship that we have read, and as we have come to expect, Jesus is rejected. "When he heard this," Luke writes, "he became quite sad, for he was very rich," and his wealth prevented him from dropping everything and following Jesus.

Notice that the rich man falls into desolation and sadness. This is what happens to all who reject Jesus, the gospel, and God. Wealth prevents our happiness. It makes us sad, and we do not even realize it. We end up preferring sadness and desolation because we are stuck in our addiction to money and possessions. We were created to follow Jesus and serve God wholeheartedly; that alone brings happiness, peace, and joy.

"How hard it is for those who have wealth to enter the kingdom of God!" Jesus says. "It is easier for a camel to pass through the eye of a needle than for a rich person to enter the kingdom of God." As we heard in Mark, Jesus's warnings reach their natural conclusion: we cannot enter God's reign if we are wealthy. We need to be as poor, as vulnerable, as innocent as a baby in a manger or a nonviolent revolutionary on a cross.

"Then who can be saved?" they ask. "What is impossible for human beings is possible for God," Jesus answers. This doesn't mean that we should keep our wealth and walk away from Jesus in the hope that God will later do the impossible and save us. It means that God is greater than our understanding—but we are still called to obey the commandments, to drop everything, sell our possessions, give the money to the poor, and follow Jesus on the path of universal love, if we want treasure in heaven. The choice is ours. The consequences of our choice are also ours.

"We have given up our possessions and followed you," Peter says. "Amen, I say to you," Jesus answers, "there is no one who has given up house or wife or brothers or parents or children for the sake of the kingdom of God who will not receive back an overabundant return in this present age and eternal life in the age to come." Here is the promise of discipleship: we will be given, during our lifetimes, many more blessings, many brothers and sisters and houses, because we will be part of the growing community of love and peace, the grassroots church of nonviolence, and learn to share all our resources in common. Indeed, we will be poor but live like the rich, wanting for nothing, loving everyone, celebrating our life in God every day. We will have the fullness of life now and eternal life after our deaths. This is the promise of Jesus to the early church and to us today if we dare the impossible and give up everything in discipleship to the nonviolent Jesus and his Gospel of peace.

I'm hoping we can rise to the occasion and do what those first apostles did, what the rich official was unable to do. Having heard everything Luke has taught, I hope some part of us wants to follow Jesus wholeheartedly, to be happy in our radical discipleship, to pursue total nonviolence in his footsteps, to do our part to welcome God's reign here on earth and know God's blessings here and now.

"Behold, we are going up to Jerusalem and everything written by the prophets about the Son of Humanity will be fulfilled," Jesus tells the Twelve. This is a specific addition to Luke; Jesus is the greatest prophet and the fulfillment of the prophets, and that means he is headed toward martyrdom. Everything that started in the synagogue at Nazareth is coming to fruition—both the proclamation of good news to the poor and the beginning of the great Jubilee, and the rejection and the determination to crush Jesus. "He will be handed over to the Gentiles and he will be mocked and insulted and spat upon; and after they have scourged him, they will kill him, but on the third day he will rise."

These words are shocking. After all the talk of universal love, boundless compassion, the innocence of children, the faith that moves mountains, the glories of the kingdom of God, the boundless compassion of God, even the abundance of life in community—Jesus himself is to be handed over, mocked, insulted, spat upon, tortured, and killed. We still cannot take this in, so we turn the page and try to ignore it.

"They understood nothing of this," Luke writes. "The word remained hidden from them and they failed to comprehend what he said." The male disciples, the Twelve, have no idea what Jesus is talking about, how his message of love and peace has been rejected, how he will be brutally killed, how such an outcome is inevitable in a world of violence and empire. Question: Dare we try to understand this? Is this word hidden from us as well? Do we comprehend what Jesus is telling us—that we too are called to love everyone, resist wars and injustice, speak out for justice and peace, practice total nonviolence, and face rejection and defeat? Do we have the faith to keep going and trust in him anyway, as Gandhi and King did? Might we give our lives to his grassroots campaign of nonviolence, knowing that he rose, trusting that if we share in his paschal mystery, then we will share in his resurrection and God's reign of peace will be fulfilled?

Jesus's statement hangs in the air. The disciples are dumbstruck and uncomprehending. So they walk on and come across a poor blind beggar who calls out, "Jesus, Son of David, have pity on me!" We notice now that he goes far beyond calling Jesus a "good teacher." He names Jesus as the Son of David; he is heir to the throne! The greatest in our midst! We're told that people walking up front rebuked the blind beggar. Of course, that would have been the male disciples. They try to control Jesus and every situation he finds himself in, as if they were his bodyguards, press agents, public relations staff, advance men. They are still clueless about the depths of his nonviolence and compassion.

Jesus has come to fulfill the oracle of Isaiah, to bring good news to the poor, sight to the blind, and the Jubilee redistribution of land and wealth upon the whole earth. And so, Jesus stops in his tracks. He orders the disciples to bring the blind beggar to him, and then he puts the most beautiful question ever to the poor homeless soul: "What do you want me to do for you?"

Here we see the episode in the synagogue at Nazareth fulfilled. Jesus places himself at the disposal of the poor, the blind, the hungry, the helpless. He does not force himself upon the poor beggar. He places himself at the man's service. He will do whatever the poor blind beggar wants, for that is why he has come. That is his mission. That is what it means for him to be the nonviolent Messiah, the beloved of God, the Son of Humanity. Note that, while Mark names the beggar Bartimaeus, Luke keeps him anonymous so that he symbolizes all the poor of the earth.

"Lord, please let me see," the beggar asks. "Have sight," Jesus tells him. "Your faith has saved you." The beggar immediately received his sight and followed him, giving glory to God. "When they saw this," Luke notes, writing as if suddenly the entire crowd was now healed of blindness and could see, "all the people gave praise to God." In this fulfillment of Isaiah and his mission, Jesus helps everyone to see and so everyone praises God. The personal encounter has a global effect. It bears tremendous, good fruit.

We may be bored with the story—and this book!—so it is good to pause and recall what Luke is trying to tell us: each one of us needs to go through life as if we are a blind beggar calling out to Jesus for the gift of sight. Until we have rooted out every trace of violence in our hearts, as Matthew's beatitude instructs, we cannot see God. Until we get rid of the two-by-four sticking out of our heads, and stop following blind guides, we will never see, much less be able to lead others. Until we recognize our blindness, we will never ask Jesus to give us the gift of sight, and we will remain stuck where we are, in the culture of violence, the blindest of the blind. In our blindness, we cannot see Jesus around us in our neighbors, in the poor, in the enemy, in creation, in the face of every child, in every person in need, everyone who is different. We are blind as long as we cannot see Jesus and follow him on the path forward into God's reign of peace.

With this comparison between the rich man who rejects Jesus and his call to radical discipleship and walks away sad, on the one hand, and the blind beggar who is freely given vision and follows Jesus on the discipleship journey to Jerusalem, on the other, Luke adds a new story, not found elsewhere, that combines parts of both caricatures to emphasize the call to discipleship, the need to renounce wealth, and the blessings that come if we do.

Jesus is walking through Jericho, the site of his parable of the Good Samaritan. The chief tax collector of the town, a wealthy man named Zacchaeus, wants to see Jesus as he passes, but he is short and cannot see over the crowd. So Luke tells us that Zacchaeus runs ahead, climbs a sycamore tree, and stands there to see Jesus as he passes by. "Jesus looked up and said to him, 'Zacchaeus, come down quickly, for today I must stay at your house.'" Zacchaeus came down "and received him with joy."

When the crowd sees that Jesus has gone to the home of the tax collector, they grumble. They hate this rich man because he doubles, sometimes quadruples their tax bill and keeps the overflow for himself. That's why he's rich. But Zacchaeus, Luke reports, says to Jesus: "Behold, half of my possessions, Lord, I shall give to the poor, and if I have extorted anything from anyone, I shall repay it four times over." "Today salvation has come to this house," Jesus answers, "because this man, too, is a descendant of Abraham. For the Son of Humanity has come to seek and to save what was lost."

Zacchaeus is able to do what the rich official earlier was not able to do—to give away his wealth to the poor so that he can follow Jesus freely. Because he does this, Luke adds, this public sinner, a hated tax collector and rich man, is saved and welcomed immediately into eternal life with Jesus. Even this sinner, Luke adds, is a Son of Abraham. Jesus has saved him, like the shepherd who found his lost sheep or the woman who found her lost coin or the compassionate father of the story of the prodigal son who welcomed back his lost son. Jesus is looking for and saving those who are lost. He has done the impossible by saving Zacchaeus. He truly is the savior of the world, the universal savior, just as Luke has been telling us all along.

But there is more to this beautiful story than meets the eye. We have long been told that this is a story of conversion. Jesus encounters a hated sinner, calls out to him, stays at his house, and inspires the sinner to convert and give half of his money to the poor. In doing this, Luke teaches us about conversion. Not exactly. According to the original Greek, when Zacchaeus announces his intentions, he uses the present tense! Luke Timothy Johnson, Joseph A. Fitzmyer, and other scholars say that a better translation of Zacchaeus's announcement would be: "Behold, half of my possessions, Lord, I am giving to the poor, and if I have cheated anything from anyone, I am restoring it four times over." Zacchaeus is not pledging to do something now that he has met Jesus; he has been doing this already! If this is so, then we can understand why Jesus addresses Zacchaeus and goes to his house. Jesus is teaching the crowd that this hated, marginalized person is actually way ahead of them on the discipleship journey of compassion and generosity to the poor. In other words, it is not Zacchaeus who is called to conversion—but the crowd, the male disciples, and us, the readers!

And so, before Jesus enters Jerusalem, Luke presents us with a final parable, and it is quite profound. Here Luke takes Matthew's parable of the pounds or ten gold coins and sets it before the arrival in Jerusalem, because Luke tells us, "They were expecting the kingdom of God to appear there immediately."

> "A nobleman went off to a distant country to obtain the kingship for himself and then to return. He called ten of his servants and gave them each a gold coin. 'Engage in trade with these until I return,' he instructs them. His fellow citizens, however, despised him and sent a delegation after him to announce, 'We do not want this man to be our king.' But when he returned after obtaining the kingship, he had the servants called, to whom he had given the money, to learn what they had gained by trading."

With this first part of the parable, Luke is telling us something about a despised heir to the throne who has come to claim his kingship. The people do not want him; they reject him, but he becomes king nevertheless. Luke uses this twist to tell us what is about to happen in Jerusalem. The crowd thinks that the kingdom of God is about to appear right before them. They expect the noble Jesus to be acclaimed the new Jewish king when he gets to Jerusalem, to become like every other king, ruler, general, or emperor in history—a king of violence who will lead his armies to defeat their enemies, protect his people through violence and militarism and rule with the sword. Luke is alerting us that something completely different is about to happen, something that has never happened before in history: Jesus will claim his kingship, but unlike any king who ever lived, he will be the king of nonviolence.

The parable continues. The first servant comes forward and announces that, with his gold coin, he has earned ten additional ones for the king. "Well done, good servant!" the king tells him. "You have been faithful in this very small matter; take charge of ten cities." Then the second servant reports that his gold coin has earned five more for the king. The king is pleased and places him in charge of five cities. The unwise third servant, however, returns the gold coin and confesses that he "kept it stored away in a handkerchief," for he was afraid of the king. "You are a demanding person," he says. "You take up what you did not lay down and you harvest what you did not plant."

This response does not go over well with the king. "With your own words I shall condemn you, you wicked servant," he says. "You knew I was a demanding person, taking up what I did not lay down and harvesting what I did not plant; why did you not put my money in a bank? Then on my return I would have collected it with interest." Here we get to the point of the story: do not waste your life. If you serve God and invest your gifts in God's work of justice, compassion, and peace, you will be welcomed, praised, rewarded, and given great honors and assignments in heaven, and even begin to live in God's reign of peace here and now. If, on the other hand, you live in fear and do not use your gifts to assist God's reign, you will not be in God's reign starting right now; you will not know the rewards of God's way and reign of universal love, compassion, nonviolence, and peace. Your gold coin will be given to the person who has ten gold coins, Luke explains, much to the chagrin of everyone else. "I tell you," Jesus's king in the parable concludes, "to everyone who has, more will be given, but from the one who has not, even what he has will be taken away."

As we sit with the story, it begins to make sense. Those saints who spent their lives doing God's will, serving God's reign, practicing God's way of love, compassion, and peace, investing their gifts in the poor and the global struggle for disarmament and justice, will receive more, and then more on top of that. Mother Teresa, St. Francis, Dorothy Day, Gandhi, Dr. King, Archbishop Romero—these great saints will be greatly rewarded, and then rewarded even more beyond everyone's expectations. And rightly so; what they did with their lives was extraordinary, beyond measure.

But the story does not end there. Luke adds one terrible line, perhaps the most violent of the four Gospels: "Now as for those enemies of mine who did not want me as their king, bring them here and slay them before me." With that the parable ends; the king kills all his opponents.

This image of the king as a king of violence who slays all those opposed to him goes totally against Luke's image of God as infinite compassion, universal love, and total nonviolence, as well as of Jesus himself as a person of total nonviolence. So I presume that this is NOT an image of God; rather, something else is going on. We know this because Luke uses the loaded word "enemies." In his Sermon on the Plain, Luke goes farther than Matthew's much more complete Sermon on the Mount and has Jesus command us twice to love our enemies. We know that "love for our enemies" is the hallmark of Christian behavior (Lk. 6:27–35), but, even more importantly, we know now that this is the very nature of God. God loves everyone universally, God has no enemies, God doesn't kill anyone but welcomes everyone into God's life of universal love. Luke's Jesus has already taught us that if we love our enemies, and do not kill them or "slay" them (or bomb them or nuke them), "our reward will be great" and we will be sons and daughters of "the Most High, for God is kind to the ungrateful and the wicked, [so] be merciful just as your heavenly God is merciful" (Lk. 6:35–36). This is the most important teaching in the entire Gospel of Luke, and we cannot hear it enough. It's one we need to ponder every day for the rest of our lives.

Therefore, a new, post-supersessionist reading hears this verse as a general warning about the consequences of our actions and what we do with our lives. If we are hostile to God and God's reign, and support killing and the culture of death, then we are not entering God's reign now, in this life, nor will we dwell with God in God's reign in the next life. In fact, the more we resist the God of peace and support the culture of violence and killing, the more it will all come back upon us. We have to get with the program of God's nonviolence and live according to God's way of love, compassion, and peace. We have to choose this life that God offers us, instead of our own selfish will and the selfish anti-God culture of violence. Our rejection of God's nonviolence and support of the culture of violence and death is destroying us and keeping us from God now, and will continue to keep us away from God as long as we continue to reject God's way of love, compassion, and peace. We will not enter the presence of the God of universal love because we have chosen not to.

What we do with our lives has consequences here and now, and for the long term, for our souls. If we use violence, one day it will come back upon us. We have been cautioned and have been taught and pleaded with to practice the nonviolence of Jesus, and to trust that, if we do, we will live right now in our discipleship to the nonviolent Jesus in God's reign of universal love and total nonviolence, and we will live on forever in God's reign. If we thoroughly reject God's reign here and now, and practice radical discipleship to the ways of death, then we will get what we wish for. It's our choice. That's the gift, grace, and challenge of free will.

Duly warned by the Gospel, we all can choose not to be selfish, fearful, violent, faithless people who oppose God, Jesus, or God's reign. Instead, we all—every human being on earth!—can choose to live according to Jesus's way of universal love and follow him on the path of nonviolence into God's reign starting now and lasting forever. We do not want to be wicked servants. We want to hear God say to us, "Well done, good servant. You have been faithful. . . ." And so we try to do God's will, to help God in God's project of disarmament and justice. Therefore, we will spend our lives, like Jesus, in the grassroots campaign to proclaim God's reign and create a new world of nonviolence and justice. We will try to win everyone over to this campaign, so that everyone will invest their gifts in God's project of justice and peace, and the culture of death and killing will end, and everyone will enter God's peace here and now by living within the Gospel boundaries of loving nonviolence.

I can hear Luke whispering across the centuries: "Try with all your might to do God's will now, to turn away from the culture of violence, greed, and war, to pursue Jesus's teachings of nonviolence, justice, and compassion, to surrender yourselves to your loving God and invest everything you have in God's reign of peace, to follow Jesus, and everything will turn out well." That's the message to take from this parable.

"If This Day You Only Knew What Makes for Peace": The Campaign Reaches Jerusalem (19:28–21:36)

The grassroots campaign of the nonviolent Jesus and his peace-movement followers have reached their goal. The long march to Jerusalem has reached its climax. For over a year, he has walked the countryside from Galilee, south along the border with Samaria, now to the Mount of Olives. Everyone has been talking about him. Crowds have gathered along the way. Word of mouth has spread like wildfire. A holy rabbi and prophet is outside the city. Is he the Messiah? What will he do? Will he establish the kingdom of God? Will he raise an army and crush the Romans and restore Zion?

On the outskirts of Jerusalem near Bethany, Jesus sends two disciples ahead of him to the home of one of his underground contacts to get a donkey. They get the donkey and help him sit on it, and he begins his procession into the city. Using brilliant street theater, as we have seen before in Matthew and Mark, Jesus fulfills the oracle of Zechariah 9:9–10, claims his kingship, and rides into Jerusalem, not like Pilate on his warhorse with six hundred armed soldiers but on a donkey: humble, quiet, gentle. He is the king of peace and nonviolence, and he brings with him his kingdom of peace and nonviolence, free and available to everyone who wants to live in God's reign of peace. As Zechariah says, he dismantles every weapon of war and, in doing so, he will abolish war itself. He is the embodiment of peace and nonviolence.

The disciples and the crowd shout for joy, just as Zechariah foretold. Their cry of peace and glory echoes what the angels first proclaimed to the poor shepherds of Bethlehem at the birth of Jesus. Here is the king that Gabriel foretold to Mary.

Shout for joy, O daughter Jerusalem! Behold: your king is coming to you, a just savior is he, Humble, and riding on a donkey, on a colt, the foal of a donkey. He shall banish the chariot from Ephraim, and the horse from Jerusalem. The warrior's bow will be banished, and he will proclaim peace to the nations. His dominion will be from sea to sea, and from the River to the ends of the earth. (Zech. 9:9–10)

People spread their cloaks on the road as he passed, and all the disciples began to praise God, saying, "Blessed is the king who comes in the name of the God of peace. Peace in heaven and glory to the highest." For me, this remarkable, hopeful march and demonstration led by Jesus would have held the kind of joy, exhilaration, and celebration we see two thousand years later, first in the black-and-white silent film footage of Gandhi's celebrated Salt March, and Dr. King's great March on Washington on August 28, 1963, when he proclaimed his dream of justice, equality, freedom, and peace to the nation, a day filled with joy, consolation, and wonder according to those who were there.

No other Gospel names Jesus as "the king." Earlier, the angel told Mary that she would bear a son who would have a kingdom that would never end. In the previous parable, we were told of an heir who went to claim his kingship, only to be opposed by many people; and when he returned as the new king, he discovered one servant who had not done his will, and he had his opponents slain. Now we know that such cruelty and violence do not represent Jesus. He is a king of nonviolence. There can be no doubt that the last parable was warning us of the consequences of our own behavior, our own injustice, our own opposition to the life of peace.

John's Gospel, written decades later, will take this recognition further, when the tortured Jesus is asked by Pontius Pilate himself if he is a king. There, John's nonviolent Jesus explains everything clearly: "My kingdom does not belong to this world. If my kingdom did belong to this world, my attendants would be fighting to keep me from being handed over to the Judeans. But as it is my kingdom is not here" (John 18:36). The only difference between the kingdoms of this world, from Rome to America, is that this world of empire uses violence and war; Jesus's kingdom of peace and love is totally nonviolent, non-dominating, non-coercive. No one is violent in that kingdom, beginning with King Jesus.

No other Gospel specifically praises God for "peace in heaven." Both of these shouts of praise for the new king and peace in heaven are immediately denounced by the Pharisees. Watching this demonstration, the appalled Pharisee tells Jesus, "Rebuke your disciples." "I tell you," he answers, "if they keep silent, the stones will cry out!" They probably saw Jesus earlier "rebuke" his disciples for wanting to call hellfire from heaven. They want him to rebuke them for calling him a king and for referring to "peace in heaven." Everyone knows that Caesar alone is king and that there is "war in heaven." Hellfire comes from heaven, they think, in their warped theology of violence. But that's precisely the point: hellfire comes from hell. Violence, killing, and warmaking are hell. Heaven is eternal peace and universal love and can send down only blessings of peace and love. This heaven invites us to the way of peace.

What happens next is one of the most heartbreaking scenes in the Bible. This story appears only in Luke, and it demands serious reflection and meditation. As he drew near and saw the city of Jerusalem, Luke writes, Jesus breaks down sobbing. "If this day you only learned the things that make for peace—but now it is hidden from your eyes," he says through his tears. "For the days are coming upon you when your enemies will raise a palisade against you; they will encircle you and hem you in on all sides. They will smash you to the ground and your children within you, and they will not leave one stone upon another within you because you did not recognize the time of your visitation."

The people of Jerusalem have refused his teachings of peace. They cannot believe that, if they trust in the God of peace and practice creative nonviolent resistance to the Roman military and its rulers, somehow they could diffuse the situation, get the Romans to leave as friends, and welcome a future of peace for the holy city. Instead, they turn to the violence of terrorism, kill Roman soldiers, and threaten the Roman occupiers. If Luke was written in 72–75 CE, as most scholars hold, then he is referring to the total destruction of Jerusalem by the Roman soldiers in the year 70. The city was razed to the ground and its people slaughtered. Jesus is the embodiment of peace and bearing the gift of peace, but no one actually wants it, so they reject his path of peace, his reign of nonviolence. He can see how their deeply rooted violence will try to outdo the violence of Rome and end in death and destruction, so he weeps. It is too late for them to learn the things that make for peace. They are blinded by their violence and hatred of their enemies. Had they taken his teachings to heart, learned to love their enemies, turned the other cheek, and sought a nonviolent resolution to their predicament, Jerusalem would have remained standing, and the children would not have been killed.

What does this dramatic moment mean for us two thousand years later? Today, Jerusalem has become the world, and we are on the brink of destroying it through systemic injustice and violence toward people and creation itself. Every city will be destroyed. Entire nations will be laid waste. Parts of the earth will burn down because of drought; other areas will be flooded and frozen. Bangladesh, for example, will be completely flooded; the small island nations will disappear. The earth will react according to the laws of nature. By heating the atmosphere, warming the oceans, and raising the sea level, we are destroying everything, including our children's future.

What can we do? We can become the people who finally learn the things that make for peace. We can take Luke's Jesus at his word and commit ourselves to universal love, universal compassion, justice for the poor, and a lifestyle of nonviolence. We can try to fulfill the vision of Zechariah and abolish weapons of mass destruction and war itself, and stop digging up fossil fuels and use only clean energy. We can educate every human being in Jesus's way of nonviolent conflict resolution, as Gandhi and Dr. King urged. We can determine to see one another as sisters and brothers, called by God to live in peace.

That means that we must unlearn the things that make for war. We do an about-face and work for the abolition of war and the causes of war and invest in nonviolent conflict resolution, just as we stop digging up fossil fuels and invest in alternative sources of energy. We get rid of our guns, abolish nuclear weapons, and stop preparing for and spending for war. We will refuse to join the military, send our young people into the military, or support the military. Instead, every nation will start to create nonviolent civilian defense systems and peace teams so that global nonviolent conflict resolution with its infinite tools of resolving conflict peacefully will become the norm. If the world is to survive, the days of war have to end now.

Most will agree with each other that this is a beautiful but impossible dream, that when push comes to shove, in the real world, war is a necessary evil. For followers of the nonviolent Jesus, however, there are no more necessary evils. The pattern for centuries has been that Christians go to church and say their prayers, but as soon as war breaks out, they rally round the troops, forget their faith in the nonviolent Jesus, and turn to the gods of war for victory. As we approach the destruction of the planet, we have to break our common addiction to war. Instead of adhering to the propaganda of the necessity of war and justifying warfare, we say no, we will not support war or resort to it ever again. There is no just war. There are a million ways to resolve conflict. Nonviolent conflict resolution is infinitely creative, from dialogue and negotiation to nationwide organized nonviolent resistance, as Gandhi proved. Christians remember the tears of the nonviolent Jesus, so we refuse to participate in the things that make for war. From now on, we are people who have learned the things that make for peace and, rather than wage war with the warmakers, we weep and take nonviolent action with the nonviolent Jesus.

If Christians learn the things that make for peace and unlearn the things that make for war, then the churches need to lead the way in calling for the abolition of war. Every church in the world needs to become a training center of nonviolence, where nonviolence is preached, taught, trained for, and required for membership. This is what the celebrated monk and author Thomas Merton called for in his famous essay in the *Catholic Worker* in 1961:

> The duty of the Christian in this time of crisis is to strive with all our power and intelligence, with our faith and hope in Christ, and love for God and humanity, to do the one task which God has imposed upon us in the world today. That task is to work for the total abolition of war. There can be no question that unless war is abolished the world will remain constantly in a state of madness and desperation in which, because of the immense destructive power of modern weapons, the danger of catastrophe will be imminent and probable at every moment everywhere. The church must lead the way on the road to the nonviolent settlement of difficulties and toward the gradual abolition of war as the way of settling international or civil disputes. Christians must become active in every possible way, mobilizing all their resources for the fight against war. Peace is to be preached and nonviolence is to be explained and practiced. We may never succeed in this campaign but whether we succeed or not, the duty is evident. (cited in Dear, *Thomas Merton, Peacemaker,* 27)

As the horrors of the world and our insane systemic violence continue to play out, however, we followers of the nonviolent Jesus will also have to break down and weep over the impending destruction of the world. We must learn to grieve as Jesus does, to mourn our lost futures, the extinction of the creatures, the poisoning of the oceans, and the destruction of the land. We have to grieve our failure to stand up and organize a grassroots global movement of nonviolence to disarm the nations, dismantle our militaries, and ensure a future of peace for every person. It is time for us to stop and weep over our world just as the nonviolent Jesus does.

"My House Shall Be a House of Prayer, but You Have Made It a Den of Thieves" (19:45–48)

Unlike the rest of us who give up once we fall into grief and despair, notice that the nonviolent Jesus instead takes action. His grief and tears lead to nonviolent direct action! He does not stop, he does not give in to despair, he does not become paralyzed or numb. He is more energized than ever. His grief and broken heart lead to even greater compassion, which leads to active nonviolence. And so, he takes deliberate nonviolent action to confront injustice and call upon everyone to turn to the God of peace in prayer.

Luke writes that Jesus then entered the temple area and "proceeded to drive out those who were selling things, saying to them, 'It is written, "My house shall be a house of prayer, but you have made it a den of thieves.'" "Every day he was teaching in the temple area," Luke adds. "The chief priests, the scribes, and the leaders of the people, meanwhile, were seeking to put him to death, but they could find no way to accomplish their purpose because all the people were hanging on his words." As we know, the faithful believed that God dwelt only in the temple, but we readers know that God is present and acting through Jesus of Nazareth. Jesus is a person of prayer and he is 100 percent devoted to the God of love and peace. God's house of prayer has become a den of thieves: he has to get rid of the banking system; it's an insult to faith and trust in God. God's house of prayer should be free and open to everyone.

Notice again that, when he undertakes nonviolent civil disobedience to protest the systemic injustice of the temple system, he does not hurt anyone, whip anyone, yell at anyone, or kill anyone—he is not motivated by anger! There is no sign that anyone is afraid that he will attack them; on the contrary, they're all amazed and hanging on his every word.

We now know that Jesus is motivated by grief. He is grieving, and so he takes action. This makes all the difference in the world. Jesus is not being violent; he is being nonviolent, but his nonviolence is not quiet passivity but active, daring, and dramatic. His nonviolence has been confused with violence and used by the culture of war down through history to get Christians to support wars. Rather, in his civil disobedience, Jesus is meticulously nonviolent. We can tell because after the action, which might have lasted all of three minutes, he spent the rest of the day teaching them the things that make for peace and justice.

But doesn't he take a whip and start whipping the people? No. There is no mention of a whip here or anywhere in the Synoptic Gospels. Only in the Gospel of John, written many decades later, is there mention of "rope." Remember, John's Gospel could have been written as many as fifty years after Luke. He rewrites the entire story presented in the Synoptics. There is no longer a grassroots campaign of nonviolence. Instead, John *begins* his Gospel with Jesus's nonviolent action in the temple, where he portrays Jesus as a prophet like Jeremiah. There, we're told, Jesus made a rope out of some cords to "drive them all out." This is the only time in the Bible when a specific obscure Greek word for a type of hemp is used. To get thousands of sheep and oxen into this enormous five-story temple structure, they used this particular type of hemp to lead the animals up the massive walkways. Jesus simply took those hemp cords, which the cattle, sheep, and oxen would have recognized, to lead the animals out. He does not take a rope or a whip and start striking people. If anything, according to John, Jesus is an animal rights activist. He saves the animals from being slaughtered! (Those interested can find my more detailed commentary of John in my books *Walking the Way* and *Lazarus Come Forth!*)

Jesus is thoroughly nonviolent at every level in his civil disobedience, and Luke's Gospel confirms it. He is not angry or violent but grieving and pleading with us. But the question remains: If Jesus was upset because of the unjust temple system, how does he feel about our plans to destroy the planet through global warfare, nuclear weapons, digging up fossil fuels, and bringing on catastrophic climate change? He must be overwhelmed with grief and wondering why his so-called followers are not grieving as well and taking bold public nonviolent action to stop the destruction of the planet. Luke's account of Jesus's nonviolent direct action in the temple challenges everyone who dares claim to be a follower of the nonviolent Jesus to join the global movement to pull humanity back from the brink of destruction, to non-cooperate with this unprecedented systemic evil, so that we show that we are people who have learned the things that make for peace.

As we face the reality of catastrophic climate change, Jesus's statement during his nonviolent civil disobedience in the temple takes on new meaning. With his "cleansing" of the temple, Jesus announces that God is now free and available to anyone, everywhere, at all times, for all time. As the Gospel of John will later make clear, God is spirit and truth and loves all people everywhere. Mother Earth herself has become the temple of God, the "mountain" of God that Isaiah speaks of, the universal house of prayer where every human being can worship the God of peace, in peace. We can step outside, look at the sky, listen to the birds, study the trees, even climb a mountain, swim a river, or gaze out at the glorious ocean, and feel our spirits lift in praise and worship of the Creator. Creation, we know now, leads us to God. It is the ultimate place of prayer and worship. We make peace with Mother Earth, live at one with all of creation, and there pray to the creator and adore the God of peace.

But no! As Jesus said in the temple, we have now turned this glorious house of prayer into a den of thieves. This is one way to understand what we have done through our destructive use of fossil fuels and rampant militarism. We are destroying the planet and causing its climate chaos so that the oceans will roar, the heat will rise, the fires will burn, and some places will be entirely flooded. All of this will mean unparalleled suffering and death. Why is it happening? Because we have let the rich elites and their corporations dig up Mother Earth's natural resources regardless of the consequences. Their greed, and our silent complicity with their corporate greed and the militarism that goes with it, has brought us to this impending doom. Jesus goes to his death resisting it and naming this global injustice in clear language for all of us to hear. If we want to follow him, we must unpack the meaning of his words for us today, apply them to our global predicament, and take similar nonviolent direct action to return creation to its rightful place as our universal house of prayer.

"What Then Does This Scripture Passage Mean?" (20:1–44)

Every day, Jesus returned to the temple area and taught the enormous crowds and then, at night, retreated across the Kidron Valley up the Mount of Olives to rest among the olive trees in the Garden of Gethsemane. He has disrupted the religious banking system and stirred the whole population with his talk of God's kingdom of justice and peace. The authorities are now dead set against him and ready to spring at their first chance. The problem is that he has become so famous. As we shall see, the only way to get rid of him is to "disappear" him, to capture him at night.

So they approach and interrogate him: "Tell us, by what authority are you doing these things? Or who is the one who gave you this authority?" As we saw earlier, he responds with a question of his own: "I shall ask you a question. Tell me, was John's baptism of heavenly or of human origin?" When they refuse to answer, he refuses to answer. He is not intimidated by them. He does not let them ruffle his feathers or scare him into submission or force him to back down. He is in full militant nonviolence mode. He is the only true authority because he is, as we secretly know, the Author of life itself.

With that, he tells a long parable about an absentee landlord and the tenant farmers who revolt against him, reflecting, as many commentators note, the growing social and economic unrest in rural Palestine in the first century. They attack and beat the landlord's servants, and when he sends his son, they throw him out of the vineyard and kill him. Luke's version is slightly shorter than Mark's or Matthew's, which we have already discussed from a post-supersessionist perspective. Luke adds this detail to foreshadow how Jesus will be led outside the city and killed. In the end, the vineyard owner will return, put those tenant farmers to death, and turn over the vineyard to others. The vineyard owner represents God, the vineyard is Israel and all of creation, the servants are the prophets, and the beloved son and heir is Jesus, who will be taken out of the vineyard and killed. That means the tenant farmers in charge of the vineyard who attack the prophets and kill the son are none other than the religious authorities.

"What will the owner of the vineyard do to them?" Luke's Jesus asks. Once again, that is the question we should focus on. Luke answers by saying the vineyard owner will return, put those tenant farmers to death, and turn over the vineyard to others." When the crowds hear this, they object as one: "Let it not be so!" They cannot imagine such an outcome—that the religious authorities will be replaced by "others." It is one of the only times when the listeners object to Jesus's teachings. Led by the religious leaders, they dismiss his parable outright. As we have discussed elsewhere, a post-supersessionist reading leads us beyond the question of Jewish versus Gentile leadership and helps us remember that God is not violent, that God practices universal nonviolent love, that violence leads to further violence and destroys violent people even as they engage in violence upon others (often without their knowing it). Once again, we are being presented with an urgent appeal to hear God's call to peace from God's prophets and witnesses and, most especially, from the nonviolent Jesus, and thus to serve God, God's people, and God's creation through God's way of nonviolence.

Today, the vineyard represents Mother Earth, and the world's rulers continue to attack and kill prophets and activists everywhere who try to protect her, just as they killed the prophets and the nonviolent Jesus. What will the owner of Mother Earth do to them? That is the question. It hangs in the air. What are the consequences for our crucifixion of the world's poor, its creatures, and Mother Earth herself? Luke insists that there are consequences for every action and that it is never too late to side with the vineyard owner and get to care for the vineyard, God's people, and all creation.

With this hard-hitting parable and a warning to the religious authorities, Jesus leads a scripture study. Luke says that Jesus looks at them. In that look, he has infinite compassion for them and a deep passion to share the truth with them. So he asks them, "What then does this scripture passage mean: 'The stone which the builders rejected has become the cornerstone'? Everyone who falls on that stone will be dashed to pieces, and it will crush anyone on whom it falls.'"

Here we see Jesus use another tool in his arsenal of nonviolent communication to engage those who disagree with him. Just as Jesus uses stories to teach people, he also asks them questions about various scripture passages to make his point. We can do the same. For example, we can ask questions to those who disagree with the Gospel of peace about specific Gospel verses. "What does this scripture passage mean?" we could ask, and then quote "Love your enemies," or "Blessed are the peacemakers," or "Offer no violent resistance to one who does evil." I have done this repeatedly throughout my life and through this Jesus technique I have spent my life discussing the Gospels with hundreds of thousands of people. This is what Jesus does. Instead of pointing to himself and calling himself "the cornerstone rejected by the builders," he questions them about the verse and draws the answer from the crowd, and from us too.

Jesus is the cornerstone of the new temple, the reconstituted Israel, the "church" of universal love and active nonviolence. He is the presence of God in the new temple, the new global church of peace. If people reject the way of love and peace, then they will fall and not be able to enter his community or God's reign.

The religious authorities cannot take this talk any longer and want to seize Jesus. They know his stories are aimed at them, but Luke reports that they feared the people. "They watched him closely," Luke writes, "and sent agents pretending to be righteous who were to trap him in speech, in order to hand him over to the authority and power of the governor." This is what ruling authorities have done ever since. Government officials wiretapped and followed Dr. King, for example, in an effort to catch him and discredit him, until finally they killed him. That is what happened to the nonviolent Jesus. Despite all his truth-telling, loving-kindness, and peacemaking actions, Jesus faced total rejection and possible arrest just as he predicted.

So, pretending to be righteous, these agents approach Jesus and flatter him with praise, trying to appear friendly, when actually they are wolves in sheep's clothing. "Teacher, we know that what you say and teach is correct, and you show no partiality, but teach the way of God in accordance with the truth." What they say is true, but they want to trick him into saying something they can use against him. Their hearts are full of violent intentions, and so their lips drip with malice and murder. It is important to note that Jesus does not take the bait and respond to flattery. He has no ego attachment. He is centered on God alone and can smell lies from a mile away.

"Is it lawful for us to pay tribute to Caesar or not?" As we have seen elsewhere, this was a critical question, especially at the time of Luke's writing. During the First Jewish Revolt, between 66 and 70 CE, rebels called upon the Jewish people not to pay taxes to the empire, and this movement of tax resistance was one of the main reasons for Rome's swift destruction of Jerusalem and the temple. Jesus asks to see a denarius, a Roman silver coin, and then asks his questioners whose name and face it bears. They show him the coin with Caesar's face and name carved on it, and answer, "Caesar's." So, he says to them, "Then repay to Caesar what belongs to Caesar and to God what belongs to God." Luke reports that they were "unable to trap him," "were amazed at his reply," and "fell silent."

Jesus's answer is brilliant but often misunderstood. To repeat Dorothy Day's interpretation, Luke tells us that, once we give to God what belongs to God, there is nothing left for Caesar. Everything belongs to God. Our bodies, minds, hearts, and souls, our speech, our vision, our hearing, our hands, all that we are, all that we do, our very existence belongs to God. We need to give everything we have to God. There is nothing left for the empire, then or now.

Just then, some Sadducees appear and challenge Jesus with a long-drawn-out, absurd question about a man who married a woman and then he died, an episode we heard in Mark and Matthew. The dead man's brother married the widow, then he died, and so on, with five more brothers. Intending to ridicule his idea of resurrection, they ask, "Whose wife will she be at the resurrection?" "Those who are deemed worthy to attain to the coming age and to the resurrection of the dead neither marry nor are given in marriage," Jesus answers. "They can no longer die, for they are like angels. They are the children of God because they are the ones who will rise." This profound answer stuns us as it did his critics. As we ponder its meaning, we hear clues about life after death. If we are worthy, if we live into resurrection, then we will be like angels. We will no longer have earthly bodies but will live in the presence of God and be the sons and daughters of God, who we know is peaceful and universally loving. This is where we are all headed: repent and surrender our lives to the will of the God of peace.

Jesus goes on to speak about resurrection, using the story of Moses and the burning bush, calling God, "the God of Abraham, the God of Isaac, and the God of Jacob," saying that God is "not the God of the dead, but the God of the living, for to God all are alive." The notorious scribes were listening too, and Luke reports they said, "Teacher, you have answered well," and "no longer dared ask him anything."

God is the God of the living, Jesus announces, which means that the prophets and the saints are alive and well with God in the new life of resurrection peace, and we are called to believe in the living God and to start living now as if we are already in the eternal life of resurrection. The problem with Jesus's teaching is that it requires us not to have anything to do with death. We do only the things that serve life, promote life, and save life.

Jesus takes the initiative, questions the scribes, and starts another Bible study. "How do they claim that the Messiah is the Son of David? For David himself in the Book of Psalms says, 'The Lord said to my Lord, "Sit at my right hand till I make your enemies your footstool."' Now if David calls him 'Lord,' how can he be his son?" Jesus's questions are problematic for these know-it-all scripture authorities and literal fundamentalists. He quotes the Psalms, which he knows better than the scribes do. He challenges their fundamentalism and raises a question about the nature of the Messiah, which reduces them to silence. They cannot respond to his questions because they do not understand him or the scriptures. He nonviolently exposes their ignorance.

"Stand Erect and Raise Your Heads Because Your Redemption Is at Hand" (20:45–21:36)

And so, as we have heard elsewhere, Jesus turns to warn his disciples: "Be on guard against the scribes, who like to go around in long robes and love greetings in marketplaces, seats of honor in synagogues, and places of honor at banquets. They devour the houses of widows and, as a pretext, recite lengthy prayers. They will receive a very severe condemnation." Do not be like religious leaders who draw attention to themselves, he advises, who keep the focus on themselves, not on God or the poor, who recite long prayers to impress, who are narcissists seeking power, fame, and money. We readers notice that Jesus does not seek attention for himself or any place of honor for himself. He puts all his attention on those that no one cares for—the poor, the lame, the blind, the mute, the deaf, the leper, the beggar, the sick, and the dead. His attention is set on God's reign and God's will. Luke contrasts the humble, selfless Jesus with the religious leaders, and in doing so, he underscores Jesus's call to focus our attention on serving the poor, working for justice, and seeking God and God's reign.

Jesus watches the wealthy put their money in the temple treasury, and he grieves the transformation of God's house into a bank that rips off the poor. Just then, he sees a poor widow drop two small coins into the treasury. She has given away her entire livelihood to the rich religious leaders, he tells his disciples, just so she too could offer a prayer to God. This is precisely the injustice he had just warned his disciples to guard against. He does not want any poor person, any widow, ever again paying money to religious leaders in order to worship God. He does not want greedy, phony, powerful religious men to devour the houses of widows, to make money off poor women, to profit from serving God by robbing the poor. This is why he turned over the tables of the money changers, to transform this den of robbers into a house of prayer, open and free to all, beginning with the poor and women. Jesus is determined to fulfill the mission he announced in the synagogue in Nazareth, to bring good news to the poor and the Jubilee Year of global redistribution of wealth. His campaign, civil disobedience, and direct action are first and foremost good news to this poor widow, for the days are coming when she will never have to pay a penny to visit God's house ever again, because, as he taught in his sermon, the kingdom of God belongs to the poor.

The religious leaders refuse to learn the things that make for peace, to practice justice for the poor, and to make God's house a house of prayer, and so, Jesus says, it will inevitably fall and crumble. How could it not? Everything corrupt and unjust, everything built on a false spirituality of violence and greed, everything that serves the empire and not the reign of God, will fall. "All that you see here," Luke's Jesus tells them, "the days will come when there will not be left a stone upon another stone that will not be thrown down." Luke is explaining to his community how Jesus foresaw everything that they just survived: the inevitable destruction of Jerusalem by the Romans as a consequence of injustice and violence. "Teacher, when will this happen?" they ask him. "What sign will there be when all these things are about to happen?"

Luke's eschatological discourse is like Mark's and Matthew's. Because Jesus wants his disciples, and Luke wants his readers, to be people who learn the things that make for peace, Luke encourages them and us to stand firm in the practice of Jesus's teachings, to remain unflinching in the hurricane of violence that unfolds around us. As disciples of the nonviolent Jesus, we stand steadfast in nonviolence. We live in the present moment of God's reign of peace. We are not afraid or worried or anxious about anything. In a concluding statement that occurs only in Luke, he will call us to stand erect and raise our heads because we know that, with Jesus, our liberation, our redemption, and God's reign of nonviolence are at hand.

"See that you not be deceived, for many will come in my name, saying, 'I am he,' and 'The time has come.'" False leaders and prophets will even imitate him and use his language to draw you into their web of greed and idolatry, he says. "Do not follow them!" Luke raises the question, Whom do we actually follow? We could conclude that today we Christians have all been deceived, that we follow everyone but the nonviolent Jesus. We follow politicians, celebrities, and media stars. We follow preachers, priests, and ministers who call us to be pro-life and lead us down the rabbit hole of nationalism so that we end up supporting war, executions, and racism, so that we end up pro-death people and don't even know it. We might think we follow Jesus, but at best we are his fans. We like him as we like Elvis. In reality, we follow the leaders of the culture of domination and have become their devout disciples.

"When you hear of wars and insurrections, do not be terrified, for such things must happen first, but it will not immediately be the end," he continues. "Nation will rise against nation, and kingdom against kingdom. There will be powerful earthquakes, famines, and plagues from place to place; and awesome sights and mighty signs will come from the sky." Luke of course is describing the end of Jerusalem and the impending second coming of Jesus, which his community now realizes is delayed. Jesus sees not only the destruction of Jerusalem and his own destruction but, because of our deep allegiance to the systems of this broken world, the inevitable destruction of people and all creation. Two thousand years later, after countless wars, empires, earthquakes, famines, plagues, genocides, nuclear explosions, and catastrophic climate change, we know how right Jesus was, and if we dare get sober, we must try to take up again his commandments of universal love and nonviolence and stand in God's peace. We are not terrified, afraid, anxious, or worried. We remain centered in Christ's peace, in mindfulness, in our breath and prayer, in community, and in the Holy Spirit. We take Jesus seriously, so we are ready for anything. We already know the ending, that the worst has happened, that life holds a slight edge over death, that God's reign of universal love and infinite peace is at hand for us, and so we stand tall, on alert, keeping watch, on the lookout for the nonviolent Jesus.

"Before all this happens, however, they will seize and persecute you, they will hand you over to the synagogues and to prisons, and they will have you led before kings and governors because of my name," he explains.

> "It will lead to your giving testimony. Remember, you are not to prepare your defense beforehand, for I myself shall give you a wisdom in speaking that all your adversaries will be powerless to resist or refute. You will even be handed over by parents, brothers, relatives, and friends, and they will put some of you to death. You will be hated by all because of my name, but not a hair on your head will be destroyed. By your perseverance you will secure your lives."

The key here is that these persecutions will offer us the opportunity to give *testimony*. This is an important word for every disciple of nonviolence. Testimony is what a witness gives under oath in a courtroom drama. The witness declares, "I saw this happen. I heard him say this. I know that this is true." That is the vocation of nonviolence: to give testimony to the way of peace in a culture that resists peace. If we dare follow the nonviolent Jesus today, we need to be people who give testimony, who take the stand for our own civil disobedience to systemic violence and proclaim that God's reign of nonviolence is at hand. Luke will conclude his Gospel with a commandment by the risen Jesus to go forth as his witnesses to give testimony.

"Not a hair on your head will be destroyed," he promises. "By your perseverance you will secure your lives." This, too, is a critical teaching for all those who aspire to the heights of

Gospel nonviolence. We trust in God that, despite the insanity of the world and its hurricane of violence, we will be safe and secure, that we will remain unharmed, that our lives will be held in God's hands. If we surrender in absolute trust, total fearlessness, and blind faith, if we commit ourselves 100 percent to God's universal love and total nonviolence, we will persevere on the journey, knowing that God will protect us, that our survival is already guaranteed, because we have surrendered to God. Our lives are not in control (if they ever were!). God now has complete control of our lives.

What? How can this be? we think. On the one hand, Jesus is saying, if you follow me and speak out publicly as I do against the entire culture of violence and war and for God's reign of nonviolence and peace, you can be sure that you will be rejected and harassed, that you will lose friends and relatives and jobs and houses, and that some of you will even be arrested, tortured, and killed. At the same time, as we heard earlier, "No harm will come to you." "Not a hair on your head will be destroyed." We are summoned to live in the tension that Jesus lived in every minute—to speak out and take risks for justice, disarmament, and creation, and to trust in God even as things fall apart around us. Most of us will not be assassinated like Gandhi and King, but we will have setbacks for our social, economic, political, spiritual, racial, and environmental nonviolence. The trick we learn from the Sermon on the Mount and the Sermon on the Plain is not to be afraid, to live in the present moment, to let go of fear, worry, and anxiety, and to surrender, surrender, surrender to God every hour of the day, while walking to our own Jerusalems. This is the life of creative tension that nonviolence brings, that Dr. King described in his "Letter from Birmingham Jail." In the end, we learn to be so surrendered that we can stand in peace as Martin did, on April 4, 1968, on the balcony of the Lorraine Motel, and remain nonviolent, at peace, and giving testimony to the culture of violence, come what may.

The other key word here is *perseverance*. We must stay faithful to the way of nonviolence, even if everyone else falls away and gives in to the culture's brainwashing propaganda of fear, hatred, and war, even if all seems lost. We stand erect in the wisdom and way of nonviolence and go to our deaths refusing to kill, willing even to be killed, surrendering our lives, our bodies, our wills to the God of peace. We stay faithful even if we're the last one standing.

"When you see Jerusalem surrounded by armies, know that its desolation is at hand," he tells us. Notice that Luke does not feature the "abomination of desolation" in the holy sanctuary; instead, he focuses on the impending destruction of Jerusalem by the Roman soldiers, which Luke's community would have witnessed. "Those in Judea must flee to the mountains. Let those within the city escape from it, and let those in the countryside not enter the city, for these days are the time of punishment when all the scriptures are fulfilled." Luke's community probably did flee to the mountains and hide away safe and unharmed. This "time of punishment" simply refers to the natural consequence of systemic violence, injustice, greed, and warmaking, which inevitably turn back on those who uphold the culture of violence. (This thinking explains the violence of the king in the parable of the gold coins.) Violence in response to violence always leads to further violence; that's what lies ahead, Jesus says, and that's what we see unfolding to this day. For Luke, the end has come with the destruction of Jerusalem, but for us, the end has widened and spread to the ends of the earth and continues to unfold by the minute. As humanity refuses to learn the things that make for peace, as it continues to reject Jesus's methodology of nonviolence, violence and war continue to reap their harvest of death and destruction and lead us toward annihilation through nuclear war and catastrophic climate change.

If you follow the logic of violence, which Jesus would have thought through, then we understand how this contagion of violence could spread across the planet and down through history until the very last days of catastrophic climate change when even the oceans, the sky, the heat, and the storms seem to unleash cosmic violence. But once again, it's not creation's fault; it is the fault of everyone who refused to learn and institutionalize the things that make for peace. Death and destruction will touch everyone who rejects Jesus's way of peace. He continues:

> "Woe to pregnant women and nursing mothers in those days, for a terrible calamity will come upon the earth and a wrathful judgment upon this people. They will fall by the edge of the sword and be taken as captives to all the Gentiles; and Jerusalem will be trampled underfoot by the Gentiles until the times of the Gentiles are fulfilled. There will be signs in the sun, the moon, and the stars, and on earth nations will be in dismay, perplexed by the roaring of the sea and the waves. People will die of fright in anticipation of what is coming upon the world, for the powers of the heavens will be shaken. Then they will see the Son of Humanity coming in a cloud with power and great glory. When these signs begin to happen, stand erect and raise your heads because your redemption is at hand."

In reading these apocalyptic words today, we can respond in a variety of ways. We can turn the page, numb to their warnings, and shake our heads, saying, "That's too bad. If only he could have done something." We can be fundamentalists of violence, misunderstand the entire Gospel and conclude that Jesus *wants* the destruction of humanity and the planet, and that a faithful response to these words is to speed up its destruction, to hasten the second coming of Christ by destroying the planet.

Or, we can put on the mind of the nonviolent Jesus and read these warnings as Luke's community understood them—as a lamentation of humanity's rejection of Jesus's way of peace, and an urgent admonition to remain nonviolent come what may, to trust in the God of peace, surrender our lives to God, and pursue peace with every breath, every step, every day of our lives. Moreover, we can choose to live in total confidence and boundless hope in God, so that no matter what, we stand up straight and lift our heads, knowing that one day we will be with the nonviolent Jesus in God's reign of peace, and all will be healed, all will be disarmed, all will be well. This verse, found only in Luke, is sometimes translated, "Stand erect, raise your heads because your liberation is at hand." The prophet who pledged in the Nazareth synagogue to liberate the oppressed will one day come to liberate all of humanity from its slavery to violence and death.

"Consider the fig tree and all the other trees," he teaches. "When their buds burst open, you see for yourselves and know that summer is now near; in the same way, when you see these things happening, know that the kingdom of God is near." This is consoling. Study nature, consider the fig tree, look at all the trees, Jesus advises; they will show you the plan of God and reveal the coming of God's reign of peace in your midst.

"Amen, I say to you, this generation will not pass away until all these things have taken place," he concludes. Luke tells his community that Jesus foresaw what has happened from his own death to the destruction of Jerusalem, but he also foresaw the coming of God's reign and humanity's liberation. He says even if heaven and earth pass away, his words will not pass away, that even if our violence consumes us and destroys the planet, God's word of universal love is eternal. So, stay alert, be centered and mindful at all times, Luke advises. Live and breathe in God's peace, so that your nonviolence will overcome even the worst violence.

"Beware that your hearts do not become drowsy from carousing and drunkenness and the anxieties of daily life," Jesus warns, "and that day catch you by surprise like a trap. For that day will assault everyone who lives on the face of the earth. Be vigilant at all times and pray that you have the strength to escape the tribulations that are imminent and to stand before the Son of Humanity." These are Jesus's last teachings in the final days of his life, Luke reports. He pleads with everyone once again to repent of any participation in the culture of violence, to learn the things that make for peace, and to seek God's reign of peace with all our hearts. Be vigilant! Be mindful! Be centered in prayer! Surrender completely to the God of peace and trust in God, so that when God comes, you will be ready. His warning, his invitation, extends to us readers today.

As with Mark's and Matthew's version, we can read these apocalyptic warnings as if Jesus was raging mad or just plain crazy, but if we imagine him as kind and gentle, like Gandhi, Dr. King, or Thich Nhat Hanh, then we know that he continues to grieve for Jerusalem and the world, and he aches for us to disarm and embrace his way of nonviolence and universal love. His words are dramatic, but so are the teachings of all peacemakers. "There is no escape from the impending doom save through a bold and unconditional acceptance of the nonviolent method with all its glorious implications," Gandhi said on the eve of World War II. "I am uttering God's truth when I say that unless there is a return to sanity, violent people will be swept off the face of the earth," he said at the end of the war (*Mohandas Gandhi: Essential Writings,* ed. Dear, 188). "Those who have their hands dyed deep in blood cannot build a nonviolent order for the world" (172). "Humanity has to get out of violence only through nonviolence. Hatred can be overcome only by love" (146).

In his Riverside Church speech against the Vietnam War on April 4, 1967, one year before his assassination, Martin Luther King Jr. spoke similarly of these end-times and the urgent need to choose nonviolence before our global violence destroys us. "We still have a choice today: nonviolent coexistence or violent co-annihilation," he said. "Let us rededicate ourselves to the long and bitter but beautiful struggle for a new world. This is the calling of the sons and daughters of God, and our brothers and sisters wait eagerly for our response" (*A Testament of Hope*, ed. Washington, 243). A year later, the night before he was killed in Memphis, Dr. King put it this way:

> We have been forced to a point where we're going to have to grapple with the problems that people have been trying to grapple with through history, but the demands didn't force them to do it. Survival demands that we grapple with them now. For years, people have been talking about war and peace. But now, no longer can they just talk about it. It is no longer a choice between violence and nonviolence; it's nonviolence or nonexistence. That is where we are today. (280)

With Gandhi and King, the world's two great apostles and prophets of nonviolence, we hear echoes of the eschatological nonviolence of Jesus and the same apocalyptic warnings. Some fifty-five years after Dr. King's death, as we move closer to nuclear war and into climate chaos, his warning remains our one last-ditch hope. As Luke's Jesus has been saying from day one, we need to repent and get on with the new life of total nonviolence in God's reign, or we are doomed.

"Father, Forgive Them, They Know Not What They Do" (21:37–23:56)

The end has come for Jesus, Jerusalem, and the world. Humanity has chosen a violent apocalypse instead of a nonviolent way out. With Luke's account of the passion and death of Jesus, we see the consequences of the mission he first proclaimed long ago in the synagogue in Nazareth. Jesus spent his life bringing good news to the poor, vision to the blind, liberation to the oppressed, and the Jubilee of global justice to humanity. He offered the things that make for peace, and we rejected them outright. He organized a Gandhian/ Kingian grassroots campaign of nonviolence to wake up everyone and summon them to the new life of God's peace. Even when he cleansed the temple and called for its return to being a house of prayer, the religious leaders sought to kill him. His days were numbered from the get-go, even though he was meticulously nonviolent and infinitely patient and compassionate. He tried every nonviolent means possible, through word and deed, to call humanity to conversion and disarmament. In Luke's telling, even as Jesus undergoes torture and death, he models perfect nonviolence and opens the door of hope.

It's Passover, and the chief priests and scribes are seeking to kill Jesus, Luke writes. People had been getting up early each morning to gather in the temple to listen to him. He would teach the crowds all day long, then rest peacefully at night on the Mount of Olives. He probably would not have been captured and killed because of the crowd's attention and praise. He might have continued this retreat work for weeks, even undertaken another nonviolent direct action, but he was betrayed from within his own community.

Luke puts it bluntly: Satan, the evil spirit of empire and death, enters Judas Iscariot, who approaches the religious leaders and, for money, offers to hand Jesus over to them and the empire under cover of night. Meanwhile, Jesus sends Peter and John out to prepare the Passover meal, telling them that, when they get to the city, they will see a man carrying a jar of water. Since no men ever carried water—that was women's work—we know this signal is part of Jesus's underground connections. They follow the man, and he offers them a large upper room for their Passover meal. We note how Jesus continues to form Peter and John through selfless service, so that one day they will become servant leaders. They make plenty of mistakes, but in the end, they learn the lesson and pass it on.

Finally, when everything is prepared and "the hour" arrives, Jesus takes his place at table with the apostles. We can contrast the table of injustice that the religious leaders set up for their banking exchange in the temple, which Jesus overturned, with this new table of justice, where all are welcome, where Jesus celebrates his last meal as an eternal feast of peace with God. Notice, too, that Luke has not included the story of the woman anointing his feet;

instead of preparing his disciples for martyrdom by anointing them as she anoints him, he focuses entirely on the Passover meal.

Luke slips in a unique line. Jesus has "eagerly desired to eat this Passover with them before he suffers," saying, "I shall not eat it again until there is fulfillment in the kingdom of God." The focus of Luke's Passover account remains the kingdom of God as an everlasting banquet with God in God's reign of life and perfect peace. With that in mind, we can ponder how Jesus "eagerly desired" to share this Passover meal. He must have thought about it for months, for years! If so, then, he knew all along what he was going to do. It was not a spontaneous gesture but long prayed over, thought out, and discerned. He would transform the Passover meal of the Old Covenant of violence into a permanent Passover in the New Covenant of nonviolence, using his own body and blood as the Lamb of God, inviting humanity to share in his life, his Passover, his paschal mystery, and his transforming nonviolence through small, faith-filled communities of grassroots nonviolent resistance! What a brilliant idea, to say the least.

Luke's Passover has Jesus taking a cup and sharing it, saying, "From this time on I shall not drink of the fruit of the vine until the kingdom of God comes." Then he offers his body and blood as the new covenant of nonviolence. "He took the bread, said the blessing, broke it, and gave it to them, saying, 'This is my body, which will be given for you; do this in memory of me.' Likewise, the cup after they had eaten, saying, 'This cup is the new covenant in my blood, which will be shed for you.'" As I pointed out before, Jesus calls us to live in the nonviolence of God's reign, to enter God's new covenant of nonviolence, and he models it by doing the exact opposite of the culture of violence. Instead of requiring the bodies and blood of others in a global anti-Eucharist of war and destruction, Jesus initiates the true Eucharist of nonviolence by offering his body and blood broken and shed for all, and he invites us to join in his campaign of giving our bodies, our blood, our very lives for the coming of God's reign of peace.

"I Confer a Kingdom on You" (22:21–34)

Just as he offers up his life for his disciples and invites us to join in this new covenant of nonviolence, Jesus announces that one of them would betray him. "Woe to that man by whom he is betrayed," he says. He does not curse Judas or even condemn him. He simply says that woe will befall him because he has betrayed and participated in Jesus's murder. The consequences of this evil act will be terrible. But the male disciples pay no attention to this announcement of betrayal or the news of Jesus's impending death. They focus only on themselves. To be fair, they are in a state of confusion, fear, and high stress, given their proximity to Jesus's enemies there in the city. Since entering Jerusalem, they have watched their master and teacher cause trouble and stir up murderous feelings among people who have the power to cause much harm to him and any of his followers. We can say that the disciples don't really care about what Jesus is going through, how he must feel, his inner devastation and grief. We can also surmise that they are unable to focus on anything outside themselves because of their distressed state of mind. Whatever the case, Jesus's friends are not "there" for him in this painful and difficult hour. Their deep fear for him and themselves triggers their egos and so they start focusing on themselves and move into out-of-control grandios-ity, self-righteousness, and narcissism, even as Jesus moves deeper into sorrow.

First, the disciples debate about which one of them would do such a dastardly deed as betray their leader. Then they argue about "which of them should be regarded as the great-est." They show no empathy or concern for Jesus, who is about to be betrayed and killed. At this most intimate moment, when Jesus is the most vulnerable he has ever been with them, they argue among themselves and fail to become available to him.

But Jesus has infinite patience and compassion for them, and for us, so he starts teaching them all over again, as if they were back at square one, which they seem always to be.

"The kings of the Gentiles lord it over them and those in authority over them are addressed as 'Benefactors,' but among you it shall not be so. Rather, let the greatest among you be as the youngest, and the leader as the servant. For who is greater: the one seated at table or the one who serves? Is it not the one seated at table? I am among you as the one who serves."

As we have read elsewhere, Jesus applies his upside-down way of life all over again and insists that anyone who would follow him become a servant of others. The word rendered "Benefactors," could be translated as "Rulers." So here we read that no Christian can be a ruler, can "lord" it over others, can dominate anyone, boss anyone, or bully anyone. We are servants, at best servant-leaders, who out-do one another in humble service, loving-kindness, gentleness, and compassion.

They have been with him all this time and still they do not understand Jesus's methodol-ogy of life. They argue about who is greater even as he sits in their midst—humble, gentle, serving, quiet, peaceful. Yet he does not lash out in frustration or exasperation. He has compassion on them. Indeed, he sees through this minor blip to the far horizon when they will be faithful, even martyred for their discipleship to him. He trusts them, affirms them, and gently encourages them with his kindness and friendship. "It is you who have stood by me in my trials," he says, in an unusual affirmation and recognition of their fidelity. "I confer a kingdom on you, just as my Father has conferred one on me, that you may eat and drink at my table in my kingdom, and you will sit on thrones judging the twelve tribes of Israel." This promise that they will dwell with him in his kingdom and sit on thrones stops them in their tracks. They are all headed toward greatness, but the journey to his kingdom remains one of humble service and utter nonviolence, and it goes by way of the cross. He is faithful to them. And so, we can conclude, if we remain faithful to Jesus and his way, then we too will share in his kingdom.

Then he turns to Peter, whom he calls by his pre-discipleship name. "Simon, Simon, behold Satan has demanded to sift all of you like wheat, but I have prayed that your own faith may not fail, and once you have turned back, you must strengthen your brothers." This too is remarkable because he can see the trouble that Simon and the disciples will have with their faith, as he himself is led away to the slaughter. The evil one, the empire, will go after these missionaries of Gospel nonviolence. That is inevitable, he says. But Jesus affirms Simon, saying that he has prayed for him, and then missions him to strengthen his brother disciples, and the rest of us as well. They will not be sifted like wheat by Satan, by the empire, because he has prayed for them, and his prayer will be answered, which means they will continue to follow him, they will be faithful to him, practice his nonviolence, and go to their own crucifixions knowing that one day they will share in his kingdom. This is how we must approach our own lives, too, knowing that Jesus has prayed for us, that we will be steadfast in our discipleship. We can call upon St. Peter to pray to strengthen us, and then determine that no matter what, we will be faithful to the nonviolent Jesus, and do what we can to proclaim God's reign of peace and justice, even as we fail and the world deteriorates into ever worse violence.

"Lord, I am prepared to go to prison and to die with you," Simon tells Jesus. For all his bluster and bravura, Simon testifies that he is willing to be killed for Jesus, to lay down his life witnessing to Jesus. It is an extraordinary pledge. Can we say this? Does our faith in the nonviolent Jesus run that deep? Are we willing to give our lives as Simon pledges to do?

Yet Jesus can see through poor Simon's weakness, his boasting, his ego, his ambition. He knows the test Simon will undergo, and he has prayed for him. He trusts that Simon will indeed stay faithful and give his life for him. His heartfelt gentleness toward Simon models the way all Christians should relate to one another—with affirmation, trust, gentleness, and kindness. We should encourage each other to go deep in nonviolence and stay faithful to the nonviolent Jesus, despite the difficulties and traumas of life in the world.

"I tell you, Peter," Jesus responds, "before the cock crows this day, you will deny three times that you know me." Now Jesus calls Peter by his discipleship name but knows that they are all in denial about the events that are to unfold. They have not heard a word he said. He has been coaching them in nonviolence, and they have not understood the lessons, but soon, when he reveals the extent of his nonviolence in just a few hours, it will shock them, and they will all run away. They will fear for their lives and run away from him. Jesus is not so much predicting the future as stating the obvious. "Peter, you will deny you even know me, and not someday, but in a few hours, because you still don't understand the depths of my nonviolence." Yet even as he warns Peter, he speaks not with anger or bitterness but with gentleness, heartfelt love, and compassion. Jesus embodies gentleness and nonviolence even as they head for the door.

"It Is Enough!" (In Other Words, "Oh, Forget It!") (22:35–38)

The exchange that follows appears only in Luke, here at this climactic moment in the narrative. The long march and grassroots campaign of nonviolence has brought them to this moment. Even though they have not understood Jesus or his civil disobedience in the temple, they have stayed with him. They remain focused on themselves. Luke's Jesus starts using dramatic, figurative language to explain how he is fulfilling the scriptures, telling them to grab what they can and head for the hills. It goes right over their heads—and our heads, too.

"When I sent you forth without a money bag or a sack or sandals, were you in need of anything?" he asks them.

"No, nothing," they replied.

"But now the one who has a money bag should take it, and likewise a sack, and one who does not have a sword should sell his cloak and buy one. For I tell you that this scripture must be fulfilled in me, namely, 'He was counted among the wicked.' Indeed, what is written about me is coming to fulfillment."

"Lord, look, there are two swords here," they said to him.

"It is enough!" he answered.

What? Has Jesus finally realized that his way of nonviolence doesn't work, that violence is inevitable, that the disciples might as well get some money, buy a sword, and join the culture of violence (and someday carry handguns, electrocute people, drop bombs, build nuclear weapons, and vaporize other sisters and brothers)? Has he renounced nonviolence? Is Jesus violent after all?

No! The entire Gospel of Luke is one long testimony and summons to total nonviolence. It begins with the announcement of the coming of peace on earth and concludes with the king of nonviolence riding humbly on a donkey entering Jerusalem as an image of the ultimate peacemaker claiming his throne in his eternal reign of peace. He has commanded us to love our enemies, rebuked us when we wanted to call down hellfire from the heavens, taught us to forgive one another, and summoned us to believe in a God of wild, unconditional, universal love.

Twice he sent his followers out ahead of him and instructed them to take nothing for their journey. First, he sent the Twelve, told them not to take anything with them but to go forth and proclaim God's reign of peace. Then he sent the seventy-two ahead of him to prepare for his coming, in classic grassroots movement building, telling them not to take anything with them, not even a walking stick. They were to be as nonviolent as lambs in the midst of wolves, offering peace to everyone who welcomed them, inviting everyone into God's reign of eternal peace. They might well be killed, but they were not to lift a finger in retaliation. He practices steadfast nonviolence, teaches steadfast nonviolence, and sends them out in steadfast nonviolence.

So, what's going on here? Why does he say, "Sell your cloak and buy a sword!"?

The key to the whole passage lies in the next verse: "For I tell you that this scripture must be fulfilled in me, namely, 'He was counted among the wicked'; and indeed what is written about me is coming to fulfillment." Who are the wicked? A better translation of that word would be "violent revolutionaries." He will be arrested, treated, killed, and counted among the wicked, the Zealots, the violent revolutionaries trying to overthrow the Roman occupation. No one understands that he is a nonviolent revolutionary; even the scriptures can foresee that the spectacular peacemaking Messiah will be totally misunderstood. For two thousand years, he continues to be misunderstood and presumed to be violent, to be wicked, like other violent troublemakers and revolutionaries.

This is important to try to grasp. He's trying to explain to his disciples what is about to happen to him, and what will eventually happen to them. Because of his radical, revolutionary grassroots nonviolence which threatens the empire, he will be treated like all those wicked people who threatened the empire. He will be arrested, tortured, and publicly executed as a deterrent to show the public what happens if you agitate for political and social change. He will hang on the cross between violent revolutionaries who murdered Roman guards. In fact, he sides with them, even though he is perfectly nonviolent.

He's been trying to teach his disciples—and us—every day about the consequences of his great sermon, his way of active, creative nonviolent resistance, but they never understood a word—and neither do Christians today. Who can comprehend his resistance to empire, or his meticulous nonviolence even unto death?

So his teaching goes right over their heads, and they take him literally and produce two swords, to which he responds, "Oh, forget it!" He was saying, "I'm going to be treated as if I was a Zealot leader, hiding out at night, raiding and killing Roman soldiers, and so will you—even though we are totally nonviolent. So get ready to be misunderstood, to go to your death accused and treated as a violent criminal, even though you are gentle as a lamb and innocent as a dove."

"Look, Lord, here are two swords," they say. Poor Jesus! They have no idea what he is talking about. "It is enough!" he says. In other words, "Oh, forget it!"

I have always looked at this exchange as a moment when Jesus is trying to tell the disciples the way it's going to be, and, in the process, like every great spiritual master, he is testing them to see whether they are really learning the lesson of total nonviolence—and they fail miserably! In the process, Luke is testing us, his readers, too, and for two thousand years we, too, have failed miserably!

Instead of grabbing two swords with breathtaking excitement and saying, "Lord, look, here are two swords," they should have said, "Lord, we are with you on the journey of peace, love, and nonviolence. We don't want money or swords. We want to be as nonviolent as you, even if we too are completely misunderstood and counted among the 'wicked.' We will surrender ourselves completely to you in the spirit of peace, faith in God and nonviolent resistance to the culture, and even go to the cross with you while maintaining our nonviolence as steadfast as you." They should have embraced him, held him in his grief, and encouraged him. They should have said, "We don't count you among the wicked or the violent. You are the face of the God of peace for us; you are gentleness, nonviolence, love, and peace personified, incarnated!" They should have knelt down before him, worshiped him, and offered their unarmed lives to him all over again. They should have promised to live out his Sermon-on-the-Plain teachings of universal love and compassion, come what may. But they do not.

They jump at the chance to resort to violence, just as we still do every time we misunderstand the scriptures.

"Oh, forget it! It is enough!" If we read these words from the perspective of a grieving, nonviolent person, like Gandhi or Thich Nhat Hanh, then the episode begins to make sense. Jesus was telling them about his death in a few hours, offering them his body and blood, announcing the new covenant of God's way of nonviolence, explaining that he is about to be betrayed and handed over and go to his death completely misunderstood by everyone and all humanity—and they start arguing about which one of them is the greatest. Once again, he says, "The scriptures will be fulfilled that I am to be accounted among the wicked, the violent," and they jump at the opportunity to resort to violence. By producing two swords, they show the depth of their addiction to violence and their inability to be nonviolent. So, he sighs and says, "Oh, forget it." As if to say, "Never mind. Forget what I said. You cannot understand what I am talking about."

Of course, few of us understand what he is talking about, and that is precisely Luke's point. "Only later," Luke's Jesus continues, "when the Holy Spirit comes upon you at Pentecost, will you begin to accept the way of total nonviolence and walk the path of universal love into the paschal mystery." So, he drops the metaphor, stops pushing them, realizes he is on his own, and heads off to pray and sob alone in the Garden of Gethsemane. They will follow him but fall fast asleep, and he lets them. He does not try to control them. He knows there is no way he can teach them or convince them about nonviolence and its consequences except through the example of his own nonviolence. His nonviolence unto death, even in all the misunderstanding that it will cause, becomes the only way he can teach them—and the rest of us—about the fullness of God's nonviolence and universal love.

Since the fourth century, when Constantine legalized Christianity and invited Christians to join the imperial military, Christians have rejected Jesus's nonviolence and have happily taken up the sword. We created the just war theory to give ourselves permission to support the empire's wars. We have waged our own wars, our own crusades, to kill in the name of Jesus as if that's what he wants us to do. Today, Christians are to blame for the world's development, use, and maintenance of nuclear weapons; for extreme poverty, systemic racism, and environmental destruction. We have gone way beyond two swords. We built a nuclear sword, and tens of thousands of them. "Look, Lord, here are thousands of nuclear swords!"

We think we are following Jesus, but we're not even fans anymore. We are so far from him that we no longer recognize him. We might consider ourselves his followers, we might think of ourselves as liberal and open-minded or conservative and devout, but the minute our leaders and the media tell us to support the troops and bless the latest war, we rush ahead in a demonic spirit of nationalism and warmaking, as if we never heard a word about nonviolence or the nonviolent Jesus. We're like the alcoholics or drug addicts who get sober for a while but then fall off the wagon at the first moment of weakness, and then go on a binge and die in their addiction. We have been dabbling in the sobriety of Jesus's nonviolence, but when push comes to shove, we eagerly take up the sword and rush off to war. We still do not know what he is talking about. We do not have faith in the living God of peace, but we turn to the false gods of dominance and war. Like the disciples, we are not yet disciples of the nonviolent Jesus. He just shakes his head, realizes we are not ready, and heads off on his own to the cross and his death.

If we study the lives of Gandhi and King, we find similar experiences toward the end of their lives. Gandhi had taught what he called "the nonviolence of the brave" for thirty years to the people of India, but in the end, when independence from Britain came, Hindus and Muslims literally took up the sword and butchered each other to death. At least one million people were brutally killed, but recent studies claim as many as three million were murdered, most of them dying horrifically by the sword. Gandhi went to his death feeling rejected and sad that no one had understood his teachings of nonviolence. He felt he was a failure, and he was. Imagine giving his whole life toward the nonviolent liberation movement, only to watch in horror as millions of people charged at one another with swords. He was depressed till the very end, and almost longed for assassination, knowing, like Jesus, that there was nothing else he could do.

Similarly with Martin Luther King Jr. Though he was only in his late thirties, he continued to broaden his vision of nonviolence to the point that he connected the dots and spoke out dramatically against the Vietnam War and incurred the wrath of everyone—beginning with other leaders of the civil rights movement who publicly denounced him. The media thoroughly trashed him, his friends argued with him, and no one could understand why he would wreck his good reputation as a civil rights leader by speaking out against the Vietnam War. They wanted civil rights and racial equality, of course, but we have to support the troops, we must support the president's war, we need to kill those commies. He was thoroughly committed to nonviolence, and so he did not want African Americans killing people of color in Vietnam. His nonviolence was consistent, and that meant that he had to stand against war and nuclear weapons—and be totally misunderstood as the culture of violence killed him.

Few go the distance in their nonviolence to denounce warfare, especially the latest war, whether the U.S. war on Iraq or Ukraine's warring resistance to Russia. Dr. King went to his death completely misunderstood, and he remains misunderstood today. He organized the Poor People's Campaign with the goal of mass civil disobedience at the U.S. Capitol to gain racial and economic justice and then intended to lead poor people in mass civil disobedience at the Pentagon until the Vietnam War was ended. When he joined the Memphis sanitation workers' strike and marched with them, the FBI paid local gang youth to disrupt the march, throw bricks at store windows, and spread the image of Dr. King as a violent movement leader. And so, the night before he was killed, he could say, "I may not get there with you. . . . But tonight, I'm not fearing any man. I just want to do God's will." He knew that God's will was nonviolence across the board, nonviolence even to the people of Vietnam, and he was determined to take that stand to the bitter end, even if everyone around him misunderstood him and did not want to go with him into the vision of universal nonviolence. He would make the connections between racism, poverty, and war, and risk participating in the paschal mystery of the nonviolent Jesus, even as everyone else supported the Vietnam War. Both Gandhi and King went to their deaths misunderstood and alone just like the nonviolent Jesus.

You could argue, as billions of Christians have done throughout history, that, in fact, a literal reading of this passage does allow us to take up the sword. Yes, Jesus was totally nonviolent up until this point. He taught nonviolence, practiced nonviolence, and commanded nonviolence of his followers—but that's exactly the problem. At the last minute, even he said in effect, "They're going to get me, so you might as well get some money, buy a sword, and get ready because from now on you're on your own." I'm convinced that is *not* the message of this passage, that instead Jesus was trying to teach them what it's going to be like to be his disciple—you will practice total nonviolence and resistance, be killed by the empire, and no one will understand that you are actually an innocent person of peace, love, and nonviolence. He dropped it and moved on to Gethsemane, knowing that he was on his own.

But if you disagree with this interpretation, with this intense teaching on nonviolence and its difficult consequences and insist on a fundamentalist, literal reading of this text, then we can agree: we are allowed to have only two swords on the entire planet! That is enough! We are not allowed to have three swords, or any guns, or any bombs or any nuclear weapons. Period.

"Pray That You May Not Undergo the Test" (22:39–46)

The disciples were probably stunned by his dismissive words, "It is enough." They had been rebuked before when they wanted to resort to violence, so they probably felt rebuked. Jesus heads off down the Kidron Valley and up the Mount of Olives to the garden, where he rests every night. When he gets there, he turns to the disciples and says, "Pray that you may not undergo the test." He has just tested the depth of their nonviolence, and they failed miserably. They are eager to take up the sword. He sees that they have no commitment to nonviolence, that they do not understand what it means to be a nonviolent peacemaker, that they are as violent as everyone else. He himself will have to undergo the ultimate test of being tortured and executed yet remaining nonviolent, not retaliating, not getting angry, even forgiving his executioners. He urges the disciples to pray, and to pray that they may not be tested to the limits of nonviolence. No matter what, no matter how nonviolent we are, no matter even if Jesus prays for us as he prayed for Peter, the culture of violence and death will react to our public nonviolence and test us, perhaps grievously unto death.

This was exactly what was happening to Jesus. His faith and nonviolence were tested to the very limits. Luke writes that he withdrew "a stone's throw from them," knelt down and prayed, saying, "Father, if you are willing, take this cup away from me; still, not my will but yours be done." It is the prayer he taught his disciples, a prayer he learned from his mother, who said that to the angel Gabriel. It is, in the end, the only prayer, the prayer of the mature Christian.

"Not my will, but your will be done." This prayer means total surrender of one's life, soul, body, and will to God, even if you do not fully understand God, and so it is the most demanding of all prayers. It is a prayer that needs to be said, like a mantra, a hundred times a day until we die.

In response to Jesus's prayer, Luke adds that an angel from heaven was sent to him to strengthen him. We see his prayer being answered. He would do God's will, but he was not left alone. God encouraged him to go all the way, just as Moses and Elijah did during his transfiguration. "He was in such agony and he prayed so fervently," Luke writes, "that his sweat became like drops of blood falling on the ground." He is grieving because he has been betrayed, his disciples have completely misunderstood his teachings, and he is about to be arrested, tortured, and killed; and, despite all his efforts to build community and form disciples of nonviolence, he is alone. Because of his fidelity unto death, God sends the angel so that Jesus is not alone, and so he can go forward trusting in God, centered on God, his face set against the inevitable.

Notice the verb that comes next. "When he rose from prayer and returned to his disciples, he found them sleeping from grief." His prayer was like a crucifixion, so much so that his sweat became like drops of blood. But after he surrendered himself to God, after he felt strengthened by the angel, he was renewed and consoled by God to go forward, and so he *rose*. This word is deliberate. It foreshadows his resurrection. He will go all the way to his death, trusting in God and in his resurrection because he prayed. He surrendered to God's will, and so he can stand his ground in steadfast nonviolence. "Why are you sleeping?" he asks the disciples. "Get up and pray that you may not undergo the test." While the other Gospels report that he found them sleeping three separate times, Luke records only this one time, which involves this new commandment: "Get up and pray."

Here is a commandment for the ages: *Get Up and Pray!* Jesus is in agony as he prays for strength to undergo arrest, torture, and execution, and his disciples sleep tight about a stone's throw away. Only an hour ago they were arguing about which one of them was the greatest. They slept through his transfiguration, and now they sleep through his agony in the Garden of Gethsemane. And so he orders them to get up and pray. It is they who are almost dead, paralyzed, like the man on the mat whom Jesus ordered, "Get up, take up your mat, and go home." This is an order to rise and pray. He keeps telling us: you are no longer dead; rise and pray. Now, in this last hour, the prayer has a specific intention: may we not have to undergo the test. In other words, may we be faithful to God's way of nonviolence, surrender to God and do God's will, just like Jesus in the Garden of Gethsemane.

"Stop, No More of This!" No More Violence, No More Killing, No More War! (22:47–53)

As he is speaking to them of resurrection, prayer, and doing God's will, all hell breaks loose. A crowd approaches, led by none other than Judas Iscariot. He approaches Jesus. As was their custom as a peaceful community of Mediterranean men, Judas greets him with a kiss. "Judas, are you betraying the Son of Humanity with a kiss?" Jesus asks. Judas has turned the most intimate gesture of friendship and love, the custom of the Jesus community, into a signal for his arrest. This is what violence does. It destroys everything and everyone, even the intimacy of human friendship and love.

Imagine: they are in the garden, several dozen armed soldiers surround them with fiery lanterns, Judas appears out of nowhere, kisses Jesus—and the sleeping male disciples wake up, stand up, and suddenly realize what is going on. They panic. They are terrified. What do they do? They do what they've always done instinctively, what we all do instinctively: we resort to violence. They reach for a sword to kill!

"Lord, shall we strike with a sword?" they ask the nonviolent Jesus who has been praying in agony. Here, too, is a great betrayal.

The teaching of Jesus comes down to this: do not strike with a sword. Do not retaliate with violence. Thou shalt not kill. Instead, love one another, love your enemies, turn the other cheek, be as compassionate as God, forgive, seek God's reign of peace, be like lambs among wolves, walk in my footsteps on the path of nonviolence into resurrection peace. Yet all they can think of is striking back with a sword and killing those who threaten them. In this scenario, Jesus is the lamb surrounded by violent wolves, not only Judas and the armed soldiers, but even the disciples, who are now armed and ready. If Jesus had time, he would have broken down and wept again. He would have turned to his disciples and said, "If this day you too had learned the things that make for peace, but they are hidden from you."

And so, one of the disciples takes up the sword, charges the soldiers, and strikes at someone to kill him. Only Luke gives us the details of their violence. This unnamed disciple cuts off the right ear of the servant of the high priest. John will later name this disciple as Peter himself. Note that the "servant" would have been an enslaved person, someone forced to be there in the middle of the night, to attend to, and probably protect, the high priest. He too is a victim of the culture of violence and domination.

The servant would have screamed. Blood would have poured out of him. The soldiers probably charged at the disciple. Another second and it would have turned into a massacre. And so, the nonviolent Jesus intervenes. He jumps right into the mayhem and stops his disciple from attacking the enslaved person and threatening the high priest and the soldiers. He might have saved their lives; that is, he saved the life of the high priest, who might have been killed. He saved the life of the soldiers and other religious leaders, whom all the disciples might have killed. And he definitely saved the lives of the disciples, who would have been killed by the well-armed soldiers and temple guard. "Stop, no more of this!" Jesus says to the disciples and to everyone else. Then Luke reports that he touched the servant's ear and healed him.

"Stop, no more of this!" This is Jesus's answer to the violence in the Garden of Gethsemane, to the violence of his disciples, to the violence and killing that people have done down through the centuries right up to this very hour.

"Stop, no more of this!" Jesus forbids violence. He will not let them kill to protect him. He will not let them defend him or themselves with further violence. He will not retaliate; he would rather turn the other cheek. In saying this, he forbids everyone who would ever follow him to engage in violence. After this climactic nonviolent intervention in this violent moment, we know now that Jesus has forbidden us all from ever again taking up the sword, striking at another, retaliating with violence, killing another, preparing for war, building weapons intending to kill others, much less waging mass murder through warfare and nuclear annihilation.

"Stop, no more of this!" Suddenly, with this commandment, with this healing of the servant's ear, the violence stops. The disciples turn and look at the unarmed, peaceful Jesus. He has just stopped them in the midst of a sword fight. He has ended the violence. Perhaps even the scared soldiers pause for a moment and look at him, caught in classic cognitive dissonance. For a moment, everyone turns to Jesus. He has just ended their sword fight and saved everyone from getting hurt or possibly killed. Perhaps they are dumbfounded, but they all quickly regain their senses. Jesus is a tower of strength, nonviolence, and truth, and for a brief moment, he has the attention of the chief priests, the temple guards, the elders, and the soldiers, so he asks them a question, "Have you come out as against a robber, with swords and clubs? Day after day I was with you in the temple area, and you did not seize me; but this is your hour, the time for the power of darkness." A robber was a name used to describe violent revolutionaries. Jesus is reminding them that there is no need for swords or clubs against him. But they are people of violence and murder, starting with the chief priests and the temple guards.

Luke puts it figuratively: they live in darkness, meaning they are in the dark, blind, and therefore violent. This is the hour of the power of darkness—the power of violence, killing, death, and destruction. With that, they arrest the nonviolent Jesus and lead him away.

The disciples are not mentioned again. Why? They have all run away. Mark says so explicitly. Here, they simply vanish from the narrative. They were terrified. They had just awakened from a deep sleep to find themselves surrounded at night by death squads armed with swords and clubs, and they take up the sword to kill those who came for the arrest and to defend Jesus, who intervenes and stops their violence. Now they get it. For the first time in the Gospel, they know that Jesus is dead serious about nonviolence, and they can't take it anymore. They run away and throw Jesus to the wolves. From now on, he's on his own.

Except for Peter. And except for the women.

"The Lord Turned and Looked at Peter" (22:54–62)

Luke gives a detailed story of Peter, who tags along at a distance. Earlier Peter bragged that he would be willing to be arrested and killed for Jesus. So now he follows the soldiers and Jesus, who is tied up, to the chief priest's house. The religious authorities get to work and start calling an emergency council of the elders for first thing in the morning so they can put Jesus on trial and hand him over to the Roman governor for execution. They want him dead because he threatens their power, control, indeed the entire temple system. While they send out messengers to gather the council, the armed soldiers ridicule, mock, and slap Jesus. This is the courtyard of "the power of darkness."

Where was Peter? We're told that the soldiers built a fire in the middle of the courtyard. It was dark and cold, and people began to warm themselves around the fire. Peter would have drawn close too, to warm himself—while only a few feet away, his friend, the embodiment of peace, love, and compassion, was being mocked and hit. And there, in the warmth of the fire, some of the people recognize Peter as one of the followers of this notorious rebel leader from Galilee.

First, a maid sees him, "seated in the light" of the fire, warming himself, Luke writes:

She looked intently at him and said, "This man too was with him." But he denied it saying, "Woman, I do not know him." A short while later someone else saw him and said, "You too are one of them," but Peter answered, "My friend, I am not." About an hour later, still another insisted, "Assuredly, this man too was with him, for he also is a Galilean." Peter says, "My friend, I do not know what you are talking about." Just as he was saying this, the cock crowed, and the Lord turned and looked at Peter and Peter remembered the word of the Lord, how he had said to him, "Before the cock crows today, you will deny me three times." He went out and began to weep bitterly.

What a heartbreaking scene. Another moment of betrayal. Peter wants to follow Jesus and tries to stay close. He witnesses Jesus's interrogation and beatings, but he is scared to death. When three people recognize him, accuse him of being part of the Jesus movement, and threaten to tell the authorities that they should arrest and torture this "Galilean" too, Peter denies it. He does not say, "Yes, Jesus is my friend! Arrest me! I am with him. He is my Lord. Let me go with him." Instead, he tries to befriend the people of the courtyard of the house. "My friend," he calls those who accuse him. He has turned on Jesus and now sides with those under the power of darkness. Just like the time he took his eyes off Jesus while walking on the water, lost faith, and started to drown, he takes his eyes off Jesus, loses his faith, and gives way to fear and terror, which always leads to denial, betrayal, violence, and death. But notice: Jesus never takes his eyes off Peter, or us.

At that moment, Luke paints a tragic scene. The unarmed, mocked, tortured Jesus turns and looks at Peter. What a moment—that glance of Jesus! He sees through the eyes of compassion, love, and peace. He is humiliated, suffering, being tortured, and there, his best friend sits warming himself right in front of his eyes, denying their friendship, denying he ever met him. "I swear I do not know this man," Peter says. Jesus knew this breakdown was inevitable, but he must have been hurt and crushed. His last friend has denied him. Jesus is now all alone, left to be tortured and killed. Luke concludes that, when Peter saw poor Jesus looking directly at him, he walked off and "wept bitterly." Peter is the best of us, and he cannot stay faithful to the nonviolent Jesus.

Every Christian needs to meditate on this tragic scene. Here Luke challenges us to notice where we are in the story, to study the gaze of the tortured Jesus, to let him look at us as we warm ourselves in the courtyard of empire, in the time of the power of darkness. Each one of us has rejected the nonviolence of Jesus, denied that we know him, betrayed him, and run from him. We run from the way of nonviolence at the first sign of violence, danger, or terror. We do not want to go all the way with the nonviolent Jesus. And so he turns and looks at each one of us with the sad eyes of suffering love, innocence, compassion, and forgiveness.

We need to let Jesus look at us. His long and sorrowful look of compassion is a blessing. It is our only hope. Therein lies a lifeline back toward him. He does not deny his friendship with us. If we dare let Jesus look at us in our moments of denial, betrayal, and abandonment, when we are possessed by fear and violence, then his compassionate eyes will disarm and melt our hard hearts. We will recognize what we are doing and weep for what we are doing and begin the process of turning back to Jesus. Then we will finally begin the discipleship journey. The key here is to notice how Jesus is feeling and to attend to his needs, regardless of the cost to ourselves.

Decades later, John will build his resurrection account around this scene (in chapter 21). He will describe Jesus sitting at daybreak by the Sea of Galilee, beside his own charcoal fire in his own courtyard of nonviolence, in the power of light. There, the risen, nonviolent Jesus will ask Peter three times if he loves him and, in doing so, heal and restore Peter's faith, hope, and discipleship. It is there, at the end of John's story, for the first time, that Jesus invites Peter to discipleship.

But for now, the nonviolent Jesus is alone, the Lamb of God led away to the slaughter. Think of the many nonviolent followers through the ages who did follow Jesus all the way to the end, in their lonely martyrdoms, and we get a sense of what Jesus underwent: Sophie Scholl being led to the execution chamber to be beheaded by the Nazis for distributing leaflets on the Munich university campus calling for resistance to the Nazis; Matthew Shephard, beaten almost to death for being gay, tied to the wooden fence on the prairie outside Laramie, Wyoming, and left in the bitter cold all night to die; Steven Biko, beaten to death by white South African police in a cold prison cell for daring to teach "Black Consciousness," the Gospel truth that Blacks are equal to whites, that we are all human, that apartheid is evil; Sister Dorothy Stang, shot and killed while walking alone down a dirt road in Brazil because she dared to oppose the ranchers who were tearing down the Amazon. We could name hundreds of thousands of others who have been disappeared and killed like the nonviolent Jesus. We could, if we dared, aspire to their legacy.

We know that Peter did come around, that he did follow the nonviolent Jesus to his own martyrdom for peace and resistance to empire. Now we know the power of redemptive suffering love, that nonviolence works and will eventually bring down the empire and win us all over to the way of universal love and God's reign of peace. Luke will go the farthest to tell us the rest of the story in book 2, the Acts of the Apostles.

"From This Time On, the Son of Humanity Will Be Seated at the Right Hand of the Power of God" (22:63–23:25)

Jesus is beaten, mocked, reviled, and blindfolded. They question him, "Who struck you? Let's see you prophesy!" They call him every name in the book. He is helpless, innocent, and perseveres in his total nonviolence—that is, he refuses to respond with hatred, anger, words of vengeance, or even, I dare say, to resentment. He does not threaten "holy" violence or revenge or a prayer that his persecutors and torturers get what's coming to them. Jesus remains focused on his beloved God, clings to God, and even prays for his torturers. He has surrendered completely, 100 percent, to his beloved God, so he is entirely centered on God alone.

It is now daylight. Luke records that the full council convenes—all the chief priests, scribes, and elders—and the badly beaten Jesus is brought before them. He has not slept in over twenty-four hours. He has not eaten anything, used the bathroom, or rested. He has been tied up, forced to stand all night, and endure the pain of his beatings. He is exhausted and shivering from the cold. In this condition, he is brought before the religious authorities in all their pomp and power—their "power of darkness."

"If you are the Messiah, tell us," they demand.

Despite his pain and exhaustion, he retains his dignity as God's beloved, and so he remains nonviolent. He answers quietly, peacefully, without anger, resentment, or condemnation, with reason and respect. "If I tell you, you will not believe, and if I question you, you will not respond. But from this time on, the Son of Humanity will be seated at the right hand of the power of God." Jesus tells the truth but does not attack his accusers with vindictive words. Can you imagine how you might respond? "Just wait and see," we might say if we were him. "Come judgment day, you're gonna get it!" Rather than speak in anger or vengeance, Jesus gives *testimony*. He is humble and faithful to his beloved God and to his own true identity as God's beloved, "the Son of Humanity," the true Human Being, the Nonviolent One. The Human One is that close to God. Notice the use of the word "power." They think they are the most powerful people in the region, near the power of the emperor's representative. They must also think this is the most powerless, misguided troublemaker ever. Jesus tells them honestly that, on the contrary, he is close to True Power, Real Power, the Divine Power of Peace, Truth, and Love Itself.

"Are you then the Son of God?" they ask.

"You say that I am," he answers. In other words, "You said it!" Unlike Peter, Jesus cannot deny himself. He is faithful to the very end. He has come for testimony, and he gives it.

"What further need have we for testimony?" they say. "We have heard it from his own mouth." They now have the evidence they wanted. He has blasphemed in front of them, they think. This beat-up, no-good, rabble-rouser revolutionary thinks he's the holy Messiah of God. Let's take him out and kill him.

But they need to follow the letter of the law because, first and foremost, they are law-abiding servants of the empire. So they take him to the representative of the Roman Empire, which has the power to kill any treasonous revolutionary.

"The whole assembly of them arose and brought him before Pilate." Here, in the only instance in the four Gospels, Luke names three specific capital charges leveled against Jesus: "We found this man misleading our people; he opposes the payment of taxes to Caesar; and he maintains that he is the Messiah, a king." Each capital crime comes with the penalty of capital punishment. We need to reflect upon them if we want to understand Jesus the criminal—and follow him.

First, Jesus is capitally charged with misleading the people and presumed guilty. Some translations say "stirring up the people," "agitating the people," "disturbing the peace"—in short, leading the people to revolution. We readers know that Jesus is totally nonviolent and is offering the leadership of visionary nonviolence, pointing humanity to welcome a whole new world without empire and war, but justice, disarmament, and peace. He's the only sane leader in history. So we know that he's not guilty of any crime, but rather he is the best of humanity. What's so ironic is that in fact it is the religious authorities and the Roman authorities who are misleading the people. They mislead the people to accept their powerlessness and poverty under occupation and empire, the hopelessness that things will never change. They mislead people to kill for the empire and go along with their fate, their early and unjust deaths. If Christians start teaching and preaching the Sermon on the Plain as Jesus did, and following his true leadership of visionary nonviolence, we too can expect not approval and applause but rejection, and possibly criminal charges. We too one day might be charged with misleading people, disturbing the peace, and causing trouble, as I myself have been many times by the U.S. government.

Next, Jesus is capitally charged with opposing payment of taxes to Caesar. If there was any doubt about his teaching, "Give to Caesar what is Caesar's and to God what is God's," now we know for sure that Jesus did not want people to give one denarius to Caesar. He is charged by the authorities for calling people throughout the land not to pay taxes to the empire. What the religious authorities do not understand—and we don't either—is that this opposition to the payment of taxes is actually a call for a renewal of faith in our beloved God, for total trust in God, for giving all we have to God—and not the empire. No emperor, ruler, or warmaker deserves our allegiance or support in any way. Only the God of peace deserves our total support.

And so, if Jesus did not want people back then to pay taxes to Caesar, he does not want us to pay taxes today. He would not want us to pay one dollar to any nation that builds and drops bombs on human beings, that builds and maintains nuclear weapons with the intent of vaporizing human beings, that maintains a massive military and a permanent war economy for the benefit of the wealthy elite one percent while starving the poor and destroying creation. He would want our total non-cooperation with the culture of death, as he did then. Dorothy Day was right. North American Christians should no longer pay war taxes. She advised Christians to live under the poverty line as we follow Jesus so that we don't give one dime to the American war machine.

Finally, he is capitally charged with claiming to be a king, the Messiah. Everyone knows that there is only one king, one ruler, one emperor, and that is Caesar. Daring to claim to be a ruler means you are in opposition to Caesar. Following anyone who claims to be the true ruler, as opposed to Caesar, means that you are in opposition to Caesar and the empire. In the 90s, Emperor Diocletian will issue an edict saying that, from now on, under penalty of death, he is to be addressed as "My Lord and my God." If you dared to call anyone else by that title, you were to be executed immediately. John will take this phrase and put it in the mouth of doubting Thomas, showing the early church—and the rest of us—the true cost of discipleship.

Jesus does not go around calling himself a king or the Messiah. He refers to himself as the Son of Humanity, the name given to the mysterious figure who appears in the book of Daniel in the fiery furnace alongside Shadrach, Meshach, and Abednego, the three nonviolent resisters sentenced to death by King Nebuchadnezzar (see Daniel 3). When he rides into Jerusalem on a donkey, fulfilling Zechariah's oracle of the coming of the king of peace, the crowds hail him as a king. Before the Sanhedrin he was asked if he was the Messiah, and he replied, "You said it." That was enough to charge him with daring to be greater than the emperor.

Throughout all of this, of course, Jesus has a completely different idea of being a king and messiah. For him, the Messiah is not a military leader but a nonviolent Messiah, a suffering servant, the ransom of the human race. As a suffering servant of total nonviolence, Jesus had no intention, desire, or call to hurt or kill anyone, much less lead a violent, armed, military coup. He is the embodiment of peace and universal love. He sees himself as the True Human Being whose messiahship of total nonviolence saves the world by calling every human being to put down the sword, become nonviolent, join his growing global grassroots movement of nonviolence, and work for a new culture of peace, God's reign at hand. Because he has attracted such a massive following, the powers that be feel threatened by the power of his personality and grassroots movement, just as the British did under Gandhi and Ferdinand Marcos did under the People Power movement in the Philippines. But they completely misunderstand Jesus because they understand only violence and killing, and so they can respond to him only with violence and the threat of capital punishment.

So, imagine the tortured, nonviolent Jesus standing before Pilate. Jesus is centered in God, totally present and aware in his nonviolence, truthful, grieving, and compassionate, and living in full surrender. "Are you the king of the Jews?" Pilate asks. "You say so," Jesus answers. "I find this man not guilty," Pilate concludes. But the religious authorities continue to denounce Jesus and demand his punishment and execution. "He is inciting the people with his teaching throughout all Judea, from Galilee where he began even to here," they say. From the standpoint of domination and empire, Jesus *was* inciting people from Galilee to Jerusalem, but not inciting them to violence, which makes all the difference. He was guilty of misleading the people and riling them up, urging people not to pay their taxes, and claiming to be the Messiah. He was shaking people out of their complacency and complicity, building a grassroots movement of nonviolence, calling people out of empire, freeing them into God's reign of peace and universal love. His nonviolent movement is growing and spreading, as all true grassroots movements of nonviolence do, and it threatens their power and control over the population, so the religious leaders are determined to put a stop to it by killing him. But of course, we readers know now, from Luke's perspective of nonviolence, that Jesus is not guilty of any crime, any violence, any military threat—they are the guilty ones! He is the only sane person in the world, the only true leader calling humanity back to its spiritual bottom line of nonviolence; the rest of us are insane, possessed by violence, nationalism, greed, fear, ego, the lust for power, empire, and the demonic willingness to kill others, even destroy the planet.

Pilate is not fazed by this religious figure and his grassroots movement because he trusts his cohort and the power of the empire, and he knows the corruption of the religious leaders—or at least that's the way Luke portrays him. When we remember that Luke and Acts are written for a prominent anonymous Roman citizen whom he addresses as "Theophilus," then it makes sense that Luke would go easy on this Pilate. Fifty years after the events, we can imagine that Luke is perhaps tweaking the story just a bit in an attempt to win over his Roman audience.

So, Pilate sends Jesus to Herod because Galilee falls under his jurisdiction. Luke's Gospel is the only one that features Jesus before Herod, the murderous ruler of Galilee who is glad to see him. Luke writes that Herod wanted to see him perform some sign, some miracle. But Jesus remains silent. Herod questions him over and over again, and Jesus stands there, refusing to answer, a tower of strength, a pillar of truth and nonviolence.

Remember that earlier Jesus called Herod "that fox." Here Jesus is presented as the silent Lamb of God standing before a violent fox who can't wait to devour him. In his silence, however, if we notice, Jesus becomes the judge, the ruler, the real king, looking down from his throne of nonviolence at Herod who accuses him mindlessly, who is filled with malice and evil. In fact, if you look closely, Jesus does offer a sign: the miracle of someone embodying peace and nonviolence standing in front of a brutal tyrant who screams and yells at him because he does not know how to respond to a person of total nonviolence and he cannot force this person to do what he's told. Jesus refuses to obey Herod, Pilate, Caesar, or any worldly ruler. He is the only ruler.

Imagine the nonviolent Jesus as the God of peace in human form—gentle and humble of heart—standing before the religious, political, and military elites of Jerusalem, being attacked and mocked. "The chief priests and scribes, meanwhile, stood by accusing him harshly," Luke continues. "Even Herod and his soldiers treated him contemptuously and mocked him, and after clothing him in resplendent garb, he sent him back to Pilate. Herod and Pilate became friends that very day, even though they had been enemies formerly." As we read through these passion accounts, we notice how Jesus acts and ponder how he feels. Certainly, he grieves for everyone. But he is also a tower of truth and nonviolence—as Gandhi said, the greatest person of truth and nonviolence ever. Jesus remains faithful to God and to the truth of his identity and to God's way of peace. He never flinches. He does not blink. He does not cave in or relinquish his obedience. He resists to the end. He practices permanent nonviolent civil disobedience.

This scene and all the trials of Jesus should force us to question the way we relate to our own political rulers, military leaders, and religious leaders. Are they violent? Do they support war and killing? Do they lie and humiliate others? The demonic spirit of violence continues to possess all those who run the culture of dominance. If we want to stand with the nonviolent Jesus, we must be freed from the spirit of violence and stand our ground in truth and faith. If we go all the way as Jesus did in public nonviolent resistance to the culture of war, then the political rulers, warmakers, military people and their guards, even other religious people and leaders, will attack us. Jesus does not get triggered by their threats or violence and teaches us how not to be triggered and retaliate in the face of threats or violence. He models how to stand firm without giving in to any form of violence toward others, including our persecutors.

Jesus is brought before Pilate a second time, which does not happen in Mark and Matthew. John will do the same later. "You brought this man to me and accused him of inciting the people to revolt," Pilate tells the authorities. "I have conducted my investigation in your presence and have not found this man guilty of the charges you have brought against him, nor did Herod, for he sent him back to us. So, no capital crime has been committed by him. Therefore, I shall have him flogged and then release him." By stressing Pilate's declaration of Jesus's innocence a second time, we see how Luke emphasizes the religious authorities as the main force behind Jesus's death.

These supposedly dignified religious leaders start shouting at Pilate. "Away with this man! Release Barabbas to us." Luke tells us explicitly that Barabbas is a violent revolutionary who is in prison for leading a rebellion against the Roman occupation and for murdering at least one Roman soldier. In the mindless "logic" of violence, they call for the release of this notorious revolutionary and murderer and the execution of the one who demonstrates and teaches peace and nonviolence. Pilate still wants to release Jesus, but the religious leaders shout, "Crucify him! Crucify him!" A third time, Pilate asks, "What evil has this man done? I found him guilty of no capital crime. Therefore, I shall have him flogged and then release him."

The question is addressed to us: what evil has Jesus done? None. He has not done one evil deed, said one evil word, or thought one evil thought. He has healed the sick, the lepers, the blind, the deaf, and the mute. He has raised the dead, invited people to understand that God loves us all, called everyone to practice universal love, and showed us how to share our resources with one another so that everyone has enough food to live in peace. It all goes back to the synagogue in Nazareth: Jesus has fulfilled his mission according to the book of Isaiah. The spirit of God has been upon him, and he has brought good news to the poor. Is this allowed in a culture of injustice and war? Do empires allow movements of positive social change to grow and spread? Do religious leaders support efforts for peace, justice, equality, and disarmament? "With loud shouts," Luke writes, the religious leaders "persisted in calling for his crucifixion, and their voices prevailed. The verdict of Pilate was that their demand should be granted."

The religious leaders demanded the execution of Jesus, and the Roman procurator granted it. Both are guilty of killing the nonviolent Jesus. Again, the question for us as readers is, Where are *we* in the story? Whose side are we on? If we claim to be on the side of the nonviolent Jesus, then we need to ask ourselves: Are the political, military, and religious leaders who run the culture of violence, injustice, and war today trying to stop us from disturbing the peace and building a grassroots movement of nonviolence for justice and peace? In our religious zeal, do we try to stop those speaking out for and working for disarmament, creation, and global justice?

"If These Things Are Done When the Wood Is Green, What Will Happen When It Is Dry?" (23:26–32)

Barabbas is released and Jesus is handed over to be crucified. Luke also names Simon, a Cyrenian, who is picked from the crowd and forced to carry the cross behind Jesus as they are led outside of the city. Note the detail: Simon is described in the language of discipleship. He follows Jesus by taking up the cross literally and walking in his footsteps. Simon is forced into discipleship, but Luke calls us readers to choose discipleship, to take up the cross of nonviolent resistance to empire and walk forward in Jesus's footsteps freely.

Notice that Luke does not include the story of Jesus being tortured by the whole Roman cohort in the praetorium. There is no crown of thorns. Instead, Luke takes time to describe Jesus carrying the cross. He notes that "a large crowd of people followed Jesus." In particular, Luke adds an original detail of "many women who mourned and lamented him." These women also followed him as he carried his cross. This detail distinguishes Luke's Gospel: women followed Jesus and were faithful to the end. There is no mention of the male disciples. They are gone. But the women are faithful. They love him, they follow him, and they are sobbing with grief.

"Daughters of Jerusalem, do not weep for me," Jesus tells them as he walks to his execution. Luke's Jesus then adds a final teaching and a heartbreaking question: "Weep instead for yourselves and for your children, for indeed, the days are coming when people will say, 'Blessed are the barren, the wombs that never bore and the breasts that never nursed.' At that time people will say to the mountains, 'Fall upon us!' and to the hills, 'Cover us!' If these things are done when the wood is green, what will happen when it is dry?" With his description of Jesus as "green wood," which is difficult to burn yet here is tortured and crushed, Luke asks, Where will humanity's addiction to injustice and death lead? What does the future hold?

We need to listen carefully to Jesus's instruction to the grieving women of Jerusalem. The days are coming, he says, when people will want the mountains and the hills to fall down and kill them. Why? Because the suffering and violence we are headed toward will be unimaginable. Luke addresses this to his community, which has seen these words come true in Nero's horrific persecution of Christians and then in Rome's complete destruction of Jerusalem and massacre of its people. But two thousand years later, after centuries of slavery, empire, warmaking, mass starvation, extreme poverty, and genocide, we have unleashed a whole new level of unimaginable violence with our nuclear arsenal.

I read Jesus's last words in light of the horrors of the twentieth century: Auschwitz, Dachau, Dresden, Tokyo, and later, the U.S. carpet bombing of Vietnam and Iraq, the U.S. drone raids over Afghanistan, and the U.S.-backed death squads and military juntas in El Salvador, Guatemala, Chile, Argentina, South Africa, Israel, the Philippines, Mexico, Nicaragua, Colombia, and Brazil. If you read the details of the U.S. atomic bombing of Hiroshima and Nagasaki, the suffering is beyond comprehension. Over a hundred thousand were vaporized immediately, but tens of thousands found themselves suddenly walking around with their skin falling off, their eyes melting, their bodies burning, their stomachs retching from radioactive poisoning. They were dying of thirst and jumped into the river and drowned. These suffering people were the people who wished the mountains would fall on them, the hills to cover them.

Today, with our thirteen thousand nuclear weapons at the ready, the human race plans to vaporize everyone. Unless we undertake and enforce nuclear disarmament treaties and dismantle every nuclear weapon and redirect those trillions of dollars toward human resources and education for nonviolent conflict resolution, sooner or later, we will all say to the mountains, "Fall on us!" and to the hills, "Cover us!" This is not despair; this is not fatalism. This is the reality of our addiction to violence and death. If we want to live, we have to break the cycle of violence and become sober people of nonviolence. This is the mission Jesus calls us to as he walks the way of the cross, and it means we will have to weep and grieve for ourselves as we suffer, endure, and resist the world of destruction and death. Jesus does not want humanity to destroy itself; he does not want one person killed in violence and war. He has given his life nonviolently to stop the violence. But if this is what they do when the wood is green, what will they do when the wood is dry? he asks.

As we observe the world as it is today, with its ceaseless wars, millions of innocents starving and dying, and the natural world systematically destroyed—we can see that we are now in the time of dry wood. As we hear his words in light of the horrors of today, Luke invites us once again to obey Jesus's teachings, to work with him in the life-giving ways of God's reign.

"Father, Forgive Them, They Know Not What They Do" (23:33–38)

Luke reports that two other "criminals," probably convicted for violent revolution and killing Roman soldiers, were also led outside the city. Luke writes that they came to the place called the Skull, stripped Jesus and the other two, nailed their hands to crosses, erected those crosses on a scaffold system, and finally nailed their feet to the crosses. Luke then adds two other points not mentioned in any other Gospel.

In this horrific moment, as Jesus hangs on a cross, bleeds in agony, struggles to breathe, and is mocked, Luke writes that Jesus says, "Father, forgive them, they know not what they do."

"Father, forgive them, they know not what they do."

Here at the end of Luke, the end of the Synoptic Gospels, we witness the height of nonviolence. Jesus asks God in heaven to forgive the people who are killing him and mocking him because they do not know what they are doing. He goes to the ultimate extreme of nonviolence.

How is Jesus able to forgive his executioners and the people who mock him? Long ago he taught his followers to forgive everyone who ever hurt them, to let go of judgment and condemnation and move into universal compassion, to look at everyone, even those obsessed with violence, through the eyes of compassion. Jesus did this every day, every hour of his life, because people were constantly attacking him, laughing at him, mocking him, doubting him, and criticizing him. He forgave them all and let it all go, over and over again, minute by minute. He did not take the bait and let their violence build up layers of resentment, hostility, anger, and hatred within him. He let it all go.

Jesus saw every human being as sick, as possessed to varying degrees by the demons of violence in the culture of violence. People are addicted to violence, killing, and death and don't even know it. They are out of their minds, like raging alcoholics and out-of-control drug addicts. They are insane and cannot be reasoned with. From the perspective of the nonviolent Jesus, every human being has gone insane with violence to varying degrees. He has come to call us all to the sanity of nonviolence, and some people have started the hard work of disarmament. Of course, most think he's crazy and so they mock him and kill him, because that is what insane, violent people do. They don't know any better. They don't know what they are doing. None of us do.

Because Jesus has been forgiving everyone and showing compassion to everyone, even in his silence before Herod, Pilate, the religious leaders, and his torturers, Jesus has moved into a liminal space that the rest of us have never known. He has become the embodiment of peace, love, and compassion. He is the ultimate Bodhisattva of nonviolence. He is totally focused on the God of peace who called him "My Beloved." In his agony, he speaks to his beloved God and appeals to God to forgive those who mock and kill him. If we look at this stunning moment of nonviolence and forgiveness within the broad scope of salvation history, we see that every person, at one time or another, has rejected, mocked, and crushed the way of love, and so the crucified Jesus asks God in heaven to forgive every one of us, every human being who ever lived, for the violence we do against God.

This is the greatest moment of nonviolence in history, the greatest accomplishment in history, the most profound spiritual achievement in history—and it is lost on the human race. No one sees it or gets it, much less aspires to these heights of forgiveness and nonviolence.

Gandhi tried, deliberately and consciously, to be as forgiving as Jesus, as he headed toward his inevitable assassination. Gandhi knew his assassins for decades. He had met them, understood their Hindu fundamentalism and hatred for him, pleaded his case with them, and knew that as independence and civil war broke out, he would be assassinated. In the weeks before his prayer service was bombed and then his assassination, he confided with Muslim friends that he hoped he would be able to forgive unconditionally as Jesus had. He asked them to pray for him that he might forgive those who killed him just as Jesus had forgiven those who killed him. In this way, Gandhi tried to reach the heights of forgiveness and nonviolence set by Jesus. I think Dr. King, Archbishop Romero, and other martyrs did as well.

No one understands the mystical depths of nonviolence that Jesus plumbed as he reached the climax of his public campaign of active nonviolence. The religious leaders, soldiers, and crowd mock him to his last breath, saying, "If you are the Messiah," "If you are the Son of God," "If you are the king." Just like the demon in the wilderness who tempted him long ago to reject his identity as the beloved son of God, now again Jesus is told to reject his true identity, to be inhuman. He will not let go of his human nonviolence. They have killed him. He cannot come down from the cross because they have nailed him to it. They are possessed by hatred and insane with violence. He, on the other hand, truly is the king of peace, and through his universal compassion for them and everyone in history, he saves all of us by showing us a way out of violence.

"Amen, I Say to You,
Today You Will Be with Me in Paradise" (23:39–43)

After Jesus's prayer of forgiveness, Luke reports another exchange that does not appear in any other Gospel. Jesus hangs on the cross in the center, with a crucified person on his left and another crucified person on his right. He is in tremendous pain and bleeding and struggling to breathe. Down below, a crowd of people watch his suffering. They are probably held back by soldiers. The women weep as Jesus slowly dies in front of them. Meanwhile, Luke reports, the soldiers divide his garments by casting lots. The rulers and religious authorities "jeered" at him, saying, "He saved others; let him save himself if he is the chosen one, the Messiah of God." The soldiers put an inscription over his head that reads, "This is the King of the Jews," and offer him wine on a sponge on a stick, saying, "If you are the King of the Jews, save yourself."

One of the crucified men starts mocking Jesus, along with the crowd, saying, and "Are you not the Messiah? Save yourself and us." The other crucified man, however, rebukes him, saying, "Have you no fear of God, for you are subject to the same condemnation? We have been condemned justly, for the sentence we received corresponds to our crimes, but this man has done nothing criminal." Then he says, "Jesus, remember me when you come into your kingdom." And Jesus whispers back, "Amen, I say to you, today you will be with me in Paradise."

Elsewhere, we heard how James and John wanted to be at the right and left hand of Jesus, but he could not promise that. Now, Luke tells us who is at the right and left side of Jesus—violent revolutionaries executed for the capital crime of murdering Roman soldiers. Jesus dies as one of them, on the side of revolutionaries in opposition to the empire, only he is a nonviolent revolutionary, and nobody understands that, then or now. As one of them mocks him, the other defends Jesus and "rebukes" the one who mocks him. Notice, Luke here uses the same word, *rebuke*, which he used to describe Jesus's response to James and John when they wanted to call down hellfire from heaven upon the hated Samaritans. The one who is defending Jesus sounds like Jesus and acts like Jesus! "Have you no fear of God?" he calls out and asks the other crucified man. It is a question that lingers in the air. As we kill, wage war, execute people, and plan the destruction of the planet, the revolutionary who is crucified next to the crucified Jesus calls to us across the centuries: "Have you no fear of God?" Do you not care what you are doing? Do you not realize that one day you will die and stand before the God of peace? Are you not concerned about the consequences of your violence, or your silent complicity with the culture of violence?

The crucified revolutionary goes further and declares that Jesus is innocent of all crime. He has not done anything wrong. This criminal is the first and only person in the Gospel to say this. Earlier we wondered about the three capital charges brought against Jesus, and all the false accusations, but now we know: Jesus is completely innocent. Nonetheless, the powers declared him guilty of capital crime, guilty of violence, and so they're killing him. After defending Jesus, the crucified man speaks directly to Jesus, saying, "Jesus, remember me when you come into your kingdom." It is perhaps the greatest statement of faith in Jesus in the Bible. And Jesus answers, "Amen, I say to you, today you will be with me in Paradise."

This exchange is one of the most painful, most beautiful, most hopeful exchanges in human history. The dying revolutionary's last words can become the prayer of every human being. "Jesus, remember me when you come into your kingdom." Each of us can ask for this gift, even though we do not deserve it. We can ask Jesus, who now reigns in God's kingdom of eternal peace, to remember us and welcome us, too. If we pray this with the crucified revolutionary, perhaps we will deepen our nonviolence, turn away from complicity with the culture of violence, and focus solely on the nonviolent Jesus and his reign of universal love.

Luke emphasizes the words of the dying Jesus. "Amen, I say to you. . . ." This is the honest-to-God truth: "Today, you will be with me in Paradise." Jesus has found someone who truly believes in him, who has heard his message about God's reign and wants to be at his side forever. He promises the man that he will be with him in paradise. The force of the statement means that right now, the crucified revolutionary is in paradise with the nonviolent Jesus simply because he takes Jesus at his word. He will be with Jesus in death, and with Jesus in resurrection. The dying criminal models how to side with the nonviolent Jesus by speaking up, defending him, honoring his reign, seeking his kingdom, and looking to him. Perhaps in the end that's all we can do, even if it costs us our very lives. But the promise is clear: if we side with the crucified Jesus and call out to be with him in his kingdom, one day—maybe today!—we too will be welcomed into the paradise of resurrection peace.

"Father, Into Your Hands I Commend My Spirit" (23:44–56)

"It was now about noon and darkness came over the whole land until three in the afternoon because of an eclipse of the sun," Luke writes. The end of the world is at hand. "Then the veil of the temple was torn down the middle." With that, the temple system has collapsed. You no longer have to pay to get in to be with God. Jesus cries out in a loud voice, "Father, into your hands I commend my spirit" (a line from Psalm 31:6). Then, Luke concludes, he breathes his last.

The culture of war and empire, with all its false spiritualities of violence and institutionalized religious injustice, has come to an end. Jesus dies trusting in his beloved God and surrenders himself again completely to God. In doing so, he concludes his teaching. He has taught us how to live, how to love, how to serve, how to pray, how to be compassionate, how to be nonviolent, how to forgive, and now how to die. Not once does he teach us how to be violent, how to kill, how to wage war, or how to dominate others.

"Father, into your hands I commend my spirit." These words are the new Christian mantra. These are the words we can whisper to God every day for the rest of our lives. These are the words we want to pray as we practice nonviolence, take public risks for justice and disarmament, get harassed and persecuted, even face arrest and jail. These are the words we want to say as we die, for they are the words of the Master of nonviolence. He trusted in God until his last breath. That is how one lives and dies nonviolently: complete surrender to the God of peace. Forget my will, my control, my priorities, my desires—"Into your hands, I commend my spirit. Take me, receive me, welcome me into the paradise of peace."

As we sit in silence before the crucified Jesus and dare to grieve with the women, then we feel ourselves disarmed. Our hearts are broken before the horrific suffering of the nonviolent Jesus. As we dare feel his suffering love, we can begin to forgive everyone who ever hurt us, show compassion to all people in their violence, and surrender ourselves to God and God's way of peace. The death of the nonviolent Jesus is an explosion of universal love and compassion that crosses time and place, touching and disarming every human being. It is the ongoing work of redemptive love and salvific nonviolence. His explosion of nonviolence has inspired billions of people to undertake the way of peace, compassion, and love, to form movements of nonviolent resistance, to seek God's reign of peace.

Luke reports that the Roman centurion who oversaw the execution of Jesus glorified God and said, "This man was innocent beyond doubt." The crowds returned home "beating their breasts," but Jesus's friends "stood at a distance, including the women who had followed him from Galilee and saw these events." Luke hints that Jesus has touched the symbol of the Gentiles, that even the Roman centurion can be touched and converted. But he focuses again on the faithful women. They have been with Jesus every step of the way, from Galilee to Calvary. They saw these events. They witnessed Jesus's crucifixion, heard him forgive, and prayed with him as he surrendered himself into God's hands. These holy women of Jerusalem are the greatest disciples of all time.

Luke ends by telling us about Joseph of Arimathea, "a virtuous and righteous man, a member of the council who did not consent to their plan of action, who was awaiting the kingdom of God." Luke does not question Joseph's motives, but we presume his primary motivation is to observe the law of the sabbath, to make sure the dead body is safely put away. So he goes to Pilate, asks permission to claim the dead body of Jesus, gets permission, has the body taken down from the scaffolding, takes the nails out of the body, has the body carried away to a tomb, wraps the body in a linen cloth, and seals the tomb with a rock. The sabbath will begin any minute, and Joseph has observed the letter of the law. If he had not buried the dead body of Jesus in the tomb of rock, Jesus's body would have hung on the cross and been picked at by the vultures.

Luke gives the last word to the faithful women. "The women who had come from Galilee with him followed behind, and when they had seen the tomb and the way in which his body was laid in it, they returned and prepared spices and perfumed oils." They rested on the sabbath, but they intended, on the first day of the week, to return and anoint the dead body. They are overwhelmed with grief but not paralyzed. Their fidelity continues. They would care for him even in death.

And so, Jesus's grassroots campaign of nonviolence from Galilee to Jerusalem is crushed and destroyed. The men have scattered in fear, the women grieve and will care for his dead body according to tradition, but there is no hope. There is no future. Nonviolence has failed. Jesus has failed. The kingdom of God is but a dream. We are left with the nightmare of imperial domination, a pool of blood and death on Calvary. The empire has won. The greedy, mean, malicious religious leaders have remained in power and have had their way. Their lies have been bought. Indeed, death itself has won. Death rules the world. The power of darkness has overcome, and the last light of hope, the burning light of the nonviolent Jesus, has been put out. He is locked away in a tomb, silent as the grave. The culture of violence has won and can run wild now. Next up, the global crucifixion of the poor, the creatures, and Mother Earth herself. We destroyed the God of peace, so now, we are free to destroy the world's poor and all its creatures, and one day, Mother Earth herself.

There is no hope. Death gets the last word. The end of the world has come.

"You Are Witnesses of These Things" (24:1–53)

Luke began his narrative of Jesus's public campaign of peace, love, and nonviolence in his hometown synagogue. Earlier, we heard how the angel Gabriel announced to Mary that her son Jesus would be a king and that his kingdom would be a realm of peace that would never end. We heard how the angels appeared to the poor of Bethlehem after his birth, praising God and singing about the coming of peace on earth. We heard John the Baptist call people to repent of the culture of violence and war and to get ready for the coming Messiah. Then in Nazareth, Jesus took up the book of Isaiah and stunned the crowd by reading how "the Spirit of the Lord is upon me and has anointed me to bring good news to the poor, liberty to captives, sight to the blind, and the Jubilee of justice to humanity." There he said the scriptures were now fulfilled. How did the hometown faithful respond? They tried to throw him off a cliff!

From day 1, the culture of violence and death has rejected the nonviolent Jesus and his way and has motivated people to kill him. They have finally succeeded and silenced his voice permanently. With him now gone, they have killed his grassroots movement of peace, love, and nonviolence as well, so that things can stay the way they've always been. The religious authorities remain in power. Rome is in control. The elite rich minority own all the resources and money while the poor suffer and die in oppression with no hope. The hopelessness of darkness, empire, and death rules the day. There is nothing that can be done.

But we turn a page and there is another chapter. Those persistent women again! They were determined to stay faithful to the nonviolent Jesus, so the minute the sun rose on the first day of the week, they set off back to that tomb. They are not afraid. They take the spices they have prepared and are determined to anoint the dead body of their poor teacher.

But what's this? The stone in front of the tomb has been rolled away.

What does this mean? The women walk into the stone cave and, lo and behold, it's empty. The body of Jesus is not there. Oh no! Someone probably stole his body! They stand there "puzzling over this," when Luke adds, "Behold, two men in dazzling garments appeared to them." The women are terrified and bow their faces to the ground.

"Why do you seek the living one among the dead?" the two men in dazzling garments ask. It is a question for the ages. Why do we continue to seek the living nonviolent Jesus among the dead, on the path of war and empire?

"He is not here, but he has been raised," they announce. "Remember what he said to you while he was still in Galilee, that the Son of Humanity must be handed over to sinners and be crucified, and rise on the third day." With that, Luke writes, the women remember Jesus's words.

The angels leave, and the women immediately set off back to the hideout where the eleven male disciples and the rest of the community lie low. They announce what happened, and the whole group thinks the women have gone crazy. It seems like "utter nonsense," Luke reports. As in the other Gospels, Luke records the names of the faithful women: Mary Magdalene, Joanna, and Mary the mother of James (probably Mary of Nazareth, the mother of Jesus), and "the others who accompanied them." "The apostles refuse to believe the women," we're told in no uncertain terms. But, Luke adds, "Peter got

389

up and ran to the tomb, bent down, and saw the burial cloths alone; then he went home amazed at what had happened."

"What Are You Discussing as You Walk Along?
What Things?" (24:13–35)

With that, Luke launches into an amazing account of the resurrection of the nonviolent Jesus, his unique story of the appearance on the road to Emmaus.

> Now that very day two of them were going to a village seven miles from Jerusalem called Emmaus, and they were conversing about all the things that had occurred. And it happened that while they were conversing and debating, Jesus himself drew near and walked with them, but their eyes were prevented from recognizing him. He asked them, "What are you discussing as you walk along?" They stopped, looking downcast.

These two shattered disciples walk away from Jerusalem after Jesus's horrific execution. They are destroyed, wiped out, grief-stricken, and afraid. All their hopes were in Jesus, and now all their hopes are dashed. They're leaving town, heading for the village of Emmaus, leaving behind Jesus's community and grassroots movement of peace and hope. They walk in despair.

But their story takes a turn. Someone sidles up to them. "What are you discussing as you walk along?" he asks them.

They stop and turn. "Are you the only person in Jerusalem who does not know the things that have happened in these last days?"

The risen Jesus then asks, "What things?"

Twenty years ago, I wrote a book called *The Questions of Jesus*. Jesus asks well over three hundred questions in the four Gospels, but he gives answers to only two of them. In other words, while Jesus is the one with all the answers, he's also the one with all the questions. Of all the amazing questions throughout the four Gospels, this one has always been my favorite.

If it were me, and I was betrayed, denied, and abandoned by my friends, then arrested, interrogated, tortured, and brutally killed—well, first of all, I would never have come back. I would be angry and resentful for a thousand years. "How could they have done that to me?" I'd think. But, let's say I did rise from the dead and appeared to my friends. I would not ask them, "What are you talking about as you walk along?" I'd launch into a dramatic tale of my supernatural adventures: "You wouldn't believe what happened to me! They brought me before the Sanhedrin, Pilate, and Herod, they interrogated me, tortured me, mocked me, made me carry a cross, and then executed me—and now, I've just risen from the dead! I'm alive! I'm back!" I would talk non-stop. I would talk about myself. My narcissism, egotism, and self-centeredness would have a field day.

But the risen, nonviolent Jesus? The two downcast disciples stop in their tracks, turn to him, and ask, "Are you the only one in Jerusalem who doesn't know the things that have happened these last days?"

"*What things?*" he asks. Jesus is as humble, peaceful, gentle, and nonviolent as ever, totally centered, the risen Christ.

"What things?"

Think about this question. He asks us to tell him what happened to this nonviolent Jesus. As I consider it, *I think Jesus wants us to tell him his story in our own lives.* He wants to hear our experience of him, our experience of nonviolence, our experience of the power of the God of peace in our lives. He wants us to share our journeys with him so he can show us how he is right there beside us. This, he knows, is how hope is reborn.

"The things that happened to Jesus the Nazarene, who was a prophet mighty in deed and word before God and all the people, how our chief priests and rulers both handed him over to a sentence of death and crucified him," they tell the stranger.

"But we were hoping that he would be the one to redeem Israel; and besides all this, it is now the third day since this took place. Some women from our group, however, have astounded us: they were at the tomb early in the morning and did not find his body; they came back and reported that they had indeed seen a vision of angels who announced that he was alive. Then some of those with us went to the tomb and found things just as the women had described, but him they did not see."

We were hoping!

"We were hoping he would change everything. We were hoping this prophet mighty in deed and word before God and all people would redeem Israel. We were hoping God would intervene and justice would come. We were hoping humanity would live in peace. We were hoping in Jesus of Nazareth. Once we had hope, but now we have no hope."

This moment is critical for Luke. He wants us to feel the despair of the two downcast disciples. They have hit the rock bottom of total despair, of no hope whatsoever. Once there was hope; now we know there is no hope. Our best hope was killed. All hope is gone. It was all a dream. He was mighty and great, but they killed him, he's gone, he's dead; the movement he started is over, there's nothing we can do, end of story.

Luke wants his community—and us his readers—to feel their despair and recognize that same despair, that no-hope-whatsoever, in us. For starters, we can recall the past pluperfects of our own lives, the times we said, "We were hoping. . . ."

Think of those moments of despair when we said, "We were hoping . . ." that life would get easier; that the world would get better; that our politicians would become compassionate and wise; that justice would flourish; that food, clean water, healthcare, and education would be available to every person; that the nuclear threat would disappear; that racism, sexism, and gun violence would vanish; that peace would rule the day; and that everyone might serve God's reign of peace. We were hoping that humanity would learn from past mistakes and create more just, more nonviolent social structures and nations. We were hoping that the church would become more welcoming, more peacemaking, more celebratory, a place where God sends us forth to proclaim God's reign of peace. Alas for such high hopes. We were hoping . . . but no longer.

The stranger listens to them and to us, and then he speaks up. "How foolish you are!"
"What?"
"How slow you are to believe all that the prophets spoke!"
"What?"

"Was it not necessary that the Messiah should suffer these things and enter into his glory?"

"Was it not necessary . . . ?" we say in response to the stranger's odd question. "The world is brimming with injustice, violence, starvation, killing, and warfare. We hang on the brink of nuclear war; billions suffer and die in extreme poverty, and climate chaos is roaring down upon us. Meanwhile, with a few notable exceptions, the church has sided with the status quo of wealth, nationalism, and domination, justifying and blessing war in your name. The way of nonviolence has been thoroughly rejected. Greed and violence rule the world. Death has won out. Things are worse now than during your days on earth."

We might think "these things," and the two downcast disciples might have wanted to argue with the stranger, but he will not hear of it. He will not cooperate with despair. This unusual person who refers to the prophets seems filled with hope. He is hope personified. He practiced total nonviolence, built a movement of nonviolence, challenged the ruling structures of violence, was killed for it, and is now alive and well, raised from the dead, out and about, carrying on his underground grassroots movement. (Note that Luke's reference to a suffering Messiah is the only time that phrase occurs in the Christian scriptures. This image refers to the prophet Isaiah and his vision of the Suffering Servant in chapter 53.)

So the stranger explains his position to the dumbfounded disciples, and to us. The risen Jesus does the most astonishing thing: he holds a Bible study right there on the road to Emmaus.

"Beginning with Moses and all the prophets, he interpreted to them what referred to him in all the scriptures," Luke writes. We don't realize it, but Luke is slowly teaching his community and us that the risen Jesus appears to us when we break open the word together, and when we break bread together.

Thus, the risen, nonviolent Jesus explains all over again the story of salvation. He reviews the journey of faith in the God of peace and progressive nonviolence in Moses through the prophets and the Psalms to himself. He tutors them on the biblical path of nonviolent resistance—the very path that leads to the cross. And then to new life and glory. He invites the two of them—and the rest of us—to understand the wisdom of the paschal mystery as the doorway to peace, the fulfillment of active nonviolence, the way into God's reign of universal love.

The Christ has not failed his mission, he explains. Death and empire are tumbling down. The culture of violence, injustice, and war is crumbling. The old world is falling away. Nonviolence works. It is the way forward. The God of love and peace is alive and glorified. The new realm of God's peace and justice is at hand. Even creation will be renewed. Suffering accepted in love, in the pursuit of truth and justice, bears immeasurable fruit, if one only believes and holds out for the long haul. As Dr. King would later say: truth crushed to earth will rise again. The Christ lives on. The revolution of nonviolence continues. The grassroots movement will spread across the planet and down through history and disarm and transform everyone!

It's as if he said to them: active, creative, loving nonviolence through grassroots, people-power movements—from Jonah and Isaiah through the early church to Francis and Clare to Gandhi and Dorothy Day, from the Abolitionists and the Suffragists to the civil rights movement and the anti-apartheid movement, from the feminist movement to the environmental movement, from the fall of the Berlin Wall to the Arab Spring to Black Lives Matter—is giving birth to a new world of justice, disarmament, equality, and environmental sustainability. This way of nonviolence, through the paschal mystery of steadfast resistance and truth-telling, becomes contagious and wins out, bears good fruit, and leads to new breakthroughs for God's reign of peace here and now. This way of Jesus works. It always works, if we are faithful to the end.

The two disciples are mesmerized. This stranger's hope, his faith, his vision are contagious. They have reached Emmaus, and he acts as if he is going on, so they invite him to join them for a meal. "Stay with us, for it is nearly evening and the day is almost over." So he joins them and, while he is with them at table, "he took bread, said the blessing, broke it, and gave it to them. With that their eyes were opened and they recognized him, but he vanished from their sight."

Jesus, you're alive! It's you! We should have known. You always explained the scriptures to us; you always "took, blessed, broke and gave" bread to us. "Were not our hearts burning within us while he spoke to us on the way and opened the scriptures to us?" they ask each other. They get up and set out at once back to Jerusalem, to the eleven and their friends. "The Lord has been raised," they say, "and has appeared to Simon!" Finally, Luke concludes the story, saying, "Then the two recounted what had taken place on the way and how he was made known to them in the breaking of the bread."

Luke's brilliant story assures his community that the risen nonviolent Jesus is present among them. He comes disguised as a stranger, a refugee, an immigrant, an outcast, a homeless person. He's present when they break open the scriptures, reflect on the presence of God moving through history bringing justice and peace, and carry on his grassroots movements of nonviolence for the coming of God's reign of peace on earth. He's among them when they bless and break bread together. He will never leave them. He is always present in the Word and the Bread.

With the story of the road to Emmaus, they know—and we readers know—that the risen Jesus is alive and well among us in our communities of faith, hope, love, and nonviolence. They realize that their hearts were burning within them when he explained the scriptures to them. They are on fire. They have been given new hope. They turn around and run back to the community. The road of despair has become the road of hope. The road of imperial defeat has become the road of daring, revolutionary nonviolence. The road of death has become the road to new life. The road of fear has become the road of daring love into God's reign of peace.

Like the despairing disciples, we too encounter the risen Jesus when we study the Gospels and break bread in Eucharist. We too can reverse our tracks, forsake the road to despair, return to our peace community, and rejoin the global grassroots movement for justice, equality, disarmament, and creation. We can share our encounters with the risen Jesus, the hope he gives us, the fire that burns within us, and the new energy we receive, and we can inspire each other to build anew his campaign of revolutionary nonviolence. He lives on in us—in our hope and faith, in our nonviolence and resistance to empire, in our fearlessness and universal love, in our trust in the God of peace and in our determination to follow in his footsteps, come what may. Nothing can stop us. Jesus is alive, all is restored, and God has affirmed all his teachings of universal love and eternal peace.

Luke's story of the road to Emmaus invites us to ask ourselves, When have we encountered the risen nonviolent Jesus on our journeys? How does Jesus come to us, in which people? How seriously do we want to believe the vision of the prophets? What gives us new hope? How do we encounter the risen Jesus in the Eucharist, when we break bread, pass the cup, and turn in prayer to God? What makes our hearts burn within us? What makes us turn around? What fills us with new energy to rejoin the community, to recommit to the grassroots movement of Gospel nonviolence, and to restart Jesus's work of proclaiming God's reign of peace at hand? What inspires us to join the work of resurrection, the life of active nonviolence? How can we rise up with new energy to resist the culture of death and carry on Jesus's campaign of life?

"Peace Be with You!" (24:36–53)

Just then, as they share their excitement with one another, Jesus appears right in front of them, saying, "Peace be with you." Here is the Jesus we know: smiling, gentle, humble, as nonviolent as ever. After all he's done and been through, here he is, alive and well, full of peace, offering us peace. They were startled and terrified, Luke writes, "and thought that they were seeing a ghost." So, he asked them, "Why are you troubled? Why do questions arise in your hearts? Look at my hands and my feet, that it is I myself. Touch me and see, because a ghost does not have flesh and bones as you can see I have." He showed them his hands and his feet, and they were overwhelmed with joy and amazement. He asked for something to eat, so they gave him a piece of baked fish, and he took it and ate it in front of them.

Then he explained everything to them: "These are my words that I spoke to you while I was still with you, that everything written about me in the law of Moses and in the prophets and psalms must be fulfilled." He opened their minds to understand the scriptures, and they understood his teachings as if for the first time and recommitted themselves to follow him all over again on the narrow path of Gospel nonviolence.

"Thus it is written that the Messiah would suffer and rise from the dead on the third day and that repentance, for the forgiveness of sins, would be preached in his name to all the nations, beginning from Jerusalem," Jesus said. With that, he sent them on mission. "You are witnesses of these things. Behold, I am sending the promise of my Father upon you. Stay in the city until you are clothed with power from on high." He led them out to Bethany, raised his hands, blessed them, and was taken up into heaven. They did him homage, Luke concludes, and returned to Jerusalem "with great joy." They returned to the scene of the crime, the temple, where they were continually praising God. (Luke ends his Gospel with the ascension of Jesus on Easter Sunday, but then takes up the story in part two, the Acts of the Apostles, which begins with forty days of appearances by the risen Jesus before he ascends into heaven.)

"Peace be with you. Go forth and preach repentance, forgiveness, and peace to all the nations. You are witnesses to these things." It seems beyond belief, but that's the point: believe and go forth and give witness. As readers, we too are missioned to be witnesses of "these things." Now we testify to our encounters with the risen Jesus, how he lived and taught the way of universal love and peace, was killed, rose, and continues to send people forth to build his global movement toward peace and life for all.

Luke's story of resurrection calls us to take up where Jesus left off, to enter the stream of grassroots nonviolence flowing through history, the holy lineage of Gospel peacemaking, the long struggle of organized movements that are methodically disarming the world. From now on, we are his witnesses. We stand up, speak out, testify, take to the streets, sit in, and announce the coming of a new world of nonviolence. We resist death and the culture of violence and war. We welcome Jesus's resurrection gift of peace, walk forward in his footsteps of nonviolence, trust in the God of peace, and proclaim the good news: *death does not get the last word.* Justice, peace, nonviolence, and love win out. God was present in the life and work of the nonviolent, civilly disobedient Jesus, and God is present among us as we carry on his mission to disarm the world, bring justice to the poor, and welcome God's reign of peace on earth.

We do this because, like the first apostles, we have witnessed the end of the world in the crucifixion of Jesus, the culture's execution of the God of peace, but we have also witnessed the beginning of God's reign here on earth in Jesus's resurrection and through his resurrection gift of peace. He was totally nonviolent in life up through his death, and came back totally nonviolent, so from now on, we too live in his total nonviolence and go forth into the culture of violence as public witnesses to a whole new way of living, the beginning of a whole new world without war, nuclear weapons, racism, poverty, killing, and destruction, the creation of a new culture of justice, peace, and environmental sustainability—God's reign of nonviolence breaking through right now here on earth.

As we come to the end of Luke, again we pause, take a deep breath, and offer a prayer of gratitude for Luke's majestic Gospel. Now we know that Mary taught Jesus the life of contemplative, active, and prophetic nonviolence; that Jesus came to fulfill Isaiah's vision of justice, vision, liberation, and Jubilee; that Jesus's Sermon on the Mount in Matthew is taught and played out again in Luke in the Sermon on the Plain, this time with a sharper bite; that Jesus builds a grassroots movement of active nonviolence in Galilee that marches to Jerusalem; and that he sends out unarmed messengers, organizers, and peacemakers ahead of him, as any campaign strategist does. We hear the depth of Jesus's compassion in the parables of the Good Samaritan, the prodigal son, and Lazarus and the rich man. We witness Jesus's brave nonviolence in Jerusalem, at Gethsemane, and on Calvary, and meet him with the despairing disciples on the road to Emmaus. Like them, we have heard him lead us in a Bible study through the salvation story as God's movement of creative nonviolence down through the history of violence, and our hearts burn within us as we return to the community of peace. There we too meet the risen nonviolent Jesus, as meek, gentle, and humble as ever, and hear his commission that we go forth and carry on his peace and nonviolence movement. So we join the ongoing global grassroots movement of nonviolence in pursuit of justice, disarmament, and creation, and decide like Luke's community, to give our lives to his way of peace, compassion, and nonviolence and his kingdom. We do this with joy because we know he is alive, he is with us, and from now on, as we surrender our hearts and lives to the God of peace, we dwell in the presence of the nonviolent Jesus, in God's reign of universal love and peace, now and forever. Amen.

CONCLUSION

As we read Matthew, Mark, and Luke from a perspective of nonviolence, any vestige of violence that we might imagine in the storied life of Jesus falls away. Jesus is unarmed, and disarmed, in this new Gandhian/Kingian perspective. We discover a Messiah of universal love and total nonviolence who invites and welcomes everyone into God's reign. He's more generous, more gentle, more welcoming, more healing, more political than we ever imagined. With this shocking realization, we hear good news beyond our wildest dreams. We notice how far we have strayed from his nonviolence and the true God of peace, but more, we see a new horizon of universal love and peace opening for every person, every nation, every creature, beginning today for each and every one of us.

The Jesus we meet in Matthew, Mark, and Luke has not a trace of violence in him, and therefore, not a trace of ego, anger, fear, resentment, hatred, narcissism, untruth, or selfishness. He is completely surrendered to his beloved God, whom we now understand as the living God of universal love and peace. With this revelation, everything we know about God is turned upside-down. God is not a God of judgment, anger, hellfire, and damnation who can't wait to punish us all. Instead, the living God is the God of infinite peace, tender compassion, and unconditional love, a non-coercive, nonviolent God who by definition grants humanity free will, the freedom to reject God and God's reign and God's way, which we have all done with a vengeance. Nonetheless, the nonviolent Jesus has opened the door to God's reign and called us all back to the fullness of life in God's reign of universal love through the methodology of total nonviolence.

As we conclude the stories by Matthew, Mark, and Luke of nonviolence in a world of violence, read from the perspective of Mahatma Gandhi and Dr. Martin Luther King Jr., we could be overwhelmed, even paralyzed by the enormity of the message and its implications. But no, we're not. If we read the Gospels from the perspective of nonviolence, we are transformed like the first disciples to imitate the nonviolent Jesus and join his ongoing global grassroots movements to disarm the world. Like the Galilee 72, we are sent "as lambs into the midst of wolves" to proclaim peace and nonviolence to those near and far and to welcome God's reign of peace here on earth. We have been liberated into the new freedom of total nonviolence and universal love. We are free not to hurt or kill others, free from fear, anger, victimhood, ego, and selfishness; free from nationalism, militarism, greed, racism, sexism, warmaking, and the entire culture of violence and empire. We are free in our total surrender to the nonviolent Jesus. The days of violence are over, as also are the days of fear, worry, anxiety, anger, greed, and ego. We have been liberated from the culture of violence and are free to take the Gospel of peace and nonviolence personally and claim our citizenship in God's reign of peace and universal love.

As we surrender our hearts and lives to Jesus and the living God of peace and take up his mission of active nonviolence, we go forward, calling everyone we meet to turn away from the culture of violence and war, to be healed of violence, and to welcome God's reign of peace in their hearts and lives. Moreover, we join and build grassroots movements of nonviolence, as Jesus, Gandhi, and King did, to tear down the structures of violence, greed, and war and build new cultures of justice, compassion, and peace that serve the poor and the least and protect and sustain creation. In our commitment to the nonviolent Jesus, we now receive new grace to go all the way, to share his paschal mystery, to take up the cross as permanent nonviolent resistance to the culture of violence and war, to live already in the eternal present moment of resurrection peace. We do our part to herald the coming of a whole new world—a world without war, guns, weapons, nuclear weapons, corporate greed, racism, sexism, or environmental destruction.

Like the disciples on the road to Emmaus, our hearts are burning within us. We are witnesses of the nonviolent Jesus, the power of transforming nonviolence, and the disarming action of God in history through people following Jesus's way. We willingly give our lives to God's ongoing movement of disarmament, justice, and nonviolent transformation for the coming of peace on earth.

Every day is Easter Sunday for us because we are now people of resurrection, people who practice resurrection, who are preparing for resurrection. Each day, we hear the great commission again: "Go forth and make nonviolent disciples of all the nations, that God's reign of universal love and total nonviolence might come to all, that God will reign on earth through my way, as God reigns in heaven." Like the early community, we rejoice knowing that death does not get the last word; that the culture of violence, war, empire, and death itself is falling away; that God's reign is coming through the steadfast grassroots movements of peace and nonviolence; that Jesus lives on among us as we build these contagious movements; and that one day, as we welcome a new culture of justice, disarmament, peace, and nonviolence, he will reign among us here on earth as he does in heaven forever.

From now on, we go forth as apostles of Gospel nonviolence and proclaim the Gospel of peace.

RECOMMENDED READINGS

Ackerman, Peter, and Jack DuVall. *A Force More Powerful: A Century of Nonviolent Conflict.* New York: St. Martin's Press, 2000.

Beck, Robert R. *Nonviolent Story: Narrative Conflict Resolution in the Gospel of Mark.* Maryknoll, NY: Orbis Books, 1996.

Berrigan, Daniel. *To Dwell in Peace: An Autobiography.* 1987. Reprint, Eugene, OR: Wipf & Stock, 2007.

Binz, Stephen J. *Peacemaking and Nonviolence.* Threshold Bible Study. New London, CT: Twenty-Third Publications, 2018.

Borg, Marcus. *Jesus, A New Vision: Spirit, Culture, and the Life of Discipleship.* San Francisco: Harper & Row, 1987.

Butigan, Ken, with Patricia Bruno. *From Violence to Wholeness: A Ten-Part Process in the Spirituality and Practice of Active Nonviolence.* Corvallis, OR: Pace e Bene Press, 2002.

Chenoweth, Erica, and Maria J. Stephan. *Why Civil Resistance Works: The Strategic Logic of Nonviolent Conflict.* Columbia Studies in Terrorism and Irregular Warfare. New York: Columbia University Press, 2012.

Crosby, Michael. *House of Disciples: Church, Economics, and Justice in Matthew.* Maryknoll, NY: Orbis Books, 1988.

Dear, John. *The Beatitudes of Peace: Meditations on the Beatitudes, Peacemaking and the Spiritual Life.* New London, CT: Twenty-Third Publications, 2016.

————, ed. *Daniel Berrigan, Essential Writings.* Modern Spiritual Masters. Maryknoll, NY: Orbis Books, 2009.

————. *The God of Peace: Toward a Theology of Nonviolence.* Maryknoll, NY: Orbis Books, 1994. Reprint, Eugene, OR: Wipf & Stock, 2008.

————. *Jesus the Rebel: Bearer of God's Peace and Justice.* Franklin, WI: Sheed & Ward, 2000.

————. *Lazarus Come Forth! How Jesus Confronts the Culture of Death and Invites Us into the New Life of Peace.* Maryknoll, NY: Orbis Books, 2011.

————. *Living Peace: A Spirituality of Contemplation and Action.* New York: Doubleday, 2001.

————, ed. *Mohandas Gandhi: Essential Writings.* Modern Spiritual Masters. Maryknoll, NY: Orbis Books, 2002.

————. *The Nonviolent Life.* Corvallis, OR: Pace e Bene Press, 2013.

————. *A Persistent Peace: One Man's Struggle for a Nonviolent World.* Chicago: Loyola Press, 2008.

———. *The Questions of Jesus: Challenging Ourselves to Discover Life's Great Answers.* New York: Doubleday, 2004.

———. *Radical Prayers: On Peace, Love, and Nonviolence.* Corvallis, OR: Pace e Bene Press, 2018.

———. *Thomas Merton, Peacemaker: Meditations on Merton, Peacemaking and the Spiritual Life.* Maryknoll, NY: Orbis Books, 2015.

———. *Transfiguration: A Meditation on Transforming Ourselves and Our World.* New York: Doubleday, 2007.

———. *Walking the Way: Following Jesus on the Lenten Journey of Gospel Nonviolence to the Cross and Resurrection.* 2015. Reprint, Eugene, OR: Wipf & Stock, 2022.

Douglass, James W. *Gandhi and the Unspeakable: His Final Experiment with Truth.* Maryknoll, NY: Orbis Books, 2013.

———. *Lightning East to West: Jesus, Gandhi, and the Nuclear Age.* 1983. Reprint, Eugene, OR: Wipf & Stock, 2006.

———. *The Nonviolent Coming of God.* Maryknoll, NY: Orbis Books, 1991. Reprint, Eugene, OR: Wipf & Stock, 2006.

———. *The Nonviolent Cross: A Theology of Revolution and Peace.* New York: Macmillan, 1968. Reprint, Eugene, OR: Wipf & Stock, 2006.

———. *Resistance and Contemplation: The Way of Liberation.* Garden City, NY: Doubleday, 1972. Reprint, Eugene, OR: Wipf & Stock, 2006.

Easwaran, Eknath. *Gandhi, the Man.* 2nd ed. Berkeley, CA: Nilgiri Press, 1997.

Eig, Jonathan. *King: A Life.* New York: Farrar, Straus & Giroux, 2023.

Fischer, Louis. *The Life of Mahatma Gandhi.* New York: Harper & Row, 1954.

Forest, Jim. *All Is Grace: A Biography of Dorothy Day.* Maryknoll, NY: Orbis Books, 2011.

———. *At Play in the Lions' Den: A Biography and Memoir of Daniel Berrigan.* Maryknoll, NY: Orbis Books, 2017.

———. *Living with Wisdom: A Life of Thomas Merton.* 1991. Reprint, Maryknoll, NY: Orbis Books, 2008.

Francis, Pope. *Against War: Building a Culture of Peace.* Maryknoll, NY: Orbis Books, 2022.

———. *Nonviolence: A Style of Politics for Peace.* Message of His Holiness Pope Francis for the Celebration of the Fiftieth World Day of Peace, 1 January 2017. www.vatican.va.

Garrow, David J. *Bearing the Cross: Martin Luther King, Jr., and the Southern Christian Leadership Conference.* New York: W. Morrow, 1986.

Holmes, Robert L., ed. *Nonviolence in Theory and Practice.* Belmont, CA: Wadsworth, 1990.

Howard-Brook, Wes. *Becoming Children of God: John's Gospel and Radical Discipleship.* Bible and Liberation. Maryknoll, NY: Orbis Books, 1994.

Kidder, Tracy. *Mountains beyond Mountains.* New York: Random House, 2003.

King, Martin Luther, Jr. *Strength to Love.* New York: Harper & Row, 1963.

———. *Stride toward Freedom: The Montgomery Story.* New York: Harper & Row, 1958.

———. *Where Do We Go from Here: Chaos or Community.* Boston: Beacon Press, 1967, 2010.

King, Mary E. *Mahatma Gandhi and Martin Luther King, Jr.: The Power of Nonviolent Action.* Cultures of Peace. Paris: UNESCO Publishing, 1999.

Lawson, James M. *Revolutionary Nonviolence: Organizing for Freedom.* Berkeley, CA: University of California Press, 2022.

Long, Michael G., ed. *Christian Peace and Nonviolence: A Documentary History.* Maryknoll, NY: Orbis Books, 2011.

Lynd, Staughton, and Alice Lynd, eds. *Nonviolence in America: A Documentary History.* Rev. ed. Maryknoll, NY: Orbis Books, 1995.

McKenna, Megan. *Blessings and Woes: The Beatitudes and the Sermon on the Plain in the Gospel of Luke.* Maryknoll, NY: Orbis Books, 1999.

McSorley, Richard. *New Testament Basis of Peacemaking.* 3rd rev. ed. Scottdale, PA: Herald Press, 1985.

Merton, Thomas, ed. *Gandhi on Non-violence.* New York: New Directions, 1965.

———. *Passion for Peace: The Social Essays.* Edited by William H. Shannon. New York: Crossroad, 1995.

Moore, Charles E., ed., *Following the Call: Living the Sermon on the Mount Together.* Walden, NY: Plough, 2021.

Musto, Ronald G. *The Catholic Peace Tradition.* Maryknoll, NY: Orbis Books, 1986.

Myers, Ched. *Binding the Strong Man: A Political Reading of Mark's Story of Jesus.* Maryknoll, NY: Orbis Books, 1988.

Nhat Hanh, Thich. *Being Peace.* Edited by Arnold Kotler. Berkeley, CA: Parallax Press, 1987.

———. *Creating True Peace: Ending Violence in Yourself, Your Family, Your Community, and the World.* New York: Free Press, 2003.

———. *Peace Is Every Breath: Mindful Eating, Mindful Life.* New York: HarperOne, 2011.

———. *Peace Is Every Step: The Path of Mindfulness in Everyday Life.* New York: Bantam Books, 1991.

Nouwen, Henri. *Peacework: Prayer, Resistance, Community.* Maryknoll, NY: Orbis Books, 2005.

———. *The Road to Peace: Writings on Peace and Justice.* Edited by John Dear. Maryknoll, NY: Orbis Books, 1997.

Oates, Stephen B. *Let the Trumpet Sound: The Life of Martin Luther King, Jr.* New York: Harper & Row, 1982.

The Power of Nonviolence: Writings by Advocates of Peace. Boston: Beacon Press, 2002.

Powers, Roger S., and William B. Vogele, eds. *Protest, Power, and Change: An Encyclopedia of Nonviolent Action from ACT-UP to Women's Suffrage.* New York: Garland, 1997.

Putz, Erna, ed. *Franz Jägerstätter: Letters and Writings from Prison.* Maryknoll, NY: Orbis Books, 2009.

Rohr, Richard. *Jesus' Plan for a New World: The Sermon on the Mount.* Cincinnati, OH: St. Anthony Messenger Press, 1996.

Rosenberg, Marshall B. *Nonviolent Communication: A Language of Compassion.* 1999. Reprint, Encinitas, CA: Puddle Dancer Press, 2003.

Rynne, Terrence J. *Jesus Christ, Peacemaker: A New Theology of Peace.* Maryknoll, NY: Orbis Books, 2014.

Schüssler Fiorenza, Elisabeth. *In Memory of Her: A Feminist Theological Reconstruction of Christian Origins.* New York: Crossroad, 1985.

Sharp, Gene. *The Politics of Nonviolent Action.* 3 vols. Boston: Porter Sargent, 1973.

———. *Waging Nonviolent Struggle: 20th Century Practice and 21st Century Potential.* Boston: Porter Sargent, 2005.

Soelle, Dorothee, and Luise Schottroff. *Jesus of Nazareth.* Translated by John Bowden. Louisville: Westminster John Knox, 2000.

Thurman, Howard. *Jesus and the Disinherited.* Boston: Beacon Press, 1996.

Trocmé, Andre. *Jesus and the Nonviolent Revolution.* 1973. Reprint, Walden, NY: Plough Books, 2014.

Vanderhaar, Gerard A. *Active Nonviolence: A Way of Personal Peace.* 1991. Reprint, Eugene, OR: Wipf & Stock, 2013.

———. *Personal Nonviolence: A Practical Spirituality for Peacemakers.* Washington, DC: Pax Christi USA, 2006.

Washington, James M., ed. *A Testament of Hope: The Essential Writings of Martin Luther King, Jr.* San Francisco: Harper & Row, 1986.

Wink, Walter. *Engaging the Powers: Discernment and Resistance in a World of Domination.* Minneapolis: Fortress Press, 1992.

———. *Jesus and Nonviolence: A Third Way.* Facets. Minneapolis: Fortress Press, 2003.

———, ed. *Peace Is the Way: Writings on Nonviolence from the Fellowship of Reconciliation.* Maryknoll, NY: Orbis Books, 2000.

Yoder, John Howard. *The Politics of Jesus.* Grand Rapids: Eerdmans, 1994.

ACKNOWLEDGMENTS

I thank all those who helped me with this project, starting with my friend Vinita Hampton-Wright, who worked so hard editing the manuscript and making it presentable. Thank you so much, and God bless you always, Vinita!

I also thank my friend and publisher Robert Ellsberg of Orbis Books for agreeing to this big project, for taking a leap of faith with me in this exploration of the Gospels from the perspective of nonviolence. Thank you so much, Robert, for your support and friendship!

I also thank my friend David Bellefeuille-Rice, who graciously proofread the manuscript and made many recommendations especially in light of nonviolence. Thank you, David! Your hard work made a big difference. Thanks also to Cornel West for his gracious encouragement, and a special thanks to Larry Purcell for his contribution to this project

I thank my assistant Kassandra Souza and all those who are part of the Beatitudes Center for the Nonviolent Jesus, especially my board members, Terry Rynne, Cathy Crosby, Ray East, and Sharon Halsey-Hoover, and our friend, Mike Matteuzzi.

I thank Laura James for the use of her beautiful artwork, "Jesus the Peacemaker," on the cover.

And I thank my friends for their support and help during the years I worked on this: Jim Lawson, Ken Butigan, Marie Dennis, John Wester, Chris Bremer, Danny O'Regan, Cyprian Consiglio, Maureen O'Connor, Chris Bryant, Mark Deats, Jeff Harbour, Bud Ryan, Steve Kelly, Dennis Appel, Tensie Hernandez, Richard Rohr, Natalie Goldberg, Jon Fogleman, Dar Williams, Patty Smythe, Jackson Browne, Brad Wolf, Janet and Martin Sheen, Shelley and Jim Douglass, Jamie Raskin, Harry Geib, Joe Sands, George Regan, Ethel and Kerry Kennedy, Carole Powell, Eric Stoner, Sherrill Hogen, Wes Howard-Brook, Emmanuel Katongole, Anne McCarthy, Gerry Straub, Bill Wylie-Kellermann, Frida Berrigan, Matthew Fox, Zoughbi Zoughbi, Kazu Haga, Ron Rolheiser, Rajmohan Gandhi, Tom Gumbleton, Peter Turkson, Michael Curry, Mariann Budde, Malcolm Young, John Stowe, Chris Ponnet, Ryan Hall, and Rosie Davila.

To you, dear reader, I invite you to join me in this campaign to promote the nonviolence of Jesus. If you are able, please tell others about this book, give copies to priests, ministers, and bishops, and urge teachers, theologians, and churches to use it. Check out videos about it on the free YouTube channel "JohnDear/Beatitudes Center," and talks about it at www.beatitudescenter.org. Thank you. It is the culmination of a series of books about Jesus: *The Questions of Jesus; Jesus the Rebel; Lazarus Come Forth!; The Beatitudes of Peace; They Will Inherit the Earth;* and *Walking the Way,* which might also be of interest.

I hope and pray that someday, every theology and spirituality book will come from the perspective of nonviolence and every commentary on Jesus and the Gospels will emphasize his nonviolence and the requirement of nonviolence for discipleship. I hope every church, seminary, and university will teach the nonviolence of Jesus, that every priest, minister, and bishop will preach the nonviolence of Jesus, and that every Christian everywhere will study and practice the nonviolence of Jesus and break out of the culture of violence and war into the freedom of God's reign of peace, nonviolence, and universal love.

I dedicate this book to Mahatma Gandhi, Rev. Martin Luther King Jr., Coretta Scott King, Glenn Smiley, Dorothy Day, Muriel Lester, Andre Trocmé, Walter Wink, Mairead Maguire, Marie Dennis, Ken Butigan, Gerry Vanderhaar, Mary Lou Kownacki, John Lewis, Adin Ballou, Ben Salmon, Franz Jägerstätter, Peter Cicchino, Cesar Chavez, Vincent Harding, Jim Douglass, Jim Lawson, Dorothy Cotton, Diane Nash, Hildegard Goss-Mayr, Richard McSorley, Robert Ellsberg, Thomas Merton, Daniel Berrigan, Pope Francis, and all those who teach, practice, and promote the nonviolence of Jesus. May you live forever with Jesus in the resurrection peace of God!

And may the God of peace bless us and the whole human race all over again to reclaim and do God's gracious will of loving nonviolence, to follow the nonviolent Jesus faithfully, and to proclaim the Gospel of Peace to the ends of the earth!

Amen. Alleluia!

ABOUT THE AUTHOR

Rev. John Dear is an internationally recognized voice and leader for peace and nonviolence. A priest, activist, and author, he served for years as the director of the Fellowship of Reconciliation, the largest interfaith peace organization in the United States. He has two master's degrees from the Jesuit School of Theology in Berkeley and has taught theology at Fordham University.

After September 11, 2001, he was a Red Cross coordinator of chaplains at the Family Assistance Center in New York, and counseled thousands of relatives and rescue workers. John has traveled the war zones of the world, been arrested some eighty-five times for peace, led Nobel Peace Prize winners to Iraq, given thousands of lectures on peace across the United States and the world, and served as a pastor of several churches in New Mexico. He arranged on many occasions for Mother Teresa to speak to various governors to stop impending executions. He is a co-founder of Campaign Nonviolence and the Nonviolent Cities Project and founder and director of the Beatitudes Center for the Nonviolent Jesus, www.beatitudescenter.org. He is on the national committee of the Selma Jubilee annual march and the National Board of Advisors for Veterans for Peace, and the literary executor for Daniel Berrigan (see www.danielberrigan.org).

His thirty-five books include *The Beatitudes of Peace; They Will Inherit the Earth; The Nonviolent Life; Radical Prayers; Walking the Way; Thomas Merton, Peacemaker; A Persistent Peace; Transfiguration; You Will Be My Witnesses; Living Peace; The Questions of Jesus; The God of Peace; Jesus the Rebel; Peace behind Bars; Lazarus Come Forth!, Disarming the Heart*, and, most recently, *Praise Be Peace: The Psalms of Peace and Nonviolence in a time of War and Climate Change*.

He has been featured in the *New York Times,* the *Washington Post, USA Today, The Sun,* National Public Radio's *All Things Considered,* and elsewhere. For eight years, he wrote a weekly column for the *National Catholic Reporter* and the *Huffington Post* and is featured regularly on the national radio show *Democracy Now!* He is the subject of the DVD documentary *The Narrow Path* (with music by Joan Baez and Jackson Browne) and is profiled in *John Dear on Peace: An Introduction to His Life and Work*, by Patti Normile.

He has received many awards, including the 2022 Beyond Duke Award, the Pacem in Terris Award, and the Courage of Conscience Award, and been nominated many times for the Nobel Peace Prize, including by Archbishop Desmond Tutu. See www.johndear.org. To invite him to give a talk, workshop, or retreat on this book, contact him at www.beatitudes center.org.

Milton Keynes UK
~ram Content Group UK Ltd.
AW031816100124
5810UK00009B/531